TRAVEL
LITERATURE
and the
EVOLUTION
of the
NOVEL

TRAVEL LITERATURE

and the

EVOLUTION

of the

NOVEL

Percy G. Adams

THE UNIVERSITY PRESS OF KENTUCKY

Publication of this book has been assisted by a grant
from the National Endowment for the Humanities.

Library of Congress Cataloging in Publication Data

Adams, Percy G.
    Travel literature and the evolution of the novel.

    Includes bibliographical references and index.
    1. European fiction—Renaissance, 1450-1600—History
and criticism.   2. European fiction—17th century—
History and criticism.   3. European fiction—18th century
—History and criticism.   4. Travel in literature.
5. Voyages, Imaginary—History and criticism.   6. Voyages
and travels.   I. Title.
PN3432.A32   1983   809.3   83-19683
ISBN 0-8131-1492-6

I propose ... a new science ... strictly tied
to literature, concerned with human travel ...
"Iterology." *Michel Butor*

We shall not cease from exploration
And the end of all our exploring
Will be to arrive where we started
And know the place for the first time.   *T. S. Eliot*

CONTENTS

PREFACE

Perhaps as ageneric as a critic can be, Samuel Johnson believed that "Definitions" in literature, as in law, "are hazardous," that they are "indeed, not the province of man," since "every new genius produces some innovations, which, when invented and approved, subvert the rules which the practice of foregoing authors had established" (*Rambler* 125). And since I agree on this point with Johnson, I shall not now try to define either of the generic terms in the title of this book, partly out of cowardice in wanting to avoid Johnson's "hazards," partly out of desire to keep my readers. By the end of Chapter One, however, perhaps my use of "novel" will be clear enough, and perhaps by the end of the book my use of "travel literature" will be acceptable. Right now, taking a cue from Abraham Cowley, who in his wonderful ode on wit defines it only by negatives, I can suggest that the travel narrative, the *récit de voyage,* is not just a first-person journal kept by a traveler. Nor is it simply a photograph in words of what a traveler observes. As the patient reader of this book will perhaps see, the traveler, like the "noveler," has a thousand forms and formulas from which to choose when writing the account of a trip, whether he intends to publish his account or not. Likewise, the reader will soon discover that the "evolutionary" process here followed extends to about 1800, although one cannot avoid an occasional glance ahead to a Howells or Henry James, to a Céline or Butor. And finally, the reader must know from the outset that the book's title refers not just to British novels and travels but to the literature of all western Europe, sometimes to early America, even though the emphasis is on Britain and France. The point is that readers before 1800, perhaps more than today, knew the writers of other nations. In the case of travel literature they knew them in the original language, in quick translations, in the hundreds of gigantic collections that appeared after 1530 and that regularly crossed national boundaries in one form or another.

This book is longer than certain other books and has been long in the making—the publisher, in fact, as well as my friends, came to believe it a myth. But anyone who attempts to write on the "novel," so elusive and so often studied, must read much—both fiction and criticism. Similarly, anyone who wishes to treat travel literature must look into an unbelievable number of volumes of travels—there are more of them than there are of fiction before 1800, but there is much less criticism or history of travels. And anyone wanting to put the two together requires even more time. Nevertheless, as any patient reader will soon see, this book is flawed by omissions, by apparent inconsistencies, surely by my own lack of talent. And yet it may partially fill a huge gap in the study of western literature. A few readers such as Victor Sklovsky have long known the importance of the récit de voyage to the evolution of the novel, and there are significant rumblings today from such people as William Spengemann and John Tallmadge, but the gap is so big that hundreds of hands are needed just to fill it partly. How much has been said about how the novel relates to the epic, the drama, or the autobiography, but how little about its connection with travel literature!

The organization of the book will pose a problem to the less-than-patient reader. Such a reader, glancing at Chapter One, may wonder how anyone can possibly say anything new about the early novel; but in that chapter I have tried to combine theories about British fiction with those of other nations, particularly France, and to leave the reader with a perspective into which the whole study may be fitted. And Chapter Two, a survey of travel literature to about 1800, should be most revealing, since it attempts something yet unattempted, since the subject is not of such common concern as fiction is, and since it too provides a frame into which the rest of the book will fit more easily. Other chapters, and their arrangement, should need no defense, but each of them, it is to be hoped, will provide new material and offer new ideas for any student—not just of the novel but of all literature and intellectual history.

To me this book has been a rewarding approach to two great literary forms, not a "labor," but a vocation and an avocation, of love. It is a love relationship that began long before my *Travelers and Travel Liars* (1962; 1980) and has resulted in something that, in Chapter Three, is distantly related to that book but which, in its consideration of the wedding of realism and romanticism, of structure, of themes and motifs, of style, has taken different roads and gone much further. If it entices readers to try those roads, perhaps to repave them or to take a road not taken, I shall be pleased. Most travelers prefer companions, especially compatible companions.

Only a few pages of this book have appeared in print—some ten pages on the coach in fiction and travel literature—although certain other sections are reworkings of ideas which I first presented in addresses or published articles. For permission to reuse these pages and ideas, I thank the editors of *Modern Language Notes*, especially Edna Steeves, and Antoinette Shalkoff, who edited the volume of addresses delivered in Alaska in 1978 and entitled *Exploration in Alaska: Captain Cook Commemorative Lectures, June-November 1978*.

While my gratitude to other students of the novel extends to so many people that I cannot name them all, I feel especially grateful in working with travels to point out how valuable to me have been such historians as George Parks, D. B. Quinn, and Boies Penrose for the Renaissance and Edward Heawood and H. W. Frantz for the seventeenth and eighteenth centuries. I feel particularly indebted also to Maximillian Novak and Paul Hunter, whose work with the backgrounds of the novel is a constant source of inspiration; to John Livingstone Lowes, most enthusiastic of admirers of travel literature; to recent scholars such as Charles Batten, Thomas Curley, and Paul Fussell; and to all those who write for *Exploration, Terrae Incognitae*, and the James Ford Bell Library's *The Merchant Explorer*, three journals that do so much with the literature of travel.

And since the writing of this book has taken so many years, it has been expensive and a number of institutions have helped support the cost of the time and travel that have been required. Through the years, for this and related projects, the American Council of Learned Societies has been consistently generous with summer grants; The University of Tennessee has just as consistently helped with travel money from the John C. Hodges Better English Fund; and, most important, the National Endowment for the Humanities provided a Senior Fellowship (1976-77) that assured the completion of my research. To all these I am deeply grateful.

Also through the years I have enjoyed unbelievable assistance from a number of libraries that make the pleasures of research even greater. The Newberry Library, with its wonderful directors Stanley Pargellis and, after his death, Lawrence Towner, was of most help in the early stages of this project. But later I was able to work at the Huntington Library and, many times, at the Bibliothèque nationale and the British Library, while for the past few years I have spent much of every summer at the Yale libraries. All of these institutions, of course, are well equipped with anything having to do with early travel literature or the early novel. And the library at the University of Tennessee, always quick to support my interests and those of other scholars, now has a fine collection of seventeenth- and eighteenth-century travel accounts.

Finally, and as always, I thank my wife Polly for her card filing and note taking, her patience, her willingness to listen and advise and encourage, and, most of all, her ever-keen editorial eye.

CHAPTER ONE

The Amorphous, Prodigious, Evolving Novel – Now and Then

Liberty of the imagination should be the most precious possession of a novelist. To try voluntarily to discover the fettering dogmas of some romantic, realistic, or naturalistic creed in the free work of its own inspiration is a trick worthy of human perverseness which, after inventing an absurdity, endeavors to find for it a pedigree of distinguished ancestors. It is a weakness of inferior minds when it is not the cunning device of those who, uncertain of their talent, would seek to add lustre to it by the authority of a school. *Conrad*[1]

In the fifth chapter of Joyce's *Portrait of the Artist as a Young Man,* Stephen Dedalus, going as far back as Aristotle and the Socrates of the *Republic,* and with help from Hegel and Schelling, divides literature into three "forms"— the lyrical, the epical, and the dramatic—an ancient tripartite division antedating the great nineteenth- and twentieth-century works of prose fiction that have so conditioned our search for an aesthetic of the "novel." But that Stephen's creator did not exclude the novel from membership in his triumvirate and expected it to partake of the nature of each of his "forms" is evidenced by Joyce's 1902 review of a book on George Meredith, who to him lacked both the "lyrical impulse" and the "epical art."[2] And there has been and continues to be a large school of critics that will not allow us to speak of the "novel" as a genre, indeed, that will sometimes refuse us that term for any kind of literature. Austin Warren, for example, questions whether literary kinds are to be differentiated "by their subject matter, their structure, their verse form, their magnitude, their emotional tone, their *Weltanschauung,* or their audience."[3] Croce, perhaps the most extreme of ageneric critics, insists not only that "the distinction of works of literature into kinds [is] an illusion" but also that "Brunetière wasted his brain writing a book on their evolution."[4] As for long fiction, Leonard Lutwack speaks

of the "three genres" of which is composed—"narrative, essay, and drama";
while E.M.W. Tillyard holds that "the novel is not a literary kind but a
vague term denoting at most a prose medium, some pretense of action, a
minimum length, and a minimum of organization."[5] Similarly, the British
fiction writer Basil Creighton has concluded that the novel is no art form
at all, for it has no rules and like Milton's Sin "is continually giving birth to
itself as the last outrage."[6]

In spite of the agenericists, however, readers of literature have tried for
well over three centuries to develop a set of terms, an approach, a poetics
that would permit them to talk intelligently about that long fiction which
most of us call the novel. Recently the journal entitled *Novel* provided four
approaches to the intelligent talk: Malcolm Bradbury's was through structure (1967), David Lodge's through language (1968), Barbara Hardy's
through narrative (1969), and Robert Scholes's through genre (1969).
Scholes, convinced that generic investigation is both "a rigorous intellectual
discipline" and "the most precise and legitimate way into the vexed question
of the intentionality of a work,"[7] finds deficient such "monistic" critics as
Henry James, Booth, Auerbach, and Frye and provides a neat geometric
pattern to describe the evolving, "modal," "ideal" novel, its forms, and their
relations. Based on the theory that there are three chief fictional worlds, "the
degraded world of satire, the heroic world of romance, and the mimetic
world of history," his pattern starts as a straight line:

Satire   history   romance
_____

Then to account for subforms, relationships, and certain evolutionary
changes, Scholes turns his straight line into an acute angle pointing to
history and bisected by the "novel":

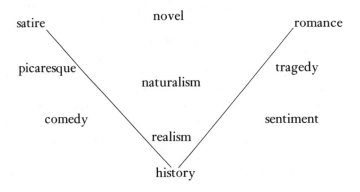

Such diagrammatic analyses are intriguing, but, like any system, this one offers problems. For example, it seems to ignore technique; it omits a favorite historical subform, allegory, as being possible only for the future—somewhere between satire and romance; and it makes no allowance for the contributions of the epic, the drama, or extraliterary forms.

A quite different generic system, and one that has had time to draw even more attacks than that of Scholes, is Northrop Frye's division of fiction into four categories—anatomy, confession, romance, and novel.[8] Like Scholes after him, Frye belabors the Jamesian "novel-centered" approach, hopes his scheme will have the advantage of offering "a simple and logical explanation" for certain works of fiction, and continually demonstrates that nearly any prose fiction is a combination of two or more of his genres, *Ulysses,* for example, being all four as well as "a complete prose epic." Frye's categories have perhaps been talked about and used as points of departure more than they have been adopted.[9]

In defining "novel" any generic critic—no other needs to define it—must employ either an inductive or a deductive method, or a combination of the two. Frye, for example, and Maurice Shroder[10] start with the assumption that certain works of fiction are novels: For Frye, the works of Defoe, Fielding, Austen, and James are central, while *Gulliver's Travels* is not; for Shroder, *Don Quixote, Madame Bovary, The Egoist,* and *The Ambassadors* are "unquestionably novels" while *Pilgrim's Progress* and *Finnegans Wake* do not seem to qualify. Scholes prefers not only to select specific works, as Arnold chose his touchstones, but by resorting to history he would make a collection of empirical facts before arriving at any kind of aesthetic for his "modal" type. But if for Scholes "mode" is all-inclusive and "genre" is reserved for, say, the comic novel or the romance, for other readers there is a problem with terms when we talk about, say, the picaresque, which has so far eluded many of us. After pointing out limitations in three recent prescriptive theories of the picaresque, Maximillian Novak, for example, argues that the picaresque is not a genre but "a universal mode."[11] Furthermore, in selecting touchstone "novels," there is less than unanimity of opinion, as *Tristram Shandy* will illustrate. For Frye, *Tristram* is peripheral, belonging rather to the anatomy; H. R. Steeves and Ian Watt hesitate to call it a novel; Wilbur Cross and others believe its publication set the novel back a hundred years; but the Russian formalist Victor Shklovsky calls it "the most typical novel in world literature."[12] Obviously there is difficulty in defining "novel," even in approaching it.

The schools of criticism that have tried to do so in the twentieth century, and that have succeeded enough to attract intelligent rebuttal and leave an impression, are legion. Some of them need to be examined, even if only briefly, at the beginning of any new study of fiction. One of the most important, from Aristotle to Dryden to now, is that school which has concerned itself primarily with the imitation of nature, with the relating of the artist's techniques to his conception of reality, that is, the mimetic school. Eric Auerbach's seminal *Mimesis* (1946; 1957 in English) provides the term, while Ian Watt's *The Rise of the Novel* (1957), just as seminal for Americans, made famous the expressions "realism of assessment" (Fielding) and "realism of presentation" (Richardson) and provides the most nearly typical mimetic criticism—"philosophic realism" is his term—of the novel, especially the eighteenth-century English novel.[13] For France the extreme mimetic approach has been taken by English Showalter, Jr., who, correctly criticizing Watt for ignoring French fiction, concentrates not on realism, which he wisely believes hard to define, but on five elements of realism the presence of which helps to explain what he calls the evolution of the French novel in the early eighteenth century.[14] In general the mimetics, Watt or Showalter or W.J. Harvey,[15] select their ideal novelists from the nineteenth century —Balzac, Flaubert, and Tolstoy, for example. And almost always they react to, and disagree more or less with, the American formalists, the autonomists, those critics such as Mark Schorer and William Handy who attempt to transfer to fiction the techniques of Brooks and Ransom and other "New Critics" of poetry in order to stress the autonomy of the artifact as art rather than as day-by-day experience.[16] Related to, often overlapping, the methods of the mimetics and the autonomists are the diachronic approach—a dependence on history, background, evolution, and genre—and the syncretic—an emphasis on the whole novel, on its parts, and on individual novels rather than on periods or developments. There are of course other quite different kinds of schools, one of the most influential being the rhetorical, led surely by Wayne Booth, who is neither a mimetic nor a teleologist.[17] And there are also those critics who try, sometimes with pronounced success, to combine methods, perhaps scholarship and criticism, as with E.D. Hirsch, or to emphasize neither form nor content, as with a structuralist such as Tzvetan Todorov, who believes that structuralism has "ceased to isolate a form as the only valuable quality of a work while remaining uninterested in content. A work of art is not a form and a content but a structure of significations whose interrelationships must be understood."[18] If, after noting so many schools of criticism and so many individual critics, we still do not know what a novel is or agree on a way to approach it, we may at least realize that the search for an aesthetics of fiction is now attaining the distinction earlier achieved by the criticism of poetry and drama.

One other problem that has made it difficult for us to define the novel is the debate over the so-called "novel-centered" view of Henry James, in particular his later concern with "playing the game" and using the third-person narrator as a limited center of revelation—a debate that has aroused little interest in non–English-speaking countries, since they have hardly experienced the influence of James. First analyzed and praised inordinately by Joseph Warren Beach (1932) and, particularly, Percy Lubbock (1921) as the ultimate in the evolutionary process, James's concerns were then adopted by those New Critics and formalists who wrote of the novel, such as Mark Schorer. But as early as 1942 Austin Warren cautioned against accepting James's method as the best, or most artistic;[19] and now Wayne Booth and the genre critics, especially those stressing the evolution of what they prefer to call long narrative fiction, are attacking not James's novels themselves but the enshrinement of certain of his theories. These same rebels are in general the ones who also refuse to permit the "novelistic" bias of the mimetics, that is, the notion that nineteenth-century novels are greater art than eighteenth- or even seventeenth-century long fiction. Frye has been such a rebel.

Perhaps the best full-length study to show that the novel is only one form of fiction, and not necessarily the best, is *The Nature of Narrative*, by Robert Kellogg and Robert Scholes.[20] Indebted especially to Frye and Auerbach these two learnedly and wisely trace narrative types through history—oral, mythic, sophisticated—combining studies of form with studies of content and finding that out of the epic, apparently for them the chief ancestor of modern fiction, came two antithetical types of narrative that fed into the novel, the empirical—that is, the historical and mimetic—and the fictional—that is, the romantic and didactic. Unlike Ian Watt, for example, who assumes a sudden birth for the novel in the eighteenth century, treats only the British novel, and is narrowly mimetic,[21] Kellogg and Scholes have demonstrated the slow evolution of fictional forms, have not, like Brunetière, believed change necessarily equivalent to progress, have pushed the emergence of the novel back before 1700, have continually pointed to the international character not only of the novel but of its antecedents and close relatives, and have stressed the fact that the long prose narrative has many faces and many forms.

These conclusions seem most useful as starting points for any new review of the evolution of fiction and the rise of what, hesitantly, is called the novel, especially if one adds to them certain other recent wise conclusions, those, for example, of Ralph Freedman.[22] Like Kellogg and Scholes, Freedman stresses the epic backgrounds and the evolutionary process. He points to specific roots of the novel that "reach down to different layers of soil," its "many strands [that] reach to the most varied layers of time," among these roots and strands being, for example, *The Golden Ass* of the second century, the early prose romance that had its origins in the epic, the picaresque novel, Elizabethan fiction, French romances as different as those of Scudéry and Mme de La Fayette, the English realistic novel, and the Ger-

man romantic novel of Goethe's day. Not only does Freedman reject the
"novelistic" bias but he reminds us at length that when applied to Continental fiction the terms novel and romance become even less clear than for English and American fiction, and he urges, with Schlegel, that the French *roman*, the German *Roman*, and *the novel* be employed in each case as a term for a sort of giant, amorphous genre. This is approximately what Kellogg and Scholes mean when they say that the "novel" is "capable of greater extremes than other forms of literary art, but pays the price for this capability in its capacity for imperfection."[23] And it is also what Henry James meant when he asserted that "The novel remains still . . . the most independent, the most elastic, most prodigious of literary forms."[24]

   If clear terms for this prodigious fiction are hard to find now, they were even more uncertain in the seventeenth and eighteenth centuries, when sociological changes in western Europe—Puritanism, new economic classes, the settlement of the Americas—and a variety of literary types were at work altering the form, the objectives, the content, and the quality of that fiction perhaps as much as they have been altered since. In France *roman*, of much older vintage than *novel* in England,[25] was long employed for any of several literary kinds and was, like the Italian *romanzo*, written either in prose or verse; it was an old type of this early fiction which Tasso compared to the ancient epic romanzo with its shipwrecks and reunions of lovers.[26] Although the earliest long romans were in verse, by the seventeenth century France preferred the term for prose tales of adventure, many of which, from Gomberville's *La Carithée* (1621) to La Calprenède's *Cassandre* (1642-45) to Madeleine and Georges de Scudéry's *Clélie* (last vol. 1660), were of tremendous length, widely read, and quickly translated into other languages, especially into English. But by 1670 Bishop Huet[27] was still, like Tasso, able to differentiate between the old romans and the newer ones. The French *nouvelle*, which for a hundred years competed with *roman* as a term for prose fiction, is, like the Italian *novella*, derived apparently from the plural vulgar Latin *novellus*, perhaps meaning "news" or "noteworthy sayings." And the plural use dominated: Boccaccio in the fourteenth century called his stories *novelle*, for example; and in 1461 the most famous of French collections of short tales was entitled *Cent Nouvelles nouvelles*. For France the impetus to employ the word occasionally for longer fiction and for less romantic fiction came after the first impact of Cervantes, especially of his *Novelas ejemplares*, a collection of tales. Cervantes's bent to burlesque and his use of ordinary people of his day as characters led, for example, quickly to Charles Sorel's imitations in *Nouvelles françaises* (1623) and *Le Berger extravagant* (1628), to a continued use of the term *nouvelle* for noncourtly prose, and to attacks on romances such as the pastoral *L'Astrée* and the courtly *Clélie*. Nevertheless, by the time of Lesage, *nouvelle* meant a short tale, usually in the Cervantean tradition, and *roman* persisted not just as a term in the titles of antiromances such as Scarron's *Le Roman comique* (1651, 1657) or Furetière's *Le Roman bourgeois* (1666) but as the common, generic term for all long fiction of whatever sort, whether used by its detractors—Boileau, for example, in *Les Héros de roman* (written 1665)—or by its defenders—from the Scudérys (1641) to Fontenelle (1687) to Lenglet-Dufresnoy (1734).

In England *romance* was the ancient word that corresponded to *roman* and *romanzo*, and not until late in the seventeenth century did *novel* cross the Channel. At first it was pronounced, as in French, without the stress on the first syllable; and at first it apparently could refer to a short tale or, in the plural, to a collection of short tales, as in the Dedication to a 1656 issue of *Painter's Palace of Pleasure*.[28] There were also late seventeenth-century English uses of the word for long works, just as Mme de Villedieu in France was at the time vacillating between *roman* and *nouvelle* for her book-length stories, which were well known in England. By 1692, for example, Congreve in the Preface to his *Incognita* was attempting to distinguish between *romance* and *novel* and believed his own book-length story to be a novel. But Congreve's word *romance*, pointing to exalted "heroes," "lofty language," "miraculous contingencies, and impossible performances," is really a term one must take back to the distant *romans héroïques* and not to the tales of love and intrigue so popular in the seventeenth and eighteenth centuries. And Congreve's "novel," defined vaguely as "more familiar," with "intrigues in practice," is by no means different from the massive romans as defined by Scudéry or Villedieu. In fact, while Congreve's attempt to create two genres is often compared favorably to that of Clara Reeve (1785) nearly a century later, one sees that his terms are unsure for his day and misleading for ours, especially when we read his words with our biases and when we read his "novel" *Incognita* and find that it is a romance of love and intrigue.[29] At any rate, by 1700 *novel* was a popular, if vague, term and was already feuding with *romance*. For example, in the same year as *Incognita*, Richard Bentley published a collection of short tales which he called "modern Novels," while in the first three years of the eighteenth century each of three collections of long fiction used the word *novel* in its title.[30] But no one seemed to know that "novel" was different from "romance." Often the two were grouped together, as when Shaftesbury, Defoe, and Richardson attacked both; and often when someone like Eliza Haywood called her book a novel, the story is one of marvelous adventures in exotic places, with all the accoutrements of ancient Greek romance except that the characters and places are said to be of the author's own time.[31] The uncertainty over these terms, the feud between them, is often said to have subsided by the time Clara Reeve in the *Progress of Romance* made her now-famous distinction in 1785;[32] but while "novel" has today been accepted by most English readers as all, or almost all, inclusive, there have been in twentieth-century England and America, and continue to be, heated academic debates about "novel" and "romance."

To complicate the problem is the fact that because of all the uncertainty over roman-nouvelle and romance-novel, other terms were found—much as in the twentieth century—that were supposed to help readers and critics speak more clearly of long fiction. While from ancient times the majority of titles of fiction contain no generic word—*Metamorphoses, or The Golden Ass, Utopia, Amadís de Gaula, Arcadia, El Ingenioso Hidalgo Don Quijote* . . . —often some descriptive term was added, especially after the Renaissance when more and more prose tales were being published.[33] One term, *The Life of . . .* , as with the anonymous *La Vida de Lazarillo de Tormes* (1554), was surely given impetus by the early seventeenth-century rash of biographies, especially in France, where *La Vie de Cléopatre, La Vie de Brute,* and lives of other ancients were popular. This generic word is found through the late sixteenth and the seventeenth centuries in such picaresque tales as Quevedo's *La Vida del Buscón* (1626) but also in moralizing tales such as Bunyan's *The Life and Death of Mr. Badman* (1680). In the eighteenth century the word retained its popularity, being used even by Marivaux and Fielding in two quite different kinds of books, *La Vie de Marianne* and *The Life of Mr. Jonathan Wild the Great.*

Certain other terms were sometimes even more popular. With the widespread interest in amorous romances of intrigue and travel, for example, many works of fiction in every European language began with the word "adventures," from the second translation of Heliodorus's *Aethiopica* into French as *Les Adventures amoureuses de Théagenes et Chariclée* (1619) to *Der abenteuerliches Simplicissimus* (1669) to *The Adventures of Roderick Random* (1748). Closely related are other terms, "Travels," "Voyages," even "Rambles," as in the anonymous English *Don Tomaso, or the Juvenile Rambles of Thomas Dangerfield* (1680). And with the rise of biography, autobiography, and first-person narratives—actual and fictional—in the seventeenth century, other terms were included, for example, "Memoirs of . . . ," "Letters of . . . ," "Confessions of . . . ," "The Journal of. . . ." But by far the most popular of generic terms to be found in titles from the Renaissance on was "History," the reason for which will soon be apparent. Of the ten seventeenth-century English stories in a modern collection made by Charles Mish, one title page has "Voyages," one has "Tale," one has "Life," but six title pages have "History." And as one would expect, authors and publishers were not always content to employ just one such term in the title. Quevedo's *La Vida del Buscón,* for example, became in English *The Life and Adventures of Buscon the Witty Spaniard* (1657); in France there were "Mémoires de la vie de . . ." and

"Mémoires pour servir á l'histoire de ..."; and even Fielding wrote *The History of the Adventures of Joseph Andrews*. Yet, in spite of the fact that popular and influential writers such as Defoe and Prévost preferred titles with some identifying—or advertising—term, the great diversity of such terms, coupled with the fact that most titles of fiction went without them, points to the conclusion that long fiction had not only many forms and subforms that were "virtually indistinguishable"[34] but also an uncertain aesthetic.

The forms and subforms were often named then and have often been renamed and reordered since. In 1664 in *La Bibliothèque françoise* Charles Sorel found eight kinds of "romans" for the seventeenth century—fables, allegories, chivalric romances, pastorals, realistic romans, nouvelles, and romans Héroïques ou Comiques. Over a century later, between 1775 and 1789, the largest and most significant of more than 160 eighteenth-century collections of novels in Europe, the *Bibliothèque universelle des romans,* devoted about 30,000 pages of its 224 volumes to seventeenth- and eighteenth-century fiction of many countries and, although erratically, placed each novel in a category.[35] In the twentieth century F.C. Green (1929) in a well-known survey discusses at least ten types of French "novels" for the two centuries. And A.J. Tieje (1912), concentrating on France and England but glancing at other countries, finds six types of prose fiction after 1579 and before 1740 —"the romance, the realistic narrative, the letter-novel, the chronique scandaleuse, the voyage imaginaire, and the frame-work conte-de-fée"; then he divides the "romance" into seven subforms.[36] None of these systems is, of course, satisfactorily inclusive or logical. For example, Green lets the "erotic novel" encompass all amatory fiction; Sorel's category "realistic romans" could include both his "nouvelles," which were not always short, and his "romans comiques," which—as with Scarron's *Roman comique*—were perhaps the most realistic fiction of the time; and Tieje not only classifies by both content and form but at least once combines "realism" with "romance": His "letter-novel" and chronique scandaleuse, for example, could be and often were the same, while the "satiric romance"—*Le Berger extravagant* or *The Female Quixote*—is really a burlesque of romance, an antiromance. Such a variety of fiction, with so many kinds of generic terms in titles, with overlapping and often indistinguishable types, with so much confusion as to what particular writers were trying to do—especially if we note Vivienne Mylne's distinction between a broad "representation" as opposed to a more narrow "realism"[37]—all this would of course make it difficult for critics of the seventeenth and eighteenth centuries to offer, certainly to agree on, a satisfactory poetics of prose fiction.

Nevertheless, there were dozens of writers who between the Renaissance and the nineteenth century made serious, often thoughtful, attempts at analysis. Cervantes was sure that all literature should instruct and that instruction could be combined best with pleasure, but he went further and was just as sure that literature should imitate real, not false, nature. Although he never put all this into a formal poetics, his demonstration in two great works and his opinions found scattered through those works were so widely read and imitated that critics who did try to explain prose fiction formally found him to be one of the best of teachers.[38] An early attempt at such an aesthetic, and one directly indebted to Cervantes, is that of Regnault de Segrais, who in his *Nouvelles françoises* (1656) has a group of ladies distinguish between the nouvelle and the roman, praise certain elements in the roman (meaning the contemporaneous fiction from d'Urfé to Scudéry), list the chief characteristics of the nouvelle, name Cervantes and the Spanish as models, and then end up telling each other "nouvelles" that employ recent incidents, French names, ordinary people, and "things as they are and not as they ought to be."[39] Among the numerous other seventeenth-century writers about fiction as a genre, possible genre, or group of genres were Frenchmen such as the moralist Chapelain, the Scudérys, and Mme de Villedieu, each of whom wrote fiction too, and Bishop Huet and Du Plaisir, who did not—all in addition to Boileau and his satire of the heroes of the roman. England in the sixteenth century had less theory than fine fiction— translations from Greek and Latin, Italian and Spanish; picaresques such as Nashe's *Jack Wilton* (1594); romantic tales such as Sidney's *Arcadia* (1590) and Lodge's *Rosalynde* (1590); and Deloney's histories combined with low- or middle-class life such as *John Winchcourt* (1597) and *Thomas of Reading* (1600). Then in the early seventeenth century England had little of either good fiction or good theory. But after 1650 its prefaces to prose narratives began to imitate the French by trying to explain the author's purpose or defend his book, just as Dryden's dramatic prefaces imitated those of Corneille. There were, for example, the critical prefaces of the two Boyles, Roger (1655) and Robert (1687), of George Mackenzie (1660), and of Congreve (1692).[40] The eighteenth century made this opening comment a practice, both for individual books and for the many large collections; and if the author wrote no preface, the publisher was likely to, especially for reprints or collections of still-popular seventeenth-century fiction. And finally, as eighteenth-century fiction attracted more and more of the better writers— from Lesage and Defoe to Richardson and Rousseau—it attracted more and more critical attention.

From the Renaissance on, criticism of fiction was often part of an attack on or a defense of the romance, the roman, or, when its name had arrived by 1700, the novel. The attack took at least four routes—prose fiction was plain trifling; it was lacking in moral value, even immoral; it was not true, either in reality or in imitation, that is, neither vrai nor vraisemblable; and it confused real history with invented history.

Among those critics who took the first route Sir Philip Sidney feared that *Arcadia* would ruin his reputation, called it "a trifle" he was "loth to father," and, in fact, permitted it only a posthumous birth.[41] A large number of early seventeenth-century French authors of romans refused to acknowledge their works, or signed their initials only, or insisted that they were writing simply for their own amusement or to kill time between more serious occupations. The père de Marcassus, for example, composed *La Clorymène* as "relaxation" between labors on a work of real history, and about the same time the sieur de Claireville wrote *Amelinte* (1635) as a "diversion" while informing us that romans "are never found in libraries."[42] Unlike Sidney, that other great critic Boileau scorned to write prose fiction, which, like Sidney, he called "frivolous."[43] Although by 1721 Jeremy Collier, apparently referring to amorous romances, could still claim that fiction stuffed "the Head with Rubbish," when the best writers took to the form this kind of charge almost completely disappeared, even though early in the eighteenth century it can be found in the translator-editor Desfontaines's apologizing for reviewing romans in his paper—a "genre . . . frivole et Même dangereux" (1731)—and even though later in the century it can be remotely connected with Goldsmith's humorous parody of the "Eastern tale," where "every advance towards sense is only a deviation in sound," or found directly in Jane Austen's young lady ashamed of reading "a novel" (1798).[44]

The charge that prose fiction not only was lacking in moral value but was even immoral has been frequently and thoroughly documented. Often the charge is explained, at least in part, by the rise of Puritanism in England. But while the Puritans did influence attitudes to both drama and fiction of all kinds, countries other than Protestant England, especially Roman Catholic France, produced just as many such attacks. Furthermore, these attacks are ancient, as with Plato's ideal Republic or Boccaccio's regrets in old age that he had written licentious tales, and can be found in the Renaissance when Roger Ascham (1570) denounced translations out of Italian fiction as "enchantments of Circe" any one of which did more harm than "Ten sermons at Paul's cross" did good.[45] In France, Bishop Camus (1620s) wrote prefaces for his many romans urging other writers to turn from immoral, unchristian fiction and to follow his lead in publishing only exemplary stories, while de Grenailles (1640) condemned vicious, "seductive" love plots.[46] As time went by, this particular attack was more and more restricted to individual works of fiction or to certain types of fiction, usually the amatory ones. Thus *Pamela*, with its erotic scenes and its heroine's supposed hypocrisy, brought on a rash of anti-Pamelas, while the erotic scenes in *Tom Jones* caused the followers of Richardson, including Samuel Johnson, to berate Fielding as lewd. Thus in 1728 the marquise de Lambert could warn in *Avis d'une mère à sa fille* that "The reading of romans is dangerous"; Montesquieu could find *Manon Lescaut* full of wicked acts; Rousseau in his first preface to *La Nouvelle Hélöise* could say that "no chaste girl has ever read a roman"; and Voltaire, even if facetiously, could condemn the secret desires aroused by such stories.[47]

That prose fiction was considered by its detractors—and its supporters —to be a lie has been documented even more thoroughly and will be a matter of major concern in a later chapter, but the charge that its use, or misuse, of history caused readers to become confused has not been so thoroughly demonstrated. Although people such as Roger Boyle with his *Parthenissa* (1654-69) wrote fiction with confused history, this charge is not found so often in England as in France, which from the early seventeenth century produced a mass of romances ostensibly or actually based on history. The most important example of concern over a misuse of history is probably that of Pierre Bayle, who, as Paul Hazard has been only one to note, was campaigning hard at the end of the seventeenth century for a new philosophy of history, one that would check sources, eliminate hearsay, and destroy superstition, lies, and credulity.[48] Bayle's chief target among the romance writers was his contemporary Mme de Villedieu, who, he complained—forgetting the earlier Gombervilles and Scudérys—"opened the door to a license being abused more and more every day," that is, the license of "mixing" love intrigues with "facts that have a slight foundation in history." Such a practice, Bayle was sure, made it easy for young people to be seduced into believing that falsehoods are real—as if, he said, the "real" historians from Herodotus on had not caused enough trouble.

Each of these charges of course elicited a defense—in fact, many defenses—since so many people wrote fiction and so many more read it. If, for example, Chapelain might claim that romans were for "women and courtiers," other seventeenth-century Frenchmen—including priests, even bishops such as Camus and Fénelon—would write them and still others defend them.[49] By the eighteenth century, English Showalter demonstrates, all French novelists read many "novels" and defended their own. The defenses were, of course, seldom born out by what followed in the books. Lesage gave "man's life as it is"; the abbé Prévost offered only "real" autobiographies that inculcated virtue and Christian principles; and Marivaux's *La vie de Marianne*, which Fielding and Richardson knew so well, was a "true" story —not a roman—that arrived in its editor's hands by strange circumstances, a claim, a device, popular for a hundred years, as with Mme de Villedieu and Swift and as with Mackenzie in *The Man of Feeling* and Chateaubriand in *Atala*.

In England also many people read fiction—Samuel Johnson and Joseph Warton even recommended "romances"—and the chief apologists for its various kinds were writers of fiction themselves.[50] The spectrum of such apologists had a broad range. There were compilers of criminal stories, such as Francis Kirkman (1673) and Richard Head (1674), who argued the advantages of exposing vice. There were the authors of historical romances, such as the Boyles (1655, 1687), who claimed to present "bright ideas of heroic virtue" and, somewhat like Bayle later, believed that histories themselves are "for the most part mixt-Romances." And, finally, there were those first-rate eighteenth-century writers who defended their own special brand of writing—not, of course, they insisted, to be confused with "romances" or "novels." Among these last were Defoe (1722) with his true "private histories," Fielding (1742) with his "hitherto unattempted species of writing" where "every thing is copied from the Book of Nature," and Richardson (1751) with his attempting "something that never yet had been done" and complaining (1748) when Warburton called *Clarissa* "fiction."

Especially in France and England of the seventeenth and eighteenth centuries one can find hundreds of statements about prose fiction, from short notices to prefaces of varying length, to formal essays associated with no particular book, some of which are attacks, far more of which are apologia, and all of which provide a considerable body of commentary from which a serious, if primitive, poetics of fiction can be extracted.[51] It is, of course, a poetics that evolves, that differs in some ways from person to person depending on national or religious or philosophical background, or on the subform being considered; but it is also one that is surprisingly consistent for readers and critics of two countries so unlike as England and France. Among the most frequently advanced theories, certain ones stand out as being either popular for that period or intriguing for our own.

First, in spite of the commonplace dismissal of fiction as trifling, there is the pleasure principle; that is, pleasure is a good in itself. Maurice Magendie offers us telling examples that this was an acknowledged and accepted aim of the roman in seventeenth-century France, as with Le Vayer de Boutigny, whose Epistre to his *Mithridate* (1651) "establishes that, even if the roman contributes only to our pleasure, it is worthy of our esteem."[52] A little later, in England, the prominent and brilliant Dorothy Osborne was consuming all the French and English romances she could lay her hands on and, what is more, sending them on to her brilliant friend Sir William Temple: "If you have done with the first part of *Cyrus* [by Scudéry]," she told him, relay it on to "Mr. Hollingsworth," and, she continued, "let me assure you that the more you read of them you will like them still better." Of course, Bussy-Rabutin's *L'Histoire amoureuse des Gaulles* (1665), Hamilton's *Mémoires de la vie du comte de Gramont* (1713), and all such chroniques scandaleuses had no other aim than pleasure even if Hamilton might suggest that a second motive was a desire to set the facts straight about his famous brother-in-law. By 1770 Charles Jenner, a better theoretician than a novelist, could sum up the pleasure principle most adequately, first by sneering at the "sour critics" who bemoan "this trifling, novel-reading age," and second by asserting that when life is so "full of cares and anxieties" one is justified in regarding novels simply as "pleasing and innocent amusements."

Pleasure was for many readers not only a good intrinsically but one that led to others—for example, instruction and moral edification. Instruction to some theorists, especially in the seventeenth century, meant the teaching of history by putting it in an attractive romance, from Gerzan and his "short" *Histoire africaine* (1627-28) to the authors of the romans de longues haleines to, say, George Mackenzie and, in Defoe's day, Mary Manley. Mackenzie speaks for this group when he writes in his preface to *Aretina* (1660), "I am confident that where Romances are written by excellent wits and perused by intelligent readers that the judgement may pick more sound information from them than from History." For, he continues, paraphrasing Aristotle, history "teacheth us only what was done, and the other what should be."[53] But even before the seventeenth century, instruction had more and more to do with the presentation of contemporaneous, and not ancient, history— that is, with manners, with the imitation of nature in the perennial sense of the word, and, consequently, with moral values. Erasmus and Vives, for example, in addition to Ascham, disapproved of prose fiction unless its function "was the direct presentation of ideal modes of conduct"; and later Elizabethan fiction, including the "anatomy" of "wit" or "fortune" by such writers as Greene and Lyly, was often intended—it said—to show the reader what not to do.[54] In the 1620s Bishop Camus, an extreme example, published some thirty exemplary novels with settings in his own century, while the pious Bunyan later allegorized the Christian's journey to salvation and the Badman's descent to hell. Most didactic fiction was of course not so blatantly thesis-ridden as Bunyan's: Even Bishop Camus over and over pointed out that the mass of people could be led and taught more quickly by sermons disguised under ingenious plots of love and adventure. This emphasis on a moral aim survived through the eighteenth century with nearly all the writers then and now well known. Defoe and Richardson in England are only two who averred that their novels taught the horrors of vice or the rewards of virtue, and even the erotic novels of Mrs. Manley are prefaced by such claims as "they have some tract of morality which may engage virtue" or "although vice be not always punished, yet 'tis described with reasons which shew to deformity" (1705, preface to *Queen Zarah*). Likewise, as Georges May and others have shown, Prévost, Mouhy, Marivaux, Crébillon, and Rousseau are only some eighteenth-century French "novelists" who professed a moral intent.[55]

But another kind of instruction was becoming popular and, at the same time, attractive to theorists. The attack by Cervantes on *Amadis de Gaula* and its fellows had been preceded by attacks of Vives and Erasmus on the bawdy and blood and the larger-than-life Lancelot of the *Morte d'Arthur*. The ridicule of the unreal pastoral romances that is found in the last part of *Don Quixote* was quickly followed by Sorel's burlesque *Berger extravagant* (1627), which ridiculed the false life of his contemporary d'Urfé's *L'Astrée* much more than it did the excesses of ancient pastorals such as *Daphnis and Chloë*. The English heroic drama, which flourished vigorously for fifteen years after the Restoration, claimed Achilles as a model, borrowed heavily from French prose romances, and hoped to arouse "admiration," but its lack of reality was quickly exposed by *The Rehearsal* (1671). Molière's internationally prominent bourgeois plays and the Restoration British comedy burlesqued extravagancies in life and art on the one hand and staged life as it was on the other. And, finally, fictionized criminal and rogue biographies, especially after 1660 and especially in England, more and more supplanted tales of heroism, just as, at the same time, the supposedly middle-class nouvelle was waging a war with the courtly roman before being absorbed by it. All of this is part of the long history of the classic theory that art must imitate nature.

That is, it must be realistic, vraisemblable; it must depict the normal acts, motives, emotions of people who are real or at least believable. Such a theory of literature is closely related to the demand for instruction, whether in secular or religious matters, since it was felt by the Erasmuses, the Cervantes, the Sorels, and the Samuel Johnsons that, on the one hand, readers of fiction are contaminated by extraordinary adventures that seduce them into fantasy but that, on the other, they are informed about the true world, its customs, virtues, and vices by their vicarious existence in fiction that is credible, immediate. Because of the influence of Cervantes and Sorel, so strong in French fiction after 1620 but not fully felt in stirfe-torn England until after 1660, by the middle of the seventeenth century almost every author of a roman or a nouvelle paid at least lip service to the demand for realism. With some writers, such as the Scudérys, who proposed (1641) vraysemblance as the chief aim of a writer of romans, the word meant a superficial use of historical names and settings and perhaps a placing of the author's contemporaries, thinly disguised, in the fiction as characters.[56] Chapelain (1647), in fact, argued that a writer of fiction should "represent" his characters as "conforming to the customs and beliefs of" the writer's own century.[57] As so many historians have noted, however, the most realistic—that is, representational—seventeenth-century works of fiction are to be found in popular, and sometimes excellent, subtypes, among which are the burlesque or anti-roman such as Sorel's *L'Anti-roman, ou le Berger extravagant* (1627), Scarron's *Roman comique* (1651, 1657), or Furetière's *Roman bourgeois* (1660), the picaresque, such as Quevedo's *El Buscón* (1626), Grimmelshausen's *Simplicissimus* (1668), or Head's *The English Rogue* (1665); and the criminal—usually worse

than rogue—"biographies" that led in England "down" from the Jack Wil-
tons (1594), the Mary Carletons (1673), and Thomas Dangerfields (1680) to
Defoe's denizens of Newgate and pirates of Madagascar. Such a realism, as
Ronald Paulson shows, is of course almost as special as the superficial historical realism of a Scudéry, since it "attacks idealization by means of a counter-
reality based on exaggerated probability. . . . Thus the ugly and gross, the
sensual and fecal, are real in contrast to the beautiful and harmonious."[58] But
while such an exaggeration has continued through "Naturalism" to our own
day, with the nouvelles of the late seventeenth century and the "histories"
of Marivaux and Fielding, the bourgeois and commonplace, although themselves often gross and fecal, substituted more and more for the noble and
extraordinary.

The display of, the claim for, a strong move to closer representation in
fiction has often been linked to the "steady and universal move toward a new
science, a new realism, a new middle-class stage audience and reading public."[59] That is to say, whether or not the word "nouvelle" had ever been
thought of, one may conclude that fictional protagonists would have
steadily descended to the bourgeois class and become the thousand eighteenth-century versions of what we now call the antihero. Furthermore, in
all this confused movement, the time-honored literary forms were also being
affected by changes in theory and practice. Voltaire, for example, attacked
(1727) rigid theories of the epic, including the idea that heroes should be like
Achilles, as did Samuel Johnson, who was perhaps as ageneric as a critic can
be. And George Lillo in the seminal preface to *The London Merchant* (1731)
argued against Aristotle's highborn hero and for a hero like ourselves, one
with whom we can empathize, an argument found in other eighteenth-
century plays, including one by the Spaniard Solano y Lobos. It is this
demand for a new realism that Georges May sees as encountering the old
demand for morality and producing the "dilemma" which he finds fiction
facing about 1700. And it is this new science, this new realism, that has led
some critics to a false notion of the age and of its art.

That is to say, we have been told, far too often and not just by William
Blake, that from Dryden and Descartes to Voltaire and Hume western
Europe promoted reason so much that the imagination was stifled. A corollary has been that fiction was striving so hard to be "true" that it especially
eschewed imagination. A.J. Tieje, who knew perhaps as much as anyone
about early prose fiction, was one victim of that theory when—like A.D.
McKillop—he argued curiously that "non-fictionists apparently believed in
the imagination" but fictionists seldom upheld it,[60] and he cited Sidney's
Defense of Poesie as a starting point.

But, in fact, fictionists then, as always, not only had imagination, with
all its elements, but talked about it constantly and defended it openly. Surely

Sidney's praise of the poet's "invention" and "wit" can be applied to his own *Arcadia*, and a survey of the seventeenth-century French roman shows that nearly every writer of romans and every critic of them employed the word "invention."[61] The sieur de Gerzan described his historical romances as "inventions" made to conform to "true history"; La Calprenède applauded his own "inventive skill"; the Scudérys defined the stories they wrote as "webs" of "falsehood and truth" woven by "a dexterous hand," a mixture of history and invention; Chapelain used the word "inventer"; and Bishop Camus insisted on the *véritable* in his romans but believed that his "artifices" and "inventions surpass by far" whatever was actually borrowed. In England, as in France, "imagination," or "wit," or "invention," or "fancy" was an important behest from Quintilian and Longinus via numerous Drydens and Popes, or via Hobbes with his "celerity of imagining." So it would be surprising if one did not find Mackenzie praising the Scudérys for their "invention," or Mrs. Manley (1705) composing "History" to her "fancy," or Mrs. Davys (1725) calling "invention" an "advantage," or Fielding listing "invention" along with "judgment," "learning," and "a good heart" as essential to the "genius" who writes "histories" such as his. Even when a defensive writer of fiction such as Grandchamp asserted that the "gallanteries" of his *Guerre d'Italie* (1710) "owe nothing" to his "imagination," he meant in fact that they owe all to it.

And on into the eighteenth century went the French as well as the English appeal to the imagination. The Chevalier de Mouhy was sure that "of all genres [preface to *Le Financier*, 1755], that of the novel is most difficult since it demands great imagination and originality," while Johnson everywhere insisted that "imagination" and "invention" were the first and absolute prerequisites for that ideal "genius" whose memory is stored with images from books and "life."[62] The writers of fiction, then, like all critics of the time, were proud of their inventive powers and believed them indispensable even before their medium was beginning to achieve a respect comparable to that accorded epic and drama. Nor is there a dilemma here, a conflict between the imagination and the attempt to represent reality; for the harder one strives to create something lifelike, the more one's inventive skills are taxed: It is not just the fictionizer dealing with fairies or giants who exercises an imagination.

The ability to provide pleasure, moral edification, and instruction in history and manners, the talent to represent current reality, and the possession of invention, wit, imagination—these are the chief ingredients of the aesthetic of fiction as it left the seventeenth and traveled on through the eighteenth century, but there are others. From the 1620s theorists promoting or simply recognizing current trends argued about, or analyzed, the differences between the "old" and the "new" romantic tale. Or they fought over the merits of the "former" and the "present" fiction. These debates reflect not only the concern over what long fiction should be called but also the changing nature of long fiction. Also, closely related to theories about verisimilitude and the "new" fiction were the new, sometimes conflicting, theories about style. As early as 1610 an anonymous author of a love story attacked "affected diction" because it "destroys belief"; George Mackenzie (1660) discoursed at length on four kinds of style before commenting on his own; Robert Boyle (1682) defended his dialogue as being derived from the historians; Perdou de Soubligny wrote an apologia (1671) for French rather than classical names; while Mrs. Manley begged for "sweet" sounding rather than "barbarous" names; and almost every bourgeois first-person narrator in an age of such narrators defended or extolled a simple, homely way of writing, that is, the voice of "plain truth."[63]

All such minor ingredients of the poetics of early fiction, coupled with those more nearly universal or significant ones, lead to an intriguing and, for any period of history, an expected fact: As the seventeenth and eighteenth centuries were searching for names for an evolving, elusive fictional form, producing examples of it, discussing its elements, attacking or defending it, there arose early and continued late the cry for a set of rules by which it should or could operate. The epic had rules supposedly known to everyone, and so did tragedy and comedy. And it was the epic to which the rule seekers or givers most often referred, from the Scudérys to Fielding. Bishop Huet near the end of the seventeenth century, for example, announced that the "regular" roman conformed to the "règles du poéme héroïque" [the epic].[64] But then Fielding made comparisons with dramatic comedy also, as did Sorel before him and Johnson after him.[65] Seventeenth-century French fiction consistently shows this early longing for a set of rules, for over and over one meets its authors speaking of "les règles des vrais romans," "les préceptes des vrays romans," "les romans parfaits," "les règles du roman."[66] Such a persistent belief that prose fiction should be a genre with a set of standards was, of course, a natural product of centuries of training that emphasized Aristotle and Horace. But since Aristotle and Horace had not pontificated about prose fiction, the seventeenth and eighteenth centuries were forced to seek their own rules for an old but freshly burgeoning and popular form with a Joseph's coat of many changing colors.

The search and the longing were there, but they often seemed futile: The fault, or the glory, of this elusive genre—if it was a genre—was its inability to conform to restrictions, lie quietly in confinement, obey rules. In the mid-seventeenth century Corneille in the second *Discours* to his works (1660) complained, not much to be sure, that while drama has certain controls of time and place which it must recognize, the roman has none of these "restraints" to worry about. Even earlier a French writer of fiction was

admitting that he had refused to follow the "rules" of the "true roman"—
whatever he thought they were—because he preferred to observe a pure
"vérite."[67] Some French writers even suggested certain of these rules.
Georges and Madeleine de Scudéry (*Ibrahim*, 1641), who often compared
their romans to epics, believed that characters should observe decorum in
their speech and that "among all the rules that these works must observe,
vraisemblance is without doubt the most important," while the author
of *Axiane* (1647), although urging the necessity of "imagination," wanted it combined with "judgment" and "reason." These "rules," of course,
go back to the ancients and would have served for any mode of literature, but that very fact shows that many seventeenth-century writers
of romans were trying to associate their creations with forms well established.

That was true also of the prose fiction of the eighteenth century,
whether in France or England, although less so since it was attaining more
respectability as it attracted more great writers. Or were the great writers
attracted because it was more respectable? In 1725, for example, the prolific
Mary Davys, with Cervantes, Mme de La Fayette, Defoe, and a host of other
critics of fiction before her, was able in the first edition of her collected
works to set down her own prescription, even though the last clause may
not apply to her amorous stories so well as it could. "I have," she said,
borrowing from Aristotle on the epic, "in every Novel proposed one entire
scheme or plot, and the other adventures are only incidental or collateral to
it, which is the great rule prescribed by the criticks, not only in tragedy and
other heroic poems but in comedy too. The adventures, as far as I could
order them, are wonderful and probable; and I have with the utmost justice
rewarded virtue and punished vice." In 1739 d'Argens, author of fiction as
well as criticism, in an essay that in part echoes the late-seventeenth-century
Du Plaisir (1683), pointed out the limitations of the nouvelle while at the
same time stressing its freedom.[68] The anonymous British author of *Constantia* (1751), appealing to the example of "the wise" Cervantes and referring to six critics of the seventeenth century—all French—wrote a fine
critical preface based on the theory that "there is certainly no kind of
writing ... that does not fall under some sort of rules," among which, we
are told, are these: the "novel" is "a sort of artificial experience"; its "principal object" is to entertain so that "the judgment may be the better disposed
to receive instruction"; it should impress "right principles, with respect to
virtue, good sense, and good manners"; and as a form it is permitted certain
"liberties" that, however, should be kept within "due bounds."[69] There were
others, such as Charles Jenner (1770), who tried lengthy poetics of the novel
without admitting always to those "liberties" that from Corneille to the
author of *Constantia* the fiction writers seemed to take.

But while they often, and as with "virtue" and "vice" sometimes monotonously, overlapped, the elements of these poetics did not become crystallized. Each new successful author was likely to alter the pattern some readers may have begun to accept, for the great "rule" of Pope and Johnson was—as with any period—not only the wisest but the most popular:

> If, where the rules not far enough extend,
> (Since rules were made but to promote their end)
> Some lucky License answer to the full
> Th'intent proposed, that License is a rule.
> *Essay on Criticism* (146-49)

Thus, the satiric allegory of a Cervantes gave way to La Fayette's soul searching and that to the secret mémoires of Courtilz and d'Aulnoy and those to Lesage's picaresque and that to *Manon*, Prévost's tale of the world well lost for love, and that to many different types of novels by such writers as Marivaux and Rousseau and Diderot. Thus, Defoe's first-person studies of whores and criminals gave way to Richardson's letters from besieged virgins and these to Fielding's third-person analyses of manners or Smollett's many kinds of traveling protagonists. Finally, all these made room for the most nearly unique of all, Sterne and his "digressive" but "progressive" *Tristram Shandy*—"anti-novel" or "most nearly typical"? And so, as these players in the game of fiction came and went, it was impossible for the ground rules to remain the same; for each of these players, whether great or mediocre, wanted his "liberties" more or less. By the time of Rousseau and the late Smollett, then, it is not at all surprising to find Elizabeth Griffith, author of *The Delicate Distress* (1769), admitting in her preface, "I know not whether novel, like the épopée, has any rules peculiar to itself"; or, two years later another novelist happily chortling, "I hug myself when I think ... how fortunate it is for us ... Life-writers, that no modern Aristotle has stept forth, and laid down Rules ... like the Unities of Action, Time, and Place, prescribed by the Ancients to all dramatic Writers"; or, at the end of the century (1795), the well-known dramatist Richard Cumberland, who also wrote novels, declaring that he will handle his fictional "puppets" as he sees fit because "it is only in the professed department of the novel that true and absolute liberty is enjoyed."[70] Obviously, then, while it may not be quite true, as it has been said, that by 1700 the world of fiction was in chaos,[71] neither novelists nor critics of the seventeenth and eighteenth centuries, although they tried, could agree completely on what had happened to fiction or was happening. And in spite of our twentieth-century sophistication, in spite of the sometimes brilliant exponents of one or another of the modern schools of poetics, the world of fiction inhabited by Sterne and Diderot was probably no nearer chaos than our own.

A number of facts are now apparent, one being that any study of the "novel" of the seventeenth and eighteenth centuries cannot, any more than for the twentieth, restrict itself to a single country. No one of course can hope to know all fiction of all countries for a given period, but from Cervantes to Goethe, the fiction of Spain, Germany, and Italy is relatively inconsiderable even though there are noteworthy exceptions, an occasional Grimmelshausen or Villaroel (1743 ff.), for example. With France and England, however, the story is different. Louis XIV, Charles II, and their successors not only fielded great armies and launched huge navies but led Europe in fashions, transportation, and the arts. It was perhaps in the sciences that the Low Countries, Germany, Italy, even the Scandanavian nations were able to compete best. And between France and England there was a lively exchange of works of fiction, an exchange that has often been, and is still being, documented.[72] Without doubt it was the Spanish *Don Quixote* that was most widely read and that influenced more fiction writers than did any other work.[73] Often its influence operated in mysterious ways, not just directly on a Sorel or a Fielding but indirectly, as when Mrs. Lennox wrote *The Female Quixote* (1752) by making some use of Marivaux's *Don Quichotte moderne* (1712; 1737), not the original French but the translation by John Lockman, called *Pharsamond, or the Knight Errant* (1749).

The prevalence of this kind of cross-Channel exchange of fiction can be easily suggested: Mrs. Haywood, author of nearly forty novels, early in the eighteenth century translated not only Bandello but six French "romances"; Mme d'Aulnoy's works were translated into English more than fifty times after 1690 and were known not only by Mrs. Manley and Defoe but by Mrs. Radcliffe much later; Daniel Mornet's analysis of 392 private libraries shows that in France the fiction of England was more popular than was French fiction for the two middle decades of the eighteenth century; in *Tom Jones,* Fielding (XIII, i) named eight masters, six of whom were not English and one of whom was the French novelist Marivaux; and the influence of Goldsmith, Sterne, and Richardson in France is as well known as that of Scudéry, Prévost, and Rousseau in England. Maximillian Novak is only one to emphasize that "The kind of nationalism we carry into the study of literature has little place in the period between 1660 and 1730," a conclusion that is just as apt for the rest of the eighteenth century.[74]

Another apparent conclusion is that fiction was experiencing important changes in content, technique, and theory after Cervantes and before 1800. And in fact the thesis that the "modern novel" came into existence during the eighteenth century is as standard as almost any thesis concerning the evolution of literary forms. The historians of the novel have consistently advertised it, in France from Le Breton to Green to May and in Britain and the United States from Cross to Baker to Wagenknecht, the last of whom echoes most of the English-speaking world when he says that "With Richardson and Fielding the eighteenth-century novel is firmly established."[75] This is the assumption behind H. R. Steeves's contention that "At the beginning of the eighteenth century there was no novel. By the end novels of every description were being published"; and it is the assumption behind Ian Watt's *The Rise of the Novel*—the title really means, one should note, just the English novel.[76] And for France, Maurice Magendie had long before pointed out that no important French writer of the seventeenth century had produced a *roman*.

There have, however, always been rebels who protested the thesis. In spite of Ian Watt's assuming, he says, "as is commonly done, that [the novel] was begun by Defoe, Richardson, and Fielding" (p. 9), two generations earlier A.J. Tieje (1912) had thought that "at the present day few historians of literature adjudge *Pamela* to be the first of English 'novels.'" But for his own day Tieje was of course not agreeing with, say, Walter Raleigh.[77] Since then, with writers such as Frye, Paulson, and Kellogg and Scholes, the protests from English-speaking critics have increased in number and intensity. Usually the protests assume one of two forms—the English did not write the first "novel"; or the novel is only one kind of prose narrative that can be traced far back and that in fact is not even necessarily the best of fiction or the culmination of some teleological process. Although historians of Continental fiction have been as insular as the English and Americans, the French have correctly pointed out that not only did Marivaux precede Richardson but that Lesage preceded Defoe. Moreover, a fine case can be, and often has been, made for Mme de La Fayette as the first modern novelist, since her *Princesse de Clèves* (1678)—sometimes dismissed as a "nouvelle" or a "romance"—is such an attractive psychological analysis of the anguish of a married woman in love with a man other than her husband. Far less tenable is the thesis of one prominent French historian of the late nineteenth century who began his book with the dogmatic assertion that d'Urfé's *L'Astrée* (1610 ff.) "is truly our first novel; it is the ancestor, the source of all the others."[78] Here is an opinion that has never caught on or caused the conflict in France that is found in England and America as to whether Defoe wrote "novels" or not. And of course the historians of ancient literature, even if they agree that the *Aethiopica* and its huge family are romances, will argue cogently that at least Apuleius's *Metamorphoses, or The Golden Ass* and Petronius's *Satyricon* must be called novels.[79] Such arguments often lead us back to the defensive term "the first modern novel."

The most popular current contender for that title is *Don Quixote*, perhaps for four reasons. First, its intrinsic merit was recognized even in its own day; and since then its genius for realism, satire, sentiment, and allegory has become more and more apparent. Second, because of its instant success with all classes of readers, it became for two hundred years by far the most influential prose fiction work ever written, even competing early with the *Aethiopica* and such epics as *Gerusalemme liberata* (1581) and perennially with those of Homer and Virgil. Third, it satisfied the search for a model to fit the theory of critics such as Ortega y Gasset that the "novel" was born of a conflict between the tradition of romance and the tradition of realism, a conflict that transformed each. And fourth, it also fits the thesis—supported by Ronald Paulson and, before him, by certain Russian formalists such as Eichenbaum—that history, as in a cycle, produces some great pieces of literature, then there is a decline, then parodic forms arise to expose the decline, then, as a result, a fresh approach is opened up that permits new life, new forms.[80]

To promote *Don Quixote* as the first modern novel, however, still offends such historians as Lionel Stevenson (31), who denies it that title because he says it lacks unity and a "primary purpose of creating an illusion of reality"; and while its enthronement satisfies some of the other theories about the sudden birth, the renaissance, the rebirth, the rise, or the beginnings of the novel in the seventeenth and eighteenth centuries, it does not satisfy them all. One modern novelist is sure that the novel "is the child of the epic, not the offspring of the theatre," which has too many unities to worry about, a theory that is one of the most popular, as with E.M.W. Tillyard.[81] Just as certain is Ortega y Gasset that to derive the novel from the epic is to misunderstand the changes that took place in the eighteenth century, that in fact "the novel and the epic are poles apart." Maurice Shroder also, but hesitantly, rejects the epic and derives the novel from "the romance of the Middle Ages and the Renaissance," while Austin Warren finds the novel "polar" to the romance. Gustave Kahn and Walter Raleigh turn from the romance, in one case, to favor the contes philosophiques of Swift and Voltaire and, in the other, to say that the great influences of the seventeenth century, "the foundations it laid for the coming novel, are to be sought, not in the writers of romance, but in the followers of other branches of literature, often remote enough from fiction, in satirists and allegorists, newspaper scribes and biographers, writers of travel and adventure, and fashionable comic playwrights. For the novel least of all forms of literature can boast a pure extraction; it is of mixed and often disreputable ancestry," coming not just from literature but from "life" (108).

This wise old conclusion of Walter Raleigh, if we forget its dismissal of the "romance" and note certain omissions, is still the most nearly acceptable one for most students of the novel. For it allows room for those historians who, like Steeves, believe that "the history of the novel is a history of quick growth, quick because in some respects it is no more than the adaptation and fusion of other and well-matured forms . . . an assembled rather than

an invented artistic form" (2); and it can make room for both the mimetics
and American formalists, even for those who, like Watt, would emphasize
sociological rather than literary antecedents. It will not, however, please
certain other historians, for example, Kellogg and Scholes, who in *The Nature of Narrative* (16) insist that their intention is not, in fact, "to view the
novel as the final product of an ameliorative evolution, as the perfected form
which earlier kinds of narrative—sacred myth, folktale, epic, romance, legend, allegory, confession, satire—were all striving, with varying degrees of
success, to become." Their hope, they conclude, is to put the "novel" in its
place as only one of many forms of narrative. But actually the thesis of *The
Nature of Narrative* is not so far from that old one of Raleigh or the new
one of Steeves, for it does dwell at length on the types of fiction—if not so
much on the nonfiction—that preceded the seventeenth- and eighteenth-
century varieties.

From all these facts and theories we may now suggest three on which
we hope to have some measure of agreement. First, the novel can include
many kinds of narratives—"romantic," allegorical, epical, dramatic, even
lyrical. Thus, not only are *Don Quixote*, *La Princesse de Clèves*, and *Robinson
Crusoe* novels but so are *Clarissa*, *Tom Jones*, *Tristram Shandy*, *Ulysses*, and
The Castle, and so are *The Golden Ass*, *Lazarillo*, Robbe-Grillet's *La Jalouise*,
and Nabokov's *Pale Fire* with its forty pages of verse couplets. It is indeed
past time to stop whipping the dead horse called the "novel-centered" theory
attributed to Henry James.[82] Second, as in science, "evolution" means simply change, formation of new species from old, and not progression toward
a more advanced species.[83] Thus, *Clarissa* or *Tom Jones*, surely *Don Quixote*,
may be as "great" as anything by Melville, Dostoevsky, Mann, or Faulkner.
And third, as Eichenbaum and Shevierev, the Russian formalists, as well as
Raleigh and Maximillian Novak and English Showalter, agree, the hundreds
of seventeenth- and eighteenth-century novels had hundreds of contributing
antecedents in the literary and extraliterary forms of their day and earlier.
One of the most important and most neglected of the forms that fed this
"insatiable organism" was the literature of travel, which could be either
literary or nonliterary or both. Before demonstrating that fact, however,
one needs quickly to glance at those other contributing forms and subforms,
the contributions of most of which have been studied. Such a glance may
help one to maintain a perspective and to remember that contributions
frequently overlap or make their way by indirection.

The first of these forms is the epic, which has had much to do with the
evolution of both ancient and modern prose fiction. We need not agree that
Don Quixote was the first modern novel, but we do need to remember that
Cervantes, echoing his countryman El Pinciano, believed an "epic can be
written in prose as well as in verse," that Byron called *Don Quixote* a "real

epic," and that the term "epic" has become firmly entrenched as a common-place of literary criticism dealing with certain kinds of novels.[84] For exam-ple, from James Beattie to Thackeray to the twentieth century, dozens of readers have agreed with its author that *Tom Jones* is a prose epic; and many of us, with the Hegel-Lukacs school, have no doubt accepted that term, not just for *Tom Jones* but for *War and Peace, Moby Dick, Ulysses,* Sholokov's Don trilogy, and Faulkner's trilogy of the Snopes family.[85] But there is confu-sion. Not only do we remember Ortega y Gasset's "The novel and the epic are poles apart," but Tillyard in his full-length study of the "Epic Strain" in British fiction denies that *Tom Jones* is an epic, preferring to apply the term to *Robinson Crusoe,* while at a famous three-day gathering of the agrarians in 1956 Cleanth Brooks announced, and then defended, the star-tling opinion that for America Hemingway "is about as close to being an epic as we have."[86]

The really great disagreement as to what the epic may have done for the novel, or to which novels, can be attributed to at least three facts: first, the arguments over whether the novel was born, or fused, in the seventeenth and eighteenth centuries or whether it slowly evolved through many centu-ries; second, the so-called novel-centered view of the novel that often limits the term to writers in the La Fayette-Richardson-James tradition, that is, to those who are never associated with the epic; and third, our perennial inability to determine what the epic itself is. Recent scholarship like that of Parry and Lord has placed so much emphasis on the oral, bardic qualities, the formulaic nature, of the *Iliad* and the *Odyssey* that the reigning fashion, at least during the 1950s and 1960s, almost denies the term epic to anything put down on paper by a sophisticated writer, even the *Aeneid* being reluc-tantly included.[87] The fact that there is a recent fashion is typical of our literary heritage, for we now know how theories of the epic have changed, how—like the novel—it has evolved, how elusive the term has been and still is: Virgil was no slavish imitator, the sixteenth-century Italians made their own tradition, Milton's Christian epic is yet more original, Dante's *Divine Comedy* was an epic to the nineteenth century, and even the *Iliad* and the *Odyssey* are marvelously unlike each other.[88]

What is important for the study of seventeenth- and eighteenth-century long fiction is that the period had well-developed theories and a lively debate as to what "epic" meant and what its connection with prose fiction was. From 1660 to 1780, from Dryden and Boileau to Johnson and Voltaire especially, readers knew that Aristotle spoke of four kinds of epics and that he discussed the elements of epics as he found them in Homer; but that period of English and French history, as it often did, disagreed with Aris-totle by usually placing the epic above tragedy. The theories about what an epic should do were phrased in England by Dryden, Addison, Pope, and

Dennis, all of whom preferred to talk of the human nature, the fire, the genius of Homer, the "music" of Virgil, or the sublimity and didacticism of Milton, and not so much of rules for the epic. Among the theorists in France were Le Bossu, Rapin, the Daciers, and Voltaire.

Of all these, English or French, Le Bossu was most significant, and it was he whom Fielding called his favorite modern critic.[89] Writing first in 1675 and then translated and widely read in Europe, Le Bossu—following common sense and not rules, hardly aware of the great Germanic epic tradition but knowing Virgil, Tasso, Camões, Ariosto, and Boiardo almost as well as he did Homer—discussed the epic under six headings: its nature, its action, its form, its characters, its machinery, and its thought and poetry. He believed that the tradition called for a grave and important subject in verse, a hero great of soul but not necessarily a warrier, a use of history and myth, the presence of divinities, a truth to life combined with the marvelous, and a veiled allegory that is didactic. In fact, he believed that the epic poet selected his moral first and then his fable and characters to inculcate that moral, a theory that prevailed more or less in European criticism for a century, in other words until after the novel became a significant and respected art form.

The interest in the epic about 1700 was indeed so great that the new art form not only had to compete in critical circles with the prestige of its elder brother the epic but often sought to bask in reflected glory by comparing itself with that elder brother, as the Scudérys did in the Preface to *Ibrahim* (1641) and as Fielding did almost exactly a hundred years later in the Preface to *Joseph Andrews*. After the disappearance of the long roman of the seventeenth century, the French—with the possible exception of Lesage and Prévost—were less and less inclined to associate prose fiction with the epic or to make use in fiction of standard epic elements. They remained closest to the more respected form in matters of human nature, the probable, the moral, interpolated or ornamental episodes, and elevated language for certain situations; they strayed farthest from it in the direction of low and bourgeois characters and contemporaneous rather than historic or legendary characters.[90]

Fielding, of course, claimed to be working in the comic-epic, or mock-heroic, tradition that from *The Margites* to *Le Lutrin* to *The Rape of the Lock* was so popular by the time *Joseph Andrews* appeared in 1742; and it is no doubt these relatively unimportant burlesque epic elements that for some readers stand out in *Joseph* and in *Tom Jones*—the Homeric simile, the mock-epic battle over Molly's sullied reputation—but the new novel as Fielding apparently saw it depended even more on the serious epic. There is, for example, not only his famous emphasis on "epic regularity," or unity or plot, but Parson Adams's lecture to Mr. Wilson on how the structure of the *Iliad* matches its content. There is, even better, the opening chapter of Book Eight of *Tom Jones,* which not only refers to Homer and the *Odyssey* but provides a long essay on the artist's duty to probability even as he leans to the lure of the marvelous, this being one of the most important of epic problems, from Aristotle to Le Bossu, Addison, and André Dacier, the last of whom Fielding even names here. And while we know how dependent Fielding's *Amelia* is on the *Aeneid*[91] and that the consensus—in spite of Tillyard—likes to call *Tom Jones* an epic, we can note that Martin Battestin has shown[92] That *Joseph Andrews* is even more in the epic tradition. There are at least five reasons for placing it there: first, the Christian, benevolent hero appropriate for the Shaftesburyian segment of the eighteenth century—Voltaire was at the same time attacking Achilles as a bloodthirsty fighter unsuitable for the eighteenth century;[93] second, the veiled allegory of Joseph-Abraham, the search for a father, and the return to a country paradise; third, the all-important moral embodied in the action; fourth, the spice and variety to be found in the integrated episodes that, from Aristotle to Ariosto, to Lesage and Smollett, were deemed necessary and decorative; and fifth, the mirroring of an age, which in our century seems to be one of the most important requirements for a serious epic. But Fielding and his followers, such as William Jenner, are not the only British novelists both to admit and to show that the epic tradition influenced them. Even a Richardsonian, a minor one, such as William B. Guthrie in his *The Friends, a Sentimental History* (1754), could call his fiction "An Epic in lower life." For the seventeenth and eighteenth centuries, then, many kinds of British and French writers believed their prose tales were close to epic poetry or owed much to it or had usurped a large number of the western islands it once laid claim to.

One of the most complicating factors in any attempt to find how and when the epic affected the novel is to note that it first affected what is popularly called the romance, beginning with the Greek romance, which is so often stressed as a second chief elder brother of the novel. The oldest extant Greek long prose fiction, Heliodorus's *Aethiopica,* not only alludes often to Homer's epics and employs pseudohistory—as Aristotle decreed for the epic—but has a single combat like that of Achilles and Hector as well as *Odyssey*-like wanderings, the Telemachian search for the parent, and even the identifying strawberry birthmark, or, if one prefers, the scar of Odysseus. And it is this older kind of fiction, the roman héroïque—out of the Greeks, the Arthurian and Charlemagne cycles, and the fifteenth-century Spaniards—that from Bishop Huet's *De l'Origine des romans* (1678) to the twentieth century has often been thought of when the term "romance" has been used. Northrop Frye in *The Anatomy of Criticism* is only one recent reader to insist that "romance" deals with heroes and is intermediate between "myth," which deals with gods, and the "novel," which deals with men; and now he enters the debate once more to elevate the "romance" over the "novel."[94]

But again there has been much confusion. The great Arthurian Arthur Vinaver, condemning critics since 1700 for bringing their modern bias—their demand for the use of "thought, reasoning faculties"—to their analyses of "romance," declares the term difficult to define because "its most important distinguishing feature is inseparable from what we normally understand by 'literature' "; and he concludes that the twelfth-century Chrétien de Troyes and his contemporaries, by drawing on "exotic traditions, written and oral," founded the "genre" so "misleadingly called 'Romance.' " F.E. Guyer, on the other hand, calls Chrétien the "inventor of the modern novel."[95] Obviously, however, Chrétien's type of fiction, even if different from, perhaps better than, that of Heliodorus, is only one of many related types of romance. Passing on by others just as original, short fictions such as the satiric *Aucassin and Nicolète* and long ones such as *Amadis* and the *Morte d'Arthur*, we can arrive at Sidney's *Arcadia* (1590), which is artistically composed of traditional elements from various "romances of adventure," and in which, Virginia Woolf believed, "all the seeds of English fiction lie latent."[96] Passing on still further, by the seventeenth century with its long *romans* of adventure and intrigue as well as its realistic burlesque romances, we note the eighteenth-century English feud over the terms "romance" and "novel." Then we arrive at the great diversity of the nineteenth century— the dreamy *Wuthering Heights* and the comic, ironic *Emma;* the romantic, passionate Balzac and the realistic, documentary Balzac; the exotic idylls of Pierre Loti and the clinical Rougon-Macquart series of Zola; Hawthorne's *Blithedale Romance* and the "poor Real Life" of Howells. Then, finally, we reach the curious theory that the long prose fiction of America is to be called "romance" while that of Britain is the "novel."[97] But we can also retreat a bit and listen to Henry James's ironic attack on such tags: "The novel and the romance, the novel of incident and that of character—these clumsy separations appear to me to have been made by critics and readers for their own convenience, and to help them out of some of their queer predicaments.... The French, who have brought the theory of fiction to remarkable completeness, have but one name for the novel, and have not attempted smaller things in it, that I can see, for that. I can think of no obligation to which the "romancer" would not be held equally with the novelist."[98]

Although some of us find this a wise conclusion, we can still agree that most pieces of prose fiction before 1700—and many after that date—contain some or many of the elements, the formulae, of what has popularly been called the "romance." The *Aethiopica*, translated into English in 1569 and issued in French eight times between 1547 and 1626, has been considered, by Huet, Magendie, and Mylne, the most influential single prose work for the development of the seventeenth-century serious French fiction.[99] Not only does it imitate the more ancient Greek epic but it contains certain patterns that become standard—ships, travels, exotic lands, pirates, shipwrecks, handsome lovers separated and remarkably reunited, feats of bravery and strength almost superhuman, and recognition of the aristocratic birth of supposed commoners. These and other such features can be found in the eighteenth century and later in the tales of Prévost, Fielding, Smollett, and a hundred other novelists.[100] Still another "romance" tradition that became a permanent and important part of the novel is that of Apuleius's *Golden Ass,* with its picaresque wanderings of the metamorphosed hero, the allegorical search for the roses that will restore him to manhood, the satire, the Cupid and Psyche interpolation that parallels the main allegory—all to go with the usual love intrigues, robbers, villains, even magic. *The Golden Ass,* translated by west Europeans even earlier than the *Aethiopica,* is found subtly everywhere, as in the muted allegory of the *Arcadia,* and openly, as in Don Quixote's fighting the wine bottles, or in the early chapters of *Gil Blas,* and through them to *Roderick Random.*[101] For the novel, then, the significance of the various romance traditions lies in the fact that writers of the eighteenth century and later knew them well and retained them, perhaps in combination with features derived from other forms of literature or life. The novel did not permit the romance—any more than it did the epic—to die in 1700.

A third literary form that contributed much to the evolution of the novel is history. History and prose fiction, in fact, have always been close, the earliest historians, such as Herodotus, often recounting myths and legends or recording hearsay and a salacious or gruesome anecdote as fact or for entertainment. Moreover, the struggles to find and tell the real truth and to decide what the rules of history should be are intriguingly like the struggles for verisimilitude and self-definition of long prose fiction. Historicists from Jean Bodin and Bacon in the Renaissance, to Bayle, to Lenglet-Dufresnoy, Bolingbroke, and Voltaire in the eighteenth century not only followed Cicero by complaining about the superstitions, mistakes, or lies in what passed for history but urged the truth, the full truth, and freedom from bias.[102] Such goals were not easy to achieve, however. Not only did Bayle condemn false use of history by authors of romans and urge truthfulness for both the historian and the romancer, but Voltaire found all ancient historians, except perhaps Thucydides, Xenophon, and Polybius, to be romancers, anecdotists, or liars, that is, fictionizers.[103] Certain writers of fiction—Roger Boyle (1655) and Charles Jenner (1770) in England; the early seventeenth-century authors of romans historiques, Lenglet-Dufresnoy (1734), and Restif de La Bretonne (1786) in France—found romans, romances, or novels to be more beneficial, less harmful, than history. Boyle, for example, said history

was really "mixt-Romance"; Jenner, recognizing that no two historians tell
the same story, suggested that novels, recounting what ought to be, might
be more affective than history, recounting what was; Lenglet-Dufresnoy
gave four reasons why the roman was superior; and Restif, like his contemporary Baculard d'Arnaud, insisted that the roman was more truly historical
than history. Moreover, if one historiographer, the Englishman Manwaring
(1739), could offer thirty-three rules for the reading and writing of history,
a fine historian such as the Frenchman Rapin de Thoyras (1727; 2d ed.) could
still claim that rules for the art were vague or useless.[104] Nevertheless, in
spite of its search for identity and for more credibility—all part of its
evolutionary process—history was firmly entrenched as a respectable
branch of learning long before the word "novel" was current, a fact true also
of its many subforms such as biography, autobiography, memoirs, and letters. As a result, by the end of the seventeenth century, most writers of
fiction were associating their works with one or more of these kinds of
history, the objects being several—to gain prestige by the association, to
appear more verisimilar, and to attempt to avoid the oft-repeated charge of
lying. The association was frequently announced not only in the title—*The
History of . . .*, *The Life of . . .*—but almost as often in an apologetic, even a
militant, preface that claimed historical accuracy, a device as old as Chrétien
and the twelfth century.

But the relations between history and fiction went further than mere
announcements or claims.[105] First, historiographers from the Renaissance to
1800 were urging a moral theme for history at the same time that Le Bossu
and other epic theorists were calling for the moral first and the fable second,
a theory to which by the time of Defoe and Prévost nearly all writers of
fiction were paying at least lip service. Second, by the eighteenth century,
history was becoming not just a collection of facts about princes and wars
but an analysis of human nature, of the manners of a people and a time. Even
in the seventeenth-century romans historiques, the tendency grew—and
after 1660 became dominant—to present ordinary people in real situations.
And well before 1750 Voltaire and Fielding were in perfect agreement that
Achilles and Jonathan Wild were not heroes and that manners were the true
subject for the writer of history, whether it was called *Charles XII* or *Tom
Jones*. Third, with its moral theme and its emphasis on manners, history was
to be edifying, a chief element in the poetics of eighteenth-century fiction.
George Nadel lists dozens of historians and historiographers from 1579 to
1800 who advocated and explained this exemplar theory of history. Among
them were the Oxford professor Degory Whear (1622), Lenglet-Dufresnoy
(1713), and Saint-Réal (1671). The first of these thought history should
provide examples of good men to be emulated and others of evil men to

avoid. Lenglet-Dufresnoy not only produced two essays on the roman but a huge study of history, the purpose of which, he said, was to instill virtue by displaying men who possessed that virtue to an eminent degree. And Saint-Réal—at the very time fictionized rogue-biographies were being offered, their authors claimed, as examples of what not to do—urged that since men are governed more by their evil natures history should provide more examples of vice than of virtue. Fourth, by the time of Voltaire and Hume, Gibbon and Robertson, one of the chief criteria for successful history was that it be artfully written; and here perhaps the novel, more respectable than formerly, may have affected the evolution of history, for the great historians of the eighteenth century were no more conscious of style than were their fellow chroniclers of life who employed the novel as a medium. Fifth, and finally, since historians of the seventeenth and eighteenth centuries—less scientifically than now perhaps—selected a subject as well as examples, discarded others, organized their materials, and drew universal truths from them, they in fact, like the novelist, adopted a mask, as Swift did in the *Four Last Years of Queen Anne's Reign* or Voltaire did in *Essai sur les moeurs.* So, in spite of obvious differences between the two modes, the novel was, and still is, close to history, evolving with it, and indebted to it. The consanguinity of the two has in fact been the chief motivation behind the most nearly mimetic school of fiction, from Lesage's "tableau des moeurs du siècle," Fielding's "Everything is copied from the book of Nature," and Richardson's "this History . . . a well-drawn Picture of Nature," to James's "as the picture is reality, the novel is history" or his friend Conrad's "Fiction is history, human history, or it is nothing."[106]

As prose fiction was moving toward more respectability in the eighteenth century, drama was contributing as much to its evolution as did the epic, the romance, or history. And since drama is so different from those forms, its contributions are easier to segregate and have often been described, for prose fiction in general and for individual novelists in particular. While the novel was gaining a name and moving close to reality after 1660, its practitioners had immediately behind them the great French "classical" theater and the British Restoration comedy. From the century before, they knew the Spanish comedy of intrigue and the Elizabethan stage. And in their own day they lived with sentimental comedy and a new bourgeois tragic hero as recommended by George Lillo and Diderot, but they also lived with fine comedy and, what may be more important, with great actors and actresses to keep them involved in theater—the Anne Oldfields and the Bettertons, the Wilks, the Lekains, and the Garricks. It is a telling fact that no important dramatist in the seventeenth century wrote fiction of any significance while in the eighteenth Lesage, Marivaux, Fielding, and Goldsmith all produced good comedies as well as good fiction, and other novelists —Mrs. Manley and Mrs. Haywood, even Smollett and Diderot—attempted writing for the stage.

Furthermore, especially before 1750, novelists were invoking great dramatists as their models, remembering the rules for comedy and tragedy, borrowing devices and scenes from the stage tradition or from individual playwrights, and comparing their narratives with stage plays, both to add luster to their new form and because they were still searching for their own poetics. Congreve explains of *Incognita* (1692) that as a dramatist he is to a certain extent conforming to the unities as he writes his "novel." In the preface to her *Works* (1725) Mrs. Haywood offers a "new" theory of the "Novel" based, as her master Congreve's had been, on the rules of drama, while Marivaux's preface to *Les Egarements du coeur et de l'esprit* (1736), like so many prefaces of his day, insists on the analogies between the roman and the comédie. All of this precedes Fielding's high praise of Ben Jonson in the preface to *Joseph Andrews* or Richardson's postscript to *Clarissa* in which at length he compares his novel to dramatic tragedy.

The debts of individual novelists to individual plays or to the stage tradition, or at least the parallels between them, are incalculable. Lesage's comedy *Turcaret* (1709), which preceded his great novel, is much like the bitter satires of Molière and is perhaps as fine as some of them, and it is to Molière's plays that *Gil Blas*, as well as *Le Diable boiteux*, owes much. Prévost, who admired Racine but praised English tragedy even more, has had his fated heroes and passionate love traced to the tradition of stage tragedy in England as well as in France. Fielding's debt to Congreve and Molière, the latter of whom he rendered in part into English, is easy to find both in his own comedy and in his fiction. With Richardson and Sterne, instead of looking for parallels with particular plays, we study the gestures and stage settings so important to drama.[107] This enormous influence of drama on prose fiction can be inadequately summarized by speaking of stock characters such as the fop, the faithful servant, the patient wife, the wit, the rake; of scene settings in inns, on stagecoaches, in bedrooms; of dialogue such as that of Don Quixote and Sancho entering Tobaso at dawn, Lady Booby and Mrs. Slipslop discussing Pamela and Fannie, the coachman and Mme Dutour quarreling in Marivaux's *Marianne*, all written by dramatists; and of unity of plot, as with *Tom Jones*, the plot of which in Coleridge's opinion was to be classed with that of two plays, *Oedipus* and *The Alchemist*. Realism of presentation and realism of assessment are of course only two ways of distinguishing among the many kinds of novelists inhabiting the rising house of fiction, but they all, from Lesage to Rousseau and Richardson, demonstrate how prose narrative can be, and always has been, aware of the tradition of drama.

And it has been aware of so many other forms of writing that one can select only a few more and hurry by them. There is the Theophrastian character, for example, which during the seventeenth and eighteenth centuries underwent an evolution amazingly parallel to that of fiction.[108] There is also allegory, which was an established mode before 1700 as well as an important ingredient of the epic and the romance.[109] And it entered prose fiction in a dozen forms—religious, with Bunyan; erotic, with Manley; vulgar, with Richard Head; political, with Swift; philosophic, with Voltaire; and epic, moral, mythic, with Cervantes and Fielding. And there is the picaresque—genre, form, or mode? Whatever we call this elusive and fascinating type of fiction, it probably did not appear full grown with *Lazarillo* (1554), and no two of the favorite picaresque stories are really alike any more than any two great epics are alike. That is, *The Golden Ass* of the second century belongs as much to the tradition as does *Roderick Random* (1748), perhaps as much as Grimmelshausen's *Simplicissimus* (1669). Although a discussion of the picaresque is reserved for a later chapter, what may be noted now is that, by whatever definition, this "mode" is one of the closest to the literature of travel, in persona, theme, and structure, and, as a result, it will necessarily be an important referent in relating that literature to the early novel.

Of the other important contributory forms to consider, apart from the literature of travel itself, one may stop with journalism. As with history, the character, the picaresque, it is an intriguing fact that while European fiction was becoming so much more representational after 1660 the literature of journalism was undergoing an even greater change that would both parallel that of the novel and help it contribute to the novel. In France the *Journal des scavans* came early and offered not only book lists and some literary criticism but, by 1681, a conversational style. Almost as important was Bayle's *Nouvelles de la république des lettres* of the 1680s. In England, John Dunton, Ned Ward, and Peter Motteux all published journals that preceded the first daily newspaper in 1704, while the most important and internationally influential of periodicals, Defoe's *Review* and the *Tatler* and *Spectator*, were all published before either *Gil Blas* (1715) or *Robinson Crusoe* (1719). This periodical literature not only offered contemporaneous realism but borrowed techniques from drama and fiction that it refined and repaid. Among these were the question-and-answer device; dialogue; satiric, comic, contrasting character sketches; interpolated tales that served as examples, taught morality, and added spice—all to go with foreign news, topics of local interest, and, as with the novel and history, an emphasis on manners.

But there is more. First, a number of eighteenth-century writers of fiction were also journalists, among them Defoe, Manley, Swift, Fielding, and Johnson in England and Prévost, Rousseau, and Diderot in France.

Second, a good case has been made for the fact that real and pseudo "lives" of rogues, criminals, and pirates penetrated journalism before 1700 and helped lead to the rise of the "low" in prose fiction. Third, scholars such as Maximillian Novak have shown how newspaper and periodical accounts of wars, people, celebrations, returned sailing expeditions, freaks of nature, storms and other natural catastrophes all became important ingredients in the new fiction, ingredients that were both real and exciting. And finally, as the newspaper became more and more important it included novellas, and after 1720 it began not only to serialize long fiction, that of Defoe being especially popular, but also to publish reviews of travel accounts, those of Samuel Johnson for Edward Cave, for example.[110] The mass media that rose to importance so fast about 1700 were, then, invaluable friends of the novel. John Wain, a journalistic-oriented critic as well as a biographer and novelist, is, like Marshall McLuhan, one who has recognized the affinity of the two forms. "The novel," Wain says, "grew up at roughly the same pace as the newspaper, and its function has always been to give the private history which could be presumed to lie behind the public history reported in the newspaper.... Once the newspaper press, and the improvement in communication generally, had aroused an interest in the surface eventfulness of life ... the flood-gates of realistic fiction opened."[111] The argument is, of course, simplistic, since the demand for verisimilitude came from every direction and permeated every literary form. As we shall see, for example, the literature of travel has a far older tradition of verisimilitude than does journalism, and its importance in the evolution of the novel is even greater than that of certain other chief contributors to that form.

During the past dozen years or so, scholars have been calling for a reevaluation of the reasons behind the rise of the novel. Decrying the critical emphasis on theme and structure, A.O. Aldridge in 1969 called for studies of narrative that include a consideration of the epic, the historical novel, history, biography, and travel literature.[112] Noting that Lévi-Strauss found that "History is ... never history but history-for"—that is to say, the study of history is a study of discontinuous figures, against a continuity barely good enough to be used as a backdrop—Maximillian Novak (1973) urged "a history of fictional forms to replace" our present "history of the rise and progress of the novel."[113] In the same year, Jerry Beasley, agreeing with William Park and John J. Richetti, concluded for English fiction that "we stand to learn a good deal about the achievements of Richardson, Fielding, and Smollett by examining certain aspects of the eighteenth-century literary surroundings."[114]

And many of those aspects have been examined well—the sociological conditions, a dozen forms of literature that preceded and fed into the novel —but others have been neglected, partly because the warnings of certain critics of the Russian formalist tradition such as Boris Eichenbaum and Roman Jakobson have been popularized only since 1965. Jakobson, explaining his theory of the Dominant as opposed to the Subsidiary in the evolution of literary forms, argues for "a shifting Dominant"; that is, he says, elements formerly considered primary in the development of literature tend at other times to become secondary. It is a theory close to, but by no means the same as, E.D. Hirsch's distinction between the Sinn and the Bedeutung—the permanent "meaning" as opposed to the relevant "meaning"—in a piece of literature.[115] "Genres which were originally secondary paths, subsidiary variants," Jakobson expands, "now come to the fore. . . ." All this of course is a product of the Russian formalist teaching that the evolution of criticism parallels the evolution of "genres." Such a poetics includes the belief that certain forms once considered extra- or nonliterary are at another period found "to fulfill an important literary function because they comprise those elements which are about to be emphasized by belles lettres. . . ." For the evolution of the novel, Eichenbaum, like Shklovsky, like Shevirev (1843), whom he quotes, and like Jakobson, emphasizes the importance of "history, travel narratives, and other marginally literary forms."[116] Of the non-Russian historians of the European novel, only Walter Raleigh, and he long ago, has even suggested that the literature of travel is of real significance.

In fact, the neglect of travel literature as a contributor to and a relative of the novel has until recently been almost uniform, as Morris Bishop complained in 1965: "The literature of exploration, travel, and adventure has been little regarded by scholarly critics." Typical of that neglect is Claude F. Jones, who in his "list" of "the major writings which fed into the novel proper up to the eighteenth century" (1956) includes no reference to travels except for one entry, Hakluyt's great Elizabethan collection.[117] Typical also is the excellent study of the eighteenth-century French novel by Vivienne Mylne (1965), which never mentions travels, not even for Lesage and Prévost at the beginning of the century or Diderot and Bernardin de Saint-Pierre at the end of the century.[118] It is true that E.A. Baker cites travel accounts used by Aphra Behn in the seventeenth century and reviews A.W. Secord's study of Defoe's sources for three novels,[119] but even his now very old gigantic history of British fiction looks at travels only as a source for incident and scene, as do certain historians of French fiction who know Claire Engel's study of Prévost as a student of travel literature. The history of prose fiction has, in fact, long needed books such as *The Road to Xanadu* (1927) by John Livingstone Lowes, whose wonderful study of the inspiration Coleridge received from travel literature has surprisingly not had the effect on knowledge it might have had.

But there are now significant attempts to "shift" the récit de voyage to the position of "Dominant." Perhaps the best such attempt for a single writer, the closest to *The Road to Xanadu*, is Thomas Curley's demonstration (1976) of the importance of travels to the mind of Samuel Johnson, and not just as that mind produced *Rasselas*, a fiction, and *Journey to the Western Islands of Scotland*, a travel account.[120] Easily the most nearly successful attempt to relate the novel in general to travel literature is that of William Spengemann, whose *Adventurous Muse* (1977) is intriguingly subtitled *The Poetics of American Fiction, 1789-1900*.[121] Surveys of travel literature have always been considered the property of geographers and historians such as Boies Penrose for the Renaissance and E.A. Heawood for the seventeenth and eighteenth centuries, or George Parks, Gilbert Chinard, and Geoffroy Atkinson, humanists turned historians, for the Elizabethan voyages and the seventeenth century; but certain students of belles-lettres are beginning to help us discover that the récit de voyage is perhaps something more than a "marginally-literary" form.[122] Lionel Casson (1974), for example, has an excitingly attractive book on ancient travels; Christian Zacher's *Curiosity and Pilgrimage* (1976) has a subtitle, *The Literature of Discovery in Fourteenth-Century England*, which has several meanings for the student of belles-lettres; Charles Batten in *Pleasurable Instruction* (1978) concentrates on such aesthetic matters as "form and convention" for eighteenth-century English travels; and Paul Fussell's *Abroad: British Literary Traveling between the Wars* (1980) is not history so much as excellent literary criticism of dozens of volumes of fine literature published during one-quarter of the twentieth century.

These books give some indication of the importance that travel literature is now assuming for the novel, for belles-lettres, and for intellectual history in general. It is an awakening prepared for by centuries of interest on the part of individuals who read travels with pleasure and profit, from Herodotus to Hakluyt, from Shakespeare and Camões to Donne and Milton, from Prévost the novelist-compiler of voyages to Johnson who reviewed them, from the ebullient John Livingstone Lowes to all those other students and admirers of James Cook who became so enthusiastic about him during the bicentennial that began in 1968 and lasted for ten years. It is an awakening also prepared for by all those thousands of readers who, without knowing the long history of travel literature, received with pleasure the books of individual travelers, as, in the United States of the nineteenth century, readers welcomed not only the accounts of travel by Hawthorne, Twain, Stevenson, Howells, and James but also those by writers who sometimes excelled their now more famous colleagues—Edward Everett Hale, W.W. Story, F. Marion Crawford, or James Jarves with four first-rate travel books and Bayard Taylor with ten. While the reception of such books was a literary phenomenon, until 1981 there was no full-length treatment of any of these as a travel writer or of nineteenth-century American travels as a whole.

Finally, one can see that the current increase of interest in the literature of travel has been prepared for by such critics as Michel Butor, Germaine Brée, and Donald Keene,[123] no one of whom perhaps knows the history of travel literature but each of whom discerns its importance as a form of belles-lettres. The novelist-critic-traveler Butor (1972; 1974) takes departure from what he calls the "intense bond" that exists between his travels and his writing to speak at length of the relationships among authors, travels, books, and readers and to urge the development of a science to be called Iterology. Brée, the scholar-critic, speaks of the voyage as genre, mode, motif, metaphor, even theme and notes that "the voyage as principle for the elaboration of fiction is tending today to become prevalent." And Keene (1977) as historian-critic of Japanese literature concludes that the Japanese novel derives not so much from early picaresque forms as it does from seventeenth-century travel diaries such as the six wonderful ones by the poet Bashō, the most famous of which is *The Narrow Road of Oku*. Such opinions may not be enough to convince us of the importance of travel literature to the history of the novel, but they may persuade us that the matter is worth investigating. Before beginning that investigation, however, we may be wise to review the story of travel writing to about 1800 so that we can see better its connection with the evolution of the early novel.

CHAPTER TWO

Travel Literature before 1800 – Its History, Its Types, Its Influence

> ... that crucial moment in modern thought when, thanks to the great voyages of discovery, a human community which had believed itself to be complete and in its final form suddenly learned ... that it was not alone, that it was part of a greater whole, and that, in order to achieve self-knowledge, it must first of all contemplate its unrecognizable image in this mirror. *Lévi-Strauss*[1]

Like the epic, like history, like the novel, the literature of travel has evolved through the centuries. Like them it has existed since the beginnings of oral and written literature. As with them some of its authors have been bad, others have delighted and informed their readers, and many, from the earliest times, have been popular, influential, even brilliant. As with other forms of literature its quantity and nature have varied because of political, religious, economic, and other social and human factors. And like them it includes countless subtypes that continually approach each other, separate, join, overlap, and consistently defy neat classification.

If the classification is by content, there is at one extreme the guidebook, of which by 1800 there had been hundreds, from Pausanias in Ancient Greece, to itineraries for pilgrims headed for holy shrines, to road and river maps, to city plans, to lists of antiquities, to routes for the seventeenth- and eighteenth-century Grand Tour. These are of course sometimes monotonous, often depending heavily on their predecessors, usually concentrating on distances, inns, transportation facilities, costs, warnings, recommendations; but often too they were published as part of—perhaps a supplement to—the account of someone who had made a real journey. By two hundred years after Christ, tourists and other travelers were being supplied, but in manuscripts too bulky for long trips, with every kind of local guidebook, the most prolific compiler of them being Polemo of Ilium, who covered Athens and its environs thoroughly but even produced a *Guidebook to Troy*. The only early guidebook to come down to us, however, is that of Pausanias, who in the second century traveled the Mediterranean countries, went up the Nile, and visited the Dead Sea before writing a guide for all Greece that took advantage of earlier such books, of his own extensive travels, and of information collected from interviews with people who had been to parts of the world he had not himself seen.[2] Pausanias set high standards for accuracy, liveliness, and credibility, describing monuments exactly, avoiding tall tales of which he was skeptical, but including legends and other stories that made his book more than a mere itinerary.

With the rise of Christianity, guidebooks were even more in demand. In the early Christian era Jerusalem and its environs became popular for pilgrims in spite of its being destroyed in 70 A.D. After the beginning of its restoration under Constantine in 326, the Holy Land regained its attractiveness, and by 333 a man from Bordeaux made his pilgrimage and wrote a combined itinerary and guidebook that is extant.[3] And through the Middle Ages and early Renaissance few types of literature were so often found, on scroll and then in print, as the itineraries and local guides that covered every important land and sea route, and the cities along them, from western Europe to Rome, Jerusalem, and other shrines, such as Saint James of Compostela. In the time of the Venerable Bede a French bishop spent nine months in the Holy Land and then dictated his account to the Abbot of Iona, who reworked it into a kind of textbook.[4] There was even a *Crusader's Manual*, while the author of *Sir John Mandeville* described four routes to Jerusalem; and at almost the same time, in 1358, Petrarch composed an itinerary for friends visiting Jerusalem, advising them however to see Rome and its monuments first.[5] The most important of all pilgrim guidebooks, and one filled with curious and fascinating suggestions for traveling, came after the Crusades and with printing, when Caxton's successor, Wynkyn de Worde, compiled *Informacion for Pylgrimes unto the Holy Land* by gathering most of his facts from William Wey's manuscripts of two journeys taken in 1458 and 1462.[6]

By 1575 the long tradition of guidebooks led to a sharp increase in their number as travel became even more popular, especially in England and on the continent of Europe. Led by German compilers such as Hieronymus Turlerus (1574), whose work was translated into English as *The Traveiler of Jerome Turler* (1575), and Theodor Zwinger (1577), each of whom thought erroneously that he was doing something new, the English and French produced countless volumes to aid the tourist. The first guide for England is really Chapter XVI of Holinshed's *Chronicle* (1577), "Of Our Inns and Thorowfares," while John Norden produced a pretentious one in 1625,

called *An Intended Guyde for English Travailers.*[7] The best-known of the
seventeenth-century English guidebooks for the Continent is James Howell's *Instructions for Forreine Travell* (1642), which went through numerous
editions and was still useful in Samuel Johnson's day. And in France it was
matched in popularity by the Jesuit de Varenne's *Le Voyage de France* (1639),
which enjoyed at least nine editions by 1687. To go with these instructions
for land journeys, there were others for the sea, most of which appeared in
prefaces to the many collections of voyages from the early Renaissance on.
Hakluyt alone has a number of such instructions, among them being the
ones he wrote for "certaine Gentlemen that went with" Martin Frobisher
in "his northwest discoverie" in the 1570s (V, 165-70). By 1665, then, it was
by no means surprising to have the Royal Society publish three essays giving
"Directions to Seamen" or by 1698 to have the Italian lawyer Gemelli Careri,
just back from a tourist's circumnavigation of the globe, include in his *Giro
del mondo* a long essay filled with advice for travelers going by both land
and sea.[8] All these guidebooks, directions, instructions, antiquities, délices,
itineraries, even volumes of maps for travelers, such as that wonderfully
detailed one by John Ogilby (1674) for England and Wales—all these may
not be belles-lettres but some of them are more attractive than others, more
imaginative, sometimes fascinating; and even the most pedestrian aided travelers, perhaps only in making their journeys easier, perhaps also in providing
information for their own books. Sterne was not the only novelist and travel
writer who knew Sanson's maps or the Jaillot family's *Liste générale des postes
de France.*[9]

Closest to the guidebook in content and most dependent on it is the
account of a journey by land, or chiefly by land, or of a series of such
journeys. Through the centuries one of the most popular books of land
travels has been Xenophon's *Anabasis,* the story of how in 401 B.C. he led
ten thousand mercenaries northward to the Black Sea after the defeat of
Cyrus the Younger at Cunaxa. Among the widely traveled early Asiatics
was the learned Buddhist Hsüan -Tsang, who left his home in China in 629
A.D. and wandered Asia for sixteen years keeping a journal that, in spite of
his losing much of it, is still one of the great travel books of all time.[10] He
describes the Himalayas and Buddhist monasteries, tells of his studies in
libraries and with wise monks and other scholars, records the intrigues in the
court of Harsha the poet king of northern India with whom he stayed a
year, and concludes with his triumphal welcome home. This great book was
not known to the western writers of fiction in the seventeenth and eighteenth centuries, but it demonstrates the permanence and universality of that
kind of travel book that is so close to the novel. Many later such books were
well known in Europe, however, such as that of the Italian Lodovico di
Varthema of the sixteenth century.[11] Varthema's talent for languages en-

abled him to change his dress or his religion at will and to become involved in adventures that caused his book (1510) to go through countless editions throughout Europe. Often the traveler supplemented his land journey by taking a boat on a river or a ship from one port to another, as with Varthema in the East and his near contemporaries Álvar Núñez Cabeza de Vaca and de Soto in the New World.[12] De Soto did not himself write up that famous journey across North America, but one of his companions, the "Gentleman of Elvas," did (1557), and Hakluyt translated him into English in 1609.

The continent that attracted most attention from authors of land travels was of course Europe; and after the invention of printing, such accounts appeared by the hundreds.[13] For example, there was Roger Ascham, who in the early 1550s stopped at every large city on the Continent to hear lectures and write home about them; or Montaigne, who visited Italy for his health in 1580-81; or Thomas Coryat, whose walking tour of the Continent early in the seventeenth century furnished material for his curious and famous *Crudities* (1611) and whose love of travel took him then to Asia Minor, where he died before publishing a second book but not before writing travel letters home that were published. And then, later, there was the young John Evelyn completing his education on the Continent in the 1640s and marrying his child bride in Paris; or Albert Jouvin de Rochefort (1672), who knew as much about Europe as anyone of his day and wrote as well about it, his first volume dealing with his own country, from Brittany to Provence, describing fêtes and towns, distinguishing among wines, and recounting escapes from highwaymen. And, finally, there were any number of eighteenth-century travelers on the Continent, in Britain, in America who by that time were finding roads smoother and inns more inviting.

Until the nineteenth century travel by water was usually far more comfortable than walking, riding horses, or sitting in jolting wagons or coaches on rough and dusty roads. Nevertheless, the fear of storms—in spite of some notable exceptions—restricted the number of long voyages until sailing ships were improved, the compass was invented, America was discovered, the route around Africa to the East was opened, and Magellan's *Vittoria* completed the first circumnavigation of the globe. There were of course famous boat trips down great rivers—Orellana's down the Amazon as described by Jesuit priests accompanying him, La Salle's on the Mississippi as told by his companion Joutel—but the longest and most significant accounts of water trips are by sailors or supernumeraries who may have seen much land but whose home for months was a ship. Although one can start in the days of Prince Henry, written records of sea voyages became more frequent and important after Columbus's first Letter was translated and went all over Europe. Vespucci's equally popular Letters, in modern times often not recognized for their true value, gave much information about the coast and people of South America, led to his name being affixed to the New World, and supplied Thomas More with facts and hints for his *Utopia.* In the same year that Vespucci sailed first for the New World (1497), da Gama began the voyage that took him around Africa to the Orient and back. Although much is known about this venture, one of the most significant of all time, only one firsthand account of it, an anonymous one, remains; but the Portuguese annual expeditions that followed in da Gama's wake would lead to other fine travel books that would ultimately induce the poet Camões to take the voyage himself and, after years, to return and write *Os Lusiadas* (1572), the best of all verse epics of the sea.

Often a long voyage resulted in several different accounts.[14] For Magellan's that of Antonio Pigafetta is the most nearly complete of four by eyewitnesses, while the first published version of Drake's even more exciting circumnavigation was by his nephew, who put together a book largely by editing a manuscript version by Francis Fletcher, Drake's chaplain. During the buccaneering days of the late seventeenth century, William Dampier, a buccaneer himself, a ship captain more than once, a circumnavigator three times, stands out also as one of the great authors of ocean voyages, his first and finest book, *A New Voyage round the World,* overlapping or being supplemented by a number of accounts by his associates, including Doctor Lionel Wafer and Captains Cowley and Sharp. And in the eighteenth century so much in demand were manuscripts of any long voyage that the British Admiralty followed the practice of confiscating all journals written on government-sponsored sailing expeditions so that an official version could be produced by careful editing. The regulation was impossible to enforce, however, for officers, even plain seamen, were able to get ashore with their notes or diaries, perhaps written in the margins of a Bible or some other book. In the 1740s, for example, besides the official narrative by Chaplain Walter, there were some eight different volumes published dealing with Anson's circumnavigation, four of which were by men on Anson's own ship the *Centurion,* the only one to complete the voyage and capture a Spanish galleon, while others were by crewmen of Anson's storeship *Wager* who survived a mutiny and other marvelous adventures after it wrecked off southern South America. And the volumes that came from the pens of Captain Cook and his associates during ten years of exploration are legion; besides his own three journals, there are all those by his officers, astronomers, botanists, chaplains, painters, and marines. The literature of sea travel has been as popular as that about land and, if possible, even closer to the development of the novel.

One can also classify travel literature according to form, and it appears in as many forms as does long fiction. It has often been found simply as notes, as with the seventeenth-century English botanist John Goodyer, who as early as 1618 was jotting down brief observations on short walking tours;

but by 1621 he was riding a horse, traveling all over England, discovering varieties of local names for flowers, and even including anecdotes, none of which he ever wrote up in book form.[15] Often a traveler did not record his own story but told it to someone else—a friend, a relative, a secretary, a reporter—who wrote it out in third or in first person, perhaps for a family or religious order, perhaps for publication, as with Saint Willibald, Niccolò de' Conti, and Álvar Núñez Cabeza de Vaca.[16] After his eighth-century pilgrimage to Rome and the Holy Land, Willibald dictated his experiences to a Saxon nun. Conti left Venice in 1419 to wander Asia for twenty-five years as a merchant, much of the time with his Indian wife and children, before returning to Italy, where as penance for having changed his religion he was requested to dictate his long story to the papal secretary, Poggio Bracciolini, himself a noted traveler. And Cabeza de Vaca, while in jail in Paraguay, dictated to his own secretary, Pero Hernández, the tale of his journey across South America.

One of the three most prolific kinds of travel narratives, whether informal or formal, has always been the letter. Roman soldiers stationed in Egypt, for example, sent notes to mother by anyone headed her way.[17] Columbus wrote letters to Ferdinand. The poet Tasso went in the train of Cardinal d'Este to France in 1571 and wrote home about his experiences, as did Henry Wotton, British ambassador in Italy for many years early in the seventeenth century. One of the best of letter writers, Mme de Sévigné, traveled throughout France but especially Brittany and Provence in the late seventeenth century and sent back her literary masterpieces to her daughter and friends. In fact, the written works of almost any important person after 1550 —Ascham, Fox, Boyle, Locke, Buffon, Voltaire, Franklin—may contain any number of travel letters. Sometimes these letters have been collected and published, perhaps by their author as with Charles de Brosse's *Lettres écrites d'Italie en 1739 et 1740.* Sometimes they were collected by an editor finding them in manuscript or selecting them from a body of correspondence, as with Lady Mary Wortley Montagu, whose early letters from Turkey to Pope and other friends were put with those late ones from Italy to her daughter Lady Bute and published as an account of her . . . *Travels in Europe, Asia, and Africa,* or as with all those thousands of letters written throughout the world from the mid-sixteenth century on by Jesuit priests and then collected, edited, translated, and run through countless popular editions. But most often, especially during the eighteenth century, the epistolary form was simply a device, as with Samuel Sharp or Tobias Smollett, two doctors publishing in the same year (1766), neither of whom wrote to a particular person.

A second popular form of travel narrative through the centuries has been the diary or journal. Sometimes, as with John Evelyn, the original brief dairy was considerably expanded by its author before being published; or it was edited, as John Fielding, out of prudishness or a fear of hurting people still alive, edited his dead brother Henry's *Journal of a Voyage to Lisbon* (1755).[18] Apparently Montaigne and George Berkeley, however, did not tamper much with their journals about Italy (1580–81; 1717–18).[19] Books about sea voyages were in journal or diary form even more often than those about land journeys, one reason being of course, that the captain's or mate's log could be reworked or consulted. Although Basil Ringrose's buccaneering experiences are at times obviously more elaborately detailed than a log demands, his published "log" is for days at a time simply a short report of the weather.[20] The well-kept journals of Dampier and Anson's Chaplain Walter are, in their published form, often interrupted by an essay on the history and manners of a place visited or a description of plant or animal life, while Robert Challe's lively journal (1721) of his voyage to the Orient (1691-91) sometimes skips many days of activities while lingering for pages on some long conversation or on one day's adventures.[21]

A third most usual form assumed by the literature of travel is surely the simple narrative. By no means always written in the first person, it customarily gives dates and names of places, normally leaps and lingers while moving inexorably forward with the journey, and often includes an essay on the nature or advantages of travel. There is, for example, Thomas Coryat's translation for his own *Crudities* (1611) of an "Oration in Praise of Travel" by the German Hermann Kirchner, while Thomas Nugent has even more ecstatic praise in the preface to his oft-reprinted *The Grand Tour* (1749).[22] Coryat wrote a first-person narrative and Nugent used the letter form, but any number of travel accounts are in the third person, among them the first part of Montaigne's, perhaps by the secretary who accompanied him to Italy. One of the best of such accounts is the Jesuit Father Trigault's rewriting of the journals of his superior in China, Matteo Ricci (1616), while the great editors of travel collections from Ramusio and Hakluyt to Prévost and Smollett consistently rewrote original journals.[23]

Finally, the literature of travel can be found in a number of atypical, even surprising, forms. It occurs, more often than one might think, wholly or partly in dialogue form, as with a long section of Lahontan's treatment of Canada (1704).[24] It can be part of an autobiography or biography— Anthony Nixon's life of the three notorious and world-famous Sherley brothers (1607), for example, or Anthony Hamilton's *Mémoires* of his even more notorious and famous brother-in-law, the chevalier de Gramont (1713), or Rousseau's wonderful relation of his walking and carriage journeys found in the *Confessions* (1766).[25] And travel literature was written even in the form of poems, or in prose that contains some poems.[26] John Smith, for example, inserted terrible little jingles in his account of Virginia, as did the humorous Water Poet John Taylor (c. 1630). Much better are the delightful verses mixed with the prose of two poets, Chapelle and Bachaumont (1656), writing a travel book about France at the same time and in much the same way as the great poet Bashō wrote of his late seventeenth-century Haiku journeys in Japan. And then there are two works (c. 1700) by Jean Regnard, the world traveler and fine writer of comedies, about two real trips in France, one "Voyage de Normande" consisting of a "letter" in prose passages alternating with clever stanzas of verse, the other "Voyage de Charmont" entirely in verse, witty, detailed, with a refrain, set to music, one stanza running thus:

> Hotêsse de la Bussière
>   Au lieu d'argent,
> Tu baiseras mon derrière
>   Assurement:
> Tu n'a pas seulement de pain.
> Vive du Vaulx et le bon vin,
>   Et le bon vin.

Evidently all these minor forms of the travel account were published often enough to warrant attention, since even the book of Bachaumont and Chapelle found imitators. Nevertheless, when one considers the history of the literature of travel, one concentrates most of all on letters, journals, first-person narratives, and the countless third-person rewritings that were so popular from about 1530.

That history of the literature of travel has yet to be written, however, in spite of many volumes about exploration and discovery or about travel in a particular country or period.[27] And here one can take time for only a bare summary that concentrates largely on movements and books known in the seventeenth and eighteenth centuries. The summary conveniently includes five periods of history, and, as with long prose fiction, one must note that a travel writer of an early period may be as attractive or as influential as one contemporaneous with Cervantes in the early seventeenth century or with Goethe, Radcliffe, and Chateaubriand in the second half of the eighteenth century, when the novel was finally accepted as an important literary type.

To writers and readers of 1700 the ancient world was well known and admired for its literature and for its importance to the Christian religion. If we turn from the Hebraic tradition with its stories of travelers from the time of Abraham and Joseph to that of Paul and Silas, or from the numerous Chinese and other Asiatic travel writers—Chang Ch'ien (c. 130 B.C.), for example[28]—now known to us but not to Charles II or Louis XIV, we can begin with Herodotus of the fifth century B.C., who has been called the "first travel writer."[29] He was not, of course, since there are extant travel accounts more ancient than his, one being a readable narrative of a business trip in the Mediterranean countries made by an Egyptian priest of the twelfth century B.C.[30] But Herodotus makes an ideal beginning because his history, the earliest extant of Greece, is so important to the history of the novel and also because it depends so much on its author's travels. He knew personally all of the Mediterranean lands, especially Egypt, intereviewed other travelers, checked sources, related anecdotes, included myths, and ended with a book that is more than fish and fowl—a travel-novel-history.

And his method of gathering materials is typical for early historians.[31] Thucydides, a traveling general in the Peloponnesian War, was exiled in 424 B.C. and for twenty years wandered about like Herodotus viewing famous battle sites, collecting eyewitness accounts, and adding personal observations and experiences that make his history invaluable. "I have," he says, "described nothing but what I either saw myself or learned from others of whom I made the most careful and particular inquiry," a claim that would go echoing down the centuries from travel writer to travel writer. It was the method of Xenophon (died 354 B.C.), not just in the popular *Anabasis* narrating the journey of the Ten Thousand but also in *The Hellenica,* a history of Greece in his own day; and it was the approximate method of the Romans Polybius, Strabo, and Julius Caesar. Polybius (c. 205-123 B.C.), an important official and friend of the Scipios, was sent on diplomatic missions, but he also traveled the entire Mediterranean area scientifically checking his facts and going out of the way to see battle grounds or to collect material for his history of events surrounding the First Punic War. Although Livy and Tacitus were more nearly fireside historians, Strabo (died c. 21), rediscovered in the Renaissance, a geographer but also a historian, saw more of Asia, Asia Minor, Africa, and Mediterranean Europe than perhaps any other important writer of ancient times. Like Ptolemy (died c. 160), that later and more influential geographer, but less credulous, Strabo depended as much as possible on what he saw and heard and was able to devote one book to the Arabian countries, another to Persia, and one even to the Far East, which he did not visit but which was already carrying on a thriving silk trade with the West. And finally there is Caesar, brilliant statesman and military tactician, a man of vision, great orator and writer, whose finest set of *Commentaries, De Bello Gallico,* is a sort of travel book as well as a history of the campaigns in Gaul and Britain. Truly to the ancient Greeks and Romans the two kinds of literature were often indistinguishable even though all their travel accounts were not formal histories. There were, for example, Cicero's letters about trips to one or another of his six vacation villas; other letters or accounts by ship passengers—Saint Luke telling of Paul and the Mediterranean storm, or the chatty letter which the Bishop of Ptolemais sent back to his brother in Alexandria (404 A.D.); and that greatest of all poems about

a real journey, Horace's *Iter Brundisium,* which is modeled on a less famous
travel poem, the *Iter Siculum,* by Lucilius.[32]

For the period 600 to 1400, if one reads the records of travelers one
discovers that this medieval period, the "dark age," was one of much movement, much gathering of experience, in many ways much "light."[33] Although narratives of the lively intercourse among the Asiatic nations were
not always known to the western world—for example, that of the Arab
Suleyman's visit to the emperor of China in the ninth century[34]—after the
Moors took Spain in the eighth century the two continents became more
closely associated, in peaceful ways as well as in war; and so a great Arab
map maker-travel writer such as Idrisi (c. 1100-1154) might know both Asia
Minor and western Europe, and his works, based on his own travels and
those of previous travelers, were available to westerners. Not so well known
in the seventeenth and eighteenth centuries were the sagas that told of the
travels of the Vikings (c. 750-1000), although those daring seamen not only
left a broad imprint on all the british Isles and even on the continent of
Europe but one of their number, Othere (c. 890), recounted his voyages to
Alfred the Great and was included in Hakluyt's collection.[35] Nevertheless,
since much of Europe was ravaged by war from 800 to 1200, and since
pirates often controlled the Mediterranean, those centuries leave relatively
few valuable travel accounts for us to read. But warriors and pirates have
never killed travel entirely, and so there was continual trade between the
West and East, the ports of Venice, Genoa, and Marseille especially sending
their ships to Alexandria or the Black Sea, where most of the eastern produce
was loaded. Moreover, we have learned much from Jewish travelers such
as Benjamin of Tudela, German merchants in the Baltic region, and trade
embassies sent to Byzantium from Italy and Germany in the mid-tenth
century.[36]

In the second half of the period, certain important events took place that
promoted travel and broadened knowledge. One was the tenth-century
restriction placed by the conquering Seljuk Turks on the 12,000 pilgrims a
year who had been making their way more or less peacefully from Italy and
Marseille to Jerusalem. As a result of the harsh restriction, the next two
centuries brought not only thousands of warring Crusaders to Asia Minor
but more religious fervor to Christian Europe and consequently an increased
desire to see the Holy Land.[37] The best, certainly the most famous, firsthand
accounts of a Crusade are that by Villehardouin, a leader of the so-called
Fourth Crusade whose *Conquête de Constantinople* (1198-1207) is as absorbing
as fiction, and that by Joinville, who accompanied Louis IX, Saint Louis, in
1248 and completed his *Mémoires* only in 1309.[38]

The second important historic event to affect travel literature and bring
two worlds closer together was the Tartar inundation of China, Tibet,
Russia, and all northern Asia that led to the great Khan empire (c. 1206-

1360), to its peace with India, to eastern toleration of westerners, to the opening of more trade routes, and to the sending out of European missionaries by the hundreds to attempt the christianizing of Asia.[39] Hardly had Ghenghis Khan and his successor built their empire and died when Pope Innocent IV sent a friar, Giovanni de Piano Carpini, as an envoy to the next khan in Peking. This land trip, which took two years, resulted in a narrative that opened up new worlds; but four years after Carpini's return, Louis IX, then in Asia Minor, sent another friar, William of Rubruquis, on a similar mission that lasted three years and produced an even better and more personal account that was addressed to Louis in the form of a report. These two were followed immediately in 1260 by the Polo brothers, who, led on by curiosity and a desire for trade in jewels, wandered eastern Asia before returning to Venice for a short time and then setting out again with son and nephew Marco, whose twenty years in Asia produced one of the half dozen seminal travel books of all time, one that would go all over Europe, first in manuscript and then in print.

After 1290 a long succession of traders, envoys, and missionaries went out, many to keep journals, write letters, or publish books about their observations and experiences in lands once unknown, dark, too marvelous. There is, for example, John of Monte Corvino with his two letters (1305-1306) to the Pope that would lead to his being made Archbishop of Peking. Shortly afterward, Friar Odoric of Pordenone (c. 1324), traveling largely by water, saw nearly all of the coastal countries of Asia and Asia Minor, added facts that escaped Marco Polo, dictated his valuable account to a brother friar, and later became a chief source for the author of *Sir John Mandeville*. There are also the Dominican Friar Jordanus in India (1329) and the Venetian merchant Pegolotti (c. 1340), the first with his great interest in Hinduism and his lust to take India forcefully for Christianity, the second with an account that turns out to be a guidebook, a text, for European merchants traveling the East as far as Peking. Of the travel accounts written after 1200, perhaps only Marco Polo's can rival that of the great Arabian traveler Ibn Batuta (c. 1324-54), who explored his own country before wandering all Asia Minor, the eastern coast of Africa, and finally even Spain but who was not generally known in Europe until after the eighteenth century. With the fall of the Tartar empire in the middle of the fourteenth century, China was again closed to outsiders, this time for more than one hundred years, but much of the rest of Asia as well as North Africa remained open for European traders and missionaries.

And during the fifteenth century the opportunity was taken advantage of, for hundreds of travel accounts, short and long, exist to tell us not only of English and other travelers moving about Europe[40] but of Europeans in the regions of the Caspian and Black seas, in Persia, in the Arab countries, in Egypt and Abyssinia, and on ships exploring the coast of Africa and finally heading for the New World.[41] Of the two best of those from the beginning of the century, both well known in Europe, one is by Clavijo, a Spanish monk sent in 1403 as envoy to Timur—Marlowe's Tamerlane— while the other is by a German named Schiltberger.[42] Clavijo went by the Mediterranean and along the Caspian Sea, through the hottest of countries to Samarkand, noting the excellent courier system and postal service maintained by the Tartars and, as with travelers of later ages, pausing to give the biography of the ruler Timur as well as to recount Timur's wars and personal pleasures. Schiltberger's *Reisebuch* tells of his years (1396-1425) of captivity under the Ottoman Bajazet and then under Timur and other masters, all of whom forced him to wander the East from the Black Sea south.

By the third quarter of the century, in spite of the Turkish threat to Europe, travel books of all kinds were being written and were among the first to be printed. There were, for example, three Venetian embassies to Persia in the 1470s, headed by Caterino Zeno, Josafa Barbaro, and Ambrogio Contarini, whose narratives were the last about that country for a while because a new line of rulers was less friendly.[43] There was also a Viennese merchant, Santo Stephano, who between 1493 and 1499 went to Cairo, down the Red Sea, and to southern India and the Malay countries, gaining and losing fortunes but all the time observing and living so well that his report is to be classed with the report Conti dictated to Poggio Bracciolini, the Pope's secretary, and that of Varthema, who traveled and wrote at the very beginning of the next century and whose adventures all over southern Asia were famous in Europe.[44] And while by the fifteenth century much of the piety of pilgrims to holy places had been supplanted by curiosity or other motives, there were still pilgrim accounts, among them the two by William Wey, fellow of Eton, who went twice to Jerusalem (1458, 1462); one by Dürer's friend Hans Tucher, who went in 1479; and one each in the 1480s by two companions, the Dominican Felix Faber and the Canon of Mainz, Bernard of Breydenbach, the account of Breydenbach being called the "most lavishly illustrated" of all fifteenth-century travel books.[45] Finally, toward the end of the century began the great age of sea voyages and voyage literature.[46]

Because the literature of the sea was so new and so important in the sixteenth century, it overshadowed other kinds of travel accounts then and, for popular opinion about the period, has apparently continued to do so. There is, of course, enormous reason.[47] The Portuguese who followed Prince Henry and da Gama produced innumerable books and letters about their voyages around Africa, their conquering and ruling of an eastern empire, and their trade, the most significant perhaps being the account of the great sailor-soldier-viceroy of India Affonso de Albuquerque, who arrived in the East in 1509 and who wrote even more of the land than he did of the sea. The Spanish sailors or passengers who went with or followed Columbus were just as prolific, from Dr. Chanca and Columbus's natural son Ferdinand, each of whom narrated a voyage of the discoverer, to an unknown supernumerary, Alonso Enrique de Guzmán, who crossed the Atlantic in 1534 and kept a journal of personal experiences. Among the almost countless relations of Spanish explorers in the Strait of Magellan or along the South American coast in general, one of the best is that of the learned and attractive Pedro Sarmiento de Gamboa, who while trying to intercept Drake was captured and taken to England, where his stories of South American wealth inspired people such as Ralegh and Hakluyt. In the same century, there were the French, with Cartier writing two exceptional accounts before 1550 to go with his three important voyages to Canada and up the St. Lawrence. The English and Dutch, far behind the Portuguese and Spanish, hastened in the second half of the century to catch up, with narratives of voyages to the Russian coast for the Merchant Adventurers or the Muscovy Company. Among these are the various accounts, especially one by George Best, of Frobisher's three expeditions to the northwest Atlantic in the 1570s. And there are others of the three voyages to the same seas made by William Barents in the 1590s, who was accompanied twice by Jan van Linschoten, the author of the great three-part *Itinerario* (1596), one part personal travels, two parts sailing routes for India and America. Just as varied are the accounts of the fatal voyage to Newfoundland of Sir Humphrey Gilbert in 1588 and of the other many English failures in the sixteenth century to find the Northwest Passage. Finally, there are the Spanish and, again much later, the English and Dutch in the Pacific, all following the circumnavigation of Magellan (1519). And the firsthand accounts of circumnavigations in the sixteenth century form not only one huge collection of travel literature but one of the most gripping. Starting, for example, with the stories of Drake (1577), who ravaged the western coast of South America and returned via Africa to bring home a cargo of riches for Elizabeth, one may turn to those of Cavendish (1586), who also captured a Manila galleon, and then one may stop, if possible, with the Portuguese Pedro Teixeira, who instead of returning home from India via Cape Horn sailed across the Pacific on a treasure galleon and then across the Atlantic to be the first person, apparently, to go around the world from west to east. Although such ocean activity would become even more significant by the time of Lesage and Defoe, the fact remains that ships have been, and always will be, a means to get from one land mass to another; and it was the new lands opened up by sailing ships or old lands made more accessible that produced, and still produce, most of the world's travel literature.

In the sixteenth century, travelers were on every continent except Australia, not yet really discovered, although of course most of Africa and most of North America were also still dark areas for map makers and historians.[48] With pilgrimages to the Holy Land and to Rome less important for Protestant England, Englishmen found other reasons for going to the Continent —for study, for trade, for picking up new languages and fashions, for diplomatic service. In fact, the great scholars of the period all traveled— Grocyn, Colet, and other Oxonians to Italy, the Cantabrigians to Luther's and Melanchthon's Germany, or Erasmus south to Italy and north to Britain writing letters about his observations and his love of the erudition and travel that took him to learned friends. Sir Thomas Hoby, who never startled the world of learning, still was typical in pursuing it (1547-64), especially hoping to gain the pure Tuscan language. Edward de Vere, Earl of Oxford and one of Elizabeth's favorites, journeyed from great city to great city for pleasure and perhaps to escape his wife, all the time writing letters home (1573-76) to his father-in-law, Elizabeth's minister Burghley. And Elizabeth is reported by Sir John Davies to have "had many Secretaries that have been great Travaylers."[49] Ambassadors to European countries often left important, sometimes entertaining, records. Among them were England's Sir Amias Paulet and, far better, Venice's Jerome Lippomano, both in Paris in 1577, the first of whom left a volume of travel letters, the other an absorbing journal. There were so many such travel accounts of Europe, in fact, that most of them were not published in their own day, something not true perhaps for travelers to other continents.

In the sixteenth century, Europeans continued to go east and southwest in even greater numbers, early from Portugal, which by the end of the century actually had the majority of its men in Asia, and all along from other countries, especially from England and Holland after 1550. There were, for example, at least three accounts of Abyssinia, the best being that of a priest named Francisco Alvarez who accompanied Roderigo de Lima on a mission there from 1520 to 1527.[50] Alvarez's book describing the customs of that strange and most often cited home for Prester John, went all over Europe in many editions and was included in Purchas's huge collection (1625). One of its best features is the story of how Alvarez and his companions found waiting for them a countryman named Covilhan, who thirty years before had left Portugal bearing the king's orders to find Prester John. They heard not only how he had wandered over north Africa and south Asia before ending up in Abyssinia to be transformed into an Abyssinian but also how along the way he had encountered a Jewish countryman by whom he sent back a written report of his wanderings, a report that was destined to become an important document for the Portuguese dreams of empire. The seventeenth century was to produce other volumes about Abyssinia, including that of Father Lobo, the translation of which was to be Samuel Johnson's first published work. So with travelers such as Alvarez and Lobo before them, novelists of the eighteenth century would know far more about Africa than what they had learned from Herodotus and Strabo about Egypt.

The sixteenth-century literature of travel for Asia and Muscovy is vast and was often well known. After the very popular Varthema early in the period, the Portuguese official Tenreiro enjoyed just as exciting a life in Persia; and his countryman Mendes Pinto, in China and then in Japan with Francis Xavier in the 1540s, had his marvelous adventures come out only in 1614, although two *Lives* of Xavier had already appeared narrating that great missionary's far travels.[51] And for only two more examples—these among the best—one can turn to the English traders Anthonie Jenkinson and Ralph Fitch.[52] Jenkinson, Chief Factor of the Muscovy Company, after 1553 opened a trade route across Russia and the Caspian Sea to Bokhara and Samarkand, made a number of trips, and proved himself a supremely fine diplomat with both the Tsar of Russia and the Shah of Persia. Fitch became thoroughly acquainted with India and the Malay countries during his eight years of moving about there (1583-91) and has one of the best journals ever kept by a merchant. Both of these writers were included by Hakluyt, who added Jan van Linschoten's eyewitness story of Fitch's escape from imprisonment at Goa.

Ships that sailed west to the New World in the sixteenth century brought Europeans who explored all of South America and Mexico and much of North America while seeking gold, colonizing, searching for a Northwest Passage to Cathay, carrying Christianity to the natives, and, even before 1600, building great cathedrals and universities.[53] The accounts of the Spanish Conquistadores—Cortés, Coronado, the Pizarros, and a hundred others—are among the most thrilling and closest to fiction. By the middle of the century the French were briefly in Brazil, as we read in the books of Thevet the Catholic and de Léry the Protestant, who were there. French Huguenots were somewhat longer in Florida (1580s), as reported by Laudonnière, who dedicated his account to Ralegh; by Jan Ribaut, who also published his in England; and by the artist Jacques Le Moyne, whose report and drawings from memory ended up in the de Bry collection.[54] Following the three voyages of Cartier in the 1540s, the great day of the French came in Canada with the exploits and journals of Champlain and the poet-lawyer Lescarbot at the very beginning of the next century; for with them went the first waves of missionaries, and after them the exploration of the Mississippi was completed by 1700, all told in unforgettable journals, letters, histoires.[55] Similarly, the accounts of Englishmen in Virginia and New England would wait until the seventeenth century, except for the first-rate one by Thomas Hariot, *A Briefe and True Report of the New Found Land of*

Virginia (1588).[56] In fact, land travelers in the New World from Germany, all in South America, outnumbered those from either England or Holland in the sixteenth century. Two of them, Hans Stade (1557) and Ulrich Schmidt (1567), each returned with a stirring, often personal, account of Indian wars and Dutch-Portuguese politics that went through various editions before being included in de Bry.[57]

De Bry and Hakluyt, although among the best known, were by no means the only collectors of voyages in the sixteenth century.[58] In fact, their collections came at the end of the century and extended into the next, having been preceded by dozens of others, some of which were translated into several languages, went through a number of editions, and were among the most popular of books in the first full century of printing. One of the earliest of these, and one of the most influential works of all time, is the Italian Fracan da Montalboddo's *Paesi novamente retrovati* (1507), which concentrated largely on voyages to America—those of Columbus, Vespucci, Cabral, for example—went through five editions in Italy in fifteen years, six in French, and countless others in whole or in part for other languages. For the continent of Europe, Montalboddo would of course be more important than Hakluyt would be. He was also a chief inspiration for the great Italian geographer Ramusio, who spent thirty years collecting accounts of voyages for his three volumes (1550, 1559, 1556), the first two of which deal largely with the East and Africa, the third entirely with the New World. Ramusio ransacked previous collections, translated his own version of Marco Polo, included the most popular travel writers, such as Varthema, Conti, Pigafetta, Cortés, Cabeza de Vaca, and Coronado, and was to be in turn a chief inspiration for Hakluyt.

The story of Richard Hakluyt is well known to English readers, and his influence on Elizabethan and later literature has often been assessed.[59] After learning geography from his cousin at Oxford and spending five years in Paris learning still more, after inspiring a translation of Cartier by Florio, and after publishing a volume of voyages to America in 1582, Hakluyt in 1589 brought out his one-volume *Principall Navigations . . . of the British Nation*, which would grow to three large volumes by 1600 and be one of the glories of Elizabeth's England.

Between Montalboddo and Hakluyt, however, there were important collections in Spain, Portugal, Germany, the Low Countries, but not in France. Spain, for example, had Pietro Martire d'Anghiera, an Italian who lived at Lisbon. Granted access to state documents, Martire began his *Decades* early in the century to tell the story of the discovery and conquest of the Spanish New World; and by 1530 he had compiled eight *Decades*, entitled *De Orbe Novo*, a book that was to be translated by John Eden in 1555 and become the first collection of voyages for the English to read in their own language. Two works about Spanish America by Fernández de Oviedo y Valdés—*Historia natural de las Indias* (1526) and *Historia general de las Indias* (1535)—show much firsthand knowledge of the subjects, for Oviedo traveled widely as a public official and knew important actors in Spain's drama, actors such as Orellana, Pizarro, and people who had talked with Columbus. A similar book, by José de Acosta, came out at the end of the century (1590) and very shortly was in French, English, and other languages for Francis Bacon and his contemporaries to read. In fact, by 1600 books about the world were likely to be histories combined with firsthand travel books or rewritten accounts of travelers, a practice that had been started early in the century by the great Portuguese historian-collectors Barros and Castanheda. The German Münster and the Spanish Gómara were to improve on the practice, one with his *Cosmographia Universalis* (1544), a "geography" that combined history and travels for all known continents and that received forty-six editions in six languages, the other with his *Historia general de las Indias* (1552), which was almost as popular. And the practice would extend into the next century with collectors such as Antonio de Herrera (1601-1615) and the great Inca Garcilaso de la Vega, whose *Royal Commentaries of Peru* was known in every European country. And that brings us back to the time of de Bry.

If Breydenbach's is the best-illustrated travel book of the fifteenth century, the most tastefully and expensively illustrated collection of travels begun before 1600 was that of the de Bry family of engravers in Frankfurt-am-Main. Starting with Theodore de Bry, who enlisted the aid of great geographers and collectors like Hakluyt, the family produced two sets of *Voyages*, called *Grands* and *Petits*. Publishing continuously between 1590 and 1634, first in Latin and then in French, the de Brys included not only the most important and attractive travel accounts of both East and West but also original drawings such as those of Le Moyne, the Huguenot artist who escaped Spanish massacres in Florida, and John White of Virginia.

There are of course many other sixteenth-century collections important for any study of travel literature or fiction, although few original ones appeared in the next hundred years. Two notable exceptions are the volumes of Samuel Purchas in England (1625 ff.), the chief disciple of Hakluyt, and those of Melchisedec Thévenot (1663-72) in France.[60] The seventeenth century, however, did continue to read the earlier great collections. An appropriate example is Levinus Hulsius, who began publishing in 1598. His voyages, largely English and Dutch, were almost as beautifully illustrated as those of his fellow townsmen the de Brys, and they were so popular that the project extended to 1663 with sixty-nine volumes. Toward the end of the century the trend was away from collecting original travels to compiling "geographies" that described the world by quoting or paraphrasing travelers, that of Oliver Dapper (*Africa,* 1668), for example, or those of John Ogilby (*America,* 1674, e.g.) and Athanasius Kircher (*China Illustrata,* 1676), or those early ones of the eighteenth century, among them being the *Description de tout l'univers* (1700) by the Sanson family, the huge English *Atlas Geographus* (1717) in one volume, and the French *Atlas historique* (1719). But by then travel collections had again become the fashion, for the eighteenth century was to equal the sixteenth in producing them.

There is one other kind of collection of voyages and travels important by 1600 and so important subsequently that it must be treated separately and for a period of two hundred years. That is the unbelievably large body of letters, journals, and summaries of travels written, collected, and published by the members of the Society of Jesus between 1540, the date the Society was chartered, and 1773, when it was dissolved by papal decree.[61] These publications began as letters from foreign missions sent back to the Pope or some other superior, a fine example being that very early one written by Saint Francis Xavier in 1544 from southwest India. Soon the letters, often one hundred pages or more in length, were being collected, two of the first such collections coming from Portuguese India, both in Italian, both published in 1559, one consisting of nine reports and the other of eighty-nine. Saint Francis moved about in India and China for years, but in 1549, accompanied by the renowned lay travel writer Mendes Pinto, he was the first Jesuit to reach Japan, which had been discovered by Europeans only seven years before. For the rest of the century Father Louis Froës was the leader of the Japanese missions and wrote some sixty-six "letters" from the East by himself or in collaboration with other priests in Japan and China. That these "nuovi avisi . . .," "Diversi avisi . . .," "Brevis Japaniae . . .," "Zeitung auss Japonia . . .," "Cartas que los padres de la Compañía de Jesus . . . escrivieron" —that these annual letters were widely read is evidenced by the speed with which they were translated throughout west Europe, including even Protestant Germany and the Low Countries. Twelve letters from Froës, for example, received nineteen printings in France by 1602, easily a record for any travel writer of the time, and a Spanish collection of ninety letters from Japan appeared in 1575. Of course Froës, Xavier, and the hundreds of other Jesuits in the East often in their writings concentrated on their missionary methods and their successful conversion of pagans, but they also told of their frequent movings about, the customs, agriculture, and cities of their adoptive countries, the intrigues and obstacles they encountered, court progresses, changes in rulers, and, finally, of their bloody expulsion from Japan.

And so they became for Europe the best regular source of information about the East, even the Protestant nations often, if with some jealousy, admiring their persistence and especially their success.

But in general the sixteenth-century annual Jesuit letters from the East are not so literary, so attractive, as those *Jesuit Relations* out of Canada and South America in the seventeenth century. The Jesuits were not the only missionaries in Canada, however, for Champlain had four Récollets sent to him in 1615, and the Récollets were to remain, although in small numbers, for a hundred years. Nor were the Jesuits by any means the only ones to describe upper North America, for Champlain's first journal appeared in 1603 and that of his companion the lawyer-poet Lescarbot in 1609. But after Jesuit Pierre Biard arrived in 1611, one of the first of his order there, and five years later published his important *Relation de la Nouvelle France* describing the Red Man, the country, and its natural history, more and more Jesuits came to evangelize, to explore, to brave great dangers from nature and natives, often to be cruelly tortured and put to death, and to send back their reports to be published by superiors who consistently edited what was written. Decade after decade these Relations were added to as France strengthened its hold on Canada and went around the Great Lakes and down the Mississippi, so that now the standard edition in English, that of R. G. Thwaites (1896-1901), consists of seventy-three large volumes. There were other Jesuit letters, from Father Páez in Abyssinia, for example, who after one failure was able to penetrate that country and remain for years, sending back reports as late as the 1620s. And the reports came from South America, especially from the Peruvian side, from the Paraguay Jesuit "kingdom" on earth, and from the Amazon, which the German Jesuit Samuel Fritz descended, wrote about, and mapped during his forty years in the region after 1684. In 1628 Sebastien Cramoisy, awarded the privilege to publish the Jesuit letters in Paris, brought out an attractive volume summarizing the order's activities; and in Italy another devoted to Paraguay appeared in 1636.

Nor were the Annual Letters the only important travel accounts of the Jesuits, for many of them supervised the publication of their own books or had their travels edited or written for them, sometimes after they had died. And among these in the seventeenth century are some of the most readable and influential of all time. After Father Trigault's great translation of Matteo Ricci's memoirs of his years in China (1616), there are Martino Martini's *Bellum Tartaricum* (English and Dutch 1654; Latin 1655), which reported for Europe the fall of the Ming dynasty; Ferdinand Verbiest's wonderfully detailed relation of his *Voyages* (1685) as astronomer to emperor K'ang-hsi; and any number of excellent, influential narratives of Jesuit embassies to Siam and China at the end of the century and on into the next. Nor did the Annual Letters cease with 1700, for the eighteenth century saw the many volumes of the *Lettres édifiantes* last so long that the first editor père le Gobien had to be supplanted by another, Jean Baptiste Du Halde. John Lockman translated many of these accounts into English in 1743, and between 1728 and 1755 a huge collection of 780 Jesuit letters appeared in German. The number of Jesuit teacher-missionaries of the sixteenth, seventeenth, and eighteenth centuries is perhaps so great as to be incalculable, and even more incalculable is the influence on European ideas of their widely read travel biographies, letters, journals, and memoirs.

But then, the total body of the literature of travel for the seventeenth and eighteenth centuries, while the novel was maturing rapidly, is so much more vast that to consider its history in a few pages is an awesome challenge. Avoiding chronology, an approach impossible to organize satisfactorily, and avoiding as well a division according to continents or countries visited and written about, an approach often taken by students of exploration or of the influence of one part of the world on another—Italy on England, China on France, for example—one may choose to show the wealth and variety of travel literature from 1600 to 1800 by noting the kinds of travel writers and their motives for going where they went.

Through the centuries a chief, if not the chief, reason for traveling has been for trade; and, after 1600, merchant groups in England, France, Holland, and Germany organized and proliferated as the nations of Europe competed with each other for the Asian trade once monopolized by Portugal and for the American and Pacific trade once belonging to Spain. The English East India Company, formed in 1600, tried annually to send expeditions to Asian waters. Perhaps the best of its many travel accounts of success and failure is from the eighth voyage, that led by Captain John Saris, who in 1611-13 sailed not only in the familiar waters of the Red Sea to the Moluccas, meanwhile fending off the troublesome Dutch, but all the way to Japan, where he established a factory, took presents to the emperor, viewed the huge cities and beautiful mountains, and kept a journal that both aided other merchants with information about monsoons, tides, ports, and trading techniques and is attractive to the historian and general reader for its observations about people and places, expecially of Japan.[62] About the same time, the French were building up their trade in the Far East and writing as many first-rate travel books about it as the English were. One expedition sailing from Saint-Malo in 1601 and backed by a merchant company included François Pyrard de Laval, who experienced more than one shipwreck, learned the language of the Maldive Islands, stored up information about a number of countries not described by the Portuguese, and returned ten years later with a tale not only gripping but also of great value for the places and the time.[63] Just as attractive, if not so celebrated, is the account written by his countryman Augustin de Beaulieu, who commanded three ships sponsored by Paris and Rouen merchants, visited and explored the African coast, including Madagascar, faced off the Dutch near Sumatra, and arrived home after three years (1622) with two ships still intact and a rich cargo to go with the journal that would later appear in Thévenot's important collection of voyages.[64] Two of the most influential books by merchants who stayed largely on land are those of the diamond experts Jean Tavernier (1677-79) and John Chardin (1686).[65] Tavernier joined a caravan to Persia in 1631, traveled much of Asia and Russia, and died in Moscow. Chardin made two extended trips to the East (1665-1677), knew Persia even better, learned its language, became an English citizen, and was knighted by Charles II before publishing his seminal and literary *Travels* that not only describes geography, agriculture, and climate but tells of eastern tyrants, intrigues, banquets, and customs in general. One sea merchant of the eighteenth century not connected with a chartered company was Nathaniel Uring, who sold slaves, cut logwood, and carried mail from Falmouth to the West Indies before ending up as governor of one of its islands and publishing his *Voyages and Travels* (1726), popular enough to have three editions in twenty-four years.[66]

Closely related to merchants who fought off foreign competitors or sold human beings were those many more or less unprincipled sailors who usually took their plunder wherever it could be found. Among them were Barbary pirates who owed nominal allegiance to an African ruler and raided ships promiscuously, pirates who owed allegiance only to themselves, buccaneers who ostensibly had letters of marque from the French government to prey on Spanish shipping and colonies even in peaceful times, and privateers who—backed by merchant combines—claimed respectability by raiding the Spanish in times of war. Seldom did a pirate publish his own story, but in the early eighteenth century pirate "lives," narrated by compilers such as Defoe, formed one of the most horrifyingly readable branches of the literature of travel and made household words of the Teaches (Bluebeards), Averys, Kidds, and Gows.[67] The buccaneers—often stealing their first ship, often organizing themselves into small navies under leaders such as Captain, later Lieutenant Governor, Henry Morgan—thrived between 1640 and the Peace of Ryswick in 1697 and were far more prone to publish their journals or memoirs, perhaps with the help of ghost writers or editors. The archetypal book for the Raveneau de Lussans, Wafers, Dampiers, Sharps, and Cowleys is *The Buccaneers of America* (1685), the first part of which was by buccaneer Captain-Doctor Alexandre Exquemelin (Dutch 1678), the second by Captain Basil Ringrose (1685).[68] This body of travel literature, larger even than for piracy, concentrates on Mexico, the West Indies, and South and Central America. It tells of the democratic elections of captains and divisions of spoils, the bloody rapes of coastal towns, the dangerous marches across Central America, the sailors left on and rescued from desert islands such as Juan Fernández, and the flora and fauna encountered by the bucca-neers. Especially attractive is the *New Voyage and Description of the Isthmus of America* (1699) by Dr. Lionel Wafer, perhaps as detailed, exciting, and important as Raveneau's *Journal* (1689) or Dampier's *New Voyage* (1697), the last of which, a favorite with Masefield and Lowes, records the death of Dampier's friend Ringrose in a Spanish ambush in Mexico.[69] Privateering expeditions of course flourished under Queen Elizabeth, but of those after 1700 two are most famous. One was backed by Bristol merchants and headed by Woodes Rogers aboard the *Duke* and accompanied by Edward Clarke, in command of the *Duchess*.[70] Each captain wrote an important book (Clarke 1711, Rogers 1712) giving his version of raids on the western coast of South America, the taking of numerous small Spanish ships, the rescue of Alexander Selkirk from Juan Fernández, and the lucrative capture off California of the first Manila galleon taken since Cavendish. And it was the last such capture until George Anson, who commanded the other great privateering voyage of the century.[71] His was another circumnavigation, one that brought him in contact with the treasure galleon near the Philippine Islands; and his *Centurion* and its store ship the *Wager* spawned a shelf full of popular volumes that read like novels.

In some ways it may be a long step from the merchant, lawful or unlawful, to the missionary; but converting the heathen, east or west, continued to be one of the several most compelling reasons for Europeans to move about in the seventeenth and eighteenth centuries. And the Jesuits were by no means the only ardent evangelists to write of their travels and trials or of the places, people, and natural history they observed. The Capuchins, in fact, were far more numerous in the regions near the Congo, the most significant of these—a traveler of many years, a narrator of his own experiences, and a collector of other travel accounts to Africa—being the Italian Cavazzi da Montecuccolo (1687).[72] Two Spanish Franciscan friars, after narrowly escaping death many times while making the third recorded descent of the Amazon, turned around to ascend it with the great explorer and world traveler Pedro de Teixeira (1637-38). A much more important travel account, however, is that of the Jesuit Acuña (1641), who also made the return trip with Teixeira.[73] In Canada the most notorious of missionaries is surely père Louis Hennepin, a member of the Récollet branch·of the Franciscans, who published two books about his exploits. It is the second of these (1697) in which he falsely claimed—and at great length and in inordinate detail—to have preceded La Salle to the mouth of the Mississippi.[74] The most prolific writers among Protestant missionaries were English, and most of them were in North America. They represented a variety of sects. There was the gentle, pious Cambridge Anglican Alexander Whitaker, who loved the Red Men and reported his *Good Newes from Virginia* in 1613. There were the Quakers, who went to America especially in the last quarter of the seventeenth century and who are perhaps best represented then by two men —John Archdale, governor of Carolina in 1694 and author of the *New Description . . . of Carolina* (1707); and George Fox, whose readable *Journal* of his travels in the New World appeared in 1694. Finally, there were the Methodists. One was John Wesley, whose amazing *Journal* tells far more than how many people he converted on his 250,000 miles of travels and how intractable he found the Auld Kirch natives of Scotland or the Indians of Georgia. Another was George Whitefield, who traveled just as far and whose various journals reveal not only much about human nature, transportation, and living conditions but about a saint who—in spite of Fielding's ridicule—could make even a Benjamin Franklin love him. All of these innumerable missionaries, Church of Rome or Protestant, were more or less literate; and since they were urged by superiors to keep records or impelled by practical considerations or vanity, they may have produced more books, even in proportion to their numbers, than did any other group of travelers of the time.

Close to this group, but during the seventeenth and eighteenth centuries far less numerous, were the pilgrims. In fact, England, Germany, and the Low Countries, no longer Catholic, sent almost no one to Rome for religious reasons; and with the sensual excesses that arose in pilgrimage groups by Chaucer's time, even the Catholic hierarchy almost ceased promoting them. There was, however, a steady stream of Christians who continued to visit Jerusalem and write about it, although seldom did a European's piety compel him to brave robbers on mountain passes in Europe or fight off marauding bands along caravan routes in Asia Minor unless the trip to the Holy Land was only one leg of a much longer journey. That was true for the Catholic Pietro della Valle, who left Venice in 1614, wandered Asia for ten years with a Circassian wife, and had his journal published (1652) only after his death.[75] It was true of George Sandys, who left home in 1610 to escape a bad marriage and traveled over Europe and the Near East before returning to England and watching his *Relation* go through four editions.[76] And it was still true in the 1730s when Thomas Shaw, sent by his government to Algiers, visited Egypt, Tunis, and the Holy Land before publishing his thoroughly documented and illustrated travel book-history-natural history (1738-46; 1757).[77]

Of all the literature of travel, that of exploration has been most thoroughly examined by the historians of geography and cartography. Edward Heawood's volume (1912), still the most helpful for the seventeenth and eighteenth centuries, refers to more than 125 different travel books by explorers themselves, only a small percentage of the total. Their authors went, of course, to the relatively unknown continents and oceans and wrote books similar to those by missionaries and traders but quite different from those by people who moved about in more sophisticated Europe. These explorers include the English and Dutch searching for the Northwest Passage—Baffin, Hudson, and Captains James and Foxe, both in 1631. They include the English on the coast of Virginia and New England, John Smith being only the most vigorous in investigating, in mapping, and then in writing the accounts of his adventures and observations. They include the French, not only Jesuits and Récollets but laymen such as Champlain at the beginning of the period and La Salle at the end of the seventeenth century, all of whom, with others such as La Salle's faithful friend Tonty, were constantly keeping an official eye on the English in their attempts, finally successful in the eighteenth century, to claim the Mississippi region. They include Virginians such as Robert Fallam and Colonel George Chicken, the first of whom went west into the Appalachians in 1677 and kept records, read before the Royal Society, that supported the early English claims to the back country, the second of whom twice led expeditions west and south into the Tennessee-Kentucky country (1714, 1725) and wrote two of the most ungrammatically fascinating of journals.[78] The great family of explorers includes père Páez, who gazed at the source of the Blue Nile in 1613, and James Bruce, who, after assuming incorrectly in 1770 that he was the first European to find those same fountains, returned home to write a most useful and literary five-volume history of himself and Abyssinia.[79] It included dozens of Portuguese and Dutch in eastern South America, as well as Spanish in the west, all still searching for the elusive El Dorado and navigating and mapping the tributaries of the Amazon, the best of these accounts perhaps being those about Teixeira and that by Johan Nieuhof, a Dutch official who also wrote a beautifully illustrated volume about China that John Ogilby put into English in 1669.[80] And, for only one more vast area, the explorers include that host of sailors in the Pacific, the one ocean still relatively unknown to Europeans, sailors such as the Dutch Tasman or the Portuguese Quirós sailing with the Spanish early in the seventeenth century and Bougainville and Cook and Bligh in the last half of the eighteenth century.

Often of course these explorers were also leaders or members of colonizing expeditions, Champlain at Quebec and John Smith at Jamestown, for example. But other colonists, permanent or semipermanent, also wrote travel literature. In addition to the religious groups, especially the Jesuits, that helped lead new colonies in the America, there were such people as John Winthrop with his detailed, often passionate, letters from New England to the wife who was to join him; the lawyer Thomas Lechford, who wrote an unflattering account (1642) of the Puritans after his three years of practice in Boston; and John Josselyn, who made two extended visits to New England and tried to settle there but instead wrote two books, partly about his voyages, partly about farming, largely about flora and fauna (1672, 1674).[81] The indentured servant George Alsop wrote a curious volume about Maryland, in it giving instructions for poor people wanting to emigrate to America (1666), while John Lawson, colonist in Carolina, surveyor, explorer, was killed by Indians, but not before writing perhaps the best travel book (1709) out of the southern British colonies.[82] And for other parts of the Americas, one may turn to Richard Ligon, an adventurer who worked on a Barbados plantation for some years before publishing one of the best of a number of books written about that island (1657); or, much later, to Edward Bancroft, overseer of a plantation in South America, whose account (1769), written on his return to England, concentrates on the native Indians and, even more, on plants and animals.[83]

Travelers who wrote or were written about also went to war. All of the three famous Sherley brothers early in the seventeenth century fought in Asia, especially Robert, who married the niece of the Emperor of Persia and led Persian armies against the Turks much as in the eighteenth century Alexandre de Bonneval, after going from one European army to another, ended up as both a commander in chief and a sort of secretary of state to the Sultan of Turkey.[84] Baron Lahontan, whose books about Canada were popular and influential, fought the Indians at Fort Michilimackinac and the English at Newfoundland. Governor Oglethorpe of Georgia attacked the Spanish moving up from Florida and told about it in his letters of the 1730s and 1740s, while Francis Moore's *Voyage to Georgia* (1744) is even more detailed about those same wars. Captain John Knox fought twice at Quebec (1757-60) and recounted his experiences, and any number of French and English officers wrote of their movements in the American Revolution—the comte de Rochambeau with his *Mémoires* (published 1809) and British Colonel Tarleton with his *History of the Campaign of 1780 and 1781* (1787), for example.

The seventeenth and eighteenth centuries sent out traders, missionaries, explorers, colonizers, and warriors but also an amazing number of ambassadors, not just within Europe but from European countries to Russia, Asia, Asia Minor, and Abyssinia. Perhaps without exception each embassy included at least one person who wrote of the journey. Most of these embassies were of course designed to promote trade or Christianity, perhaps to help one country compete with another.[85] Sir Thomas Roe, for example, representing England as a good-will ambassador to the Great Mogul, arrived in India in 1615 and spent three years negotiating trade relations before returning home to have his journal—only one of at least four written about his voyage—come out in Purchas's collection in 1625. In the 1630s, when the little German municipality of Holstein was granted the right to send an embassy to Moscow and then on to Persia, two groups from there actually went to Russia, the first of which the scholarly Adam Olearius served as secretary, the second of which completed the journey to Persia with Olearius as counselor. His book—about the Russians, the Persians, the hazardous trip with its two shipwrecks and its threatening Cossacks, and the geography and natural history along the way—came out in 1647 and then was enlarged in 1656 to become one of the most useful travel books of all time as well as one of the most popular, with at least nine German editions before 1700, four in French by 1680, and three in English in the 1660s alone. Later in the century Russia sent a number of embassies, usually unsuccessful, to China before, during, and after the time these two nations were warring over the Amur basin. One in 1678 produced a first-rate journal by the leader Spathary, and in 1689 the Chinese mission that met with the Russians to sign a treaty was accompanied by the widely traveled Jesuit Jean François Gerbillon, whose accounts were published by Du Halde in the *Lettres édifiantes*. Even more significant for the literature of travel was the Russian embassy to China in 1692, which went by way of Manchuria and Tibet and was led by Everard Ysbrantz Ides, whose journal was almost as attractive, generally useful, and important in the history of fiction as that of the German Olearius. In the very period China and Russia were ceasing their wars, Louis XIV dispatched an ambassador to China and Siam named de Chaumont, who was accompanied by a party of Jesuits selected for their erudition and who ultimately became famous travel writers, among them being Gerbillon and Louis Le Comte in China and Pierre Tachard with his two books about Siam and the voyage there. All such official government embassies were of course more than matched by others representing the great trading companies, such as that of Roe for the East India Company or those sent out by the Pope, as when Innocent XII sponsored an expedition to Abyssinia in 1700 that included Friar Thomas Krump, who returned two years later and in 1710 published his account of the embassy.

There were other kinds of officials serving their nations who belong to the history of travel literature between the time of Cervantes and that of Fanny Burney. Among the English governors who wrote about North America were William Bradford and John Winthrop in Massachusetts, John Archdale in Carolina, and Oglethorpe in Georgia. Among the French colonial officials were Etienne de Flacourt, Governor of Madagascar in the 1640s, with an account of the island and of his experiences there that remained standard for many years, and N.G. Léonard, Lieutenant General of the Admiralty for France in Guadeloupe, who published his *Idylles* of that island in 1766.[86] Then there were traveling officials such as William Byrd of Virginia, who sent letters and kept diaries during his years in England in the 1710s and 1720s as representative of his colony and who wrote an attractive "secret" *History* and then a published *History* of the surveying trip which he led to establish the line between Virginia and North Carolina in 1728. Toward the end of the century, Arthur Young represented the British Board of Agriculture on trips to France and throughout the United Kingdom that led to five travel books in the 1780s and helped make him one of the most admired of travel writers.

Travel writers between 1600 and 1800 worked for their religious order, their trading company, or their nation, but they also represented almost every occupation imaginable no matter who paid them.[87] There were secretaries, such as the great poet Tasso in France (1571) with an Italian embassy, or Olearius with the Holstein embassy to Russia, or Nieuhof, whose well-illustrated account (1665) of a Dutch embassy that left the East Indies for China in 1655 is not only one of the most attractive books to look at but one of the most useful for its day and now. Nearly every group of any size that went somewhere—an embassy, a ship's crew, a trade expedition—took along a chaplain, Protestant or Roman Catholic, who because he was educated often wrote of his journey, as did Edward Terry, an Oxford graduate with Ambassador Thomas Roe to India in 1616 whose book supplements that of his superior, or pére Joutel with La Salle, or Richard Walter with Anson's *Centurion*. Sometimes an ordinary seaman or inferior officer competed with his captain, his chaplain, or some supernumerary by keeping a journal and publishing it, perhaps with an editor's help, as did Lieutenant John Rickman whose volume beat by three years the official three volumes of Cook and King for the fatal last voyage of Cook (1776-80), or the marine John Ledyard with his version of that same voyage.

Medical doctors seemed to travel and write more than did the members of other occupations. In addition to buccaneers like Wafer and Exquemelin they include such eminent people as François Bernier in the East, a far traveler who served Aurengzebe three years as physician and then published (1670-71) a volume recounting his adventures, including information about Kashmir not found elsewhere in his day; or Engelbrecht Kaempfer, doctor-naturalist who went with a Swedish embassy and saw much of Persia, Batavia, India, and Japan before returning home in 1693 and doing two important books; and Sir Hans Sloane in the West Indies as a governor's physician gathering notes and specimens that would lead to his famous two volumes about the islands and also to the beginnings of the natural science collection at the British Museum.[88]

Other kinds of scientists also wrote travel books. Among them were engineers such as Amadée Frézier attacking the Jesuits in his *Relation* (1716; English 1718) and drawing plans of fortifications along the western coast of

South America; or the eccentric and energetic J.W.G. de Brahm, a German telling of the Indians in Georgia, Tennessee, and Florida and of his engineering the construction of famous Fort Loudoun on the Little Tennessee River in 1756.[89] There were geologists such as William Coxe, whose dry book about Switzerland (1789) was translated by Ramond de Carbonnières, another geologist but one whose account of his own travels among the Pyrenees (1789) is anything but dry. There were map makers everywhere, such as John Smith with his *Map . . . Description of Virginia* in 1612 and his *Description* of New England in 1616. There were surveyors, among them the Jesuits who were assigned early in the eighteenth century to survey much of China; John Lawson about the same time in Carolina; William Byrd's party on the Virginia–North Carolina line a little later; and St. Jean de Crévecoeur with Montcalm and then in Pennsylvania and New York. There were astronomers, Halley off South America (1700), for example, or Wales and Bayly on Cook's second voyage, all taking lunar observations and all keeping journals. And, finally, there were botanists by the hundred, including the great John Ray (1673, e.g.) or the Swedish Peter Kalm in America (1753-61) and Daniel Solander with Cook, two of Linnaeus's traveling disciples.

There were yet other occupations the travel writers represented. One can, for example, find magistrates such as Charles de Brosses (1739-40) on his way to Italy, even secret agents such as Defoe and François Michaux the elder.[90] The first of these two toured Britain for years as an undercover man for Robert Harley while collecting notes for the best and most often reprinted travel book about the British Isles (1724-26). The other botanized in Kentucky and Tennessee in the 1790s while serving Genêt in the interest of the French Girondists. Scholars went from library to library looking at rare manuscripts and at the same time keeping unusually personal and complete journals of their peregrinations, among them being the two Benedictine monks Martine and Durand (1717-24). English philosophers such as Berkeley and Locke wrote of their experiences on the Continent; the latter was in France twice, once for three and one-half years (1675-78), traveling widely, especially in the south, and keeping journals and writing letters that would eventually be collected as *Locke's Travels in France*. And any number of tutors accompanied their young charges on a Grand Tour—Locke himself with the son of Sir John Banks (1678), or the Roman Catholic Richard Lassels, who toured many times before writing *The Voyage of Italy* (1670), which with *Voyage d'Italie* (1691) of the Huguenot F.-M. Mission, another tutor, was one of the two or three most popular guidebooks for people on the Grand Tour.

And these tutors, recommended by Bacon in "Of Travel" and employed by wealthy parents for more than two hundred years, had charge of many young members of one of the largest groups of travelers, the students or pseudostudents on the Grand Tour or studying at a Continental university.[91] Their numbers of course varied with political or religious conditions: Louis XIII's war with the Huguenots in the 1620s, for example, spoiled travel across France, just as Roman Catholic persecution, even forced conversion, of Protestants in Italy and Spain caused a decline in the number of tourists during James I's reign. If the Grand Tourists were English of the seventeenth century, they preferred France and Italy for learning, for languages, and for social graces, although they often found their way to the Low Countries and Spain, especially after Charles II returned to the throne of England, after Spain and Italy became more tolerant of and friendly to Protestants, after Louis IV could be counted on to remain peaceful, and after transportation improved. By the 1630s and 1640s the Earl of Cork insisted on sending all six of his boys to the Continent, in pairs, each pair accompanied in turn by their "governor" Marcombes and their servants. The greatest of these sons, Robert Boyle, even in his teens wrote letters about and kept a journal of what they saw and did and whom they visited, while Marcombes's letters to the Earl are most revealing of such matters as clothes, transportation, problems, and studies.[92] The French of the same time also preferred Italy, the minister Colbert, for example, sending his son, the future minister, marquis de Seignelay, across France to Italy accompanied by both an architect and a painter as tutors. The great naturalist Buffon, at age twenty-three (1730-31) and without a tutor himself, joined up with the young English Duke of Kingston, who did have one, and journeyed over southern France and Italy writing letters home to his friend the président de Ruffey. All such young travelers were of course not so well attended. George Sandys, for example, went alone early in the seventeenth century and kept going to Asia; in 1650 at age twenty-two Sir William Temple traveled in France and the Low Countries unattended and stayed three years at Brussels learning the Spanish language and much besides, all of which later helped to make him an ambassador and one of the most admired statesmen of Europe; and Joseph Addison at the beginning of the eighteenth century also spent more than three years on the Continent, but at government expense, preparing himself for a diplomatic career. The book he wrote became standard fare for any Englishman headed for the same countries. The Grand Tour remained popular until the nineteenth century and, in fact, has always existed in one form or another, and it has always produced a great body of literature to be read and imitated, to be used as a guide and an inspiration, or to be satirized. The seventeenth and eighteenth centuries, however, are still thought of, and with reason, as the age of the Grand Tour.

When travelers of the time were not following the call of religion, occupation, or education, they could be visiting or accompanying spouses, other relatives, or friends. Often the members of these groups wrote letters about their journeys, and sometimes the letters grew into, or were collected as, books.[93] The young scientist Christiaan Huygens, who visited London correspondents in 1661 and again in 1663, is one whose letters were later published as his *Reyseverhael.* Horace Walpole's letters from Italy in 1740 show that he stayed in Florence for weeks partly because his new friend Horace Mann resided there, was so hospitable, and caused him to fall in love with Italians. Benjamin Franklin, an inveterate traveler, letter writer, even keeper of journals, visited friends constantly, in Boston, New York, Britain, France. One of the greatest of women letter writers, Lady Mary Wortley Montagu, accompanied her diplomat husband to Turkey (1716-18) and was inspired to pen some of her most delightful correspondence, while another, Mme de Sévigné, was similarly inspired when her daughter moved with her governor husband to Provence and for years needed to be told of the mother's life, not just at her hôtel in Paris but on the trips to Brittany which she took before ending up at Aix-en-Provence with the daughter and writing other people. One of the most influential of travel books—known so well by Defoe when he wrote the continuation of *Robinson Crusoe*—was that by J.A. von Mandelslo, who in 1635 went along as a friend of Olearius when the Holstein embassy was sent to Persia; becoming addicted to travel, Mandelslo parted with his companions to see other parts of Asia before returning via Italy and making another voyage, largely by sea, to the East Indies. After his death his journals were edited by Olearius (1645). In somewhat similar fashion John Ray traveled for three years on the Continent with his pupil-friend Francis Willughby, Ray concentrating largely on plants and the younger man on animals; the trip resulted in Ray's best travel book but also in his having to edit, add to, and publish the two books Willughby completed before dying.

Still other kinds of travel accounts resulted when people fled litigation, family problems, persecution, or unhealthy climates and sought safer, happier, or healthier countries.[94] The two giant, warrior-lover cousins Franz and Friedrich von der Trenck, one dying young about 1749, the other guillotined with the poet André Chénier in 1794, left memoirs of their exciting lives on the Continent as they went from one court or amour or duel to another, often one step ahead of the law or of irate parents or husbands, even of Frederick the Great. Claude Le Beau, claiming to have been estranged from his father, took refuge in Canada and wrote two volumes of a fanciful *Voyage curieux parmi les sauvages . . .* (1738). Perhaps even more numerous than those men fleeing the law after seducing a woman or killing a man in a duel were the religious refugees, especially the Huguenots after the revocation of the Edict of Nantes. Not only did Huguenot François Misson get into the business of tutoring Englishmen on Grand Tours and of writing real and fake travel books after having to leave France, but his brother Henri left a splendid account of his observations of England. Ill health, even vacationing, was an abundant source of travel literature. In 1634-35, for example, Sir William Brereton, later a leader for Parliament in the civil wars in England, took his children to see doctors in Leyden and apparently used the trip as an excuse to continue touring the Low Countries, attending church services, buying paintings, "enrolling" at the University of Leyden for a few pennies, and ending with one of the best of journals. And in the eighteenth century three great English novelists wrote journals of the travels they made primarily for the sake of health—Fielding, Sterne, and Smollett.

And finally there are those travelers who are not only among the most intriguing but whose stories are also among those closest to certain forms of the novel—the adventurers and the lovers of travel for the sake of travel. By no means, however, should one forget that members of these groups have always existed and have always been found not just alone but often inspiring or corrupting, leading or following other groups of travelers. The lust for money, whether in elusive El Dorado, in the pockets of the gullible in Europe, or in the holds of Spanish treasure ships; the thirst for glory, perhaps in the armies of Marlborough or Prince Eugene, perhaps in expeditions to new continents or new oceans headed by already famous travelers such as Teixeira in Brazil, La Salle in French America, Morgan in the West Indies, and Cook in the Pacific; or, quite simply, the fascination with the unknown, the distant, the exotic—all these and other reasons attracted travelers who had a purpose or wanderers who perhaps had none. And if they wrote, their accounts were a source of information and pleasure for the sedentary by his fireside or sometimes the magnet that pulled him from his chair and onto ships or highways. Of many possible illustrations one may select three subgroups that are typical.

One of these adventurers is the curious traveler who must see every-thing, perhaps in his own country, or in more than one country or continent, and who may take time to record his observations. One such person was Mandelslo, who left his friend Olearius in Persia and kept going to follow his gleam. Another was the dramatist-novelist Jean Regnard, who as a young man left Paris to see the Mediterranean region, was captured by pirates, served as a slave, and then after being ransomed was, like Ulysses, unable to stand a quiet life at home and set out again to see those parts of Europe he had not yet seen—Belgium, Scandanavia, even Lapland and Russia. Still another was the young chemist Henry de Rouvière, who went all over France and Switzerland in 1703-04, was almost ecstatic about certain parts of his homeland, especially Lyons and Montpellier, and left four long essays detailing his impressions and describing towns, roads, industries as Defoe at the same time was doing for the United Kingdom.[95] Each of these travelers was published in his lifetime or shortly afterward and was read by seventeenth- and eighteenth-century novelists and readers of novels.

There were countless others, however, whose sometimes first-rate journals could have had little or no direct influence on the intellectual history of their own time since they were published only later—for example, the English Celia Fiennes (c. 1687-1703) and the French P.-T. du Fossé (1657-91).[96] Fiennes, traveling by horse, by water, infrequently by carriage, and even on foot, made dozens of short journeys in England and a long one to the north in 1697 before writing most of a journal in 1702 that is now an indispensable companion to Defoe's *Tour through the Whole Island of Great Britain* (1724-26) and John Macky's *A Journey through England*, which was written in prison in 1709 and published five years later. Du Fossé, a well-known Jansenist writer, also had to see all of his native land and over a period of thirty-four years managed to do so; and like Fiennes he described not only the industry and agriculture, the monuments, castles, and chateaus—Saint-Michel being one of the best described—but also his trip on the Loire, which Mme de Sévigné enjoyed too, his inns and food, and his coach stuck in the mud. But while such journals as these two were not available in print until the nineteenth century, they help demonstrate that while the novel was evolving people were avidly traveling and writing about their travels.

There have always been opinions as to which nation or which period of history produced the greatest proportion of these travel-hungry people. In England, for example, there is a time-honored tradition that the English have been the greatest travelers. No doubt the pilgrimages and then the Crusades helped to foster that belief. At any rate, by Chaucer's day Gower, Wycliffe, Higden, and the author of *Mandeville* note the Englishman's inordinate wanderlust, a national characteristic attributed to the fact that the moon ruled the "seventhe clymat," that is, England; and so, in Mandeville's words, since "the mone envyrouneth the erthe more hastyly than any other planete," it pulled the English here and yon frantically seeking "strange thinges and other dyversitees of the world."[97] And, of course, with the rise of Britain as the greatest sea power and with the spread of its vast empire, that reputation was even strengthened. But Germany has also had its tourists. In the fourteenth century Gower noted that "Alemaigne" was ruled by that same "mone" that controlled England, and Clare Howard has estimated that in the Renaissance the English were known as the greatest travelers "next to the Germans."[98] Smollett in the Preface to *Fathom* (1748) found the Scotch "addicted to traveling." But of what country and of what age has the same opinion not been offered? Lionel Casson in his fascinating *Travel in the Ancient World* demonstrates clearly that men have always traveled and traveled much, no matter how slowly or with what difficulty, although certain ages may seem to stand out, for example, the first two hundred years after Christ, which, he says, "were halcyon days for a traveller."[99] And if we accept the English, Scots, and Germans as travel addicts, we must surely find even a greater proportion of Spanish and Portuguese moving constantly over the world during the time their small nations controlled such enormous parts of it. Furthermore, for so many centuries what nation sent out more travelers than Italy, the home of the Polos, Varthema, Niccolò Conti, Columbus, Vespucci, Pigafetta, Benzoni, all of whom were known throughout Europe before Shakespeare died? Perhaps it is the nature of man, of all nations, to be restless, to wander.[100] The reason may be the one offered by the early Church fathers, who blamed such restlessness on original sin, an unholy urge to use the eye; or humanists from Petrarch on may be right when they attribute it to curiosity, a healthy desire "to seek, to find," to enter that "arch wherethro' / Gleams that untravell'd world"; or perhaps the opinion of W.B. Carnochan (1977) can be considered when he argues that because Europeans of the eighteenth century felt confined by their environment they were compelled to flee it and travel the face of the earth like Cain or the Wandering Jew. At any rate, this Ulysses Factor supplies us with our first kind of obsessed traveler of the seventeenth and eighteenth centuries, when, one German of the time insisted, travel was so popular it was an "epidemic" that spread its germs by means of countless books.

A second typical kind is that person who not only followed his curiosity, his penchant for observing and experiencing, but who became involved in the experiences of those other travelers who had been to places he was unable to see. Hakluyt at the very beginning of the seventeenth century is one who stands out in this group. Although he saw little of England, he did visit France for five years before spending the rest of his life reading and collecting the journals of other travelers and even directing and advising them before they set out. Melchisédec Thévenot, although not the traveler his famous nephew was in Asia and Europe, still traveled widely before starting his collection of voyages in the 1660s, as did the novelist Prévost, who was actually inspired by his visit to England, by his position as secretary in the home of the leading merchant of London, and by his subsequent reading of English travels to spend years translating and editing one of the great travel collections of the eighteenth century. It is an intriguing fact that none of these three, as with nearly all travel collectors, published an account of his own travels, each being content to enjoy the experiences of others vicariously. A notable exception is Tobias Smollett with his *Travels through France and Italy* (1766) to go with his huge *Compendium of Authentic and Entertaining Voyages* (1756).

The third obsessed traveler is the adventurer par excellence, a man of action who seldom takes time to write; and the eighteenth century has been called by Peter Wilding the Age of the Great Adventurers, those who, Montesquieu claimed, move the world more than do rulers of great empires.[101] One cannot be sure if the two would agree that Wilding's five famous showpieces were all politically world shakers—John Law, the brilliant Edinburgh mathematician and banker who gambled his way over Europe and controlled the French bank; Alexandre de Bonneval, the warrior and statesman who ended up helping to rule Turkey; Theodor von Neuhoff, solider of fortune, briefly "King" of Corsica, and one of the six deposed rulers Candide met in a Paris boarding house;[102] Casanova, the irresistible, moving from the boudoirs of one nation to those of another; and Giuseppe Balsamo (Cagliostro), complete charlatan, quack doctor, magician. But certainly they were significant and certainly they traveled far and often, although only one, Casanova, left memoirs that tell of his travels. Each of the others inspired countless books about his adventures, however, and Bonneval had the distinction of having spurious autobiographies published.

But great adventurers, or "honored adventurers" as Goldoni called them, have always existed, some have been more honored and honorable than several of Wilding's five, and some of them have written their own travel accounts. Surely there were no greater adventurers and lovers of travel than Marco Polo in the thirteenth century, ibn-Batuta of the fourteenth, John Cabot in the fifteenth, or in the sixteenth the "swaggering . . . universal Renaissance genius Dom de Castro"[103] as well as dozens of the Conquistadores who flocked to South America and Mexico. But the seventeenth and eighteenth centuries had more than their share, so many in fact that one could supplement Wilding with several volumes of biographies as fascinating as those he selected. Starting with John Smith, all over the New England coast, Virginia, and Asia, and the three Sherley brothers in Asia Minor, Persia, and the Mediterranean country, one could move forward to the comte de Gramont, who flitted or ran between France and England arousing courts, forcing exile on himself, breaking hearts, and marrying against his will. Then one could look at a bucanneer such as Dampier, who sacked cities and ships, was befriended by Sir Hans Sloane and introduced to Queen Anne, led government expeditions, and sailed around the world three times; or at the baron Lahontan, soldier of fortune in Canada who offered to spy on his native France for Spain or any country that wanted him, friend of Leibnitz, and self-professed authority on American Indians.

One could next move into the eighteenth century to the French fake Psalmanazar, who went to England, ingratiated himself in high places, taught "Formosan" at Oxford before being exposed, became a hack writer, and ended up a friend of Johnson.[104] And there is that other but much more successful fake, the Spaniard genius Torres y Villaroel, who led a wild university life terminated by mad pranks and who mixed poems, satires, and fencing, sold contraband, became a chemist and dancing master, was appointed to the chair of mathematics and astrology at Salamanca, correctly foretold the death of King Louis I in 1724, studied medicine for thirty days and became a doctor, spent a long exile in Portugal, and during his seventy-seven years lived, as he himself said, the life of a picaro. But Germany seemed to produce any number of unbelievable stories of real adventurers. For example, there are the cousins von der Trenck, both barons, who lived all over Europe not just by their giant strength, their swords, and their love making but by their obvious intelligence and quick thinking; or that other baron, von Pöllnitz, self-styled "cavalier of wit and distinction" and "adventurer of the first rank, a regular Proteus: courtier, gambler, author, scandalmonger, Protestant, Catholic, canon, and what not," who changed his religion six times and was a confidant of two kings, a soldier in three armies, and a political spy; or, better still, Rudolph Erich Raspe, another universal genius, a "scholar, linguist, scientist, mining engineer, poet, librarian, coin expert, editor, and hoaxer," who fled to England after robbing his patron the Landgrave of Hesse, became a friend of Horace Walpole and other notables, implored Captain Cook to take him on the third voyage, and died in Ireland after failing to convince a rich landowner that there was gold on his property. Nearly all these adventurers, from Smith and the Sherleys on, wrote travel accounts of some kind, the exceptions being Gramont, whose *Mémoires* are by his brother-in-law Anthony Hamilton; Psalmanazar, who wrote a fake history of Formosa as if he had been there; and Raspe, who wrote not of himself but of Baron Munchausen, a satirical composite of such real travelers as Abyssinian James Bruce and the Baron de Tott. Without exception the accounts by or about these men have been accused of being fictionized. And, to be sure, their lives are usually larger than life, the stories of middle- or upper-class picaros who need and know no home. With them the literature of travel approaches all of Northrop Frye's types of long narrative fiction—the romance, the novel, the confession, and, with geniuses such as Villaroel and Raspe, the anatomy.

And their stories lead us to the outer edge of the literature of real travels where, on the edge and mingling with them, sits another huge shelf of books that have been important to the history of travels, of ideas, and of the novel.[105] These are the books that are partly or wholly fabricated by real travelers, by their editors, or by writers who needed only a good library and an imagination. Their spectrum ranges from books whose authors were sometimes too credulous and repeated gossip, false reports, or old wives' tales, to books that contain much truth but also certain embellishments or exaggerations, to others whose authors occasionally falsified their adventures or their facts, and finally to those that are almost or entirely concocted out of whole cloth—or other men's books. Few travelers, in fact, even the most important, escape being placed in the first of these four groups, from Herodotus, who repeated legends, to Defoe, who augmented his *Tour* by borrowing from Camden's *Britannia*, to Linnaeus's student Peter Kalm (1753-61), who let his American friends pull his leg with a good bear story. And almost as many honored and necessary writers—even in the seventeenth and eighteenth centuries—have been prone to embellish or exaggerate what they saw or heard on their journeys—the height of Niagara Falls, the length of the manatee, the size of the Patagonian "giants," the curative powers of New World plants, the beastly or the admirable qualities of the Red Man.

Closest of course to the novel is the story put together by a real traveler, or by a fireside traveler, who employs accounts already published and creates a narrative partly or wholly fake but at the same time so realistic, so much like other books, that he is able to deceive readers for a few years, perhaps for a century, perhaps forever. The number of these fictitious, or partly fictitious, travel books is so great that one can merely suggest a few significant variations. The name of the author of *Sir John Mandeville* (c. 1356) will probably never be known; but his book—no matter how much we praise his genius—is certainly a fabrication that may have failed to fool a few educated people but that for perhaps three hundred years fooled most and was even considered genuine when Marco Polo's story was not.[106] This unknown author borrowed from contemporaneous encyclopedias and from travelers, perhaps more nearly real than he, such as William of Boldensele (c. 1336) and Odoric of Pordenone (1330)—Sir John even starts his journeys on the same day William set out!—and put together such an attractive book that not only do more than three hundred of its manuscripts still exist, but after printing was invented it remained popular, in spite of being frequently condemned by writers such as Robert Burton and Sir Thomas Browne. In 1725, in fact, the year before *Gulliver's Travels*, the manuscript of the first of *Mandeville's* English translations was discovered and printed.

But the authors of *Mandevilles* have always existed. Lucian, for example, attacked them in the *True History*, concentrating most perhaps on Herodotus. In his early edition of the *Principall Navigations* Hakluyt printed the story of David Ingram's impossible hike from mid-Mexico to Canada in less than a year, but in 1598 the great editor, by then less gullible, omitted it. About the same time, Vicente Espinel, inspired largely by the great traveler Sarmiento de Gamboa, invented both *La Vida de Marcos de Obregón* and much "geografía fantastica" about South America; and an unknown Frenchman invented the story of "le sieur de Combes" (1609) by borrowing from Champlain's six-year-old book and using his own vivid imagination.[107] Nearly a century later, another Frenchman, the baron Lahontan, augmented his real travel experiences in North America with fake ones, including, first, the account ("Letter" 16) of a nonexistent river and the impossible people living along it and, second, a dialogue between a most learned Red Man and a badly outmaneuvered European. Each of these inventions would be later increased to more than twice its length and help Lahontan's works become incredibly popular and influential.

By the eighteenth century there were, in fact, a surprising number of creative writers and editors making a practice of producing such books, among them being Mme d'Aulnoy, François Mission, Gatien de Courtilz, and Daniel Defoe. The first of these wrote a fake *Relation de voyage d'Espagne* (1691); the second, after producing his standard Grand Tour guide, *Nouveau voyage d'Italie,* published his amazing invention—not by any means out of whole cloth—the *Voyage et avantures de François Leguat* (1707); the third was notorious for his wholesale production of pseudobiographies and autobiographies of soldiers, even women, who traveled Europe; and the fourth was just as notorious, not so much for his novels such as *Moll Flanders* but for his pseudotravels such as *Captain Singleton* (1720), *A New Voyage round the World* (1724), and probably *Robert Drury's Journal* (1729), all three of which were accepted as authentic for some time, and the last of which is still giving scholars trouble.[108] That such books were more or less successful in deceiving readers can be discovered in many ways. One may, for example, note that in 1759 the sophisticated *Journal des savants* listed four of them as authentic.[109] Or, for a quicker reference, one may check the pages of Philip Gove's seminal study, *The Imaginary Voyage in Prose Fiction* (1941), which includes not only supranatural or extraordinary voyages but those fabricated realistic ones that had been exposed by Gove's time. Furthermore, the fact that travelers could embellish real accounts or that they and nontravelers did invent some or all of what seemed to be authentic is one indication that the literature of travel was popular.

It was indeed popular well before and during the time long narrative fiction was becoming respectable. Even before *Don Quixote* appeared, the early letters of the Jesuits and the great Renaissance collections of voyages were found in every important language except English and were known to most educated men, while individual fascinating accounts by real or supposed travelers went through many editions, among them *Mandeville* and the books of Marco Polo, Varthema, Benzoni, Cartier, Hans Stade, Ulrich Schmidt, Pinto, and the Sherleys. Such literature not only remained popular but the eighteenth century itself produced more than one hundred new collections of voyages and travels, over twenty-five in English alone, from the Churchills at the beginning to Adams at the end. And obviously these books were widely read. Although one may to a certain extent discount as prejudiced the claims of popularity and importance made in prefaces by nearly all editors of the collections, such as Thévenot (1663-72), Harris (1744), Prévost (1746 ff.), and Smollett (1756), one needs also to know that when Prévost, for example, began his ambitious *Histoire des voyages* by translating from John Green's collection and with the intention of adding to Green's natural history in order to supplement Buffon, he was so successful that his first two volumes had three editions in two years and were translated immediately into Dutch and German.

There is an abundance of other, perhaps completely disinterested, evidence. Chapelain the literary critic, for example, writing in 1663, a year before Thévenot, believed that French reading taste had changed, that "instead of 'romans,' which have fallen with La Calprenède, travels have been elevated and now hold the highest place in the court and the city."[110] Richard Steele in *Tatler* 254 (1710) extolled the reading of travels, in particular praising *Mandeville*, which had more than twenty editions in the eighteenth century; and a year later the Earl of Shaftesbury was pointing out the good and bad results of the great appeal of the récit de voyage.[111] In the Preface to her novel *The Accomplished Rake* (1727), Mary Davys echoed Chapelain by asserting that "for sometime ... novels have been a great deal out of use and fashion ... ladies have been taken up with amusements of more use and improvement—I mean history and travels." And if the newspaper serializations of real and false and imaginary travels that became so popular in England after 1720 are any indication,[112] Mrs. Davys's estimate is tenable for that nation. And it is just as appropriate for France or Germany. As late as 1786, for example, the editors of the great monthly *Bibliothèque universelle des romans*, begun in 1775, were still able to say, "The taste for travels has always piqued the curiosity of readers ... we derive more pleasure indeed from the abbé Prévost and Captain Cook than from the most attractive book on morality"; and in October of 1784 C.M. Wieland's *Der Teutsche Merken* had an article, "Ueber das Reisen," which claimed that "In no age of this world was travel so common as ours ... it is no wonder ... that so many descriptions of travel are written.[113]

By now this sketch of the history and types of the literature of travel should have made certain facts obvious. One of the most important is that, like the novel, it was always more or less international. In the ancient world, the writings of Herodotus and those other traveler-historians concern the whole Mediterranean and often more. In the Middle Ages, the volumes rifled by the author of *Mandeville*, who by some scholars is considered English, are nearly all Continental. The letters of Columbus and Vespucci were translated into many languages immediately, while the great collection of the de Brys—published in Latin and French but in Germany—favored the literature of no nation. And, finally, the collections of the eighteenth century, such as those of the Churchills and J.-F. Bernard, were in each case non-nationalistic. Perhaps because of the vastness of the subject, however, most students of travels other than the historians of exploration have not ventured into languages other than their own, or even into translations of foreign books. Such a limitation mars the effectiveness of studies by R.W. Frantz (1932-33) and A. Lytton Sells (1964),[114] who consider only English travelers, and of Gilbert Chinard and his disciple Geoffroy Atkinson, whose various books—in spite of their excellence—seldom consider any but French travelers.

But the historians of ideas, including students of the novel, must know that those many readers in the seventeenth and eighteenth centuries—and of course long before—had access to and knew well the travel literature of many nations. In England, Swift's mentor Sir William Temple read foreign travelers more than he did those of his own country; John Locke not only kept a journal of his trips on the Contenent but in a treatise on morals cited four travelers not one of whom was English; the *Spectator* used the English Robert Ligon's book on Barbados more than once, but it borrowed more often from the French Chardin, Tavernier, and père Le Comte; and Samuel Johnson's first published work was a translation of a French version of the Portuguese Lobo's account of Abyssinia (1735).[115] As for the French, Mme d'Aulnoy, probably without ever going to Spain, as she claimed, was able to write realistically about it because of her reading; and since the abbé Prévost first became interested in travelers while living in London, it is not surprising to find that his great collection of voyages was begun as a translation of an English collection. Not only then were people of the seventeenth and eighteenth centuries traveling in their own countries, into other countries, and across vast seas writing generously of their experiences, but their knowledge of other languages permitted them to read travel books from other countries as soon as they were off the press or, failing that, to read them quickly in translations, not just in the many collections but also individually. Mme d'Aulnoy's *Relation du voyage d'Espagne* (1691), for example, was for thirty years more popular in England than was the translation of Galland's very popular *Arabian Nights*.[116] Even the erudite A.-F. Frézier's *Relation* of his voyage to South America (1716) was available in English translation in less than two years. Similarly the French J.-F. Bernard paraphrased the English Royal Society's "Directions for Seamen" and placed them in his collection of voyages to the north,[117] which included Dutch and English narratives as well as French, while Prévost, like Churchill before, printed in his eleventh volume (1750) the "Advice" to travelers written by the Italian Careri in 1698. Truly there was an enormous interchange of books and ideas among the nations of western Europe, a fact noted with pleasure by Voltaire in 1748: "One sees among all nations a mutual corre-spondence; Europe is like one great family."[118]

With all this wide reading of the literature of travel, the influence of that literature on every phase of the history of ideas was incredibly broad and deep. Geographers and students of exploration have long been aware of it, but now that influence is being estimated and described more and more in special studies in other realms of thought. A book such as Frank Manuel's *The Eighteenth Century Confronts the Gods* (1959) considers the effect of travel literature on religion, while dozens of studies depend on travel books for their information, studies such as William W. Appleton's *A Cycle of Cathay: The Chinese Vogue in England during the Seventeenth and Eighteenth Centuries* (1951) or Albert Lortholary's *Le Mirage Russe en France au XVIIIe siècle* (1951). There are likewise dozens of articles, like those in *Terrae Incognitae*, that consider such matters as the effect of travels on seventeenth-century Dutch culture, or like those inspired by the Captain Cook bicentennial. The current renascence of interest in early travels and voyages extends, in fact, to every broad area of ideas in the seventeenth and eighteenth centuries. The reasons for that interest are as many as the realms of thought affected by travelers.

First, just as trade inspired businessmen and ministers of state to send out expeditions overseas or embassies to other nations, the books and letters produced by these groups not only made it easier for others to follow but inspired a longing for exotic goods that quickly became necessities. As a result, accounts written by men engaged in such travel were often propa-gandistic. A chief motive for Hakluyt, for example, was the desire to estab-lish not just a British empire but good trade relations, to discover new commodities of trade, to arouse the interest of English statesmen or business-men.[119] Similarly, in his reports La Salle moved the Mississippi west so it would be closer to Spanish gold; Defoe lost no opportunity to propagandize for British trade when he composed his fake travel accounts such as *A New Voyage round the World;* and Theodore Drage, voyager, explorer, merchant, travel writer, persuaded Benjamin Franklin and others to finance two expe-ditions to look for the Northwest Passage.[120] All such books help to explain most of the embassies to foreign countries, John Law's crash and the South Sea Bubble about 1720, and the formation of all the great trading companies after 1600. As propaganda for international trade and for colonization, travel accounts had no equal.

Second, no one depended more on the récits de voyage than did the geographers and cartographers.[121] Almost every sailing expedition from Prince Henry and Columbus on included mathematicians and draftsmen who could take sun shots and determine latitude and, less well, longitude and then make sketches of ports, islands, and coastlines, all of which cartographers might consider. The Jesuits were particularly helpful, even being assigned the task of surveying and mapping great areas in China. Some accounts of course were not always trustworthy, since they included either outright distortions or the results of wishful thinking—the fabled city of Manoa in South America or Lahontan's fictitious "rivière Longue" in North America—but gradually the true was sifted from the false, and map makers in Defoe's day such as Herman Moll and Guillaume Delisle were able to draw better and better maps.

Third, although the debt of geography to the literature of travel is immense and well documented, the debt of science is just as great even if that story has yet to be told.[122] In spite of the exaggerations and secondhand incredibilities in early travel journals,[123] their authors—including the author of *Mandeville*—also recorded facts that belong to the real, the valuable, world of science; and as time went by travelers became more and more accurate as they could more easily expose each other or expect less gullible readers. The discovery of America gave great impetus to the search for and dissemination of facts about man and nature; for, from Martire's *Decades* (1511-30) on, hardly a letter was sent from the New World or a book written about it that did not speak of its flora and fauna, of its inhabitants and their customs, of its geography, tides, and hurricanes. All this information was spread far and wide, as with the excellent book (1565) on botany by the Spanish medical doctor Nicholas Monardes, a book translated into French (1572) and then into English by John Frampton (1577) as *Joyfull Newes out of the Newe Founde Worlde* before being used by Thomas Hariot in Virginia when he wrote the first English account of America (1588).[124] Volumes such as that of Monardes did much for the rise of modern science, for Bacon, experimentation, and scientific utilitarianism.[125]

In fact, from the beginning, travelers were urged to keep notes, make drawings, report observations. Ferdinand's court wrote out such instructions for Columbus, Hakluyt provided them for Frobisher's first voyage in 1576,[126] and by 1665-66 they were standard procedure when the Royal Society published its famous "Catalogue of Directions" to travelers that concluded with Robert Boyle's "General Heads for a Natural History of a Countrey, Great or Small."[127] Such directions were not only often reprinted in collections of voyages, as with the Churchills (1704; again 1732) and J.-F. Bernard (1725),[128] but they were burlesqued by Swift in nearly every one of Captain Gulliver's voyages. Furthermore, great scientists themselves traveled, kept their journals, and helped organize that universal Republic of Science envisaged by Bacon. The close association of the newly established academies of science in England, France, and Italy is in fact nowhere better shown than in the travel diaries and letters of Evelyn, Boyle, Ray, Sloane, Christiaan Huygens, Samuel Sorbière, Count Magalotti and dozens of other well-known scientists of the seventeenth century as they recorded their trips abroad, especially their visits with each other.[129] Perhaps, however, the influence of the amateur scientists and other lay travelers was even greater. When Prévost, for example, advertised his huge collection of travels as a supplement to Buffon's classic *Histoire naturelle* and John Ogilby's big one-volume *Africa* (1670) stressed on the title page its section on "the wonderful Plants, Beasts, Birds, and Serpents," both men were working in a tradition dating back to Martire, Hakluyt, and de Bry. And by 1700 another tradition was firmly established, that of sending trained scientists on official embassies or voyages of exploration. Thus, Louis XIV's embassy to Siam and China in the 1680s had Tachard, author of two travel books, and five other trained scientists, a distinguished group that foreshadowed by nearly a century the botanists, astronomers, mathematicians, and physicians who accompanied Cook and Bougainville and reported their observations. All this gripping, yet untold, story—travel literature and the evolution of science—is one of the most important for the history of ideas.

And it is closely related to a fourth influence of travel literature, one well documented, that on religion. To demonstrate this influence, three points can be made. First, science helped the traveling Jesuits to evangelize the pagan world. After Ricci was able to arouse the admiration of the Chinese by setting in operation four pieces of astronomical apparatus their ancestors had built and then forgotten, and after Tachard and his fellows successfully observed the moon's eclipse in 1682 in a performance attended by the wide-eyed King of Siam, Leibnitz was convinced that the success of the Jesuits in Asia was due "solely to the wonderment aroused by their introduction of European inventions and discoveries" in science.[130] Second, the Jesuits more than any other religious group were so eager to convert pagans that they found closer and closer ties between Chinese ethics and Christian practices—Confucius became almost a Christian saint—or between the gods of Canada and the god of Europe. So far did certain Jesuits go in fact, especially Louis Le Comte and Charles Le Gobien in the 1690s, that they led to the notorious "Rites" controversy of about 1700 and to their own official condemnation, even though Le Comte and the Jesuit letters from Canada would continue to be read for a century.[131] Third, travelers other than Jesuits or Protestant pastors affected religious thought in many ways, but as Frank Manuel and others have shown, they were especially important to philosophers proving the universality of religious beliefs, to deists attacking revealed religion, or to the adherents of one religious sect arguing with those of another.[132] That is, by resorting to the travelers, Leibnitz could propose a universal system of natural theology, Bayle could prove that pagan nations did not have an innate conception of a divinity, or Sir William Temple could praise Confucius and attack the orthodox

Bishop Burnet.[133] For the seventeenth and eighteenth centuries, then, travel literature was both a source of revolution in religion and a sourcebook to be drawn on by biased readers searching for evidence to support their preconceived notions about religion.

The importance of travels, in fact, extends to every realm of thought, to every significant business, political, religious, academic, or creative enterprise undertaken during the centuries when the European novel was maturing so fast. What has been demonstrated here for science and religion can be shown for political science, for philosophy, or for the visual arts. It is well known that Montesquieu's *Les Lettres persanes* (1721), a fiction, owes much to books by travelers to the Orient; it may not be so well known that his *Esprit des loix* (1748), the political science bible of the eighteenth century, made use of a far wider range of récits de voyage, and not just for the famous section on the influence of climate on laws.[134] Such theories as those of Montesquieu lead to the far broader subject of relativity in general, as well as to the closely related philosophical optimism of Leibnitz, Pope, the early Voltaire, and Goethe. Obviously travelers as far back as "Mandeville," with his liberal contrasts of English with Arabs and of Christianity with other religions, were instrumental in leading Europeans to consider satisfactory not only a plurality of religions for a given country and for the world, or political systems, or languages but also to recognize their own insularity. It is indeed true, as Lévi-Strauss argues, that, beginning with the Renaissance, western Europe experienced "that crucial moment . . . when, thanks to the great voyages of discovery, a human community which had believed itself to be complete and in its final form suddenly learned . . . that it was not alone, that it was part of a greater whole, and that, in order to achieve self-knowledge, it must first of all contemplate its unrecognizable image in this mirror."[135] Furthermore, just as J.L. Lowes and a few others have been aware of the effects that travel and travelers have had on poetic imagination, scholars such as Barbara Stafford are recognizing the significance of travel volumes for art history, not just because they were often so exquisitely illustrated but also because they fired the artistic imagination in ways such as those Coleridge experienced.[136] For each of these and many other worlds that would have suffered without the travel writer, volumes of explanation are needed. And perhaps none is needed more—as Michel Butor and Germaine Brée might agree—than one showing the close relationship between the récits de voyage and the early, evolving novel.

CHAPTER THREE

The Truth-Lie Dichotomy

A man will lie more plausibly if he will mix in some actual truth. *Strabo*[1]

Although much has been written about the artist as deceiver, as liar, much is left to be written, and that in spite of one recent American's hope that Continental Europeans will stop belaboring the subject since "English and American readers and critics [have] learned with their mother's milk that art is prevarication."[2] As a matter of fact, English-speaking writers seem more concerned with art as prevarication than are Europeans. Even as the hope was being uttered (1977), for example, Richard Kamber was attempting as a philosopher to combine—or separate—"Liars, Poets, and Philosophers," and within the decade William Nelson had done a survey called "The Boundaries of Fiction in the Renaissance: A Treaty between Truth and Falsehood," a survey which he was to turn into a book.[3] Moreover, the authors of the best long studies of eighteenth-century French fiction—each by an English-speaking scholar—are forced to spend much time on the subject, and one of them is entirely devoted to the charges made about lying in art, to the defense against those charges, and to a study of the novelist's devices for creating the illusion of truth, all to go with earlier treatments of the same problems for British fiction.[4] It is, then, a topic not just of perennial and abiding interest in general but an important one for understanding the evolution of "fiction."

It is just as important for the study of travel literature. And here there are also certain scholars who consider deceitful writers or those falsely accused of deceit, that is, their methods and their reasons for deceiving or appearing to deceive. Marjorie Nicolson (1936) and Geoffroy Atkinson (1920; 1922) are two who have done seminal books on imaginary voyages that could not have deceived any reader, those voyages invented by Bishop Godwin (1638) and Cyrano (1657), for example, who like Defoe in his *Consolidator* sent their protagonists to the moon.[5] But Philip Gove's admirable bibliography of the *Imaginary Voyage* (1941) concentrates perhaps less on such blatantly impossible voyages and more on books about apocryphal travels that were realistic enough to fool some, most, or all readers for a period of time, those such as William Sympson's *A New Voyage to the East Indies* (1715), Defoe's *A New Voyage round the World by a Course Never Sailed Before* (1724), the anonymous *Richard Castleman* (1725), or Peter Longuevil-le's *The English Hermit* (1727).[6] And it is that kind of travel fabrication, realistic and believable, that is exposed, dissected, explained, and followed through history by my *Travelers and Travel Liars: 1660-1800* (1962), which also records the tradition, stated gently in 1739 in a letter from Turin by Pope's friend, the traveler Joseph Spence, that "all travellers are a little noted for lying" or more certainly by Farquhar's Scrub, who in *The Beaux' Strate-gem* (III.iii.89) boasts that he "tells lies as if he had been a traveller from his cradle."[7] The tradition of traveler as liar is, in fact, as old as that for belletris-tic writers in general and for authors of long prose fiction in particular.

Almost at the very beginning of the eighteenth century, Pierre Bayle in his influential *Dictionnaire* (1697) argued that "Everybody is deceived" by writers: "the Ancients, who lied . . . spontaneously; the Moderns, blinded by the prestige of the Ancients; the best, the most respectable of authors are deceived . . .";[8] and over fifty years later David Hume, whether seriously or not, declared poets to be "liars by profession."[9] Bayle and perhaps Hume are in one branch of the tradition that thinks of the creative writer as prevarica-tor. Nor was Plato the first limb of that branch when in the second and third books of the *Republic* he banished Homer and Hesiod for dealing in illusion, for imitatiing appearances rather than reality, for teaching falsehood through false subjects and methods. Before him, according to Plutarch, the great lawgiver Solon contended that if Thespis lied on the stage in sport he would teach others to lie in earnest; and after him Lucian, while pretending to damn Odysseus, Ctesias the historian, and the fictive travel liar Iambulus, nevertheless took the position "that a tale must be judged true or false, the story-teller an honest historian or a liar."[10] Today a medievalist scholar can say truthfully that "from St. Augustine to Boccaccio poetry was branded as attractive lying," and a Renaissance scholar can successfully demonstrate that fact for his period;[11] but from Solon and Plato to Bayle to Hume to Picasso, not just poets but dramatists, narrators of prose fiction, and all artists were often considered deceivers, and by 1700 that tradition was especially thriving.

And obviously artists of all kinds were thriving too, in spite of their reputation, for through the centuries they had instructed and pleased and managed a successful defense that was aided by critics and even sometimes by churchmen. Aristotle, for example, may have described both poets and dramatists as "skillful liars";[12] but no one of such influence ever praised good writers more, and in the *Poetics* he argued against Plato by asserting that the artist "represents" a greater truth than Plato's real. For that matter even Plato supported literature that told "salutary fictions," and his own "myths" in the *Republic* were considered edifying.[13] Cicero, Quintilian, and Plutarch defended the poet as one who, although "not greatly concerned with truth," was able to invent facts without misleading anyone who could read him. The Christian era, in spite of opposition such as that of the old Boccaccio, who wanted to burn all his salacious stories, continued to perpetuate and defend the lies of belletristic writers. St. Augustine himself apparently argued for stories so openly false they could not deceive anyone and knew the value of parables that expressed universal truths, while the many apocryphal and popular biblical narratives of the medieval period, such as the Troy stories and the chronicles of Charlemagne and Arthur, encouraged writers of all kinds to emulate their success in pretending to be real. Boccaccio humorously defended the *Decameron* as history, and Chrétien playfully warned the readers of his story of Yvain to beware of sequel writers who would tell them "lies." Similarly, but much later, Cervantes would write the second half of *Don Quixote* to tell the "truth" about his knight and give the lie to the fake sequels that had sprung up, while Lesage in the early eighteenth century found it convenient to keep *Gil Blas* going for years to protect himself against literary thieves.

In the Renaissance one of the best perpetrators of deceitful literature was Sir Philip Sidney, whose *Arcadia* he allowed to be published only after his death; but he was also one of the best defenders of "The Poet," who, he argued,[14] comparing him with the historian, the medical doctor, and the astronomer, "is the least lier" because "he nothing affirmes, and therefore never lyeth. For as I take it, to lye, is to affirme that to be true which is false." That is, the poet writes allegorically and figuratively and, "looking for fiction," uses the narration only "as an imaginative groundplot of a profitable invention." Thus, Sidney agreed with his contemporary Tasso, who believed that "the poet does not spoil truth, but he seeks it in a perfect form, supposing in place of the truth of particulars that of universals, which are Ideas."[15] And these two would have agreed with their predecessor Juan Luis Vives, the great Spanish humanist who in 1522 wrote a dialogue, "Truth Dressed Up, or Of Poetic License: To What Extent Poets May Be Permitted to Vary from the Truth." Here Vives offers ten articles of behavior for "poets," to whom he gives free license to compose instructive apologues and to use metaphor and other rhetorical figures for embellishment; but then he urges them not to change history after the time of the Olympic games and to make sure that all their embellishments of truth "be characterized by verisimilitude, consistency, and decorum."[16] It is intriguing to note that, as William Nelson points out, such Renaissance theorists did grant the writers of "new comedy," because they could not be proved false, the "right to set fictional stories about private people in the contemporary scene," a privilege not accorded writers in other forms of literature.[17] It is intriguing because well before the end of the Renaissance the Italian novella, the early French nouvelle, and the English prose fiction of Dekker and Greene and Nashe were apparently not considered a reputable genre; for, like the dramatic new comedy, they employed contemporaneous characters in Renaissance settings. Vives, while convinced that his restrictions would have little effect, was writing before the author of *Lazarillo* and before Dekker, Bandello, and Cervantes, some of whom may have helped Sidney, Ariosto, and other late Renaissance critics to be more lenient and offer better defenses for the deceitful "poet."

The defense and the success continued into the eighteenth century. Along the way John Dryden, after condemning outright lies as unacceptable to "the understanding," quoted Aristotle on the pleasures of creative imitation. The "means of this pleasure," he believed, "is by deceit." The pictorial artist "imposes on the sight," while the poet imposes on the understanding and, as Sidney and even St. Augustine had argued, paradoxically provides "a true story by a fiction."[18] In "Advice to an Author" in his widely read *Characteristics* of 1711 the Earl of Shaftesbury quoted with approval Aristotle's praise of Homer—"above all others he understood how TO LYE"—and in the tradition of Sidney, Ariosto, and Dryden argued that "facts unably related, though with the greatest sincerity and good faith, may prove the worst sort of deceit [,] and mere lies, judiciously composed, can teach us the Truth of things beyond any other manner."[19] A few years later Swift would in verse sum up the tradition of defense for the creative aritst:

> Unjustly Poets we asperse;
> Truth shines the brighter, clad in verse,
> And all the Fictions they pursue
> Do but insinuate what is true.[20]

More than poets who wrote in verse, more than authors of any other form of literature in fact, writers of long prose fiction and writers of travel accounts were accused of lying. For ancient times, for the medieval period, and for the Renaissance the accusations for prose fiction have been documented at length,[21] and by the decades just before Lesage and Defoe they were legion. In the 1690s Bayle attacked the popular Mme de Villedieu for her bastard genre, half roman and half "history,"[22] while Congreve in the preface to his romantic tale *Incognita*, after expressing concern that readers might become too emotionally involved in "romances" or "novels," concluded that they would eventually recognize their error upon being "convinced that 'tis all a lye." In the very beginning of the eighteenth century the abbé de Bellegarde (1701), noting, like Dryden, that the proper nourishment of the understanding is "Truth," warned readers of the danger they faced in learning to love "the false," that is, in reading novels; and even Marivaux quoted his readers as expecting falsehoods in a novel that is only a novel.[23] Such charges continued on into the century, sometimes directed at all prose fiction, sometimes at individual authors. Voltaire, for example, thought Courtilz, prolific about 1700, "one of the most guilty of the writers of this genre" for "he has inundated Europe with fictions he called history."[24] Lady Mary Wortley Montagu was just as hard on Courtilz's contemporary, the Mme d'Aulnoy. "Would you," she asked in a letter, "have me write novelles like the Countess D'Anois? And is it not better to tell the plain truth?"[25] And Diderot, a novelist himself, satirized the novelist's claim to authenticity, just as today certain well-known critics continue to argue that prose fiction "cannot be construed as embodying claims to tell any truth about the real world."[26]

Similarly travel writers have always been condemned as embellishers of the truth or as plain liars. Lucian did not find their lying particularly reprehensible since, he said, it was traditional; what bothered him was that travelers were so naive as to think no one would find them out, and so he began his burlesque récit de voyage by announcing proudly, "I will say one thing that is true, and that is that I am a liar."[27] In the Middle Ages, Marco Polo and the author of *Mandeville* were by no means the only travel writers to be found guilty of falsehood. In fact, since pilgrimages attracted so many travelers, they also produced many who were accused of reporting falsely. The Prologue to Langland's *Piers Plowman* (11. 48-49) concerns palmers and pilgrims who return home to lie about their journeys; Chaucer's *House of Fame* (III, 1032-33) always "Was ful of shipmen and pilgrimes, / With schrippes bret-ful of lesinges [lies]"; and William Thorpe, speaking to Archbishop Arundel of Canterbury in Chaucer's day, concluded his complaint about pilgrim excesses, "And if these men and women be a moneth out in their pilgrimage, many of them shall be an halfe year after, great janglers, tale-tellers, and liers."[28] So strong was the tradition that these and other medieval travelers, afraid readers would think them liars, often denied they were and in the denying simply confirmed the general opinion.

The Renaissance, with even more authors of travel accounts, many of whom are indispensable for history, geography, science, and belles-lettres, was totally unable to alter this traditional opinion. About the year 1500 Arnold von Harff claimed a long journey to Jerusalem, Mecca, Madagascar, and India that was recorded, read, doubted, and now known to be more than a little apocryphal.[29] At the same time a far more valuable account, that by the linguist, lover of women, and lover of travel Lodovico di Varthema, is so broad in its coverage of Asia, so replete with keen observations, and so personal that it reads like a novel and was reissued countless times. Often suspect in Varthema's own day, however, it has a long section about a journey to the Spice Islands that would have been impossible. Just as important as Varthema and, if possible, even more entertaining as a writer, Mendes Pinto left Portugal in 1537 and returned over twenty years later to tell a story so fabulous about his wanderings in Asia—he claimed to have been sold into slavery seventeen times—that, while he was widely read, he was not always truthful, and that in spite of his friendship with St. Francis Xavier. But now we know that he did not at all deserve his nickname of "Mendax." Such Renaissance travelers are too numerous to count, still others are totally unreliable, and all helped to solidify the popular opinion that travelers were not to be trusted.

Even after the formation of merchant companies, after the journeys of Christian evangelists, and after the success of great compilations of travel accounts in the Renaissance, that reputation lingered on. William Biddulph (1609), an English Protestant, divided his description of Jerusalem into the "Apparent Truths," "Manifest Untruths," and "Doubtfull Things" as recorded about the city by his predecessors, concentrating however on the "absurdities of Roman Catholic visitors."[30] Among the Roman Catholics, the Society of Jesus received most of the attacks by far, largely because its missionaries were the busiest and most productive; and consequently they contributed much to the general notion, reportedly summarized two centuries later by Macaulay, "Liars by a double right, as travellers and as Jesuits."[31] While the novel was becoming popular and respectable in the seventeenth and eighteenth centuries, then, general observers were finding travel accounts to be something less than history and much like fiction. Samuel Butler in his character of "A Traveller" condemns his archetype for returning home to scorn the ignorance of his untraveled acquaintances even though "little Credit is to be given to his own Relations and those of others, that speak and write of their Travels."[32] Shaftesbury, while praising "judiciously composed" lies, had no patience with stories of monstrous brutes and men.[33] Steele, in *Spectator* 136, after letting a correspondent explain at length how much of a fireside travel liar he is, concludes that the correspondent and his kind "might rather be called *The Historians,* for Liar is become a very harsh Word." About the same time Ned Ward gleefully repeats the amusingly incredible stories told by such "Historians" back from sea voyages.[34]

The charges continued well after the publication of the first great novels of the eighteenth century. In France the abbé Jacquin, considering the origins of the novel, seriously excluded not only certain histories more fabulous than true but also all travel tales, since their authors, "persuaded that one must report marvels when one goes abroad, have filled their relations with gross lies and unbelievable wonders"; and Voltaire, just as seriously, also condemned all travelers because, he said, it is among them especially that one finds most of the lies that are printed.[35] That was in fact almost the opinion of a fine collector and editor of travel accounts, J.-F. Bernard (1725), who defended those he published but who inveighed against the generality of such books for their exaggerations and "falsehoods."[36] Nor is it surprising to hear so many complaints in a period that produced such authors of travel books as d'Aulnoy, Courtilz, Hennepin, Lahontan, François Misson, Defoe, Psalmanazar, Pöllnitz, Dr. Brickell, Benyowski, Jonathan Carver, and Chateaubriand, as well as dozens of others whose works are wholly or partially fake.[37]

Often travelers themselves, both the truthful and untruthful ones, ironically contributed to the bad reputation of their fraternity by attacking the credibility of all travelers, or just those who preceded them to a particular spot, in order to claim uniqueness as dependable reporters. That kind of claim is of course ancient and can be found from Lucian to pilgrims in Jerusalem to, say, Hakluyt, where, for example, Thomas Nichols minutely describes the Canary Islands after maligning not just the account of it by the Frenchman André Thevet but all accounts of it, for, he says, "I find such variety in sundry writers."[38] By the time of Dampier and Defoe, of Lesage and Prévost, this brotherly backstabbing had become common. Captain Nathaniel Uring (1726), one of the more trustworthy sort, begins by modestly claiming that he "should not have troubled the World" with another travel book if his "Friends had not almost obliged" him to do it because, he says, "The Falsities and Inventions that are too often found in Books of this kind, . . . made [his "Friends"] desire to see One on which they could rely."[39] F.-M. Misson (1688), Gilbert Burnet (1687), and François Deseine (1699) all went to and wrote about Italy, and each defended his own observations while deploring the credulity or errors of his predecessors.[40] Similarly every eyewitness account of Anson's famous voyage in the 1740s showed that its author—or his editor— was concerned about the company he was keeping. The preface to the volume by Bulkeley and Cummins, who sailed on Anson's store ship *Wager*, is typical: "It has been a Thing, usual, in publishing of Voyages, to introduce Abundance of Fiction; and some Authors have been esteemed merely for being marvellous. We have taken to deviate from those, by having a strict Regard for Truth."[41] Late in the century Thomas Jeffreys, the King's map maker in America and author of a travel book, complained of "the carelessness of travellers, who have taken many things on trust"; and James Adair, one of the most respected of American Indian authorities, sounds like Captain Uring when in the preface addressed to his friends and patrons he over and over asserts, "truth hath been my standard," but only after reminding his friends, "You often complained how the public had been imposed upon either by fictional or fabulous, or very superficial and conjectural accounts of the Indian nation—and as often wished me to" write a book that could be trusted.[42] Truly, before 1800 the récits de voyage, like novels, were by their readers and their authors frequently and perennially charged with telling lies.

Nevertheless, for both novel and travel account, just as frequently and just as consistently there were defenses erected against these charges; often the defense erected by the friends of one form is like that for the other; and often the defense leads to an awareness that travel account and novel are much alike and that sometimes they become one form. For the French eighteenth century it has been concluded[43] that novelists had three ways of vindicating their "lies"—by justifying fiction as fiction; by maintaining that fiction could improve "history," that is, help its readers avoid boredom; and by claiming that novels are not fiction at all but true stories. By adding to these three and recombining, one can suggest four popular defenses offered about 1700 by novelists and readers of novels everywhere.

In the first place, it has often been said, in order to be touched, improved, or pleased, seventeenth- and eighteenth-century readers needed to be assured that what they had was not a novel at all but the truth; and so, convinced of that fact, or of the gullibility of the public, or of its willingness to suspend disbelief, the novelist discarded the "once upon a time" beginning and opened by simply stating that his story was true.[44] After Thomas Nashe, Cervantes, Bishop Camus, and other late Renaissance creators of ficiton with contemporaneous characters and settings, the assertion became standard. Nashe had in fact in his first work, *The Anatomie of Absurditie* (1589), pretended that it was true and belabored the romancers of his day for indulging in the "Legendary license of lying."[45] By 1664 Charles Sorel, critic and novelist, thought readers were preferring "modern" novels, those that included not only "truth-like" events but what really passed for the truth; and Gabriel Guéret in 1669 believed readers were demanding that they be guaranteed the truth.[46] Thus, at the very beginning of the eighteenth century, Mme de Villandon in the preface to *La Tour ténébreuse* (1705) insisted that she had "followed exactly the truth"; the publisher of the *Mémoires de la comtesse de Tournemir* (1708) claimed, "I know" that "these little Mémoires" are "very true"; and Burnet de Brou announced in his preface to *Le Tendre Ollivarius* (1707) that his tale was both true and autobiographical.[47] It is this kind of desire to allay the public's fear of "romance" or "novelistic" lying that caused Prévost and Marivaux to carry on the pretext and that forced Richardson to admonish his friend William Warburton for sending him a preface to *Clarissa* that spoke of the novel as fiction, for, Richardson explained, he wanted "the air of Genuineness" to be maintained, not for the purpose of deceiving readers with lies but "for fear of weakening ... that kind of Historical Faith which Fiction itself is generally read with, tho' we know it be Fiction."[48] It is the same motive that impelled Fielding to say in *Tom Jones*, "We determined to guide our pen ... by ... truth." And it is the same motive that led to Henry James and his famous exclamation at the "terrible crime," the "betrayal," by Trollope and other writers who admit that their stories do not happen, for such an admission "implies that the novelist is less occupied in looking for the truth ... than the historian."

For, in the second place, when an age of writers called their stories "histories"—or used in their titles a term for some subtype of history, such as "life," "letters," "memoirs," "journal," "travels," "voyage"—those writers wanted to achieve the appearance, the techniques, the reliability of history at its best, the same reliability that Herodotus had hoped for. By the last quarter of the seventeenth century Aphra Behn was striving hard for that illusion when in the opening sentence of *Oroonoko* (1688) she said she had been "an Eye-witness to a great part of what" she was telling and that the rest came "from the Mouth of the chief Actor in this History," a claim she echoed at the beginning of *The Unfortunate Happy Lady, a True History* and other novels.[50] Almost at the same time Mme de Villedieu, Mme d'Aulnoy, and Courtilz de Sandras were perfecting this already popular method of authentication—Villedieu with the *Mémoires de la Vie de Henriette-Sylvie de Molière* (1672), which, advertised as authentic autobiography, was so successful it led one biographer erroneously to believe it based on the author's own life; d'Aulnoy by employing real names and places for scandalous court intrigues in London; and Courtilz, the master of the type, by avowing that not only did he know the protagonists of his many fictional *Mémoires*, some of whom had real names, but that other people knew them, had helped supply facts, and would verify what he wrote.[51]

It was a method that would immediately be adopted by even greater novelists whose influence would extend through the century, among them Challe, Defoe, and Prévost, and by lesser ones. Authors of rogue stories used it for pseudolives of adventurers and criminals, some of whom never lived. In the decade after 1663, for example, more than twenty sensational books were published purporting to be autobiographies or biographies of the notorious Mary Carleton, the "German Princess." Then in 1673 the best of them appeared, called *The Counterfeit Lady Unveiled* and written by Francis Kirkman, author also of a continuation of Head's *The English Rogue* and described as "the most talented" of "the criminal biographers who disguise their fiction as fact."[52] After loosely authenticating his scholarship and his sources, Kirkman (12) stifles any final suspicions by sharing this "confession" with his readers: "If I should promise to give you a true account of her whole life I should deceive you, for how can truth be discovered of her who was wholly composed of falsehood." His was the method of the author of

The Highland Rogue: or . . . Rob Roy (1723), another notoriously "veracious" biography, and of *The Matchless Rogue: or . . . Newgate Tom* (1725), the preface to which insists "That all the Facts herein recited, are literally true."[53] Again, Defoe, along with Courtilz, would be among the most successful writers of this type of fictional biography, from the completely fictitious *Moll Flanders* and *Roxana* to the partly true *History of the Pyrates* and more nearly authentic *History of Jonathan Wild.* But later writers, the chevalier de Mouhy and Eliza Haywood, for example, would learn from Defoe and all the others. One of Haywood's many successful novels, a term she often used, is called *The Fortunate Foundlings* (1744) and subtitled in Courtilz's fashion "The Genuine History of. . . ." In her preface she sums up the tradition, exposes it, and continues it thus:

> The many Fictions which have been lately imposed upon the World, under the Specious Titles of Secret Histories, Memoirs, etc., etc. have given but too much room to question the Veracity of every Thing that has the least Tendency that way: We therefore think it highly necessary to assure the Reader, that he will find nothing in the following Sheets, but what has been collected from Original Letters, Private Memorandums, and the Accounts we have been favoured with from the mouths of Persons too deeply concerned in many of the chief Transactions not to be perfectly acquainted with the Truth, and of too much Honour and Integrity to put any false Colours upon it.

There are so many varieties of "true" fiction after 1650 that one need call attention to one unique type only—that which purported not just to rectify the errors of some previous publication but to answer the lies of real or supposed enemies of the protagonist. Although the type is often found in England, as with *Rob Roy* (1723), which condemned as unauthentic the just-published and soon-to-be-popular *History of the Lives and Robberies of the Most Noted Highway-Men . . .* (1720), it was even more common in France. There it can be traced at least to Villedieu's *Henriette-Sylvie de Moliére* (1672), the protagonist of which, falsely accused of leading a scandalous life, must clear her reputation by publishing her *Mémoires* and dedicating them to the unnamed noble lady who has asked that she write the apologia. The reputed author of Courtilz's *Mémoires de Madame la marquise de Frêne* (1701) —there was a real marquise de Frêne—writes to expose the lies of her terrible husband, who sold her to pirates. In the "Advertisement" of *L'Infortuné Napolitain, ou les Avantures et mémoires du signior Rosselly* (1704), attributed to the abbé J. Olivier, the "editor," knowing how the public considers "all writers of *mémoires* to be imposters," assures us that "Those people who knew Signior Rosselly in France and Italy can witness to the truth of these *mémoires,"* and then on page 3 Rosselly offers this *raison d'être* as an author: He would never have written if a woman had not threatened to "expose" him; and so, always studious of the truth, he has taken pen in hand "to confess publicly to all the world" the terrible circumstances of his life—that is, like Rousseau after him, he will not color the truth. And the narrator of the fake *Mémoires* (1737) of the comte de Bonneval, one of the famous real adventurers of the eighteenth century, is publishing the true facts in order to forestall, he claims, any ambitious fictionizer who might want to profit by stealing Bonneval's name. This last is exactly the reason for publishing that, two years later, the prolific chevalier de Mouhy puts in the mouth of the real Ann-Marie de Moras in her fictive *Mémoires* (1739).

Such defenses against lies of the past or lies that might come were of course employed by even the best writers. One was Anthony Hamilton, whose *Mémoires* of his brother-in-law the comte de Gramont, were designed to rescue Gramont's reputation from the calumnies of the real Bussy-Rabutin and the real Saint-Évremond. Another was Diderot, whose Suzanne of *La Religieuse* escapes a convent and must with her memoirs prove to her potential protector that she is a heroine and not an antiheroine. All varieties of this particular device for allaying suspicion and creating illusion were concerned with two sorts of "lies," those indulged in by the novelist as imitator of what was sometimes called a spurious kind of biography and those he invented for his protagonist to expose or forestall. And after 1740 few novelists felt compelled to use the device: Even in 1736 Crébillon fils, although he was only an "editor," would—unlike Defoe, Prévost, or Marivaux—spurn all pretense at history or "truth"; Richardson could play the game straight, in the Jamesian manner; and Diderot was to spend his life being concerned with more sophisticated techniques of illusion than the one involving his *Religieuse.*[54]

A third defense that novelists erected against charges of lying, and a time-honored one for all creative writers from Aristotle to Sidney to the twentieth century, was that they were in fact telling the truth, an allegorical or general truth, even though their characters and plots might be partially or wholly invented. It was the pretense, the simulation, of writers such as Villedieu that caused Bayle to attack their false history; and it was such attacks that led not just to novelists often calling themselves editors, as with Courtilz, Defoe, Prévost, and Richardson, but to their sometimes urging that they told this higher truth. And Defoe, in spite of the deceptions he foisted on the world as real biographies, was one who persistently employed this defense. It is true that in the often-cited *A New Family Instructor* (1727) he permitted the "Sister" to condemn both writing and reading of any "Story which we know to be false, but related as if it were a Truth," since such a story is "what the Scripture meant by *making a Lye.*" But then Defoe gave the "Brother" a rebuttal that is obviously supposed to be the final word: What we call a novel is a pleasurable way to provide instruction. "Fables, feigned Histories, invented Tales, and even such as we call *Romances,*" the Brother argues, are, when handled well, "the most apt to make Impressions upon the Mind, and open the Door to . . . just Inferences and Improvement."[55] It was a defense close to that of St. Augustine for teaching through parables, and Defoe often resorted to it. In the preface to Part II of *Robinson Crusoe,* for example, he argues that "The just application of every incident, the religious and useful inferences drawn from every part, are so many testimonies to the good design of making it public, and must legitimate all the part that may be called invention, or parable in the story." And again, in the preface to *Colonel Jack*, he says, ". . . whether the Colonel hath told his own story true or not; if he has made it a History or a Parable, it will be equally useful and capable of doing good."

This defense became stronger and more sophisticated as the century moved along. Jerry C. Beasley, although incorrectly assuming that earlier novelists had only the "mimetic," or realistic, defense, shows clearly that for British novelists of the 1740s "truth to life" included "moral" reality—that is, they recognized two truths, "the ethical and the mimetic."[56] In the preface to his *Polyandre* (1648) Charles Sorel had said that "Good comic or satirical novels"—meaning those of Furetière and Scarron as well as of Cervantes—are close to history, "to the truth," because "they take as their subject the common actions of life" and not the uncommon adventures of "romance." After quoting Sorel, Beasley concludes that Richardson, Fielding, and Smollett not only attack the romance tradition, as Sorel had done, but demonstrate that "allegorical history," a fictional "life," might, without concealing or denying the function of the imagination, justify itself as a "true" account of the general experience of mankind rendered in particular terms. And in *Tom Jones* (XII.xiii) Fielding does refer his readers to Shaftesbury on profitalbe lies and vigorously assert that his stories are a new kind of "true" history or "biography." He is so vigorous that one twentieth-century reader has concluded that he was impatient with the "standard" view that history was "Supposed to record the truth, while a fiction presented only a pleasing lie," that, in fact, for Fielding, "The truth value of history was not necessarily greater than that of a fiction and it might be less." [57]

In France not only did Crébillon fils reject the purely mimetic argument and openly confess to writing fiction, but in 1754 the noveliist La Solle in a forty-four-page prefatoral defense went so far as to say that "The novelist is the creator and master of his subject; the historian is the slave of his"; and another novelist, Béliard, went the further step to place long fiction above history, for, he said, "Novels . . . under the appearance of fiction, contain a great many truths, and [histories], under an air of truth, contain many fictions."[58] La Solle and Béliard were by no means alone, for their freedom from history was exactly like that of their countrymen Lenglet-Dufresnoy and Baculard d'Arnaud or that of their contemporary across the Channel Charles Jenner.[59] Imaginary history, guided by art and an ethical system, such belletrists believed, had been, was, and could be more useful, certainly more attractive, than what was generally agreed to be "real" history.

The fourth defense acknowledged the values of both history and fiction, claiming the novel to be partly the first, admitting it to be partly the second, and challenging the world to separate the two. Georges May concludes that the early French novelists succeeded so well in confusing fiction and truth that "readers no longer knew where one stopped and the other began."[60] The Scudérys said it in the preface to *Ibrahim* (1641): "When the lie and the truth are mixed by a clever hand, one not only has trouble separating them but hesitates to destroy something so pleasing." Desfontaines (1724) and Prévost (1735) agreed that the novel was defined and made useful by such a mixture, one of them explaining that, because pure history is often dry, readers can through fiction be led to acquire historical information, the other contending that the wise author employs the adroit mixture because "the truth alone does not always please and stories of pure imagination [meaning fantasies] do not satisfy readers of intelligence."[61] Any number of novelists admitted to some invention, the weakest admission being that all was true except the names. At the start of *Roxana*, for example, Defoe insisted that he told the "substantial" truth but with different names, for to use real names would have the result that "many a pleasant and delightful history would be buried in the dark, and the world deprived both of the pleasure and the profit of it." Gaillard de Bataille in the preface to *Mémoires de . . . Kermelac* (1741) was still more definite, his story being "exactly true" except for the names.[62] Although she did not admit to false names, Mary Davys in the first paragraph of *The Accomplished Rake* (1727), after announcing that she was "delivering nothing but plain fact in the fundamental part," satirized the whole half-and-half tradition, first, by confessing that "by way of episode I may intermix now and then a pretty little lie," and, then, by challenging the reader to find her out and "convict" her "if he can." But there were novelists who were serious followers of the tradition. Seigneux de Correvon (1728), for example, would still define the novel as something between fable and history, a "mélange" of the two, since a fable is only a "tissue of fictions" and history "contains only the true." And Fielding, quoting Pope, believed that "the great art of poetry is to mix truth with fiction, in order to join the credible with the surprising."[63]

Whether *Don Quixote* is the first modern novel or not, it is archetypal in many ways, not the least of which is its importance in the long and continuing tradition of attempting to create illusion, to represent life, and then either fighting to avoid the charge of lying or teasing the whole tradition. Robert Alter, Carlos Fuentes, and many others have demonstrated how Cervantes is forward looking in two special ways: first, he looks to the mimetic and philosophical realists as he sends his "pâpier-maché" knight riding across the plains of a very real La Mancha; and, second, his many artifices foreshadow those employed by self-conscious novelists as they "play the game," manipulate characters, and force a suspension of disbelief.[64] Three examples will show his playful, and yet his serious, concern with whether the novelist is artist or liar. In one episode of *Don Quixote*, the character Ginés de Pasamonte contends that his own "La Vida de Genés de Pasamonte" is superior to *Lazarillo de Tormes* and gives as his reason the fact that the lies of other writers cannot equal his kind of realism: "no puede haber mentinas que se igualen."[65] In another episode, in Part II, the Knight meets and talks with Don Alvaro Tarfe, a character in Avellaneda's spurious second part of *Don Quixote*. It is enough, Alter suggests, to "induce ontological vertigo" when the "true" fictional character confronts the "false" fictional character. The third scene is that in which Don Quixote enters a printing shop in Barcelona and "is thus sent by Cervantes to his only reality: the reality of fiction."[66] Here, Fuentes decides, is an example of how "art brings truth to the lies of history." And it is one explanation for Dostoevsky's opinion that *Don Quixote* is "a novel where truth is saved by a lie."

Many a travel account was also saved, or damned, by a lie, and the defenses of travel writers against charges of deceit were just as frequent as those of novelists, very much like theirs, and, if possible, better established by the mid-eighteenth century. Since they were often thought to write more for instruction even than for pleasure, they early had to authenticate their facts, especially for a Renaissance public thirsty for knowledge of the greatly expanded earth. By the time of Columbus the traveler was already consistently providing a preface or some other opening that would vouch for his reliability. *The Travels* (1510) of Lodovico di Varthema of Bologna,[67] relating a six-year journey with exciting adventures in the East, was deservedly and widely read in translations, in collections of voyages, and in abridgments. One German translation of 1515 ends its long title by claiming that "all of this" Varthema "has seen." Ramusio's translation (1550) from the Spanish claimed, truthfully enough, that Varthema's account "is so fully and so correctly narrated as to transcend all that has been written" about Persia and India. Then in his own dedication to the Duchess Taglicozzo, Varthema explains that he gives "a faithful description" of his voyage because "one eye-witness is worth more than ten heard-says" and informs his patron that the "truth of the facts" will shine through even his clumsy writing.

Jumping over a century and a half and hundreds of declarations of honesty by travelers, their editors, or their translators, one can pause over the apologies of John Chardin and the buccaneers. Chardin, jeweler, Huguenot, linguist, member of the Royal Society, and an English knight by the hand of Charles II, had the first volume of his *Travels* to Persia published in 1686 in both French and English.[68] The English translator dedicates the *Travels* to the Duke of Chandos, tells him that Chardin's "sincerity . . . is not very common in a Traveller of good Invention," and then in a preface adds that he himself has in no way altered the original since it contains only authentic facts one can "give into," except perhaps for a typographical error. About the time Chardin was publishing, the great age of buccaneer adventures and journal keeping, so important to the eighteenth-century novel, was at its height. The English translator of Exquemelin, author of most of *The Buccaneers of America* (1678 in Dutch; 1684-85 in English), assures us of Exquemelin's having been "an eye-witness," of his "candour and felicity," and of "the truth and sincerity wherewith everything" is written, "there being no greater ornament . . . to History . . . than Truth."[69] William Dampier (1697), described by his admirer Coleridge as "Old Dampier, a rough sailor, but a man of exquisite mind," in the dedication to Charles Montagu offers him a "plain piece," since, "without the vanity of a Traveller," he is not "fond of telling stories"; then in the preface Dampier defends his retention of a running account of his fellow buccaneers by saying, "I would not prejudice the Truth and Sincerity of my Relation" by any omission. Finally, Dampier's colleague, surgeon-buccaneer Lionel Wafer, said it succinctly (1699): "I have been most especially careful . . . to say nothing but what . . . is the very Truth." Such affirmations of honesty by travelers went on for another century.

Because so many travel accounts were indeed wholly or partly fictitious, a second defense forced upon their authors or their admirers was the popular one—sometimes satiric, often serious, and even heated—that pointed out how collectively or individually they were falsely accused by suspicious or ignorant stay-at-homes. About the same time that Antonio in *The Tempest* (III.iii), after witnessing marvels, was exclaiming, "travellers n'er did lie / Though fools at home condemn 'em," Ralegh (1596), who had reported "men in Guiana with eyes in their shoulders and mouths in their chests," was concluding that Mandeville's reports, long held to be false, had often been proved true following the discovery of the East Indies.[70] Henry Timberlake (1603) and William Biddulph (1609), the former one of the most popular of travel writers about the East, were only two of dozens who, in order to attack it, quoted the old proverb "Travelers lie by authority."[71] Biddulph, unhappy with readers who "will hardly believe anything but that which they themselves have seen" and who smugly dismiss anything strange with "Travellers may lie by authority," concludes bitterly, "but they are liers themselves which say so."[72] William Wood, in New England twice in the first half of the seventeenth century, was quite upset by the common opinion concerning travelers. "I would," he said at the start of his *New England's Prospect* (1634), "be loath to broach any thing which may puzzle thy belief, and so justly draw upon myself that unjust aspersion commonly laid on travellers, of whom many say, They may lie by authority, because none can control them." And then he explodes, "There is many a tub-brained cynic [like Diogenes], who because anything stranger than ordinary is too large for the strait hoops of his apprehension, he peremptorily concludes that it is a lie," and so Wood rejects "this sort of thick-witted readers." More than a hundred years later the great French circumnavigator and explorer Bougainville would be just as upset. In his *Voyage autour du Monde* (1771), after the first report of Tahiti [New Cythera] had reached Paris, been published, and attracted blame as well as praise, he began his Preliminary Discourse, "I am a traveller and a mariner; that is to say a liar and an imbecile in the eyes of that class of lazy and arrogant writers who in the shadow of their study philosophize endlessly on the world and its inhabitants." Diderot was, of course, one of those fireside "arrogant writers" when in his famous *Supplément au voyage de Bougainville* he answered the mariner by letting an old Tahitian order Bougainville off the island in order to leave the natives their own customs, which "are wiser and more honest than yours." Samuel Johnson, in spite of harboring certain reservations about individual travelers —Abyssinian James Bruce, for example— summed up the tradition of defending travelers by attacking their accusers: "Many relations of Travellers have been slighted as fabulous, till more frequent voyages have confirmed their veracity" (*Idler* 87).

A third defense for travel writers provides what Defoe's "Sister" or Diderot would say is a case of the pot calling the kettle black; that is, travels were frequently more rewarding, because more truthful, than novels. In spite of his "Brother's" able defense of novels, Defoe consistently rated travel books and history over "romances, playes or diverting stories," just as Fielding, after having praised his own type of historical and biographical novel with its higher truth, would in the preface to his *Voyage to Lisbon* first attack travel lies and then insist that he "still" preferred travel-historians, such as Herodotus, to authors of fiction, such as Homer.[73] A writer in the *Critical Review* (1756), believing novels the fashion, said it thus: Travel accounts "for the most part afford us much more rational entertainment than the fashionable study of idle novels and romances"; but the novelist Mary Davys (1725), believing fiction less fashionable, had put it differently: "for some time . . . novels have been a great deal out of fashion and . . . ladies . . . have been taken up with amusements of more use and improvement—I mean history and travels, with which the relation of probably feigned stories can by no means stand in competition."[74]

A fourth and final defense, not, as with novels, normally offered openly, was that a travel account was a mixture of pleasure and profit and therefore must at times be a mixture of the false with the fact. Since any writer of travels other than pure guidebooks must of course include secondhand information, personal adventures, reflections, interpretations, and emotions, he must often approach the boundary between the existent and the uncertain, between facts for facts and facts for pleasure.[75] Defoe, in his *Tour 'thro the Whole Island of Great Britain*, presented a useful picture of England in a fictional framework; Challe, in a travel journal accepted as authentic, has long sections of conversation and speeches that are obviously written after the fact and in the same way he wrote his "fiction"; and Smollett, to make his *Travels in France and Italy* more pleasurable and more nearly complete, altered whatever journal he had kept on the spot.[76] One seventeenth-century traveler willing to admit the possibility of mixing subjective with objective reporting was named Brunel. In Spain in 1655, ten years before his account appeared, Brunel, who praised traveling as the "grande école," promised to tell only what he saw or took for truth; but, he went on, it will be a marvel if he does not perhaps "tell a lie without lying" ["diray peut-estre des mensonges sans mentir"].[77] The same admission was made more than one hundred years later by Henry Swinburne at the beginning of his *Travels through Spain* (1779): "I may be detected in many mistakes ... but I shall never be detected in a wilful perversion of the truth."[78] What Brunel and Swinburne meant was that like all good travel writers they might succumb to a false report too easily or let their bias or emotion color their observation, all to add more dulce to the utile. And of course since the beginning of time travel books have varied widely in the amount of subjectivity they include. That is, the less they have, the more they seem like a guidebook; the more they have, the more they approach the novel and seem to be lying.

For a long time before and after 1700, then, both travel book and novel had to respond to all these charges of lying, the defenses for one form very often being amazingly like those for the other.

To begin to understand this fact, however, one must first recognize that what Georges May and others agree on as being true in France about 1700 was just as true in England and other countries: The novel-reading public wanted to believe that what it read was true, or at least it wanted to be told that stories were real. And so not just pseudomemoirs and journals and autobiographies, such as those of Kirkman and Villedieu and Prévost, but third-person fiction, that of Mme de La Fayette's *Princesse de Clèves*, for example, normally began with a preface or other opening statement that provided the proper assurance. But travel books such as that of Varthema had been doing it long before the seventeenth century. Each of these two popular forms of literature needed to give the appearance, or the illusion, of being some sort of biography or autobiography, of being "history."

The assurances were of several kinds and were often ingenious. Sometimes a statement simply claiming truth was deemed sufficient, as with the novelists Mme de Villandon (1705) and Henry Fielding and the travelers Gemelli Careri (1698) and William Dampier (1697). Sometimes the writer or publisher agreed that others had lied but not this writer: Cervantes had to contend with authors of "false" sequels and Nashe with "lying" romancers, while not only Renaissance voyagers such as Timberlake but also Bulkeley and Cummins, on Anson's *Wager*, claimed to be truthful in spite of the tradition travelers had acquired. Others, the novelist Mme Villedieu and the traveler Uring, for example, were publishing their books only because a patron or a friend urged them to give the world a true account. Still others were responding to particular or general charges of lying. Thus, among the novelists, Courtilz's Mme de Frêne is simply answering her terrible husband, while Diderot's Suzanne is clearing her reputation; and, among the travelers, the buccaneer Wafer in his second edition is carefully pointing out that other travelers have just proved his facts about "white Indians" in Central America not to be false, while midshipman Alexander Campbell in a *Sequel to Bulkeley and Cummins* (1784) is giving an apology for his own actions and proving his former companions on the *Wager* to be liars.[79]

Many novelists pretended to be merely editors or translators of a journal, a volume of letters, or other manuscripts; and so did many travelers. Among the novelists, Richardson, Marivaux, Defoe, and Courtilz followed that practice, as of course did Gabriel Foigny, who pretended to have recovered the manuscript of *La Terre Australe connue ... par M. [Jacques] Sadeur* (1676) from the very hands of its dying author. Among the travelers and pseudotravelers Pierre Bergeron apparently edited the largely spurious *Voyages fameux du sieur Vincent Le Blanc* (1648); Defoe, or someone, apparently pieced together the *Journal of Robert Drury* (1729); and Crèvecoeur "discovered" the water-soaked manuscript of his *Voyage dans la haute Pensylvanie et dans New York* (1801).[80] "Editors" such as the novelist Marivaux and the traveler Crèvecoeur offer anecdotes telling how their manuscripts ended up in their hands; or, like Courtilz and Bergeron, they explain how well they know their protagonists. These "editors" could also point to individuals, imaginary or real, who would verify something or everything. This device was a favorite with authors of the popular fake memoirs. Francis Kirkman, for example, in *The Counterfeit Lady Unveiled* (1673) assures his readers that the protagonist's husband will vouch for his version of the Mary Carleton story. But the technique was even more popular with authors, publishers, and translators of both fake and real travel books. Thus, the "publisher" vouches for the reputation for truth acquired by Gulliver among his neighbors at Redreff; in the preface to *Robert Drury*, the author calls on Captain William Mackett to verify the existence of the traveler-protagonist; the French "editor" and the English translator of Dubois-Fontanelle's *Naufrage de M. Pierre Viaud* (1769, 1771) offers "authentic" certificates that attest to the marvelous facts presented; and—the only trustworthy one of these four —John Chardin's English translator vouches for the truth of the great French traveler to Persia and cites another important traveler, Tournefort, who gives Chardin "the Character of an author of great exactness." Similarly, if the protagonist of the fictive memoirs or the pseudo or actual travel account had the name of a real person, the publisher might argue, as the novelist Thomas Holcroft did in his translation of the autobiography of the notorious traveler Friedrich von der Trenck (1786; 1788), that "the memory of the several exploits . . . is so recent, the scene of action so near, the facts so public, and the character of the illustrious writer . . . so universally known, as to exclude the least appearance of fable or fiction."[81]

One clever way for "editors" to lull suspicion was to admit either to a suppression of some fact or to a failure to suppress it. With novelists this device permitted asterisks in place of all but one or two letters in names, but it also permitted the changing of names completely, as Defoe in *Roxana* and Gaillard de Bataille in *Kermelac* claimed to have done. Few travelers, on the other hand, could use such alterations, Smollett in the "letters" he wrote about France and Italy being one of the few to employ asterisks. They found other ways of suppressing facts or confessing to facts, however. For example, in writing the completely fictional *Les Voyages du capitaine Robert Lade* (1744), which is more in the tradition of travel literature than of the novel, Prévost first points out how the Englishman Lade withheld information about the coasts of Africa, where he amassed his fortune, and then adds, "But one can regard this suppression . . . as a sign of good faith for the rest of the work, since with less regard for truth [than he has] it would be easy to fill the gap with imaginary suppositions." [82] A generation later Doctor John Moore, after being attacked for novelistic, subjective elements in his *View of Society and Manners in France* . . . (1779), published a second edition and confessed that because the first two letters of the original, with their "assumed character and feigned situation," give too much "an air of fiction" to the rest, he is now restoring "those two letters to their original form."[83]

Admissions such as these, usually in the editorial apparatus, were designed to create reader faith in concocted or marvelous stories, just as "editors" of novels and travels, afraid of possible attacks on their content, wrote essays to point out that time had often proved a lie to be truth. In travel literature that defense was standard. But two examples will show how close the fiction writer was to the travel writer in using this defense. In *Tom Jones* (VIII.i) Fielding, agreeing with Dacier and other theorists of the epic, laments those readers who "believe nothing to be either possible or probable ... which hath not occurred to their own observations." His words are almost exactly those of travelers like William Biddulph who long before Dacier complained of stay-at-homes who "will hardly believe anything but that which they themselves have seen" (see note 71 above). An even better example, since it fits both forms of literature directly, comes from Prévost, who as "editor" to his novel *Cleveland* argues at length, like travelers such as Ralegh before him, Wafer in his own time, and Bougainville and Johnson after him, that readers are too suspicious of "surprising incidents." For, he says, "how many famous authors have been accused of writing untruths, which afterwards have been proved to be matters of fact. *The travels of ... Sir John Chardin* were considered in [this] light by multitudes, till several persons of undoubted credit, who have since visited the same countries, assure us of his veracity."[84]

Such defenses of the marvelous, or the different, are part of the larger problem that both the novel and the travel account faced because of the demand placed on each for pleasure as well as for profit. The writers of each form, such as novelists Prévost and Fielding and travelers Brunel and Swinburne, admitted to giving the marvelous and argued that what some readers insisted on as incredible was really only marvelous and was needed not just for providing entertainment but for recording the full truth, that, in other words, each form was in varying proportions a mixture of truth and invention. In fact, certain defenders in each group insisted that the pleasure principle was paramount, as did Charles Jenner (1770) the novelist and the anonymous writer of the *Critical Review* (1756) with his greater "rational enjoyment" for travels. As a result, writers in each form were accused of mixing lies with facts, distorting history, as Bayle attacked the novelist Villedieu or Biddulph attacked Jesuit visitors to Jerusalem.

But writers of each form constantly insisted that they were teaching history, from novelists Bishop Camus in the 1620s, George Mackenzie in 1660, and François Béliard in 1765 to almost every traveler, or his editors, the editor of that most popular *Buccaneers of America* being only one when he described its author Exquemelin as an eyewitness recorder of Morgan's exploits in Central America. Indeed, it was a standard argument, on the one hand, that novels were more truthful, as well as more pleasurable, than history and, on the other, that *récits de voyage* were more pleasurable, as well as more truthful, than novels, although each had to be adroitly or artistically put together, as Scudéry and Defoe said for the novel and Shaftesbury and Fielding said for the travel account. For either, truth was said to be more marvelous often than fiction, Abysinnian Bruce's story of having eaten steaks cut from live cows ultimately proving the age-old maxim stated by Maupassant, "Le vrai peût quelque-fois n'être pas le vraisemblable."[85] Perhaps John Taylor the "oculist," in the fictionized version (1761) of his "Travelling-Doctor" father's life, said it for both traveler and novelist when he contended that his hero's exploits "founded upon Facts so manifest, so illustrious through all Europe, exceed, in Number, and entertaining Incidents, the most fertile Romance, that Invention has hitherto produced."[86] William Nelson (see note 3 above), in concluding his study of the Renaissance, believes that by the seventeenth century the way was open "for fiction set in the far away . . . to take the form of history without pretending to be history, to present itself as a work of the imagination." One can just as safely conclude that by that time and on through the eighteenth century the way was open for a travel account set in the faraway to take the form of fiction without pretending to be fiction, to present itself as a work of fact by employing the imagination.

In fact, if one starts with the apparently truthful but relatively dull travel account such as that of William Bromley's *Remarks in the Grande Tour . . .* (1692), goes to the many apparently truthful and fascinating ones such as those of Chardin, Olearius, Dampier, and Careri, and then to the fascinating but partly untruthful ones by Marco Polo, von Harff, Varthema, Pinto and Le Blanc—all published before anything by Lesage or Defoe—if one goes through all these one needs only a short trip to arrive at *Mandeville*, the sieur de Combes, Foigny's *Sadeur*, and Veiras's *Sévarambes*, all written before 1700 also and all more or less vraisemblable but never vrai. To make that journey from Bromley to Veiras is to encounter, with much other artistry of course, examples of "ontological vertigo" to rival those of Cervantes. One needs, however, to continue the journey on into the eighteenth century, when the novel was evolving further and faster.

First, there is Veiras (1675) in his preface comparing his "real" travel book with "false" ones such as Plato's *Republic*, More's *Utopia*, and Bacon's *New Atlantis*, always to their detriment.[87]

Second, there is Steele in the *Tatler* (1710; No. 254) saying, "There are no Books which I more delight in than Travels, especially those that describe remote countries, and give the Writer an Opportunity of showing his Parts without incurring any Danger of being examined or contradicted. Among all the Authors of this kind, our renowned Countryman Sir John Mandeville has distinguished himself, by the Copiousness of his Invention, and Greatness of his Genius. . . . One reads the Voyages . . . with as much Astonishment as the Travels of *Ulysses* in Homer, or the Red-Cross Knight in Spenser. All is enchanted ground and fairy-land." *Mandeville*, with ten editions in the seventeenth century and over twenty in the eighteenth, was also praised in the *Dictionary* (1755) by Johnson. In other words, a real lie, one intended to deceive, if adroitly, judicially composed, is not only, with Shaftesbury and Fielding, more instructive but with many readers more successful and more admired than the truth![88]

Third, there is Defoe in his fake travel books, as well as Swift in *Gulliver's Travels,* teasing his friend, the great cartographer Herman Moll, about Moll's false geography.[89]

Fourth, there is F.-M. Misson putting together the fireside *Voyage . . . de François Leguat* (1707), in which one of his inventions is a bird, the Gelinotte, a composite of three real birds found in previous real travel books, a bird later classified by the *Cambridge Natural History* as *Erythromachus leguati* but dubbed "extinct," while Newton's *Dictionary of Birds* gives this "singular rail" the title *Miserythrus leguati!*[90]

Fifth, and last, there is Swift, who in the Dublin edition not only gives Gulliver a supreme reputation for truthfulness with his neighbors and a "cousin" named William Dampier but lets him address a prefatory letter to another cousin, Sympson, the reputed author of *A New Voyage to the East Indies . . .* (1715) but who, as Swift may well have known, was as nonexistent a person as Gulliver.[91] Here is an example of a fictitious protagonist facing a "real," but just as fictitious, protagonist, another fictional Don Quixote confronting his illegitimate alter ego. Truly the adroit travel writer or novelist could make lies aid the truth or the truth aid lies. Under such conditions, then, it should not be surprising to discover the two kinds of writers facing the same charges of falsifying and then responding in the same ways to those charges: Each was forced to learn "the manner whereby to convince others of the truthfulness" not only "of his lies" but of his truths.[92]

CHAPTER FOUR

Realism and Romanticism:
Local Color and Exoticism

The décor is verifiable, one must not lie. . . . By the exactitude of the décor the novelist makes credible the human
verity of his characters, he makes a success of his lies.
Aragon[1]

One of the best examples of ontological vertigo out of the early eighteenth
century demonstrates how the novelist's imagination can create so well that
his creation becomes reality for other people. In 1744 the abbé Prévost, after
writing a number of his best novels, including *Manon Lescaut,* and after
living in England and reading dozens of travel books, published his two-
volume *Voyages du capitaine Lade,* which, the title page claimed, was "Tra-
duit de l'anglois." The *Journal de Trévoux* immediately praised the new book,
and Prévost himself referred to it as an authority when in the twelfth volume
of his huge *Histoire générale des voyages* (1754) he pointed to a "détail curieux" found in "le voiage de Robert Lade" as well as in the *New Voyage*
(1697) of William Dampier. By 1896 certain doubts about Lade caused
Henry Harrisse in a study of Prévost to declare a "strong" belief that the
Captain and his travels were apocryphal. Then twentieth-century scholars
not only proved the *Voyages* to be fake and Lade a myth but showed how
Prévost put his novel together. He had created a captain and, using his vast
knowledge of travels, two volumes of voyages for the Captain; and then ten
years later, while wearing his editor's cap, he had, side by side with one of
the most respected of voyagers, cited his invention as an authenticating
witness.[2]

Swift's Yahoos provide an entirely different example of the artist's imag-
ination at work with facts taken from the literature of travel. William
Bonner prefers to think that the filthy female Yahoos come from Dampier's
New Voyage, but long ago R.W. Frantz demonstrated how the Yahoos derive
from a number of accounts Swift certainly knew, in particular of the south
African Hottentots and Central American monkeys.[3] From travelers such
as Thomas Herbert (1638), Dampier, Edward Cooke (1712), and especially
John Ovington (1696), the descriptions of the Hottentot women with ugly,

dangling breasts led to the Yahoo females with "their dugs hung between their Forefeet." Similarly the Yahoos in trees dropping their excrement down on Gulliver are obviously like those Central American monkeys which, Dampier wrote, "scattered their Urine and Dung *about* my Ears," or, as his buccaneer friend Dr. Lionel Wafer said (1699), skipped "chattering" from tree to tree "pissing down purposely on our heads."[4] As with Coleridge later, Swift's mind was stored with images from travel books, and, as with Coleridge, his imagination worked those images into forms that fitted his purpose.

The oft-repeated notion that the imagination was "profoundly mistrusted" before the middle of the eighteenth century has a corollary false notion that less imagination is needed for a Defoe, working with a real life, perhaps a real journal, surely with certain real publications, to produce a travel story called *Madagascar: or Robert Drury's Journal* (1729),[5] or for a Prévost, working with a library of books and an invented person, to write the "Voyages" of Captain Lade. For example, William Nelson, reluctantly, to be sure, cites Murray Bunday's study of the "Classical and Medieval Theory of the Imagination" (1927), which arrives at the first conclusion; and A.J. Tieje (1913) offers the second conclusion for the seventeenth and early eighteenth centuries, although he allows creative writers other than novelists some trust in and use of the imagination.[6] Yet surely Joyce is right in believing that imagination, along with its elements or close relatives—invention, genius, fancy plus reason, wit plus judgment—has always been as important in one century as in another; that is, "The human mind," as J.R.R. Tolkien argues, "is capable of forming mental images of things not actually present. The faculty of combining the images is (or was) naturally called Imagination. But in recent times, in technical not normal language, Imagination has often been held to be something higher than the mere image-making, ascribed to the operations of Fancy (a reduced and depreciated form of the older word Fantasy); an attempt is thus made to restrict, I should say misapply, Imagination to 'the power of giving to ideal creations the inner consistency of reality.' "[7]

Tolkien would agree with Locke's theory of images collected by the senses, stored in the memory, redistributed and recombined by reflection, and—as Johnson explained in his *Preface* to Shakespeare—called up by the imagination of a genius as the stuff of creative writing, whether in an *Iliad*, a *Don Quixote*, a *Crusoe*, or a *Rasselas*. Curiously, no matter what the phenomenon is called or related to, or how it is defined, the very essays by Nelson and Tieje in which they help perpetuate a myth demonstrate over and over how much the geniuses before 1750 were endowed with imagination, just as do all the studies of earlier prose fiction.[8] The myth, the confusion, may stem in part from the fact that when historians recognized the slow and powerful trend to verisimilitude in a fiction that became better with Lesage, Marivaux, Richardson, and Fielding, they concluded erroneously that to produce such "representation" requires a higher kind of imagination, a Coleridgean kind that goes beyond image producing and extends to a broader arranging of patterns in the mind to fit patterns considered "real," like the experience of the creator and his audience. Hence, at least for large segments of Britain and the United States, we arrive at the mimetic "novel" displaying powers of imagination and the allegorical, dreamy, historical, and/or adventure "romance" stemming more from fancy.

But where does the novel start and the romance stop? Did the "new" realism of the seventeenth and eighteenth centuries separate itself from the old methods or longings? Or was it a combining, as Philip Stevick would have it when he argues that Borges and other great writers have just given us a new "mock-fact" fiction by superimposing their "myth-making imagination" on the dry data of a "fact-glutted age"?[9] That is, just as the new realism gave us a nouveau fiction about 1700, Borges and his colleagues have now reversed the trend and given us still another nouveau fiction that stresses "imagination." Yet, as with Robbe-Grillet, Butor, and their French nouveau roman of a generation ago, is it new for any reason other than that a genius, by letting his invention play over his knowledge, created people, events, images that attract us? And are the tales of Borges and Butor novels or romances? In a now old essay Albert Thibaudet offered *Robinson Crusoe* as the "most extraordinary" adventure roman of all time, an opinion with which Martin Green agrees even as he is sure that Defoe's adventure "novel" is no romance, since that term should be reserved for stories such as *Amadis*. [10] And others, Green being one, are still trying to keep fictional genres and subgenres neatly catalogued, one critic asserting that "the distinction between romance and realistic fiction was clearly recognized" by the "intelligent" reader after 1700, another believing the novel to be "adult" and the romance to be "childish."[11] Each of these two opinions needs to be examined.

In Chapter One we saw how the epic and the romance—Greek or medieval or seventeenth-century French—contributed to the kinds of prose fiction published in the eighteenth century, how from Congreve to Johnson and Clara Reeve the English were not sure about what was a novel or a romance, and that on the Continent nouvelle gave way to roman for all long prose fiction. Congreve called his own *Mourning Bride* a novel, even though it is filled with intrigue, eroticism, and exoticism, while Johnson and Reeve carefully distinguished between the old and the new romance, which they also called novel, that is, between the incredible tales of superhuman heroes "formerly written" and those credible but marvelous ones being told in the eighteenth century. But the old-new distinction was current more than a hundred years before Johnson made it, as indicated by the title and contents of Chapelain's *De la Lecture des vieux romans* (1647; published 1870) and, even earlier, by Bishop Camus in the 1620s writing, and asking others to write, exemplary love intrigue tales with contemporaneous settings and characters.[12] Sometimes eighteenth-century England accused the French of setting a bad example with their romantic fiction. In the preface to her 1725 collected works, Eliza Haywood was one English person to make that charge. John Macky was another when in 1724 he attacked both the travel accounts and the "Novels" of France, at the same time throwing in yet another use for "old": "The French are certainly the unfittest People ... to write Descriptions of Countries; for if they don't mix something Romantic in their accounts, it is thought flat and insipid and does not go down with them. As most of their modern Memoirs, like their Novels, are but a new way of Romancing, since *Don Quixote* laughed Scuderys old way out of Countenance; so their Voyages and Journeys are much the same."[13] Still another such accuser was the anonymous author of the 1751 *An Essay on the New Species of Writing Founded by Mr. F——*, who believed his countrymen then to be tired of the "Romances" imported from France. "Nothing," he wrote, was formerly "received with any kind of Applause, that did not appear under the Title of a Romance, or a Novel; and Common Sense was kick'd out of Doors to make Room for Marvellous Dullness." Now, however, he thinks Fielding gives "not a mere dry Narrative, but a lively Representation of real Life" in "the several Stages of his History," which "Mr. F—— ... metaphorically calls a Journey" and which never disobeys Horace's dictum —freely translated by the 1751 critic—"The Life-wrought Tale should ne'er advance / A Line that savours of Romance."[14] "Intelligent" readers of the eighteenth century, then, were quite confused about the difference between romance and realistic fiction. In France roman served for both, just as Schlegel employed Roman for both as late as 1800.[15] And in England "Novel" was consistently not distinguished from "Romance," of which there were apparently at least four kinds—the kind "now being written"; two "old" kinds, one for Greece and the Middle Ages, that is, the fabulous kind, and one, more nearly credible, for the seventeenth-century Scudérys; and, finally, one for almost any contemporaneous tale out of France.

There are now two important points to be made for fiction in general and, in particular, for the eighteenth century, when travel literature was such an aid to what Aragon calls the "décor" of fiction. First, the Auerbach-Watt mimetic approach which has for a generation dominated English-language criticism of prose fiction has led to a false separation of that fiction into two opposing genres, the "adult" novel overshadowing the "childish" romance. And, second, it is today apparent that this "novel-centered" view, after contributing so much, is at last being relegated to a common-sense position. The evidence is all around us. Starting with the admirers of the nouveau roman and its dreamlike, fantastic characters and techniques—as in Robbe-Grillet's *Jalousie*—one can add the many voices that have recently been raised not simply to attack the mimetics but to set the record straight. Critics such as Kellogg and Scholes, for example, by reminding us to avoid the term "novel" because it has come to imply that long fiction cannot as an art form go farther than "realism," are attempting to counter Fiedler's "Death of" and Wain's "Decline of" the novel, meaning the realistic long tale. Ralph Freedman supplies the positive, and even more common-sense, proposal that "any comprehensive perspective of the novel, roman, or *Roman* must take into account the multiplicity of its points of view and of the directions of its development." And other critics, such as Quentin Kraft, argue that the novel has no future if one expects it to be merely realistic, that, in fact, as with Stevick writing about Borges, the mimetic must be subordinate "to the creative."[16]

Still better evidence that the "novel-centered" view is in danger is the fact that in the past decade critics have been attacking "realism," redefining it, or promoting the cause of "romance." The most important of these critics is Northrop Frye, who has just now gone well beyond his earlier theories of the novel-romance-confession-anatomy and of what romance is by devoting a full-length book, his Norton lectures, to "romance," to what he considers the four primary narrative movements in fiction—each a journey—and to what Paul Hunter correctly says are "perhaps the most radical claims for the superiority of romance to the novel as a form."[17] And so, following Frye's lead or without knowing of his extreme stand, readers are again finding romance elements in almost all eighteenth-century novelists, not just the obvious ones such as Prévost, Rousseau, and Bernardin but Defoe, Richardson, Smollett, and Fielding. One such reader is H.K. Miller, who in *Henry Fielding's Tom Jones and the Romance Tradition* concludes that both *Joseph* and *Tom* "are romances and both exhibit the same narrative and dramatic elements that had been the mark of the romance tradition for almost two thousand years."[18] All of this leads, at the moment, to an excellent essay by Terrence Doody in which, one, he quotes Erich Heller's "The Realistic Fallacy" and Nietzsche's scornful opinion that "Realism in art is an illusion, all the writers of all the ages were convinced they were realistic"; two, he notes Joyce's recognition of the polarity experienced by the novelist striving to stay "down to facts" and, at the same time, resist the objective by using imagination; and, three, he concludes, "The novel has flourished in this ambivalence, at least since *Don Quixote.*"[19]

A better theory, in fact, is that the modern novel was in great measure produced by this ambivalence, by a conflict and an alliance between realism and romance in which each was and is being so transformed that neither can with ease be separated from the other.[20] It is the duality in man that is found in Dorothy Richardson's statement that "the few masterpieces of realism are pure romance."[21] And for the seventeenth and eighteenth centuries it is confirmed by the allegorical mating—not the opposition—of the ideal and real in *Don Quixote* and by the great discussion about the necessary conjunction of the credible and the marvelous in the epic and in fiction in general, a discussion that, stemming from Le Bossu, Rapin, Dacier, and Addison, is found in Mrs. Davys's "wonderful and probable" (1725) and Fielding's "Probable" and "Marvelous" (1749).[22] There should be, then, no further need to say that the marriage of realism and romance, of the vrai and the merveilleux, in, say, Aphra Behn's *Oroonoko* (1688) is "curious"[23] when, as with Pope's "Wit" and "judgment," the marriage is necessary—an ambivalence, not a dichotomy.

And the ambivalence is found in a marvelously similar way in travel literature. Throughout history that literature has been a combination of the objective and the subjective, of details of setting, history, and customs to go with the traveler's own experiences, adventures, and reflections. He could be almost totally objective, as with Nieuhof (1669) describing the Chinese landscape and people while serving a Dutch embassy as secretary, or William Coxe (1779) recording his geological and other observations while in Switzerland. The traveler could be entertainingly personal, recounting his own exciting adventures, his love affairs, his opinions of religious customs or food, his judgments of national traits, as with the Renaissance travelers Ambrogio Contarini in Persia (published 1487), Pyrard de Laval in Goa (published 1619), and Pietro della Valle in Arabia (published 1650-63), or as with later travelers such as J.-F. Regnard on his way to Scandanavia and the Barbary coast in 1681 and Lady Mary Montagu with her sprightly letters from Turkey in 1717. If he was almost totally objective he was likely to be called dull, as with Coxe, who recorded geologic formations rather than grand scenes or curious manners; but if he preferred to talk of himself and his extraordinary life, he might be judged a liar, perhaps inappropriately as with Captain John Smith, "Mendax" Pinto, or James Bruce, perhaps with real justification, as with Father Hennepin pretending to have seen the mouth of the Mississippi before La Salle, or Psalmanazar claiming to be a Formosan and teaching an invented Formosan language at Oxford.

Such authors of travel books, and countless others, combined the objective and the subjective in various proportions to achieve success or fame, perhaps notoriety, as Béat de Muralt (1728) did when he wrote what for a century was one of the best accounts of England by a Continental but which included such volatile opinions about the English and French that it upset both nations.[24] The notoriety of a Muralt or a Pinto, or the general success of a Brunel (1655) in Spain, a Richard Ligon (1657) in Barbados, a Misson or Addison in Italy, or a Gemelli Careri or a Dampier around the world, would stem in great measure from an artful mixture of empirical and subjective data ranging from almost all history or topographical facts to controlled judgments about or reflections on people and places to fanciful exaggerations and even inventions. Margaret, Duchess of Newcastle, recognized the need for this desirable mixture in travels when at the beginning of her *Description of a New Blazing World* (1666) she prepared the reader for the fact that, since "The end of Reason, is Truth [and] the end of Fancy, is Fiction," she will join Truth and Fiction "as two Worlds at the ends of their Poles"; for, she said, one aids the other.[25] And like Lucian and Cyrano before her and Swift after her, she did combine travel descriptions—of strange animals, of Aztec sun worship—with her fantastic voyages and utopias.

That nearly all travelers who hoped to publish, and perhaps most of their readers, were, like the Duchess, aware of the need to mix dulce with utile is reflected in the many complaints of seventeenth- and eighteenth-century reviewers and other readers who found travel books often going too far in one direction or the other. Concerned about too much dulce an Anglican bishop wrote in the *London Journal* that "books of Voyages and Travels, filled with monsters and incredible Stories," were then popular because they satisfied a "morbid taste for extravagant fiction"; upset about too much utile, Smollett developed "the headach" from reading J.G. Keyssler's encyclopedic and impersonal *Travels through Germany . . .* (1740).[26] The tension between these two extremes, the two chief elements in travel writing, is reflected also in the exclamation of a very recent student (1977) of the literature of New World explorers when he wonders how anyone can "convey that subjectively true sense of the marvelous and at the same time keep the reporter's cardinal goal of conveying objective truth"; it is a chief theme in Curley's *Samuel Johnson and the Age of Travel* (1976); and it is found in the thesis and stated in the title of Batten's new book (1978) on eighteenth-century travels—*Pleasurable Instruction.*[27]

This tension between the personal and the impersonal, the romantic and the realistic, the fanciful and the useful, is as important in the evolution of travel literature as it is in the evolution of the novel, and to study it in one form is to study it in the other. Furthermore, the récit de voyage, well established long before Cervantes, was ready to supply the nouveau roman of 1700 with the realistic, yet often romantic because exotic, details that pure fiction employed in increasing amounts and with increasing scientific accuracy.

There are several routes to choose from in setting out to demonstrate, first, the close relationship between fictional methods of achieving concreteness and those established ones of travel literature and, second, the fact that the novel borrowed so many of its details from travel narratives or from the histories and geographies that depended on them. One could, for example, determine the geographic regions most popular with early novelists and then note not only that the details about those regions were normally borrowed from travels but that, with novelists and their readers, the popularity of a country depended in great measure on trends in exploration or on currently popular or important travel books. Thus, seventeenth-century Jesuit accounts of China, from Ricci in Shakespeare's day to Le Gobien and Le Comte at the very end of the century, provided science fiction writers —Bishop Godwin and his successors—with inspiration for their theories of a musical international language.[28] Or one could follow individual travelers and note the importance of each to novelists—Cartier in Canada as he is being read and used by Rabelais; Richard Ligon in the Barbados as he inspires Mr. Spectator and others to retell a version of the Inkle and Yarico story; or the baron Lahontan in North America as he helps not only Leibnitz and the Encyclopédistes but also Swift and Prévost. Or, finally, one might consider, perhaps chronologically, the individual novelists and their debts to travel literature, whether in a given novel or in all the novels of each writer, as A.W. Secord has done for Defoe or Claire Engel has done for Prévost. Here, however, we can employ a less encyclopedic fashion of demonstrating not only the dependence of fiction on travels for facts and color to be used creatively but also the parallels between the ways the two forms employed them. That is, by selecting not certain countries to go to or certain travelers or novelists to follow chronologically or nationally, we can combine the three methods and be selective. First, then, we should note how Renaissance and earlier storytellers developed the tradition and, next, consider some of the many types of fiction in the seventeenth and eighteenth centuries.

The search for an aesthetics of the early novel, while revealing that seventeenth-century fiction did not evoke a colorful, living, external realism, notes that even the authors of long French "romances" claimed exactness in their documentation, one (1648), for example, insisting that his geography and history are exact, another (1633) that his characters—whether displaying the talent or not—know the languages of countries they visit. Most writers tried to let names of characters—in Egypt, India, America—help with local color; Bishop Camus, from rugged Savoy, had traveled in Spain and was able to describe mountains; and Gomberville in 1637 added an appendix to the fifth part of *Polexandre* (1632) in which he cited authorities for an invisible island and attacked certain historians for their lack of faith in travel and other accounts.[29] Perhaps most admired of such attempts at local color, if still weak by eighteenth-century standards, is Gomberville's fanciful, exotic, but more or less detailed description in *Polexandre* of the costume of a Mexican princess with its highly decorated skirt and its sleeves of silver gauze and diamond buttons.[30] The relatively crude local color of the French romancers, combined with the much greater ability, or need, of the picaresque writers for exact details, we have been saying, led not just to Defoe and Marivaux and apt description of people and places but also to what has been called the evocation of the artist's "world"—"the dimension necessary for a perceiving consciousness to apprehend" the quantitative data in the description of a setting.[31] Such attempts would lead also to that range of novels which Frye calls the anatomy, those narratives that stress the cognitive value, the encyclopedism, of fiction sometimes more than they do the aesthetic or pleasure principle.[32]

This providing minute and varied details has of course been a chief end of travel books from the beginning of literature. And their titles, when not abridged as they so often are by modern commentators, reflect not only their factual content but the desire of their authors to attract a prospective reader's attention and, at the same time, place their books in a popular tradition. The adventures of the traveler were not enough. He had to give facts, preferably unique, perhaps amazing, about places and people. Even before 1550, for example, almost every edition and translation of one of the most subjective and popular of Renaissance travel books, that by Lodovico di Varthema, emphasized on its title page the fact that a reader would here learn about the people, how they lived and thought, and the animal life of Africa and the Near East.[33] A sixteenth-century history-guide-narrative such as that of "Johannes Boemus" was called *The Manners, Lawes, and Customes of All Nations* (1539). Robert Harcourt, with Ralegh in South America, published a volume, as much anatomy-promotion tract as narrative, that he or his publisher called *A Relation of a Voyage to Guiana. Describing the Climat, situation, fertilitie, provisions and commodities of that Country* (1613). Very often such composites—as with the novel—would be named "Histories." The Jesuit Joseph Acosta, who traveled in South America for many years, wrote a *Historia natural y moral de las Indias* (1590; English 1604). By the end of the seventeenth century such titles as these were the rule. The French doctor Pierre la Martinière's *A New Voyage to the North* (1671; translated 1706) adds the promise, *A Particular Relation of the Court of the Czar; of the Religion and Customs of the Muscovites.* And two of the most widely read of early eighteenth-century travel books, one by A. F. Frézier (1712-14) on South America, the other Defoe's three-volume *Tour Thro' the whole Island of Great Britain* (1724-27), made similar promises, the first offering the "Genius and Constitution of the Inhabitants. . . . Their Customs and Manners; their Natural History, Mines, Commodities . . .," the second, as part of an even longer title, announcing "The Customs, Manners, Speech . . . of the People . . . With Useful Observations upon the Whole."

The effect on fiction of such books and such titles can be seen immediately if one glances at the titles and contents of the volumes in that huge body of literature usually called the Imaginary Voyage. The title page of Gabriel de Foigny's influential *La Terre Australe connue* (1676) offers us the "moeurs" and the "coutumes" of that hitherto "unknown country"; the anonymous *The Lunarian* (late 17th century) promises to describe to "the Lunaticks of this World" the moon's "Citties, Towns, Countries, and Provinces" as well as its "hills, Plains, Promontories, and Forrests"; and the title page of the three volumes of "William Sympson's" Mandeville-like *A New Voyage to the East-Indies* (1715) advertises itself as describing "Products, Trade, etc.," "Religion, Manners, and Customs," as well as "Directions for Travellers." All of this is a tradition followed by Chetwood in his two fictions *Falconer* (1720) and *Boyle* (1726) and by Defoe in *Captain Singleton* (1720), Defoe's title including *An Account of the Customs and Manners of the People* of Africa. Even in his biographical-fictional *History of the Pyrates* (1724-28) Defoe employed a title for the second volume which informs the public that this "History" is "Intermix'd with a Description of" the "Laws, Manners, Customs, Government and Religion" of Ethiopia, including an account of tombs and religious ceremonies, all taken from pirate journals, "The Whole instructive and entertaining."[34]

And no matter how fantastic or how believable the fiction was, no matter whether or not its title claimed some of the accoutrements of travel literature, writers who invented characters and sent them on journeys—and that means the great majority of authors of epics, romances, historic and other long narratives—satirized the details of travelers, employed such details imaginatively, perhaps fantastically, or actually transferred real ones from travel books. Lucian (c. 180 A.D.), in a fabulous account that teases Herodotus and other "lying" voyagers, describes horse-vultures and horse-ants on one island, the aromatic air of another, and the mating customs on the moon, where "marriages are of male with male" and "where to be beautiful ... is to be bald and hairless."[35] About the same time Apuleius opens *The Golden Ass* with "As I fortuned to take my voyage into Thessaly," then tells of a juggler he watched in Athens, lets friend Socrates recount his adventures in Macedonia, gives facts about foods and prices in the markets as he goes along, and—at great length and exactly in the fashion of some travel books—describes a house in Hippata, including statues of Diana, her dogs, and Acteon.[36] The author of *Mandeville* (c. 1356), now often called a wonderful romance and not a fake travelogue, claims to have traveled in India, China, Egypt, and the Holy Land but borrows all his copious details —real and extravagant—from actual travelers such as Marco Polo, Odoric of Pordenone, and William of Boldensele.[37] Thomas More's Hythloday accompanies Amerigo Vespucci, crosses South America with other travel-

ers, and sails west to Utopia, where, as in the first travel accounts of the New
World, no one distinguishes between *meum* and *tuum*, land is held in common, gold is despised, there is a plethora of religions, and, exactly as with
Vespucci, each home has behind it a beautiful garden open to all.[38] In the
later books of *Pantagruel*, Rabelais also sends his hero to the New World
and mixes fantastic facts with real ones, the real ones borrowed from Jacques
Cartier, who sailed out of Rabelais's native Saint-Malo; and in exactly the
same way an anonymous author sends his fictional "sieur de Combes" (1609)
to Canada, adapting facts from Champlain and inventing others—carriages
on wheels, for example. All of these and dozens of other examples from fiction written before 1630 attest to the ancient and perennial thirst for exact
details—whether recognizably real, merely marvelous, or obviously fantastic.

Nor is Gomberville's description of a Mexican costume in *Polexandre* the
best example of local color in an early novel employing a foreign setting.
Clarence Rouillard[39] has demonstrated not only the real and permanent
influence on western Europe of sixteenth- and seventeenth-century travelers
to Turkey and Persia, those before Chardin and Tavernier, but also the fact
that Montaigne and the Church fathers—as with Montesquieu, Defoe, and
Voltaire later—used these travelers to make comparisons and to draw moral,
philosophical, or religious conclusions. Their influence on fiction was great.
Rabelais's Panurge, for example, has been a captive in Turkey and, in telling
of his experiences there, provides a feeling for place, chiefly with names and
words from the Koran but also by noting such customs or facts as the
injunction against wine and the great number of dogs; and *Gargantua* shows
its author's knowledge of oriental geography, of the Turkish belief in "the
sanctity of madness," and of Jean Thénaud's colorful description of a caravan with which, in the company of a Persian princess, he traveled from
Jerusalem to Cairo in 1511.[40] Moreover, Gomberville's *Polexandre*, not in the
first edition of 1609 but in the later editions of 1629 and 1637, has much more
than a Mexican costume; it contains real Turkish, as well as Islamic, local
color—the battle of Lepanto; a Moslem funeral; a visitation, apparently
taken from traveler-botanist Pierre Belon, of Black Angels in a tomb; the
Turkish system of military promotion based only on merit; a royal wedding;
and the fiery passion of the Turks.[41] But Gomberville and Rabelais, as well
as less important writers, were outdone by Madeleine and Georges de Scudéry in their treatment of the story of Ibrahim in a novel (1641) and a
tragicomedy (1643). In the novel Madeleine was precise in names and titles,
provided exotic descriptions from her reading, was careful to distinguish
between seraglio and harem, gave authentic details of Soliman's reception
of ambassadors from Genoa, and knew that the Sultan was an avid gardener.
All of this information she could have found in travel books of the time or

in books depending on them, the last two touches, for example, coming from the *Peregrinations* of Palerne (1606).[42]

To learn that well-known authors of prose fiction before 1660 made use of travel information and techniques should not be surprising if one remembers that other forms of literature were doing it too. Robert Cawley and Clarence Rouillard are only two, for example, who have made the point for Renaissance drama.[43] But for a type of literature even closer to the novel of adventure, intrigue, and exoticism, one goes to the long narrative poem. Homer, it has been well argued, was dramatizing the reports of sailors when he wrote of Polyphemus throwing rocks from a volcanic island and of Scylla reaching out from murderous cliffs; and Lois Whitney showed sixty years ago how much Spenser depended on travel accounts when he wrote *The Faerie Queene* (1596 ff.) and interwove "the mythical and the real," the exotic and the fabulous with the believable.[44] He knew about Amazons in South America from such real travelers as the Huguenot Thevet and from such collections of real voyages as the *Decades* of Pietro Martire. From Marco Polo or *Mandeville* he took large-lipped and long-eared wild men, as well as Tartars (or Parthians?) shooting backward as they fled. From Thevet, Duarte Barbosa, or the *Decades* of Richard Eden, a reworking of Pietro Martire, he was able to describe the costume of the kings of Malabar. And much of the Bowre of Blisse episode in Book Two imitates the legendary voyage of Saint Brandon, while any number of hints for the same adventure came from Lucian's satiric travel book or from accounts of real travelers in Spenser's own time. Camões's *Os Lusíadas* (1572) and Ercilla's *La Araucana* (1569, 1589), each no doubt the best long narrative poem in its language, are, however, even closer to the literature of travel than is *The Faerie Queene:* One depends on its author's voyages to India almost as much as on the accounts of Vasco da Gama; the other is by a statesman-warrior who traveled in Chile and Peru before putting their geography and history into verse.[45]

Better than other forms of literature such long narratives, in poetry or in prose, lend themselves to parallels with and borrowings from the literature of travel. Whether the intent was to supply fresh adventures and exotic marvels or merely real facts about a real world, Rabelais, Spenser, Cervantes, Gomberville, or Scudéry—as with Homer or Apuleius in ancient times— hoped to be more successful with their attempts at illusion, at local color, at parodying unbelievable, or believable, travels. It was, then, a well-developed tradition that the eighteenth-century authors of the "new" novel accepted and continued to improve on. The fictional models were there and the travel accounts, old and recent, were there, informative, readable, accessible. To make the point for fiction after the Scudérys, we need for convenience to look only briefly at some of a dozen types of novels that, as in any scheme, will often overlap.

The story with a naive but astute foreign observer was one of the most popular of fictional forms of the eighteenth century, from J.P. Marana's *L'Espion turc* (1684; English 1689; 26 eds. by 1770) to Irving's tales of Mustapha Rub-a-Dub Keli Khan in the *Salmagundi Papers* (1807). Although normally satiric and therefore dealing largely with the author's own country, the type nearly always shows its author's wide reading of, and even imitation of, those travel books written about the fictitious observer's homeland. Montesquieu's *Lettres persanes* (1721) not only is one of the best of the type but was perhaps the most influential. In it Montesquieu was sharpening his wit and collecting those ideas he would develop in the great political science document of the century, *L'Esprit des lois* (1748). And in it he made practical and imaginative use of a number of travel books, real and fictional.[46]

His chief fictional sources were Marana's *L'Espion turc* and Dufresny's *Amusements sérioux and comiques* (1699), which has a man from Siam in Paris and which was itself inspired by accounts of the embassies sent by Louis XIV to Siam in the 1680s; and while Montesquieu's knowledge of the Orient was derived from that long tradition of travelers known by Rabelais and Montaigne, it was more directly dependent on late seventeenth-century travelers such as John Chardin (1686), J.-B. Tavernier (1676), François Bernier (1699), Thévenot (1663), Olearius (1659), and Mme d'Aulnoy with her fireside *Relation du voyage d'Espagne* (1691).[47] From Tavernier's book on Turkey and Chardin's primarily on Persia, Montesquieu took seraglio and harem customs—for example, the roles played by white as opposed to black eunuchs. In Chardin and Olearius he found the method of conveying wives in "cages" or hampers on the back of camels. Tavernier supplied distances and itineraries and Chardin a description of the holy city of Qum, although Montesquieu—but not Chardin— confused the Fatima venerated in the great mosque there with the daughter of Mohammed, somewhat as he erred in transcribing the Persian calendar, copying Chardin's months Rebiah and Cheval as Rebiag and Chalval. From Mme d'Aulnoy he learned that Spaniards were grave and that Spanish women were reserved and often wore spectacles. From any of these he borrowed an anecdote here or there and fitted it to his story; for example, from Olearius he took the report—hearsay which Olearius did not himself believe (III.ix)—that a Muscovite woman feels unwanted if she goes twenty-four hours without a beating from her husband. And often he altered facts or exaggerated them, as in accounts of the number of eunuchs in a seraglio or a shah's exercising his rights to the life and death of his subjects. Thus, in a hundred ways Montesquieu took what he found in the travelers to the Orient, worked it over imaginatively, and incorporated it in a book which he was happy to call a roman and which, he noted, was widely popular and read for pleasure more than for instruction.[48] And what is true of *Les Lettres persanes* is true also for dozens of other stories with a fictitious foreign observer, among them Goldsmith's *Citizen of the World* (1760-62), which, in addition to taking its inspiration from Marana, Montesquieu, Lord Lyttelton's *Letters from a Persian in England* (1735), and especially the *Lettres Chinoises* of the marquis d'Argens (1739), made use of the real travels and observations of père Le Comte and the letters of those other well-traveled Jesuits as found in J.-B. Du Halde's popular *Description . . . de la Chine* (1735).[49]

Close to the first-person story of a foreign observer is the novel with any foreign setting, and of this kind there are many varieties after the great day of the seventeenth-century French *romans*, which normally placed their characters in exotic if often vague locales. In 1656 Margaret, Duchess of Newcastle, was sending her heroine Travelia on voyages that combine the fantasy of Lucian with the realism, often marvelous but based on fact, of Renaissance travel accounts.[50] While dressed as a man and serving on a ship headed for "new discoveries toward the South," Travelia observes customs and animal life, including a strange beast made up of hawk, parrot, and unicorn. Her marvelous animal is in a tradition that extends to François Misson, who in the fake *Voyage et avantures de François Leguat* (1707) combined features of real birds in real travel accounts and created the "gelinotte," a bird scientists accepted for two centuries.[51] And Travelia visits an island inhabited only by Amazons, who mate annually with the inhabitants of another island inhabited only by men. This was a story passed on by Columbus and other voyagers to Pietro Martire (1511, 1530), after whom it would be repeated for two hundred years, as in the popular *Atlas Geographus* (1717).[52]

Another, but more realistic, type of fiction with foreign setting is the colonial novel. The many examples of this type include Aphra Behn's *Oroonoko* (1688), set in Surinam; Defoe's *Moll Flanders* (1721), with incidents in the British North American colonies; Prévost's *Manon Lescaut* (1731), whose heroine ends up in Louisiana; N.-G. Leonard's *Idylles* (1766), which takes place on the island of Guadeloupe, where he lived for some years; Arthur Young's *The Adventures of Emmera; or the Fair American* (1767), which is set largely in New York; Charlotte Smith's *Old Manor House* (1793), the hero of which fights in the British army in the colonies; and Chateaubriand's *Atala* (1801) and *René* (1802). Each of these provides a kind of imitation travel account, and some are by actual travelers to the spots described.

Oroonoko, or The Royal Slave, partly because it is early, has had its colonial realism studied most. Whether or not Behn went on to Surinam after her governor-father died en route, as she claimed, is less important than the fact that in *Oroonoko* her local color is often verifiable even if sometimes inaccurate. Although literary historians such as Steeves and Wagenknecht

accept her claim, Ernest Bernbaum (1913) long ago argued rather convincingly that she had not been to Surinam, that some of her facts about its flora,
fauna, native customs, and places are wrong, and that whatever facts she has
right could have come from contemporaneous news releases and travel
accounts such as George Warren's *Impartial Description of Surinam* (1667).[53]
And E.A. Baker (III, 91) is one who with A.W. Secord (12) accepted the
conclusions of Bernbaum and other doubters, asserting that Behn's "romance" is "full of blunders and misunderstandings" derived from hearsay
and a "hasty" reading of Warren. But an imposing line of scholars have come
to her defense,[54] all of them showing that she described correctly not only
the Koromantins of the African Gold Coast, the tribes from which
Oroonoko and his beloved Imoinda came, but also Indian costumes of the
Guianas and horrible punishments of slaves unique to the West Indies. If,
then, with all these and certain other details Behn was not reporting what
she saw, she found them in seventeenth-century travel books, both French
and English—for example, the practice, recounted in Du Tertre's *Histoire
générale des Antilles* (1667) and elsewhere, of slave traders enticing blacks
aboard and then sailing off with them.

Oroonoko was prodigiously popular, even more on the Continent than
in England, Daniel Mornet's now well-known study of reading tastes in-
dicating that Behn, Richardson, and the Fieldings supplied eight of the nine
most widely owned English novels in France about 1750 and that her novel
was even more popular there than Prévost's *Manon Lescaut.* It was, in fact,
important to many French writers, translators, and critics, including Rousseau, Voltaire, and Saint-Lambert, who imitated it in *Zimeo* (1769).[55]

Again, however, for a study of the evolution of the novel, the question
of Aphra Behn's having been to South America—or the West Indies, or the
Gold Coast of Africa—is not so significant as the realization that she learned
so much from travelers, combined her learning with her imagination, and
composed a novel that inspired not only a tradition of colonial novels but
much other European fiction. In that tradition the most influential eighteenth-century writer is perhaps the abbé Prévost, who because of his up-to-
date reading of accounts of North America was able to send his fictional
Manon Lescaut to Louisiana as one of the several hundred girls—most of
them debauched, some even criminals—actually sent there in 1719-20 by
John Law to be married off. And, like many of them, Manon dies of fever
in the French colony. Also in that tradition is Chateaubriand, who like his
mentor Prévost mixed great quantities of the romantic with certain portions
of the real[56] and whose stories about America—*Chactas, René, Atala*—were,
over a hundred years after Behn, more inaccurate at times than hers and just
as idealized. And while we know that he traveled in North America (1791)
before writing them and that he later published an account of that trip
(1827), we know also that Chateaubriand depended far less on what he

observed than he did on the books of other travelers, among them William Bartram, the marquis de Chastellux, père Lafitau, Jonathan Carver, and Gilbert Imlay.[57]

Close to the colonial novel—and perhaps the largest and most amorphous of all possible types—is the novel primarily of adventure. It could be a story of intrigue, satire, the amatory, the picaresque, the voyage, the imaginary voyage, the exotic, or any combination of these. It had so many varieties, in fact, and was so popular that one can only nod at it and note how often and how necessarily it was like a travel account and how often it depended on actual reports of travelers. A picaresque adventure such as the *English Rogue* (1665), by Richard Head, called by one reader "A modern Mandeville," could, as H.F. Watson and others have shown, make obvious and extended use of J.H. Linschoten's widely read *Voyage to the East Indies* (1598) for names and uses of animals and plants on the island of Mauritius, for details about a Brahmin woman leaping onto the funeral pyre of her husband, and for the custom—taken expert advantage of by Head's lusty hero Latroon—of the Calicut bridegroom handing over his bride for the first night's deflowering by another man.[58]

Here Head, as with other fictionizers, was carefully selecting and rearranging the facts of travel books for their exoticism, their uniqueness, and —especially true for him—their pornographic value. Accounts of the first-night Indian custom Latroon profited from were of course popular in western Europe long before Head's time and can be traced to books written a century before Linschoten, to, for example, the *Travels* of Lodovico di Varthema (1510) and the *Journey* (1499) of the Genoese merchant Santo Stephano. The earlier, Santo Stephano, reported that at Calicut "men never marry any woman who is a virgin"; rather, if any bride is a virgin "she is delivered over before the nuptials to some other person for fifteen or twenty days in order that she may be deflowered."[59] Varthema, perhaps using his imagination as much as would Linschoten and Head long after him, dramatized the reputed custom, extending his contemporary's four lines to two pages and insisting that the king, as well as all the citizens, selected white men, either Moslems or Christians, for the ritual, which lasted only one night under pain of death. Varthema also claimed that his companion, almost exactly as with Head's rogue, acceded to a Calicut merchant's pleadings to sleep with his new fifteen-year-old wife, doing "for the merchant all that he had asked of him, ... although truly the lady would have desired that the first night had lasted a month."[60] And truly Richard Head's famous traveling creation had no more imagination and no more sense of drama than some famous real travelers who felt they needed to stress the marvelous as much as some novelists stressed the real.

The adventure novel could exploit sea voyages such as those told about in hundreds of travel volumes, especially those written after Prince Henry and Columbus, Hakluyt, the de Brys, and Purchas. Often the voyages are only a part of a picaresque plot, as when Head uses the last eleven of seventy-six chapters to send his rogue to the East Indies. But while the report of this particular journey is only one-seventh of the novel, it supplies exact details of the hard, unattractive daily life of the ship's crew—dirty hands, tangled hair, stinking water, beef and pork that "stirred as if it had received a second life, and was crawling out of the platter to seek out the rest of his members"[61]—just as the journal of a sailor or of a ship's supernumerary might have suggested. Other late seventeenth-century tales have still more voyages, one example being another rogue story, *Don Tomazo, or the Juvenile Rambles of Thomas Dangerfield* (1680). In it the protagonist takes ship to Cádiz and then to Africa and the Orient; on the voyage home his ship is wrecked and he is rescued by the Dutch; he buys a vessel and sets out to "bring destruction to the whole Guiney trade"; finally, after being shipwrecked on the coast of Ireland he is successful as a pirate until shipwrecked again, this time off Holland. All these events are of course second to the protagonist's life on land, his amorous exploits, and his counterfeiting of money. By 1720, imitating and borrowing from voyage literature, especially from Ned Ward's *Trip to Jamaica* (1698), the author of *The Jamaica Lady* could write a better sea novel that would provide ship scenes, sea talk, and a lifelike captain,[62] thereby looking ahead to Defoe, Smollett, and Shebbeare in England and to important French novelists such as Prévost and the later Lesage.

Defoe's adventure-voyages include pirate fictions such as *The Life, Adventures, and Piracies of the Famous Captain Singleton* (1720) and *Of Captain Misson* (1728), as well as the stories of more nearly law-abiding sailors, for example, *A New Voyage round the World by a Route Never Sailed before* (1724) and the *Four Years Voyages of Capt. George Roberts* (1726). Of the many students of Defoe's techniques Arthur Secord has shown best how for *Singleton* Defoe was often inspired by and maneuvered details from his own biography of the pirate Avery (1719), from the books of his favorite traveler the buccaneer William Dampier, and from accounts of other travelers such as Mandelslo and Flacourt, both of whom had been to Madagascar, where Singleton spends much time.[63] The French Captain Misson, now known to be totally fictional—just as, in fact, much of Defoe's material on other, real "pyrates" included in the *General History* is invented[64]—sails in the Mediterranean, along South America and the West Indies, and on both side of Africa. He engages in a number of ship-to-ship combats and always wins, is always popular with his crew, and is consistently generous to his prisoners. All of this is the product of Defoe's vivid imagination working on places and directions out of books by the buccaneers Exquemelin, Ringrose, Dampier, and Wafer and on their versions of buccaneer democracy, the taking of prizes, and the detailed lists of goods found on those prizes. Even the French Misson's generosity and humanity are not unsurprising when one reads the *Journal* of the more or less admirable buccaneer Captain Raveneau de Lussan (1689), which was published with the accounts by Exquemelin and Ringrose, and when in Dampier's *New Voyage* one finds another sophisticated, hospitable French buccaneer captain in the West Indies who several times invites Dampier to dinner and urges him to join with the French.[65] The origins of Defoe's Misson are suggested of course in the third sentence of the "biography," where, we are told, the pirate captain was as a boy "much affected with the Accounts he had read in Books of Travels." Somewhat as with Singleton and Misson, for *Roberts* Defoe nourished his imagination on his own account of the real pirate Ned Low and even more on *Ashton's Memorial* (1725), which was published the year before and which provided details about ship and pirate life as observed by a young colonial held captive in the West Indies by Low's crew.[66] *A New Voyage* is a more complex problem than *Roberts* when one considers Defoe's expansive invention as it was fed by his great store of geographical knowledge, his library, and his ambitions for Britain's takeover of Spanish trade.

And *A New Voyage round the World by a Route Never Sailed before* has had a recent revival, not just in scholarship dealing with it but in critical appreciation. Peter Earle and Pat Rogers, for example, are enthusiastic about this fake travel book as a good novel, an opinion concurred in by Benton Fishman;[67] and for Defoe's methods in putting it together, both Fishman and Jane Jack have added to the old study made by the geographer J.N.L. Baker (1929; 1963).[68] Defoe's title is an extension of that of Dampier's first book, *A New Voyage round the World*, which was always an inspiration for Defoe the novelist. Here, however, his protagonist-captain, unlike Dampier, sails east around the world after reaching the southern end of South America and quelling a mutiny on the very spot where Drake a century before had quelled another. Passing the Cape of Good Hope and coming east across the Pacific, the captain skirts Australia as Dampier had done, refers to the Dutch circumnavigators Schouten and Le Maire, and at the high latitude of 67°S records in his log, "[This], I suppose, is the farthest latitude that any European ship ever saw in these seas," words almost exactly those of the real Woodes Rogers, who in 1709 had reached merely 61.53°S.[69]

This novel, like all Defoe's sea novels, really has more to do with masses of land, and one of its chief incidents is the crossing made of South America by part of the ship's crew. Obviously Defoe was obsessed with the crossing of little-known or totally unexplored continents. In *The Further Adventures of Robinson Crusoe* he sent Crusoe across Asia, letting him reverse the journey made by Ysbrant Ides in 1692; in *Singleton* the intrepid buccaneer and his crew hike all the way across Africa carefully following, as far as possible, rivers and lakes and mountains then shown on maps in Dapper's *Africa* (1668) or Ogilby's *Africa* (1670), until finally Defoe was forced to invent names and topography for that great section of equatorial Africa not to be mapped until the time of Livingstone and Stanley more than a hundred years later; and in *A New Voyage* the hikers also follow much unexplored territory near the Andes, although Defoe was able to make imaginative use of the sixteenth-century Alonso de Ovalle (1646) as found not only in the travel collection of the brothers Churchill in 1704 but also in Herman Moll's *The Compleat Geographer* (1709). And for both *Crusoe* and *Singleton*, Defoe borrowed from his collaborator Moll, who like Defoe depended on travelers and who provided maps for Dampier and many other navigators known to the novelist.[70] But these inspirations for Defoe's creativity constitute only a fraction of the total. For example, as the crew in *A New Voyage* crosses South America, it is fascinated with the same roaring torrents Ovalle saw; and where the Renaissance Spaniard merely spoke of volcanoes, Defoe dramatizes a volcanic eruption witnessed by his fictional explorers. No other novelist, in fact, every made such broad, such specific, such creative use of so many travel accounts.

Smollett and his bête noir Shebbeare are sea novelists of another kind, Smollett with Roderick Random's voyage (1748) to the West Indies and, in *Peregrine Pickle* (1751), with Commodore Trunnion and his memorable crew, and Shebbeare, in *Lydia* (1755), with his heroine and his noble savage Cannassetego crossing the Atlantic to England on a British man-of-war. The ugly life in the hold of Roderick's ship bound for Carthagena is obviously like the one Smollett himself must have experienced on the Chichester man-of-war in 1740-42 in that same Carthagena expedition, but the ugly life in *Roderick*, as well as the press gangs, the shipwreck, and the officers, is to be found in embryo in the accounts of George Anson's circumnavigation of the world made at exactly the same time and reported later, as in the official version credited to Chaplain Walter.[71] And just as obviously Shebbeare also knew that circumnavigation, for twice in *Lydia*, and at length, he attacks Walter's very popular book[72] while at the same time recounting scenes aboard ship and introducing characters much like those of *The Jamaica Lady* (1720). Although all such novels are important parts of the tradition of English sea fiction, any English novelist, from Richard Head to Smollett, learned less about the sea from previous novelists than they did from their own sailing experience or from that great mass of accounts of actual sea voyages from Hakluyt to James Cook.

Lesage's one important contribution to fiction of the sea is *Avantures de M. Robert Chevalier, dit de Beauchêne, capitaine de flibustiers dans la Nouvelle France* (1732).[73] Claiming that he was merely the editor of travel memoirs

given him by the widow of Beauchêne, Lesage lets his scoundrelly hero tell
of his career as a companion of the Iroquois in Canada and, about 1707-08,
as a youthful buccaneer in the Antilles. The author had to tell us himself,
however, of Beauchêne's later life as gambler in France and of his death in
a quarrel at Tours at the hands of "des Anglais." In reality the buccaneer-
adventurer's career was invented in the fashion of Head, Courtilz, and
Defoe, the chief travel-book inspirations being those of buccaneers such as
de Lussan, Exquemelin, and Dampier for the sea portions and the baron
Lahontan for Canadian geography, the Red Man, French life in Canada, and
episodes such as the romantic one of Mlle Laclos sent to the New World.
Although the last name of Lesage's hero has been found on a seventeenth-
century baptismal record in Montreal, no one has any record of an active
life led by a "Robert Chevalier, dit de Beauchêne." Nor was Lesage's character ever in the same part of the world as the real Captain de Beauchene-
Gouin who, according to Woodes Rogers (1712), was in the South Seas in
1699-1701 leading a French naval expedition and helping map makers locate
islands more precisely. Lesage's invention was so successful that the editor
of the 1824 edition echoed the author: "This is not a fiction but the unique
history of a buccaneer captain"; and that in spite of the fact no such Beauchêne has been found outside the pages of Lesage, who in his later volumes
admitted he was writing a roman.[74]

Lesage knew and used the buccaneers, Lahontan, and, for *Gil Blas*,
travelers in Europe such as Mme d'Aulnoy, but Prévost knew far more
about travel accounts in general and books about the sea in particular. He
had been tutor to the son of the leading London merchant, Sir John Eyles,
in the 1720s, had studied Defoe, perhaps F.M. Misson, the author of the fake
François Leguat, and in 1746 began publishing his colossal twenty-volume
Histoire générale des voyages. His one complete sea novel is the *Voyages du
capitaine Lade* (1744), although he left unfinished another, to be called the
Monde moral. For his English Captain Lade, who sails in many seas and, like
Beauchêne, listens to a number of stories told by other travelers, Prévost
employed what Claire Engle and others call "une imagination féconde et
souple" and a library of travel volumes rivaling that of Defoe but, unlike
Defoe's, one should add, nearly all English.[75] And by fueling his imagination
with Dampier, Exquemelin, Rogers and Cooke, Robert Ligon and his *Barbados* (1657), Daniel Coxe and his *Carolana* (1741), Thomas Gage and his
New Survey of the West Indies (1648), Hans Sloane (1707; 1725), and other such
popular travelers, Prévost was able not only to provide details about the
Hottentots of South Africa, the geography of Cuba, hurricanes in Mexico,
or a gold hunt in Guinea but also to find support for his methods of putting
a book together, for his sentimental primitivism, and for his attacks on
European civilization when compared with that of China as described by

French Jesuits.[76] And while he naturally committed certain errors in geography, Prévost kept his exotic details plausible enough that a contemporaneous reviewer wrote admiringly, "One does not see in the *Voyages de Robert Lade* those unbelievable oddities which are so often found in the imagination of travelers more attentive to arousing the reader's curiosity than to respecting the truth."[77]

Of the many traditions about fiction of the sea that provide both romance and realism and that stem directly from travel literature, four stand out in the seventeenth and eighteenth centuries—the use of shipwrecks, of pirates, of episodes of slavery, and of desert island castaways. The accounts of real shipwrecks make up one of the most fascinating branches of voyage literature and are found as far back as the Renaissance collections of voyages, those of Ramusio and Hakluyt, for example. In 1552 and 1554 the *São João* and the *São Bento* were wrecked off the coast of Natal and caught the attention of all Europe, the latter tragedy being written up by Manuel de Mesquita Perestrelo (1564), "the hero of the ordeal," in an account that makes vivid the terrors of the storm, the helplessness of the crew and of the ship itself, the actions of people on board in such horrible times, and the reactions of those who were fortunate enough to survive.[78] The first important English collection of such disasters—twenty-seven of them by James Janeway—appeared in 1675, while a classic one, by Bernardo Gómes de Brito, came out in two volumes in Lisbon (1735) and gave the stories of twelve shipwrecks important in Portuguese history between 1552 and 1602. These are nearly all first-person narratives, and many of them give the sense of immediacy expected in the first-person novels of a Defoe or the letters of a Richardson or a Rousseau. Keith Huntress lists some five attractions the narratives of sea disasters seem to have for readers, three of which stand out for students of fiction—the "obvious" appeal of the exotic scenes, language, and events; "the religious and moral lessons to be learned," since most of the narratives stress divine providence, prayer, and repentance; and the experiencing of an "Aristotelian catharsis," that is, enjoyment without danger.[79]

From ancient times fiction in prose or poetry has exploited the storm at sea and its aftereffects—the shipwreck, the actions of captain and crew and passengers, often the rescue by another ship, the drifting in a small boat, or the life on a desert island to which survivors come. The moving story of the wreck of the *São João* off Natal was made into one of the great Portuguese epics, *Naufragio de Sepulveda* (1594), by Jeronymo Corte-Real, two of whose relatives had died in a similar disaster near Newfoundland.[80] Passing over Ariel's rescue of Ferdinand and his shipmates in *The Tempest*, as well as the storms and shipwrecks found in the seventeenth-century tales of La Calprenède and the Scudérys, none of which is vivid or horrifying, we encounter more and more use in fiction of such incidents. By the time of *The English Rogue* (1665), Richard Head was able to employ all of the exact and frightening details by then so popular in narratives of real sea disasters—dark, portentous skies, great winds and huge waves, praying crews, parallels with Jonah, frightening cries, the crash between two rocks, the drowning of some people, the slow and painful escape of others, the splitting and sinking ship, the rescue. In fact, Head not only describes such a wreck off the Isle of Man but gives a detailed, convincing account of a leaking ship that sinks, an escape in a long boat, the tantalizing agony of a drawn-out rescue by another ship, and then a storm and wreck on the way to the Canaries.[81] Only Defoe in *Crusoe* was to equal him in such graphic and violent scenes at sea, but then Defoe had practiced well with his exciting reports of real ships and men in *The Storm* (1704).

And in the eighteenth century such episodes were to become routine for novels of adventure. Penelope Aubin has three of them—in *The Strange Adventures of the Count de Vinevil* (1721), in *The Noble Slaves* (1722), and in *Count Albertus* (1728). Two others are found in novels by Eliza Haywood: one is *Philidore and Placentia* (1627), in which a "Christian Eunuch" tells how he and his companions returning from Contantinople suffer two tempests, have their boat sunk, and undergo experiences similar to those of Head's Meriton Latroon in a long boat; the other is *Idalia* (1742), in which the heroine rides a plank to shore in the Mediterranean after a violent storm shatters her ship. Such scenes are just as standard for the "Imaginary Voyages" listed by Philip Gove. For example, Chetwood's *Falconer* (1720) has several shipwrecks, and his *Boyle* (1726) has Richard Castleman's story of another; Gulliver is the only survivor of the wreck in Voyage One (1726); and the protagonist in Paltock's *Peter Wilkins* (1750) is shipwrecked near the South Pole. But then, authors of novels that are never called imaginary voyages, without necessarily exploiting all the sufferings and lamentations of the tradition, have found it convenient or appropriate to indulge in or make use of a shipwreck. H.-F. Lasolle in *Mémoires de Versorand* (1752) lets the playboy hero sail on a merchant ship so that he may be wrecked on an island off the west coast of Africa and spend four years learning from the natives how to work. And Smollett in *Roderick Random* wrecks his erring hero so that he may be robbed by his mates and yet discover his true love.

Pirates—but not buccaneers normally—often accompany slaves in seventeenth- and eighteenth-century fiction. There are a number of well-known episodes involving both, among them Crusoe's Sallee adventure; the experiences of Aubin's four lords and ladies in North Africa as recounted in *The Noble Slaves;* her other stories of slavery in the same place found in *Charlotta Du Pont* (1723); and Chetwood's account of Captain Robert Boyle (1726) and his escape from Barbary slavery with Mrs. Villars. And there are other episodes involving Europeans enslaved in eastern palaces—for example, Haywood's Christian eunuch in *Philidore and Placentia* and his life in the harem of a Bashaw. All such stories were popular in France too. In the fifth part of Lasolle's *Versorand* the hero is captured by Mediterranean pirates, is sold as a slave in Algiers to a master with a beautiful daughter Irene, gives up Christianity for Islam in order to marry her, but then, when they flee, loses her by drowning and escapes alone. Such plots in French fiction were standard long before Lasolle, however, for in 1736 Crébillon fils had attacked those romans with too marvelous adventures that take the hero over many seas to be captured by Turks and to end up in seraglios where sultanesses are guarded by eunuchs.[82]

Slaves and pirates were popular in travel literature long before *Robinson Crusoe*, however, even before *Don Quixote*, which has its "Strange Adventures of the Beautiful Morisca," a Christian who has lived in Algiers in disguise and witnessed the treatment of slaves.[83] By the seventeenth century, Mediterranean corsairs had made a lucrative business of selling white captives to north Africans either to be retained as slaves or to be ransomed through the intermediaries found in Tripoli, Algiers, and other cities on the coast. In 1610 George Sandys, poet-traveler-statesman, witnessed a scene in the Mediterranean in which Christian slaves unsuccessfully tried to escape in a captured galley, and at the home of ambassador Thomas Glover in Constantinople he met the self-styled Prince of Moldavia, who had actually been a slave for years before escaping.[84] Purchas in his collection of travels (1625) included the stories of Englishmen who suffered such captivity and added his own horrified appraisal of North Africa as the "Stinke of Slavery."[85] Among the best-known stories of Europeans enslaved in the seventeenth and eighteenth centuries were those of the Englishmen Francis Knight (1640), William Okeley (1675), and Thomas Pellow (1740), while in 1721, only months after *Crusoe* and just before Aubin's *The Noble Slaves*, London witnessed a procession of 280 Englishmen ransomed from African captivity.

Every European nation, however, had its problems with the corsairs, one of the most intriguing examples being that of the French dramatist-traveler Jean Regnard, who as a young man was captured by pirates, sold in Algiers, and ransomed in 1681. Years later he romanticized his experiences in a novelette, *La Provençale*, published in 1731 after his death. The fictional account, using a Decameron-like story-within-story framework, has Zelmis (Regnard), his beloved, and her husband captured, each sold in Algiers, she into a harem. Zelmis, because of his talents as a chef, endears himself to his "patron" and becomes a favorite in the owner's harem. When, however, he insists on remaining true to his "belle Provençale," disappointed harem girls inform on him. Then, just in time, the French consul intervenes with ransom money, and Zelmis and his beloved return to France only to have her escaped husband show up in time to spoil a marriage. Regnard's story is typical except that it lacks the usual long account of an escape.

G.A. Starr,[86] concentrating on the narratives of Barbary escapes as told by Englishmen or their editors, has pointed out not only the favorite formula for these narratives and how important they are for historians of North Africa but also how close to the novel they are in dramatic incident, tormented characters, the epic moral, and the providential design of the whole. The details of the real escape in *Eben-ezer* (1625)—the plan to construct a collapsible boat, the hiding of the sections and provisions, the frantic rowing at night, the frustrations all along the way—are, Starr shows, as realistic as Crusoe's attempts to build an escape boat as told generations later.

These Barbary captivity tales continued to inspire writers of fiction long after Regnard and Head, Defoe and Aubin, Chetwood and Lasolle. In 1797 Royall Tyler learned enough from his friend David Humphreys—United States Commissioner in Algeria and contriver with Joel Barlow of a treaty to free American prisoners—to write *The Algerine Captive*, the sensational second part of which tells of the hero's life as a slave. In his preface Tyler pretends to attack "novels" that attempt to paint "the manners, customs, and habits of a strange country," believes that Americans have given them up in order to quaff "wine with Brydone in the hermitage of Vesuvius" or to sport "with Bruce on the fairy land of Abyssinia"—that is, to read travel books—and insists that he himself is writing a travel book.[87] Starr is obviously correct in arguing not only the close relationship between true and fictional captivity accounts but also the impossibility of separating truth from fiction in one or fiction from truth in the other; for each form of narrative, so often and so well, mixes the realistic and the marvelously exotic with drama, suspense, amorous intrigue, misery, morality, and the clash of religions and cultures.

The fiction of desert island castaways is gigantic, greater even than that of pirates or African slavery or shipwrecks, and it is also even more a part of the literature of travel. *Robinson Crusoe*, the great archetype for the castaway novel, has its roots in every direction, as A.W. Secord, especially, has shown. For Crusoe's twenty-six years on his island off eastern South America, Secord does most with Defoe's use of Dampier and of the travels of Robert Knox (1681), nineteen years a captive on Ceylon.[88] As important an inspiration as any other, however, is *The Cruising Voyage round the World* (1712), the account by Woodes Rogers of his circumnavigation aboard the *Duke*, which was accompanied by the *Duchess.*[39] The journal of Rogers provided a chief impetus for Defoe's ambitions to open a British South Sea trade, but it also contains the first and basic account of the most famous of all real island castaways, Alexander Selkirk.

Selkirk's startling appearance to the first of the *Duke*'s crew who landed on Más a Tierra, largest of the three islands in the Juan Fernández group west of Chile, his manner of being left there over four years before by the buccaneer Captain Stradling, his way of life on the island, his being taken aboard and given the position of mate—all these details are given first and best by Rogers's journal. That this portion of the journal created quite a stir in Europe is evidenced by several facts. The second edition of Edward Cooke's companion account of the voyage, for example, which appeared after Rogers's volume, on its title page took advantage of the current interest by advertising Selkirk as its chief attraction. Within a year there was published an anonymous *Providence Displayed or a surprising Account of one Mr. Alexander Selkirk* purporting to be "written by his own Hand and attested by most of the eminent Merchants on the Royal Exchange," a booklet that drew its facts from Rogers and used Selkirk to promote moral and religious lessons. And about the same time Richard Steele devoted all of Number 26 of his *Guardian* (December 3, 1713) to Selkirk. While Steele reported talking with Selkirk more than once and drew certain sentimental conclusions from Selkirk's life on Juan Fernández, his account is very close to that in *A Cruising Voyage*. Furthermore, Steele's next *Guardian* advertised Edward Cooke's journal of Rogers's circumnavigation. Defoe himself, so busy with other matters at the time, gave no immediate attention to Selkirk; but in 1719, the year after the second edition of *A Cruising Voyage*, he published his own famous story of a fictional desert-island castaway, the first of many books he was to write about supposed or real or partly real voyages.

The adventures of Alexander Selkirk on Juan Fernández were not the only such adventures that might have inspired Defoe. There were, in fact, many other real castaways who, alone or in small groups, had left their impression on islands throughout the world. One of the best known was Pedro Serrano, whose story is to be found in Garcilaso de la Vega's classic *Royal Commentaries of Peru*, translated into English in Defoe's lifetime by the travel writer Paul Rycaut (1688). Serrano, about the time of Cortés, was washed ashore on a small cay between Panama and Cuba and spent three years alone in a more primitive condition by far than that known by Selkirk or Robinson Crusoe. He had no clothes, food, or firearms to begin with, as Selkirk and Crusoe did, and existed by drinking rainwater and turtle's blood. Later he was joined by another refugee from a shipwreck, who did not live long, while Serrano was eventually rescued and brought back to Europe to be briefly lionized. Nearly a hundred years later, in 1614, three Englishmen were stranded off the coast of Scotland, where two died, one by suicide, the remaining one being rescued after eleven months by a Captain Pickman. Then there was Henry Pitman, a surgeon with the Duke of Monmouth's abortive rebellion in 1685, who was imprisoned and sent to Barbados. With seven other prisoners he escaped to the island of Tortuga, so well known by the buccaneers, and lived like a Crusoe for some months before being taken off.

But no other small island has had so many such castaways, or been so well advertised by voyagers and their journals, as the one on which Selkirk lived, Más a Tierra, largest of the islands that make up Juan Fernández, as it has always been popularly called. Discovered by Spaniards in the third quarter of the sixteenth century, this tiny oasis of about fifty square miles became a favorite stopping-off place for scurvy-ridden sailing vessels, especially for those of the seventeenth-century buccaneers, who, unlike the Spanish, had no home bases in that part of the world. The first report of men left on Juan Fernández is from 1624, when the Dutch Admiral Jacob le Hermite, on his way around the world, left three gunners and three soldiers there at their own request because they were weary of the voyage. No one knows when or how or if they were rescued. Toward the end of the same century Basil Ringrose's journal was published in *The Buccaneers of America*, and under the entry for 3 January 1681 he records that on that day the ship's Spanish pilot told the crew how "many years ago a certain ship was cast away upon this island, and only one man saved, who lived alone . . . five years before any ship came this way to carry him off." The best known of Selkirk's predecessors, perhaps because William Dampier told us about him in *A New Voyage round the World*, was a Mosquito Indian named Will. In 1681 Dampier was with Captain Watling off Juan Fernández when three Spanish ships of war appeared and forced the English buccaneers to leave in such haste that they had to abandon Will, who was away hunting goats. The fleet-footed Indian, with only a gun, some powder and shot, a knife, and the clothes on his back, lived alone for three years and eleven months, eluding the Spaniards who sought him, making fishhooks from his gun barrel, which was used also to strike fire from flint, eating seals, fish, and goats, and building a rock hut half a mile from the sea, which he lined with goatskins. Then in 1684 Captain John Cook, another buccaneer, sailed in to Juan Fernández and rescued Will. William Dampier was also on that ship and on 22 March 1684 recorded in his journal how on that day they "went ashore to see for the Moskito Indian" whom they had left there. The journal also tells how Will, recognizing the friendly ships, welcomed the crew with three cooked goats, how he was tenderly greeted by another Mosquito named Robin, and how he thought the ship had come expressly to rescue him.

Will was the most Crusoesque of Selkirk's predecessors, but he was not the last. The Captain John Cook who took him off in 1684 was succeeded on the same ship by Edward Davis, who a little over two years later returned to Juan Fernández and, at their own request, put five English buccaneers and four blacks ashore and sailed away. Again Dampier tells us how the nine men defended themselves successfully against the Spanish who came to take them, how because of disagreements and personality conflicts they lived apart from one another, how one of them went over to the Spanish, and how nearly three years later the remaining eight were finally taken off by Captain John Strong, whose manuscript journal in the British Library confirms the story. Although a group of French buccaneers stayed on the island for ten months and reportedly trained some of the goats to come at milking time, the next Englishmen who lived there alone came just before Selkirk.

In 1703 the ubiquitous William Dampier sailed from England in command of two ships, the *Saint George* and the *Cinque Ports,* on one of the most unsuccessful raiding voyages ever undertaken. He kept no journal of that circumnavigation, and so we obtain our information from other sources. The captain of the *Cinque Ports* died early on the voyage and was succeeded by Captain Stradling, who quickly began alienating his crew. At an island off Brazil nine of his men left him in disgust, and at Juan Fernández more than forty more abandoned the same ship, returning to their posts only when Dampier went ashore to reason with them. Nevertheless, when a large French ship suddenly appeared, the two English ships had to make such a quick departure that they left behind five of the crew of the *Cinque Ports* and a black from the *Saint George,* as well as a long boat and other supplies. The French not only prevented Dampier and Stradling from coming back right away but captured four of the stranded men and took the supplies, the remaining two men staying alone, apparently with some comfort, for more than six months before Stradling (now separated from Dampier) was able to return for them. It was at this time that Selkirk, unhappy with his captain, perhaps knowing from Dampier of Will's experience, or perhaps having heard from their own lips the story of his two fellow crew members, asked Stradling to leave him on Juan Fernández.

Nor was Selkirk the last lonely occupant of that little island. John Clipperton, mate on the ill-fated *Saint George,* returned in 1719 as captain of his own privateer and abandoned two of his men, who stayed two months before the Spaniards took them off. And the next year George Shelvocke, after his man Simon Hatley had shot the albatross that was to inspire Coleridge, wrecked his ship on Juan Fernández. There his crew took five months to build a small boat and then had to leave twenty-four men when they sailed away. Apparently the marooned sailors were "rescued" by the Spaniards, since the Dutch commander Roggewein found no one when he visited Juan Fernández two years later. Many of these stories of castaways and shipwrecks, on Juan Fernández and elsewhere, would have been known to Daniel Defoe, so widely read in the voyage literature of his day.

There were other sources of inspiration for him, however, from apocryphal and legendary literature, for the Crusoe myth has always existed. He could have known of Philoctetes, who was said to have existed alone on the island of Lemnos, supporting himself with his bow and arrow. And he was surely familiar with the third book of the *Aeneid,* which tells of Achaemenides, left on Sicily by Odysseus and rescued by Aeneas. Even Odysseus spent seven years on Ogygia, not quite alone to be sure, for there was the beautiful Calypso to keep him company. It may be, however, that the legend most likely to have been an influence on *Robinson Crusoe* was that of Hayy ibn-Yakzan. Originally in Arabic of the twelfth century and, in its best form, by ibn-Tufail, this often-told story related how the boy Hayy was sent to an idyllic deserted island in the South Indian Sea, how he grew up and conquered nature, and how he was later joined by his father, who taught him to speak as Robinson Crusoe taught Friday. The story of Hayy was first translated into English in Defoe's lifetime and then twice again before *Robinson Crusoe* was written, the most popular translation, that of Simon Ockley in 1708, being republished in 1711 just before Woodes Rogers brought Selkirk back to civilization. All such legends flowed into the stream of the Crusoe myth, which was further swelled by accounts of fictional Europeans thrown up on inhabited utopias, such as Tyssot de Patot's Jacques Massé, who came before Crusoe, or Swift's Gulliver in the land of the Houyhnhnms, who came shortly after him.

Nevertheless, it seems obvious that Woodes Rogers's Selkirk, even more than Robert Knox on Ceylon, was the chief fountainhead for Defoe's novel, which is itself the greatest tributary to join the Crusoe stream. There are, of course, many differences between the real and the fictional castaways. One was shipwrecked and able to take many supplies from his wrecked ship while the other was left on Juan Fernández at his own request and with very limited supplies; one spent twenty-six years on his island while the other spent less than five; one had his Friday and feared cannibals while the other lived alone and feared only the Spanish; one was marooned in the Atlantic, the other in the Pacific; one tamed goats or set snares for them while the other outran them and took them by force. Yet the similarities are just as striking. Each was about twenty-seven years old when he began his solitary life; each went through a period of despondency; each feared captivity, if not death, by some enemy; each had goats and cats on his island; each replaced worn-out clothes with garments of goatskin; and each built a home and used goatskins for wallpaper. From the stories of Selkirk's predecessors on Juan Fernández and other islands Defoe could have found other hints for his fully developed novel. For example, the French buccaneers who spent two months on Juan Fernández tamed goats as Crusoe did; the nine men left on the same island by Captain Davis in 1688 were reported to have grown more religious, as both Selkirk and Crusoe did; and in the same year the surgeon on Tortuga was making pottery, as would Defoe's hero later. It may be that Will the Mosquito Indian was as close to Crusoe as anyone, but we know less about his life and comparatively a great deal about Selkirk's because of Woodes Rogers's account.

Selkirk himself has inspired three biographies since 1800, one of which —by the Reverend H.C. Adams—is sometimes republished with editions of *Robinson Crusoe*. This coupling is indicative of the relationship between the real and the fictional castaway, a relationship so close that many writers accused Defoe of stealing his story from Selkirk while others thought Selkirk to be the real author of *Robinson Crusoe*. It is true, however, that the eighteenth century usually kept the castaways apart, as two examples will illustrate. First, some years after his death and thirty years after he was rescued by Woodes Rogers, Selkirk was restored to life by the often-reprinted account of Lord Anson's circumnavigation. In it Chaplain Walter tells at some length how he and others encountered gray-bearded, venerable goats on Juan Fernández whose ears had been slit by the fleet-footed Selkirk, who often outran the goats for pleasure and then left his mark on them. Second, it was Selkirk rather than Robinson Crusoe whose name was in the title of the poem by William Cowper beginning "I am monarch of all I survey." Cowper's notion of the solitary ruler could have come from Woodes Rogers, who not only tells how the crew nicknamed Selkirk "Governour" but suggests that he was also "absolute Monarch" of the island. Walter's travel book and Cowper's poem represent the two chief elements in the Crusoe myth—the realistic, material everyday existence of a solitary man fighting for survival, and the moral, religious, social lessons to be derived, that is to say, the allegorical nature of the myth.

For like the Wandering Jew, Odysseus, Faust, and Don Juan—like all myths—the Crusoe story has been treated allegorically, depending on the prejudices or inclinations or nationality of the writer who retells the story. Steele and the anonymous author of *Providence Displayed* emphasized the notion that man separated from society turns to religion for comfort. Cowper, finding no "charms" in a life of "Solitude," let Selkirk confess that it is better to "dwell in the midst of alarms, / Than reign in this horrible place." Steele adopted the contrary view that Selkirk was never happier than when he was alone on Juan Fernández, where the simple regimen "conduces to the health of the body" and where Selkirk had proved "Necessity to be the Mother of Invention." Perhaps Rousseau, who often read travel books and just as often read into them evidence for the same kind of primitivism, shows best the myth-making possibilities in the Selkirk-Crusoe story. *Robinson Crusoe* is the first and chief book his Emile is to read, for it teaches the lad how to be self-reliant, how to face nature, how to know his own passions. And all his life Rousseau himself posed as the solitary man who preferred semilonely retreats near mountains and lakes to crowded, sophisticated cities. Fascinated by Crusoe's—or Selkirk's—costume, he even affected a peasant costume in old age and once threatened to remain for the rest of his life on a tiny island in a Swiss lake, until the government ordered him to leave. Actually Rousseau was myth-making, since Robinson Crusoe was an unwilling solitary and like Selkirk left his island at the first opportunity. Maximillian Novak has argued well that although a majority of writers have stressed Crusoe as "an embodiment of the enterprising, fearless economic man," Defoe's hero, like Selkirk, was afraid, cautious, and longing for the society he had left. The most allegorical of all the interpretations of the Crusoe-Selkirk myth, and a popular one, has been that which explains the experience as a return to paradise. Here the story is brought close to that of Hayy ibn-Yakzan, the most allegorical of the early versions of Crusoe.

Neither Defoe nor Woodes Rogers may have recognized the innate myth-making possibilities in the lives of their castaways, but both of their heroes have long since become part of the memory of the human race; and if Virginia Woolf was right in believing that *Robinson Crusoe* "resembles one of the anonymous productions of the race itself rather than the effort of a single mind," then one can also say that of the countless "anonymous" authors who have contributed to that composite production, Woodes Rogers is second only to Defoe himself. Since the time that Defoe wrote down what the race dictated to him, there have been many other fictional castaways, all part of the myth, all at least indirectly indebted to Rogers's Selkirk. There are Crusoe's immediate successors like Philip Quarll (1727) and Masterman Ready (1727), later ones such as Tennyson's Enoch Arden and Wyss's popular Swiss Family Robinson, and recent ones such as the lads in the very allegorical *Lord of the Flies*, which, quite unlike the story of Hayy, Steele's essay on Selkirk, or Rogers's *Cruising Voyage*, attests that a desert island brings out all the Calvinistic evils man is heir to, an interpretation far from the one derived by millions of youthful followers of the Crusoe-Selkirk tradition dreaming of their very own island utopia.

To get from Rogers's *Voyage* and Defoe's *Crusoe* to Golding's *Flies*, however, is to go through nearly three centuries of travel journals and novels that often exploit the desert island even more than the fictions recorded in Hermann Ulrich's bibliography (1898).[90] And as each new novel in the tradition flaunted or betrayed its kinship to *Crusoe* and the Crusoe myth, it was likely to demonstrate its author's imitation of Defoe's imaginative use of travel accounts. Defoe himself followed his success by taking advantage of the more-or-less real account of Philip Ashton (1725) when he wrote the story of Captain Roberts (1726), who was marooned "near two years" on "the Unfrequented Island of St. John."[91] In the same decade Peter Longueville in *The Hermit* (1727) produced the most popular imitation of *Crusoe* ever written, telling the story of Philip Quarll, fifty years on an island off Mexico, reworking "many passages unblushingly from Dampier,"[92] and pleasing other novelists such as Thomas Day and Dickens. One can hasten by the fictitious Dutch sailor who died and left his journal on Ascension Island (1728), or J.G. Schnabel's well-known *Insel Felsenburg* (1931), or all the other German, Nordic, Danish, American, French, Italian, Spanish *Robinsonaden* such as *Joe Thompson* (1750) and *John Daniel* (1751) and come to a stop with what is now called the first novel written in the United States, William Williams's *The Journal of Penrose, Seaman.*[93]

Williams, a Welsh painter, arrived in Philadelphia at the age of twenty after a brief life aboard ship, lived there for thirty years, became renowned enough to be Benjamin West's teacher, and returned to Britain in 1776 carrying the manuscript of *Penrose* with him. After an intriguing history the fictional journal was posthumously published in 1815 by John Murray in a bowdlerized form, the original manuscript not being discovered and published until 1969. It is a gripping story of a castaway on the coast of Central America who falls in love with nature and the simple life, loses one native wife and marries another, rears children, surrounds himself with a small and changing colony of natives and Europeans, and on dying leaves his journal to posterity. Scott recommended it for publication, and Byron was fascinated by it. So real in fact did the journal appear that long after Williams's death his English patron, Thomas Eagles, and his old art student, Benjamin West, insisted that it was authentic, or at least highly autobiographical, a claim discounted by Murray the publisher and now easily disproved.

For, whatever suggestions William Williams took from his life as a sailor before settling in Philadelphia at the age of twenty, or from his one year spent painting in Jamaica, his account of Penrose is another attractive fiction that employs techniques necessary for inventing a Crusoe or a Quarll; that is, he had a library of travel books and a lively tradition to work with. All of his best local color, in fact, comes, or could have come, from that library. From Lionel Wafer, Dampier, Captain Nathaniel Uring (1726), or any other well-known traveler to Central America, he could have learned about land crabs and the navel on the back of the wild hog they all called "peccary" (123). The antics of Penrose's parrot (127) were inspired perhaps more by the seminal Nieuhof in South America than by Wafer. When Penrose claims (308) that he saw "some spiders which would spread the full extent of a man's finger or thumb when expanded," he was echoing an oft-repeated claim, as made, for example, in Knox's *New Collection of Voyages* (1767): "One of these spiders extended, takes up the space equal to that of a man's hand with his fingers spread out" (II,231). After Penrose ate a prickly pear the first time, he was shocked to discover that his urine came out red, an experience Thomas Gage and others had been reporting for 200 years. And Penrose's four kinds of "tortoises" (348 ff.) turn out to be Dampier's four kinds of turtles (77 ff.). The point is not, however, that Williams, even more than

Aphra Behn, made use of travel books or other sources for his natural history but that he has so much of it, it is so accurate, and he was so artful in working it into a narrative that appeals because of its verisimilitude, its exoticism, and its reflection of one of the most important myths in fiction —the castaway in a distant, lonely place.

But then, any novel with a foreign setting anywhere in it was likely to need travel accounts for authentic local color or for an imaginative reshaping of reality. Perhaps the best evidence for that fact is to be found by turning to the abbé Prévost, who learned his methods and stored up his images from novelists such as Courtilz, d'Aulnoy, Lesage, Defoe, and Aubin, from his merchant patron in England, and from all those travel accounts Defoe also knew and used, many of which went in some form into Prévost's magisterial *Histoire générale des voyages* (1746 ff). Prévost serves well in another way since few novelists of the eighteenth century were so widely read in Europe or so often imitated: Just as he followed and used Defoe and Aubin, his *Doyen de Killerine* (1736) was admired and used by Sterne and Fanny Burney; his *Cleveland* (1731 ff.) was said to be Diderot's favorite fiction; Rousseau and Chateaubriand learned from him, as did Frances Sheridan and Ann Radcliffe; and he was translated and read everywhere, his *Cleveland* having a dozen editions in England alone in the eighteenth century.[94]

Prévost's training and imagination permitted him to employ travels not just in *Robert Lade* but throughout his career. In the fifth book (1731) of *Homme de qualité* he followed the practice of certain travel books and included such detailed descriptions of Bristol, the English countryside, St. Paul's, and London in general that, as Philip Stewart says, the reader gets the impression that "the writer was 'really there.' "[95] Such a conclusion is not surprising when one learns not only that Prévost had traveled in England but that some of his scenes have been traced to Defoe's *Tour thro' the Whole Island of Great Britain* (1724-27), which saw the first of its many printings the year before Prévost began his stay in England. Again in the fashion of certain travel books he described the colony of Louisiana where Manon is sent. "The details on the absolute power of the governor, on the life of the colonists, on the poor mud cabins like those that sheltered" Manon and Des Grieux—all these, Gilbert Chinard believes, are so well verified by "geographers" that Prévost must have had "first-hand information."[96] Captured by Turks, the marquis in the *Homme de qualité* escapes with the beautiful Selima only to lose her to death. Here Prévost's scenario is more than a little like that of Regnard's *La Provençale* (1731), published in the same year, and the Barbary tradition in general. And in *L'Histoire d'une Grecque moderne* (1740), Prévost was inspired by the true story of a famous Circassian beauty bought out of slavery by the French ambassador at Constantinople and dead of tuberculosis in 1733. Nearly all of his novels, in fact, involve tortured men and women who travel—Spain, Constantinople, Italy, France, and England in the *Homme de qualité*, or all over the world in *Robert Lade*.

Both Engel and Chinard have sometimes smiled at Prévost's geography,[97] but Paul Vernière now defends the geographical details of the long North American section in *Cleveland* by showing that Prévost carefully followed geographies and travel accounts for the first and last parts of the episode, inventing only for the middle portions, where Cleveland, Fanny, and their retinue disappear into and live in the wilderness and then make a trek through unchartered lands of the Tennessee-Florida region.[98] It is, in fact, a journey much like those journeys which Defoe's Crusoe, Singleton, and merchant captain make across uncharted lands in Asia, Africa, or South America. In the same episode Cleveland's wilderness utopia belongs to the deistic utopian tradition for North America that is reflected best in the *Voyages* of the baron Lahontan (1703; 1705); even the advanced "kingdom" of the Noplandes discovered in southeastern North America by Mme Riding and Cleveland's daughter Cécile was invented in much the same fashion that Lahontan had invented his tribes of bearded Mozeemleks and "Pythagorean" Essanapes.[99]

Just as Mme Riding tells Cleveland of the Noplande democracy, his half-brother tells him the story of a French Huguenot semiutopia on an island near Saint Helena in the Antilles, where the climate is always mild, all people are healthy and handsome, and there is no distinction between *meum* and *tuum*. Actual reports such as these, and of the same part of the world, began with Columbus and Vespucci and are found in Martire's *De Orbe Novo* (1533) and other great collections of voyages. Engel believes the Huguenot colony to have been inspired by the story—told best in the fabricated travel account by François Misson in *Leguat* (1707)—of a small band of Huguenots on the island of "Eden," that is, Rodriguez.[100] The invention of an island, whether for a utopia or for an adventure, is of course a fictional device as ancient as the *Odyssey* and the *Aethiopica;* but real sailors created islands too. For example, about the time Lahontan "discovered" the rivière Longue in North America and was successful in getting it placed on maps, buccaneer Captain Ambrose Cowley "discovered" and described an attractive island in the South Seas convenient for refueling. Called "Pepys' Island" it was placed on the "General Chart" of the scientist Halley, who checked variations of the compass in the South Seas in 1701 but who took Cowley's word, as did the geographer Moll. Byron, Carteret, Cook, de La Pérouse—all these looked for it in vain through the century until finally maps began to call it "Pepys' Imaginary Island," for, it was argued correctly, no one could be so far off in latitude, even in longitude, as Cowley had been.[101] Prévost himself was a victim of such invented islands, for in his *Histoire générale de voyages* he retold the story not only of a fake island reported by

Captain J.-B. Loyselle in 1730 but of the "Isle of Pines" on which sailor George Pines and three women were supposed to have begotten a whole race and provided evidence for new laws of genetics.[102] Prévost, then, following with his heroes in the wake of famous travelers, reworked from those travelers both geographic details and philosophic ideas such as deism, free love, and democracy; like them he described places and recounted incidents of piracy and slavery; and like them he discovered nonexistent islands. In short, as Jean Sgard correctly says, Prévost created heroes, sent them wandering and searching, and let them "all . . . mix the ideal with the real."[103]

With the examples before them of Head, Grimmelshausen, and the Scudérys, of Behn, Lesage, Defoe, and Prévost, eighteenth-century novelists continued to need real travels for inspiration and local color. If, in fact, they had not been to places their characters visit, and yet wanted to provide details of geography, scenery, or flora and fauna, they were totally dependent on writers who had been to those places. Even before Prévost's description of St. Paul's and the English coast in *Homme de qualité* or Defoe's exact pictures of the streets of London in *Colonel Jack*, some novelists were interrupting their narratives to describe places visited. Grandchamp in *La Guerre d'Italie, ou Mémoires du comte D*xxx (1702, 1710), for example, paused for three pages to tell of *L'Hopital générale* and other buildings of the "rich city" of Milan, and the abbé Olivier in *L'Infortuné Napolitain* (1704) described Geneva.[104]

Although not all novelists were so detailed, in the second quarter of the century Ramsey in his *Travels of Cyrus* (1727) insisted that, like Xenophon, he was making his hero travel in order to let him teach "history and geography" to the reader, while the English translator of the *Peruvian Tales* (1736) was as sure as Aragon would be in the twentieth century that "In laying a scene of a romance, the geography of a country must be as well preserved . . . as if the adventures represented therein had really happened."[105] Thus, Thomas Amory depended on his own earlier travels for the lakes, waterfalls, and grottoes of England found in *The Life of John Buncle, Esq.* (1756); and in *Memoirs of Several Ladies of Great Britain* (1755) he let his first lady, Mrs. Marinda Benlow, tell of her tour of the Hebrides and provide exact details of monuments, ruins, and plant and animal life,[106] as Martin Martin had already done for those islands and as other travel writers such as Pennant, Boswell, and Johnson would do after her. Similarly, Frances Brooks, the popular novelist friend of Samuel Johnson, went with her chaplain husband to New York state and Canada and put into her novels the scenery she saw, especially describing the St. Lawrence and the Falls of Montmorency for *The History of Emily Montague* (1769).[107] Charlotte Smith and Ann Radcliffe, not having traveled widely enough, however, were, like many novelists, forced to depend on writers who had. Smith went to William Beckford's *A Descriptive Account of the Island of Jamaica* (1790) when she wrote the "Story of Henrietta" and set its scene in Jamaica, the same William Beckford who composed that fictional masterpiece *Vathek* (1786) after steeping himself in eastern lore and history by using a dozen travelers such as Chardin, Thévenot, Hasselquist, Tavernier, and Pococke.[108] And for *Celestina* (1791) Smith also needed the traveler-geologist Ramond de Carbonnières's "sublime" descriptions of the Pyrenees.[109] For majestic scenes and many other details reworked from travel accounts, Ann Radcliffe is an even better example among later eighteenth-century novelists.

And while much has been said about Radcliffe's knowledge of travelers, much is still to be written. As with Mrs. Smith, her favorite writer for mountain settings was Ramond de Carbonnières, whose grand scenes in the Pyrennes, Gascony, and Languedoc she used when describing the same scenes in *The Mysteries of Udolpho* (1794); but she liked them enough to put them in other novels such as *The Italian* (1797) and *A Sicilian Romance* (1790), where her Alps look like Ramond's Pyrenees. More than fifty years ago J.M.S. Tompkins demonstrated how much Radcliffe enjoyed Ramond's mountain fogs, his sunsets, rushing torrents, old towers, and his perfume-laden air, how in *Udolpho* Emily St. Aubert's first view of the mountains is, like Ramond's, of "a chain of blue and white summits along a southern horizon," and how her "terrible mountain road, leaping chasms on a single arch," is like one Ramond traversed also.[110] But for Italy and for facts and scenes not provided by the lyric geologist, Radcliffe needed other travelers, one of whom, another Frenchman, Pierre-Jean Grosley, Tompkins also discovered. In *Udolpho,* he shows, Emily enters Italy by Mont Cenis, as Grosley did, observes the same flowers he saw, rides in a handbarrow as he did, and listens to Montoni and Cavagni dispute about the place and nature of Hannibal's passage over the Alps, their argument being a short version of Grosley's long essay on the subject.[111]

For all her stories with foreign settings, in fact, Radcliffe obviously read the travelers. For example, although she knew Mrs. Piozzi[112] and any number of other visitors to the Mediterranean, her chief inspiration for Italy and Sicily in both *The Italian* and *A Sicilian Romance* was without doubt the best known of contemporaneous accounts of those regions, Patrick Brydone's *A Tour through Sicily and Malta in a Series of Letters to William Beckford, Esq.* (1776).[113] Brydone, one of those true travelers applauded by Royall Tyler in the Preface to *The Algerine Captive,* visits convents and meets beautiful but sad nuns who, although they were forced to take vows, refuse to admit their lot is bad (I,61-62, e.g.); he describes the Strait of Messina with Sicily on one side and the Calabrian Apennines on the other and notes that

Messina is twelve miles from the entry to the Strait (I, 45-47); he tells at length of the Prince's use of "banditti" as guards (25) and of the many mountain caverns on Sicily, including those "vast subterranean apartments" with niches in the walls "all filled with dead bodies" (II,108); and three times he reports displays of fireworks (I,206,212-15,237). In Radcliffe's *A Sicilian Romance* Julia meets the fleeing daughter of a nobleman who is trying to force her into a convent (214-15), and while taking refuge at the Abbey of St. Augustin she finds a beautiful, unhappy nun, named Cornelia, who—like Brydone's nuns—"appeared perfectly reconciled to her fate" (21-27); she looks out of the window of her governess's apartment and "views the straits of Messina, bounded on one side by the beautiful shores of the isle of Sicily, and on the other by the mountains of Calabria" (60), and in the distance— Brydone's twelve miles—she sees Messina; Julia's father, the marquis, comes from a family that, like Brydone's "Prince," has always employed "banditti," and while pursuing the escaped Julia he and she are separately captured by "banditti" living in caverns some of which, Julia and Ferdinand observe, have niches in the walls where bandit victims have been buried (I,120; 189-196; II,140-50); and near the beginning of this novel, as at the beginning of *The Italian*, there is a display of fireworks like the three such displays found in the récit de voyage. For both novels, Radcliffe could have taken many other hints from Brydone—a "sublime" morning scene over the Strait, with a kind of aurora borealis; smoking Mount Etna; more abbeys and convents; lustful priests (also in Mrs. Piozzi, II,30-31); and cruel relatives.[114]

In fact, there is undoubtedly no other British novelist of the late eighteenth century who was more inspired by travel writers than was Radcliffe. She and others among the landscape novelists knew writers of fiction who in the fashion of some real travelers described idyllic scenes they really saw —Léonard on Guadeloupe, Lennox in Canada, Chateaubriand in North America, Bernardin on Mauritius. Or they were inspired by travelers who wrote no fiction but described lyrically and sentimentally, as did Ramond de Carbonnières in the Pyrenees and Brydone in Sicily.[115] Or for scenery they combined travelers with landscape painters, as Radcliffe did,[116] although for more than a century well-known travelers had been describing magnificent scenes and sometimes letting their publishers supply illustrations that were grand and sublime, from Ralegh to John Dennis, and from Nieuhof to Captain Cook's artists. And by using travelers the novelists even moved scenes from one part of the world to put them in novels set in another part, as Radcliffe moved the Pyrenees To the Alps and as Thomas Amory transferred Bishop Pontoppidan's "Norwegian grandeur" to Lancashire and other parts of the Fell District of England.[117] But she and others of the sublime landscape school needed travel and travel literature for more than mountain scenery: As creative writers they required all kinds of real facts about countries foreign to them, facts to be found quickest in recent or perennially popular travel accounts; if they had seen the places their characters visit, they for a moment became both travel writer and novelist; and, perhaps most important, they profited from the inspiration that accounts of places exotic or familiar afforded the imagination.

And those are facts true for almost every novelist of the eighteenth century and for many kinds of novels. Mme de Graffigny's *Lettres d'une Péruvienne* (1747; English 1748), which went through at least four different English translations in forty years and was one of the most popular of fictions, begins, for example, with a thirty-six-page historical preface about Peru, the Incas, and South American customs in general. And throughout her novel she describes sentimental landscapes to go with the sentimental plot and includes dozens of footnotes to explain such terms and manners as "cacique" and "hamas." For all these terms she was heavily dependent on writers who had been to South America, the best known being the Inca Garcilaso de la Vega, whose *Commentarios... de los Incas* (1609) and *Historia general del Peru* (1617) had been pillaged by travelers and novelists for a century and a half.[118] Likewise, the chevalier de Mouhy follows the tradition when in *Les Délices du sentiment* (1753) he supplies copious erudite footnotes about Tartary, where the stories are set, although nearly all of his information is invented.[119]

An even more obvious example is François Béliard's *Zelaskim histoire amériquaine* (1765), which closely imitates Prévost's *Cleveland* in that it is set in North America, has a Frenchman who takes his family there and serves as "empereur" of an Indian nation, invents several kinds of strange utopias, brings in character after character to tell a tale, indulges in incest or hints of incest, and makes use of both real travel accounts and much imagination. And when it employs Indian terms and customs, like the novels of Mouhy and Graffigny it provides footnotes, gives plain facts in context, or dramatizes them. That is, the "grand calumet de paix," or peace pipe, is explained in detail in the body of the story (I,17); "Kichi Manitou," or "grand esprit," is defined in a footnote (I,18); and the custom of blowing on the "allumette," or firebrand, is dramatized for fifteen pages (I,42-48).[120] And in the case of the fascinating "allumette," somewhat as novelist Richard Head treated first-night marriage customs of India as reported by travelers Santo Stephano and Linschoten, novelist Béliard took the custom of blowing on the firebrand and added much sex. That is, where Lahontan, Charlevoix, and other travelers to Canada for one hundred years reported merely that to accept a proposal of marriage an Indian maiden blew out the firebrand offered by her sweetheart, Béliard at length tells how Zelaskim's father finds Indian males bringing firebrands to be blown out nightly in order to enjoy sex promiscuously, how he passed laws forbidding the practice except on two stated feast days a year, and how on one of those occasions the beautiful Zelaskim spends hours turning away burning firebrand after firebrand until her true love Zédomire appears, succeeds in having his "allumette" extinguished, and happily spends the night in her arms.

For yet another fictional use of travelers, one turns to Rousseau and discovers him in 1757 borrowing Mme d'Epinay's copy of Chaplain Walter's *Anson* in order to write Saint Preux's letter telling of his circumnavigation with the English commander.[121] Domestic, sentimental novelists like Rousseau, and like Richardson and Mme de LaFayette before him, normally, however, had little need for exotic or any other kind of facts from travelers. But after *Emile* (1761) and the *Confessions* (1788) Rousseau exerted throughout Europe a great influence on writers of fiction who depended on their own travels or on those of someone else. The wanderings recorded in the *Confessions* were combined with those in Sterne's *Sentimental Journey* (1768) and inspired any number of pseudo-travel accounts, or travel novels, from the German Bretschneider in England in 1772 to the Russian Radischev in 1790, each of whom produced a highly sentimental narrative.[122]

More dependent on travelers other than themselves for reports of customs, geography, animal and plant life in distant places were those writers dealing in the sentimental education fiction that sprang especially from *Emile* and the *Confessions*. This group is represented in Britain by Edward Bancroft and his *History of Charles Wentworth* (1770), whose English hero is educated to natural goodness by the Arrowauk Indians of South America; by the eccentric Henry Brooke and his *Fool of Quality* (1765-70); by authors of books primarily for children, such as those by Maria Edgeworth at the end of the century; and by Charlotte Smith with *The Young Philosopher* (1798), whose heroine Medora has been reared in America according to nature and marries George Dumont, who has been reared in Europe in the tradition of Emile. Perhaps the best example is Thomas Day, who in *Sandford and Merton* (1783-89) lets Mr. Barlow combine the Socratic method with common sense and travel lore to educate Tommy and Harry. Not only do the boys learn temperance, humility, and all the cardinal virtues, but at length they hear of the Laplanders and their simple life from their well-read tutor; they find out from a well-traveled Scots soldier about the manners of American Indians as well as the plant and animal life of America; and they listen to the story of a black boy from Africa. Although Day—but not Bancroft—was often superficial, he and his contemporaries who wrote educational novels were often forced to resort to geographies and anthologies dependent on travelers, or to the travel books themselves, for facts, for local color. They realized that if their heroes and heroines were to learn about the world, they had to become fireside travelers, that is, with the hero of

Ramsey's fictional *Travels of Cyrus* (1727), travel the world in order to learn "history and geography."[123]

And now, at last, there is that fascinating branch of long fiction often called the conte philosophique, so important to the seventeenth and eighteenth centuries and to the history and theory of the novel. Normally placed in the category which Frye calls the anatomy, the conte philosophique is a story of adventure with a foreign setting, usually a burlesque travel-romance, and nearly always a satire close to the tradition of *L'Espion turc* and the various Persian, Chinese, and Jewish *Letters*. Unlike the foreign observer, however, or the countryman writing home from the city, the protagonist of the conte philosophique does not normally employ the letter form, although he does travel and he is usually naive. This form has many antecedents and mingles with nearly every other fictional form, especially that dealing with utopia; but in the eighteenth century perhaps the best representatives of it are *Gaudentio di Lucca* (1737), long attributed to Bishop Berkeley but now known to have been written by Simon Berington; Swift's *Gulliver's Travels* (1726); Voltaire's *Candide* (1759); and Johnson's *The History of Rasselas, Prince of Abissinia* (1759).

For *The Memoirs of Signior Gaudentio di Lucca*,[124] two years after Johnson's translation of Father Lobo's *Travels in Abyssinia*, one may start with four important and intriguing facts. First, like nearly all imaginary and real voyages it has the proper authentication of its contents, some of which is original. The narrator, a Roman Catholic doctor living in Bologna, is investigated by suspicious officers of the Inquisition, is asked for his background, and produces his memoirs, which tell a long and almost unbelievable story. As a young man accompanying his merchant father on a voyage, he was captured by Algerine pirates after a fight at sea, sold to a merchant at Cairo, and taken on a march hundreds of miles into the interior of Africa, where for twenty-five years he lived in a utopia called Mezzoramia, returning to Cairo only after his native wife and son died. The Inquisition, so impressed by Dr. Gaudentio's learning and bearing, send his manuscript to Signor Rhedi, librarian at St. Mark's in Venice, who confirms its history and geography as far as possible, even contacting M. Godart, the ship captain from Marseilles who brought Gaudentio back to Italy. Shortly thereafter, the English editor is given a copy of the manuscript by the librarian and publishes it.

Second, on his long journey into the interior of Africa, Gaudentio, like the heroes of Defoe and Prévost, follows known geography as far as possible, in this case to the upper reaches of the Nile. Then, with the master who bought him in Cairo, he goes many days west and south and finally up to the elevated utopian country of Mezzoramia, which he describes in all its fruitfulness, peace, and happiness, and which he locates in the then un-mapped part of central Africa known only to Defoe's fictional Captain Singleton, who had preceded him there.

Third, the title of *Gaudentio*, like that of many travel books, promises *A Discovery of an unknown Country in . . . Africa. . . . With an Account of their Antiquity, Origine, Religion, Customs, Polity, etc. . . . Faithfully translated from the Italian.*

And fourth, although its sources in and parallels with travel accounts have not been carefully worked out, one student's statement will show how close its contents are to those of real and imaginary voyages: "voyagers and explorers had awakened a strong popular interest in the far places of the earth—in races and peoples, manners, customs, flora, fauna, in the changes and chances of foreign travel, in all the concrete facts and experiences of life in remote regions. This interest Berington undertook to satisfy. The earlier utopias lacked concreteness. . . . Berington's Mezzoramia, on the other hand, is as real as Mexico or Peru."[125] And, in fact, the tone of Berington's novel is closer to that of More and Plato than it is to that of the satirists Swift and Voltaire. Gaudentio is, then, a traveler-discoverer-commentator and not a naive observer, although his travel-romance is carefully put together in the fashion of the best of contes philosophiques. Gulliver, Candide, and Rasselas are, on the other hand, all naive—at least in the beginning—and their close connections with travel literature have been carefully, if not completely, studied.

Gulliver was a voyager to all oceans of the world, although his four discoveries of strange lands—two in the South Pacific near Australia and two in the North Pacific between Japan and North America—were in waters uncharted at the time. But even though Swift carefully selected uncharted oceans for his settings, just as Defoe and Prévost selected un-mapped continents for some of their novels, his knowledge of geography and travels has often been praised and just as often condemned. Among those who cite Swift's accuracy in details of direction, place, and winds are A.E. Case, Arthur Sherbo, and especially W.H. Bonner, while J.R. Moore and Frederick Bracher, concentrating on the maps in *Gulliver's Travels*, are the chief fault finders.[126] And recently it has become fashionable to say not only that Swift was playful about his sailing directions and careless in allowing his publisher Motte to employ amateur engravers for the maps but that in fact he had a "disdain for the kind of knowledge embodied in maps, voyages, and geographical works. Quite apart from their lies and errors, which Swift noted so scornfully, the voyages represented increments in that kind of 'modern' knowledge, so dear to members of the Royal Society, which, while increasing man's knowledge of the external world, was blandly indifferent to his moral improvement. Swift did not take geography more seriously than was necessary to satirize it."[127] These words of Bracher (1944) are much like those of J.R. Moore a bit earlier, and they are echoed by John Richetti (1969) and Clive Probyn (1974). Probyn asserts that while Swift wrote in the "genre" of travel literature he "attacks the insularity and prejudiced condescension of the travel-book"; Richetti, stressing Swift's "reactionary" nature, believes that Swift, "aware of the peculiarly modern, and therefore hateful and dangerous, implications of travel literature and its popularity," held a "contempt for the vulgar credulity that nourished" such a popular form and that as a result, he made Gulliver a "malicious caricature" of the "ideal hero-traveller."[128]

Swift did not, however, in *Gulliver's Travels* satirize travel literature any more than in *A Tale of a Tub* he satirized religion or learning. There, as he says more than once, he was attacking only the "abuses" in religion and learning; and one can show that his attacks on travel literature were not directed at it as a form but rather at certain of its features and certain faults of some of its writers. For example, there are in the "Letter . . . to his Cousin Sympson" and elsewhere the prefatorial authentication, the avowal of truth, the defense of the "simple" style, the reference to boring lists of sailing and wind directions, the "I shall not trouble the Reader" apology—all to be found in the fake Sympson as well as in the real voyagers Ringrose and Dampier, whom Swift admired.[129] Then there is Gulliver's bringing back tiny sheep and cows from Blefuscu, as far travelers were urged to do by the Royal Society, although he had to explain, as Lahontan had done for his invented kingdoms in North America, why he was unable to return with any natives. And, perhaps best, there are the last chapter of the Fourth Voyage and Gulliver's—not Swift's—attack on other travelers because they did not, as he did, "strictly adhere to truth."

Nevertheless, his imitations of the style and form of travel accounts— as well as his borrowing of images from them for the ugly Houyhnhnms —do not indicate that Swift was contemptuous of travel literature or of imaginary voyages. His patron-teacher Sir William Temple had a library stocked with real voyages, knew and praised them, and drew on them for moral and political lessons.[130] While he was in Temple's library in 1697-98, Swift compiled a list of thirty-six books he was reading, including six of travels; at that time Dampier's *New Voyage* appeared, and in *Gulliver* Swift shows that he knew it and at least one other volume by the widely respected Dampier.[131] His correspondence with Vanessa in 1722 speaks of his reading travels with delight; and to Stella at the same time he says, "[I have read] I know not how many diverting books of history and travels." And finally, although his own library had "only" two maps in it—something J.R. Moore finds unusual—it was well stocked with voyages.[132] For Swift, then, as with Fielding later, travels were close to history and not, as some readers have thought, to be classed with the productions of the Royal Society. Far from being contemptuous of travel accounts, he could tease "Cousin Sympson," who never existed, but he could read with profit the books of Dampier, Sir Thomas Herbert, or Lionel Wafer and from them store his mind with facts for local color and images to be used creatively.

And even J.R. Moore, who finds fault with the Pacific geography of *Gulliver,* grants much—that Gulliver "has the solemn spirit of inquiry into strange lands," as travel writers did; that, like them, Swift provided maps and records of distances, directions, and winds; and that for the Yahoos he was indebted to travelers among the Hottentots and in Central America. There is, of course, more than that—Swift's use of Sanson the French geographer, for example; his teasing, in Gulliver's Fourth Voyage, of Moll the cartographer, whose maps are in any number of real travel books; his teasing of himself when in the Third Voyage he lets Gulliver explain how he formerly read travels with profit; his borrowing from the *Mariner's Magazine* in the First Voyage; and his careful following of the structure of travel accounts.[133] Swift, as he himself said without sarcasm, read real travels; and, as we all know, he read those writers who like himself invented imaginary voyages—Veiras and his *L'Histoire des Sévarambes* (1679), Foigny and his *La Terre australe connue* (1676), Lucian, Rabelais, Cyrano—all of whom, like Swift, read real travelers. He mixed fact with fantasy in *Gulliver's Travels* not to satirize voyage literature but to employ that popular and instructive form to attack the evils and stupidities of that "little odious vermin" called man. But much more than that, however, as Steven Cohan has shown so well, by "making Gulliver a wandering traveller . . . Swift [exposed] him to many different kinds of experience, building a series of contrasts as the book's organizing principle."[134] That is, Cohan concludes, as with real travelers "each voyage threatens Gulliver's psychological equilibrium" and he is forced to shift his perspective, "his values and concerns, even his moral and physical impulses, until his inner balance is restored." Swift may not have been overly concerned about the maps Motte supplied for that first edition of *Gulliver's Travels,* but—like Temple or Addison or Fielding—he read travel books for profit and inspiration.

Candide (1759), three decades after *Gulliver's Travels,* also attacks the stupidities and moral weaknesses of man even as it unfairly ridicules the school of philosophical optimism that runs from Plotinus through Spinoza, Shaftesbury, Leibnitz, and Pope and that includes Voltaire himself until he was about fifty years of age.[135] Like Swift, Voltaire invents a candid observer who journeys far—to the Mediterranean, France, Germany, England, South America—not, as with Gulliver, largely for love of travel or gain but in search of his beloved Cunegonde and the best of worlds, a traveler who, like Gaudentio, Gulliver, and Rasselas, gradually learns through experience to recognize the shortcomings in European and other "ordinary" societies.

Voltaire's *ur-Candide*, a few pages long, was published in 1756 as *Histoire des voyages de Scarmentado* and hints at much that is developed in *Candide*—characters, themes, and places visited—and each of the two plots is in many ways that of a romance-voyage. Candide experiences a storm, a shipwreck, an American utopia called El Dorado, and he sees natives of South America in subjection to Jesuit priests. At an inn in the mountains of Sierra Morena, he listens to Cunegonde's old waiting woman tell of her capture by pirates and of her experiences in a seraglio and as a slave in Morocco and Algiers; and in his hotel in Venice he hears six former kings tell their stories to illustrate the vanity of human wishes—all in the tradition of the novels of a Cervantes or a Prévost and the travel journals of a Montaigne or a Sandys.[136] For the South American scenes visited by his naive passive observer, who is learning that the optimism of Leibnitz and Pangloss and the primitivism of Rousseau are foolish, Voltaire studied Garcilaso de la Vega, as Mme de Graffigny had just done for her *Lettres d'une Péruvienne* (1747), but he also read Walter Ralegh's *Discoverie . . . of Guiana* (1596), well known in France after being published there with the fake travels of François Coreal in 1722.[137]

And for a tradition to work in Voltaire went to the fictional observer, that is, the naive country person in the city or the traveler who leaves one civilization to encounter another quite different civilization; but he went even more often to that great body of imaginary voyages that includes the novels of Foigny, Veiras, and Tyssot, as well as *Gaudentio* and *Gulliver's Travels*. Like all the writers in this tradition, for example, and especially like Swift, he played the real traveler's game of authentication. Just as Swift in the 1735 Dublin edition had let Captain Gulliver write to his equally fictitious Captain Sympson and refer to their "Cousin," Captain Dampier, Voltaire in 1762 published in the *Journal encyclopédique* a letter dated April 1, 1759—a poisson d'Avril, or April Fool's joke—in which, tongue in cheek, he wrote, "Gentlemen, You say, in the March issue of your journal, that some sort of little novel [roman] called *Optimism or Candide* is attributed to a man known as Monsieur de V. . . . I do not know what Monsieur V. . . . you mean; but I can tell you that this book was written by my brother, Monsieur Demad presently a Captain in the Brunswick regiment."[138] Furthermore, Voltaire insisted, he and his "brother" had just returned from Paraguay where they had spent some months observing the Jesuit "pretended kingdom" there. And, just as Swift and Defoe had teased Moll the geographer, Voltaire grandly discounted the Jesuit Charlevoix's history of the French settlements in America, a book heavily dependent on travelers and one on which they and novelists depended.[139]

Voltaire wrote other voyages imaginaire—*Micromégas* and *Zadig*, for example—or *Lettres d'Amabed* (1769) with its eastern Brahmin wandering Europe in amazement, or *La Princesse de Babylone*, in which Amazan, lover of the Princess, travels the world looking for her, somewhat as Taji in Melville's *Mardi* will search the world over for the elusive Yillah; and in *L'Ingénu ou l'Hermite* (1762) he invented a Frenchman, reared him among Canadian Indians, and brought him to France to be educated, or corrupted, by civilization. None of these stories shows a great knowledge of specific travel books or employs much local color from them, but each one, including *Candide*, has travelers reacting to new civilizations, commenting on them, growing with them, or succumbing to them. For Voltaire exoticism was not so important as it had been for Berington or Montesquieu; for him the travel-book plot was primarily a method for attacking the infamous.

In *Rasselas* (1759) Samuel Johnson attacked the infamous too, with much less satire, to be sure, but with much more local color and far more indebtedness to real travel accounts. And no conte philosophique has had its author's sources of inspiration studied more, the latest and most thorough such study being Thomas Curley's "Mythic and Historic Travel in the Creation of *Rasselas.*"[140] Besides using the journey structure, Johnson employed travel accounts in his novel in at least three ways.

First, there is the North African setting—Egypt, the Nile, Abyssinia. For his knowledge of these countries Johnson drew from his amazing memory much that he had learned while translating and abridging (1735) the *Voyage to Abyssinia* of Father Jerônimo Lobo, who was in east Africa in the 1620s and 1630s.[141] But Johnson also knew those other Portuguese Jesuit accounts found in Balthazar Téllez's *Travels of the Jesuits in Ethiopia* (English, 1711)—for example, those by Fathers Alvarez, Páez, and Fernández. And he knew well the popular travelers George Sandys (1621), Richard Pococke (1743-45), and the French medical doctor Charles Poncet (1698-1700). Some of these accounts of North Africa he had consulted while translating Lobo, and some he had found helpful in writing the Emperor Seged sequence in the *Rambler*. For the "luxury, learning and power politics" of Cairo, for the Grand Pyramid, and for the convent of Saint Anthony to which Pekuah wants to return, he drew imaginatively on Pococke and Sandys. Pekuah's capture by lawless Arabs reminds us that Pococke almost lost a servant to them and that Lobo was actually captured by Turks. For the travels up and down the Nile, Johnson had a dozen accounts before him.

Second, the Happy Valley from which Rasselas and Imlac and their party escape, although it has complex origins, was inspired by the Jesuit Alvarez, by Lobo, who considered the east African district of Ligonus a paradise, and by Téllez, who described the Abyssinian emperor's palace, which Johnson adopted and moved to his Happy Valley before embellishing it.

Third, even the names of Rasselas and Imlac, as with Seged in the *Rambler*, were derived from the Portuguese accounts. "Seged" came from a line of "Segued" rulers in Abyssinia but especially from that unhappy sultan (1603-32) known by Fathers Páez, Fernández, and Lobo. "Rasselas" was derived from the name of Segued's brother Ras Sela Christos; and "Imlac" was the name of an ancient emperor, although as a character he is amazingly like Gregorius Abba, an Abyssinian world traveler and philosopher whose dialogues are sometimes the same as those discussed by Johnson's Imlac and Rasselas.[142] There is in fact no other important conte philosophique—perhaps no other eighteenth-century novel of significance—more dependent on travel accounts for local color, for incidents, for names, for geography, for characters, even for tone than is Johnson's *Rasselas,* which is at the same time one of the most imaginative and original of fictions.

One can, then, while demonstrating the close relations between early fiction and the literature of travel, start with the stories of foreign observers whose primary purpose, as with Montesquieu, is to preach relativity while satirizing the faults of western Europe; and one can end with that other, closely related, kind of fiction that sends a protagonist traveling in order to prove that happiness though unattainable must be sought for, as with *Rasselas.* Or one can use the traveler to argue that since philosophic optimism is an illusion we must cultivate our garden, as with *Candide;* or that civilized man's pride in his scientific and material progress needs to be more than matched by moral and ethical advances, as with *Gulliver.* Or, as with Berington's Mezzoramia, the traveler may find a utopia that is a counterpoint to Europe, one that is inhabited by people "the most Ingenious and Industrious in the World," one "where there has been no War for near Three Thousand years."[143] But along the highways and over the oceans one encounters nearly all the other kinds of fiction imaginable, the great exceptions being those novels—some of our best, to be sure—that can be called domestic, such as *Clarissa* and *La Nouvelle Héloïse,* or city-bound, such as Marivaux's *Le Paysan parvenu* and Fielding's *Amelia.* The novel that is like certain travel books in form, however, is a gigantic class that often employs the author's observations made on some journey, or that still more often borrows places, animal life, people and customs, even incidents, from travel literature, all helping to make the fiction seem authentic and at the same time inspiring the author to invent more easily, that is, to achieve one of the perennial aims of the novel—a blend of the real with the romantic.

CHAPTER FIVE

Structure: The Hero
and His Journey

The man who writes his own journey, is under a necessity
... of making himself the hero of his own tale. *Edward Ive*[1]

In a key passage in *Biographia Literaria* Coleridge, indebted most to Schelling, describes imagination in one way as "the balance of opposite or discordant qualities";[2] and by now it is obvious that much of fiction results from, or is molded by, this tension between two extremes, two modes of man's mind, the realistic and the romantic, and that the same tension in great measure shapes the *récit de voyage*. But the architects of the many houses of fiction are related to those of travel literature by more than concern with a common tension: The structural principles of their two forms are often remarkably alike and always have been, each drawing on a common tradition and each inspiring or learning from the other. By perhaps universal agreement the journey plot, whether real or allegorical, is the most nearly basic in imaginative literature.[3] And yet the fictional journey of whatever sort surely came after and, for its inspiration, depended heavily on those prior real journeys experienced vicariously or directly and passed on orally by the earliest forms of humankind, whether they were watching flights of birds or animals, engaging in short or extended hunting trips, riding on logs in a rushing river, or simply walking to the top of a hill. Michel Butor agrees with W.D. Howells that they were travelers before they were novelists.[4]

There must have been also, however, ancient oral tales of actual love triangles, obedient and rebellious children, family discord, and problems with animal food in the local jungle or fruit in the nearby wild orchard; and so we arrive at two chief kinds of fiction, the domestic narrative and the adventure narrative, the static and the dynamic. One, represented by early novels such as *La Princesse de Clèves, Clarissa,* and *La Nouvelle Héloïse,* as Ronald Paulson says, "is usually indoors, in drawing rooms, hallways, and bedrooms—the 'close, hot, day-dream' world Coleridge noted." The other, such as *Don Quixote, Tom Jones,* or *Candide,* is often "out of doors, on roads, in inns, in coaches, on horseback," aboard ship, or, these days, on trains or airplanes, in automobiles or space ships—that is, "the wide world of epic with all classes and all manner of locales."[5] Frye's archetypal scheme describes the two forms by opposing the "idyllic" fictional world "associated with happiness, security, and peace" to the "demonic or night world" of exciting adventures; while Manfred Kusch, Bottiglia, Dalnekoff, and—for the medieval period—Pearsall and Salter prefer the Garden and River metaphors for these two complementary structures. That is, in *La Nouvelle Héloïse*, Wolmar advises Saint Preux to "settle down," to be content with a cultivated Swiss garden; but Candide, who says, "it is necessary to travel," leaves the Garden of Westphalia, journeys along the River of the world and of history, descends an actual river that leads into El Dorado, leaves this paradisal Garden in pursuit of Cunégonde, and ends, like Wolmar but perhaps not so contentedly, cultivating his symbolic Garden.[6] Nevertheless, *Don Quixote* and *Tom Jones*, for example, include much to be called domestic, and from *The Golden Ass* to *Tristram Shandy* to the international novel of Henry James to *As I Lay Dying*, novels have combined the two kinds of fiction. Few indeed are the writers who do not at some time send their characters journeying, actually or allegorically: In *La Nouvelle Héloïse*, a Domestic or Garden novel, Saint Preux circumnavigates the world with George Anson and writes a letter from a distant desert island; and even Clarissa, imprisoned, moving in a sharply defined space, is expelled from her earthly home and undergoes torment in her quest for a father.

To understand, to explain, this journey—physical or metaphorical—this "basic" image, we have tried any number of roads. Some are well traveled; others parallel, cross, or coincide with the worn-out ones; and some—new, perhaps circuitous, perhaps poorly paved, often attractive to the adventurous traveler—are to be followed with caution. Northrop Frye, who has been improving his explanatory superhighway for years, now insists in *The Secular Scripture* (1976) that "the marvellous journey ... the one formula that is never exhausted" is the "romance" plot; that Borges's story of the ship forever searching the Mediterranean for a lost island "never seems to come to an end"; that there are "four primary narrative movements in literature" as well as two for the "quest"; that the "novel"—that "realistic" myth of the nineteenth century—depends on the "Romance" tradition for all those plots; and that with "romance, Westerns, murder mysteries, and science fiction," we are undergoing "a change of taste" that was "fostered by the prestige of a [now] displaced and realistic tradition."[7] This "realistic" fallacy that Frye attacks is the same "traditional fallacy" that Arthur Vinaver deplores in *The Rise of Romance*.[8] Frye and others, then, would replace the old novel-myth with a romance-myth. Whether or not the attempt is successful, the journey structure so important to that great mass of long fiction often called "Romance" is marvelously like the form of the *récit de voyage*.

Building on the roadbeds of the earlier Frye and of critics such as Jessie Weston (1920), Mircea Eliade (1949), and Joseph Campbell (1968), many scholars are at the moment saying much about the journey plot of "Romance," among them Kathryn Hume, Dan Vogel, and Norman Friedman.[9]

Hume lists three stages of the typical romance: first, the Hero's Departure following the call to adventure, supernatural aid, and crossing the threshold; second, the Initiation—the great middle of the story—with its road of trials, its temptresses and temptors, its atonement with the Father; and, finally, the Return of the Hero as Master of Two Worlds. Such a system is, of course, highly traditional.

Vogel simply isolates and defines what he considers to be the six basic movements in literature—the Journey (*Tom Jones* but not *Don Quixote*), the Wandering (*Huckleberry Finn* and Byron's *Don Juan*), the Quest (*Sir Gawain* but not *Catcher in the Rye*), the Pilgrimage (*Pilgrim's Progress* and Joe Christmas in *Light in August*), the Odyssey (*Typee* and *Grapes of Wrath*), and the Going-Forth (*The Red Badge of Courage* and *A Portrait of the Artist*). Vogel's scheme is highly suggestive even as it provokes disagreements or modifications. The Odyssey, for example, he defines as having "no mission in the spiritual or moral sense" when the archetypal Odysseus surely is striving to reach his Penelope, his Telemachus, and his kingdom; the wagon ride of the Bundren family as it takes Addie's body to Jefferson in *As I Lay Dying* has been described not only as a Pilgrimage, a Journey, and a Quest but especially as an Odyssey with a moral mission; and in Godwin's *Caleb Williams* (1794) Caleb flees to many places pursued by the hounding Falkland in a plot where Flight and Pursuit are distinctly unlike any of the six motifs in Vogel's system.

Friedman, often inspired by anthropologists such as Roland Barthes, mythologists such as Frye, and psychologists such as Jung, is concerned with all fictional archetypes—for example, "the hero as sun-god or fertility figure or vegetation force" and "the hero as questing psyche" (p. 314). And while he has much to say about fertility and other images of the natural cycle, Friedman discerns three patterns to plot—the birth and creation phase involving imagery of childhood and gardens and including the hero's rise and early triumphs; the initiation and death phase with imagery of the journey, quest, descent, contest, exile, and other trials; and the rebirth phase stressing imagery of return, ascent, success. It is again the Garden-River, the Domestic-Adventure, the Static-Dynamic polarity, with "plot" implying movement or journey in all its possible forms. Such categories and systems go far toward explaining the structure not just of "Romance"—whether Greek, Roman, medieval, seventeenth-century French, "naive," or "sentimental"—but also of the "Anatomy" such as *Gulliver's Travels*, the "Confession" such as *Moll Flanders*, and the "Novel" such as *The Ambassadors*.[10]

And they go just as far in explaining the form of the *récit de voyage*. In fact, the most obvious tie between travel literature and the novel is this

"Romance" journey structure. For, by any hypothesis of the evolution of society, it is the form, more or less, of all those real journeys, short or long, that preceded the first imaginary journeys told about in tales that may have been merely a mutation—an exaggeration, a combination—of real experiences. And it has been the form of written travel accounts since writing was invented. Some of these, in all their parts, may in fact be as much like "romance" as any piece of fiction. The setting forth and the return, as with fiction, may be marvelous, even heroically incredible—wrecks at sea, frightening animals or people, captivity in strange lands, tortures and narrow escapes. Torquato Tasso, writing his great epics after the *Odyssey* but also after the marvels and embellishments of "Mandeville" or St. Brandon or the real traveler Fernão Pinto, knew that to avoid the charge of lying he and other romancers must set their scenes "among distant lands in unknown countries" so they could "easily feign many things without taking away the authority of the story"; a reader in 1750 knew that certain travel journals "generally looked upon as truth," have "a much stronger claim to the reader's attention, than the most striking incidents in a novel or romance"; and Garnier in his gigantic collection of prose fiction (1787-89) included the real *Relation du naufrage de Madame Godin* as told by her husband-companion because, Garnier argued, her experiences were so wonderful that any reader, if told that this truth was fiction, would "accuse the author of the novel of lacking vraisemblance."[11]

And the journey structures of countless travel volumes are based upon quests and other adventures commonly thought to be romance in nature but which were real in the reports of travelers or of editors and compilers of travel literature. Such travels-to-romance structures were known to fictionizers from Lucian, to Chaucer, to Spenser, Ariosto, and Camões, to Cervantes, and to all the eighteenth-century novelists.

An important phase of this structure is the Hero's Call to Adventure. In fiction it takes the form of voyages to the unknown, the lure of excitement in adventure, the fascination of travel, all of which are found in the Ulysses Factor, in Borges's Mediterranean ship sailing forever, in Gulliver's inability to stay home after the first voyage. But they are found also in Poggio's account of the real Niccolo Conti as he leaves home; as he walks, rides, sails, rows over more of the East than any European before him; as he marries an eastern wife and takes her and their children on countless other exciting and enlightening trips; as he forswears his Christianity in order to continue his quest; and as he makes and loses money as a trader before finally returning to Italy and dictating his compelling story that would be repeated over and over during the Renaissance and later.[12] And the Call to Adventure is found in thousands of sailor-explorers from Vasco da Gama and Columbus to James Cook. The lure of the unknown and the fascination of travel make up the Ulysses Factor, but they are also the Ishmael theme as expressed in the first pages of *Moby Dick:* "I am tormented with an everlasting itch for things remote . . . to sail forbidden seas, and land on barbarous coasts." It is the knight's call to adventure, the Amadís motive, and it is found not just in men but in Erskine's fictional protagonist in *Mme de Richelieu* (1744), who opens her story by telling how her aunt, a Parisian prioress, instilled in her a thirst for travel which, through three volumes, she was unable to quench.[13] But like the Ulysses Factor, the Ishmael archetype was real before it was fictional. It lived in Marco Polo; in ibn-Batuta (c. 1325-65) wandering east Africa, the Niger region, and Spain; in Father Lobo penetrating Abyssinia in the 1620s; and in Mandelslo leaving his friend Olearius (c. 1650) to travel on through India and sail back around the Cape. Such real people inspire books about themselves but they also inspire creative writers to find in them the probable and the marvelous.

Freud believed that "if one motive for traveling is curiosity, a stronger motive is that which impels adolescent runaways."[14] Although it would be difficult to show that the runaways outnumber the curious wanderers, the fictional hero's call does indeed often come only after some kind of rejection. That is, he is driven from home or forced to take flight from an unbearable situation, as Candide is "expelled" from Westphalia "with great kicks in the behind" (Chap. 1); as Tom Jones is sent away by Squire Allworthy and leaves "determined to go to sea" (VII.ii); as Simplicius, surrounded by soldiers raping, murdering, and robbing his people, is successful "in escaping to the woods" and to his kind hermit before being "overcome by a desire to look at the world" (Chaps. 5, 13); and as all picaros and antiheroes of whatever kind are continually running from bad masters, pregnant lovers, vengeful husbands, jailers, army sergeants, or other constricting or menacing people or situations.[15]

And like the protagonists of novels, a host of well-known travelers, whether they wrote their own stories or were written about, left home and started their journeys to avoid unpleasantness, that is, to take flight from danger or from some kind of prison. When in 1610 George Sandys set out from England on the travels over Europe and the Near East which produced a journal that would see nine editions in fifty years, "probably an impelling motive," his biographer says, was "the desire to get away from a most unhappy marriage and all the litigation succeeding it."[16] Four years later, Pietro della Valle undertook a pilgrimage to the Holy Land when a lady of Venice rejected his offer of marriage, the result to be years of satisfied wandering, business successes and failures, narrow escapes, and a passionate romance before he returned in 1626 to produce a best-selling travel book.[17] In 1681, resolved to settle quietly in France after suffering slavery in Morocco, J.F. Regnard, the dramatist-to-be, took to the road and traveled through some eight eastern and northern countries because, he said, his marriage was prevented by the return of the beloved one's husband.[18] And in 1738, the year before Richardson began *Pamela,* well before Marivaux stopped writing *Marianne,* and seven years after Prévost's *Cleveland*—each a novel in the romance tradition—a travel volume appeared in Amsterdam that reputed to be the story of his life with Indians in North America of one Claude Le Beau after he was expelled, he said, by a father tired of paying his gambling debts in Paris.[19] Le Beau's tale of his beautiful Indian maiden and their life together in the wilds of Canada is as adventurous and exotically sentimental as the tales of travelers such as John Smith and della Valle. So far only Gilbert Chinard has even mildly questioned the existence of Le Beau, not only because his life and book, as Chinard implies, have obvious biographical and stylistic parallels with Lesage's Beauchêne, invented three years before, but because—as with Beauchêne—the "voyage curieux" attributed to Le Beau depends for all its facts on the mendacious Hennepin (1697), the inventive Lahontan (1703, 1705), and the more nearly reliable père Lafiteau (1724). But even if someone eventually proves that "lawyer" Le Beau lived and went to Canada, the fact remains that his story, like that of the real della Valle a century before, is as close in form to the fictional romance as to the real travel book.

Whether the hero or heroine of romance took the initial departure after being driven from home, after escaping an undesirable environment, or after succumbing to curiosity or a restless nature, the continuance of the journey nearly always involved some kind of quest. Seven sorts of quests can with ease be singled out as common to the novel and the récit de voyage—quests involving religion, war, a golden or social utopia, exploration, monetary gain, a person, and knowledge of the world or oneself. Some of these, however, are found more often in one of the literary forms than in the other; and as with real travelers, the goals of fictional protagonists vary through the centuries with historical or literary fashions.

The religious quest—the search for the Holy Grail, the pilgrimage—is one of the most enduring in fiction, from Gawain and Percival to Bunyan's Christian. The books about real travelers seeking holy objects, people, or places—Jerusalem, Rome, Compostela—would fill a large library, and they were still being read in the seventeenth century. In the first decade of that century, for example, when Henry Timberlake, William Biddulph, and George Sandys all went separately to Jerusalem, each produced a popular book about the pilgrimage; and ten years before *Pilgrim's Progress,* when Chardin was publishing on Persia and when Newcastle was writing her travel fiction, Bishop Simon Patrick, depending on the tradition of William Wey and other travelers and guides to the Holy Land, published a *Parable of the Pilgrim* (1667), in which the Bible becomes a travel guide for the

Heavenly City and the *Parable* itself claims to have the form and function
of a real travel account; that is, allegorically it provides "an exact Description of the Situation and Nature of the place; of the Quality of the Inhabitants, of the imployments wherein they are ingaged, of the Fruits of the Soil,
of the Way that led to it, of the Travels of several Persons that had gone
thither. . . . [20] In the later Renaissance, however, and until the time of Sterne
and Diderot, the real religious quests were more and more the militant search
for souls to be rescued from paganism, that is, the evangelistic missions of
St. Francis and Father Ricci in China or Japan, of other Jesuits in Canada,
South America, or Africa, and of the S. P. G., the Quakers, or the Methodists. And such evangelistic quests were often turned into satiric fiction. In
Spain, for example, Padre Isla's protagonist in *Historia del famoso predicador
Fray Gerundio de Campazas* (1758 ff.), called "the Don Quixote of the pulpit,"
ridicules the itinerant purveyors of pulpit bombast; and in England, Richard
Graves's Geoffrey Wildgoose in *The Spiritual Quixote* (1772) is employed to
attack John Wesley and the traveling Methodist preachers.

If he or she did not seek religious goals, the romance protagonist could
go forth armed physically and emotionally to search for and to war with
the enemies, whether human or in nature, of people, of country, of self.
Thus, in Book Four of *Amadis* the hero fights for his country against King
Lisuart of Great Britain; Don Quixote and Spenser's Sir Guyon set out to
right wrongs in society; Pamela and Clarissa, in a fashion different from that
of medieval and Renaissance Amazons, fight for their lives against male
attackers; and all the heroes and heroines of romance, from Ulysses and
Beowulf to Crusoe and Ahab, war against sirens or cyclops, dragons or
demons, storms or white whales. And if real travelers make their encounters
with such human or natural or unnatural enemies seem fictional, readers
must remember that travel writers have the same imagination, the same
traditions, and the same techniques as those of the fictionizers. Joinville and
Froissart journeyed to the Holy Land and told of the Crusaders warring for
Christ and country; Bernal Díaz (1632, posthumously), Pizarro's secretary
Francisco de Xérez (1534), and other Spanish and Portuguese soldier-observ-
er-travelers recorded the dangerous conquest of Peru and Brazil and Mexico;
both French Protestants and Spanish Roman Catholics gave versions of the
bloody battle for Florida in the 1560s; and Captain Best (1612-14) and other
East India Company commanders kept journals which show that they set
sail for the East not just for trade but to vanquish the Portuguese off Surat.

The accounts of travelers warring with other men are legion, but the
stories of their battles with nature are just as stirring, from the sailors who
perhaps inspired Homer's one-eyed monster throwing rocks at ships, to
Jonah's whale, to now. Among the most gripping before 1600 is the account
of Álvar Núñez Cabeza de Vaca's grubbing for rodents and seeking meager

shelter from sun or frost on his epic journey between Florida and Mexico (1528-36). Over and over, however, the voyagers valiantly battled hunger, dysentery, and stormy seas, as Gilbert did before he was drowned off Newfoundland (1583). And, just in time for the eighteenth-century novelists to know about him, Alexander Selkirk for five years outran his supper in the form of wild goats before he was taken off Más a Tierra Island by Woodes Rogers in 1709. In fact, although the Call to Adventure was not always inspired by wars and rumors of wars with man and nature, the hero's search in early fiction and travels often involved him in such wars.

The third quest common to fiction and travel literature concerns that most ancient of romance ideals—the golden Atlantis or the social utopia. Here the mythical Mediterranean ship ceaselessly searching for an island blends with the myths of the ancient Garden of Hesperides, the medieval land of Cockaigne, the medieval and Renaissance Kingdom of Prester John, the Renaissance El Dorado, and all those ideal states of Plato, More, and Bacon. But it was the real travelers who continually inspired the theorists and fictionizers by actually searching for these marvelous places, or by reporting that they had indeed found them or had heard more and still more rumors of their existence, or by pretending to find them or something like them. Marco Polo and Friar Odoric, as well as the author of *Mandeville*, repeated attractive hearsay about Prester John, while dozens of far travelers sought him throughout the East and Near East and even in America. Before dictating his plausible account to the Pope's secretary, Niccolò Conti told another travel writer, Pero Tafur, a false story of how he stayed a dazzling time at the court of Prester John; and so other searchers were sent out, including Pero da Covilhan in 1487, who found his Prester John in Abyssinia and stayed over thirty years to greet later searchers, such as the priest Francisco Alvarez (1520-27), who wrote one of the best of those early accounts of North Africa that would lead to Berington's *Gaudentio* and Johnson's *Rasselas*. Another kind of utopian questor was Ponce de León, who sought the Fountain of Youth in 1513 and became the archetype for the "search for prolonged youth," which is "still a theme of romance."[21] New World lands of fabulous wealth were as attractive as Prester John, and so Cabeza de Vaca inspired de Soto, who inspired Coronado to search (1540-41) for the Seven Cities of Cíbola and thereby give birth to the thousand elusive Coronado's children.[22] Then, guided by this tradition and by tales told in London by the captured Sarmiento de Gamboa, Ralegh twice (1596, 1617) sent his Captain Keymis to search for El Dorado in Guiana and twice went himself, a book coming from each of them that would influence other searchers and be read into the eighteenth century. And enough gold and silver and pearls were found in the New World to verify the fact that such quests were, or might be, successful. If the search for, or discovery of, a social utopia was sometimes more important than Atlantean gold, Columbus and Vespucci could help inspire Thomas More's *Utopia;* Acosta and other New World historians and travelers could feed Bacon much for the *New Atlantis;* "the golden world" natives of Pietro Martire's *Decades,* a book of travel reports translated by Richard Eden (1533), could lead the young Hungarian poet Stephen Parmenius to write an epic in Latin eulogizing the ideal New World and then sail with Gilbert to drown off Newfoundland;[23] and, after 1700, the inventions of Lahontan, aided by facts from dozens of other travelers, could inspire Prévost's utopias in *Cleveland* as well as Le Beau's idyllic Indian life in Canada.[24]

The quest of the fictional hero perhaps comes closest to that of the real traveler when one considers the history of the exploration and discovery of new lands in general. Discoveries normally led to explorations and were inspired by political, religious, scientific, or monetary reasons—or by a combination of such reasons. It was true, for example, that pilgrims like the real Odoric and the unreal Mandeville "inevitably and historically develop into curious wanderers: pilgrimage converts to exploration."[25] Columbus sailed west driven by that same curiosity, a desire to prove the earth round, as well as to find a new and easier route to the silks and spices of the Orient. Prince Henry and da Gama, Magellan and Orellana, John Smith and La Salle, Cook and Bering, all discovered and explored new oceans, new river beds, the coasts or interiors of continents, and each was impelled more or less by the thirst for national honor or personal glory, by religious enthusiasm, perhaps by greed. Hakluyt and the Royal Society, as well as King Ferdinand long before, wrote out elaborate instructions and advice for voyagers setting out for new lands. This spirit of discovery has always been a chief source of travel literature, which in turn has given birth to all kinds of fictional quests and discoveries and explorations, among them Rabelais's heroes in Canada and Morocco, Newcastle's Travelia on her "Voyage of Discovery to the South," the crossing of three unexplored continents by Defoe's protagonists and of another by Prévost's Cleveland, and, of course, Gulliver's four discoveries in uncharted oceans.

Quests for fortune, whether realistic or allegorical, pervade literature. The hero seeks the dragon guarding a golden hoard or simply sets out to find his fortune, or a poor hero or heroine eventually discovers an inheritance and so can marry a loved one. Such stories were told from the time of Heliodorus and Longus to the seventeenth-century French river fiction to the eighteenth-century novels of Lesage, Haywood, Aubin, Marivaux, Fielding, and Smollett. But the Seekers of fortune in travel literature have also always existed and were especially well known in the seventeenth and eighteenth centuries, with the great merchant combines of England, France, and Holland sending ships everywhere and attracting adventurers hoping to become rich. Chardin and Tavernier, independent and wise, made fortunes on their travels in Persia; the buccaneers found willing converts to a life of pillaging Spanish towns in South America or ships anywhere; and the fabulous Spanish galleons taken in the Pacific by Cavendish, Woodes Rogers, and George Anson were even more exciting to the imagination than any invented story of discovered treasure. Haywood's fictional Philidore, however, unlike Smollett's fortune-hunting heroes, was one young man too sorrowful to set out to make money: "he was in reality embarked for Persia, not out of any hope of making his fortune with an uncle, who could have easily put him in the way of doing it; for he, alas! was dead to all considerations of interest."[26]

The search for a person—a father or other relative, a sweetheart, someone lost—is perhaps the only quest more common to fiction than to the literature of travel, which has few accounts of missing parents or lovers separated. Nevertheless, travelers from Italy and Spain in the Middle Ages and Renaissance sought the person Prester John almost as much as the ideal kingdom he was supposed to rule; Governor White in 1590 and others searched for Ralegh's "Lost Colony" at Roanoke Island; and there have always been Stanleys looking for Livingstones, as in 1791-92 Captain Edwards in the *Pandora* and d'Entrecasteaux in the *Recherche* and the *Espérance* sailed the Pacific, one searching for the mutineers of the *Bounty,* the other for the lost La Pérouse. The fictional search for a father—Telemachus in the early books of the *Odyssey;* Simplicius and countless other picaros; Stephen Dedalus and Joe Christmas—is more often allegorical than realistic. But the tale of lovers trying to rejoin each other is a favorite romantic plot device, with pirates often being used as the separating agent. In the earliest of Greek prose novels, Theagenes and Chariclea are parted and must travel long before being reunited, and the seventeenth and eighteenth centuries could hardly have done without this standard plot. In *Isabelle, ou Le Jeune amoureux d'Espagne* (1675), for example, Mme Villedieu has Ramir cross the Mediterranean looking for his wife Isabelle only to be killed rescuing her from her captor corsairs; Haywood's Placentia takes ship for Persia to follow Philidore; C.M. Wieland's Agathon (1773) searches long for his beloved Danae, a former mistress of Alcibiades, and finds her in time to have his story end happily; and Gothic novels of the late eighteenth century thrived on parted lovers pursuing and finding each other.

Finally, there is the quest for knowledge or wisdom, for oneself, for happiness. And while it may involve all the adventures and problems of other kinds of quests, those for war or monetary gain especially, it can be described best with plots of theme in a later chapter, plots in which the hero is a Grand Tourer or a Bildungsheld.

One way to show how closely all these quests are related in real and fictional travel literature, as well as to demonstrate how the two kinds can blend, is to read, first, the letters of Cortés and the account of his exploits as related by Bernal Díaz; second, to consider the wandering life of the eighteenth-century Alexandre de Bonneval; and, third, to place the first-person account of the Renaissance traveler Lodovico Varthema beside that of one of Eliza Haywood's characters.

Cortés,[27] like so many Spaniards of the sixteenth century, was an avid reader of romances and was inspired to seek the marvels described in them. The popularity of *Amadis* and *Palmerin* after 1508 paralleled the popularity of the letters of Columbus and Vespucci or the *Decades* of Martire, and just as the romances told of giants, Amazons, dwarfs, and El Dorados, the "real" accounts contained stories of giants, golden isles, noble savages, and enchanted places *más allá*. Cortés, as addicted as Don Quixote, read *Amadis* to his soldiers around the campfire, Spaniards were easily persuaded to join expeditions to an America that might be the ideal land for valorous action as well as rich treasure, and descriptions of Mexico City or Peru sent home to Spain often sounded like the literary romances themselves. In 1510 Montalvo published the fifth volume of his *Amadis* cycle, *Sergas de Esplandián*, which went through six Spanish editions during the century. In it is told the story of Calafia, queen of a race of Amazons who reside on a craggy island named "California," celebrated for "its abundance of gold and jewels."[28] All of this literature had an incalculable influence on Cortés and the Pizarros. For example, Cortés's fourth letter to the King tells how an expedition he sent out looking for Amazons and gold returned with the exciting news that ten days beyond their stopping point, the soldiers were told, there was an island rich in treasure and inhabited by women. This "island" Cortés's men would soon discover in reality and name "California," and it would until 1700 remain an island on nearly all maps of the New World. Thus it was, and continued to be, that romance traveled west, travel literature went east, and each traveled with or crossed the path of the other.

Bonneval's story is almost as intriguing, if less celebrated by historians.[29] Early in the eighteenth century, after following the call to adventure and serving against the English at age thirteen, he became one of the most daring and successful of military men, being pardoned for killing a wronged husband in a duel, fighting for France and then for the Holy Roman Empire, and living a gay and expensive life. At first a close friend of Prince Eugene and then his competitor for honors, Bonneval could easily have succeeded the aging Prince if he had been content to wait a few years. After moving about Europe, fathering illegitimate children, studying sciences, and engaging in social imbroglios that helped kill the time while nations were at peace, he ended up in Turkey as Achmet Pasha, for ten years general of the armies and a kind of secretary of foreign affairs for the sultan. One of the most munificent of hosts and fanatic about his beautiful homes, he was admired by his soldiers, by statesmen all over Europe, and by Voltaire; and until his death in 1747 he was a successful questor for glory and fame and success. And while he wrote no travel journal, no autobiography of any kind, his career was so filled with romance that others took some facts, more rumors, and much imagination and produced accounts of his nomadic life that he looked at and found boring.[30] Like the Spanish Cortés, the Portuguese Pinto, the English John Smith, and the French Lahontan, the restless Bonneval, always seeking or running or living fast, was real and yet incredible; and like them he was both inspired by fictional heroes and adventures and a source of inspiration to people who wrote fiction.

The story of Varthema's travels (1510) and that found in Eliza Haywood's *Philidore and Placentia; or L'Amour Trop Délicat* (1727) come close to each other not so much in the manner of the hero's departure—one has an insatiable curiosity; the other follows custom and takes a Grand Tour to be an accomplished gentleman—or the quest involved but in the trials the hero undergoes.[31] Varthema's account, one of the most popular during the Renaissance, is found in collections from Ramusio to Purchas to Prévost; and while there is apparently no way to know if Haywood read it, its episode in the harem and prison of the chief sultan in Arabia Felix is so graphic, so incipiently romantic, so widely read that it became a part of the romance tradition. Certainly it is closer to Haywood's long interpolated tale told by the Christian Eunuch of his experiences in a Persian seraglio than is any of the several sad stories of eunuchs found in *The Persian Letters* published just six years before.

Varthema, captured and imprisoned in southern Arabia, is saved from death by a beautiful "wife" in the sultan's harem, whose love he gently, diplomatically, and persistently repulses knowing what a violent fate will be his if he succumbs, but whose money and help he accepts in order to escape and tell of his fascinating experience. Haywood, of course, has her fictional eunuch fall so deeply in love with the most beautiful of the bashaw's wives that he accepts the offer of his adored one's bed only to be caught, unhappily, as he prepares to enter. The sixteenth-century Varthema feigns madness to escape punishment and be invited into the harem by the love-smitten queen; Haywood's hero pretends to be a mute in order to roam the seraglio and be near his loved one. Each hero is handsome, with a white skin that fascinates the lover; each has made himself a master of the native language; each "Queen" invites him apart and offers herself; each provides him with money that permits an escape, Varthema making his cleverly after some weeks, the fictional protagonist, after sadly lingering "on about six years," being rescued from pursuing janissaries by Philidore. The striking difference between the two stories is that Varthema has the ability to play mad so long and to resist his impassioned rescuer, that is, to overcome temptation as Sir Gawain and Spenser's Sir Guyon do, whereas Haywood's hero succumbs to the temptress, in scenes no more erotic than those in Varthema, and suffers a tragic emasculation. Nevertheless, either conclusion satisfies the romance tradition, which honors a hero wary in the boudoir but loves the hero who, like Tristan or both the real and fictional traveler Mark Antony, gives all for love.

The trials of such heroes lead back to the fact that all the emphasis here on reasons for the hero's departure may have obscured the many other similarities between the journey structure of fiction and the journey structure of travel literature. No matter what the initial impulse for the real traveler was in fact—Montaigne seeking health, Sandys fleeing a wife, Orellana turning from his superior to strike out on his own, or Cook bent on southern discoveries—he often had the experiences of the hero of fiction. That is, the real traveler, whether a questor from the start or perhaps turning from a motiveless going forth to a quest or pilgrimage, engaged in contests that were more or less frightening, descended into physical or mental hells, and finally underwent rebirth or resurrection to make the ascent or return journey on the river, across the ocean, or through the wilderness. Only in the most fanciful romances could a hero face cannibals in New Zealand or return from a frightening hell off the reefs of Australia, as Cook did; or find himself for six months descending deeper and deeper into a primeval wilderness, fighting rapids and starvation, battling women warriors and wild beasts, as he crosses a continent on a mighty river while seeking its mouth, as Orellana did. And if he survives—as La Salle in Texas did not, or as Cook on his third voyage did not—the traveler-hero finally turns home, the conqueror of great forces, wiser, perhaps sadder, but invariably master of the world he started from as well as all those worlds he encountered during his heroic or adventurous or knowledge-seeking years of wandering. It is surely this archetypal real traveler with a thousand forms and faces who is the legitimate "romance" protagonist.

CHAPTER SIX

Structure: The Narrator

As for the Actions of the Company among whom I made
the greatest part of this Voyage, a Thread of which I have
carried on thro' it, 'tis not to divert the Reader with them
that I mention them . . . but for method's sake, and for the
Reader's satisfaction; who could not so well acquiesce in my
Description of Places . . . without knowing the particular
Traverses I made among them. . . . And as for the Traverses
themselves, they make for the Reader's advantage . . . since
thereby I have been the better inabled to gratify his Curiosity; as one who rambles about a Country can give usually
a better account of it, than a Carrier who jogs on to his Inn,
without ever going out of his Road. *Dampier*[1]

Along the way that leads to the discovery of the close relationship between
the hero who journeys in fiction and the protagonist of travel literature, one
cannot avoid recognizing other close structural similarities in the two forms.
All that has here been said about these two heroes, for example, leads to the
notion that writers and readers of both fiction and travels are concerned
with the problems of the narrator and the narrative method. To test that
notion one needs to be reminded again that travel literature is not a simple
"genre," that it is no more easily defined than is the novel.

In considering the history of travel literature, we noted how ancient the
form is, how popular it has been since the invention of printing, and how
varied are its practitioners, its fashions, its contents, and its types. But because so few writers have studied that history, it is vague in outline, incom-
plete for every century, and most difficult to theorize about. As a result,
while thousands have described prose fiction, offered its history, considered
its evolution, and more or less agreed that there is a "modern" version that
started with the seventeenth and eighteenth centuries, no one has offered us
a *Don Quixote*, a *Princesse de Clèves*, or a *Pamela* for travel literature. That
is, no one suggests Dampier's *New Voyage* (1697), Lahontan's *Nouveaux voyages . . . dans l'Amérique* (1703), or Defoe's *Tour* (1724 ff.), no two of which
are at all alike, as the first modern récit de voyage. We have made small
attempt, in fact, to treat travel writing as belles-lettres, to note how it may
have changed with changing tastes, improvements in travel conditions, or

discoveries of new lands, even to distinguish between its older forms and its more recent ones.

There are of course certain exceptions to this rule. Among the most recent are William Spengemann's study of the effect of travel accounts on the American novel and Charles Batten's book on eighteenth-century British travels.[2] The first of these, citing some of the great travelers from Joinville to Columbus to William Bradford, William Bartram, and Richard Henry Dana, finds a marked tendency to more and more subjectivity in their accounts, that is, to the narrator's increased willingness to reveal how the journey affected him or her. Batten, who believes that British readers of the eighteenth century thought the travel account to be a first-person journal or letter that recounted the author's experiences on a journey, not only argues that "the recognized generic objectives of travel literature" required its practitioners to avoid extensive autobiography but also demonstrates that by the end of the century sentimentality and landscape description, as well as more subjectivity, were important elements of the form.[3] Such proposals, tidy for the first-person narrator and for the evolution to subjectivity, are helpful starts and need to be tested in the same fashion that critics have been testing the poetics of the novel.

John Tallmadge, in "Voyaging and the Literary Imagination" (1979), using the term "poetics" and invoking Demetz, Champigny, Barthes, and structuralists in general, has indeed approached what he calls the "literature of exploration" with certain critical methods comparable to those employed for fiction and poetry.[4] Like Swift and Fielding, Tallmadge places the literature of exploration as a "genre" under history and suggests that it can be predominantly imaginative, primarily historical, or simply documentary, the first being most, the third least, personal. Best of all, he suggests the need to study not just the observations, reflections, and historical reporting of this literature but also its imagery, its rhetoric, its narrator, who is, he says, the protagonist or a companion, and the "plot," which he insists must not be invented. All of this is heady stuff that needs, as with the novel, to be grounded on the reading and analysis of thousands of books, not just of exploration reports but of all travel literature.

But when, for example, we examine the role of the narrator, we discover that he or she need not write in the first person, that a travel account is not "specialized autobiography" any more than, when classified by content, it is "geography."[5] In fact, the majority of literature about real travels has been written in the third person, and without doubt much of that portion has always been thought of as "travel literature." In this respect, then, a great mass of travel literature is biographical and, at least before 1800, shares with the novel—"still heavily dependent upon other genres"—those elements noted so well by Paul Hunter and others as being shared by biography and fiction.[6] Among these elements are the concentration on a protagonist; the concern with a set of ideas and themes; an exemplar theory of history (vice and virtue must both be shown in the protagonists and other characters); the use of a chronological order to give a life story, with the narrator's selection, suppression, ordering, and digressions; and the picture of a society.

The travel biography, the third-person account, is often by a participant, a companion, or an observer, but it can also be the work of an editor or a historian close to or far from the facts. Joinville was with Saint Louis on the Seventh Crusade and fifty years later wrote one of the most delightful of biographical-personal travel memoirs, with graphic details, an historical perspective, and a reverence for the central character Louis, all joined to personal digressions, much of it witty and humorous. Ferdinand, the natural son of Columbus, accompanied his father on the fourth voyage and then, like Joinville, years later wrote his adulatory *Historie* of the great voyager (published 1571); but, unlike Joinville, he kept himself almost entirely out of the account. The historian Oviedo y Valdés (1478-1557) traveled all over the Spanish New World meeting Pizzaro, Orellana, Quesada, and other men and women involved in conquering, exploring, and settling it, talked with people who knew still other actors in the great drama, and ended with his *Historia general . . . de las Indias* (1535), which not only recounts many of the travels of conquerors but also gives a version of Magellan's voyage. Although the accounts of Francis Xavier by Torsellino (1596) and Lucena (1600) and the heavily edited papers of Matteo Ricci in China (1616) are eulogistic biographies of two great Jesuit evangelists, they are also attractive stories of the journeyings of two of the most widely traveled people of any day. The famous Sherley brothers who lived such dangerous and romantic lives wandering the Orient and Russia were often written about: William Parry, for example, who accompanied Sir Anthony to the East, returned to tell the story of that brother's travels (1601), referring to himself perhaps no more than four times in the book; and Anthony Nixon in *The Three English Brothers* (1607) told of all three Sherleys in a widely read third-person narrative. There are, in fact, at least four important kinds of travel literature not in the first person.

The first of these is represented by the great collections after 1500 that, in addition to original journals, included translations and edited or condensed versions of travel tales. Hakluyt over and over, for example, rewrote accounts of travelers, even rewriting what previous editors had rewritten, as when he translated and put into his own words (V.87-90) the three versions of Cabot's voyages he found in Ramusio, Pietro Martire, and López de Gómara; Purchas likewise included his own imaginative reworkings of Spanish and Portuguese voyagers; and John Lockman (1743), often in the third person, condensed and altered the Jesuit *Lettres édifiantes* (1707 ff.) collected and edited by père Le Gobien and, later, by Du Halde. These collections and dozens of others like them, of which no two are alike, are a prominent and irreplaceable kind of travel account.

A second type of third-person travel tale is that, for example, written by Chaplain Richard Walter, who accompanied Anson and did the authorized version of the famous circumnavigation, which had sixteen editions by 1781. Since he left the *Centurion* in China and returned to England early, however, Walter was unable to provide any of his own eyewitness reports of the last part of the voyage, even of the famous capture of the Spanish galleon off the Philippine Islands. He, then, like Herodotus, combined his own observations with hearsay.

Third, there is the account such as John Hawkesworth's authorized edition of James Cook (1773), which is not Cook's own journal but a composite of Cook, Banks, and others on that great first voyage of discovery.

Finally, there are the thousand twentieth-century, and earlier, rewritings of the stories of travelers—Collis's *Marco Polo* (1950), Morison's *Admiral of the Ocean Sea* (1942), Maynard's *The Odyssey of St. Francis Xavier* (1936), the travelers in early North America as told about by Brebner or Parkman, or—recent and popular—R.B. Downs's *In Search of New Horizons: Epic Tales of Travel and Exploration* (1978), a rewriting in third person of the exciting stories of twenty-four favorite travelers of all time.

When readers of literature realize that all such volumes have through the centuries been considered travel literature, they will agree that Patrick Anderson is close to a vaguely proper definition when he says that "The travel book extends from the journal, which can be a novelist's technique, to the novel itself,"[7] that is, from the oral or written first account, to the more or less objective rewritings, to the realistic and / or imaginative reworkings.

Nevertheless, while there is no typical travel account any more than there is a typical novel, for many readers the first-person journal or letter, that pristine document, is still the archetypal form for the *récit de voyage*. And it is a form long in popular use before fiction exploited it dramatically. Some early writers of prose fiction, Lucian and Apuleius among them, employed the first-person persona; but after the stories told by Lazarillo and other picaros and picaras such as Simplicissimus, after the fictional autobiographies of rogues and criminals, after the spiritual autobiographies from St. Augustine to those known so well by Defoe, and after the real memoirs of Cardinal de Retz and Mme de La Fayette,[8] the first-person narrator really thrived in prose fiction. It thrived until 1750 in the many fictional *mémoires* in France, especially after Mme de Villedieu and her *Mémoires de la vie de*

Henriete-Sylvie de Molière (1672), in the very popular pseudoautobiographies of Courtilz de Sandras, in *Gil Blas* (1715 ff.), and in the novels of Prévost, Marivaux, and Crébillon. And it thrived in England at the same time with Defoe's *Crusoe, Moll,* and *A New Voyage round the World,*[9] as well as in the secret "memoirs" and secret "histories" of Manley and Haywood. Until the middle of the eighteenth century, in fact, the first-person persona was for European fiction the favorite narrative technique.

Related to this fact are a number of popular opinions. One is that autobiography began in the eighteenth century. It is a thesis that Georges May has recently defended (1978), at the same time suggesting four reasons for the phenomenon—the increasing secularization of society, the growth of inductive reasoning, the new notion that truth is subjective, and the strong move to combat rationality—and it is a thesis, one reviewer says, that "reaffirms the consensus view."[10] Second, Lawrence Formo is not the only one to argue that long fiction evolved from authentic memoirs (La Rochefoucauld) to pseudomemoirs (Courtilz) to memoir novels (Lesage).[11] And third, travel writing, it is often claimed by students of belles-lettres, is not itself a branch of literature but a form of memoir writing or autobiography. One such student, for example, calls Imlac's tale of his travels "autobiography"; others insist that Johnson's *Journey to the Western Islands* is not a travel book but historical autobiography, while Boswell's *Journal of a Tour to the Hebrides* is not a travel book but a biography of Johnson; and another, after studying more than one hundred examples of seventeenth-century "autobiography" under a variety of religious headings, ignores the fact that the lives of half the writers—Anglicans such as Sir George Courthope and Quakers such as George Fox—were more or less conditioned by their extensive travels.[12]

All of this poses a number of questions. If, for example, we agree that a travel account written in the form of a memoir or journal is a kind of autobiography, should we not, in considering the rise of autobiography, consider the rise of first-person travel literature? Students of autobiography, however, pay no attention to travel journals, even as they disagree about the origins of autobiography. Roy Pascal, Burton Pike, and others argue, with May, that there is "an absence of autobiography before 1700." On the other hand, George Misch and Karl Weintraub, in spite of May and the popular opinion, speak at length and convincingly of early autobiographies, not only by Saint Augustine and Saint Teresa but by the soldier Xenophon, the lover Abelard, the poet Petrarch, the artist Cellini, and the doctor Cardano, all before 1600; and Dean Ebner and Paul Delaney find that the seventeenth century "gave birth" to the "genre" in England.[13] None of these, however, refers to any traveler found in Ramusio, Hakluyt, de Bry, or Purchas, just as those who begin autobiography with the eighteenth century pay no attention to Joseph Banks and his long first-person account of what he did and thought on Cook's first voyage and almost no attention to the several travel journals of James Boswell,[14] all of which make up an autobiography to rival his *Life of Johnson.*

The problem is similar to that concerning the evolution of the novel. That is, if we accept one widely quoted definition of autobiography as "a search for an inner standing,"[15] we can then start the "genre" with Rousseau, perhaps nodding at Saint Augustine, just as by limiting our definition of the novel we may begin that "genre" with *Pamela,* perhaps *La Princesse de Clèves,* and not with *Don Quixote.* Writers of genius before Rousseau and Richardson did not know, however, that they should reveal all their own motives or emotions or those of their fictional characters; nor did they know that to present soul searching in a bit of self-biography or a first-person novel was more desirable than to present physical actions. Nor did they know that the word "autobiography" would be invented in the nineteenth century for a book that pretended to reveal the whole life of the author, or that "novel" would be separated, by some at least, from "romance." Nor, finally, did they know that a first-person account of a two-year, or a ten-year, journey would later qualify only as a "branch" of autobiography and would be neglected by students of autobiography. This neglect is not to be explained by saying, as some people do, that every piece of writing, including a poem or a tale, is autobiographical in the sense that it reflects the author's personality,[16] for a great body of travel literature consists of accounts of observations, adventures, and reactions experienced by the narrators themselves.

A second and closely related question arises when we note that Patricia Myer Spacks and others have begun to recognize more clearly the close relationship between fiction and autobiography, two "genres" which, Spacks says, came to "efflorescence" about the same time.[17] Hers is a fine attempt to expand what has been said about the popular spiritual autobiographies and the even more popular rogue stories and "secret" memoirs, all of which are so important in the evolution of "true" autobiography as well as of the novel. But whether we agree that travel literature is simply a branch of memoir writing or autobiography, or whether we attempt to make it a separate type and see, as William Spengemann does, that travel writing influenced American autobiography and the form of American fiction,[18] should we not go far back before American fiction, before eighteenth-century American travel writers such as Mrs. Knight (1704; published 1835) and William Bartram (1791)—in fact, even before the memoirs of more or less sedentary people such as de Retz and La Fayette of the seventeenth century—and see what must now be obvious?

That is, throughout Europe the popular first-person travel accounts would necessarily affect not only the content but the form of autobiography and fiction and would not, in fact, be thought of as a genre separate from autobiography or, often, from fiction. For the personal, subjective nature of that literature has always been one of its chief and most endearing elements, no matter how often some readers and critics through the ages have tried to eliminate it from all travel accounts as undesirable, or have failed to find it except in those published after the supposed rise of something called "romanticism." Even the eighteenth-century critical conflict over the personal and objective in travel literature, as well as the definition, often published, that attempted to limit, even eliminate, the subjective,[19] simply proves the point that, if the personal element had not already been so popular and so much desired, the purists—found in any age—would not have been so insistent on muting it and stressing the factual content of the account. The most widely read of Renaissance travelers were the subjective ones, and in the eighteenth century Johnson was obviously voting with the majority when he found Boswell's first-person narrative of his own experiences more attractive than the historical-geographical section he added to his book on Corsica.[20]

The evolution—not necessarily the progress to something better—of the first-person narrative technique in travels is a fascinatingly important part of the history of literature, and it is so large a part that one can only suggest its outline.[21] We have often been told that medieval travelers, not just pilgrims, were warned that curiosity about the physical world, the lure of strange lands—travel for the sake of travel—was sinful, derived from eye-wandering lust, and contrary to the Church's emphasis on the soul's journey through this dark world to heaven.[22] Nevertheless, the conflict between the spiritual and the earthly sides of pilgrimage was enormous, for thousands journeyed to Rome, to Jerusalem, to Compostela, to Canterbury, and to other shrines and were subjected to scenes and ideas that had exactly the opposite effect from that intended by the Church fathers. How very few of Chaucer's fourteenth-century pilgrims—the Knight, the good Parson, perhaps the Prioress and two or three others, surely not the poet himself—kept their minds on the religious object of their trip to Canterbury! And many such pilgrims—some more pious, others more secular—have left their own accounts. Some of these have been treated as partial or apparent exceptions to the questionable rule that medieval travelers were impersonal in their accounts, among them the eleventh-century Bishop Ingulphus, who went to the Holy Land; and the thirteenth-century Joinville and William of Rubruquis, who were with Louis IX on the Seventh Crusade.[23] Perhaps the best, however, of many early travel tales to display the narrator's personality is that one about Sir John Mandeville, whose travels were surely fake but whose *Travels* were long considered truthful.[24]

The author of the *Travels* provided a two-part structure that was to be popular until after the great eighteenth-century novels appeared—one part objective pilgrimage itinerary and history, one part personal, where "Mandeville" is both protagonist and author, a persona whose personality emerges vividly from the pages of a book that has come to us in more than two hundred and fifty manuscripts. This persona is most curious about people and places and plants and animals and legends—the more unusual the better he likes them. Although apparently a pious pilgrim, he is a relativist, urging Christians to remember that Moslems must be different from them in customs and religion. He is gullible but observant, a "scientist" interested in the astrolabe and sure that the world is round. He is even fascinated by language and reports that in their alphabet the Arabs have four letters "more than othere for dyversitee of hire langage and speche, for also moche as thei speken in here throtes. And wee in Englond have in oure langage and spech ii. lettres mo than thei have in hire a b c, . . . the whiche ben clept *thorn* and *yogh*" (104). It is true that the author of *Mandeville* depended on a number of real travelers for his facts and that his journey if probably fake. But the persona's personality is not false, and the popularity of the book proves that readers the world over were attracted to it not just by its pilgrim and guidebook portion—easily found elsewhere—but much more by the attractive autobiographical quality, "our awareness of the narrator's presence,"[25] that can be found in so many travel writers before the novels of Lesage and Defoe.

By the time of Columbus these autobiographical travel writers were well known. With more than 130 of its manuscripts extant, the *Travels of Marco Polo* (1271-95), although by no means so personal as Mandeville's *Travels,* stresses the narrator's motives, his adventures at court and elsewhere, his impressions, and his personality. Another Venetian, also known throughout Europe, was Ambrogio Contarini, who went to Persia as an envoy in 1474 and then told of his interviews with the king's son at Tabriz, of how the news of the capture of Kaffa by the Turks made him violently ill, and of his remarkable voyage on the Volga. And at the very time Columbus was ending his first westward journey, Hieronimo Santo Stephano, who wrote one of the liveliest of first-person accounts, was on his way to Egypt, the Red Sea, and other places in the Orient.

All of these, combined with a hundred others of the sixteenth century who told their own stories, helped to develop a strong tradition of a travel literature that included personal observations and reflections. In the sixteenth century, for example, Niccolò Conti, who left Venice in 1519 to travel the Orient for twenty-five years, tells how he learned Persian and conducted business with his Persian partners, gives his opinions of suttee, recounts his problems in a stormy passage of sixteen days from Sumatra to the Malay Peninsula, and emerges as a persona who is curious, successful at business, intelligent about strange customs, and thirsty for new sights and experiences. Varthema plays mad to escape death in prison. Cabeza de Vaca saves his life by successfully acting the part of doctor among the natives of the American Gulf coast and then in his account (1542) defends those natives as human beings with as many rights as Europeans claimed. The German gunner Hans Stade (1557) tells how the South American natives captured, beat, fed, argued over him, and shaved his eyebrows, and how he tried to comfort another captive who was to be killed and eaten. And, at the end of the century, Linschoten reveals how his love of travels and a curiosity fed by books inspired him to set out on wanderings that would lead to his widely used *Itinerario* (1596), the journal part of which becomes more personal the more he writes.

In the seventeenth century, autobiographical travel accounts not only increased in number but in many ways improved in quality. They became more numerous as travel conditions improved, education required Grand Tours, the reading public was increasing in size, and all kinds of travel literature were in demand after such popularizers as Ramusio, Hakluyt, de Bry, and Purchas. They became better often because travelers were learning from each other about technique as well as about history and geography. And sometimes, as with Pyrard de Laval and Edward Terry, the traveler's success with a first edition would cause him and his editors to bring out a later, often much more personal, account.[26] Furthermore, Pinto and Pyrard at the beginning of the century are as personal and fascinating as the best travel writers at the end of the century—Dampier and Gemelli Careri, for example. Pinto was that swashbuckling adventurer who in twenty-one years (1537-88) came to know the East from Ethiopia to China to Japan as well as any European ever has known it and who returned to publish a long journal in 1614 that is so full of himself and his fantastic life that everyone who edits him must defend his veracity.[27] He goes from stories of looting ships and towns to his association with St. Francis Xavier, to his nearly being put to death when a young Chinese prince steals his gun at night, discharges it, and hurts himself. Pyrard, a more attractive and less adventurous person, left France for the East in 1601 and returned in 1611 with an autobiography that went through several alterations. Shipwrecked in the Maldives he recorded how he learned the language, was taken in by a local family, became a favorite with the lord of the island, received special attention in a fine hospital when he was ill, and became wealthy in business with native merchant partners. Both these men are significant in the history of travels and each makes his character visible, fully enough if not so completely as a self-centered Rousseau is to do it much later.

And that is true of others throughout the century before Defoe and Lesage, others such as the excellent Dampier and Careri. Although Dampier, the favorite travel writer for such different people as Coleridge, Galsworthy, and Humboldt, was a buccaneer and avoided certain topics when he published his *New Voyage* (1697), he revealed himself wittingly or unwittingly in his journal. That is,

> while he showed that in 1697 he was on the defensive because of the life he described in his book, he also displayed many admirable characteristics. Curious, ambitious, and encyclopedic in his quest for facts, he told how he forsook Captain Davis for Captain Swan simply "to get some knowledge of the northern parts" of North America. Level headed and compassionate, he managed to pacify his piratical fellows in the East Indies and persuade them to put him ashore when they refused to follow his advice and return for their abandoned captain. Once ashore he was joined by friends who preferred to follow him in an uncertain life among savages than to follow others in a certain life as pirates. Fair minded always, he once thought his own crew "unreasonable" for not dividing Spanish spoils with another crew engaged in related adventures. Not lacking in generosity, he was willing to puff his buccaneer-surgeon friend Lionel Wafer's account of the Isthmus because, he said, "Mr. Wafer is better able to do it than any Man I know." Although Dampier's journals and other journals show that he avoided the drunkenness so prevalent aboard ships in his day, he was obviously liked and respected. He told with some pride, for example, how a sophisticated French captain and his lieutenant invited him more than once to visit them aboard their ship for dinner and urged him to leave the English buccaneers and come with them to France. After meeting Dampier in his book, one is not surprised to discover how socially acceptable he became in London.[28]

Careri, the Italian lawyer who also circumnavigated the globe, reveals himself even more than does Dampier and by some standards has a travel book just as important.[29] Widely read—the Churchills (1704) gave him 607 pages, more space than they gave any other writer—Careri in a long, six-part journal records minute details of almost every place he went (1693-98), but the great charm of his narrative comes more from the artless and uninhibited, but never obnoxious, mingling of personal matters—the reasons he leaves home; the sentimental parting with his brother's family; his curious experiences in the palace of the Grand Master at Malta; his problems getting boat passage and money; his cleverness in avoiding cheaters, thieves, and greedy customs officials; his having to run for his life when children stone him in Alexandria for venturing too close to a mosque; his problems with a leechlike janissary who drinks his wine on a boat trip up the Nile; his successes or failures and reasons for them on the many pheasant, quail, and other hunting trips he loves to take even in primitive Mexico; his being mistaken at Smyrna for someone else and then having to prove his innocence before the French consul; the churches he regularly attends; his terrible experience with food and storms while crossing the Pacific on a Spanish galleon; his reactions to an earthquake near Acapulco; the lodgings he enjoys, or puts up with, everywhere; and—as with Dampier at the same time —the problems he has transporting his manuscripts by boat, carriage, or horseback. Careri's *Giro del Mondo* is more than history or geography. It is a happy blend of personal observations and intriguing narrative, and, like its countless predecessors among autobiographical travel tales, it points ahead to the first-person technique so popular in the fiction of the first half of the eighteenth century.

And yet, it is the pseudoautobiographical travel volume that in this respect of course comes closest to the novel. To illustrate that consanguinity, one may start with *Mandeville,* now called a "romance." Next, one may turn to books such as the three *Voyages fameux* of Vincent Leblanc (1648) as rewritten by Pierre Bergeron and packed with incidents of and reflections on "piracy, shipwreck, murder, plague, poisoning, witchcraft."[30] Finally, one goes to the volumes of the lying Father Hennepin, the creative Baron Lahontan, the romantic Jean Regnard, and the curious John Dunton, all at the end of the seventeenth century. While no two of these are alike and each has no doubt been much tampered with by editor or author or both, Dunton will illustrate the close connection between the narrative technique and structure of first-person travel account and first-person novel.

Dunton, so important to the history of journalism with periodicals such as the *Athenian Mercury,* is even more important to the history of autobiography, travel literature, and fiction. After traveling in England, in America, and on the Continent, he published in 1691 *A Voyage round the World, or a Pocket Library . . . the Rare Adventures of Don Kainophilus . . . intermixt with Essays, Historical, Moral and Divine; and all other kinds of Learning. Done into English by a Lover of Travels.*[31] And indeed the persona—Don Lover-of-the-New—loves traveling. He claims to have been born in a coach and to have been on the go ever since. His favorite metaphors are those having to do with travel—rambling, jogging, sailing, voyaging, or "casting anchor i' th' arms of" his beautiful Iris. Even Fame is to him a "rambling Gypsie." In the Don's many "poetic" interpolations "His Soul (in Dreams) trots all the World around," and he warns his reader, "Nor think, Dear Friend, I ramble now from you, / My Subject Rambles, and I but pursue." But "Don-Kainophilus" warns us also that in his book "There's more truth in't than you think of, or are like to know." He rambles to Boston, to the wigwams of Indians, and to Rotterdam, part of the time with friend Philaret. He idolizes the creative inventor of Sir John Mandeville, obviously his model; he condemns travelers who witness against their fellows; he digresses, often sentimentally, on many subjects—friendship, companions, love of women, even digressions —all of which he calls mental ramblings; and he compares himself to Odysseus and his Iris to Penelope.

This long jeu d'esprit, often witty and seldom dull, comes before Dunton's *Athenian Mercury* (1691-93) and before *The Life and Errors of John Dunton* (1704), which borrows much from the *Voyage*—Boston and Indian life—but which is a most sedate autobiogrpahy of one at least temporarily religious and uninclined to irony or wit. And it is the *Voyage* that Sterne read and that is especially like the *Sentimental Journey* and Tristram's wonderful travels in his seventh volume.[32] In fact, just after Sterne had made his first splash in London and three years before the seventh volume of *Tristram Shandy* was published, Dunton's *Voyage* was reissued (1762) with editorial additions as *The Life, Travels, and Adventures of Christopher Wagstaff, Gentleman, Grandfather to Tri— Sh—*, all to prove that "Shandeism" existed "long before a well-known publication."[33] Such creative travel books are the last leg on the journey from autobiography to novels with characters who move, observe, and act.

There are third-person stories of travelers and first-person journals and memoirs of real or partially real travels, but there is yet another kind of narrative technique standard in travel literature long before it was used widely by novelists, and that is the letter. If the memoir, the autobiographical novel, predominated in western Europe before 1740, the epistolary novel was much the most popular for the following half century, as so many people have agreed.[34] While F.C. Green minimizes the influence of the epistolary *Pamela* and *Clarissa* in France, he and Mylne find that the "vast majority" of French fiction of the eighteenth century was written in the first person and that after 1740 novelists employing letters, such as Crébillon fils and Rousseau, were the rule and not the exception.[35] For England, where there were "800 odd epistolary novels" by 1790, the monopoly was just as great.[36] There are of course many foreshadowings of this phenomenon. After 1690, periodicals such as the *Athenian Mercury*, Defoe's *Review*, and the *Spectator* employed and varied the letter-to-the-editor technique; and after 1740 Eliza Haywood's *Female Spectator*, like Johnson's *Rambler*, frequently had letters from correspondents.[37] Even closer to the early novel are the popular pseudoletters—the 211 by the Duchess of Newcastle (1664) depicting London life and ostensibly written to a friend, the letters of the

"Portuguese" nun to the false cavalier (1678 in English), and those of Eloisa to Abelard or the thirteen amorous ones from a French woman to her "cavalier" (1699), all before *Gil Blas* and well before *Pamela*.[38] And then there are the "familiar letters" (1741) Richardson was working on before he published *Pamela*, a type traceable to the early seventeenth century,[39] as well as poetic "epistles," such as Pope's to Arbuthnot, and real letters, such as Curll's unauthorized edition of Pope's correspondence (1735). These are all recognized as setting the scene for the letter novel after 1740 with its "editor," its confessional tone, its "writing to the moment," its aura of intimacy even greater than that theretofore achieved by the memoir novel.

What has not been pointed out, however, is that travel letters were standard and widely read throughout Europe before Newcastle and the Portuguese nun and, although apparently unknown to Richardson, were primary models for other novelists, such as Smollett, the collector and synthesizer of travel accounts. One can begin with the four voyages of Columbus, the first resulting in that famous "Letter," abridged from the admiral's *Journal* and printed in each of four capital cities of Europe within a year of his return; the second producing a "Letter" printed in Pavia (1494) by Nicolò Syllacio and based on the correspondence of one of Columbus's sailors; and the third and fourth giving the world two more letters of Columbus himself, both addressed to Ferdinand and Isabella.[40] These set the fashion for three "Letters" by Amerigo Vespucci, including the seminal one to his friend Soderini in Florence, and for actually hundreds of others in the sixteenth century, many to be found reprinted in Montalboddo, Ramusio, Hakluyt, and other collections in the sixteenth century. Among these are letters from Caminha, who was with Cabral in South America in 1500; from Oviedo in 1543 to Cardinal Bembo about the Amazon River; and from John Whitehall in Brazil to his friend Richard Staper in 1578.[41] Among the best —as literature, as history, as personal revelation—are the letters of the educated Cortés, the first of which has been lost but three of which were widely circulated, with fourteen editions in ten years.[42] Some others are even more personal, that of Whitehall, for example, who tells of his marriage in South America to the only daughter of a rich Italian, of his ambitions as a sugar planter in partnership with his father-in-law, of the equipment he needs to have sent from England, and of why he is changing his name to John Leitoan.[43] The greatest mass of travel letters in the sixteenth century, howeve, were the merchant letters and the even more numerous Jesuit letters.

Merchants were writing home to their backers and superiors early in the century; and by the time of the various East India and other great merchant combines of the early seventeenth century, such correspondence had become a standard practice that provided material for the big collections.

There are, for example, those letters from Aleppo, Goa, and other eastern cities sent in the 1580s by John Newbery and Ralph Fitch to friends such as Leonard Poore, John Eldred, and Hakluyt himself, all published by Hakluyt.[44] Then there are the some forty-three letters from the 1570s and 1580s received by the Venetian house of Bembo from all over the Mediterranean.[45] A letter from Fitch, not at all untypical, briefly describes Goa but dwells far longer on personal matters, beginning thus:

> Loving friend Master Poore ... Since my departure from Aleppo, I have not written unto you any letters, by reason that at Babylon I was sicke of the fluxe, and being sicke, I went from thence for Balsara, which was twelve dayes journey downe the river Tygris, where we had extreame hot weather, which was good for my disease, ill fare, and worse lodging, by reason our boat was pestered with people. In eight daies, that which I did eate was very small, so that if we had stayed two dayes longer upon the water, I thinke I had died: but comming to Balsara, presently I mended, I thanke God. There we stayed 14 dayes, and then we imbarked our selves for Ormuz, where we ... were put in prison ... untill the 11 of October, and then were shipt for this citie of Goa ... where for our better intertainment we were presently put into a faire strong prison ... we found there 2 Padres, the one an Englishman, the other a Flemming. ... if they had not stucke to us, if we had escaped with our lives, yet we had had long imprisonment. (III, 280)

The letters of the Jesuits, both the annual newsletters and their personal correspondence, were unbelievably popular throughout Europe, although Protestant England seldom translated or republished them. Beginning with the founding of the Society of Jesus in 1540, but especially after the first letters of St. Francis Xavier in 1544, so popular were the annual letters that in a given year they might be translated into a number of languages and published in several European cities almost at the same time: One of two Italian collections of 1559 has eighty-nine letters; ninety in Spanish were published in 1575; and even anti-Catholic Germany in 1571 had a well-edited set of ten letters, 179 pages long, accompanied by a laudatory introduction and fine illustrations.[46] Letters from Father Luis Froës in Japan, Father Matteo Ricci in China, or the ardent evangelists in Canada brought the latest news of foreign politics, European merchant advances, and missionary successes or failures; but over and over, even after being edited in Europe, they reveal the personal life of the authors—their ambition, their use of learning, their methods of gaining favor with local rulers or of combatting the competition and jealousy of vested interests, and their problems with or simply accounts of health, friends, food, clothing, lodging. And since these Jesuits were highly educated, they were invariably articulate reporters, and often their enthusiasm or their vanity made their letters even more attractive. A Cervantes or a Scudéry would know such letters even if neither wrote an epistolary novel.

And while Protestant England, unlike Protestant Germany, translated few Jesuit letters, by the end of the seventeenth century it, as well as all Europe, had an even stronger tradition of travel letters that every reader would be aware of. The East India Company's correspondence from abroad, largely a reporting by its factors of voyages, trade, political and social conditions, and personal matters, now fill six volumes.[47] But the century had letters from abroad that were not primarily about business. Very early in the century three Englishmen traveled the Near East and to Jerusalem, each sending back letters that would appear in Purchas. Among these were three from the favorite Thomas Coryat, a spiritual grandfather to John Dunton and already widely known for his volumes about his walking tour of Europe; the second traveler's account had been published in 1609 as a small book of four letters that, the editor explained, were put together from twenty letters by William and Peter Biddulph to a relative at home; and the third account, by Henry Timberlake, was perhaps the most widely read single letter in the century. First published in 1603, Timberlake's *A True and Strange Discourse of the Travels of two English Pilgrims* saw many editions before *Pamela* appeared, and it was often referred to, as by William Biddulph, who verified its account and hoped to borrow from its prestige.[48] Timberlake is most personal, employing "I" continually, telling how his companion, but not he, escaped imprisonment in Jerusalem by pretending to be Greek, how he was saved by a kind Moor whom he once befriended and who accompanied him through perilous country back to his ship, how he paid road "taxes" to scavengers all along the way, and how he was nearly murdered. After 1693 the title invariably includes "In a Letter from H.T." or "In form of a letter from . . .," and after 1715 this oft-reprinted work was frequently illustrated.

For both Protestant England and the Continent, however, there is much more. In Purchas, to be borrowed from and imitated by the French collector Thévenot (1663) and by eighteenth-century collectors, there are other fascinating letters. Two are from William Adams (Vol. II), an English pilot with a fleet of Dutch ships who was made a captive in Japan in 1600, became a favorite with local rulers and emperor, married a native woman, and settled down to greet other English visitors. One of his letters was to the English wife he never saw again, and both were still being reprinted more than a century later.[49] Also in Purchas (Vol. II) is the deathbed letter by the old Thomas Cavendish, circumnavigator and galleon captor, who bares his soul to his friend Sir Tristram Gorges. This poignant tale of great accomplishments and few rewards was long ago described in the *Cambridge History of English Literature* as "a pathetic page in our literature."[50]

One traveler known all over the Continent as well as in Britain was Pietro della Valle, who left Rome for the East in 1614 and returned home in 1626 to travel Europe and write numerous learned letters to friends before putting the long account of his early travels into fifty-four "Lettere familiari" addressed to his friend Mario Schipano.[51] Besides enjoying many editions in their own right, including three in English, della Valle's letters were translated and inserted into Thévenot's collection and into all three of the editions of the Churchills. In fact, few travel accounts—or books of any kind—were better known, for at least two reasons: They were informative and written by a genius who spoke Turkish, Arabic, and Persian, sang, played musical instruments, and discovered cuneiform writings in Assyria; and they were among the most personal of autobiographical tales of a nomadic and romantic life. The second "Letter," from Goa, opens with della Valle's description of his new mustache and beard and new clothes in the "Portuguese mode." In the third letter, he at length observes four small boys learning arithmetic; and here, as well as throughout his letters, he shows a love for beautiful scenery—mountains and rivers especially—and records his feelings about it. The seventh letter tells of his marriage to the Georgian girl Maria: della Valle describes her ecstatically—her eyes, figure, color, hair; he mentions her frequently until her death; and he carries her remains on his travels, even back to Rome. And Letter Eleven tells how he penetrated a pyramid and sent two mummies home.

Della Valle's account could just as easily have been published as a journal, but the fact that he and his editors chose to employ the form of familiar letters is telling evidence for the strength of a tradition already long established. The tradition can be seen everywhere, as when the great traveler Olearius published his dead friend Mandelslo's travel account as two personal letters that would go into many languages and be important to both travelers and novelists, including Defoe.[52] The tradition is seen also in the twenty-eight personal letters of Careri that he posted all over Europe in 1686 to his friend Amato Danio but that were not published until after his successful *Giro del mondo* (1698).[53] It is seen in the *Lettres sur les anglois et les françois et sur les voiages* by the Swiss Béat de Muralt, a volume that was widely quoted, praised, and attacked, one that saw two editions in English within a year of its first publication in 1725.[54] And the tradition continued to be seen frequently before *Pamela* appeared, as in the "Letters" that made up John Macky's *Journey through England* (1714-23) and that were answered with what Defoe pretended were the letters of his *Tour* (1724-27).

Best of all for the early tradition of the travel letter, whether real, pretended, or familiar, were the various volumes and many editions of James

Howell, who published not only the most widely printed of seventeenth-century English guidebooks (1642) but also *Epistolae -Ho-Elianae: Familiar Letters Domestic and Forren* (1642), which, with eight editions in the seventeenth century, was easily the favorite set of nonfictional letters in England until long after the novel was an established form of literature.[55] In his guidebook Howell at length urged any traveler to write at least one letter a month, to "write elaborately and methodically," for "Letters are the Ideas and truest Miror of the Mind." He himself traveled on the Continent widely and wrote home frequently, for example, from Rouen to his father or to Dr. Thomas Richard at Oxford, from The Hague to Sir James Crofts, or from Paris to Lord Herbert of Cherbury; and when he did not have actual letters from abroad to include in his volumes, he invented them. And so the great majority of his *Familiar Letters* were travel letters, well written, learned, often chatty, often punctuated with personal reactions and anecdotes. Early on, he says to his father, "I begin more and more to have a sense of the sweetnesse, and adventure of forren travel" (22), and two years later to his brother, after a stormy voyage, he humorously apologizes, "If this letter fail either in point of Orthography or Style, you must impute the first to the trembling posture my body was in at the writing hereof, being a shipboard, the second to the Muddiness of my Brain, which like Lees in a narrow Vessel, hath been shaken at Sea in divers Tempests neer upon fourty days . . ." (39-40). Howell was a voluminous writer, publishing even more than his contemporary, the humorous, corny traveling "poet" John Taylor, and he was deservedly popular not only for his breadth, his style, and his wit but for the personal tone that causes his letters to foreshadow those of the letter novel that will dominate fiction a hundred years later.

But the last step to that novel was taken in the many fictional travel letters that after Marana's *L'Espion du Grand Seigneur* (1684) and Montesquieu's *Lettres persanes* (1721) were such favorites in western Europe. The correspondence of the Turkish "spy" that Marana pretended to translate was shortly put into English (1689) and saw twenty-six editions before Smollett or Rousseau was dead; and Montesquieu's fictional travel *Letters*, as George Healey says, "created an immediate sensation, . . . went through multiple printings in the first year, stimulated a number of inferior imitations, and remained a steadily popular title throughout" the century.[56] Among the imitations were several by the Marquis d'Argens—*Lettres chinoises, Lettres juives*—and by Fielding's friend Lord Lyttelton, all before *Pamela.* Such fictional letters not only borrowed all their local color from real travelers such as Sir John Chardin and the Jesuits but employed the on-the-spot, at-the-moment reporting by letters that Europeans had learned to favor from Columbus to Timberlake to della Valle to Howell to Defoe. Both their content and technique would be employed by Smollett and other writers of travel novels, while their technique would be taken over by

Richardson and Rousseau and carried to the extreme of psychological interpretation of character.

All three of these narrative devices common to the travel account and
the early novel—the third-person omniscient observer, the first-person narrator of memoirs or journals, and the letter writer—have for fiction been
studied in great detail; and the same kind of study can be done for travel
literature. Here one can note a few possibilities only. First, after dismissing
as least interesting the totally omniscient, highly selective editorial narrator
—Hakluyt or de Bry translating dozens of medieval and Renaissance travelers, Maurice Collis retelling the story of Marco Polo (1950), or J.B. Brebner
selecting and rewriting for *The Explorers of North America, 1492-1806* (1933)
—one has the "I" as observer-participant to contrast with the "I" as chief
protagonist and both to be considered for their reliability. Since Joinville as
reflector for the travels of Saint Louis dictated his account (1304-1309) fifty
years after returning from Jerusalem, his reliability as narrator is surely
questionable even if his account is so attractive. On the other hand, while
not so attractive, the volume by Edward Terry (1655), chaplain in India with
Ambassador Sir Thomas Roe, is by a narrator who is the central character
but who both writes thirty years after the fact and explains in the preface
how he completely revised his original journal, a brief one published in
Purchas, and how he added "very long digressions" and otherwise "enlarged
it" in order "to profit as well as delight the Reader"; that is, by making
changes, he hoped to attract readers who rebell at unadorned sermons but
who, in this case, will "be taken before they are aware."[57] Terry, embellishing his first account of how he prevented an Indian mob from attacking an
Englishman, or Joinville returning in memory to Jerusalem and perhaps
making King Louis even more saintly and heroic than he was, or William
Dampier failing to speak of his inadequacies as a ship's captain—these and
other travelers illustrate Wayne Booth's now common argument that all
narrators—first or third person—"judge, blacken, or embellish their characters."[58]

Thus, the reliability of narrators in travel literature can be tested when
they deal with geography, flora, fauna, and historical facts; but when they
arrive at the realm of Terry's "Parallel observations and inferences"—as do
those travelers who continue to be read—one must question their responses
just as readers of novels are cautioned about trusting the words, or thought,
of a fictional narrator. Moreover, as St. Augustine and Rousseau said of
autobiography, there are several reflectors involved in the composition of
any travel volume; and thus narrator opinions may undergo a change with
each new reflector. In Terry's case there are the departing voyager who
begins his journal in 1615 and writes in it whenever he can; the experienced

traveler, at home after conquering his second world, revising his manuscript for "the later King in 1622 when he was Prince of Wales"; the expectant young author invited in 1625 to send it—or a still different version—to Samuel Purchas, an editor notorious for altering manuscripts; and finally the old rector looking back with obvious vanity on his greatest accomplishment, living it over in memory, coloring it with his imagination, his learning, his increased religious enthusiasm, and then, while striving to capture readers, producing something enormously different from that pristine journal. A century and a half later, Samuel Johnson will in a much shorter time employ similar techniques by writing long letters from the Hebrides to Hester Thrale and then, after his return to London, employing those letters, books by Martin Martin and Thomas Pennant, and a phenomenal—but fallible— memory to compose his *Journey to the Western Islands of Scotland* (1775). Such teller-characters are all more or less aware of their own involvement as protagonist-narrators, just as they are in fiction. Johnson, for example, tones down his own involvement so that he is less conspicuous in his book than in his letters written on the spot, while in contrast, Terry is much more personal in his 1655 than in his 1625 version. And in fiction the highly experienced, often-married, old Moll Flanders looks back on her rambles, willingly and often makes such confessions as "I repent it with shame and horror" or "it was necessary to play the hypocrite a little more with him," but is in general no more on the defensive as a narrator than is Diderot's young Suzanne in *La Religieuse* (1760; 1796), who, although innocent and naive, is nevertheless quite aware of how artfully she is acting as she writes letters to explain to her protector why she is rebelling against life in the convent.[59]

The reliability of a Suzanne or a Moll is further complicated by the fact that the actions or opinions of each are sometimes colored by the prejudices or philosophy of the author, who can intrude without apparently intending to do so—Defoe's mercantilism or Protestantism or Diderot's antireligious feelings—a fact that is true for all travel accounts also. It is true not just of the first-person narrator but, in an identical way, it is true of the third-person limited reflector created by an editor writing of the travels of someone else. In a very broad sense, then, the terms reliable and unreliable apply to all authors of fiction and all récits de voyage, for not only is a writer in either group aware of being involved in an act of narration but that writer intrudes and thus colors the tale. When, however, we suspend our disbelief, erase the nonerasable author, and live only with the reflector in the story—whether first or third person—we can agree that "The opposition of teller- and reflector-character [Moll versus Strether in *The Ambassadors*] is of structural importance because there is an epistemological difference between a story" told in third person and one told in first person, whether a memoir or as letters.[60] With Robbe-Grillet, Butor, and other authors of the "nouveau roman" of the 1950s and 1960s, such narrator and reflector ambiguities have been carried to an extreme, and apparently they have been accepted as desirable by "advanced" readers and most professional critics of fiction. Wayne Booth, at least, thinks so when he attacks what he considers to be the myth of the unreliable narrator: " ... we have looked for so long at foggy landscapes reflected in misty mirrors that we have come to *like* fog ... irony reigns supreme ... our lines of communication have been fouled, and that is not a good thing" (372).

To go with the problems of the unreliable persona and the outside, yet intruding, author, other structural problems common to fictional and travel-account narrators may be suggested. One of them is the relationship between the narrator and the audience. The Italian Niccolò Conti in the fifteenth century, for example, runs into the gullible travel writer Tafur at Mount Sinai and gives him a tall tale of how Conti discovered Prester John; but then in Rome, while doing penance for having in Arab countries forsworn his Christianity, he is most sedate and apparently more nearly reliable as he narrates his travels to the Pope's well-traveled and less gullible secretary. Cortés, writing from Mexico to the King, does not fail to laud his own exploits and discoveries or defend himself from his enemies. John Newbery, writing back to Hakluyt from the East, is surely aware that the great collector will shortly publish his letter, while the old Cavendish writing to a personal friend just as surely does not know that years later his letter will end up in the hands of the editor Purchas. Woodes Rogers, sent out by Bristol merchants, returns with great wealth from harrying Spanish America and capturing a galleon and, much like Defoe's fictional captain in *A New Voyage*, writes a journal addressed in great part to mercantilist interests in Britain. And Boswell, touring Scotland and the Hebrides, writes the first draft of his journal with Johnson in mind; for Johnson reads it as it grows, but then, with Johnson dead, the journal becomes a document more for posterity. Of all these, perhaps only Cavendish achieves anything like total reader identification, for, as with the first-person narrator in fiction, ellipses, a greater or less degree of interiority in the teller, slanted accounts of any kind, facts added by the narrator some time after the event—all these may create tension between teller and audience, make the reader wary, even alienate the reader entirely.[61]

Finally, there is the device of the multiple point of view in fiction and the récit de voyage. In recent fiction, Faulkner in *As I Lay Dying* narrates the odyssey of Addie Bundren by means of a number of reflectors, no two alike. In the eighteenth-century *Humphrey Clinker*, Smollett uses the letters of five members of a traveling family to record their progress over England and Scotland, a structural advance over *Clarissa*, where the heroine's letters far outnumber those of other writers. Well before Smollett, or even Richardson, however, Montesquieu in the *Lettres persanes* had invented the young, amorous, satiric traveler Rica to counterpoint the older, more philosophic Usbek as the two write home from France. And yet, well before Montesquieu, the history of travel literature is a history of readers comparing the accounts of real, or supposed, travelers to a given place. Two or more travelers might go separately, even years apart—as with Marco Polo and the sources of *Mandeville* in the East; or all those voyagers read and compared by generations of businessmen and politicians searching for the Northwest Passage; or the hundreds of Jesuits writing for years from Japan or some other exotic place. Or they might go together, each keeping a journal that may or may not have been published or widely read, as the journals of Ambassador Roe and his Chaplain Edward Terry were only the best known of at least five kept during that embassy to India in the seventeenth century.[62] A hundred years before Johnson and Boswell traveled together and each published his version of the trip, Jacob Spon and George Wheler went to southern Europe and, according to the overcritical Johnson, "described with irreconcilable contrariety things which they surveyed together."[63] Perhaps even more of an inspiration for novelists seeking variety in viewpoint, for counterpointing personalities of characters, would be the collections of voyages so popular in the eighteenth century, such as Smollett's *Compendium of Voyages,* or the just-as-popular seventeenth-century geographies of Dapper and Ogilby, which followed the practice of summarizing or quoting a number of travelers to the country being considered. At any rate, if, as John Kilham says, Montaigne gives himself a created persona in his *Essais* (1571 ff.)—"I am myself the matter of my book"—"almost" as much as Addison does in *The Spectator,* and if, one may add, every writer of travel accounts creates for himself a narrative voice, then the problems of the narrator in that form—as with autobiography and the essay—are much like those of the narrator in fiction.[64] And that is true not just for the well-known novelists from Challe to Chateaubriand who also wrote travel books but also for Montaigne in his *Journal de voyage,* for Addison in his *Remarks on Italy,* and even more, for the far-traveled Jesuits, "Mendax" Pinto, and John Dunton—all part of a strong tradition that existed before Lesage or Defoe published a novel.

CHAPTER SEVEN

Structure: Action, Character, but Especially Theme

> ... take a book of geography, some one of a thousand and one compilations of natural history, a volume of sermons; hire a copyist to extract at random a few bits from first one and then another, connect these excerpts by any sort of plot you choose, and you will have a novel. *Anonymous critic, 1788*

To make certain discoveries about how the hero and the narrator of the novel relate to the hero and the narrator of the travel account is by no means to exhaust the problems of structure when the two forms are considered together. There are, in fact, so many other important similarities that one need only find a suitable way of exploring them.

One approach is through the Russian formalists and French structuralists, who have been as concerned with narrative plot as with language. A nineteenth-century formalist such as Victor Shklovsky[2] contrasts the shape of the novel with that of the short story, emphasizes the influence of oral tales on that shape, stresses—as do so many other European critics—the importance to the evolution of the novel of such "subliterary" forms as history and the travel account, and argues for two types of construction, one called "linking," the other called "framing." Framing, he says, is found in *One Thousand and One Nights, The Decameron,* and *The Canterbury Tales;* linking is usually employed in stories with only one hero; Apuleius in *The Golden Ass* makes use of both; and Gil Blas, not a developed character, is simply "a thread which connects the episodes" of Lesage's novel. Coming after Shklovsky, Vladimir Propp, in his *Morphology of the Folk Tale* (1958), isolates thirty-one functions for use in classifying plots and has inspired innumerable structuralists—Barthes, Lévi-Strauss, Bremond, Todorov, and Julia Kristeva with her eight structures—to argue with or take departure from him, all agreeing on the importance of repetition to a writer, that is, the importance of a writer's appealing to the reader's expectation and intuition.[3]

Certain structuralists divide "narrative" into story, existents, and discourse, where story is chronological events or happenings, existents are characters and atmosphere, and discourse is the means of conveying the story sequentially, that is, the employing of "process" statements to move the plot and "stasis" statements to analyze character, describe atmosphere, or convey opinions.[4] One well-known structuralist, Tzvetan Todorov,[5] talks attractively about narration as opposed to description, with one as "movement" and the other as "pause," both of which, he claims, belong to the discourse of the narrator as opposed to the discourse of the characters and as structural devices are elements of linking and embedding. And in a brilliant essay on "The Secret of Narrative," in which he distinguishes between "horizontal" and "vertical" plotting, Todorov shows at length how Henry James is the master of vertical narration, with countless substitutions, or pauses, that are both stylistic and structural. A striking expression of an old truth is his theory that "The 'unnecessary detail' is perhaps, of all details, the most necessary to narrative," his examples including Sir Galahad's taking four days to reach the coast because he did not know the road very well and so "had not taken the shortest way" (137). All of these, formalists and structuralists, may emphasize language and may have done little with character in the novel, but what they have been saying—if often moot—is often most pertinent to the study of narrative structure of any kind.

Two other approaches to plot, out of many, lead back to Aristotle. In "The Concept of Plot and the Plot of *Tom Jones*," Ronald Crane distinguishes among plots of action, of character, and of thought, types which he and others, such as Frye, take from Aristotle's first three elements in the *Poetics*—mythos or physical movement; ethos, which includes both characters and setting; and dianoia, that is, thought or theme.[6] Concentrating on the "fictional" and "thematic" aspects, Frye shows that a reader may ask two questions: How does the tale turn out (mythos)? and What is the point (dianoia)? But surely there is a third question concerning plot: A reader, especially of a bildungsroman, may ask not only about the thesis, the point, but also by what stages the hero or heroine grows or, for any novel, how character is unfolded (ethos). The other Aristotelian concern is that of whether digression, or interpolation, can be an embellishment of, perhaps a counterpoint to, the plot and not just a flaw in its unity. It is a concern about which, especially for the eighteenth-century novel, much has been written. Each of Crane's three types of plot—as well as almost any other approach to the structure of the novel, including the problem of digression—also constitutes an approach to the structure of travel literature. A consideration of that possibility becomes even more attractive when one reads the opinion of Thomas Curley that "Novelists from Defoe to Sterne habitually imitate the format of travel books to plot the development of characters, the sequence of incidents, and the evolution of themes."[7]

In considering the hero and the narrator of the two forms, we have, however, already said much about plots of action and character, less about plots of theme. As a result, it must be obvious that perhaps no narrative is of one kind, that every narrative has at least a modicum of story, existents, and discourse.

The plot of action does of course dominate many of the novels constructed around a journey, allegorical or otherwise, just as it dominates not only the real récits de voyage of a Varthema avoiding the embraces of a queen, a Cortés conquering Mexico, a Hans Stade surviving among the Indians of Brazil but also the suspect or spurious travel accounts of Defoe or of the authors of *Beauchêne* or *Le Beau*. At the moment, however, the question of how many early plot-centered novels do in fact involve journeys and movement is of some academic importance. William Spengemann, quoting John Richetti, argues that the eighteenth-century "novel" has little traveling and that "wherever travel occurs in these novels, 'the infinite possibilities and new perspectives which secular travel can imply [are] automatically qualified by the ideological limitations and restrictions which traditionally defined travel as a sobering, pious metaphor of life.' "[8] Spengemann and Richetti are speaking only of English fiction, and both are of the tradition which believes that until after the time of Defoe and Richardson "travel" was a "pious" metaphor and travel was suspect. It is a myth that no one advocates for, say, the Continental novel, and it is a myth that for Protestant England has been convincingly disputed by such scholars as Christian Zacher, who shows the great secular appeal of travel for even the thirteenth and fourteenth centuries.

One can, in fact, easily demonstrate that most of the travel writers who preceded the eighteenth-century novelists not only ignored religious restrictions but were impelled by secular motives primarily: From Marco Polo to Columbus to Ralegh to John Smith to Dampier and Careri, they were fascinated by new worlds, new people and customs, and they apparently felt no sense of guilt about that love of travel. Editors of Renaissance collections of travels were obviously as fascinated by the voyagers they included as were their many readers, and they traveled the world talking to people, ransacking libraries, and feeling no remorse. In fact, the Protestant Hakluyt learned that travel was not a pilgrimage to a religious shrine; it was itself a sermon read in the greatest of cathedrals—for travel taught the wonders of God's creation. "From the Mappe" and navigation, he says, cousin Richard "brought me to the Bible, and turning to the 107 Psalme, directed me to the 23 and 24 verses, where I read, that they which go downe to the sea in ships, and occupy by the great waters, they see the works of the Lord, and his woonders in the deepe."[9] But even this pious motive for traveling became thoroughly sublimated as other motives expanded and absorbed not only Hakluyt but all the merchants, warriors, diplomats, adventurers, and explorers whose accounts he published. Moreover, the editors of the eighteenth-century collections of travel—the Churchills, Prévost, Smollett—consistently avoided pious pilgrim literature and saved their own piety for prefatorial sectarian arguments—the Protestant Churchills arguing with Roman Catholic doctrine or with Jesuit claims; Catholic J.-B. Bernard tilting with deists or Protestants. And finally, not only does Magendie (222), like so many others, show that plots involving movement are dominant for the seventeenth-century French roman; not only is travel the chief structural principle for British fiction from Nashe's *Jack Wilton* and Lyly's *Euphues* to *The English Rogue* and *Oroonoko;* and not only is almost every important Continental novel of the seventeenth and eighteenth centuries travel oriented—*Simplicissimus, Agathon,* Torres y Villaroel's *Vida, Fray Gerundio*—but Paul Hunter, an impartial and learned observer, believes "It is well-known that eighteenth-century novels very often bear as title the name of a central character whose life they trace, and the action nearly always involves extensive movement through space, conceiving time as a journey or series of journeys."[10] And, Hunter concludes, "Prose fiction is not the only eighteenth-century art form dominated by the contemporary preoccupation with movement through space as a learning experience."[11] Even if such conclusions were only partially correct, the novels and travel accounts so far treated here would suggest that action-structured plots were of inestimable importance to each of the two forms.

Yet, while movement and action for their own sake were attractive, they often led to something more, to a character's being exposed to himself or herself and to the reader. As a result, our treatment of the hero's journey and of the narrator has necessarily said much about the relationship between the journey and the one who journeys, both in fiction and in travel literature. That is, just as the peripatetic Moll or Cleveland, Agathon or Roderick Random controls the fictional narrative, moves through space, and grows with that movement or is exposed by it, so, we have seen, does many a traveler, or a narrator of a récit de voyage, control the account or move, grow, become exposed in it. It is true for Santo Stephano, James Howell, Careri, and Dunton, all before 1700. It is true also for the sophisticated, humorous Sarah Knight riding the back roads of New England (1704), for the swaggering, philosophic Chale headed for the East Indies in 1690, for the ambitious playboy Boswell on his Grand Tour, and for the splenetic Smollett in France and Italy, all writing at a time when novelists were learning that their art form should be more concerned with the technique of presenting character.[12]

The plot that moved itself and its readers (mythos) could, then, unfold character (ethos), but it was more often designed to develop an idea, a theme (dianoia), although the ideas are often closely related to the character or characters. Among the many kinds of novels and récits de voyage whose plots are wholly or partly controlled by a thesis, one can concentrate on the bildungsroman and bildungsreise, the Grand Tour story, the satire, and the picaresque, even though, obviously, any one of these can and sometimes does overlap another.

Almost any novel can be read as a thesis about character growth or development, whether the protagonists stay at home with tutor, books, and nature, as the lads do in Thomas Day's *Sandford and Merton* (1783-89) and as Stephen does in Joyce's *Portrait of the Artist,* or whether they travel, as does the young hero in Wieland's *Agathon* (1766) or Strether in James's *The Ambassadors.* And if, as in these four, the thesis and the development are marked, we often call the novel a bildungsroman and look for the archetype to Goethe, not to his more famous *Faust,* even though it concerns the development in society of a great scholar traveling with a tutor Mephistopheles, but to his huge novel about Wilhelm Meister. In 1786-88 Goethe's travels in Italy and Switzerland inspired not only his well-known *Die Italienische Reise* (1816) but also a great number of plays and poems about the education of mankind. Already, however, he had projected *Faust* and the many parts of *Wilhelm Meisters Lehrjahre* (the Apprenticeship, 1796) and *Wilhelm Meisters Wanderjahre* (the Travels, concluded 1829). Sometimes a distinction is made between this type of moving, adventurous, search-and-growth experience—"the hero's confrontation with his environment"—and the more sedentary experience of Tommy Merton and Harry Sandford—an Entwicklungsroman as opposed to an Erziehungsroman [13]—but the education that Mr. Barlow and Mr. Sandford give Day's boys is really both, since it is supplemented by real travelers who have been to America and Africa and is often based upon travel books.

It may be unhistorical or contrary to the laws of evolution to say that only German novels like *Wilhelm Meister* are bildungsromane, and even if one insists on being so limited, that type and all its near relations are obviously close to travelers and their literature. Goethe's archetypal novel, for example, includes not only a variety of teachers, from pedagogues to men of the world, but almost every kind of traveler, real or allegorical—émigrés, traveling troupes of actors, geologists moving in the mountains, the Grand Tourer from Italy, religious pilgrims. One of the chief impulses for the real or fictional traveler—even the medieval pilgrim—is a curiosity about all kinds of life and societies, about the unknown world, about his or her personality as it encounters that world; and Odysseus is not the only ancient hero who can serve as the archetype of the bildungsheld who struggles with man, natural forces, and himself on a soul-searching journey of achievement: Every hero, in the romance sense, even Gilgamesh, must learn from his experiences, is always becoming, and is therefore forced into a permanent search.[14] Georg Lukacs describes his two chief types of novel—one with an adventurer whose soul is "narrower" than his world, that is, he says, one like Don Quixote; the other with a hero whose soul is wider than his "life-world," a disillusioned romanticist like Dr. Rieux in Camus's *La Peste*.[15] One can object to Lukacs's interpretation of *Don Quixote*, since a popular reading today makes a Christ figure of its hero—as it does of Dostoevsky's Prince Myshkin—and finds his soul wider than the corrupt world he moves in; but one can hardly disagree with the notion of two types of protagonists, and variations on them, or with Lukacs's conclusion that "The novel's heroes are seekers, but not necessarily finders."[16] This brings us back to thesis (dianoia).

To put it structurally, there are, David Richter says, three ways to complete a quest novel—success, failure, and eternal search.[17] Success, we gather, attends Apuleius's hero in *The Golden Ass* and Smollett's Matt Bramble and all his companions. Failure awaits the warrior-slave Oroonoko and Haywood's two heroes, the eunuch in *Philidore and Placentia* and Montrano in *The Fatal Enquiry* (1719), each a far-traveler who is castrated to keep him from the woman he loves; and it awaits Richard Graves's Wildgoose and Chateaubriand's René, the first of whom seeks the evangelist George Whitefield only to find him a fake, the second of whom seeks peace among American Indians but finds death. And the eternal search, the open-ended story, comes perhaps in *Gulliver's Travels*, where the protagonist never finds an ideal world or is rejected by it and left in an ambiguous state; or in *Rasselas*, where the Prince and his companions end unsatisfied, apparently pausing between quests.

Likewise, these three types of seeker-heroes help structure the travel account. Their stories end successfully if they are pilgrims to Jerusalem, such as William Wey and William Timberlake, and return not only spiritually rejuvenated but with a book about their holy and secular adventures; and they are successes if they are Xavier, Froës, and Ricci opening up China and Japan to Christianity, or if, like Dampier, they are a buccaneer carrying journals in bamboo canes and specimens instead of guns. But their stories end in failure, even tragically, if they are Ralegh looking for El Dorado, Coronado for the Cities of Cíbola, and Baffin or Theodore Drage for the Northwest Passage;[18] they are also failures, although not spiritually so, if they are Jesuits being tortured to death in Canada before their accounts end; and they can crown a most successful life with failure if they are James Cook killed on a beach in Hawaii before he can complete his explorations and his journal. Finally, they can even supply open-ended stories, as does Celia Fiennes, walking and writing until she dies; or Careri, who turns from a circumnavigation and a great travel volume to Grand Tours of Europe and more travel accounts. The questor theme shapes such novels and travels, and invariably their heroes are also shaped—by their new, their continuous experiences.

Thus, from the point of view of both the reader and the narrator, travel literature as education, as a means of structuring experience, is very close to the bildungsroman. Goethe's allegorical *Wilhelm Meister* is firmly rooted in practical education as well as in aesthetics, music, and the visual arts, all in accordance with Goethe's Masonic doctrine of bildung and with his bent as a universal genius. From the moment we enter the Uncle's Italianate villa we begin our training in the fine arts, especially those with which Goethe had fallen in love during his own studies in the south of Europe. And much later Wilhelm travels with Jarno, a geologist who urges him to adopt a profession, the entire episode reflecting the author's own practical studies in science, including geology. Through his novel with its muted allegory, then, Goethe for much of his career guides the reader on a voyage of discovery, of growth.

And that is of course what many travel writers through the centuries have thought they were doing, although their approach while practical, artistic, or both has, unlike Goethe's, not been designedly allegorical. That is, travelers with broad, inquisitive, or trained minds observed, read, listened, wrote, and then taught. Nor was Goethe the first genius among such travelers. The sixteenth-century Portuguese João de Castro, as well as the Dutch Jan van Linschoten at the end of the century, with startling success attempted almost every kind of role in government, science, war, exploration, literature, and domestic life; each was avid in the search for information; and each ended with three volumes filled with useful facts about nature, people, and geography as well as about his own growth.[19] Although John Ray, another genius, collected specimens and was the typical great scientist when he toured the Low Countries, his *Observations, Topographical, Moral, and Philosophical* (1673) is much more than a guide to scientific knowledge: It is a volume stressing experiences with people and attractive enough to help any reader develop in several ways. The brilliant Engelbrecht Kaempfer crossed Persia, joined a Dutch ship as surgeon, saw much of the Orient, published a travel book in 1712 about his experiences, scientific and otherwise, and ended doing a history of Japan using information he collected during the three years he spent there. And, for only one more, Joseph Addison's government-subsidized three years on the Continent helped educate him in languages, politics, history, religion, architecture, literature, and the arts. Then, on his return he wrote *Remarks on Several Parts of Italy* (1705), which reflects not only all these interests but how they served to structure his account by leading him to what he wanted to inspect, provided quotations to support the results of his inspection,[20] and brought him home to rewrite a series of essays on the pleasures of the imagination that would depend in part on his intellectual Grand Tour. Addison's, like many another bildungsreise, was as widely read and inspirational as any bildungsroman.

And, as we have seen, one of the chief reasons for a real-life hero of the sixteenth, seventeenth, and eighteenth centuries to travel was to follow his, seldom her, gleam—or that of the traveler's ambitious parents—and visit the principal cities and tourist attractions in Europe on what was called the Grand Tour. While thousands of young men, especially English and French, took the Tour—often with a tutor, sometimes with a whole retinue of specialized tutors and servants—the tourists best known then and later were the intellectuals, especially those who wrote accounts of their travels, such as the poet-statesman Sandys and the eccentric hiker Coryat, the admirable John Evelyn and the scientist Robert Boyle, John Locke taking Shaftesbury, the président de Brosses, Joseph Spence with his three lords, or Boswell, William Beckford, and Goethe. Invariably these actual travelers praised the Grand Tour as an institution, often effusively, as did Coryat, who translated the twenty-six-page oration on travel by Herman Kirchner to add to his own praise; as did Howell, both in his guidebook and his travel letters; and as did Thomas Nugent, whose *The Grand Tour* (1749) was designed, he says, "to contribute to the improvement of that noble and ancient custom of travelling, a custom so visibly tending to enrich the mind with knowledge, to rectify the judgment, to remove the prejudices of education, to compose the outward manner, and in a word to form the complete gentleman."[21] But from the beginning of the custom there was opposition to it from the stay-at-homes who sometimes saw their countrymen return swelled with importance, aping foreign fashions, dropping names, lisping an occasional French or Italian phrase, or exaggerating their experiences. Nearly every seventeenth-century writer of the popular books of "Characters," for example, included a satirical sketch of the "Traveller," while stay-at-homes such as Defoe and Eliza Haywood agreed that the Grand Tour "is the common error of the age."[22] There were also the critics who praised the custom but cautioned about excesses, as with Bacon in his "Of Travel"; or Shaftesbury (1711), who took the Grand Tour, learned French well enough to be mistaken for a Frenchman, and urged travel—when wisely used—as a conditioner of "taste";[23] or the Earl of Hardwicke, who in 1712, according to tradition, wrote the letter to Mr. Spectator (No. 364) that points out the advantages of the Grand Tour as the "last Step to be taken in the Institution of Youth."

Such a perennially popular institution, given such wide publicity by the returned travelers and their countless books, would of course invade other kinds of literature—poetry, for example, as in James Thomson's *Liberty,* written after the poet escorted the young Charles Talbot over the Continent, or in Byron's *Childe Harold*—but it is especially found in the early novel as a structural device. By the middle of the seventeenth century, French fiction often included heroes heading for Italy to gain polish, not just in painting, architecture, literature, and the social graces but in science and the arts of war.[24] In one such roman, aroused parents send their son on the Grand Tour in order to prevent his marrying against their wishes.[25] England, with more Grand Tourers, had even more such fictional travelers completing their education. Dorilans in Haywood's *The Fortunate Foundlings* (1744) has in 1688 just returned from the Continent as action begins, while Frankville in her *Love in Excess* (1742) takes his Tour during the course of the novel. About the same time, in *Travels and Adventures of Mad—Richelieu Who made the Tour of Europe . . . in Men's Clothes* (1744), Erskine sent out his lively, curious apoligist for women's rights who as she travels provides a brief history of places visited, describes important spots, and tells of her inns and of the people she meets in them. In one of the most sentimental scenes in Mackenzie's *Man of Feeling,* Harley's father consigns him to Montford, who as an admirable mentor is to guide Harley away from the temptations of the Continent while they travel there. And in Charlotte Lennox's *Henrietta* (1758) Squire B. has just completed his visit to the Continent when the story opens, while the heroine's brother accompanies Lord Clairville on his Grand Tour.

Perhaps *Tristram Shandy* is the best example. Sterne at first planned it as one big Grand Tour novel in which he would "travell his Hero Tristram all over Europe" to make "strictures and objections on the different Governments."[26] Then in the final version he employed the Grand Tour in a variety of ways. First, Tristram tells of having accompanied Mr. Noddy's eldest son through Europe in 1741 (24). Second, Walter, with Sanson's atlas and a book of post roads in front of him, is laying out Bobby's Tour route when Bobby dies (344). And third, Volume VII is the story of Tristram's second Grand Tour. On this one he is in the company of Death—hardly the most congenial of tutors and one he manages to leave behind; on the earlier one he was accompanied by Walter, uncle Toby, Trim, Obadiah, "and indeed most of the family, except my mother" (512). Surely the most advanced use of the Grand Tour as a structural device is Tristram's superimposing the events of one of these two journeys on events of the other, as he does in France, where he confesses to living three kinds of time at once: "I have been getting forward in two different journies together, and with the same dash of the pen—[and as a result] have brought myself into such a situation, as no traveller ever stood before me; for I am at this moment walking across the market-place of *Auxerre* with my father and my uncle Toby, in our way back to dinner—and I am at this moment also entering *Lyons* with my post-chaise broke into a thousand pieces—and I am moreover this moment in a handsome pavilion built by Pringello, upon the banks of the Garonne . . . where I now sit rhapsodizing all these affairs" (515-16). And surely few novelists have come so close to the Grand Tour format as does Sterne when he lets Tristram plan a visit to such sights as the great clock of Strasbourg, give travel rules for Lyons, explain procedures for riding post and for taking boat on the Rhone, borrow heavily from Piganiol de la Force's guidebook *Nouveau voyage de France,* and describe towns and scenes, or explain why he does not describe them, as when he arrives at "the rich plains of Languedoc" and tells us "That there is nothing more pleasing to a traveller—or more terrible to travel-writers, than a large rich plain" with "which they know not what to do" except to cross it "to some town."[27]

Just as English novelists more often than others included Grand Tours in their novels, they more frequently ridiculed them. Smollett and Shebbeare provide prime examples. The fifth section of *Peregrine Pickle* (1751; revised 1758), written after Smollett had just returned from the Continent, sends Perry to France for polish and brings him home from his Grand Tour not only vain, arrogant, and corrupt but viciously so. In the Louvre, accompanied by Jolter, a satiric portrait of a tutor, he meets Pallett the artist, who tells of his own Tour and in the telling gives Smollett a chance to ridicule all those travelers from Addison on who, Smollett thinks, feel they must look at, admire, and then describe their reactions to art.[28] The forty-third chapter of Shebbeare's four-volume *Lydia* (1755) begins an even more satirical tale of the Grand Tour. In it the doting mother decides that young Viscount Flimsey is "of proper Years and Accomplishments for the Honour of England to travel, to make Observations on Foreign Countries . . . and compare them with his own, which he never had seen; a Method generally practiced with great Success in this Nation, as may be remark'd in numberless Instances of our travell'd Lords, Baronets, and Squires." Accompanied by his Swiss tutor, M. de L'Ourse, who has made the Tour six times and has a manuscript about roads and inns which he cannot get published, the viscount learns adultery at Paris, card cheating at Turin, and atheism at Rome. Backed by scoundrelly bankers, doctors, and merchants, he bountifully rewards pretty girls for the loss of their virginity, buys "Seven undoubted Raphael's, Six Dominichino's, Five Corregio's," and bestows an annuity on the tutor before returning home penniless to lead a life far more criminal than that of young Perry. And, finally, there is for this Grand Tour "an Account of every minute Circumstance which the Lord transacted from Morning to Night, in a Series of very familiar Letters" which, Shebbeare says, he will spare us. This kind of foppish, foolish traveler on the Continent is seldom found in fiction before 1700 and is never found in travel literature itself.[29] The satiric fictional Grand Tours, however, depend entirely on the actual ones for the itinerary and for situations, people, and customs to ridicule.

As one would expect, a favorite theme of novels of education, a type that increased in popularity as the eighteenth century went on, is the theme of relativity. That theme of course is vastly important in Montesquieu's *Esprit des loix* (1748) with its concern for such ideas as the effect of climate on laws and customs and with its use of Italian art and English laws as bases of comparison. It is important in Addison's *Spectator* essays that constantly compare English speech, generals, music, clothes, taste, and personalities with those of France and Italy. Or much earlier, it is important in Montaigne's widely read "Of Cannibals" (1580). "How can anyone be a Persian!" Montesquieu's untraveled Frenchman in the *Lettres persanes* exclaims of the two visitors from the East, thereby echoing Montaigne's just-as-famous irony, "But wait! they don't wear trousers," as he concludes his comparison of American cannibals with Europeans who eat people in more sophisticated ways.[30] Addison sums up the whole literary tradition of relativity when he concludes *Spectator* 50 with a lament about the "narrow way of Thinking" that fancies "the Customs, dresses, and Manners of other Countries are ridiculous and extravagant, if they do not resemble those of our own."[31]

Each of these three writers had taken the Grand Tour and was of a tradition already strong with the thirteenth-century author of *Mandeville*, who with a remarkably liberal mind compares Christianity with Mohammedanism and the English language with Arabic. The tradition would grow stronger with three hundred years of exploration after Columbus. The "empirical tourism," the "Lockian discoveries," described for the eighteenth century,[32] were in fact well prepared for by Hakluyt and de Bry about 1600 and by the Royal Society after 1660, as well as by all those travelers whose chief concern, it often seems, was to find something new—scenes, people, animals, plants, customs—to marvel at but also to compare with what was left behind. Sometimes, as with Chaplain Terry (1655) looking back over his voyage to the East, the traveler, prejudiced by his Christianity or his English pride, might look with horror on certain religious practices or marriage customs in India. But always the traveler made comparisons, and often that traveler advertised by actions and words the benefits one gained by understanding life in other nations, either because it decreased prejudice or because it made one more satisfied with life at home. The typical advice is that given about 1700 by the well-traveled François Misson: "In proportion as one moves from country to country, one has the opportunity to note how in all things diversity reigns in the world."[33]

Inspired ultimately by such travelers, all novelists of the eighteenth century employed the theme of relativity when occasion arose, whether or not they left their fireside or whether or not they were important. The abbé

Olivier in *L'Infortuné Napolitain* (1704), an early example, lets his French Catholic hero explain how as he toured Europe he learned that Protestants in Geneva were, like his countrymen, decent human beings and that Italians had religion in their books whereas Genevans had it in their homes and shops.³⁴ In the same decade Grandchamp in *La Guerre d'Italie* (1710) not only compares one city with another as his hero travels but explains at length how women and courtship customs in Milan differ from those in Spain, France, and the Piedmont. From "They order, said I, this matter better in France," the opening sentence of *A Sentimental Journey* (1768), Sterne delights in comparison. And, not just in *Travels through France and Italy* (1766), where Boulogne is surprisingly preferred to Wapping in some ways, but in *Peregrine Pickle* Smollett continually, irascibly even, contrasts French coxcombs, dress, food, court life, and religion with what he found at home. The most extended use in fiction of relativity as a means of structuring comes of course in the contes philosophiques of the Turkish Spy tradition. In the *Lettres persanes,* for example, not only does Montesquieu contrast life in France with that in Persia but he even contrasts the viewpoints of the older Usbek with those of the younger Rica. Mme de Graffigny's *Lettres d'une Péruvienne* (1747), a popular and sentimental imitation of Montesquieu's tale, attacks the manners and institutions, as well as the "prejudices," of Europeans as seen through the eyes of the captured Princess Zilia. And, finally, many novelists liked to generalize about national character traits for any country mentioned; for example, Arcq in *Lettres d'Osman* (1753) lets his traveled Turk identify the logical but inconstant French, the ridiculously proud Spanish, and the melancholy English. This, of course, was an ancient game indulged in by nearly all real travelers, including the best educated, such as Addison, who writes, "In the court of Milan, as in several others in Italy, there are many who fall in with the dress and carriage of the French. One may, however, observe a kind of awkwardness in the Italians, which easily discovers the airs they give themselves not to be natural. It is indeed very strange there should be such a diversity of manners, where there is so small a difference in the air and the climate. The French are always open, familiar, and talkative; the Italians, on the contrary, are stiff, ceremonious, and reserved. In France...."³⁵

With this long tradition of real and fictional traveled protagonists who learn of the diversity in the world, live happily or sadly abroad, acquire languages and impressions, and constantly make comparisons, we of course arrive at a *Wilhelm Meister* and at dozens of international novels by such people as Charlotte Smith late in the eighteenth century. After living a few years in northern France, Smith wrote a number of theme-adventure novels that contrast English life with life in France or America, often to the disadvantage of her native country. In *Desmond* (1792), for example, the

Wertheresque hero writes travel letters back to the woman he cannot yet marry in which he both explains the revolutionary attitude in France and defends it against the official English attitude. And in *The Banished Man* (1794) the hero D'Alonville, blatantly modeled on Smith's far-traveled French son-in-law, is used to preach the fact that prejudice against a foreigner is disgraceful. In short, Charlotte Smith borrowed impressions from her own travels and those of people she knew and wrote fiction designed to attract readers but also, as with so many "real" récits de voyage, to display a diversity of customs and sights and to attack national prejudices.[36]

The theme of relativity—foreign customs as opposed to those at home, what is considered false or virtuous contrasted with what is thought to be true or vicious—is perhaps the chief theme of that mass of early fiction with a Lucianic, mobile protagonist who, Ronald Paulson says, "travels over the earth, or up to Olympus to question the gods, or down to Hades to question the dead, always probing appearance, idealization, myth, and custom."[37] For Frye, in fact, the "radical of [all] satire" is the narrative in which the hero descends to a lower world and reveals its absurdity and folly.[38] Whether such a protagonist becomes a commentator by attacking folly or by drifting with it, he is, as the seventeenth-century Samuel Butler knew, "a Kinde of Knight Errant,"[39] sometimes, like the Don Quixote of one interpretation, a hero above his world, more often, like Butler's Hudibras, an antihero. The Lucianic protagonists can be blatantly allegorical, as in Gracián's once famous and influential *El Criticón* [*The Master Critic*] (1651-57). Here Critilo (reason) and his young companion Andrenio (passion) travel Europe employing countless guides (hypocrisy, light, old age) as they search for Felisanda (happiness), but all the while they are forced to observe Machiavellian politicians, fickle and stupid mobs, and religious hypocrites in what the author calls a mixture of "the piquant of satire with the sweetness of the epic."[40] Fielding's Tom Jones is both a convert from evil and a touchstone for showing evil to others,[41] while Fielding's Job Vinegar in *The Champion* is a traveler who has returned home to write satiric essays that will expose and correct hypocrisy and other human foibles. Swift's Gulliver, primarily an observer, is constantly forced to compare any society he encounters with that of England, always to the detriment of his native land. And if a Grimmelshausen or a Voltaire found ingenious ways to send out the hero who would—perhaps until the end of the tale—be a part of the false life he finds everywhere, on the other hand, not only does Sarah Fielding's David Simple never become a willing participant in the evil society he tests while searching for the true friend he never finds but thirty years later Mackenzie's Harley, the Man of Feeling (1771), is the sentimentally perfect knight-errant whose guides in London are both satirists and part of the satirized. Paulson finds the two extremes in *Tom Jones* and *Roderick Random*, with Fielding's satire being "centripetal"—that is, his persona is on the periphery—and

Smollett's being "centrifugal"—his persona is in the middle of the action, and all that he observes is colored by his point of view.[42]

And if one wants to see quickly how this kind of fictional mobile protagonist is often like, perhaps inspired by, the real traveler who "recognizes, reacts, and rebukes,"[43] one can perhaps do no better than place Smollett's *Travels through France and Italy* beside his novels and note how close one of his forms is to the other in theme, tone, and structure.

The great consensus now is, in fact, that the narrator of Smollett's *Travels*, although a Lucianic voyager, is a Juvenalian satirist, a created persona more like the observer-"hero" Matt Bramble or Roderick Random than the participating antihero Peregrine Pickle. To one careful reader this "fictional creation" represents a stereotyped eighteenth-century figure, "the victim of splenetic imbalance who travels therapeutically for his condition"; to another he is a patriot whose larger "didactic purpose is directed at showing his countrymen British superiority, teaching them how to travel abroad, warning them not to be taken in by foreign practices and foreign affection"; to yet another he is the "sick satirist" who continually contrasts the Continent with England and provides "as much a guidebook to conduct as to the sights of France and Italy."[44] No doubt the best analysis so far of the satire in the *Travels* is that by Scott Rice,[45] who argues that Smollett employed "an appropriate satiric spokesman from a selective dramatization of his own literal identity as an ailing Scotch physician" and, in doing so, returned "to a device he employed in ... *Roderick Random.*" That is, he returned to "the stock image of the satirist as one who," in Alvin Kernan's words, "seems always to come from a world of pastoral innocence and kindness: ... the prophet come down from the hills...." Not only is the "chief purpose" of this spokesman, Rice concludes, "to render a Juvenalian attack upon luxury, satirizing in a foreign setting the same vices [Smollett] would later treat domestically in *Humphrey Clinker,*" but the "persona's consistent and interrelated appreciations also function to integrate the travel book materials on antiquities into the governing scheme of the satire." After noting such an emphasis on what are considered to be novelistic techniques, one can add other such techniques: Smollett's forty-one letters in the *Travels* were never sent to anyone; he completely rewrote whatever journal he kept; he shifted Roman festivals to Nice and intentionally confused dates; and—like novelists Ann Radcliffe and Charlotte Smith using Carbonnières—he pretended that certain descriptions were his own when they came from earlier travelers and from guidebooks.[46] Considering these many "fictional" devices, then, one can see how a novelist or anyone else writing a travel book can successfully succumb to a desire to add to or modify the experiences he or she "recognizes," "react" to them more intelligently or entertainingly, and, if a satirist, "rebuke" them more ironically.

But there is more. Just as Smollett's *Travels* is much like some novels in format and content, each of his novels is much like certain kinds of travel books. For *Humphrey Clinker,* Charles Batten has shown it best by stressing three important facts.[47] First, Smollett begins by calling his fictional *Humphrey* a travel account and then ironically but correctly points out that his volume of familiar travel letters is handicapped because it has such strong competition—"there have been so many letters upon travels lately published"; then he lists seven of the competitors, including his own *Travels* and Sterne's *Sentimental Journey,* all of which in his own day were considered more or less "real." Second, as Smollett biographers know, the trip taken in *Humphrey* is " 'only a history, fictitiously coloured,' of the trip he took to his native Scotland in the Spring of 1766."[48] And third, as with so many travel accounts, there are in the novel any number of actual places described —Bath, inns and roads, London courts, buildings, and streets—and actual people dramatized, not just friends and acquaintances such as the actor James Quinn but Matt Bramble himself, who is much like Smollett, or Lydia and her brother Jery, who resemble Smollett's daughter and nephew.[49] As Kahrl implies and as Batten contends, "Smollett thought of *Humphrey Clinker* more in terms of a travel book than a novel,"[50] and it is indeed a "sophisticated fictional reworking of the travel book."

To relate the fictional elements in Smollett's *Travels* and the travel book elements in *Humphrey Clinker* leads to problems if one has fixed feelings about genre, whether genre is to be determined by content or by structure. One reader of the *Travels* finds that "it is not a typical travel book" because it is not "diffuse and rambling"; another believes it to be "related less . . . to travel books than to the imaginary visits made by Orientals to Paris and London," that is to such "novels" as *L'Espion Turc* and *Les Lettres persanes.*[51] Similarly, readers of *Humphrey* are sometimes reluctant to call it a novel because of its supposed lack of unity, that is, because "it shares characteristics of both the novel and the nonfictional travel book without, properly speaking, being either."[52] Each of the two kinds of opinions needs comment. First, as we have seen, there is no "typical" travel book, and certainly "diffuse and rambling" would not describe such a type of literature any more than it would define prose fiction as a form. Second, Smollett's *Travels* is indeed related to the tradition of *Les Lettres persanes,* which is itself so indebted to real travel accounts; but then the "novel" *Humphrey Clinker* with its multiple satiric personae may be even closer to Montesquieu's conte philosophique with its two Lucianic observers. Moreover, the fact that *Humphrey Clinker* lacks the kind of structural unity found in La Fayette's *Princesse de Clèves, The Scarlet Letter,* or a "well-made" play by Scribe may simply mean that Smollett has imposed not a Greek-French dramatic unity on his fiction but a kind of form derived from travel epics such as the *Odyssey* and the *Aeneid,* from Lucian's mobile satires, from the bifocal *Lettres persanes,* and from travel literature, both his own Grand Tour book and his *Compendium of Authentic and Entertaining Voyages*. It is a form that, as with so many other borrowed elements, has been absorbed by the amorphous, prodigious novel. And finally, to deny that Smollett's *Travels* is a "real" travel account—or to call it untypical—is to forget that its use of fictional letters is a venerable tradition in the literature of real travels, one far older for it than for the novel, and that its "false" structure is less false than that of any number of other travel accounts accepted as real, the "letters" of Timberlake and Howell, for example, or Defoe's widely used *Tour*, a travel book if its many admirers are to be believed.

And while Defoe's *Tour* (1724-26), unlike Smollett's *Travels*, is not satirical, as much as any travel account it has a plot of discourse, or thought, and that plot as a vehicle has been studied well. The thesis, the load carried on the tour, has been stated as Defoe's expression, especially through images, of England's economic "increase and improvement" as opposed to its "erosion and destruction"; that is, the *Tour* is Defoe's "moral imperative pointing the way toward England's industrialization."[53] The plot itself has been described in two ways, one metaphorically, one geographically. Jo Ann Hackos, noting that in the *Tour* Defoe repeatedly refers to England as a "Planted Garden," finds him following Pope in his conception of "an artfully controlled 'naturalness' and in his imaginative attempt to recreate that natural landscape verbally"; for her the plot is described by "the concept of *ambulando*, or the progression through the Garden," with Defoe as the master gardener.[54] Pat Rogers, concentrating even more on the artistry in the *Tour*,[55] notes how often Defoe speaks of Tour, Journey, Excursion; shows that his "digressive" Progressions, his "Circular" Rambles, are related to those of Dunton and Sterne and the tradition of burlesque travels; emphasizes the relationship between Defoe's Persona-Guide and his Reader-Listener; and, finally, demonstrates that the itinerary of the *Tour* is thoroughly contrived. That is, the Guide selects London as a focal point and then leads his group of tourists out from it, first in one direction, then another, then another, frequently selecting a smaller city as a secondary focal point from which other excursions may be taken, all of which Defoe suggests in Letter One. The point is that the *Tour*, so popular for a century, was long considered to be a collection of essays which Defoe put together over the years he was traveling for the government. Now, however, we know that he was answering John Macky's travel letters, called *Journey through England* (1714-23), with fictional letters of his own, that he employed Camden's *Britannica* as much as he used his own observations, and that he organized his material in the form of a journey like none he had ever taken. Defoe's methods in the *Tour* were, in fact, more "novelistic" than those of Smollett in his

Travels, even though so far no one has apparently labeled the *Tour* untypical.[56]

Nor, apparently, has anyone argued that a hundred other such books are not "typical" or not "real." Although Sterne's *The Sentimental Journey* is now a "novel," in the eighteenth century it was a travel book and inspired a huge school of sentimental travel accounts, as many in Germany, France, and Spain as in England, none "typical" for William Dampier's day or for ours. Then, in the nineteenth century, writers in the United States, learning from Dampier, Defoe, Smollett, and Brydone, published almost every conceivable kind of book dealing directly or indirectly with a journey or with a series of journeys. Hawthorne's *Italian Note Books,* for example, reflects the author and his development as an art historian and connoisseur more than it does the countryside or people he saw, while his novel *The Marble Faun* depends heavily on his travel book and was standard reading for any American headed for Italy. Charles Dudley Warner, who wrote ten travel books, announced only half facetiously in his first that, departing from the travel tradition, "we shall go somewhere and not learn anything."[57] The travel accounts of Mark Twain are surely not "typical," for no two of them are at all alike. Besides the popular *Innocents Abroad* and *A Tramp Abroad,* he not only wrote *Roughing It,* revealingly called by one twentieth-century historian a "travel narrative that belongs properly to belles-lettres," but also *Life on the Mississippi* (1883), which the mature author put together as he rode the river again, relived his memories, reworked other memories published eight years before in the *Atlantic,* and lifted a section from *Huck Finn,* all to create another special kind of book that, like Sterne's Volume VII of *Tristram,* combines a lively imagination with several journeys. Perhaps the method of William Dean Howells, who sometimes was not sure whether he was producing a novel or a récit de voyage, is typical not just for the nineteenth century and later but for all time. After his Italian and other travel accounts, he published *London Films* and *Certain Delightful English Towns,* each put together with the help of a journal he kept, of letters and a diary he sent home to his wife, of books he read before and after the fact, and of an imagination working on memory. Like Defoe, Prévost, Sterne, and Smollett, like Mark Twain, Henry James, and Michel Butor, Howells was indeed "a Traveler long before [he] was a noveler"; and if one claims that Howells—or any other writer—employs "novelistic" practices in travel literature, one must also note that *Their Wedding Journey* (1872) is, as George Arms says, only one of a number of his novels built "closely upon the tradition of travel."[58] It is by no means, then, the Lucianic or the Juvenalian errant satirist alone who follows his artistic inclinations to touch up and restructure a "real" récit de voyage.

Of all satiric fiction the kind perhaps most closely and most often associated with travel literature is that vaguely and uncertainly called "picaresque," even though with a liberal use of the term one can argue that not all picaresque fiction is satiric.[59] Some analysts are not so liberal, however, A.A. Parker and certain Spanish critics, for example, permit no evolution of the picaresque novel, limiting it to *Lazarillo de Tormes* (1554), its Spanish imitators, and perhaps *Simplicissimus*.[60] Others, one being Stuart Miller, go further and include *Guzmán, Gil Blas, Moll Flanders,* and *Count Fathom.*[61] Others, including W.M. Frohock and Walter Allen, lament a twentieth-century confusion over the term and find that "for every novelist to write a new novel there is at least one critic waiting to find something picaresque in it."[62] Yet others, among them Watt and Ulrich Wicks, prefer that picaresque not be called a genre like epos, prose, drama, and lyric but a mode, while Claudio Guillén, after suggesting that the "picaresque tale" is a "genre," identifies three circles of picaresque—*Lazarillo, Guzmán,* and *Simplicissimus* in the center; *Gil Blas* in the next circle; and certain novels of Defoe and Smollett in the outer circle—and concludes with a "picaresque myth," that is, "an essential situation or significant structure derived from the novels themselves."[63] And then there is Paulson's mobile Lucianic satirist who as a picaro is "decidedly centripetal" in English fiction, where he is the focus of attention, and "centrifugal" on the Continent, where the society around him is the object of satire.[64]

Whatever the definition or the argument, however, perhaps most readers think they recognize a picaresque novel or, at least, the picaresque elements in a work of fiction. Among those elements one can for our purposes, and by employing an approach no more liberal than that of Guillén or Paulson, select the following three as pertinent: first, a protagonist who is a scoundrel, a rogue, a delinquent, or some sort of antihero who may be passive or dynamic, that is remain an antihero, as Lazarillo does, or evolve upward in society, as Gil Blas does; second, an ironic tone that with most picaresque novels—*Simplicissimus* but not *Moll Flanders*—leads to satire of society; and, third, movement through space, that is, travel from one occupation or kind of life to another, often over a whole nation, frequently, as with *Roderick Random* and *Fathom,* over nations and seas.[65] Since the beginning of literature this picaresque mode with its moving protagonist—from Apuleius's donkey to Huck Finn on his raft—has been part of or closely related to the satiric mode that employs a Lucianic mobile satirist. In each tradition the protagonist travels in order that the author may picture all phases of a restrictive, corrupt society that educates, perhaps seduces, the protagonist to its ways. In each tradition, as a result, there is emphasis not just on satire and adventure but on close details, even on encyclopedic knowledge that often comes from histories, geographies, compendia of all kinds, and travel writing. The traveling antihero thus becomes a bildungs-anti-held, and because he develops, learns how to conform, he is in one important sense like the romance hero, who redoes that "other" world before coming home. In fact, in a very ironic sense this antihero is just as much the conqueror of two worlds, the difference being that his two worlds are ultimately the same—the one into which he is forced is really the one to which he returns. Like the Lucianic satura the picaresque antihero is often thought of as Butler's knight-errant on a voyage to hell or Frye's on a journey of dark descent.

This association of the picaresque novel with Latin satire was often made in the seventeenth century, as by Jean Chapelain, who translated Alemán's *Guzmán* into French in 1619, and Charles Sorel, who translated Cervantes and other Spanish writers and wrote the antiromance *Francion*. [66] In fact they and apparently the great majority of the many Europeans outside Spain who knew *Lazarillo* and its Spanish successors read them with pleasure and then translated them, nearly always changing facts or opinions about religion, morality, or politics. And they wrote imitations or continuations that often lifted the protagonist out of roguery into a more admirable sphere and gave him a happy ending, as Nashe did in *Jack Wilton, or the Unfortunate Traveler* (1594), the hero of which is a gentleman who travels with the Earl of Surrey and returns to wealth and a wife; as Sorel did with his "noble-souled" Francion; as Scarron did with his "noble-hearted pica-resque hero Le Destin" in the *Roman comique* (1651, 1657); and as the French translator of Quevedo's *El Buscón* did in 1633 when he transformed the Spanish rogue and rewarded him with a true love and two fortunes. [67] The Spanish picaresque then was absorbed—as with so many other forms and modes—into the main stream of European fiction. It was, in short, combined with the sentimental, the adventurous, the comic until it no longer existed as a "genre" or a "form" but as a tradition evolving with the evolving novel. Ironically, perhaps the most important piece of literature to help in the international transformation of the picaresque was another Spanish novel, *Don Quixote*, which foreshadows, by its use of them, all the important combinations later novelists would contrive by starting with the tradition of *The Golden Ass* and *Lazarillo*.

Nevertheless, the picaresque tradition is there, however dimly it may sometimes be discerned; and, as with his Lucianic relatives, the protagonist of that tradition—a real picaro in Quevedo's *El Buscón* who drifts with the unadmirable world; a mad saint in *Don Quixote* who dies trying to reform the world; or a sane youth whose noble heart conquers the corrupt world in Sorel's *Francion*—is a traveler and his creator works close to the travel-writing tradition. Three examples will help to show that fact, all from the seventeenth century, when travel accounts and picaresque tales were being simultaneously absorbed by the novel.

First, there is James Mabbe, who did the most popular English version of a Spanish picaresque story, Alemán's *Guzmán,* and called it *The Rogue*

(1622-23). As a traveling secretary in Spain for three years, Mabbe collected dictionaries, other reference books, and his own observations. Then after combining all these with the editing of an Italian translation of *Guzmán*, he changed the text, added notes, drew "attention to peculiarly Spanish customs and religious practices," and hoped to leave the impression that his traveling rogue was, like the narrator of a certain kind of travel book, recording an "accurate picture of Spanish life."[68]

Second, after the Jesuit priest Albertinus wrote a long allegorical continuation of *Guzmán* (1615) in German that sent the rogue over Germany, Switzerland, and Austria before converting him to a repentant Christian, Martin Freudenhold did yet another German continuation (1626) in which the protagonist, after reverting to his old ways, travels all over the Orient and provides descriptions, history, and information about customs, much as the Dutch Linschoten had earlier done in his *Itinerario.*[69]

The third example, which could be added to over and over, is Grimmelshausen's *Der abenteuerlichen Simplicissimus* (1668-69), which to almost any commentator is one of the novels closest to the *Lazarillo* model. But far more than the Spanish archetype, perhaps as much as any novel in the tradition, *Simplicissimus* is a travel book too. After his initial adventures as a boy thrown out into the world, Simplicius travels and travels—Russia, Turkey, Japan, Egypt, the eastern islands—and is able to do so because his creator not only follows the routes of real travelers but borrows their information, using especially the compilations of the de Brys, including Linschoten, more especially the books of the great German travelers Olearius and Mandelslo,[70] known so well by other novelists such as Defoe. Grimmelshausen's method is like that of Richard Head in the last part of *The English Rogue*, another picaresque fiction but one that, like *Moll Flanders*, has little satire. It is the method of all fireside travelers who take the work of real travelers and invent books that, for a time at least, may be real to their readers. And it is the method of any real traveler who supplements his own observations and experiences with those of other travelers or synthesizers of travels.

Such mendacious narrators—fireside or partly real—often inspired the author of a novel to satirize them by inventing a picaresque traveler more mendacious than they, that is, a Lucianic mobile satirist, since Lucian's *True History*, so popular in the seventeenth and eighteenth centuries, is the prototypical satire of exaggerated or fabricated travel memoirs.[71] Among the older fabricators of travel stories there are Odysseus at the court of King Alcinous, Boccaccio's garrulous Friar Onion, and Rabelais's Pantagruel. For the eighteenth century, Baron Munchausen, created primarily to ridicule Abyssinian James Bruce, is easily the best known of the fictional tellers of tall tales about travels, although he is exceeded as a mendacious picaro by his brilliant and notorious creator Rudolph Erich Raspe. Almost ninety years before, however, a Leipzig student named Christian Reuter had written a kind of novel, which he called *Schelmuffsky* (1696), to satirize the marvelous adventures recorded in so many reiseromane. Schelmuffsky, like Munchausen, relates his own travels and exploits. He is a good-for-nothing who drives a wagon from London to Hamburg, sees Venice on top of a mountain, claims an impossible trip to the East, is beloved by all ladies, and all the time keeps assuring us of his veracity, just as nonsatirical novelists of the day were doing—Mme d'Aulnoy, Tyssot de Patot, and Defoe—and just as Gulliver does when he ends his last voyage with an attack on lying travelers.

The picaro or picara is the reader's guide from one spot to another, the binding element in a moving episodic plot; and if the author's motive is satire, the rogue can become an animal, an inanimate object, or a supernatural creature in a tradition that includes Lucian's Icaro-Menippus, Apuleius's donkey, and Lesage's Asmodée in *Le Diable boiteux* (1707).[72] Mrs. Manley's Justice or Virtue in one novel and Cupid in another travel and eavesdrop on scandalous and titillating scenes in a scandalous society—a "New Atalantis" or an "Island adjacent to Utopia." Charles Gildon, in a *New Metamorphosis* (1709, 1724), replaces the donkey of Apuleius with a lap dog that like Manley's Cupid can observe salacious scenes and evil politics. Even Lesage's Asmodée has models—for example, the Spanish *El Diablo cojuelo* (1641), in which the spirit lifts off roofs to expose what is below, much as Lesage's spirit and his companion hear chimneys telling of what they are privileged to see.

But it is a gigantic tradition that spawned a number of minor traditions. The *Diable boiteux* leads immediately to *Le Diable bossu* (1708) by Bruslé de Montpleinchamp, with its demons and gods lifting the veil on society; then to Crébillon's *Le Sopha*, with its sofa listening to the travelers who sit on it; and on to Diderot's *Les Bijoux indiscrets*, where a magic ring goes from scene to scene in French society.[73] The picaresque ass or lap dog leads to Addison's monkey, "who" in *Spectator* 343 tells of having transmigrated from one body to another. In fact, the *Spectator* and The *Tatler* could hardly have done without the picaresque tradition—kept women moving from man to man, rakes going down the social ladder as Fielding's Old Man of the Hill and Mr. Wilson do, peripatetic servants changing jobs, even a shilling (*Tatler* 249) starting as silver ore in Peru and going from pocket to pocket before being melted down. Then, more vulgar even than Diderot's ring, there is Smollett's atom, a vehicle for political satire. Perhaps most fascinating of all is the long list of long noses that point to Sterne's tale by Slawkenbergius in which the great nose of Diego leaves admiring men and love-smitten women in the wake of his patient mule.[74] This inanimate, or at least unparticipating, agent of satire that, as with the shilling, moves about is close to but much less intriguing than the human agents in the tradition of the fictional Turks, Persians, Chinese, and American Indians in Europe. It is close also to the naive countryman taking a tour of the city, as with the one escorted over town in Ned Ward's *The London Spy* (1698), or Sarah Fielding's David Simple, who is guided by Orgueil. And it is close to the real travelers, who may not, however, record satirical observations.

But there is a reciprocal influence too; that is, the picaresque mode affects the real travel tale when it is thought of as biography or autobiography. Not only is *Lazarillo* or *Buscón* named the *Vida*, the *Life*, of Lazarillo or Buscón, but for two hundred years the "Vida" of a real picaro was often shaped like that of the famous fictional ones. Elkanah Settle's life of the law-breaking impersonator Will Morrell (1694), for example, not only shows him to be no less admirable than the protagonist of Quevedo's *Buscón* (1626; English 1657), but Settle obviously had the Spanish picaro in mind as he let his imagination play over the life of the English criminal.[75] For the eighteenth century the best example is surely that notorious Spanish genius of all trades, Diego de Torres y Villaroel, a close relative to all those other real picaresque adventurers of the day such as Neuhof, Casanova, and the two cousins von der Trenck. Torres wrote his own *Vida* after 1743; and ever since, somewhat as with Sterne's *Sentimental Journey* in this century, it has been called a picaresque novel.[76] A fictionized autobiography in the tradition of Hamilton's "novel" about his brother-in-law the comte de Gramont, it tells of its author's Proteus-like life all over Spain and Portugal, one that Torres himself called "picaresque." Now, however, readers of the *Vida* are going beyond the picaresque tag and finding it a link between the novel and biography or autobiography.[77] The *Vida* of Torres, even better than the *Confessions* of Rousseau, illustrates the thesis of Burton Pike that "Autobiography is not simply an attempt to retell one's past life on a linear scale, but rather in effect a novel written in the present, with one's past life as its subject."[78] That is, the picaresque *Vida* of Torres is a traveler's tale full of fact flavored generously with fiction, a bildungsreise and yet a bildungsroman.

As with the real traveler and the structure of his or her book, the traveling protagonist invented by a fiction writer with a theme—the bildungsheld, picaro, or Lucianic satirist—determines the form the fiction takes by moving from one adventure or character to another; and each kind of protagonist offers the writer a chance not only to employ the structural schemes called "framing" and "linking" but also to digress, to interpolate stories told by other characters.

Framing is the device used by Chaucer in *The Canterbury Tales*, by Boccaccio, by Margaret of Navarre, with Chaucer's pilgrims being closest to the tradition of the real traveler. In the seventeenth and eighteenth centuries it is the device found in many sedentary fictions, say, Subligny's *La Fausse Clélie* (1671), a collection of nouvelles held together by a frame—one character imagining herself to be Scudéry's Clélie. And in a sense it is the device used by every novelist who finds a way to start a protagonist moving as a focal point for actions, ideas, or any kind of interpolation. There is, for example, the fictional foreign-observer frame, as in *Les Lettres persanes*, where Rica and Usbek are more or less static reactors; or Ned Ward's countryman being shown London. But the travel frame is by no means restricted to, or even found chiefly in, satire. It is, for example, the device of *The Three Princes of Serendip* [Sarendip], published first in Italy in 1557 apparently, translated into French and English in 1722 with a much longer conclusion, and the inspiration for Horace Walpole's happy accident in coining "serendipity," that is, "The gift of finding valuable or agreeable things not sought for."[79] Here the Emperor of Serendip pretends to be angry with his three sons in order to send them out in the world to tell and hear stories. In fact, the seven tales they hear, combined with those told by the princes, make up over half the volume. Framing, Victor Shklovsky says, is combined with linking in *The Golden Ass,* a fact that is true for *The Three Princes of Serendip* and for any fiction that devotes so little space to the framing structure itself.

The linking device can be a sofa that sits and listens, but nearly always it is a traveler. This traveler can be a passive character, as with Apuleius's man-donkey, Addison's shilling, or Diderot's ring. It can be a weak participant who, as Shklovsky says of Gil Blas, is the thread on which Lesage strings his episodes. Or the traveler can sometimes be a very active participant, such as Joseph Andrews, who temporarily loses his Fanny, walks and rides highways, and is robbed and beaten; and yet, at other times, he can be a passive observer, as when Joseph lies in a bed injured while, in the inn below, other characters do the acting. Framing, in its extreme form, does not attract digressions since the fiction is made up, so to speak, of digressions; but linking provides countelss opportunities for the protagonist to provide information about a new scene, idea, or person and to meet people who tell stories about themselves or other people.

Such interpolations have anciently been condemned unless they are closely related to the main plot, but, especially for the seventeenth- and eighteenth-century novel, they have also been defended in a variety of ways. One way is to show how the interpolations in our favorite novels are functional. Those in Scarron's *Roman comique,* for example, are now often considered "integral parts of the novel, functionally related to its purpose and structure"; those in *La Princesse de Clèves,* formerly attacked, are explained today as a "traditional device . . . used with such a sense of unified purpose that the integrated episodes cease to be digressions at all"; and even the story of Fielding's Old Man, an "excresence" to Ian Watt, is defended by H.K. Miller and others, who relate the Old Man to the pious hermit and "embittered traveler" of romance and find his story to be an exemplum designed to aid the young listener on his journey to maturity.[80] Such attempts to explain digressions can show them to be exempla, allegorical messages, parodies of the chief story, explanations for past events, or foreshadowings of events to come; and their appropriateness may be strengthened if their image patterns are similar to those of the main plot.

Another favorite way to explain digressions now is to show that they are a necessary part of the tradition of satire, a tradition that would include Frye's anatomies—the works of Rabelais and Burton, for example—and all those many other long fictions, prose and poetry, that overlap the anatomy, from the *Satyricon* to Swift's *Tale of a Tub* to *Tristram Shandy* to Byron's *Don Juan,* in the last of which the narrator facetiously confesses, "If I have any fault, it is digression" (III. 96). Eugene Korkowski is the most recent scholar to trace the tradition from Menippus to Lucian and through a dozen other satirists to Dunton, Swift, and Sterne.[81] Menippean satire employed the digression to satirize the various forms of philosophical discourse. That is, the satirist's persona pretended to forget his train of thought in a mock argument and then to offer excuses for the memory lapse. All this led to digressive structures considered entertaining and attractive, to mock excuses for inability to follow a prearranged plan, to explanations about lost or burned leaves in a manuscript, even to an apparently formless jumbling together of prose and verse. For the seventeenth and eighteenth centuries this Menippean digressiveness, associated with erudition, wit, and entertainment, was for satirists a normal way of writing; and since many of them were also novelists—Cervantes, Lesage, Fielding, Voltaire—their well-trained tendency to wander from the main plot naturally affected the structure of their novels.

For the twentieth century the weakest defense one can apparently offer for a digression is to suggest that it provides variety or is an attractive story in its own right. But that was a fine explanation—no defense was needed— for Aristotle and, after him, for all those other critics who judged the epic with its "ornamental" digression to be in some ways superior even to tragedy. Addison was agreeing with Rapin, Dryden, Le Bossu, the Daciers, and Fielding when he said, ". . . if we look into the Conduct of *Homer, Virgil,* or *Milton,* as the great Fable is the Soul of each Poem, so to give their Works an agreeable Variety, their Episodes are so many short Fables . . ." (*Spectator* 303). Today, however, a reader conditioned by "well-made" plots can avoid the opinions of critics from Aristotle to Fielding and, as Auerbach does in his chapter on "The Scar of Odysseus," argue that since Homeric life had meaning in every element the epic as a form has no digressions. But for readers of the seventeenth and eighteenth centuries, fumbling—as we are— for an aesthetic of the novel, tradition seemed to be enough; and since the novel was so often compared to the epic—or to its close relative the Greek-French romance—novelists needed no excuse for inserting a digression: If Homer let Theoclymenos tell his autobiography to Odysseus, if Don Quixote could stop at inns and listen to stories or watch a puppet show, all for variety and embellishment, the Scudérys, Haywood, Marivaux, or Fielding might have digressions and embedded stories too.

And yet, as important as all these reasons are for explaining the digressive structure of much early fiction, travel writing of whatever kind offered the novelist another popular model for the use of digressions. In fact, whether much or little, the traveler has customarily gone beyond his or her adventures, reactions, and feelings to add descriptions, lists, historical background for spots visited, even pictures of plants and animals indigenous to those spots, and stories of encounters with natives who relate hearsay, tell tales, perhaps describe buildings or towns the traveler is unable to visit. In other words, while it is the nature of travel literature for the protagonist to follow an itinerary, a main road, and report—or have reported—what he or she does and sees, it is just as necessary for the traveler to pause and go aside, to leave the main route, to interpolate, to digress. Just as Byron the Menippean satirist can know that his digressions are the most attractive features of *Don Juan,* so any good writer is aware that for a travel book digressions become both entertaining and functional. If it is true that without them we would not read *Don Juan,* it is just as true that without them Masefield and other readers would not be able to praise the *New Voyage* of Gulliver's "Cousin" Dampier, who himself argued that "one who rambles about a country can give usually a better account of it, than a Carrier who jogs on to his inn, without ever going out of his road." "Vertical" plotting, in short, is as necessary as "horizontal" plotting.

The place of digressions in, as well as their importance to, imaginary voyages, the fiction closest to the travel account, has been pointed out by Aubrey Rosenberg,[82] who considers three such fictions—those by Gabriel de Foigny (1676), Denis Veiras (1677; English 1675), and Simon Tyssot de Patot (c. 1714). And he is able to make his point without reference to the Menippean-Lucianic tradition or to the romance-epic tradition, each of which is important to any study of imaginary voyages, especially those that treat utopias and are satiric. Among the conclusions drawn by Rosenberg are these. First, in *La Terre australe connue, ou Les Avantures de Jacques Sadeur,* Foigny spends whole chapters describing the way of life, the religion, and the constitution of the people, as well as the topography and flora and fauna of their country, all of which is "irrelevant to the narrative framework and to the main purpose of the novel"; and yet, Rosenberg insists, "digressions are conspicuously absent" because Foigny's purpose is to provide "authenticity" and "describe a utopia" (p. 28). Second, Veiras in his *Histoire des sévarambes* not only has long essays on the historical and social background of his Sévarambian society but he provides a number of interpolations that have nothing to do with the protagonist—for example, the story of two lovers, told because their picture hung in the Temple of the Sun; and yet, Rosenberg argues, the facts about society are necessary because they describe a utopia, while the embedded tales not only "provide entertainment and a change of pace from the largely factual and realistic account of" the society but also are "padding" needed by the author to round out his second volume (29-30). And third, Tyssot's *Voyages et avantures de Jacques Massé* consists of approximately equal parts of autobiographical details, a description of a utopia, a discussion and satire of religion, and a series of "irrelevant" anecdotes; and yet, Rosenberg very correctly says, because Tyssot was using the "imaginary voyage genre" primarily as a "vehicle for the display of his scholarly and literary talents ... these digressions constituted for [him] the most important feature of the novel" (34-39).

Each of these conclusions seems to contradict the meaning of digression, and yet each is quite acceptable. What needs to be pointed out, however, is this truth: Not only are some of the facts about the three imaginary societies and their geography and products taken from travel books, as we are told, but the structure of each of the volumes, no two of which are alike, is the structure of a certain type of travel book in every way. They have, for example, the journey, direct or circuitous; the account of a country's society and of its history, geography, flora, and fauna; an emphasis on strange animals, as in Veiras, or on a peculiar religion, as in Tyssot; anecdotes told by strangers; other anecdotes that take departure from pictures or places; and the author' erudition as inspired by real places and events or by those invented to display that erudition. In short, the popular imaginary voyages—so many of which are called novels, romances, romans, as with Haywood, Defoe, Voltaire—were modeled directly on travel books written by people who actually experienced all or some of what they claimed to have experienced. It may be then that any defense of digressions in imaginary voyages can be based primarily on the fact that "digressions" are indispensable to real voyages, those being imitated by writers like Tyssot or Defoe. Another of Rosenberg's conclusions is most revealing: "Episodes [in seventeenth- and eighteenth-century novels] that were once regarded as irrelevant digressions are now considered not only relevant to the purpose of the novel, but sometimes, of the very essence of the work" (21). And they were so considered, one may add, partly because the tradition of the travel account before 1800 called for the author to step aside from some plot or itinerary considered major in order to describe, to reflect, to relate an anecdote. Swift was following that tradition in the backward-looking, "digressive" sixth chapter of "The Voyage to Lilliput" as much as Dampier was when he paused in 1686 to describe the people and customs of Mindanao.

Few travelers through history, however, have supplied all their "digressions" in the first draft of a journal or diary; such side trips, such history or geography, and such erudition or tales take time, planning, reflection, a study desk, books, and a rewriting of whatever notes were taken on the spot. The *Journal* of Montaigne's overland trip to Italy (1580-81) is a good example of the spare, largely unadorned travel account that, never published in his day, was left without the rewriting that a learned, witty, erudite Montaigne could so beautifully have given it. On the other hand, George Sandys, setting out for the East in 1610, did take time to completely rewrite his notes, to add material from histories and from other travelers, and to end with a travel account which—loaded with "digressions"—saw many editions in his own lifetime.

The methods of Coryat (1611), both unusual and typical, are strikingly attractive and influential. Like dozens of other travelers—such as Captain John Smith, John Taylor, and John Dunton, all in seventeenth-century England—he followed the Menippean tradition and inserted his own poems, in Latin, English, and Italian, even including the music for them at times. Occasionally he wrote one in Latin and then gave the English translation (I, 59). At Lyons he stopped his fascinating account of himself, his observations, his inn to give the history and physical features of the city, the number of churches, all named, and anecdotes such as one about Pontius Pilate committing suicide in the city (I, 203-12). His friend Chaplain Terry, who was with Ambassador Roe in the Orient, learned from Coryat's popular book and from others how to "digress," how to rewrite and add. Not only did Terry in the final edition (1655) of his account pause at length to condemn a pagan religious practice or eastern adultery, but Coryat's visit with him in 1613 provided Terry with the opportunity for another kind of digression, an account of how Coryat was his "Chamber-fellow or Tent mate" for some months. Here, almost forgetting himself and India, Terry told of Coryat's fluency in languages, his "itch" to travel, his eccentricities that caused Roe and Sir Henry Wotton to call him fool, and his departure and death at Surat (58-78). Within this digression there is another, the anecdote of how Coryat took on a shrewish Indian woman in her own language, answered tirade for tirade, and finally silenced her. One of the most popular hearsay anecdotes in a seventeenth-century travel account—one of many in the same book— is that of the Bermuda beauty named Yarico as told about by Richard Ligon (1657), an anecdote Steele borrowed and embellished for *Spectator* 11 before passing it on to novelists, even travel writers.[83] And like Coryat and Terry and other travelers, Ligon inserted his own poems, even his own drawings. Through the centuries, then, and into our own day, what may be called digressions in some forms of literature are for travel accounts structurally inherent: They may be primarily entertaining, as with Ligon's Yarico, or primarily instructional, as with George Sandys's bits of history or descriptions of folk customs.

By the time the novels of Lesage and Defoe appeared, traveler writers offered countless variations on these two kinds of digressions, depending on whom they were imitating, their special circumstances, and their talents. Chardin, welcomed at the Persian court as a gem merchant and political emissary, was a typical land traveler if ever there was one. He could be personal and subjective; but immediately after narrating an incident involving servants and horses sent for him by the First Minister, he provided a two-page history of how the English first came to Persia in 1613, a translation of a letter from Charles II to the King of Persia, and a one-page copy of the original letter, all short, appropriate, and intriguing (100 ff.). Perhaps Woodes Rogers would be considered "typical" of the seamen who wrote about their voyages. Although he told of incidents aboard ship during his circumnavigation and of the capture of a Spanish galleon, his book is more digression—by some standards—than it is personal narrative. After days of journal keeping he starts his first digression on page 37 and ends it on page 74. For it, after describing "The Island Grande" off Brazil from his own observations, he uses Nieuhof out of Churchill's collection to give a history of Brazil and a description of its people, including tribes and customs, and then shifts back and forth among Purchas, Churchill, and Sanson's popular geography, itself a compilation from travels, to tell at length of the discovery and exploration of the Amazon, all the time consistently naming his sources. This kind of historical and geographical information is supplemented by copies of official documents that provide instructions to all officers aboard the two ships (103-4, e.g.), regulate the handling of plunder (170-71), and in general record the actions of the committee that governed the voyage (227-28, e.g.). All in all, both Chardin and Rogers tell much about themselves—what they did and saw—but they were writing in a tradition that also encouraged the inclusion of anything the author deemed interesting and pertinent.

Yet, while they are typical, they are especially typical of two kinds of travel writers—those who collect and keep documents they themselves do not write and those who find a publisher or editor willing to help them fill out a journal with erudition gleaned from the most trusted, the most recent, or the most accessible of accounts by other travelers. Perhaps representative of a still larger group of travelers are John Ray and Gemelli Careri. Surely

one would expect Ray, the great botanist, to pause and describe a plant in
the Low Countries or Italy in the 1660s, or to list plants and animals he sees
—all to go with his personal, wide-ranging, thorough journal. So well,
however, is such erudition normally worked into the journal, so appropriate
does it seem that one is perhaps only mildly dismayed when, after learning
about "Serpent Stones and some petrified Cockle and Muscle-shells" in
Germany, one discovers that Ray has inserted an eighteen-page essay on
petrified stones, shells, and bones in England and all over the world and has
offered theories about how they come to be where they were.[84] Careri is
even less obtrusive with his digressions—an occasional bit of history, an
analysis of customs—as when a three-page account of the kings of Mexico
becomes almost incremental in a long and fascinating day-by-day narrative
of what the lawyer-sportsman-circumnavigator did in Mexico in 1695.[85]

And finally there are the dialogues and the embedded narratives, two
other kinds of digressions in travel books. Although the dialogue form is as
old as Plato and Lucian and was popular with satirists of the Menippean
tradition, it was especially important to those travelers who wanted to offer
a thesis and at the same time appear objective. By the eighteenth century
dozens of travelers had employed it. In his *Decades* Pietro Martire reports
a brief conversation between Columbus and an old West Indian, while
Lescarbot quotes a long one between Champlain and a Canadian Indian as
they talk of religion.[86] Perhaps one of the most influential users of the form
in the seventeenth century was Lahontan, whose one-sided dialogues with
the wise, philosophic Canadian Adario (1703) were expanded for later editions of the *Nouveau voyage*.[87] But not just naive Americans were permitted
to attack the traveler's native Europe. Coryat (I, 211-12) wins a heated
religious argument with a Turk in Lyons; Lancelot Addison (1674) loses out
to a Moor attacking hypocritical Christianity; Robert Drury converses with
a prince in Madagascar who calls the Christian heritage "old wives' tales";
and John Marshall (1668-72) "translates" a long dialogue he claims to have
had with a Brahmin who preaches more Thomism than Hinduism.[88]

And dialogues often become conversations the traveler overhears or
participates in. Long before Careri, who reports conversations constantly,
his countryman Varthema delighted in them, frequently giving the Persian
or Indian words and sometimes including several different conversations or
one long one in a short chapter.[89] By the beginning of the eighteenth
century, dialogues and conversations were characteristic of many kinds of
travel accounts. In 1721, for example, Robert Challe in *Journal de voyage aux
Indes Orientales* records conversations he had, especially on religion, while
aboard ship. And the next year the *Relation des voyages de François Coreal aux
Indes Occidentales*, now—but not then—known to be a fake travel book, has
any number of conversations between the supposed author and natives of

America: In one, an ironic Puerto Rican sneers at syphilitic Europeans; in another, a South American defends his people's ancient marriage customs.[90]

Such examples of dialogues and debates can be increased a hundredfold and can be paralleled in early fiction. All imaginary voyages have them, as when old Suaïns argues with Foigny's Jacques Sadeur for forty pages.[91] In 1711, in *Spectator* 50, Addison has four American Indians talk of St. Paul's and the sham elements in European religion; Robinson Crusoe, like Champlain with his Canadian, has trouble explaining Christianity to a not-so-stupid Friday; Gulliver loses debates with the King of Brobdingnag and his master in Houyhnhnmland; and Maubert de Gouvert's Iroquois Igli (1752),[92] in Paris, but like Lahontan's Adario in Canada, is allowed to win debates with priests and lay wise men. Likewise, Rousseau and Voltaire have their critical Hurons; Diderot takes over Bougainville's dialogues with Tahitians and turns them against him and all hypocritical Europeans; Bage's Hermsprong (1796) lets Great Bear exchange religious myths with Hermsprong's mortified mother in America; and in two travel novels by Lesuire (1760, 1780), long formal dialogues are set up involving several ethnic groups —French, English, Chinese—with English inns, food, and customs in general receiving the brunt of the satire.[93]

Travelers were even more prone to include embedded narratives than to report real or invented dialogues. These narratives could be biographical, as with Chaplain Terry's information about his fellow traveler Coryat and that of Woodes Rogers about Beauchene-Gouin, his predecessor in the South Seas; or travelers could repeat anecdotes they were told or that they found in books. The pristine journal of a land or sea journey is far less likely to include such anecdotes. Celia Fiennes, for example, whose seventeenth-century diary of her rambles over Britain (c. 1685-96) was not published in her lifetime, has perhaps only two short narratives told her by individuals she identifies, as when in ten lines her landlady at York tells of a Roman Catholic who made her own relic by dipping a handkerchief in the liquid that oozed from the joints of bones dug up at the old abbey.[94] Like certain other travelers, Fiennes was often content with "they say" or "I was told." Also unpublished in its author's lifetime, the sixteenth-century journal of Montaigne records hearsay, but more often than Fiennes he identifies the sources of his embedded narratives. An Italian vicar, for example, tells him the story of the miraculous cure effected on him by a stone sent from India by his father; and "le Seigneur d'Andelot" in Franche-Conte explains why half his beard and one eyebrow are white and the rest black.[95]

These kinds of anecdotes, rare in unpublished travel manuscripts, pepper the accounts of travelers who had time to edit their journals before publication. Thus in the sixteenth century Varthema reports "a very great miracle" told him by a Christian in India (187), while Dampier in the seventeenth century draws on sailor John Read for a tale of ambergris floating near his ship (58) or on "a Spanish Gentleman that had lived 30 years in tne West-Indies" and so was a "trustworthy source for certain relations" (161). The closest approach, however, to the interpolated narrative of the seventeenth- and eighteenth-century novel is Ligon's romantic story of Yarico or the one Smollett is able to insert in his *Travels* when Joseph, the native driver of the three mules pulling the big berline along the Rhone, is inspired to tell the tale of the capture and execution of a smuggler named Mandrin.[96] It is this longer kind of embedded story that Smollett works into his novels and that nearly all writers of epics and prose fiction before 1800 have included, from Homer and Heliodorus to Cervantes and Sterne.

And it is found in travels just as much. Mandeville delights in stories about the fabulous Prester John; and Father Alvarez in *A True Relation of the Lands of Prester John*—that is, Ethiopia—often interrupts his journal (1520) to relate a story. For example, he records part of a chronicle telling of the queen of Saba (sheba) and her son by Solomon, and he retells the story of Queen Candace, Saint Philip, the eunuch, and how Christianity came to Ethiopia.[97] Similarly, in the seventeenth century Coryat pauses in Switzerland to insert the anecdote of William Tell and the apple as the natives told it to him and as he found it in "the third book of Munster's Cosmography" (101-3). All such digressive tales lead to those found in the imaginary voyages of a Veiras or the novels of a Prévost. And yet, for travel literature the pause in the main narrative that comes with dialogue or with an anecdote of any kind comes less often than the break that is taken while the narrator objectively describes a scene, reports on soil or animals or plants or customs, or records a bit of history. That is, the more popular break in most récits de voyage comes when, for a time, story becomes guidebook information, process statements become stasis statements, horizontal becomes vertical plotting, and the unnecessary detail becomes the most necessary to the narrative.

Perhaps a unique, or at least suitable, way to demonstrate the closeness of structure between novel and récit de voyage, whether one speaks of narratives of action, character, or theme or of all three, is to consider certain travel motifs that the early novel could hardly have done without.

CHAPTER EIGHT

Motifs: The Coach, the Inn

> If ... I had not duties ... I would spend my life driving briskly in a post-chaise with a pretty woman [who could] add something to the conversation. *Samuel Johnson*

> ... what are the contents prefixed to every chapter but so many inscriptions over the gates of inns ... informing the reader what entertainment he is to expect, which if he likes not, he may travel on to the next.... *Fielding*[1]

As with any other term in aesthetics "motif" is difficult to employ. If a dictionary simply equates it with "theme," a critic like Boris Tomashevsky can at great length talk of a major theme as being composed of smaller ones called "motifs," decide that story is "the sum of the motifs in their causal-chronological order," and conclude that plot is "the sum of the same motifs ordered so as to engage the emotions and develop the theme."[2] So often, however, does theme become motif become metaphor, even determine image patterns, that readers confuse these terms, a fact particularly true with words connoting journey or having to do with journeys—and the borrowing of "Leitmotif" from music has helped literary critics only in a limited way. The confusion, or problem, is similar to that arising when we use "genre" for long prose fiction and then, as so many people do, call picaresque fiction or adventure fiction a "genre" rather than a "mode."[3] One student of the early nineteenth century has "voyage," for example, as a "motif," which, for the eighteenth century, he argues, "usually functions only as action" while in "Romantic poetry, on the other hand, the motif functions both as action and as a profound psychological pattern."[4] This thesis, if true, would of course controvert much of what has here been said or will be said. Moreover, Germaine Brée, in a brilliant article, "The Ambiguous Voyage: Mode or Genre," after admitting the critical problem, uses not only mode and genre for voyage but also motif, theme, and metaphor, after which she suggests that to "argue about the exact meaning" of such terms "may be creating bafflement rather than understanding."[5] Obviously, then, there are very large, perhaps plot-controlling, motifs—not only in the literary tradition but in a single piece of literature—and smaller ones that, combined with

others, can assist psychologically or emotionally or intellectually in moving
a plot or in developing a theme or character.

Of the countless motifs employed by novelists to help form their fiction,
many have already been suggested here, among them Barbary slavery,
storm, pilgrimage, exploration, or the ocean with all its parts and functions
and appendages—islands, havens, ports, anchors, ships, tides, currents—that
is, its leitmotive. Two others, each having to do with land travel, may be
selected to show again how close the novelist before 1800 was to the travel
writer. One is the coach, the other the inn motif. Each is important in
traditional literature.

"If ... I had not duties ... I would spend my life driving briskly in a
post-chaise with a pretty woman [who could] add something to the conversation." According to Boswell this was Samuel Johnson's enthusiastic pro-
nouncement made when he was nearly sixty.[6] And while she says nothing
of the request for a lone woman companion, Mrs. Piozzi confirms Boswell
when in her *Anecdotes* she notes that Johnson "loved coaches where people
were trapped to conversation."[7] Through the seventeenth and eighteenth
centuries this entrapment was recorded by many real travelers and became
a most entertaining and useful device for writers of fiction. It was, in fact,
one of the closest bonds between the established travel book and the evolving novel.[8]

Although the ancient Romans, and before them the Hittites and others,
had fine roads and chariots, the enclosed coach is said to have been invented
about 1450 in the town of Kochs in Hungary and to have almost supplanted
the heavier and more cumbersome wagon by the end of the sixteenth century, at least as a passenger vehicle.[9] By 1630 it had become a symbol of
wealth and prestige in western Europe, and by the 1660s it was so popular
that some cities were cluttered with hurrying hackney-coaches for hire and
with splendid private coaches—six horses and a brilliant equipage for a
visiting French ambassador in London and two beautiful blacks for Samuel
Pepys. In fact, by then governments found it necessary to pass stringent
licensing acts and levy taxes that forced some coaches out of Paris and
London but aided in the movement for cross-country commercial carriages
and better highway systems.

Travel writers disagree—for many obvious reasons—about the quality
of seventeenth- and eighteenth-century roads and coach service, as well as
that of roadside inns, but we do have some important facts about the development of the coach, both private and public.[10] One is that by 1610 Sully,
Henry IV's grand commissioner for highways and public works, was doing
much to make coach travel easier by improving French roads. Another is
that after the invention of leather suspension systems not only were there

public coaches between certain towns in England as early as the 1620s but in 1637 John Taylor's *Carrier's Cosmography* spoke of two coaches a week between St. Albans and Aldersgate as well as others to Hertford and Cambridge. Then in the 1650s Sir Ralph Veney was told of two coaches a week to Southampton and another to Winchester while the *Mercurius Politicus* advertised three coaches a week to Chester, each of which used relays of fresh horses to cover the 184 miles in four days. We also know that Sir Anthony Wood was one of those who in 1669 made that first "flying coach" trip from mid-London to Oxford in thirteen hours of one day in a coach with a boot on each side for extra passengers; that glass windows were in carriages on the Continent by the 1660s and in England immediately after the Restoration, with the Duke of Buckingham having the monopoly to make them; that by then the more comfortable berlin (or berline) had made its way from Germany via France to England; that wars and other political events affected the conditions of roads at a given time; that in summer months stagecoach service was normally prompt but in winter the roads often became so bad that coaches took twice as long for a trip and often gave way to wagons; and that by the end of the seventeenth century inns had sprung up along all major highways out of large cities, a fact that encouraged public coachmen to favor those innkeepers who favored them.

By the beginning of the eighteenth century there were road guides for each important country in western Europe as well as improved methods of building and maintaining public thoroughfares. The highway guides gave distances, costs of the toll roads, and information about inns and customs; and there were innumerable guides for individual cities such as London, Paris, Rome, Naples, Lyons. For English roads John Norden's guide of 1625 was popular, although it was supplanted in 1675 by John Ogilby's amazingly detailed and often-reprinted road map. Not only did France in 1716 begin a state corps of road engineers but in 1747 it opened the first college for them and through nearly the entire century produced an annual road book, the monopoly for revising it being given to the Jaillot family. By the 1770s France had many excellent roads because of the work of Pierre Trésaguet, an engineer who preceded McAdam in England by two generations but whose advances were almost equaled in his own time by the English road builder John Metcalf. And so, as early prose fiction was evolving, public stagecoaches and coach travel in general were evolving with it. The new novel, then, could hardly have avoided making artistic use of the stagecoach.

Not that fiction was the only literary form to see its possibilities. Sir Robert Howard's play *The Committee*, on stage in 1665 but set in the 1620s, opens with six passengers arriving by the Reading stagegoach. And George Farquhar's three-act comdey of 1705 entitled *The Stage-Coach* is set in an inn between London and Chester where the coachman has been bribed to stop for the night with his six passengers; and it includes a song—thereafter often reprinted—that begins "Let's sing of Stage-Coaches" and has a galloping refrain as well as this stanza,

> In Coaches thus strowling
> Who wou'd not be rowling;
>   With Nymphs on each side,
> Still Prattling and Playing;
>   Our Knees interlaying,
>   We merrily ride.

Periodical essays took advantage of coaches too. Richard Steele, writing on August 1, 1711 (*Spectator* 132), tells of Mr. Spectator's trip back to London via public coach, describes each of the five other passengers, and tells how Ephraim the Quaker taught manners to a rough soldier. Mr. Spectator concludes that stagecoaches are an ideal means of bringing out human nature. Samuel Johnson, in *Adventurer* 84 for August 25, 1753, has a much more cynical conclusion, and even a better essay than Steele's. He also describes the five companions, ironically tells of their feeble and unsuccessful early attempts at conversation, lets each of them act a part for the sake of impressing others, and, after exposing them all at the end of the four-day trip, concludes that his companions are typical frauds in the journey through life where one daily puts on a face to meet the faces that one meets.

From the mid-seventeenth century to 1800, however, the literature of travel—both real and pseudo—made far more use of coaches than did the periodical essay or the drama, which found difficulty in placing horses and vehicles on stage. John Evelyn in the 1640s describes numerous modes of travel in his several years on the Continent; and, like Robert Montagu on the Grand Tour shortly after, he praises the stagecoaches and roads of France, especially the well-built highway between Paris and Orleans.[11] In a letter to his country cousin written late in life John Dryden describes vividly his ride to London in a public coach, a ride that was ruined for him by a woman passenger so fat that to give the horses rest she frequently asked the coachman to stop so she could "go behind the hedge"; but, Dryden finished gleefully, "we got even by finally sending her into mud up to her ankles."[12] Jean Regnard, surely France's best writer of comedies between Molière and Beaumarchais (if we exclude Lesage's *Turcaret*), was also an inveterate traveler and travel writer. He tells of his stagecoach ride from Paris to Brussels in 1681, describes each stage stop as well as his five fellow passengers—one an army captain, another an amusing priest, all under age twenty-eight—and tells how a storm frightened the horses so much that they overturned the coach. The six men were thrown into the mud and forced to struggle several leagues on foot to Cambrai, where they found a warm inn and comfortable clothes.[13] Dozens of European travel writers, Henri Misson in the 1690s,[14] for example, give simple details about hackneys or other public coaches— their size, their coachmen, the prices, the regulations governing them. Others, from John Evelyn in 1643 to Samuel Sharp in 1766, compare the transportation systems of one country with those of another, each of these two travel writers finding the coaches of Rome the most ostentatious in Europe. The Frenchman Brunel (1655) is one of the best sources for seventeenth-century travel in Spain, where by law all wagons and coaches had to be drawn by mules, even at festival time when women—but not men—paraded in their finery and stopped to eat their delicacies in mule-drawn vehicles, as with modern tailgating at American football games.[15] And in Portugal, the same writer explains, only the clergy were permitted to have horse-drawn coaches or wagons. Among the many other accounts of actual coaches and coach traveling that seem close to the fictional ones is that of Joshua Reynolds's nephew, Joseph Palmer, who wrote up his four-month tour of France in 1776 and in detail described a trip by public diligence from Paris to Chalôns with "ten to twelve persons," including a surgeon, a mercer, a pretty girl, and a Knight of Malta. This group, with the aid of much wine and fine weather, had a lively time, kept comfortable, and drowned out the sound of the big wheels with conversation and with tales of actual or invented experiences.[16]

Between these real travelers and the creators of the novel are those writers who combined experience with imagination to produce pseudo-coach journeys that were models for their contemporaries. Mary Manley, William Byrd, and Laurence Sterne serve as excellent examples. Although Mrs. Manley's little volume was first published in 1696 as *Letters to a Friend* —without her permission, she claimed—it was later brought out in 1725 as *A Stage-Coach Journey to Exeter.*[17] Among her companions on the seven-day trip are a fop who ogles her and tells a story of catching his mistress in bed with another man; the wife of a major, very talkative, whose story is of her second husband; and two virgin travelers who know no better than to enjoy the trip. Mrs. Manley gives every bill of fare, from excellent trout to bad mutton, and judges every inn and innkeeper along the way. At Salisbury they must remain all day Sunday, even go to church, since public travel is illegal on the sabbath. There the coach coming from Exeter joins them and more characters are introduced, including a pregnant wife, her roving husband, and a friendly Mrs. Stanhope, who also has a story, hers sentimental, of an unfaithful lover. Although the final letters are unattractive, Mrs. Manley made much of her experience and led to novelists like Mrs. Haywood, Fielding, and Smollett.

She also apparently influenced William Byrd the Second, who both knew and admired her, for in one of those many pieces written by Byrd and discovered and published in our day is his letter to "Lucretia," whom he visits in southwest England by means of a six-day stagecoach ride and to whom he describes his companions, among them on obnoxious prelate and a boring prude.[18] The coach is apparently the Exeter-Plymouth coach, and Byrd—even though he described no inns and inserted no amorous histories —was apparently imitating Mrs. Manley's ironic character sketches and satire of human affectations and frailties.

In *A Sentimental Journey* Sterne represents a different tradition since he does not use the letter form or describe a trip in a public coach. Instead he dickers with M. Dessein, the famous master of the inn in Calais who is also owner of the yard full of chaises waiting for the anxious travelers from Britain. Sterne almost buys an old *désobligeant*—a one-passenger coach— in which he sits while writing his preface; but when a pretty woman seems to need a ride to Amiens, he purchases a chaise for two, a *remise*, only to lose her to her "brother." So Sterne, accompanied by a servant La Fleur, travels to Paris, to Lyons, to the end of his book and the foot of the Alps with his own small chaise drawn by two horses. For him, then, the convey-ance is a source first of reflections about traveling and travelers, then of conscience-striken hopes for a tête-à-tête à deux—at least as far as Amiens —then of comic incidents, and finally of moving from one inn to an-other or one sentimental scene to another. He is able in *A Sentimental Jour-ney* to provide his inimitable sketches of characters—a monk, a seductive woman, Maria, La Fleur, Janatone—without having any of them in his coach, nor does he record conversations among passengers trapped in a vehicle.

How much of these three coach journeys is fact and how much fiction no one can ever know, just as one cannot be certain whether or not Steele and Johnson were incorporating actual experiences in their accounts of journeys by Mr. Spectator and Mr. Adventurer. In fact, knowing the an-cient and persisting reputation of travelers to tell more or less than the truth, one is perhaps safe in believing that the authors of real travel books—a young John Evelyn, a young Jean Regnard, a young Joseph Palmer, even an old but admittedly biased Samuel Sharp—would be tempted to enliven, to embellish their stories of rides in coaches. It is, then, only a short post ride to the coach motif in the novel.

Although earlier novelists have horse- or mule-drawn wheeled vehicles —the cage of the lion Don Quixote wants to fight with, for example—*Le Roman comique* (1651, 1657) is apparently the first important long prose narrative to make much use of them. More than once Scarron's troupe of traveling actors are transported partly by carriage, although they have horses and wagons also.[19] Nearly always the vehicles are a source of

comedy. Once, Mlle de L'Etoile, one of the actresses, is in pain at Bonnesta-
ble and summons a two-wheeled horse-drawn litter (*un brancard*), an open
conveyance for one reclining person. La Rancune, a member of the troupe
escorting the litter, goes to sleep on it but is rudely jolted out of his siesta
when it breaks down and must be repaired. The fun made of him is compounded when by coincidence three other such litters arrive at the tiny
village, perhaps, it is agreed, all there are in France. Scarron's most amusing
incident involving a four-wheeler is that in which the foolish clown Ragotin,
drunk and robbed of all his clothes, staggers toward a coach that has been
carrying an abbess and several nuns but is now stuck in the mud after a
heavy rain. The coachman and a group of priests trying to extricate the
cumbersome vehicle shield the eyes of the nuns and drive off the naked
clown.

After Scarron and Mrs. Manley the French have other prose fiction that
employs more advanced coaches in a more artistic way. Although he is best
known for *La Vie de Marianne* (1731-42) and *Le Paysan parvenu* (1734-35),
one of Marivaux's early stories is entitled *La Voiture embourbée* (*The Coach
Stuck in the Mud;* 1714).[20] Among the best coach stories ever told, it exploits
all the possibilities the motif offers, thereby excelling Mrs. Manley and
rivaling Fielding, Smollett, and Sterne. The first-person narrator takes the
stagecoach to Nemours with four other passengers—a middle-aged mother,
her vivacious daughter, a young, self-centered bachelor, and a fat business-
man. At first the narrator pays no attention to his companions because he
falls asleep to recover from his late hours at a carnival. Waking up half an
hour before lunch stop, he takes out his tobacco, gives some to the mother,
and discovers that everybody else wants some too, including the coachman
and postilion. Since tobacco, like wine, makes friends quickly, all seven are
soon laughing and friendly. When their good lunch is over they head for
the warm fire at the inn only to have the clock-watching coachman shout
"Allons!" and all climb reluctantly back into the carriage. After providing
an amusing character sketch of each of the five passengers, including himself, the narrator gives the amorous eye to each female when the other is not
looking, and the mother starts a conversation on romance and sentiment. All
the men join in, each displaying some vanity and, the two older ones especially, much interest in women. The lively and titillating discussion is interrupted when the coach comes to a sudden stop. It seems that the coachman
and postilion have dropped behind to start cocktail hour early, and the
horses, left to themselves, have headed for green onion grass by the roadside
and are now stuck in the mud as deeply as the wheels of the coach. Since
no amount of cursing, straining, or praying, in that order, disembogues the
coach, the five set off across a field to a small hamlet while the postilion goes
for help. The rest of the story is set in the village inn with its sparse menu
or in the local curé's home, where the narrator and landlady's son go for

more food. But before the coachman comes for them at five A.M., they are able to get a round of stories told, each story designed to fit the character telling it. If one omits these stories, which are an ingredient not just of almost every eighteenth-century novel but surely of almost every tale that traps its character in a coach, then Marivaux's *Voiture embourbée* is an amusing, highly realistic early novella with well-drawn characters and impressive local color.

Other important French eighteenth-century novelists—Lesage, Prévost, Crébillon, Rousseau, Laclos—found small need of carriages. One must remember, however, that Lesage set *Gil Blas* in Spain, where cross-country transportation, for men at least, was by horseback or, lacking that, muleback or mule-drawn wagons. Two minor French writers, however, kept the coach rolling delightfully through prose fiction, one being Thomas l'Affichard in 1737, the other being Gimat de Bonneval in 1753. L'Affichard's *Le Voyage interrompu (The Interrupted Trip)*[21] has three young men start out from Paris at five in the morning in a private coach for a weekend at a country place. They pick up an older friend, amusing and intellectual, for "ballast," and after each has had a nap they engage in witty conversation that includes discussion of the amorous dreams of one of them who is a widower. Stopping for lunch at an inn they pick up, politely but unwillingly, a thirty-five-year-old talkative woman, who joins them at lunch and then in the coach while one of the young men rides her mule beside them amid much teasing and many jokes. Like Marivaux's, this coach ride is interrupted, not with mud however but with a broken wheel, the one under the heavy Mme Braille, who takes back her mule and rides on leaving them stranded. As with Marivaux the rest of the story has little to do with traveling, since the four men cross a vineyard to the home of a wealthy farmer who has not only an abundance of food, wine, and clean linen but a beautiful daughter, educated in Paris, for the poorest of the young men to marry. *Le Voyage de Mantes (The Trip to Mantes)*,[22] by de Bonneval, like l'Affichard's story is constructed around a holiday, not a weekend but a summer to be spend in a country home to which a wealthy Parisian judge, M. Hugon, takes his wife, daughter, son, servants, menagerie of pets, and apprentice clerk, all in a large carriage. Each stop at an inn is given in detail, two coachmen in one inn yard get in a fight over interlocked wheels, two dogs fight at another, a curé joins them in the coach for two days, they picnic by the side of the road, they encounter storms and good weather, and all the time the narrator-clerk and the daughter are concentrating on how to obtain privacy in order to make love. Like Marivaux and l'Affichard, de Bonneval is fascinatingly successful until he ends the journey and turns his tale into a romance, this one cynical rather than sentimental.

So by the time Fielding, Smollett, Sterne, Mackenzie, Fanny Burney, and other British novelists were exploiting the coach motif, it was a well-

established tradition in European fiction. Passing reluctantly over Mackenzie's thirty-seventh chapter of *The Man of Feeling* (1771), which imprisons
six people for two days in a stagegoach, more reluctantly over Evelina's
thirty-third letter (1778) and its account of the farcical holdup of Madam
Duval's coach by Sir Clement and Captain Mirvan, and far more reluctantly
over Sterne's famous Abbess of Andouillets and her mule-drawn calash
(*Tristram Shandy,* VII; 1765), we can concentrate on Fielding and Smollett.

Fielding had little use for coaches in his last two novels, but *Joseph
Andrews* (1742) could hardly do without them. After Joseph is beaten,
robbed, and left naked, Fielding sends along a stagecoach in order to give
us his version of the story of the Good Samaritan. The coachman, as always,
must meet his schedule and cannot stop, a hypocritical woman passenger is
prudish and wants no naked man aboard, while a lawyer argues that they
must legally take him along or be fined; only the poor postilion gives Joseph
a coat and helps him inside, where the man of wit fits his bawdy jokes to
the occasion. Later, Parson Adams and Mrs. Slipslop, riding in another
public coach, converse and listen to a fellow woman passenger's story of the
unfortunate Leonora, which Fielding interrupts with a comic scene at one
of the many inns he lets his readers enter. Adams finds the injured Joseph
at the inn but is temporarily unable to get him a seat in the coach because
Miss Graveairs refuses to ride with a servant. All is well, however, when Miss
Graveairs's father arrives to take her into his private carriage and we discover that she is herself a former servant and her father nouveau riche. The
coachman, now behind schedule, pushes his passengers into the vehicle only,
Fielding brilliantly records, that they may everyone get out again to
retrieve some article left behind, the coachman fuming all the time. Fielding,
who traveled much, knew his roads, coaches, inns, and people so well that
with the aid of his training in drama and such of his favorite authors as
Cervantes, Marivaux, and almost surely Mary Manley he was in *Joseph
Andrews* able to take advantage of the stagegoach motif perhaps as artistically and in as varied a fashion as anyone ever has.

Smollett's best coach story may be found in *Ferdinand Count Fathom*
(1753; Chaps. 27-30) when Fathom arrives in England, takes a post chaise to
Deal in order to catch the London stagecoach, pretends to know no English,
observes the flourishing countryside, judges at length each of his five companions, becomes almost fatally involved with one of them at an inn, which
produces still other characters, and ends by seducing a naive young girl
passenger on her way to the big city to start life as a mercer's apprentice.
This fictional trip is so much like that of a foreigner in a strange land that
it has been compared to the real travel account of the same road given a few
years later by the Italian Joseph Baretti.[23] But *Humphrey Clinker* (1771)
employs coaches from first to last. In it Smollett is able to let the irascible
Matt Bramble attack not only the conspicuous consumption of those people

who have expensive carriages but also the vehicle-infested highways of England and the streets of London: "The porters and chairmen trot with their burthens. People, who keep their own equipages, drive through the streets at full speed. Even citizens, physicians, and apothecaries, glide in their chariots like lightning. The hackney-coachmen make their horses smoke, and the pavement shakes under them. . . . In a word, the whole nation seems to be running out of their wits."[24] Matt, accompanied by his set of "originals," must rent a coach for the trip from Bath to London and then another for the long journey north to Scotland and back to Wales. Unostentatious, he is content with only four horses, although the coach carries himself, sister Tabby, niece Lydia, and servant Winifred, while Lydia's brother Jery and his servant ride horses.

But the coach is not just a means of transportation for the group; it is a structural and comic device. Jery early gives a character sketch of each of the four occupants, including that of the servant Win holding Chowder in her lap, Chowder, we know, being vicious enough to bite people but not so indiscreet as that other lap dog held by Lucian's stoic philosopher in another horse-drawn vehicle centuries before.[25] On the way to London, Matt's coach goes too fast downhill, causing a horse to fall, the coach to turn over, and the footman, bitten by Tabby's Chowder, to get impertinent, get fired, and make way for the hiring of "a shabby country fellow," named Humphrey Clinker, who happens to be nearby. On the way to Scotland, with Humphrey, Jery, and Jery's man on horses and two postilions handling the four pulling the coach, the travelers discover the roads to be in bad shape after heavy spring rains, a fact that gives Matt an opportunity to curse bad roads and heavy turnpike taxes. Near Stockton, while crossing a deep gutter made by a storm, "the coach was so hard strained, that one of the irons, which connected the frame, snapt, and the leather sling on the same side, cracked in the middle." All this to allow Humphrey to take over, become both smith and leather worker and repair the coach in an hour at an old abandoned smithy. Again the coach, fording a stream, is suddenly struck and overturned by a wall of water let loose by a broken mill head. And again, Humphrey, even more than Jery, comes to the rescue, snatches his sweetheart Win to safety, and then plunges back, at the risk of his own life, to save Matt and earn a spot in his master's will even before it is known that he is Matt's bastard son. Although in *Humphrey Clinker* long and lively coach conversations are lacking, as are the stories told by passengers trapped in the coach, Smollett has incorporated most of the elements traditionally afforded by the motif and added others.

And, it is now obvious, many of these elements could be and often were used artistically in a day when coaches and roads were improving, when people traveled constantly—on the Grand Tour, to the large cities, to country estates, to war—and when the evolving novel was taking advantage of every device, as well as every literary form, it found available. The coach motif, drawn from actual experiences or from the literature of travel, provided the novelist with a means of transporting his characters; of selecting them so they could be described as a John Earle or a la Bruyère would have described them; of letting them tell stories of other people or of themselves; of stopping them at inns for comedy, satire, intrigue, as well as for rest or food; of letting them see pleasant countryside or storms; of giving them a chance to note the rules of traveling or the quality of coaches, coachmen, or roads; of providing them an opportunity to break down or get stuck in the mud in order to see new people or have unexpected adventures; or of engaging them in conversation that could reveal character or be witty, bawdy, sentimental, or even intellectual enough for a Samuel Johnson. And, of course, it is a motif that has lived on in fiction—in trains such as the Orient Express, in airplanes like those flown by Saint-Exupéry in *Le Vol de nuit*, or in the wayward buses of a John Steinbeck. But from the fiction of Marivaux to that of Smollett, the fascinating horse-drawn coach was a structural tool that the new novel often needed.

When readers of English fiction think of inns, they turn first to Fielding and Smollett, perhaps to Sterne. In *Joseph Andrews* (II.i) Fielding calls his interchapters "inns," where the reader "may stop and take a glass, or any other refreshment." He makes the parallel in the last of eight chapters that relate the incidents at Mr. Tow-Wouse's inn, where we meet host and hostess, Betty the chambermaid, Barnabas the local parson, a quack doctor, and Adams and Joseph and witness the reception accorded them. It is by no means the last of Fielding's many inns, among which is one in *Tom Jones* where Justice Fielding had often stayed himself, the sign of the Bell at Gloucester, operated by the brother of George Whitefield, who, however, was "absolutely untainted with the pernicious principles of Methodism" (VIII.viii). But the account of Jones's brief stay here is preceded by forty pages that tell of his adventures at another inn, where Northerton breaks Tom's head with a bottle and Partridge enters his life. And it precedes by only a few chapters the even longer and more famous section dealing with the inn at Upton where Tom engages in battles "of the amorous kind" with Mrs. Waters and where Sophia also spends a night and leaves her muff for the conscience-stricken Tom before they all hurry off separately on the road to London. Smollett's inns are just as important to him, two of the best of his inn scenes being perhaps in *Fathom*—at Dover and on the way to London; and just as Fielding has Tom Jones at the sign of the Bell in Gloucester, Smollett opens *Sir Launcelot Greaves* with a scene at the equally famous real Black Lion at Weston on the highway between York and London. Similarly

Matt Bramble's entourage follows Smollett's own route between Edinburgh and London and occasionally spends the night at an inn he seems to know well. Novelists in fact, like many other writers of the mid-eighteenth century, were able to depend on their own travels for knowledge of and experiences at public hostelries in England.

But each of them also had ample precedent in eighteenth-century European fiction, and not just in Mrs. Manley's *Fortunate Foundling* (1744) or, better still, her *Stagecoach to Exeter* (1696) with its bills of fare and curious characters in the inns along the highway. For inns are found in Defoe's *Moll Flanders* (1722), where Moll both marries her clerk and saves her previous "husband" Jemy at an inn at Brickhill; in Mrs. Davys's *Merry Wanderer* (1725), where the narrator spends an amusing night at a public house after arriving from Ireland; and in *Jamaica Lady* (1720), where Galenicus and Holmeria rob the innkeeper and there are two pairs of late-night exchanges of bedfellows. On the Continent, Lesage in *Gil Blas* (1715 ff.) is just one of the best early eighteenth-century novelists to provide the traveler with inns of all sorts. On the fourth page he brings the protagonist and his mule to an inn (*auberge, cabaret, hôtellerie*) at Peñaflor, where he encounters a babbling host, a pretty hostess, and a parasitic "cavalier" who devours Gil Blas's omelet and drinks his wine. And Lesage, a favorite with Fielding and Smollett, was as dependent on inns as they, from Gil Blas's not-so-sumptuous *auberge* at Toledo, in which he dines and meets intriguing conversationalists between the shows put on by the acting troupe, to the Lavish "hôtel garni" where he stays in Madrid (VII.ix-xii). Nor are these early eighteenth-century novels the earliest precedents for the popular use of inns in fiction: Throughout the 1600s, and earlier, they are found in the bourgeois novels, the nouvelles, the romans comiques from Cervantes through Scarron.

Lazarillo de Tormes (1554; Chap. 34) has one delightful scene at an inn just outside Valladolid, where the chief of picaros tries to eat a whole side of goat and observes a young gallant overpower two cavaliers who expect to take their sister Claire from him; and early British poetry and drama have their Tabard Inns and Boars Head Taverns; but without question Cervantes is the great archetypal novelist for fictional inns, not just for the seventeenth century but for all times. Don Quixote's first sally takes him to the inn where two prostitutes are great ladies, his armor must be protected from muleteers, and the harried host finally knights him so he will leave. The most famous, certainly the most imitated, inn scene in literature comes at the opening of Book Three. Here after the "Rencounter" between the Yanguesian carriers, Sancho finds an inn whose kind hostess and her daughter put his badly mauled master to bed in the room where the dwarfish servant girl Maritornes, intending to sleep with a mule carrier, causes ludicrous midnight mistakes and where the sore and bruised Don Quixote and Sancho try the

Knight's "blessed medicine," which cures one and nearly kills the other. Perhaps the best inn scene of the later and more mellow Part Two is that favorite one in which the puppeteers put on their show and Don Quixote mounts the stage to demolish the cardboard Moors (III.xv-xvii).

Scarron, largely because the *Roman comique* (1651-55) is the story of a troupe of traveling actors, needed inns even more than Cervantes did, and some of his inn scenes are as masterfully comic as any in *Don Quixote*. The most ludicrous surely is that in which Rancune (Chap. 6), pretending to be afflicted with urinary problems, graciously lies next to the wall so his stranger bedfellow, a merchant, may have the open—or chamber-pot—side of the bed, then keeps his bedfellow awake for hours passing the pot, even though Rancune returns it "sans avoir pissé une seule goutte," until finally he lets loose, fills the pot, and spills it on the merchant, thereby driving him angrily away and freeing the whole bed for the actor, who comfortably sleeps away the rest of the night. Again Scarron's fool Ragotin happens to step into a chamber pot at an inn and must wait till day for an ironsmith to come and file it from his foot. But then, in this comical novel hardly four chapters go by without at least one inn scene.

Seventeenth-century British fiction also has its share of inns. Elkanah Settle's retelling of the life of *That Notorious Imposter Will. Morrell* (1694)[26] was advertised as fact but is probably more fiction. At any rate, the picaresque counterfeiter, con man, and physician Don Juan Morrell and his Sanchoesque companion Tom stop off in many inns, in one of which Morrell marries the innkeeper's daughter and absconds with her money and belongings. In his first experience with inns, however, he is able as a lad to marry the young widow innkeeper only when his old tar bedfellow privately informs the widow that her young suitor's private parts are more those of "a horse than a man." After the ceremony, the widow, having discovered that Morrell is no larger than her first husband, disappointedly pays him off and parts with him. Throughout the seventeenth and eighteenth centuries inns were popular in fiction as backdrops for such comic scenes and incidents, but they were more than that.

They also provided a gathering place for players, lovers, picaros, sailors, outlaws, travelers of all kinds—over and over each of the novels mentioned here calls its characters "our travellers"—when they need to stop not just for food and lodging but to tell their stories to each other, read books aloud, or offer disquisitions to captive audiences. Here was the place, the planned excuse, for the novelist to insert an epic, ornamental story, a digression of any kind. Thus the curate in *Don Quixote* reads aloud the romantic tale of Anselmo, Lothario, and Camilla at the same inn where the maid Maritornes had earlier visited a number of beds in one room (Pt. Two, IV.v ff.). Thus at a "hôtel garni" the actress Laura tells Gil Blas the story of that part of her life that has gone by since he saw her last (VII.vii), and Captain Chinchilla in another hotel tells his autobiography (VII.xii). Thus in *Tom Jones* Sophia, at the first inn after Upton, listens to "The History of Mrs. Fitzpatrick" (XI.iv); and, much earlier, the occupants of Marivaux's *La Voiture embourbée* (1714), stranded in a barren country inn, spend the night telling each other stories both realistic and romantic while waiting for their public carriage to be repaired. One can well believe that the early novel could hardly have done without its inns, as a structuring device but also for local color and humor.

There is, however, a parallel tradition, an even stronger one, that involves inns in travel accounts. Readers of the travels of well-known British novelists of the eighteenth century will remember Fielding's battles with his hostess in the Isle of Ryde at the beginning of *The Journal of A Voyage to Lisbon*, Smollett's dissatisfaction with most of the public houses in France as he describes them in *Travels through France and Italy*, or in *A Sentimental Journey* Sterne's first meal in France, his begging Franciscan monk, his preface written in the *désobligeant*, the sentimental scene with the pretty woman in the *remise*, the bargaining with the innkeeper for a chaise—all in the inn and inn yard at Calais and all perhaps more or less from Sterne's own experiences. Or French readers may remember that the fiction writer Challe wrote a *Journal d'un voyage fait aux Indes Orientales* in 1690-91 (1721) that reads like a novel and begins with his experiences at inns in Brest as he waits for his squadron to sail—breaking a bottle with old friends at the Image Saint-André and rehearsing a little drama at the Pavillon that will help him buy provisions for the squadron at the price he wants to pay (65-67). Now it is true that Challe, Smollett, and Fielding all knew Cervantes and Scarron almost by heart—each translated, imitated, or wrote a continuation of *Don Quixote*—but each, as well as Sterne, was widely read in travel literature and was a part of that tradition of travel writing so firmly established even before *Don Quixote* or the *Roman comique*.

As the early European novelists knew them, however, inns were not so many centuries old. Although the ancient orientals set up sheds and one-room empty huts along their highways and the Romans had post houses for the convenience of travelers, public hostelries for charge apparently were introduced in Europe only by the fourteenth century. Pilgrims in England and on the Continent were accustomed to asking for and receiving hospitality while well-to-do travelers often carried letters of introduction that procured them entrance to the homes of ambassadors, merchants, or city fathers as well as to all churches and hospices that honored St. Christopher, the patron of travelers. Thomas Coryat, for example, traveling in Italy and the Low Countries about 1610, five years after *Don Quixote*, Part One, often slept under the stars, but he also often stayed in empty houses by the road side or with people such as Sir Henry Wotton, ambassador at Rome, to whom he was recommended.[27] As early as the fifteenth century Edward IV worked not only at improving highways but at establishing better inns; and since his family badge was the white hart, a number of rest houses called "White Hart" came into existence, such as the popular one on the Exeter coach road. Many inns, especially in England, are associated with literary figures—the Ship Inn between London and Stratford where Shakespeare is said to have written parts of early plays; the George in Salisbury where Cromwell slept and where Pepys, although sleeping on silk sheets and eating well, was charged too much; or the Old Rose in Workingham where Swift, Gay, Pope, and Arbuthnot are said to have been inspired to immortalize in verse its sexy bartender, the "sweet Molly Mog."[28]

But there are more than legends about European inns; travelers regularly ate and slept in them, observed customs and experienced adventures in them, and wrote about them in letters and journals that would, whether published or not, demonstrate the strength of a tradition that preceded and then paralleled that of the early novel. The evidence is fascinating.

Although Coryat about 1610 sometimes slept in empty houses or on the ground, he stayed more often in public inns, describing their two-hour evening meals in Switzerland, Germany, and Holland as well as the custom of holding a tankard of beer in the hand all evening while drinking with friends and strangers. He quotes the long Latin inscription over the door of the Golden Winged Lion (the arms of Venice) on Saint Mark's Mountain in the foothills of the Alps in Italy, reports on the "very soft feather beddes" in all the inns of Switzerland, describes the stove in the "two Storkes" in Zurich and the baths provided by the Bear, the Crowne, the Flower, and the Oxe in Baden, and at "Brooke" near the Rhine finds "the kindest host" on his "whole voyage out of England." Easily his longest description of inn life is that of the Three Kings, the best and most patronized public house in Lyons. Coryat tells of groups who lodged there when he did, of music and dancing in the yard, of his religious debates with a curious Turk, and especially of the amusing murals on the courtyard walls.[29]

Fynes Moryson, traveling the Continent in the 1590s but publishing in the next decade, finds fewer good inns than Coryat does, but he regularly tells what they feed him, records all their prices, and has some entertaining stories about them. At Voghera, for example, he and one of his countrymen meet at an inn, each pretending to be from the Continent; but after testing each other's German, then French, then Italian, they discover they are both English.[30] Again, while traveling alone on a most expensive horse and headed for the Alpine pass into Switzerland, he stops at an inn where the host eyes his mount, notes what a splendid animal it is, and then, without asking Moryson, turns it loose with his own herd so "that the rascall might make himself sport with his covering of the mares" and of course so that he might produce fine colts for the innkeeper.[31]

And through the seventeenth century, travelers continued to be as exact and entertaining about the inns they visited. A young German bon viveur, Just Zinzerling, for example, made an enjoyable tour of France and published in Latin (1616) an attractive account in which he recorded stays at a number of good inns, especially noting their menus.[32] At the Mulberry-Bush in Saumur the wine comes from the freshest of cellars; in Picardy the innkeepers supply their guests with nothing but bed and bread—anything else has to be ordered in second-class eating places; and the public house at Blamont is the best between Strasbourg and Paris. Even more attractive is the report of the German Abraham Goelnitz, who traveled Belgium and France a decade later and whose Latin journal of 1631 had other editions in the seventeenth century.[33] Traveling on foot and by horse, Goelnitz finds certain parts of France and certain small towns to have uncomfortable inns, but he does find more elegant ones in the larger towns. His most detailed account is of a rustic inn on which he and his small party stumble late at night in a rainstorm and where the old innkeeper meets them on the road to guide them in, where the bread and wine taste like nectar and ambrosia, and where the straw pallet in front of the great fireplace is better than a bed. In the 1640s John Evelyn on an extended tour stays in the famous hotel at Saint-Cloud so luxurious that he and others pay the price just to have the experience of staying in it; and at Orleans he sleeps at an inn where during the night a cat has kittens on his bed, one of which is so deformed that it dies.[34] Brunel (1655) very early in his account compares Spanish inns with those of England and explains how he regularly left his inn in Spain in order to buy food in butcher shops.[35] Even the botanist John Ray consistently tells of the inns he stayed in on the Continent. One of the best accounts of a single inn is by the dramatist J.-F. Regnard, who, somewhat like the German Goelnitz before him but more like the novelist Marivaux after him in *La Voiture embourbée*, recounts at length his comfortable reception—the food, fire, bed, the conversation and entertainment—at the inn in Cambrai that receives him and his companions after their coach overturns in the mud during a storm.[36] Over and over such seventeenth-century descriptions of real inns are as fascinating as those of the novelists.

That travelers were telling others of their inns even by the time of *Don Quixote* can be shown by looking not only at the accounts of Coryat and Fynes Moryson but also at those written by young Torquato Tasso (1571) and a series of ambassadors to France in the 1570s and 1580s.[37] Even better is the record found in the wonderful journal kept by Montaigne on his trip to Rome in 1580-81. He always gives the name of the inn in which the company spend the night—the Angel at Plombières near Bar-le-duc, the Unicorn the next night, the Sign of the Grapes (le Raisin) at Mulhouse, the Rose at Innsbruck, the Eagle at Brixen, and so on. And the price of food for men and horses, the cleanliness of the rooms and the beds, the kinds of sheets, curtains, or windows, the quality of the food and wine, the friendliness of the host and hostess—all these he tells about. At the Raisin Montaigne learns from his host some of the history of the Huguenots in Switzerland. At the Ange he stays several days to drink the water and take the baths for his health. At Rovereto just inside Italy he praises the menu—including huge escargots, peeled truffles sliced thin and soaked in oil, oranges, olives, lemons —and describes the beds at length, even though he prefers those of Germany and France. All that is lacking here to bring the inns of his sixteenth-century journal even closer to those of the budding novel is a late-evening tale told in one of them to pass away the time or enliven the account, a spilled chamber pot, a midnight trading of beds, perhaps a servant like Maritornes in *Don Quixote* or Betty the chambermaid in *Joseph Andrews*. But all of that is the product of invention, of imagination playing on the novelist's experiences at real inns, with a reading of fiction such as that of Cervantes, Scarron, and Lesage, and with an immersion in travel literature, that primary source for exact knowledge not only of inns but of coaches and oceans and all the motive and leitmotive that relate to them.

CHAPTER NINE

Character Types

You can't put the whole of a character into a book. . . . You must select traits. You must take many traits for granted, and refer to them in a way to show that they are conventionalized. . . . No novelist can always be creating absolutely new, or fresh, characters. *Arnold Bennett*[1]

No doubt novelists have learned something from biography and autobiography—surely from drama—about selecting and developing characters. In the case of travel literature, we have seen how the narrator-persona, as with the first-person narrator in fiction, reveals his or her own personality and may be judged reliable or unreliable, as the adventurer Pinto, the buccaneer Dampier, and the swashbuckling, intellectual Challe were exposing themselves before Lesage and Defoe let Gil Blas and Crusoe tell their stories. Or, if the travel writer dealt with someone else, we have seen how he developed that person's character, as Joinville developed Saint Louis and Pigafetta reported on Magellan. Furthermore, we have noticed certain character types common to travel literature and the novel, among them the questing or fleeing hero, the picaresque protagonist, and the adventurers such as Lahontan of the seventeenth century or Neuhof and the von der Trenck cousins in the eighteenth.

If we disregard the heroic hero for having been dealt with at length, and perhaps the adventurer and the picaro for the same reason, among the more attractive characters found in both fiction and travels is the older and wiser companion, an intellectual guide, often the hero's initiator. The archetype, better than the Chiron of Achilles, is of course Mentor, who with the help of the wise Athena advises Telemachus as he searches for his father Odysseus. Mentor, as well as his pupil, was recreated in 1699 by Fénelon in *Télémaque*,[2] a piece of exemplary fiction widely read by eighteenth-century novelists such as Fielding. And, as all historians of the romance tell us, since Homer's time this character is almost necessary in the novel of search and growth. In an important way, negatively or positively, depending on the point of view, each picaro learns from each of his masters—Lazarillo from his blind beggar or his lawyer, Simplicius from his venerable hermit. Each hero of an eighteenth-century *conte philosophique* has one or more initiators

—Gulliver has his kindly gray Houyhnhnm, Gaudentio his mid-African master, Rasselas his Imlac, and Candide his optimistic Pangloss and his pessimistic Martin. He is of course a chief character, whether for satire or not, in novels with the Grand Tour, and he is often important in other kinds of novels. In Gracián's allegorical *El Criticón* (1651-57), for example, a character representing reason leads one representing passion; in Prévost's *Cleveland*, Mrs. Ryder guides her niece Cécile through North America; Parson Adams travels English roads advising Joseph Andrews; and throughout their journeys Diderot's Jacques argues with his *maître* about fatalism.

Such initiators are found in travel literature through the ages. Sometimes the informed companion appears briefly, as when the traveler stops for advice from a local guide. At other times the association is important. Pinto, for example, accompanies his beloved friend and spiritual mentor Francis Xavier to Japan in 1551; Pyrard de Laval lives with and learns much from the kindly "Lord" of the Maldive island where he is stranded in 1601; John Ray, the botanist, not only acts as the wise model for his younger companion, the ornithologist Willughby, but when his friend dies prematurely, Ray edits and publishes both their travel books (1673, 1675); Boswell travels Scotland with his teacher Samuel Johnson; and about 1790 the naive young Herman is guided through New York and Pennsylvania by the older, more experienced Crèvecoeur. For two hundred years, however, the obvious travel mentor was the tutor accompanying his charge or charges on the Grand Tour, as their "governor" Marcombes accompanied each of three pairs of the Boyle brothers and wrote letters home, or Richard Lassels went half a dozen times as mentor before publishing his guide for other Grand Tourists. And again the voyage imaginaire is a link between the more sophisticated novel and the *récit de voyage*, for it often makes use of this type of character, as in the anonymous *Épigone* (1658), where the hero is indoctrinated by a good old man; or Foigny's *Jacques Sadeur* (1676), where old Suaïns for many a page must introduce Sadeur to Australian life and ideas; or Veiras's *History of the Sevarites* (1675), in which we learn of the Sun-King Sevarias and his Grand Tour with a Christian tutor named Giovanni.[3]

Closely related to the teacher-initiator, sometimes overlapping his responsibilities, is the loyal companion, the trusted servant, the man Friday. In fiction he is of ancient vintage of course, as in the epic, where Gilgamesh travels and fights beside his close friend and one-time opponent Enkidu, or Aeneas is accompanied by his fidus Achates and Roland by his Oliver. With the tales of chivalry, when the companion becomes a squire or servant,[4] it must follow that Don Quixote has his Sancho, Will Morrell his Tom, Don Tomaso his Don Pedro, or, finally, Candide his clever Cacambo. And not only does Crusoe have Friday, but Defoe gives Captain Singleton the loyal Quaker William and to Captain Misson he assigns the deistic lieutenant

Caraccioli, while Prévost lets Cleveland find his Friday in a North American Indian named Igloo.[5] Even in the third volume of Erskine's *Madame Richelieu* (1744), the heroine persuades Arabella to accompany her on travels through Italy and Spain, both in men's clothes. So common, in fact, is this character in fiction that he or she could only be derived from real life where almost any traveler needs someone to go along for company, for support, for safety.

That notion is supported by the history of travel literature. There the companion can be a close friend, a clerical colleague, a spouse, a servant, a superior, even an enemy. While a Coryat or a Careri may travel alone in one sense, neither is really alone for any length of time on any leg of a journey; and seamen, tourists, and guides, businessmen, government officials, and priests seldom set out by themselves. Thus in South America, Cabeza de Vaca goes with his secretary, and so does Montaigne on his journey to Italy, while Father Ricci has his subordinates as companions in China, all in the sixteenth century. Thus Timberlake, leaving his ship early in the seventeenth century to visit the Holy Land alone, finds a "good Moor" who stays with him, shows him how to avoid trouble, even saves his life; and in the same decade Lescarbot agrees to accompany a friend to Canada just as, three decades later, Mandelslo accepts the invitation to go with his friend Olearius, secretary for an embassy to Russia. In this tradition, John Dunton's Don Kainophilus takes along his Philaret, who dies and is mourned in Part III of *A Voyage round the World* (1691). Perhaps nowhere are the novel and travel literature closer than they are with the companion travelers.

Almost as popular in literature, especially in the eighteenth-century novel, is the Noble Savage, nurtured and advertised by travel literature. This character comes from every part of the less sophisticated world—the Americas, Africa, the Orient, the South Seas—in fact, from any nation's farm or ranch or jungle lands. The discovery of America gave much impetus to the myth, and Montaigne's *Des Canibales* of the 1580s depended even more on voyagers to the New World than on Lucretius and his kind of primitivism. Much has been written about the Noble Savage, especially since Benjamin Bissell (1925) and H.N. Fairchild (1928) worked with the American Indian in English literature and Gilbert Chinard (1934) and his followers wrote of him in French literature of the eighteenth century.[6] And while there was a tradition out of Columbus's Dr. Chanca that made the American natives almost animals—"their degradation is greater than that of any beast"—there is the other tradition described in Martire's *Decades,* which by 1530 asserted that the American natives "seeme to live in the goulden worlde."[7] It was these handsome primitives that in the de Bry collections of voyages appeared as Greek heroes in romanticized pictures that would be imitated for over a hundred years.[8] Chinard thinks with some reason that the Rousseau-Saint Pierre-Chateaubriand philosophical and literary version of the idealized, simple, virtuous savage who knew no superiors and was puzzled by sophistication was inspired most by the seventeenth-century travel accounts of père du Tertre, which were both detailed and ornate.[9] At any rate, one can begin with a strong Continental tradition that leads from Las Casas, the de Brys, Champlain, and du Tertre and goes through père Labat and other eighteenth-century travelers. Next, one turns to those books that fostered the English detestation of Spanish cruelty—for example, the translation of Las Casas by Edward Phillips, Milton's nephew, called *Tears of the Indians* (1656). Third, one reads those English travel writers in America such as John Lawson in Carolina (1708).[10] And fourth, one adds the accounts of Bougainville and Cook in Tahiti. Then one arrives at the strong Noble Savage tradition in the novel of the seventeenth and eighteenth centuries.

It is so strong, in fact, that one can only suggest starting with Aphra Behn's prince-slave Oroonoko, a vivid pagan contrast with wicked European Christians, and Prévost's primitive Abenakis in North America, who join the sophisticated refugee Cleveland in a long utopian interlude. Then, passing over a number of the imaginary voyages in Gove's bibliography which include natives of the New World, one arrives at the second half of the eighteenth century—Rousseauism, the French Revolution, the American War of Independence, and the opening of the South Seas—when the novel exploited the Noble Savage most. Bissell is no doubt correct in believing that no fiction of that time presents the American Indian in a more favorable light than does Shebbeare's *Lydia* (1755), in which the New England Indian Cannassatego exemplifies the tradition in every way: He is the naive commentator on corrupt Europe; the ideal in simple regimen and clean thoughts; the willing defender of virtue and honor when Europeans hold back; the one cheated and scorned as stupid while maintaining his integrity in spite of temptations. He is even the handsome warrior compared, as in the de Bry drawings, with the "statue of Apollo which adorns the Belvidera."[11]

Used even more as a contrast with profligate Europeans, however, is the hero of an anonymous, slashing satiric fiction called *Memoirs of the Life and Adventures of Tsonnonthonian, A King of the Nation called Roundheads* (1763), which, while written in the "excremental" method of Smollett's *History and Adventures of an Atom* (1769), borrows not only from travel literature for the tradition of the Noble Savage but, as James Foster has shown, leans heavily on favorite French travel books—Lahontan, Lafitau, Lebeau, and Charlevoix, especially—for local color and even incidents. There are at least six direct borrowings from Lebeau alone.[12] And Foster, who rediscovered the book and calls it "truly original," concludes that "In no other English novel of the century do the Indian and his customs figure so conspicuously."[13] About the same time there were any number of such novels, not just in England but in France where Prévost's influence was perhaps no stronger than it was in England, among them Mercier's *L'Homme sauvage* (1767), banned immediately after publication, in which two noble savages, brother and sister, grow up together, love and live together without sin until civilized Europeans teach them to be sinful. In England, Mackenzie's *The Man of the World* (1773) has a hero who, after failing in Europe, goes in the army to America, is captured by the Cherokees, and in the fashion of Rousseau's Emile learns from them to love nature and seek virtue. Similarly in Charlotte Lennox's *Euphemia* (1790), the son of Euphemia and her ignoble husband in New York is taken early by savages, reared in nature, given the name "The Huron," and like Hermsprong in Bage's novel (1796) sent back to be both a model for the simple life of the heart and a foil to decadence. This Noble Savage who came from the travelers, with more than a little basis in reality, was often returned to them in the form of a bias which they took with them to America or the South Seas and which often colored their observations, as with Chateaubriand on his journey to the New World in the 1790s.

One branch of the large Noble Savage family is the presumably naive American or other character who in a debate with a European is easily awarded the palm by his creator. He is foreshadowed in the account of an old Indian Columbus talks with and in another in which the Protestant de Léry records a discussion with a Topinambou wise man in Brazil (1578). He is foreshadowed even better in Lescarbot's four-page version of Champlain's conversation with an American native about religion (1609). But this favorite in imaginative literature is fully developed only in Lahontan's popular volumes about Canada, after which he blends with the philosophic oriental created by Europeans following the great Rites controversy that grew out of the accounts of China by Le Conte and other Jesuits at the very end of the seventeenth century.[14] Lahontan's *Voyages,* two volumes in French, was published in Holland in 1703 and immediately translated into English before going all over Europe. The 1703 version in English includes a conversation between Lahontan and a Huron named The Rat. This addition became the chief attraction in the third French volume, which appeared in Holland within months. Called *Supplément aux voyages du Baron de Lahontan. Ou l'on trouve des Dialogues curieux entre l'auteur et un sauvage de bon sens qui a voyagé ...*, it was expanded by Lahontan, perhaps with the encouragement or assistance of the writer Gueudeville, for the third of three volumes (bound in two) of a 1705 French edition. It is this *Supplément,* often republished by itself, in which The Rat has become Adario; and it is the *Supplément* which so many eighteenth-century thinkers knew, including Rousseau and the *Encyclopédistes.*

Adario is the name of a real Tionontati chief of the Hurons, also called Kondiaronk and The Rat.[15] In New France he led Hurons against the Iroquois, he signed treaties with the French, and he was honored by his allies and feared by the English and their Iroquois friends. Moreover, Lahontan may have known him personally while the two were at Fort Michilimackinac in 1688. At any rate, Adario was buried in Montreal with military honors in 1701, just in time for Lahontan to use his name for the "sauvage" who, as The Rat, is permitted only a few pages of attacks on the religion, laws, and self-interest of Europeans and then, as Adario, granted more than one hundred pages of such attacks. From then on, the uncorrupted man of nature with the orator's tongue became a standard character in fiction. With the English he was usually an Iroquois, as in *Tatler* 171 (1710) and *Spectator* 50 (1711) where the four "chiefs" display the natural life and attack sham religion; with the French he was most often a Huron, the natural enemy of the Iroquois and friend of France—the protagonist of Voltaire's *L'Ingénu* is a Huron. Adario blends with Swift's Brobdingnagian king attacking the "little odious vermin" of Europe and combines with Gulliver in Desfontaine's *Le Nouveau Gulliver* (1728), where, the author claims, one sees "the censure of all the polished nations, in the mouth of a virtuous savage."[16] After the middle of the century the Huron chief's cousins are found in Tahiti, especially after Bougainville brought back Aoutourou to Paris and Cook's ship brought Omoo to England. Bricaire de la Dixemarie, for example, uses Aoutourou in 1770 as spokesman for the philosophes in an attack on French society; Voltaire in 1775 published a conte philosophique that sends Orou to Tahiti with Cook to observe life there and comment on the softness of its religion; and Diderot's *Supplément au voyage de Bougainville* (1772) borrows not only Lahontan's title but his method in letting the wise old Tahitian reject the philosophy of Europe—especially its sex mores—as represented by the great Bougainville.[17]

But the tradition of Adario and the Tahitians was constantly being strengthened by reports of other real "savages." Three times Benjamin Franklin told stories, which he claimed to be true, of European Americans debating unsuccessfully with natives, the best of the three being one (1784) in which a Swedish minister loses out to a clever Indian who sweetly turns the Christian myth of the apple into a farce and then has his own creation story rejected in disgust.[18] Similar stories of Swedish, or Moravian, or other European ministers were published in the *London Magazine* (1760), the *Scots Magazine* (1761), and the *Philadelphia Magazine* (1789), often with requests for help in answering the unsophisticated questions of the savage—and replies were forthcoming. All of these stories could have been inspired by the life of the eighteenth-century Delaware warrior Glikhikan, who, in the opinion of other Indians, refuted the Christian doctrines as argued by

French priests in Canada, debated a Moravian missionary, was converted to Christianity in 1769, and was murdered and scalped by whites in 1782. And such stories, invented, exaggerated, or truthful, obviously inspired novelists such as Robert Bage, who in *Hermsprong* (1796) lets the hero's Roman Catholic mother in America reject Great Beaver's religious myths, which, as in the Franklin-Glikhikan branch of the Adario tradition, are made to sound much like those of Christianity. Adario, with a long lineage, had a strong hold on travelers and novelists.

In contrast to the heroic hero and his relatives—the mentor, the companion, the Noble Savage, and Adario—there are any number of less admirable characters or antiheroes common to travel literature and the novel, one of which is the highwayman. He is of course found in fiction from its beginnings, as in Apuleius's *Golden Ass*, and prominent in later picaresque fiction, as in *Lazarillo*, the *Roman comique*, *Gil Blas*, and *Moll Flanders*, in which Moll's favorite husband is an elusive robber on the roads. In *Humphrey Clinker* the highwayman is sentimentally reformed, much as Tom Jones overpowers a would-be robber on the road and then talks him into virtue. And a favorite fictional rescue scene is one involving a highwayman. In Davys's *The Reform'd Coquet; a Novel* (1725), for example, Amoranda and her guardian Formator are returning home in a coach when they are attacked by masked men who are successfully routed by the valiant Formator.[19] The real highwayman is not only just as old in travel literature but even more ubiquitous. Pilgrims such as Chaucer's banded together for safety against him, and travelers as late as Smollett worried constantly about encountering him, on Continental or English roads. Late in the seventeenth century he was much written about, especially in the picaresque-like rogue biographies that were advertised as being real. One of the best of these, *Jackson's Recantation* 1674), tells the story of a notorious, highly successful highwayman with his companion, his carefully laid schemes, and his many robberies; and it even pauses for some pages to provide an essay on how to be a highwayman and how to guard against one. Defoe was not the only one to write up the lives of highwaymen such as the famous Jack Shepherd, a model for Macheath in *The Beggar's Opera*.[20]

While the highwayman in fiction was often treated as a hero, sometimes sentimentally, the amorous sea captain, often a pirate, was nearly always a villain. This character is of course found as one of the sea elements in the Greek romance formula, beginning with the *Aethiopica*, is employed in *Don Quixote* (IV.xxi-xxiv), and is popular in the seventeenth-century French *roman*.[21] The eighteenth century retained him for its fiction, especially in England; and through the century he was the seagoing cousin to the lecherous country squire found in a hundred British novels—Squire B in *Pamela*, the venal baronet in Mackenzie's *The Man of Feeling* (1771), the fox-hunting

Sindal who in his *Man of the World* (1775) seduces Harriet by using opium, and all those lords who in the novels by Robert Bage are memorable for their license in matters of sex, such as Lord Winterbottom in *Barham Downs* 1784), who even keeps a pimp. But the lecherous country squire is not a character in travel literature while the amorous captain is. Although Hakluyt, Purchas, de Bry, and other collectors have no stories of such characters, the literature of the Barbary corsairs contains a thousand of them for the romantic imagination to feed on.[22] And after 1670 buccaneer Captain, later Lieutenant Governor, Henry Morgan was notorious for lusting after female captives. In a raid on Panama, Exquemelin says, "as soon as any beautiful woman was brought as a prisoner to his presence, he used all the means he could ... to bend her to his pleasure."[23] In fact, Exquemelin, himself a buccaneer, is horrified at Morgan's attempts on the chastity of one Spanish woman who rejects his advances—first mild, then cruel—until at last he lets her go. Stories of the buccaneers and Mediterranean corsairs were combined in the early eighteenth century with other kinds of tales, those, for example, about the degenerate life in the pirate stronghold of Madagascar so well known by Defoe's Captain Singleton and by those other captains found in his *History of the Pyrates*, in which captured women are sometimes treated mercifully and at other times divided up by lot among the men.

Although Defoe, except mildly in his *Pyrates*, did not capitalize on the erotic possibilities of such situations, by his day the eroticism was well established.[24] In *The Jamaica Lady* (1720), for example, the ship's master hired to take Bavia away from England and her scheming husband attempts her virtue but is diverted by the offer of a precious jewel, and later a lieutenant on Captain Fustian's man-of-war gains the favors of both Bavia and Holmesia, each a passenger for England; in *Cleveland*, Prévost lets the villainous Captain Will on an Atlantic crossing separate the widow Lallin from Cleveland, force her to be his mistress, and then forsake her; and the maid of the irresistible Lady Villars in Chetwood's *Boyle* (1726), with the crew's help, saves her mistress from ravishment by the lusting Captain Bourn, who has tricked her aboard his ship and sailed off. Eliza Haywood puts the amorous captain in nearly every one of her many sea plots. When in *Philidore and Placentia* (1727) the heroine takes ship to follow her beloved to Persia, the captain, overcome by "lust and rage," is about to rape her when corsairs attack, capture the ship, and sell the crew and passengers into slavery; in *The History of Montrano and Iseria*, the second in a collection of novels called *The Fatal Enquiry* (1767), a Dutch captain persuades his passenger Elphania, later a "queen," to become his mistress; and in *Idalia: or, The Unfortunate Mistress* (1742), the heroine is saved in exactly the way Placentia had been —the ship is attacked by corsairs. Similarly, Harriot in Charlotte Lennox's *The Life of Harriot Stuart* (1750) must fight off the lecherous captain on her return voyage from New York to England, just as the heroine of Sheb-beare's *Lydia* also barely escapes rape when the noble American Indian Cannassatego rescues her from Captain Bounce on the man-of-war carrying them across the Atlantic. It is this entire tradition that Fielding burlesques in *Jonathan Wild* when he introduces an amorous captain lusting after Heartfree's beautiful wife, who has been entrapped by Wild into fleeing to the Continent with him.

Closely akin to Captain Henry Morgan and his fictional lustful brothers, and even more ubiquitous, is the cruel Turk of the seventeenth and eigh-teenth centuries. A "familiar romantic novelist stereotype," according to McBurney,[25] this character is important in the novels of Haywood and Aubin, as when in Aubin's *Strange Adventures of the Count de Vinevil ...* (1721) Adelissa escapes the lustful Turk Osmin with the help of a fire and an assassination. Geoffroy Atkinson provides a bibliography of French books about the real Turk, especially his harsh treatment of Christians; Starr, with evidence from narratives of the Mediterranean, concludes that such characters have "long been fabulous villains";[26] and Defoe, in the preface to his *Continuation* of *Letters Written by a Turkish Spy* (1718), defends his depiction there of the "anti-Christian Turk" as being true to the facts, that is, as he existed in accounts by travelers.

One of the most common characters in early fiction was the wicked, perhaps the merely scheming or overzealous, Roman Catholic priest or Protestant parson. He is found in a mild form as an English country curate such as Thwackum in *Tom Jones;* and he exists in an extreme form with Prévost's Jesuits in France who take Cleveland and his children captive, try to force conversion on them by any possible means, and even plan to poison the sons. Foster's *Pre-Romantic Novel in England* (pp. 50-51) contains a long list of literary works, especially from 1721 to 1759, that have such characters as Prévost's cruel pére Le Bane, but they continue to the end of the century in the novels of Radcliffe, Monk Lewis, and others. This anticlerical tradi-tion had become strong in the previous century with deistic French travelers to America like Lahontan, with Roman Catholic Spain's persecution of the natives of Chile and Peru, with vivid travel reports by Englishmen treated cruelly in Italy and facing the Inquisition in Spain, and with the growing political strength of the Jesuits throughout Europe. Then in the eighteenth century the tradition grew even stronger, first, because of the Rites contro-versy, which elicited favor for Confucious and the Chinese from people such as William Temple but aroused antagonism against the Jesuits from others such as Defoe; second, because of travel reports, both Roman Catho-lic and Protestant, of the Jesuit takeover of the natives of Paraguay and Argentina; and third, because of the increasing number of deists in England and on the Continent who decried any attempt to convert American natives, orientals, blacks, Tahitians, even people of another Christian sect.[27]

Besides Lahontan, dozens of well-known travelers aided in developing the image of the scheming, hypocritical, or time-serving man of the church, any church. For example, early Europeans in Japan—William Adams with his letters in Purchas was one—found their strongest opposition from Japanese religious leaders jealous of, or uncertain about, Christian beliefs or Christian influence on the Shoguns. In Cochin China, Pyrard de Laval and two friends were betrayed into prison by two established Portuguese priests afraid of Frenchmen in what they considered their territory (1611). Thomas Gage, a Roman Catholic priest turned Protestant, gave a harsh picture of the Church's treatment of natives in Mexico (1648). Frézier, a French engineer in South America, condemned bad priests in both Argentina and Peru (1716), as did Bougainville fifty years later, thereby aiding the *Philosophes* in their anticlerical campaign. Even James Bruce in Abyssinia found his most hostile enemy to be the jealous priest Abba Salama (1790), who would become the "baleful priest" in a novel by Haggard.[28]

So, while there are a few good clerics in early fiction—Aubin in *Madame de Beaumont* has one who appears twice, once to rescue the heroine, once to rescue her husband from prison—the bad cleric is indispensable. He is needed by the picaresque novelists, by Defoe and Prévost, by the Gothic writers, by Voltaire sending Candide into the Jesuit stronghold in Paraguay, and by satirists attacking the "hypocritical" Methodists, as Richard Graves did in the *Spiritual Quixote* (1773), or the "saints" of New England, as Ward did in his *A Trip to New-England* (1699).[29] The tradition, then, is much more than that described by Bissell (1925): "The introduction of a French priest becomes the means of exhibiting the hypocrisy of the Christians, in contrast with the credulity and simplicity of the savages."[30] It is in fact more than that of the political-minded Jesuit described by Foster as "the priestly villain that abounded in the flourishing anticlerical literature of the" eighteenth century.[31]

All of the early fictional characters created or influenced by travel literature are not men. Although Radcliffe and late eighteenth-century novelists were inspired by the sad nuns in convents written about by travelers such as Piozzi and Brydone in Italy, the nun, usually sad, had been a stock character in fiction from the middle of the preceding century, beginning with the famous *Lettres d'une religieuse portugais,* translated into two volumes by Roger L'Estrange as *Five Love-Letters from a Nun to a Cavalier* (1678) and *Seven Portuguise Letters* (1678-81) and imitated many times through the eighteenth century. Mme d'Aulnoy in her *Voyage d'Espagne* (1691) reports what are probably fictional visits to convents in Spain where she supposedly talks at length with nuns and with aristocrats retired there, but the year before she had already written the *Histoire de Hipolite,* a novel, in which the heroine Julia is kept in a convent by her jealous husband until she manages to escape to Florence. Similarly Aubin's Protestant heroine in *Madame de Beaumont*

(1721) is imprisoned in a convent by her Roman Catholic guardian until rescued by her lover. Even Marivaux in *La Vie de Marianne* (1731-41), one of the best novels of the century, must let his seductive but sad heroine take a sort of refuge in a convent from which she is kidnapped. An even better example is Diderot's *La Religieuse* (1760; pub. 1796), whose unhappy young nun must struggle long to get out of her convent after writing letters to her prospective guardian. French and other Continental novelists did not, of course, need a travel book to tell them of the sad nuns sent to convents by spouses, guardians, bigoted priests, or relatives; their religious tradition provided a direct contact that would aid the imagination. But English novelists who did not themselves travel were in need of those eyewitnesses who did. As with L'Estrange, Aubin, Manley, and Radcliffe, for the sad nun they took their facts and their inspiration from writers of fiction on the Continent or from travel books such as those of d'Aulnoy and, much later, those of Brydone and Piozzi.

One other sentimentally attractive female character exploited by early fiction and found also in travel accounts is the faithful, naive native forsaken by her man; and here, we can be sure, the *récit de voyage* comes first. Richard Ligon in his account of Barbados (1657) tells of the native girl Yarico who rescues an unnamed English sailor, feeds and loves him much as Haidee does Byron's Don Juan, is taken by him aboard a ship to England, and then is deserted.[32] Jean Mocquet, a widely traveled Frenchman, had told a similar, but much more gruesome, story four decades before, the two traditions combined leading Gilbert Chinard to believe the story "common" and "indispensable" in voyage literature.[33] In Mocquet's version an English pilot, the only survivor of a shipwreck off South America, is rescued by a beautiful savage who succumbs to his promises of eternal love. After guiding him across deserts for eight hundred leagues, she helps him find an English vessel to take them aboard. But now the pilot becomes ashamed of his native woman, puts her ashore, and sails off. Her revenge is like that of Medea dealing with Jason: Before he is out of sight she cuts their child in half, throws one part toward him, and sorrowfully carries away her half. Mocquet, as well as certain others who told the tale, used it in part to contrast the simple, trusting natives with the inhumane Europeans. Richard Steele in *Spectator* 11 (1711) let it serve another purpose. After the virtue and loyalty of women had been maligned in an earlier *Spectator* with a version of the Widow of Ephesus story as told by the cynical Petronius, Steele borrowed the tale and the name Yarico from Ligon, whose book dealt with the island where Steele owned a plantation, added Inkle for the name of the deceitful English sailor, and let the story of Inkle and Yarico expose a deceitful man and defend the honor of women.[34] Then, the eighteenth-century travelers as well as novelists kept the story alive. When Prévost, who knew Ligon well, employed his *Barbados* and other travel books to put together the spurious account of Captain Robert Lade (1744), he worked in the story of Yarico, as did the abbé Raynal in *Histoire philosophique des Indes* (1770). In England, Shebbeare borrowed the name Yarico for his Indian maiden in *Lydia* who loyally waits for her beloved as he contends with the English government, the whole episode supplying a double commentary by displaying the corrupt European as opposed to the uncontaminated savage and by contrasting the chaste, loyal Yarico with the Libidinous Rachel and her Puritan seducer Parson Mouthtext. Finally, the *Bibliothèque des romans* included a novelette entitled *Inkle et Yarico, histoire américaine* (1778; vol. 28). Primitivism, sentimentality, the defense of women—the story of Yarico served several purposes after fiction borrowed her from travelers like Mocquet and Ligon.

While there are obviously another dozen characters in fiction who are also, often earlier, in travel relations, perhaps only two more need some comment. One is the sailor, a character found in novels such as Defoe's *Singleton, The Jamaica Lady, Lydia,* and *Roderick Random.* He is found first, however, in accounts by or about such seamen as Hawkins, Gilbert, Magellan, and Drake or by supernumeraries such as Pyrard de Laval mingling with his blasphemous sailors on a voyage to India, Robert Challe consorting with his gallery of officers aboard the *Ecueil (The Reef)* bound for the East Indies, and Careri paying his fine to determined Spanish tars as they cross the Pacific. For this important character in the novel, one need only note two opinions. One is that of George Parks writing of *The Observations of Sir Richard Hawkins knight, in his Voyage into the South Sea* (Purchas, 1622): "The work is not merely a narrative. it is a reasoned account of every incident or observation, explaining errors and necessary precautions against errors in the management of ships, in discipline, in strategy and tactics, and also spelling out observations of tropical medicine and people and commodities. Altogether the book 'gives a fuller picture of life at sea than is to be found in any other Elizabethan work.' "[35] The other opinion is that of Watson in *The Sailor in English Literature* (4): "The story of the presence of the sailor in English literature should begin with the narratives of actual sea voyages, for it is from them, especially in the earlier periods, that our knowledge of the facts must be obtained."

The second of the two characters to need comment is the national stereotype, the image the traveler or the novelist gives of the natives of a country visited or a country sending visitors. In the late eighteenth century, one reviewer reports, such stereotypic images rested on the "shopworn commonplaces" of travelers. An Englishman, for example, is "serious and morose: a Scotchman proud and overbearing, an Irishman a fortunehunter: a Frenchman, a fop, with paper-ruffles and no shirt. A Spaniard, grave, stiff, and haughty: a Russian, bearish; an Italian, effeminate, a fidler."[36] Such pictures remind the reader that Smollett takes Count Fathom to Paris, where he meets "a Westphalian Count, a Bolognian marquis, a French abbé, a Dutch officer, and an English squire," and to London, where he is "thrown with Scottish Sir Mungo Barebones, Irish Major Macleaver, English Captain Miniken, Theodore, king of Corsica, and the crazed Frenchman."[37] Shebbeare also, and at great length, tries four of these types on board Captain Bounce's man-of-war. Such attempts date back, more or less, to every novelist who has a foreign character or who sends his characters into a strange environment. But they date back even earlier in travel literature, as we have seen, with Addison commenting on the French and the Italians, Béat de Muralt comparing the French and the English, or any Grand Tourist describing the nations he visits. Before 1700 Ned Ward in *A Trip to Ireland* supplies a long, facetious interpretation of the character of Irish men and women, of the Dutch in *A Trip to Holland,* and of the Welsh in *A Trip to North-Wales.* About the same time, one finds the popular Mme d'Aulnoy in large part responsible for the opinion of the French and English that Spaniards are "haughty."[38] The Turk, the Chinese, in fact almost every nationality, was dissected either directly or indirectly by a long line of travel writers, from Mandeville interpreting the Arabs, to Columbus and his colleague Dr. Chanca providing conflicting pictures of the Americans, to Varthema and Pyrard analyzing the natives of India, to Chardin reporting the Persians.[39] This fascinating tradition that attempts to separate the character of one nation's people from that of another is part of the tradition of the international novel, Grand Tour literature, and the *Bildungsroman;* and, as we shall see, it is just as closely related to the language and style of both the travel book and the novel.

CHAPTER TEN

Language and Style

> But this racy individuality of phrase and diction is not the
> whole secret of the fascination which the language of the
> voyagers exerts. If one seek farther, one will come in the
> end ... to a trait which almost all the early travellers have
> in common ... the way they have of clothing the very stuff
> and substance of romance in the homely, direct, and every-
> day terms of plain matter of fact. *J.L. Lowes*[1]

For the *récit de voyage,* the subject of language and style is as significant as
it is for the study of any other form of literature. As with other forms, in
fact, one can approach travel literature primarily from the point of view of
style, as American formalists such as Mark Schorer have preferred the
stylistic, the technical, approach to fiction rather than, say, a generic approach. Here, as we offer suggestions about the relationship between the
language of travel accounts and that of the early novel, we shall argue—
contrary to much received opinion—that the language and the content of
a travel account before 1800 are more or less inseparable, that an individual
traveler is unique and develops a unique style depending on the time, the
place, the audience, and the writer's training, talents, and inclination.

One of Auerbach's conclusions is that the trend to greater realism in
literature after 1650 was supported strongly by a breakdown in levels of
style. Agreeing with him for France, Vivienne Mylne explains what those
eroding styles were considered to be: "The doctrine of stylistic levels was
of course a commonplace of literary theory in the seventeenth and eighteenth centuries. ... In practice, it was based on three interdependent factors: the social status of the characters involved; the nature of the
subject-matter—tragic, serious or gay; and on the established hierarchy of
literary genres."[2] Closely related to the conclusion is another by Auerbach
concerning the style of memoirs, a type of literature close to travel accounts,
although less popular and less important. " ... the memoir literature of the
seventeenth and eighteenth centuries, he says, "did not conform with the
aesthetic rule that the everday and low should be kept apart from the
sublime and serious."[3] Although one cannot be sure that such breakdowns

were a chief factor in the trend to realism or were themselves byproducts of that trend, one can agree that writers of England, as well as of the Continent, were aware of levels of style and of the appropriateness of certain styles to certain subjects. Congreve in the preface to *Incognita* (1691), for example, contends that "Romances" of the former kind—not his—are written in "lofty Language" to "elevate and surprize the Reader," a conclusion supported in the same year by the English translator of Scudéry's *Arta-mène*. Two decades later, in a theory she herself did not always follow, Mary Manley announces that conversation in fiction should have a "Plainness," a "Simplicity," a "Free and Sincere Air."[4] And all critics of the epic knew that Homer, Virgil, and Milton employed an elevated style, although occasionally they might attack or defend the low language of certain of Homer's characters such as the swineherd Eumaeus in the *Odyssey*.

Not only were writers and readers aware of a move to replace an old hierarchy of literary styles with a new set, but by the beginning of the eighteenth century there was an obvious awareness that great numbers of important people were urging that prose style in general be plain, more in the tradition of the Attic style of Isocrates than in the Asianic of Cicero. Today we explain that move to a plain style by pointing to the rise of a middle class and a new reading public that included women; by noting developments in science that led to the influence of the powerful academies; and by stressing the more realistic content of literature, as in the nouvelles and the picaresque. And today, sometimes forgetting that the "plain style" of 1700 is not our plain style any more than Aristotle's "complex" plot for drama is ours, we are quite busy, often with computers, analyzing seventeenth- and eighteenth-century prose, which we have sometimes liked to divide into two types.[5] One we have called Ciceronian, periodic, ornate and trace it in English through Lyly, the divines Donne and Taylor, Sir Thomas Browne, Milton, perhaps the young Swift of *A Tale of a Tub*, and Samuel Johnson. The other we have called Senecan, terse, plain and find it in Bacon, the divines South and Tillotson, Thomas Sprat and the Royal Society, often Defoe, and the Swift of *Gulliver*. The terms in either set are of course not equivalent, nor—as we have learned—are two writers in one set necessarily alike. In fact, the notions that Bacon employed one plain style or Donne only an ornate style are now vigorously challenged. Furthermore, in spite of his praise of South's relatively plain style, Dryden is more varied, even more nearly ornate, than most good twentieth-century writers. Heavily metaphorical, he by no means ever wrote "journalistic" prose in our sense.

Another fact we may be learning is that by 1700 the concrete, the small, was as necessary as the large universal; that is, the particular came before the general, whether in Bacon's inductive logic, Sprat's history of the Royal Society, or Locke's philosophy, Thus, Mary Manley could denounce "most

Authors" of "Romances" because they "are contented to describe Men in general . . . ; they don't perceive Nice Distinctions."[6] And long before Johnson's Imlac advised the poet to store the mind with images that would bring life to the tulip, Pope said it best for all good writers:

> But it is the Images of Things as in the Characters of persons, . . .
> a small Action, or even a small Circumstance of an Action, lets us
> more into the Knowledge and Comprehension of them. . . . There
> is a vast difference between a small Circumstance and a trivial one,
> and the smallest become important if they are well chosen, and not
> confused. . . . small Circumstances, artfully chosen [make the reader
> feel] the force of them and represent the whole in the utmost
> Liveliness to his Imagination. *This alone might be a Confutation of
> that false Criticism some have fallen into, who affirm that a Poet ought
> only to collect the great and noble Particulars in his Paintings.*[7]

Yet a third fact being learned, perhaps more slowly, is that good writers then, as now, varied the style to fit the subject. In the process they employed countless forms—narration, description, dialogue, letter—but also countless sentence patterns, rhetorical devices, vocabularies, as Dryden did. Two of their sentence patterns are now talked about most: The paratactic, coordinate, or native English syntax is opposed to the hypotactic, subordinate, or Latinate syntax, although even in Bacon we are discovering a blend of the native with the Latin tradition. Writers also changed styles drastically from one subject to another, as Addison did so beautifully in the *Tatler* and the *Spectator;* or from one period in their career to another, as Swift did when he moved from *A Tale of a Tub* to *Gulliver.* Likewise, Defoe not only spoke in many "voices" but, as Bonamy Dobrée claims, had a "hundred" styles.[8]

And all that is more or less true of many authors of travel accounts, for from the beginning they had a hundred styles which have been looked at only casually. One of the most recent analysts of ancient travelers is J.A.K. Thomson in *Classical Influences on English Prose* (1956).[9] Thomson, a deservedly popular scholar, is content, however, simply to offer certain believable generalizations: "The second book of the *Histories* of Herodotus" is "the best piece of travel literature ever written," or Horace's *Iter ad Brundisium* exerted "an extraordinary influence" upon the eighteenth century, especially on "Sterne's *Sentimental Journey* and its progeny." And he says little about style except indirectly; that is, he mentions "tone," "picturesqueness," "scientific interest," "formal description" only casually.

Even more recent are the comments on style made in two essays dealing with travel writing in Elizabethan England. In *The Hakluyt Handbook* (1974), there are a seven-page analysis of "Hakluyt's Languge" by N.E. Osselton and a brief history of Tudor travels by G.B. Parks.[10] Osselton, concentrating on Hakluyt's own style as editor and rewriter of other men's travels, makes a number of intriguing observations for Renaissance prose in general. In an age, he thinks, when there was a "conscious imitation of rhythmical periodic Latin sentence structure," as well as "varieties of syntax" ranging "from the artlessly simple to the artificially complex," Hakluyt's "Language exemplifies the process by which imitation of classical models helped the vernacular ...; his own peculiar strength lies in avoiding the current excesses of embellishment both in the choice of words and the shaping of sentences." Concentrating on history George Parks has little time for language, but he does suggest that while some Renaissance travelers had an "elaborate Latinate style"—George Best on the Frobisher voyages, Ralegh in Guiana— "the characteristic form" of Elizabethan travel accounts was "a straight chronology more or less elaborated." Together Osselton and Parks think that in Hakluyt's day there was a "wide range of choices" for the writer to make in both sentence structure and vocabulary and that Hakluyt himself was an influence against "embellishment" and "overwriting."[11]

John Livingstone Lowes, although just as brief as Osselton or Thomson, does more with language. In *The Road to Xanadu* (1921), in which he shows how he fell in love with the countless travel books that fed the imagination of Coleridge, Lowes is ecstatic about the simplicity and directness, the vividness, the descriptive powers, and the homely yet colorful metaphors of all those "mariners" who "were often poets without knowing it."[12] One of his favorites is Friedrich Martens (1675), who sailed to Spitsbergen and was used by Coleridge a dozen times; but Lowes also likes the language, in translation if necessary, of Quirós, Ringrose, Dampier, Shelvocke, and a multitude of others. He quotes much, praises effusively, and loves it all.

Watson in *The Sailor in English Fiction* (1931) is just as brief on travel style, less enthusiastic, and stresses the accounts in Hakluyt and Purchas.[13] He devotes a sentence to the seminal Coryat, notes a Latin quotation in an account of the Earl of Cumberland's voyage to the Azores, and quotes a famous "succinct" report from Cavendish's second voyage—"Here l Harris lost his Nose: for going to blow it with his fingers, cast it into the fire." Next, he observes that Master Ellis and Ralegh are euphuistic and appends a list of metaphors from early voyagers. Then, going to the eighteenth century, he finds Shelvocke's description of Juan Fernández "romantic" and notes how mariners such as Dampier and Rogers claimed a simple sea language.

R.W. Frantz (1934), inspired by the enthusiasm of Lowes and interested primarily in English travelers of the period 1660-1732, concentrates on that simple language.[14] Convinced, as R.F. Jones had been, of the great influence of the Royal Society on English prose style, he quotes Edmund Hickeringill on Jamaica (1661) and George Alsop on Maryland (1666) as examples of travel writers who "Early in the period [1660-1732] ... indulge in all the diffuseness of language and extravagance of hyperbole that characterized the old prose at its worst" (57); that is, they were too early to feel the effect of the plea of Thomas Sprat (1667), speaking for the Royal Society, for "a close, naked, natural way of Speaking; ... bringing all Things as near the mathematical Plainness as they can; and preferring the Language of Artizans, Countrymen, and Merchants, before that of Wits, or Scholars."[15] "It was not long" after Alsop, Frantz argues, "until this formula appeared with marked regularity in the prefaces of the voyagers" (59), who after 1660 demonstrate "a conscious striving for brief, clear, precise utterance" (61). A second, and related, conclusion of Frantz is that also after 1660 travelers became more devoted to the aim of providing "a superabundance of specialized, detailed fact" (61). Yet a third conclusion by Frantz is that with such subjective, even "romantic," writers as George Shelvocke (1726), Nathaniel Uring (1726), and Robert Drury (1729) in the 1720s "there came into being a type of voyage account intended to please as well as to instruct" (67). These conclusions have been approved and they have been attacked.[16] Now, however, they can be modified and perhaps related to theories about other types of prose.

To begin with, one must stress the fact that Sprat and the Royal Society, while important for the history of prose style, learned from and were working in a tradition already long and well established, and not just in England. It is the tradition of John Locke, writing shortly after Sprat and well before 1700, one that stressed the denotative function of language—"observation, fact-collecting, and classification"—as David A. Givner has explained while pointing to Locke's medical, botanical, and zoological, rather than mathematical, background.[17] And it is a tradition that continued, as with Vicesimus Knox, one of the most-reprinted essayists of the late eighteenth century: "The style of voyages and travels should be plain, perspicuous, and unaffected."[18]

But it is also a tradition of the sixteenth century, of Bacon, for example, or of Montaigne, whose words could have been in Sprat's mind when he appealed for the language of "Artizans, Countrymen, and Merchants": "It is," Montaigne asserted in Florio's popular seventeenth-century translation, "a natural, simple, and unaffected speech that I love, so written as it is spoken ... a pithie, sinnowie, full, strong, compendious and materiall speech ... free, loose and bold ... not Pedantical, nor Frier-like, not Lawyer-like, but rather downe-right, Souldier-like."[19] And it is a tradition to which many travelers and travel editors belonged for at least two hundred years before Sprat, Robert Boyle, and their immediate disciples.[20]

There were reasons why after 1500 so many travelers and their publishers claimed a simple language. One is that unadorned, clumsy, hurried prose

—untampered with—was offered as evidence of truthfulness. Another is that some travelers either lacked the education to be ornate or, more often the case, while on their journeys lacked the time to do little more than record facts periodically. Thus, as early as 1510 Varthema in his dedication to the Duchess of Tagliacozzo says, "I . . . give a very faithful description of this my voyage, according to my humble abilities," speaks of his "fruitful, although, perhaps, unpolished writing," and begs his patron to forgive the "want of skill in the connection of the narrative, grasping only the truth of the facts."[21]

By the time Hakluyt was translating writers out of the early collections of voyages, these prefatorial apologies were commonplace. Not only does a typical "Commission" written for one of the many English expeditions to the Orient or Russia instruct the leaders to take "paper and inke, and keep a continuall journall of rememberance day by day . . . that it may be shewed and read" on return, but once in his own prefaces Hakluyt analyzes the "unaffected," "unpolished" style of Richard Chancellor on an ill-fated expedition "toward the mighty Empire of Cathay" in 1553. And, in yet another place, he insists that when he translated accounts like those of Giovanni de Piano Carpini or William de Rubruquis he "put them downe word for word in that homely stile wherein they were first penned."[22]

It is this kind of prefatorial apology one finds more than a hundred years later in *Gulliver's Travels,* where in his "Letter" to "Cousin Sympson" and in "The Publisher to the Reader" Swift was parodying not only Dampier's "plain piece" and his defense of "so many Sea-terms" but also *The Buccaneers of America,* the English translator of which (1684) claimed for it "such candour of style, such conciseness of period, so much divested of rhetorical hyperboles or the least flourishes of eloquence . . . that he strongly persuades all along to the credit of what he says."[23] But well before Swift, even before the *Buccaneers,* imaginary voyages parodied or, for realism, imitated such claims, as when Veiras in the preface to his *L'Histoire des sévarambes* (1677; English 1675) prepares the reader for a book "written in a manner so simple that no one could doubt the truth of what it contains."[24]

And a great many travel accounts are of course in an unadorned style with simple syntax. The account could be in journal form with limited diction and uninvolved sentences, as—for an extreme example—with Anthonie Jenkinson writing of his embassy to Russia in 1557. He could monotonously begin a number of short sentences in succession with "Then," or he could adopt longer sentences, paratactic and still simple, that employ as many as seven consecutive "and" clauses to list information in what has sometimes been glibly called the native English style.[25]

Also consistently "plain," but more varied in syntax and therefore much less monotonous, are the sentences and paragraphs of travelers such as

Henry Hawks, merchant to New Spain, who wrote a fascinatingly factual account at the request of Hakluyt in 1572. Here a typical paragraph gives his version of the myth of the Seven Cities of Cíbola: "The Spanyards have notice of seven cities which old men of the Indians shew them should lie towards the Northwest from Mexico. They have used and use dayly much diligence in seeking of them, but they cannot find any one of them. They say that the witchcraft of the Indians is such, that when they come by these townes they cast a mist upon them, so that they cannot see them."[26] From simple catalogue in several forms to a slightly more varied, coherent, and attractive "plainness," this is a kind of prose employed by dozens of travelers in the sixteenth century—Martin Frobisher (1578) writing to his followers captured by American Indians, or Sir Richard Hawkins (1593) describing dolphins—as well as by dozens in the next two hundred years, including Martin Martin writing about Scotland (1703) and, of course, William Dampier.[27] It is the kind of prose that Frantz apparently describes as "vigorous," "artless," "forcible," "clear and terse."

This kind of writing is frequently to be found in an account written on a journey but not intended—at least not readied—for publication. Often of course one cannot be sure if such an account was designed for publication or if its publisher altered it to make it more readable. The author of a letter to Hakluyt, for example, might, as John Newbery did in 1583, realize that the correspondence would be published, but the same person writing from Aleppo to his friend Leonard Poore might not know that Hakluyt would gain possession of that letter and publish it too. Nevertheless, each kind of letter was written for the eyes of an educated reader, and no doubt the traveler used his best style. At any rate, Newbery's letters are alike, their grammar and spelling are those of an educated merchant, and yet their syntax is relatively uninvolved. His is an educated, clear, more or less simple prose.[28] Quite different is the plain style of someone like Celia Fiennes, who traveled far and wide over Britain at the end of the seventeenth century, always keeping a journal, observing carefully if Whiggishly and primly, and never trying to publish, as her contemporaries Macky and Defoe did. Her style is perhaps "charming," as her twentieth-century editor claims;[29] but in spite of her social position—her father was a colonel, her grandfather a Baron—the grammar, spelling, and pointing of her journal are far below the standards of many educated men of the time. Her rough prose, the style of which remained unchanged in years of travel, can be illustrated from any page, as here:

> Thence we went to Maulton [Malton] 14 miles which is a pretty large town built of stone, but poor, there is a large market place and severall great houses of Gentlemens round the town, there was one

Mr Paumes that marry'd a relation of mine Lord Ewers [Eure's]
Coeheiress who is landlady of almost all the town, she has a pretty
house in the place; there is the ruins of a very great house which
belonged to the family but they are not agreeing about it caused the
defaceing of it, she now makes use of the roomes off the out buildings and gate house for weaving and linneing cloth . . . she supply'd
me with very good beer, for the Inn had not the best.[30]

There is, however, another "simple" style tradition for travelers as for
other writers, one in which the sentences are frequently longer, the syntax
is perhaps more involved, and the connectives *and* and *so* often give way
to *which, who, that, whereupon,* and all the other signs of the hypotactic style.
It is in fact a strong tradition with a variety of followers. His editor correctly describes the more or less educated language in the letter-dispatches
of Cortés to the Spanish emperor (1519-26) as "solid, never pedantic, controlled and forceful," although "his style is wordy and often involved."[31]
With him one can indeed find any number of run-on sentences tied together
with copious coordinating and subordinating connectives. Even more involved, however, is much of the prose of someone like Job Hortop, who
sailed with Hawkins and had adventures in Mexico. Although his vocabulary is limited and simple and he is wonderfully exact, his sentences are often
long and hypotactic to the extreme, this one, half of which is omitted, being
by no means unusual: "Then our keeper put up a petition to the Judge . . . ,
that we might be sent to the great prison house in Sivill, *for that* we broke
prison, *whereupon* we were presently led thither, *where* we remained one
moneth, and then from thence to the castell of the Inquisition . . . , *where* we
continued one yere: *which* expired, they brought us. . . ."[32]
   Such run-on, hypotactic prose was by no means written by uneducated
sailors only, for it is the kind of prose—to be put into four languages—that
the very learned Thomas Hariot always wrote in 1587 except when he was
cataloguing the "Merchantable commodities" of Virginia.[33] And this hypotactic style is the one which dozens of later travelers employed occasionally
or often. One of Defoe's "hundred" styles, it is, in fact, the favorite of his
Tour . . . of Great Britain and can be represented by this half of a normal
sentence (I, 152) in that seminal travel book:

. . . for Mr. Howard's house and garden, call'd Deaden, the garden
is so naturally mounded with hills, *that* it makes a compleat amphitheatre, being an oblong square, the area about eighty yards by
forty, and the hills unpassably steep, serve instead of walls, and are
handsomely planted with trees, *whose* tops rising above one another
gradually, *as* the hill rises at their roots, makes a most beautiful
green wall . . . at the north end, *which* is the entrance, is the house,

which closes it wholly; and at the south end ... Mr. Howard, by *what* we call perforation, caused a vault or cave to be made quite through the hill, *which* came out again into a fine vineyard, *which* he planted the same year ... and *which* they say.... [My italics]

Here is a style Defoe occasionally employed in *Robinson Crusoe,* less often in *Singleton,* and very seldom in "The Shortest-Way with the Dissenters," a satiric argument with personae, rhetorical questions and answers, and catalogues of reasons.

But by no means did all early travelers write a simple style, a fact not unsurprising in a period that produced Lyly, Hooker, Donne, Taylor, and Milton. Frantz, however, lists (54-57) as "exceptions to the rule" of simple prose those voyagers who were more ornate, quoted Latin, or displayed erudition of any kind. "In the main," he says, "they take the form of pedantry. We find traces of it in Beste.... It runs rampant in" Coryat, Sandys, and Thomas Herbert as well as in George Alsop in Maryland. All these, we are told, were pedantic and employed exaggerated language because they were too early to feel "the impact of the movement toward simplicity and precision." One can easily add to these travelers many others who displayed erudition, that is, a knowledge of language and literature. Captain Keymis in South America (1596) quotes Latin twice in three pages; Fynes Moryson (1617), a Cambridge man, talks of three Latin writers in one paragraph; Terry and other chaplains use their Latin and of course the Bible; and the great scholar-travelers from Montaigne and Lescarbot to Locke and Challe and Addison "display" their learning the way Coryat, Sandys, and Herbert do.[34] And, as we have seen, any number of them—as different from each other as are Captain John Smith, the indentured servant George Alsop, Chaplain Terry, and the voyager-novelist Robert Challe—included poems, their own, those of their contemporaries, even translations of the Greeks and Romans. There were, in fact, far, far more educated travel writers who were published—Jesuits, ambassadors, secretaries, divines, businessmen, scientists, tutors—than there were untutored sailors or servants.

Furthermore, a learned allusion or a poem or a bit of Latin does not necessarily indicate pedantry or an ornate or an involved or any other kind of style. Captain John Smith (d. 1631), one of the most prolific, subjective, and attractive of travel writers, could intersperse his narrative with his own poems or devote an entire paragraph to "the beginnings and endings of the Monarkies of the Chaldeans, the Syrians, the Grecians, and Romans." Then in one long sentence his prose could be hypotactic and involved in the extreme; in another he could be paratactic and involved, with *and, but, then, for;* and yet often in other sentences he was as "plain" as a fascinating writer could be, as in this famous and typical paragraph:

At last they brought him [Smith writing of himself] to Meronocomoco [5 Jan. 1608], where was Powhatan their Emperor. Here more than two hundred of those grim Courtiers stood wondering at him, as he had been a Monster; till Powhatan and his trayne had put themselves in their greatest braveries. Before a fire upon a seat like a bedsted, he sat covered with a great robe, made of Rarowcun skinnes, and all the tayles hanging by. On either hand did sit a young wench of 16 or 18 yeares, and along on each side of the house, two rowes of men, and behind them as many women, with all their heads and shoulders painted red: many of their heads bedecked with the white downe of birds; but everyone with something: and a great chayne of white beads about their necks.[35]

It is a paragraph as concrete, as colorful, as imagistic as one normally finds after 1660; and, in addition, it is metaphorical—"as he had been a Monster," "in their greatest braveries," "a seat like a bedsted."

Again, a twentieth-century reader may look upon George Sandys (1615) as pedantic and imply that he was not so observant as post-Royal Society travelers were,[36] and yet the travel account by Sandys, a fine poet, translator, statesman, is not only most readable and informative now but with its nine editions in half a century was even more popular in his day than Dampier was in the early eighteenth century. His language is indeed allusive and learned and metaphorical; he did embellish it with quotations; he did make use of other travelers from Herodotus to his day; and he was an intelligent collector of curios and books. Nevertheless, he was a keen observer, blending gossip and personal opinion with history and geography. And his style, like Smith's, like that of his educated contemporary Fynes Moryson, is, though sometimes involved, often neatly balanced, antithetical, and plain.[37]

All of that is true likewise for Thomas Coryat (1611) and George Alsop (1666), accused even more of false erudition.[38] It is true that in his life and in his writings Coryat was "eccentric," a favorite expletive applied to him in his own day and since. It is true that he knew Latin, perhaps as well as Montaigne, Milton, or Dryden did, and that he inserted Latin quotations and allusions in his travel volumes, as Montaigne, Milton, and Dryden did in their prose or as Addison and a hundred others did. It is also true that he liked to print his own poems—in English and Latin—and that he was personal and subjective, characteristics some readers believe they must condemn in travel writers, who, such people say, were and are supposed to commit themselves to a "style compact of vigor, simplicity, and artless charm," one designed simply to convey "specialized, detailed fact."[39] But Coryat may be the most unfairly maligned of all great travelers, for his eccentricities were often wonderful. He normally walked in a day when gentlemen rode horses; he was a genius at learning languages; he took time not only to learn local dialects but to live with natives, to participate in their customs; and his lust for travel was puzzling to the more sedentary of his readers. Moreover, after skimming one hundred pages of prefatorial material one reaches Coryat's real travel account and discovers it to be as minutely exact as any such account in the seventeenth and eighteenth centuries, as clearly and as plainly written, its "erudition" restricted largely to the transcription of Latin mottoes in public places, its "eccentricities" no more noticeable than those of other favorite travel writers of the day, for example, William Lithgow in Italy or the brilliant young Peter Heylin in France.[40] *Coryat's Crudities* is in fact a deservedly seminal book, one of the most widely read for a century, imitated by many travel writers, and by no means unattractive stylistically.

George Alsop is clearly more "eccentric" in his style than is Coryat, or even the notorious traveling Water Poet of the same time, John Taylor. In the first four pages of his *A Character of The Province of Mary-Land* (1666), he quotes French and Latin, apologizes humorously for his self-conceit—"I almost think I want none"—speaks of New World plants as "Emblems of Hieroglyphicks of our Adamitical or Primitive situation," includes three long hypotactic sentences, and records some eulogistic jingling verse.[41] Once through those four pages, however, Alsop writes with less of his opening flamboyance and can be followed easily and profitably even though he retains his jingles and his bookish metaphors—for example, "watry tenements of the deep," "fertile womb of this Land." Since 1934 when Frantz was impatient with Alsop's style, scholars have spent much time with this Royalist who was able to return to England after the restoration of Charles II. One of them, Leo Lemay, in agreement with Richard Beale Davis, Moses Coit Tyler, and other students of the "madcap, wit, poet, satirist" author of the *Character*, analyzes Alsop's entire promotion tract-travel account and says of its persona-narrator, "in fiction it would be a success; in the promotion tract, it is a triumph." Lemay concludes of the style in general:

> George Alsop's witty *A Character . . . of Mary-Land* uses the current literary fashions to win his audience: the background of the new science; the tradition of learned wit, especially the elaborately rhetorical low style characteristic of Thomas Nash; the Restoration frankness about sex; comic word-play, including paradox, pun, incongruous personification, extravagant figures of speech, and word coinages; and finally, an unusual number of folk sayings, maxims, allusions, and colloquialisms. All these make up a racy prose. Alsop's *Character* is one of the most witty and scurrilous books of colonial America.[42]

There are, then, several traditions for the prose of Renaissance and eighteenth-century travel literature, and about them it is most difficult to generalize. There is obviously a line of writers of several kinds of plain travel prose, one that starts with people such as Anthonie Jenkinson of Elizabeth's day and runs through Dampier and James Cook. And there are other groups that are ornate, or involved, or learned, or poetic. Thus, while Alsop is witty and ornate, Sandys is serious, learned, and ornate; and if George Shelvocke provides romantic descriptions of Juan Fernández in the 1740s, the young Georg Forster sailing with Cook employs biblical language and romantic imagery of the sea to describe tropical islands in the moonlight or towering icebergs in the southern seas. Furthermore, some "plain" travel writers often have involved sentences, some who display erudition are often plain, and some who consider themselves plain or are called plain by one reader may be ornate or involved to another. For example, Luke Fox (1635) and Thomas James (1633) were two ship captains searching for a northwest passage at about the same time. James, educated and attempting to be scientific, used simple language and a smooth syntax; Fox, who prided himself on being of the old school, was suspicious of education, and in his opening sentences he condemns eloquence and learning. But the way he does it is most revealing: "Gentle Reader, expect not heere florishing Phrases or Eloquent tearmes; for this child of mine [his book], begot in the North-West's cold Clime (where they breed no schollers), is not able to digest the sweet milke of Rhetorick, that's food for them."[43] Then Fox goes on with very long sentences, some paratactic, more hypotactic, and all leaning heavily to that eloquence he denies having, as in this typical set of clauses, a small part of one sentence: " . . . when they shall look forth and tremble at the rising of the wave and shall be aghast with fear to refrain those rocks and dangers which lie hid within the sea's fairest bosom." In other words, Fox, claiming simplicity, can handle involved syntax and is ornate somewhat like Alsop, more like Friedrich Martens, Shelvocke, and those other travelers who, Lowes claims, are poetic without knowing it.

Surely, then, the most important fact about travelers who wrote before the novel became an important art form is that most of them were educated and that, if they had time to revise, they wrote a varied prose. As students of classical rhetoric, like their nontraveling educated contemporaries, they either were well aware of levels of style or instinctively varied the style to fit the occasion. One cannot, for example, praise enough the colorful, grand, but varied style, with sentences ranging from involved to simple, of Walter Ralegh in his *Discoverie of. . . Guiana* (1596), which had many editions in four languages; but two other books about Guiana at the same time are almost as attractive.

One of these is by Ralegh's Captain Keymis (1596); the other is by Robert Harcourt (1609; Purchas, 1626). Harcourt's diction—"abandon,"

"expel," "slothful," "pernicious," "rarities," "incredible"—is that of an educated person, and his sentences can be run on to the extreme.[44] Keymis, far
more attractive, is also educated but his obvious love of words led him to
repetition. And he is metaphorical. Promising, in the traditional fashion, no
"enlargement of made wordes," since "single speech best beseemeth a simple
trueth," he then goes on "to remove all fig-leaves from our unbeliefe," to
argue—as do Ralegh and the Spanish—that El Dorado is no "pleasing
dreame of a golden fancy," and to conclude his propaganda with a rhetori-
cally balanced plea to his countrymen for action: "To sleepe then, because
it costeth nothing; to embrace the present time, because it flattereth us with
deceitfull contentment; and to kisse security, saying, What evill happeneth
unto us is the plaine high way to a fearefull downfall."[45] Furthermore,
Keymis asks and answers rhetorical questions and varies his syntax from
sequences of terse statements of fact to circuitous, run-on sentences with
copious subordinating elements.

Ralegh's charm as a travel writer has many sources. Although his sentences are consistently long by some standards, his account is so easy to read,
so coherent and graceful, and his adventures and comments are so intriguing
that without doubt his *Guiana* is a far more fascinating and useful book than
is his *Historie of the World*. And any analyst can select passages from it to
rival the eloquence of this one admired so much by Lowes, a sounding
account of "the Mountain of Christall" in Guiana and its river: "We sawe
it afarre off and it appeared like a white Church-tower of an exceeding
height. There falleth over it a mighty river which toucheth no part of the
side of the mountaine, but rusheth over the toppe of it, and falleth to the
ground with so terrible a noyse and clamor, as if a thousand great bels were
knockt one against another. I thinke there is not in the world so strange an
over-fall, nor so wonderful to behold."[46] In considering style, it should be
as significant to quote a genius such as Ralegh—or Montaigne, or Ricci, or
John Evelyn, or Challe, or Defoe—as to quote travel writers less talented if
sometimes as intriguing.

And wherever we turn, there are the educated travelers writing with
variety—for example, Champlain and Lescarbot, the French contemporaries
of Ralegh and Montaigne. One recent admirer of Champlain's huge *Voyages*
(1604–1632, then many eds.) correctly finds him "an experienced stylist"
who modulates his "tone range from the factual to the grotesque."[47] But
then, in spite of lapses in grammar and in spite of a liberal spelling, his syntax
and vocabulary are also varied. Part of a paragraph about a portage on the
Iroquois River ends thus in a faithful translation: "After he had passed the
rapids, which was not without difficulty, all the savages who had gone by
land over a good path and level country, although there were many trees,
again got into their canoes. My men also went by land, but I went in a canoe.
The savages held a review of all their people, finding that there were sixty

men in twenty-four canoes. After the review was completed, we kept on our way as far as an island, three leagues long, which was covered with the most beautiful pines I have ever seen. There they went hunting and captured some wild animals. Continuing some three leagues farther, we encamped to rest for the night."[48] And if one wants Champlain's "grotesque" tone in a terse style, one may turn to his graphic picture in words of Algonquins burning and torturing Iroquois captives.[49] Yet, with all these excellences, one Champlain scholar says, the style of his predecessor Cartier is superior.

Lescarbot (1609), less graphic in accounts of American natives, quotes the ancients, has variations of one style for his long history of the discovery and settlement of the New World, other styles to describe vegetation and animal life, still others for the adventures he and his friends experienced, and occasionally a whimsical style, as for this storm at sea and the heroism of the sailors: "We also had calms sometimes, very tedious and wearisome, during which we bathed in the ocean, we danced on the deck, we climbed the maintop, we sang in chorus. Then, when a tiny cloud was perceived to issue from under the horizon, we were forced to give over these exercises in order to watch out for a gust of wind wrapped in that same cloud, which on dissolving itself, grumbling, snorting, whistling, roaring, storming, and buzzing, would have turned our ship upside down if men had not been ready to do what the master of the ship . . . ordered."[50] Like Champlain, or Cartier, like later travelers such as della Valle or Defoe, the lawyer-historian-poet Lescarbot had a range of voices and styles.

With all such stylists before them, it is to be expected that by 1660, and even more so by the time of the novelist Lesage, travelers had many models to look to and much inspiration not only to publish their accounts but to write them well and attractively. And the variety of their style is great, perhaps, as with other prose writers, because of differences in their background, their personality, their audience, or the territories they traveled in. The great botanist John Ray, already famous by 1670, had surely developed his wonderfully natural, trained style before Sprat published in 1666; it was a style partly conditioned by his gregariousness, by the fame that preceded him wherever he went on the Continent or in Britain, and by his being a devout doctor of divinity. At any rate, in the Dedication to his best travel book (1673) he modestly apologizes for having, through haste, to "huddle up" the writing and make the "Phrases and Language in many places less ornate"; for, he says, "my main purpose having been to render all things perspicuous and intelligible . . . , I was less attentive to Grammatical and Euphonical niceties"—and revealingly he hopes to provide not only "Information" but "Diversion to those that abound in leisure." Similarly, Gemelli Careri, who like Dampier circumnavigated the globe, was a compulsive writer as careful to guard his manuscripts as Dampier was; and yet, unlike

Dampier, he was highly educated, a sentimental family man, and a devout Roman Catholic, all of which contributed to a manner of writing different from that of the no-more-observant buccaneer and yet as easy to read. Robert Challe, an important writer of fiction, was able in his *Voyage* (1691-92; pub. 1721) to vary his style to tell of lively parties he attended, to provide character sketches, to record business and political dealings, to marvel at the beauty of moonlight off an island, to describe the weather at sea, to quote in Latin from Lucretius and Ovid and dozens of others or in French from Montaigne, Corneille, and Racine, to reconstruct conversations he had on board ship or in port, even to write out long arguments—"digressions" to some readers—about philosophy, life, or literature. Without seeking to distinguish among the styles of the writers involved, students of the sea voyages reported in Hakluyt have contended that "Much excellent prose, strong and vigorous in character, often dignified and pervasive, is to be found in the book. Lucid and careful description, often lighted up by imagination and literary power, distinguishes many of these relations of voyages."[51] It is a conclusion conforming in every respect to that of John Livingstone Lowes, and yet that conclusion could be much broadened if it included the accounts of land travelers like Ray and Careri or of great collections other than that of Hakluyt. And by continuing on into the eighteenth century and studying the styles of dozens of travelers whose accounts left their mark on intellectual history and belles-lettres, students will discover a remarkable and influential group of prose writers who belong to their time and are still unique.

Stylistic influences are perhaps the most difficult to ascertain in literature, and such influences no doubt vary greatly during the career of any writer. Nevertheless, the relationship to and influence of the styles of travel writers on eighteenth-century novelists must have been as significant as with any group. As Cartier influenced Rabelais or Hakluyt influenced Shakespeare, so Defoe was trained in part not just on the content but on the language of Exquemelin, Dampier, and Woodes Rogers. Likewise, Lesage, Prévost, Swift, Voltaire, Bernardin de Saint-Pierre, and countless other novelists up to and including Chateaubriand burlesqued the styles of particular travelers or imitated them seriously. The problem, or the pleasure, of any analyst is compounded by the fact that such stylistic influences were returned, perhaps much altered, to later travelers, especially by fictionizers such as Tyssot and Head, Defoe and Smollett, Sterne and Swift. Walter Raleigh, William Bonner, and Michael Echeruo are only three to talk briefly of Defoe's debts in style to Dampier.[52] George Kahrl is only one to suggest that Smollett the novelist both affected travel literature style and was affected by it as he rewrote accounts for his *Compendium* of voyages with this stated aim in mind: "to clear away [the] rubbish in such a manner as to leave the narrative less embarrassed but more succinct . . . to polish the style, strengthen the connexion of incidents, and animate the narration. . . ."[53] Charles Batten is only one to recognize not only that Sterne wrote in some kind of travel-book style but that travelers after him, often admittedly, imitated his *Sentimental Journey,* one such writer being James Douglas, who in his *Traveling Anecdotes* (1782) copied many of Sterne's characteristic mannerisms in language and form.[54] And Philip Gove has noted eighteenth-century travelers who were affected by *Gulliver's Travels,* including John Bell, who for his *Travels from St. Petersburg in Russia to . . . Asia* (1763) took the advice of William Robertson, the Scot historian, studied the style of *Gulliver,* and wrote, one reviewer claimed, "the best model perhaps for travel-writing in the English language." Gove here concludes, "However much Swift's style may have been affected by his reading of true voyages, he demonstrates the simple, direct style so perfectly and with such convincing probability that his fiction could in turn teach a profitable lesson to the writers of true voyages."[55]

It is this "simple" style of one travel prose tradition—incorrectly assumed by so many to be the true travel-writing style—that would seem to be closest to that of some eighteenth-century novels, to that of far more nineteenth-century novels, and to the ideal uniform style advocated for fiction by such critics as Leonard Lutwack, Philip Rahv, W.J. Harvey, and Ian Watt, who, Robert Murray Davis sums up, believe "that plain style without ornament is the norm for the novel."[56] And it is of course often claimed to be the norm for such early English novelists as Richardson, who, like Montaigne and Locke, and like Sprat and Vicesimus Knox for travel prose, wanted a "simple, easy, natural and unaffected" style for prose of any kind, including his own.[57] Just as Richardson did, novelist after novelist in Europe, or their editors, claimed the simple and natural way of writing that so many travelers, or their editors, for two hundred years before them, had been claiming. In 1702, on the second page of his novel *La Guerre d'Italie,* Grandchamp not only pretends that he has made up nothing but claims that "the simple and naive manner" with which he tells the "histoire" suffices by itself to show that his "plan is not to write a novel."[58] Lesage in *Beauchêne* (1732) apologizes, exactly as the buccaneers and Gulliver had already done, for "the style a little too much that of the sailor"; Prévost, who knew the travel tradition even better than did Lesage, insists with travelers from Varthema to Dampier that in the *Mémoires d'un homme de qualité* he has paid more attention to "the exactitude of truth than to the ornaments of language"; and over and over the eighteenth-century novelist claims a "simplicity of style" to accompany a profession of truth.[59]

Nevertheless, before an Anglo-American myth attempted to separate novels from romances and before the rise of a notion that a uniform style for novels is best, the eighteenth-century novel, like the récit de voyage, offered variety in style. Among the French, Lesage may often have failed to fit language to a character; but, as Mylne has shown, unlike certain seventeenth-century picaresque stories, *Gil Blas* has a witty, ironic style to go with a more elevated, serious one.[60] Moreover, although Prévost was addicted to a hyperbolic manner of telling a story, he also effected "a compromise between the quasi-historical narrative of the seventeenth century, where the character's feelings and motives are . . . deduced from the outside, and the subsequent memoir-form in which the narrator displays a full knowledge from within of one person's ideas and emotions"; and in addition he could use conversation that is more lively than the indirect discourse of most early novelists—more than half of *Manon Lescaut* is in dialogue form.[61] Marivaux was in *Marianne* more adept in such matters than either Lesage or Prévost, and near the beginning of *La Voiture embourbée* he carefully explains that he has exploited a "mixture" of styles that should make the fiction enjoyable rather than soporific.[62]

For England, not only is there Defoe with his hundred styles, but Leonard Lutwack argues at length that Fielding, unlike later novelists, employed a number of different styles in *Tom Jones* and *Joseph Andrews*, at least three for narrative, one for the essay interchapters, and one for the verisimilar speech of characters such as Western, Square, and the garrulous Honour.[63] Even Richardson—endowed with a "Uniformity of style" by Lutwack[64]—over and over insisted that while employing a simple manner of writing he could at the same time provide each letter writer with a distinctive style that would enable the reader to identify that character. In short, like Marivaux, he was convinced that he gave the reader entertaining "variety" in styles.[65]

And whatever one means by claiming a "uniform style" for novelists of the nineteenth and twentieth centuries, it would seem that any number of them altered their styles as, earlier, Swift did when he moved from *A Tale of a Tub* to *Gulliver*, as Laclos did while saying of his variety almost exactly what Richardson had said of his.[66] Moreover, one needs to know that the prose of the travelers was everywhere in front of the fictionizers from Rabelais and Cervantes on, that any one of those travelers might have a variety of styles—narrative, descriptive, dramatic, epistolary—and that seldom did two of them write alike. If, then, levels of prose style began to give way before the onrush of realism, it is because those levels were artificial and inappropriate, because, aided by hundreds of travel writers and their sedentary colleagues, the new prose developed other systems of levels that were to be less artificial.

There are, of course, other ways of relating the language of travelers to that of early novelists. Like most writers, novelists are concerned with language and languages—their own, those of other nations, dialects—and travelers have always been great carriers of languages and of information about them. When in 1721 Montesquieu wrote facetiously in the Introduction to *Les Lettres persanes* that he had "spared the reader as much as possible of the Asiatic idiom,"[67] he really meant that his book provided local color partly by means of eastern terms borrowed from Chardin and Tavernier; and when Swift made up languages everywhere he sent Gulliver, he was parodying not just Dampier but a long tradition in travel literature.

First in that tradition is the fact that travelers returned either with a real knowledge of one or more foreign languages or with a smattering of some one language, a fact that in its abuse was widely satirized, as on the English stage. Careri's Preface to his *Giro del Mondo,* often reprinted after 1698, strongly urged any traveler to learn languages before leaving home; but long before him Hakluyt had advised any Englishman going to the East to learn Arabic and Malagasy in order to avoid an utter dependence on Portuguese as a lingua franca.[68] And before and after Hakluyt countless important travel writers—unlike so many twentieth-century tourists—were linguists of ability, a fact that aided them both in understanding what went on around them and in reporting facts about language. Varthema, who, like Eliza Haywood's fictional eunuch, learned Arabic and Persian as well as variations on those and other languages, includes whole conversations in a foreign language without always translating them. Álvar Núñez learned any number of American Indian languages, including dialectal variations, as he moved about near the coast of the Gulf of Mexico in the 1530s. Pinto's great success as a Renaissance adventurer in the Orient was aided by his facility with the Indian, Chinese, and Japanese tongues. Early in the seventeenth century Pyrard de Laval distinguished himself by quickly picking up the Maldive language, while about the same time della Valle went easily all over the Orient because he also learned new tongues easily. Coryat's genius for languages was a distinct characteristic, as it was with Chardin in Persia. The Jesuits, marvelously motivated, were as a group adept at languages, and the Grand Tour was designed to teach foreign speech as well as foreign manners. And on and on it went, until we hear of Lieutenant King, who succeeded Cook in command on the third voyage and whose ability to master languages was unusual even for his day.

Second, the travelers often included glossaries of foreign words and sometimes wrote comments, occasionally an entire essay, about the languages they encountered. The author of *Mandeville,* for example, used real travel volumes in order to supply equivalents for oriental words and to theorize about the differences between Arabic and English. William Wey in the fifteenth century returned from Jerusalem twice and appended to his account a "list of Greek words and phrases useful for the pilgrim." Breydenbach's, that best-illustrated of early printed travel volumes, has a list of Arabic words. In 1544 in Antwerp a Hungarian, Bartholomew Georgiewitz, published a book telling of his thirteen years as a peregrinating slave in Turkey, a book that "attained a phenomenal European popularity which continued through the seventeenth century."[69] Not only does this book employ hundreds of Turkish words and expressions but its last chapter has a vocabulary, including the Turkish system of counting, and a sample conversation. Hakluyt, de Bry, and other collectors invariably have such glossaries; Pyrard included a Maldive vocabulary; while Defoe, or someone, drew up a long list of Malagasy words for *Madagascar;* or *Robert Drury's Journal.*[70]

Almost without exception, books about the New World followed the custom, beginning with de Léry in Brazil and Cartier in Canada. Pigafetta, who sailed with Magellan, has a three-page list of important "Words of the Patagonian Giants," which, he explains, "are pronounced in the throat"; and William Piso and George Marcgraff, who published a beautifully illustrated and important work on Brazil's natural history (1648), included a similar vocabulary for the "Taupia Indians." John Smith recorded the speech of Powhatan; Lahontan made up poetic Indian names for months; and John Long supplied Huron and other vocabularies and called Lahontan's glossary a fake.[71] Working with a long tradition, then, authors of imaginary voyages felt compelled to include such information too, sometimes at length. Foigny, for example, devoted Chapter Nine in *Sadeur* to the monosyllabic speech of his natives; and Veiras has an even longer section on the language of his Sévarambians—grammar, sounds, sentence patterns, history, even prosody.

This concern of seventeenth- and eighteenth-century imaginary voyages with language is also part of a somewhat different tradition, but one still heavily indebted to travel accounts. Authors of utopian literature from the time of Sir Thomas More, whose utopians spoke a simplified language based on Greek, were quite interested in the possibilities for an international or ideal language.[72] Descartes and Leibnitz were two philosophers to advocate research leading to such a language, while Rabelais invented one for Panurge and two hundred years later Rousseau was still talking about such matters. The movement was given its greatest impetus, however, when in the seventeenth century Bishop Francis Godwin, inspired by the Jesuit Matteo Ricci's account of China, not only wrote a treatise (1668) urging an international musical language based on Chinese but earlier put the plan into his *Man in the Moone* (1638), one of the most popular of extraordinary voyages. Then, Godwin in turn immediately inspired two other influential voyages to the moon, one by the scientist John Wilkins, who also wrote two long treatises on an international language, the other being Cyrano de Bergerac's *Histoire comique ou Voyage dans la Lune* (1650), which saw eight editions in French alone in thirty years and which borrowed the musical language apparently without knowing that Godwin found it in a travel account. There was universal interest, then, both in the Lunarian-Chinese musical language— even Swift's whinneying horses are in the tradition—and in other such suggestions that paralleled both Europe's increasing awareness of the world's Babel of tongues and the desire of some Europeans to bring the speakers of the world closer to each other by means of a common language. Thus, the inventors of nations in imaginary voyages—Foigny's Sévarambians, Veiras's Australians, and Tyssot's South Pacific islanders whose simple language has seven vowels and thirteen consonants—are often in two language traditions that stemmed from real travelers: One required the foreign observer to report on the speech of a country visited; the other provided an opportunity for the observer to invent, or promote, the notion of a simplified language that might replace all lingua francas.

Although early novelists in general were uninterested in promoting a universal language, or had little occasion to do so, like those who wrote imaginary voyages they often employed foreign names, words, or sentences as travelers from the time of Mandeville and Varthema had been doing. Sometimes the attempt was and is obviously facetious, perhaps a parody of travelers; at other times it was, or pretended to be, completely serious. Rabelais in *Pantagruel* (1532) lets Panurge, escaped from a Turkish prison, use some of the author's invented Turkish words; but many others he puts in Panurge's mouth are quite authentic and came from travel books published before 1530—for example, "seraphz," the name of a Persian-Turkish coin.[73] And through the seventeenth century this was a favorite way of providing some semblance of local color to European fiction, as in Scudéry, whose *Ibrahim* (1641) has much oriental vocabulary, or Aphra Behn, who in *Oroonoko* (1688) tries a dozen or so exotic West Indian words, some of which she immediately explains. "Tepeeme," Behn says, means "numberless wonders"; "Amora Tiguamy" she glosses as "welcome Friend"; and "a little Beast call'd an *Armadilly*" is a thing which, she says, "I can liken to nothing so well as a *Rhinoceros;* 'tis all in white Armour, so jointed, that it moves as well in it, as if it had nothing on: this Beast is about the bigness of a Pig of six Weeks old."[74] All of this emphasis on exotic languages is marvelously in the tradition of the travel account, which contributed much to a more precise local color in seventeenth-century fiction than histories of literature have in general noticed.[75]

But eighteenth-century fiction has even more of it, as it has more novelists of all kinds. Some of the best of them, however, from Richardson to Laclos, by keeping characters in their native countries were not concerned with an exotic local color; and even Defoe and Prévost, with their great knowledge of travel accounts and of geography, may have kept their place names correct and used them often, but they seldom showed interest in foreign languages. Defoe's *Singleton*, for example, the novel in which he had most need of them, has in fact only two expressions from foreign languages, not counting words like "canoe," already familiar in his day: Once he has *"barcos longos"* for two Spanish boats at Cádiz, and for Africa he apparently invented a native word "Okoamo" for "help."[76] It was far otherwise with some eighteenth-century novelists. A number of them, taking their cue especially from Montesquieu, employed many such expressions taken from travel accounts, as did Mme de Graffigny in the popular *Lettres d'une Péruvienne* (1747; English 1748) with its dozens of footnotes to explain South American words used in the text. The same practice was followed for North America by Béliard in *Zélaskim* (1765) and for Switzerland by Rousseau in *La Nouvelle Héloïse*, while Mouhy, in both *Lamekis* (1737) and *Les Délices du sentiment* (1753), made up extravagant languages for Tartary and Egypt, glossing them all the while.[77] Furthermore, just as Jesuit père Ricci in the sixteenth century analyzed the Chinese language for Europeans, so Jesuit père Lafitau (1724) ends his account of Canada with a chapter on the vocabularies, the sounds, and the syntax of what he considered to be the chief American Indian languages.[78] Exactly in that tradition the author of the satirical novel *Memoirs of the Life and Adventures of Tsonnonthonian, A King of the Indian Nation called Roundheads* (1763), employing the method of Swift's Third Voyage but depending obviously on Lahontan and Lafitau, includes a chapter called "Of the Indian Idiom of Speech."

There was also a travel tradition with regard to dialects, although from Aristophanes and the Roman comedy to Shakespeare to Molière and Shadwell to the eighteenth century, the travelers and early novelists who reported or employed dialects could have been inspired by their colleagues writing for the stage. Perhaps the best report on English dialects by a traveler is that given by Defoe. While he was in Somersetshire, he says in the *Tour* (I, 218-19),

> It cannot pass my observation here, that . . . the dialect . . . is not easily understood, it is so strangely altered; . . . it is so in many parts of England besides, but in none in so gross a degree as in this part; This way of boorish country speech . . . t'is call'd *jouring*. . . . It is not possible to explain this fully by writing, because the difference is not so much in the orthography of the words, as in the tone, and diction; their abridging the speech, *cham* for *I am*, *chil* for *I will*, *don*, for *put on*, and *doff*, for *put off*, and the like.

Then Defoe relates two anecdotes to illustrate his point (I, 219-20). In the first, he visits a schoolmaster friend and listens to a boy reading from the fifth chapter of Canticles:

"I have put off my coat, how shall I put it on, I have washed my
feet, how shall I defile them?"

The boy read thus, with his eyes, as I say, full on the text.

"Chav a doffed my cooat, how shall I don't, chav a wash'd my
veet, how shall I moil'em?"

And so, Defoe concludes the story, "How the dexterous dunce could form
his mouth to express so readily the words . . . in his country jargon, I could
not but admire." The second anecdote is of a clever dog that nightly steals
meat from an inn, for at night "he was fierce as a lion, but in the day the
gentlest, lovingest creature that could be." Finally, however, the innkeeper
catches the dog in the act; but instead of observing the letter of the law and
having him executed, the "good humoured" innkeeper takes out his knife,
cuts off the dog's ears, chops off his tail, and

> having thus effectually dishonour'd the poor cur among his neigh-
> bours, he tyed a string about its neck, and a piece of paper to the
> string directed to his master, and with these witty west country
> verses on it.

> To my honour'd master———Esq;
>   Hail master a cham a'coam hoam
> So cut as an ape, and tail have I noan
> For stealing of beef, and pork, out of the pail,
> For thease they'v cut my ears, for th'wother my tail;
> Nea measter, and us tell thee more nor that
> And's come there again, my brains will be flat.

Here, with the Somersetshire speech, Defoe is obviously much better at
handling dialect than some five years earlier he had been in *Robinson Crusoe*.

Even before Defoe, however, Ned Ward in *A Trip to Jamaica* and *A Trip
to North Wales* was facetiously recording conversations that included dialects—Jamaican, Irish, Welsh—all in the way Shakespeare had done with
Fluellan or Ward's contemporary George Farquhar would do with Foigard,
the spurious Irishman, and with Count Bellair, the real Frenchman. There
is a significant difference, however. Ward was in the tradition of travel
accounts in two ways: He recorded sample speeches—as dramatists and
travelers both did—and he added linguistic analyses, humorous of course;
the Irish, he said, speak "precipitately" in a "whining tone" and their language "rather grates than tickles the ear," while the Welsh speech "is inartic-
ulate and guttural."[79]

Ward's parody of travelers and their interest in language runs through
the fiction of the next century, as with the author of *Jamaica Lady* (1720).

Whether that novelist was Ward's friend William Pettis or not, he learned from *A Trip to Jamaica*—which was so popular it saw eight editions in three years—to give his seamen nautical expressions that are more or less accurate and that would lead to Smollett's better use of sea language in *Roderick Random;* he learned also to include an Irishman speaking a poorly represented brogue—"Aragh bee mee shoul, don beesh very much to blame ..."; and he learned to let his "heroine" talk what is called "the *Negroish* Tongue" of Jamaica and then to gloss her expressions, among which is "Baccarara" (a white person), a word the author borrowed from Aphra Behn or from one of Behn's travel sources.[80] Just as humorous is a long scene in Mary Davys's *The Merry Wanderer* (1725) in which an educated Irishman headed for England arrives at an inn sixty miles from Holyhead and has fun with an ignorant English countryman who speaks a broad dialect something like that reported by Defoe almost exactly at the same time: "Noa, noa ... yo looken laik one of us; but those Foke that I mean, are Foke wi' long Tails, that have no Clothes on, but are cover'd laik my brown Caw a whom with their own Hair."[81] One of the best recorders of such country patois in the eighteenth-century French novel was Thomas l'Affichard, a dramatist who transferred his dramatic talents to his prose fiction *Le Voyage interromptu* (1737), in which a party of four men leave Paris on a holiday, have their coach break down on the highway, and are rescued by a well-to-do country family, the head of which, page after page, is endowed with an amusing peasant speech. When, for example, the young men ask for cards to kill time with, he answers that people play cards only on Sundays and holidays and so "Pargue ... charchez du divartissement à queque autre chose" ["Parbleu ... find something else to do"].[82] This kind of fun with country and other dialects is of course standard in eighteenth-century drama and fiction. Marivaux, for example, reproduces a coachman's uneducated speech; Fielding has a variety of dialects from Squire Western's to that of a Quaker; John Shebbeare in *Lydia* tries French, Scotch, Welsh, and Irish. Normally, however—as with Ward's travel accounts and, to a certain extent, with Defoe's *Tour*—such verisimilar speech in fiction was employed not so much for realism as for humor. At any rate, it is by no means true that Smollett was the first to "capture dialectal and sometimes ideo-dialectal peculiarities in the speech of his characters,"[83] for Smollett was well trained on drama, fiction, and travel literature.

One of the most fascinating of travel reports on language had to do with what was considered to be the very poetic, oratorical nature of the speech of North American Indians; and while this fascination was recognized early by travelers and their readers, it really reached its peak in the late eighteenth century, when it found its way into novels. De Bry and Renaissance travelers such as Thomas Gage had advertised the stoical Red Man with his Greek warrior appearance, his few words, and his eloquence;[84] the Jesuits in their dozens of volumes about Canada often spoke of the Indian languages; and, finally, Lahontan's too sophisticated Adario had given Europe an Indian orator who could more than hold his own in debate. But with the publication in 1727 of Governor Cadwallader Colden's *The History of the Five Indian Nations*, which went into other, enlarged editions (1747 ff.) and which included translations of Indian speeches given at peace treaties, Europe erected a myth, by no means unfounded, about the eloquent manner of speech of the Red Man. On the Continent, Colden's reports were passed on by the traveler Charlevoix (1744), who like Thomas Jefferson after him reported Indian expressions and Indian orators that would have been applauded in the assemblies of Rome and Athens.[85]

Perhaps the fullest expansion of this side of the American Indian is in *Lydia* (1755), for which John Shebbeare borrowed the name of his wise, chaste warrior Cannassatego from a Senecan chief who, Colden reported, spoke eloquently at treaty councils held at Philadelphia and Lancaster in 1742 and 1744. But Shebbeare borrowed the eloquence too. The opening scene in the novel is of Cannassatego, here an Onondaga chief, calling a council and delivering an oration closely modeled on speeches in Colden but even more ornate and metaphorical. For his orator, Shebbeare not only adapted such metaphors as the "Calumet of Peace," the "sacred Wampum Belt," and "the Kettle of War" but gave him the perennial nature metaphors, as in these lines on how he has suffered from English faithlessness: " . . . the autumnal Blast has not scattered more Leaves than I have uttered Sighs, the rushing Cataracts of the Catarakui poured more Drops of water, than I have shed Tears . . .; each day treads on the Heels of another, loaded with fresh Marks of Perfidy."[86]

Following this fictional use of reports of oratory out of North America, the literary use in belles-lettres expanded,[87] swelled with the parallel myth of Ossian after 1760, and, as often happened, returned to travel literature. Before the end of the century, English travelers such as James Adair and John Long were providing examples of Indian eloquence, as were the French Lafitau (1777), Chateaubriand (1791; pub. 1827), and especially Crèvecoeur (1801), who devoted twenty pages to the deliberations and speeches of Indians at a council reportedly held at Onondaga in New York.[88]

If for Europe one of the chief attractions of the Red Man's oratory, as with the Ossianic poems, was its simple yet stately metaphorical quality, it is that quality which was apparently one important reason why so many seventeenth- and eighteenth-century readers were drawn to travel literature. It is also the quality which John Livingstone Lowes praises most. The early "voyagers," he says, employed "vocabularies richer, and racier, and fuller flavoured than before or since"; their "expression" was "captivatingly spontaneous and naive"; they clothed "romance in . . . homely, direct, and every-day terms" which "took on enchanting connotations."[89] Among these expressions are Friedrich Martens's similes (1671) as rendered by the translator (1675): "Rose-like-shaped Slime-fish"; "numerous as Atomes in the Air"; a mass of ice "curiously workt and carved, as it were, by the Sea, like a Church with arched Windows and Pillars."[90] Another is the hyperbolic description of a red bird on Juan Fernández as written by Anson's Midshipman John Philips (1744): "the Colours in its Head so gloriously mix'd and glowing like Gold against the Sun, that it surpasses all Description, Imitation, or even Imagination."[91] One of Lowes's favorites, and a favorite with many travelers, is a description of the tiny South American hummingbird as given by Oviedo and found translated in Purchas by Coleridge and Lowes: "This Bird, beside her littlenesse, is of such velositie and swiftnesse in flying, that who so seeth her flying in the Aire, cannot see her flap or beate her wings after any other sort than doe the Dorres, or humble Bees, or Beetols. . . . And doubtlesse, when I consider the finenesse of the clawes and feete of these Birds, I know not whereunto I may better liken them, then to the little birds which the lymners of bookes are accustomed to paint on the margent of Church Bookes, and other Bookes of Divine Service."[92] Such pictures of plants, animals, and topography are of course to be counted in the thousands when one reads travel literature as Coleridge, or Defoe, or Prévost did.

Lowes, as well as Frantz and Watson, obviously thinks only of sea journeys when he quotes passages or speaks of "voyagers," but for the full story one must turn also to all those accounts, far more numerous, of land travels. And there one finds not just descriptions of buildings, reflections on history, quotations from the ancients, and information for science, religion, or politics; a number of land travelers, inspired by the Alps, Pyrenees, Apennines, by the Volga or the Rhone or an Italian lake, took time to record descriptions of nature that are metaphorical, exact, full of color. And obviously these descriptions reflect the admiration of the writers for what they have discovered. Pietro della Valle (1652; English 1665) was by no means the first European in the Orient to revel in the beauty of the out-of-doors. In Letter Three alone, written from Goa, he tells of ascending a mountain called Ghat and a river named Garsopa, each of which he describes fully and praises for its beauty, all before stopping for the night by yet another river that pleases him.

The English who visited Italy in the seventeenth and early eighteenth centuries often found its views as magnificent as Wordsworth would find them more than a hundred years later. Two such Englishmen of the seventeenth century were John Evelyn and John Dennis. Evelyn kept a diary when he was there in 1643 and in it records an admiration and respect for mountains that Patrick Anderson, for one, finds rather strange in an "Augustan."[93] The young Evelyn enjoyed views at Lake Maggiore and Lake Geneva, as well as of the Rhone; and in the Apennines he wrote metaphorically of the experience:

> As we ascended we encountered a very thick, solid, and dark body of clouds, which look'd like rocks at a little distance, which lasted neere a mile in going up; they were dry misty vapours, hanging undissolved for a vast thicknesse, and obscuring both the sun and earth, so that we seemed to be in the sea rather than in the cloudes, till, having pierced through it we came into a most serene heaven, as if we had been above all human conversation, the mountain appearing more like a great island than joyn'd to any other hills, for we could perceive nothing but a sea of thick cloudes rowling under our feete like huge waves, every now and then suffering the top of some other mountain to peepe through, which we could discover many miles off: and between some breeches of the cloudes we could see landskips and villages of the subjacent country. This was one of the most pleasant, newe, and altogether surprising objects I had ever beheld.[94]

Dennis, the critic who helped popularize the "sublime" of Longinus in England, was in Italy in 1688. Although he "delighted" in the "softer" kind of nature in England, he recognized over and over that as with "great Wits" nature's "careless irregular and boldest strokes are most admirable"; and so it is not surprising that he was overwhelmed with the rugged beauty of the Alps:

> The impending Rock that hung over us, the dreadful Depth of the Precipice, and the Torrent that roar'd at the Bottom, gave us such a view as was altogether new and amazing. On the other side of that Torrent, was a Mountain that Equall'd ours.... Its craggy Clifts, which we half discern'd thro' the misty gloom of the Clouds that surrounded them, sometimes gave us a horrid Prospect. And sometimes its face appear'd Smooth and Beautiful, as the most even and fruitful Vallies. So different from themselves were the different parts of it: In the same place Nature was seen Severe and Wanton. In the mean time we walk'd upon the very brink, in a literal sense, of Destruction; one Stumble, and both Life and Carcass had been destroy'd. The sense of all this produc'd different motives in me, viz. a delightful Horrour, a terrible Joy, and at the same time that I was infinitely pleas'd I trembled.[95]

A dozen years later the young Addison not only found the Alps and Apennines as beautiful but consistently employed superlatives for the "prospects" that he stumbled on or went out of his way to see—the river Tever-one throwing itself down precipices until "After a very turbulent and noisy course of several miles among the rocks and mountains . . ., [it] falls into the valley . . ., where it recovers its temper, as it were, by little and little, and after many turns and windings, glides peaceably into the Tiber";[96] or the river Velino, whose rapid fall of one hundred yards ends in mist: "It is impossible to see the bottom on which it breaks, for the thickness of the mist that rises from it, which looks at a distance like clouds of smoke ascending from some vast furnace, and distills its perpetual rains on all the places that lie near it" (412). "I think," he ends his long description, "there is something more astonishing in this cascade than in all the water-works of Versailles." Again, impressed with the Alban Lake lying like "some vast Amphitheatre" because of "the continu'd Circuit of high Mountains that encompass it," he believes that the scene, combined with nearby "Green Hills and naked Rocks," makes "the most agreeable Confusion imaginable"; and near Geneva "the steeps and precipices" fill "the Mind with an agreeable kind of Horror."[97]

Bishop Berkeley in another dozen years was so entranced with the same islands and rivers and "barren mountains, all thrown together in a most romantic confusion," that he wrote the young Alexander Pope urging that it was "worth a poet's while to travel, in order to store his mind with strong images"; in fact, he said, if one wants "to describe rocks and precipices, it is absolutely necessary that he pass the Alps."[98]

These are the sentiments with which James Thomson in 1730 set out for Italy accompanying Charles Talbot, future Lord Chancellor. "Travelling has been long my fondest wish, for the very purpose you recommended," he wrote Bubb Dodington. "The storing one's imagination with ideas of all-beautiful, all-great, and all-perfect Nature: these are the pure *Materia Poetica*, the lights and colours, with which fancy kindles up her whole creation, paints a sentiment, and even embodies an abstracted thought. I long to see the fields where Virgil gathered his immortal honey."[99] And while the Italian "fields" were a disappointment—the travelers found too much poverty and ignorance—the poet Thomson was rewarded by "all-beautiful Nature," for he records his impressions of Lake Geneva, "the Vale, fair-spread / Amid an Amphitheatre of Hills," in one of the best passages in *Liberty*. All these are also the sentiments of Certain other travelers, of Thomas Gray and Horace Walpole, for example, as they viewed the mountains around Grenoble.

It is an awareness of the popularity of such sentiments, and of the descriptions reflecting them, that encourages scholars such as Lowes and

Barbara Stafford to argue against the theories of George Parks and H.W. Frantz that "natural wonders appearing in travel accounts were ordinarily described in plain, unvarnished language.[100] And, indeed, there is no reason to think that any traveler, from Ralegh in South America to Evelyn in Italy to Byron at Lake Geneva, would fail to be impressed with the beauty of mountains, which—"rugged," "irregular," "romantic"—inspired travelers such as Dennis, Addison, and Berkeley to employ both metaphorical language and, long before Burke's "horror" in sublimity, expressions such as "agreeable confusion" and "an agreeable kind of horror."

Moreover, just as so many travelers have written of their fascination with the beauties of new scenes, with the uniqueness of new flora and fauna, with the attractions of exotic customs, so other writers have read them and stored their minds with images that though twice removed come surging from the memory to enliven, to color, a page of great literature. That influence has been demonstrated for poets such as Ronsard, Shakespeare, and Donne, as well as for others such as Goethe, Coleridge, and Byron, many of whom both traveled and read.[101] But it is true for novelists also, even though their image patterns derived from travels have been studied so much less. With them, as with poets, it is not just Scudéry borrowing the color of court pageantry from travelers to Turkey, or Behn borrowing the armadillo from travelers to the New World, not just Head or Defoe with their storms and shipwrecks, and not just the scene painters such as Radcliffe and Charlotte Smith adapting Ramond de Carbonnières's Pyrenees. With novelists, as with poets, it is also a more subtle question of spontaneously recalled images, a Goethe, for example, in *Die Leiden des jungen Werthers* suddenly for an analogy remembering the magnetic mountains of ancient travelers.[102] That is, just as travelers record the images they see, perhaps create analogies for them, so novelists are inspired to use those images, perhaps to create metaphors from them. A reading of travel accounts, in fact, will show that no other form of literature has had, perhaps could have had, a wider effect on the exactness of imagery, even on the metaphorical language, of early novelists. After demonstrating that fact for Diderot, whose wide reading in the literature of travel "haunted his imagination," Eric Steel concludes that it also haunts the imagination of "all readers of the best in literature."[103]

And yet, the exact images out of travel literature are perhaps no more significant for the style of novelists, for any group of writers, than the broader, more general, metaphor of travel itself, what can be called the rhetoric of travel. It is surely the oldest and largest cluster of metaphors in any language, and its pervasiveness has no doubt increased with every traveler who returned to unload his cargo of wonders. It was current even before what Joseph Addison calls "those beautiful metaphors in Scripture, where Life is termed a Pilgrimage, and those who pass through it are called

Strangers and Sojourners on Earth" (*Spectator* 289, 1712). It was found in poems long before Dante opened the *Divina Commedia* with the line "Nel mezzo del cammin di nostra vita" [Midway on the journey of our life]. It was recognized as the most popular of metaphors long before Purchas in his preface (1625), and after him other travel editors such as Prévost (1753), demonstrated its great popularity.

In fiction, the journey, or voyage, of life was useful not just for matters of the spirit but for very tangible realities. It was useful for careers, or for love affairs, long before Scudéry in *Clélie* (1654 ff.) developed her famous parallel of the lover's hope to sail past the rocks and sands that wreck true love. This was a metaphor reworked in a hundred novels, as in Manley's *New Atalantis*, where the unfortunate Charlot, seduced and destroyed by her guardian, is described as "a true Landmark, to warn all believing Virgins from Shipwrecking their Honour upon (that dangerous Coast of Rocks) the Vows and Pretended Passion of Mankind."[104] Fiction of the eighteenth century could not do without such metaphors any more than could travel accounts themselves. Paul Hunter, for example, shows how much the "rhetoric of travel" controls both the plot and the language of *Joseph Andrews*.[105] Perhaps no novel, however, depends on that rhetoric more than does *Tristram Shandy*, the story of Tristram's journey in time, his *Tristrapoedia*, with side excursions such as those in Defoe's *Tour*, with Book VII as a real journey, with travel imagery throughout. The metaphor can be serious, as in the spiritual autobiographies; it can be humorous, as with Dunton and Sterne; it can even be bawdy, as with Ned Ward's contrast of the whore and the writer. The "Jilt," he says in the preface to *A Trip to Jamaica*, "has the Advantage," for we writers "do our Business First, and stand to the Courtesie of our Benefactors to Reward us after; whilst the other, for her Security, makes her Rider pay for his Journey, before he mounts the Saddle." But to find, record, and classify such metaphors, in travels and fiction alone, is an impossible undertaking. Their prevalence in both forms of literature brings the two still closer together in style and indicates again how much the novel —a great teacher itself—has learned from the travel account.

CHAPTER ELEVEN

Conclusion

Fare forward, travelers! You are not the same people who
left that station. *T.S. Eliot*[1]

One of the closest points of contact between the travel account and the early
novel is through parody. In 1735 a large book appeared written by G.H.
Bougeant that burlesqued the romantic excesses of both the novel (*roman*)
and the travel account. Its title, *Voyage merveilleux du Prince Fan-Férédin dans
la Romancie; contenant Observations Historiques, Géographiques, Physiques, Cri-
tiques et Morales,*[2] promises that the structure will be like that of many travel
books—for example, John Ray's fascinating *Observations Topographical,
Moral, and Physiological; Made in a Journey through . . . the Low Countries*
(1673). And the promise is carried out: Chapters One and Two tell of the
"Departure for" and the "Arrival of" the Prince; Chapter Four is "Of the
Inhabitants of Romancie"; and subsequent chapters distinguish between
"Upper" and "Lower" Romancie and describe its unique plants, its workmen
and industries, its strange marriage customs, and its carriages. Furthermore,
the traveler's love of marvels and penchant for exaggeration are ridiculed.
"Most travelers," the Prince says, "love to praise the beauty of the countries
through which they go, and since the simple truth does not furnish enough
of the marvelous, they are forced to have recourse to fiction" (20, my
translation); and since, in order to avoid the suspicion of lying, one must not
suppress any truth, the Prince, as good "Historian," will relate the facts most
truthfully, "without exaggeration" (21). That means, first, unlike other travelers, he will describe the exotic plants without philosophizing about them
and, second, he must report that the air of Romancie supplies all nourishment for him and his horse, obviously the reason why heroes on a journey,
in novels at least, never refer to such mundane matters as food.

Yet, while the form of Bougeant's *Voyage merveilleux du Prince Fan-
Férédin* is largely that of certain popular travel accounts, the content turns
largely on certain of the romance-novel traditions. There is a "Forest of
Love" (Chap. VIII), and ultimately the Prince falls in love with the Princess
Rosabelle. The three kinds of horses in Romancie are quicker and more
beautiful than those of Europe, one kind having horns like those of unicorns;
a description of the sheep leads to an essay on shepherds and shepherdesses,

who are like those of fiction; and the first town Fan-Férédin comes to has only handsome young people—no children or old folks (45-60). In Romancie all strangers can speak the native language on arrival and there are two kinds of home-grown travelers, those who set out with letters of credit and those who depart with only "romantic letters of the proper sort" (137-49). And what happens? The first traveling hero goes round the world without a single adventure: He eats always at inns "at his own expense"; he becomes tired, bearded, sick; he almost dies for lack of help; and he returns home exactly the person who left. The second hero, on the other hand, has a wonderful journey: Wherever he goes, his head is turned by countless lovely women; *his* letters get him invited to sleep and eat at beautiful chateaux where there are always new adventures; he is never lost, tired, or ill; and he returns home with marvelous stories to tell. There is even some symbolism: The Prince, like Don Quixote, is reared on *romans*, sets out to find the fabulous land of the *Romans*, learns that ordinary people he meets have never heard of it, and discovers it by chance when his horse slips and he rolls down, *down*, to the *lowest* of valleys where bones of serpents, centaurs, and griffons signal his approach to Romancie, the land of his books. And continually the Prince finds parallels between the scenes, people, and adventures in Romancie and those found in favorite works of fiction. On two pages he cites *Lazarillo*, Scarron's *Roman comique*, Lesage's *Diable boiteux*, Alemán's *Guzmán*, and Quevedo's *Buscón* (212-213). He makes extravagant use of the ending of Villedieu's *Isabelle* (174-75) and refers to many other *romans*, including *Gulliver's Travels* (120). Most of all, however, he delights in the books of a newcomer (in 1735) to Romancie named Prévost: The Prince finds Prévost's Manon Lescaut to be "quelle femme," and in order to plan an escape with Rosabelle he borrows, he says, a device from *Cleveland* (231, 259).

The journey of Bougeant's protagonist follows two parodic routes then —one ridicules the excesses in travels, the other the excesses in novels. Often the two routes converge, as when the Prince "digresses" on any subject, sets out on a journey of discovery, or describes exotic plants, animals, and people. Often they parallel or diverge. When the Prince digresses to describe the sheep of Romancie, he is like a Mandeville or a Sinbad telling of marvelous animals or a Dampier pausing to describe four classes of turtles in the West Indies; but when the Prince then digresses further to dwell on romanticized shepherds and shepherdesses, Bougeant is thinking of the tradition of *Daphnis and Chloë, Astrée*, and the second half of *Don Quixote*. Moreover, when the Prince sets out to find Romancie, he is like the Italian or Portuguese Jesuits searching for the land of Prester John, Cortés for California, or Ponce de León for the Fountain of Youth; but when his horse and he need no food because the air of Romancie provides their nourishment, he is closer to those novels whose heroes and heroines never lack for the necessities of life. All in all, however, Bougeant has seen the similarities in the two forms of literature and has been able to combine his satire of one form with that of the other and to do it so well that for a time the stories of fictional travel and real travel become one.

In that respect, of course, Bougeant is not unique, or best—just most obvious. Voltaire, with *Candide,* is a wonderful example of a genius who by parodying both the romance tradition and the travel tradition—now one, now the other—is able to demonstrate the fact that the two are not only much alike but sometimes so alike the reader is not sure which form is being thought of. Most burlesquers, however, do not attack the borrowed form but use it to ridicule faults in people or society—as *The Rape of the Lock* does with the epic, or as *Gulliver* and *Humphrey Clinker* do with the travel account. The romance with its many plot devices has invited most of the parodies, but even there the parodied form is not often the chief object of ridicule: *Don Quixote* becomes more and more a satire of society and less and less an attack on stories such as *Amadis,* and Furetiére's *Roman bourgeois* (1666) is primarily an exposé of the pretensions of lower-class Frenchmen and only secondarily an attack on romantic fiction.

By no means, however, are Swift, Voltaire, and Bougeant the only writers of the eighteenth century to parody travel literature for the purposes of satire. Three other examples will show a variety of such satire. First, early in the century William King, a popular translator, published *A Voyage to the Island of Cajamai* as an attack on a particular travel book, the much-lauded Hans Sloane's *Voyage to Jamaica,* the first volume of which appeared in 1707. One passage of that burlesque has caught recent attention, that in which King's Esdras Barnivelt is given a prescription to cure him of being "a melancholy morose Husband . . . always 'drowsy and sleepy.' " The situation, as well as the prescription that follows, is taken almost word for word from Dr. Sloane's account of his experiences on Jamaica—but not the name "Esdras Barnivelt," which the Scriblerians adopted from King and which Pope used for the author of his "A Key to the Lock."[3]

Second, in 1750 the abbé Coyer wrote a satire that was published first in England as *A Discovery of the Island Frivola* and then in Holland the next year in French. The second English edition, that of 1752, has a different title beginning *A Supplement to Lord Anson's Voyage round the World,* and it is the book with this title that was amazingly popular throughout the century.[4] Coyer was not attacking the authorized account of Anson's circumnavigation, although other writers, Shebbeare for example, did. Rather, he was taking advantage of its success, which was even greater than that of his satire of European society as transferred to a Pacific island reputedly discovered by Anson. Coyer's *Supplement* to a real travel account is in the tradition starting with Lahontan's Supplément to his own *Travels* in Canada, which attacks European religion and politics, and extending to Diderot's satiric *Supplément* to the *Voyage autour du monde* of Bougainville.

And, third, there is the little *Voyage au labirinthe du Jardin du Roi* (1755) by Simon Linguet, a parody in alternating prose and verse of travel books in general. Linguet's two characters enter the labyrinth at 4:30 in the afternoon, view with distaste its strange plants and animals, and emerge at 5:30 cursing all accounts of voyagers. One of the disgruntled men concludes, "If I were a poet or a liar, I would tell you. . . ."[5]

Parody, then, may be used to attack a particular récit de voyage or the excesses of the form in general; it may employ the structure of a travel account to attack the faults of people; and it may combine the characteristics of travel literature with those of the novel in order to attack both forms or anything else. The satiric possibilities of the two forms of literature demonstrate again how much they are alike in structure and content. But the two have so many other similarities not yet discussed here that one can suggest only a few.

Carey McIntosh (1973) has noted an attractive and important one. In a fine analysis of *Rasselas* he finds Johnson making "somber fun of the quest for a secular summum bonum" but alerting us to other activities "proper to mankind."[6] Among those advanced in *Rasselas,* "One set of activities seems specially privileged, the kind of travel that encourages talk." One can add that, as with Rasselas, Imlac, and their entourage, the talk is encouraged before, during, and after the journey, whether the journey is real or fictional.

A second close relationship has to do with certain subspecies of prose fiction. One is science fiction, a form given short notice here and a form exceedingly popular through the ages from Lucian to Godwin, Cyrano, and Defoe to our day. A glance at the annual bibliography of the Modern Language Association will convince anyone of the academic as well as the mass appeal of science fiction, much of its appeal deriving from new real ways of travel, as indicated partly in a title such as "Le Voyage spatial dans la science fiction."[7] Similarly, the fairy tale, the literature of the marvelous, which became so popular in Europe after Perrault and d'Aulnoy at the end of the seventeenth century, evolved much as did the more respectable forms of literature and owes much to the movement to realism and the interest in travels and travel writings. That debt has not been worked out, but one need only start with the French writer Caylus (1692-1765), artist, archeologist, diplomat, prolific writer in several types of literature, and author of some five volumes of fairy tales almost as good as those of d'Aulnoy. Caylus was a world traveler whose best fairy tale is a supernatural voyage, and like the "true" novelist he knew not only that realism is a necessary ingredient of the marvelous but that travel is a source of inspiration for fiction.[8]

A third relationship is that surrounding the idea of the ingénu, a necessary character in both fiction and travels. Chaplain Terry and Marc Lescarbot are real travelers who leave Europe, one for India, one for Canada; Gulliver, Candide, and Bage's Hermsprong depart on fictional trips, one leaving England and going to Houyhnhnmland, one setting out for South America, one coming from a simple society in North America to a complex one in Europe. In each case the person setting out for strange lands is relatively naive, an ingénu. The travel ingénu may develop noticeably—Álvar Núñez and Lescarbot discovering American Indians to be respectable people; the youthful Robert Boyle maturing socially and scientifically in Italy. Occasionally a real traveler apparently remains naive, almost untouched by contact with other civilizations or other parts of his or her own country—Chaplain Terry retaining his British biases after visiting India; Dr. Chanca seeming, on return, to be as narrow-minded as when he sailed away with Columbus for the New World. The ingénu who travels in fiction, however, nearly always grows in some important way—positively with Agathon or Wilhelm Meister or Gulliver; negatively with the satirized Grand Tourists of Shebbeare and Smollett.

A fourth relationship, close to the problem of the ingénu, can best be explained by employing Jean-Paul Sartre's distinction (1947) between internal and external qualities in phenomena.[9] Sartre believes that Albert Camus's method in *L'Etrangère* was borrowed from Hemingway and other "American neo-realists" who, like Hume in the eighteenth century, he says, "deny the existence of any but external relationships between phenomena." But, Sartre argues, while such a denial runs counter to the findings of "contemporary philosophy," which has demonstrated "that meanings are also part of the immediate data," the world of the absurd people of Hemingway and Camus "is the analytic world of the neo-realists." And so, even as he disagrees with the philosophy, Sartre concludes that the method of the "neo-realists" has "proved its worth" through the centuries: "It was Voltaire's method in *L'Ingénu* and *Micromégas*, and Swift's in *Gulliver's Travels*. For the eighteenth century also had its own outsiders, "noble savages," usually, who, transported to a strange civilization, perceived facts before being able to grasp their meaning. The effect of this discrepancy was to arouse in the reader the feeling of the absurd."

Although one can argue with Sartre's opinion about the "neo-realists," his conclusion about the inability of early fictional protagonists to grasp the meanings of phenomena new to them is definitely a conclusion appropriate not just for those characters of fiction but for the real travelers who preceded and followed them. And without relating the fact to fictional protagonists, Wayne Franklin has observed it well for the early travelers to America, where, he wisely notes, not only was there an "initial failure of even a verbal understanding between red and white" but "the profusion of unknown natural objects in America placed an extra burden on the traveler's mind and languages."[10] It was indeed a cultural shock for the European visitors, whose vaunted sophistication was often found wanting; and so, what Sartre says of the readers of fiction in the eighteenth century was true of the readers of travels, for what they read surely aroused in them "the feeling of the absurd," especially if they were at all like those readers who, Ralegh, William Biddulph, and Bougainville complained, believed nothing they had not seen.

Franklin suggests that the accounts of these travelers to America prove that " 'Realism' is to be defined . . . according to the realities of the world which it touches" (238 n), a fact more or less true for travelers to other worlds, near or close to home. For of course reality is multilateral in exactly the ways a character of Marcel Proust is multilateral—for two people it is not alike and it changes with time, with training, and certainly with place. If, then, the readers of *L'Ingénu* and *Gulliver* felt the cultural shock experienced by their fictional protagonists, they were undergoing what had long been felt by travelers in all parts of the world and by their readers. For each of them it was "that crucial moment" Lévi-Strauss speaks of when, "thanks to the great voyages of discovery," the European community began "to achieve self-knowledge," that is, to find another realism to replace the old.[11] Goethe knew it in the eighteenth century. When Schiller asked him to collaborate on *The Journey*, in which they would describe reality by changing it, Goethe told him it was an old theme.[12]

A fifth and final relationship between travels and early fiction has to do with the effect that correspondents at home had on the letters written to them by distant travelers. And it is an important and fascinating part of the literature of travel since so much of that literature is in the form of letters. It is obvious how the tone and content of a fictional letter are conditioned by the person to whom the letter is addressed—Clarissa writing to the dear Anna Howe or to the disgusting Solmes. And while most of the letters of traveler James Howell of the seventeenth century are alike no matter who the recipient was, a letter to his father can be more personal than one to Lord Herbert; and even Samuel Johnson writing from Scotland to Hester Thrale may have told her almost exactly what he would have told anyone else. But surely some difference is to be expected depending on the sex, age, and training of the person receiving the travel letter, a fact easily accepted when one looks at the letters of Lady Mary Wortley Montagu written to Pope from Turkey. These are perhaps the best letters she ever wrote and some of the best in the history of travel literature.

Lady Mary's letters—probably much revised for publication—show her studying Turkish politics, harem customs, art, and poetry, but they also show Pope's influence on her tone and almost surely on her subject matter. Very recently Patricia Meyer Spacks offered a number of cogent observations about those letters,[13] one being that Pope tried to draw Lady Mary into a correspondence with erotic overtones, a correspondence, he said, composed by "imaginations warm and tender." His is a courtly romance tradition that, Spacks shows, can be traced at least to Vincent Voiture, whom Pope had read. Voiture, widely admired as courtier and author of vers de société, especially by women of all ages, often traveled for his king and always wrote charming letters back, usually to women, from teen-agers to dowagers, and often with slight touches of the erotic. From Morocco in 1633 he could write Mlle Paulet, la belle lionne, so called because of her golden hair, and talk wittily about her appearance more than about Africa; in 1642, writing to Mlle Rambouillet, of the family of the most famous of salon hostesses, he could still be as witty and clever but at the same time make quick, unpretentious statements about the hills and vineyards around Avignon, be facetious about water travel on the Rhone, and tell the young girl a story of the boatman who had carried 10,000 people from Lyons to Beaucaire.[14] It is this tradition, Spacks notices, into which Pope was trying to draw Lady Mary; for, he said, their correspondence "belongs only in a Romance." And for him "Romance" obviously meant both eroticism and exoticism; that is, travel letters were to feed two kinds of fantasy, one being sexual, the other being dreams of far places. And thus Lady Mary's journey would be vicariously for Pope what the fictional Strether's journey to Paris two hundred years later would be for him—"psychosexual as well as geographical."[15]

The close relationships between a great variety of travel accounts and as many varieties of the amorphous early novel are, then, many—from structure and subject matter and language to tone and philosophy, even to literary conventions and motives for composition—but certainly the two forms are often not alike and in fact can be as different from each other as prose fiction sometimes is from the best-known examples of epic or formal history, or as one kind of novel is from another. Travel literature contributed little of course to the kind of characterization done so well by certain novelists from Richardson to James, even though travelers often reveal themselves or their companions or other people as well as do some fictionizers who stress spatial movement and episodic plots rather than motives and emotions. Nor do travel writers normally take time to develop the minor characters they introduce, whereas minor characters often become important in the novel—Fielding's Partridge or Smollett's Lismahago, for example. Furthermore, the plots of most travel accounts are not of the type advocated by a Corneille or a Dryden, that is, plots requiring that careful attention be given to liaison des scènes, as in *Mariane* or *Clarissa* but not in *Tom Jones* with its travel section that sometimes may lead us anywhere and with its dozens of blatant coincidences. Nor do travel writers follow a psychological line in time, as certain fiction writers do, so much as they follow—or try to follow—a space line drawn on a chart. It is true, as Mylne says, that eighteenth-century novelists "found better methods of shaping and conveying a story" than they had formerly used, the most obvious structural development—an improvement by certain standards today—being the loss of the interpolated tale;[16] but travel writers have continued to make interpolations of all kinds ornamental, attractive, expected, necessary. In fact, when in the twentieth century an Osbert Sitwell believes he is creating the word "discursion" from two words, "discourse" and "discursive," in order to characterize his travel books with their "personal random reflections and sentiments," or a Norman Douglas describes his "personal structure" for a travel book—that is, "narrative and description interrupted by frequent interlarded essays"[17]—each of these fine writers is doing exactly what travel writers since the beginning of time have been doing. Moreover, travel writers, the early ones at least, did not knowingly incline to allegory or employ suspense and foreshadowing artfully; and while like the novelists they were all subject to selection for artistic and factual reasons, they perhaps had no need of what Henry James called foreshortening. Nor, in general, did they record dialogue realistically until after the novel did, each group then borrowing the art of conversation from drama and from each other. In spite of these and other differences, however, the important fact remains that, as certain Russian formalists have noted and as the present study has shown in detail, prose fiction and the travel account have evolved together, are heavily indebted to each other, and are often similar in both content and technique.

If, then, one wishes to pursue the early, real relationship between these two forms, can we at this point provide a manageable definition of travel literature, one that students of the novel may begin with? To be sure, we have noted how "novel," or long prose fiction, cannot itself be defined to the satisfaction of any group.[18] And to define travel literature—that is, the récit de voyage, perhaps a better term—is just as impossible. Genericists like Tallmadge will call it a "genre" and yet, as Swift and Fielding did, make it a category of "history."[19] Reuel K. Wilson, in an attractive recent study of Russian travels to the time of Pushkin, calls the form a "travelogue" written in the first person,[20] and he begins its "evolution" far too late, apparently with Defoe and the eighteenth century. But if we find any definition of travel literature historically inaccurate or too restrictive, perhaps we can, as Abraham Cowley did with "Wit," define it by negatives.

The récit de voyage is not just a first-person journal or diary. Much of it is in third person.

It is not just in prose. There are many poetic travel accounts, from Horace to the Polish poet Twardeski (1622) to Bashō to Bachaumont and beyond,[21] and travel literature is often beautifully illustrated or it may have fascinating drawings of engines and buildings and parks, as the French scientist Lalande does in the account of his visit to England (1763).[22]

It is not necessarily a story with a simple, uncontrived plot, as Defoe's *Tour* evidences.

It is not just a set of notes jotted down each day or whenever the traveler has time, as with Montaigne, Huygens, Fiennes, and Lalande; but far, far more often the account has been reworked, changed in translation, polished, edited, often with collaboration. In fact, nearly every récit de voyage published in the author's lifetime is not a pristine journal or set of notes, a fact that for the twentieth century is perhaps even more true.

It is not just an objective report, a description, of places and people seen, of inns visited, food eaten; much more often it is a subjective interpretation —"observations" is a favorite term—of scenes and of political, religious, and social events or situations. Subjectivity and selectivity may, in fact, lead to almost total disagreement among observers as to the nature of food, inns, roads, friendliness of people. It is safe to say that the lasting travel accounts are quite subjective, that—within limits—the more subjective they are, the more readable, the more "valuable" they are. Travelers, like novelists, learned long ago the truth of Todorov's statement of a universal law: "The best description . . . is the one which is not description all the way."[23] That is, the best description is combined with, cannot really be separated from, narration, reflection, interpretation.

Travel writing, in spite of what librarians and historians have often said, is not a branch of history any more than it is of geography. Its ties with history and with geography are of course real and self-evident, as titles such as *The History of Tom Jones* point to the ties between the novel and history; but most travel writers are more subjective than historians, at least since Pierre Bayle, ever admit about their work. Some such travel accounts are by botanists or medical doctors; others are by divines, businessmen, ambassadors, pirates, artists, engineers, tutors, students. Seldom does one of them have the training of a historian or a geographer. And even a geographer such as Thomas Jeffreys, the King's Geographer in the eighteenth century, may write about nature and people from a layman's point of view and perhaps say nothing of his professional interests. Frank Kermode has made the point that, while the novelist and the historian are alike in many ways, the first is concerned more with *geschichtlich* (relevance to now) and the second more with *historisch* (criticism of the past).[24] In this important respect the travel writer is much closer to the novelist, for he consistently takes departure from present scenes and events and returns to the past only as those scenes and events guide his thinking. The lasting author of travels—neither historian nor novelist—is, then, a roving, literate journalist who seeks to combine several disciplines, among which are anthropology, sociology, psychology, and of course history and geography. That journalist can be an amateur with one book—Captain Luke Fox in the North Atlantic or Lionel Wafer in Panama. He can be a professional writer in another field turning to travels—Addison, Defoe, Johnson, Goethe, and a thousand others. Or he can be a professional travel writer such as James Howell of the seventeenth century; Arthur Young and Samuel Ireland with his "Picturesque Views" of British rivers, both of the eighteenth century; Charles Dudley Warner of the nineteenth century; and, say, John McPhee of the twentieth century with his "oranges" of Florida, his beautiful studies of Alaska and New England, and his "Arch-Druids" of the Rockies.

The récit de voyage is, of course, not just an exploration report like that of Columbus or John Smith or James Cook; it can also be an account of an ocean voyage, of a Grand Tour, of a short trip from London to the Lake Country, of a Barbary captivity, of Madam Knight riding a horse through rural New England.

It is not a complete record of a journey but, as with any type of art, often carefully selective when the writer considers what to record or comment on.

It is not "subliterature" perhaps any more than prose fiction is. It is, in fact, often fine literature, as with Addison, Lady Mary, Smollett, Sterne, Beckford, and Radcliffe, or with Challe, Muralt, Carbonnières, Goethe, and Chateaubriand, all of the eighteenth century. And also, sometimes long before the eighteenth century, there are "Mandeville," Joinville, Cartier, Champlain, and there are Ralegh and Lescarbot, della Valle and Howell. But where do we draw the line? Are the subliterary travelers not just as difficult to segregate as are the subliterary fiction writers? Do we use that term for the books of the articulate lawyer Careri, the equally articulate botanist Ray, or the buccaneer Dampier and other favorites of Coleridge, Masefield, and Lowes? Are not the personal and exciting stories of Álvar Núñez and Mendes Pinto more than history, more than autobiography? If we accept Defoe's *Tour* partly because he wrote *Robinson Crusoe*, what do we do with the travel journal of that other literary genius Montaigne, who, unlike Defoe, did not revise? In later centuries, are the travel accounts of Mark Twain and Henry James not fine literature, or when they are that good do we, as with Sterne's *Sentimental Journey*, insist on calling the composition fiction or, with Boswell's *Hebrides*, call it biography? The literature of travel is gigantic; it has a thousand forms and faces. In fact, if we disregard

Don Quixote and the *Princesse de Clèves*, perhaps half a dozen of their fictional fellows, there are a hundred travel accounts of the sixteenth and seventeenth centuries that give as much pleasure to the reader, as much sense of excitement and wonder, as much instruction and aesthetic satisfaction as any one of the favorite fictions published before Lesage and Defoe. And for the eighteenth century there may be more good travel books than good novels.

Finally, the récit de voyage cannot be a literary genre with a fixed definition any more than the novel is; it is not even sui generis since it includes so many types both by form and by content. For, like other forms just as amorphous, it evolves and will continue to evolve.

Such conclusions, not all negative to be sure, will not of course be warmly accepted by everyone, for they leave us with a literary form difficult to separate from other forms, one that through change will keep on eluding us. And if critics of the récit de voyage were as numerous as those who write about the novel, perhaps there would be a school forecasting the death of travel writing, as at one time or another Ortega, Fiedler, Wain, and Walter Sullivan have talked about the death of, the "perilous" state of, the possible exhaustion of the novel, in each case "novel" apparently being used in a narrow sense, one that leaves small room for evolution. Two years after Ortega wrote his opinion, however, the Nobel Prize was awarded to William Faulkner, one of the greatest and most experimental novelists of all time —or did he write "romances"? And as Fiedler and Wain wrote, another "nouveau roman" had just reached its peak of accomplishment and in so doing suggested again that fine writers may continue to accommodate themselves to their time and, paradoxically, find new ways of continuing the tradition.[25]

Nevertheless, as with the novel, one may argue that travel writing is an exhausted literary form. One possible argument is that the twentieth century has developed so many visual means of communicating travels— Jacques Cousteau and *National Geographic* on television—that people now turn from books to screens. Another argument—this one a paradox—may be that we all travel so much now that we do not need accounts of travel by other people. Again, however, the evolutionary process may be expected to take over. As means of travel expand, writers are inspired to travel more; they thus exercise their imagination more and acquire more information; and they write more books. Likewise, as readers also travel more, the more they want to travel; and since they still cannot go everywhere, they may want to read books inspired by places they have not seen. Butor is right in a very real sense to say that, just as "travel is writing, reading is travel."[26] But surely reading often leads the recluse from his arm chair. John Harris of the eighteenth century provides the popular opinion for all times: ". . .

if so much Pleasure result from the Perusal of Voyages and Travels, there must be still a greater in Travelling itself."[27]

And as the novelist finds new topics, new themes, new techniques, so does the travel writer. The seventeenth and eighteenth centuries had few professional travel writers such as Coryat, John Taylor, Howell, perhaps Gemelli Careri, but the nineteenth century had dozens of them: James Jarves, Mark Twain, and Howells wrote four travel volumes each; Bayard Taylor and Charles Dudley Warner wrote them all their lives. Dana's *Two Years Before the Mast* (1840), Taylor's *Views A-Foot* (1846), Jarves's *Parisian Sights* (1855), Twain's *The Innocents Abroad* (1869), and Stevenson's *Travels with a Donkey in the Cévennes* (1879) are only five of the many different kinds of récits de voyage that captivated the United States before 1900.

And the twentieth century has even extended the variety. Paul Fussell's *Abroad* (1980) is a study of scores of first-rate British travel books written between the two World Wars. Then there are the pilgrimages of Thomas Merton, each a "symbolic acting out of an inner journey";[28] the Ugly American books of certain Europeans; the lyric accounts of aviators such as Saint-Exupéry; and a book like Butor's *Mobile* with its ambiguous title, newspaper headlines, and a treatment in alphabetical order of all states in the United States. Or, more recently, we can read Studs Terkel, who has traveled the United States with his recorder, taped three hundred autobiographies, and put together *American Dreams: Lost and Found*, a book that conforms to the opinion of Voltaire and Samuel Johnson that it is better "to go an hundred miles to speak with one wise man, than five miles to see a fair town."[29] And just as the eighteenth-century Grand Tourists visited ancient Italian buildings and the places Virgil wrote about, so in our century do travel writers hew out or follow literary paths, in at least three ways: Students of Greek culture have sailed the Mediterranean in the wake of Odysseus hoping to find traces of his Cimmerians and his Achaians; enthusiasts of another kind have followed the steps of Johnson and Boswell in Scotland and the Hebrides superimposing a twentieth-century time on an earlier time, as Sterne's protagonist did when he paused after a second visit to Lyons and wrote his impressions; and just now the British Jonathan Raban, author of *Arabia: A Journey through the Labyrinth*—but also of *The Technique of Modern Fiction*—has taken a sixteen-foot boat down the Mississippi River in order to follow Huck Finn and write *Old Glory: An American Voyage*—the "plot ... written by the current of the river itself"—a travel book advertised as having "the endless fascination of a wonderfully observed novel."

By no means, then, have the novel and the récits de voyage ceased to evolve, or to evolve together; for the journey motif—real or fictional—is still the most significant, whether geographical, spiritual, psychological, or intellectual. Céline's *Voyage au bout de la nuit* is a successful novel whose Ferdinand travels the world to face a hundred environments and in the second part of which the shipwrecked Robinson [Crusoe] enters as a symbolic character. Céline, Germaine Brée concludes, has employed "the voyage metaphor on several levels—in detail and as the basic structural device ordering the specific viewer—a viewed dynamic that governs the episodic unfolding of the journey, its plotting."[30] In Bellow's *Herzog* the journey is symbolic in yet a different way—with Thomas Merton it is spiritual; here and with Céline it is more psychological and intellectual. "The action which leads to the beginning of Herzog's self-discovery," Harold Mosher points out,[31] "is both a voyage in time, a descent to the underworld of the past through letters and memories, and a series of voyages in space—futile attempts to establish his identity in the present. Paradoxically these voyages, mental and physical, are attempts both to escape and find the self. Ultimately, however, Herzog ends his psychological journey [and his very real geographical journeys] facing his real self." And, finally, there are writers like V.S. Naipaul, whose novels are travel books and whose récits de voyage are novels—he has written three of each since 1969. As Lévi-Strauss in 1934 sailed to Brazil, he said, in the path of Columbus, Naipaul goes back in time to his native India or west to South America. In *The Loss of El Dorado* (1969) he retells the story of that kingdom of fabulous hopes and, as Martin Green says,[32] he tells it "in Conradian style, as a sardonic grotesque comedy," not as an ordinary historical account of all those Spanish and English travelers who sought the fabled land and created the myth. For Naipaul, Sir Walter Raleigh is the hero, and his story and his travel book are "part of the world's romance."[33] With writers such as Céline and Bellow the fictional protagonist becomes a traveler like those great travelers of all time—Marco Polo, Columbus, Pinto, Cook. With writers such as Naipaul and Raban, the travel book and the novel become one form, as they sometimes did with Challe, with Sterne, and with Smollett in the eighteenth century. Such writers are more and more numerous, as Patrick Anderson has seen when he argues that Lawrence's novel *Kangaroo* gives a better description of Australia than his travel books do of Italy, that William Beckford's *Visit to the Monasteries* is a novel more than it is a travel journal, or that, for each of these—"real" travel account or "realistic" novel—the author has achieved "a balance between an interesting personality and an exterior world imaginatively and critically seen."[34]

ABBREVIATIONS USED FOR TITLES OF JOURNALS

BNYPL	Bulletin of the New York Public Library
CE	College English
CEA Critic	College English Association Critic
CL	Comparative Literature
CLS	Comparative Literature Studies
EAL	Early American Literature
ELH	English Literary History
HLQ	Huntington Library Quarterly
JEGP	Journal of English and Germanic Philology
MLQ	Modern Language Quarterly
MLR	Modern Language Review
MLS	Modern Language Studies
MP	Modern Philology
PLL	Papers on Language and Literature
PMLA	Publications of the Modern Language Association of America
PQ	Philological Quarterly
RES	Review of English Studies
RHL	Revue d'Histoire Littéraire de la France
SEC	Studies in the Eighteenth Century
SP	Studies in Philology
SVEC	Studies in Voltaire and the Eighteenth Century
TSL	Tennessee Studies in Literature
TSLL	Texas Studies in Language and Literature
YES	Yearbook of English Studies

NOTES

CHAPTER ONE

1. Joseph Conrad, "Books," 1905. Rpt. in *Notes on Life and Letters* (1921) and in Miriam Allott, *Novelists on the Novel* (New York: Columbia Univ. Press, 1959, 1966) pp. 132-33.

2. See William T. Noon, *Joyce and Aquinas* (New Haven: Yale Univ. Press, 1957), p. 55 and p. 55n., as well as Paul Hernadi, *Beyond Genre* (Ithaca, N.Y.: Cornell Univ. Press, 1972), for example, p. 152, who refers us to Ernst Hirt, *Das Formgesetz der epischen, dramatischen und lyrischen Dichtung* (1923), for evidence that by about 1800 (the time of Hegel and Schelling) "the Germans," very generic-minded, had settled on these three as the major types of literature.

3. René Wellek and Austin Warren, *Theory of Literature* (New York: Harcourt, Brace, 1942). p. 239.

4. Benedetto Croce, *Estetica* (1901), trans. Ainslie (London: MacMillan, 1909), pp. 361, 363.

5. Lutwack, "Mixed and Uniform Prose Styles in the Novel," *Journal of Aesthetics and Art Criticism*, 18 (1960) [rpt. Robert Murray Davis, ed., *The Novel: Modern Essays in Criticism* (Englewood Cliffs, N.J.: Prentice-Hall, 1969), p. 254]; Tillyard, *The Epic Strain in the English Novel* (Fair Lawn, N.J.: Essential Books, 1958), p. 24. See Davis, p. 264 for yet more ageneric critics of the novel.

6. Creighton, in *The Future of the Novel* (1924; rpt. Port Washington, NY.: Kennikat, 1970), pp. 96-97.

7. Scholes, "Towards a Poetics of Fiction: An Approach through Genre," *Novel*, 2 (1969), 101-11; see p. 111 for the quotation. In "Towards a Syntax of Fiction," *College English*, 36 (1974), 147-60, Frank D. McConnell takes departure from this essay by Scholes to talk of certain trends in novel criticism.

8. Frye, *The Anatomy of Criticism* (Princeton: Princeton Univ. Press, 1957).

9. See Alvin B. Kernan, *The Plot of Satire* (New Haven: Yale Univ. Press, 1965), for only one attack on Frye's system, in particular, on Frye's long discussion of Menippean satire and its inclusion in "anatomy."

10. Shroder, "The Novel as a Genre," *The Massachusetts Review* (1963) [rpt. Davis, ed. *The Novel*, pp. 43-57].

11. Novak, "Freedom, Libertinism, and the Picaresque," in Harold E. Pagliaro, ed., *Racism in the Eighteenth Century* (Cleveland: Case Western Reserve Univ. Press, 1973), pp. 35-48. For much more on the picaresque, see Chap. VII below.

12. For Frye, see note 8 above; for Steeves, see his *Before Jane Austen: The Shaping of the English Novel in the Eighteenth Century* (New York: Holt, Rinehart, and Winston, 1965), p. 1; for Watt, see his *The Rise of the Novel* (Berkeley and Los Angeles: Univ. of California Press, 1962; 1st pub. 1957), p. 291: "not so much a novel as a parody of a novel"; Cross, *The Development of the English Novel* (New York: Macmillan, 1925), p. 72; and for Shklovsky, see Lee Lemon and Marlon Reis, eds., *Russian Formalist Criticism: Four Essays*, a Bison Book (Lincoln: Univ. of Nebraska Press, 1965), p. 57, and quoted also by Robert Scholes, "The Contributions of Formalism and Structuralism to the Theory of Fiction," *Novel*, 6 (1973), 137.

13. Auerbach, *Mimesis: The Representation of Reality in Western Literature,* trans. Willard Trask (Garden City, N.Y.: Doubleday Anchor Books, 1957); for Watt, see note 12 above.

14. Showalter, *The Evolution of the French Novel, 1641-1782* (Princeton: Princeton Univ. Press, 1972), p. 7. The five are "chronology, geography, money, names, and the narrator." Showalter prefers "novelistic" to "realism."

15. Harvey, *Character and the Novel* (Ithaca, N.Y.: Cornell Univ. Press, 1965).

16. Both Schorer's epoch-making essay "Technique as Discovery," first printed in the *Hudson Review* in 1948, and Handy's "Toward a Formalist Criticism of Fiction" are reprinted in Davis, ed., *The Novel.*

17. Booth, *The Rhetoric of Fiction* (Chicago: Univ. of Chicago Press, 1961).

18. For Hirsch, see, for example, his "Objective Interpretation," *PMLA,* 75 (1960), 463-79; and for Todorov, see his *Poétique de la prose* (Paris: Seuil, 1971), p. 54, as translated by Robert Scholes (see note 12 above), p. 149.

19. See Wellek and Warren, *Theory of Literature.*

20. Kellogg and Scholes, *The Nature of Narrative* (New York: Oxford Univ. Press, 1966).

21. It has of course been fashionable to "expose" this really significant study of the eighteenth-century English novel. Watt's consolation may be that a bad book would never have attracted so much profitable attention. See his response to the tribe of critics in "Ian Watt, Reflecting on *The Rise of the Novel* (1957)," *Novel,* 1 (1968), 205-19.

22. Freedman, "The Possibility of a Theory of the Novel," in *The Discipline of Criticism,* ed. Peter Demetz, Theodore Greene, and Lowry Nelson, Jr. (New Haven: Yale Univ. Press, 1968), pp. 57-79.

23. See Kellogg and Scholes saying, much like Freedman later, that "the novel is not the opposite of romance, as is usually maintained, but a product of the empirical and fictional [including romance] elements in literature." Shroder (note 10 above) agrees with Freedman and with Kellogg and Scholes, although he prefers to stress the "romance" origins rather than the epic. Walter R. Davis, *Idea and Art in Elizabethan Fiction* (Princeton: Princeton Univ. Press, 1969), adopts the theory that critics should not compare "pre-novelistic" with "novelistic" fiction.

24. James, *The Art of the Novel* (New York: Scribners, 1934), p. 326.

25. The information about terms given here and in the next paragraph comes from many sources but especially from Edith Kern, "The Romance of Novel/Novella," in Demetz, Greene, and Nelson, eds., *The Discipline of Criticism,* pp. 511-30; Werner Kraus, "Novela-Novelle-Roman," *Zeitschrift fur romanische Philologie,* 60 (1940), 21; Arthur Tieje, "A Peculiar Phase of the Theory of Realism in Pre-Richardsonian Fiction," *PMLA,* 28 (1913), 215-53, as well as his "The Expressed Aim of the Long Prose Fiction from 1597 to 1740," *JEGP,* 11 (1912), 402-33 [hereinafter cited as Tieje (1913) and Tieje (1912)]; Showalter (see note 14 above), e.g., pp. 11-37; Dieter Schultz, "Novel, 'Romance,' and Popular Fiction in the First Half of the Eighteenth Century," *SP,* 70 (1973), 77-91; René Godenne, *Histoire de la nouvelle française aux XVIIe et XVIIe siécles* (Geneva: Droz, 1970); F.C. Green, *French Novelists: Manners and Ideas from the Renaissance to the Revolution* (1929; rpt. New York: Ungar, 1964); and Vivienne Mylne, *The Eighteenth-Century French Novel* (New York: Barnes and Noble, 1965), pp. 19-24 especially.

26. Torquato Tasso, *Discorsi del poema heroico* (1594?). See, for the great influence of Tasso in France, Maurice Magendie, *Le Roman français au XVIIe siècle* (Paris: Droz, 1932), pp. 47 ff. For romanzo and roman, see p. 51.

27. Daniel Huet, "Lettre à M. de Segrais sur l'Origine des romans," appended to Mme de La Fayette's *Zayde* (1670).

28. See OED, s.v., "Novel," for this date and for the pronunciation, and Kern, p. 522.

29. Showalter, pp. 21-22, is, I believe, the first to point out this most important fact that readers of English literary history must remember.

30. John A. Clapp, "An Eighteenth-Century Attempt at a Critical View of the Novel:

The Bibliothèque Universelle des Romans," *PMLA*, 25 (1910) 60-96. There were 102 such collections in England of the eighteenth century, Clapp finds, sixty-five in France. In England "romance" and "novel" appear indiscriminately in the titles for most of the century.

31. For Shaftesbury, see "Advice to an Author," from *Characteristicks of Men, Manners, Opinions, Times . . .*, as found in Oliver E. Sigworth, ed., *Criticism and Aesthetics: 1660-1800* (San Francisco: Rinehart, 1971), p. 184 ("Romance, *or* novel" [my italics]). For Defoe, see his *The Family Instructor* ("novels, romances, and such like stuff"); this and other similar uses of the words can be found in Maximillian Novak, "Defoe's Theory of Fiction," *SP*, 61 (1964), 650-68. For Richardson, see his Preface to the sequel to *Pamela* (1741), where he hopes to avoid "the improbable and marvelous with which novels abound." For Haywood, one of several examples is *Idalia: or, The Unfortunate Mistress. A Novel*, in Vol. III of her *Secret Histories, Novels, and Poems* (1742).

32. See Kern, p. 526, e.g. E.A. Baker, *The History of the English Novel*, 10 vols. (New York: Barnes and Noble, 1950; 1st ed., 1924-39), IV, 13-14, is, I think, quite wrong in his opinions about the terms *roman* and *novel* and the "rise" to realsim in France and England.

33. Much of what follows can be checked by reading the standard histories of fiction, especially those for the seventeenth and eighteenth centuries. For France, see Magendie, *Le Roman français au XVII⁄ siècle;* Showalter; F.C. Green; Godenne; Mylne; Philip Stewart, *Imitation and Illusion in the French Memoir-Novel, 1700-1750* (New Haven: Yale Univ. Press, 1969); and Georges May, Le *Dilemme du roman au XVIII⁄ siècle* (New Haven: Yale Univ. Press, 1963). For England, see Lionel Stevenson, *The English Novel* (Boston: Houghton Mifflin, 1960); Ronald Paulson, *Satire and the Novel in Eighteenth-Century England* (New Haven: Yale Univ. Press, 1967); A.D. McKillop, *The Early Masters of English Fiction* (Lawrence: Univ. of Kansas Press, 1956). In spite of its brilliance, Ian Watt's book is of little use here because of its limited point of view and slight attention to the seventeenth century. For bibliographies that are of use especially for terms, see those by S. Paul Jones (1939); R.C. Williams (1931); R.W. Baldner (1967) [including the review by Frédéric Deloffre, *Dix-septième siècle*, no. 79 (1968), 105-107]; William H. McBurney (1960); and Charles C. Mish (1952).

34. Showalter says this of the various "subgenres" in France at the end of the seventeenth century; the statement is just as true for English language fiction then.

35. See Clapp, note 30 above.

36. For other modern classifications see Showalter or, for a quite different one, John J. Richetti, *Popular Fiction before Richardson: Narrative Patterns 1700-1739* (Oxford: Clarendon, 1969).

37. Mylne, pp. 2-3, contends that the twentieth-century term "realism," or "réalisme," is not satisfactory for the seventeenth and eighteenth centuries, and so she prefers "representation," which she defines more broadly.

38. See Paulson, *Satire and the Novel*, pp. 29-32, for a similar statement. See the preface to the anonymous *Constantia; or A True Picture of Human Life* (1751) for evidence that the eighteenth century knew Cervantes's theories well. For only one example of Cervantes's expression of his theory of verisimilitude and pleasure, see *Don Quixote* (Part I, Chap. 47).

39. Segrais, I, 146 [my trans.], Showalter, pp. 22-24, has much on Segrais and provides further evidence for seventeenth-century opinions about the nouvelle and the roman.

40. For all these and more, see Tieje (1912); Showalter; especially Megendie; George Barnett, ed., *Eighteenth-Century British Novelists on the Novel* (New York: Appleton-Century-Crofts, 1968); and Stevenson, *The English Novel.*

41. For Sidney, see the letter to his sister that accompanied the MS.

42. For Marcassus and Claireville, see the "Avertissements" to their romances as quoted in Magendie, pp. 123-24.

43. For Boileau, see his *L'Art poétique* (1774), III.119: "Roman frivole."

44. For Collier, see Appendix to *Morey's Great Historical, Geographical, and Poetical Dictionary* (London, 1721), as quoted by Arthur Johnson, "Romance Reborn," in *Enchanted Ground* (Oxford: Oxford Univ. Press, 1964), p. 38, and reprinted in Eleanor T. Lincoln, ed. *Pastoral and Romance* (Englewood Cliffs, N.J.: Prentice-Hall, 1969), p. 249; for Desfontaines, see F.C. Green, "The Eighteenth-Century French Critic and the Contemporary Novel," *MLB*, 23 (1928), p. 75; for Goldsmith, see *Citizen of the World*, Letter XXXIII; and for Jane Austen, see *Northanger Abbey*, Chap. V, quoted also by Mylne, p. 15.

45. Ascham's *The Schoolmaster* is quoted by Stevenson, p. 13.

46. For Camus and de Grenailles, see Magendie, pp. 142-49.

47. For the marquise de Lambert, Montesquieu, Voltaire, and other examples, see May, for example, p. 25.

48. For Bayle, see Paul Hazard, *La Crise de la conscience européenne (1680-1715)* (Paris: Boivin, 1935), pp. 107-11, who is analyzing Bayle's philosophy as found in the *Dictionnaire historique et critique* (1697), especially the articles on "Calius," "Capet," "Pyrrhon," and "Manichéens." For the attack on Villedieu see Bayle's article "Jardins," that is, Marie-Catherine Desjardins, the earlier name of Mme de Villedieu. For more on Bayle's campaign, see Georges May, "L'Histoire a-t-elle engendré le Roman?" *Revue d'histoire littéraire de la France*, 55 (1955), 157-59, and Mylne, p. 19. Bayle, like Voltaire, also attacked Courtilz de Sandras, a prolific precursor of Defoe, for his false "histoires," and d'Argens (1739) "detested" the mixture of fiction and history (May, *Dilemme*, p. 157).

49. Here, and in this paragraph, for Chapelain, see his letter to Scudéry (1660) found in Magendie, p. 120, who also has examples (p. 124) of readers who argued that simple pleasure, escapism, was enough; Showalter, p. 71. For Lesage, Prévost, and Marivaux—as well as many others—see their prefaces or opening words in, say, *Gil Blas, Cleveland*, or *Marianne*.

50. For Kirkman and Head, see their prefatorial claims to stories in Spiro Peterson, ed., *The Counterfeit Lady Unveiled and Other Criminal Fiction of Seventeenth-Century England* (Garden City, New York: Doubleday Anchor, 1961), p. 11, p. 144; for Defoe and Fielding, see the prefaces to *Moll Flanders* and *Joseph Andrews;* and for Richardson, see his "Postscript" to the fourth ed. of *Clarissa*, found, e.g., in Barnett, p. 76, and his letter to Warburton quoted in A.D. McKillop, *Early Masters*, p. 42.

51. Much of the information in the next several paragraphs can of course be found by a wide reading in seventeenth- and eighteenth-century literary history, but I believe that a brief survey is necessary here for what follows in this and other chapters. Note, however, that Tieje (1912) concludes that there are five "expressed aims" of long prose fiction between 1589 and 1715—the reader's amusement, his edification, his instruction, the depiction of contemporaneous life, and the arousing of emotion.

52. For France, see Magendie, pp. 124-25; for Osborne and Temple, see Stevenson, p. 33; for Hamilton, see his first chapter; and for Jenner, see Book IV, Chap. I, of his *The Placid Man; or, Memoirs of Sir Charles Beville* (rpt. in Barnett, p. 127).

53. Barnett, p. 6. See Tieje (1912) for many examples of authorial or editorial claims that fiction taught correct religion, or politics, or geography.

54. See Walter R. Davis, *Idea and Art in Elizabethan Fiction*, pp. 95, 97.

55. May, *Dilemme*, p. 248, e.g.

56. Georges Scudéry, Preface to *Ibrahim* (1641).

57. Chapelain, *De la Lectures des vieux romans*, p. 12, as quoted in Magendie, p. 135.

58. Paulson, *Satire and the Novel*, p. 24.

59. Percy G. Adams, "The Anti-Hero in Eighteenth-Century Fiction," *Studies in the Literary Imagination*, 9 (1976), 29-53. For more on this topic, see Raney Stanford, "The Subversive Hero and the Beginnings of Fiction," *Discourse*, 13 (1970), 366-78. In the rest of the paragraph, for Voltaire, see his *Epic Poetry of the European Nation from Homer down to Milton*

(London: Jallasson, 1727), which, the next year, he let the abbé Desfontaines "translate" into French as *Essai sur la poésie épique* (Paris: Chaubert, 1728), the French version being almost unrecognizably different from the English. For Lobos, see I.L. McClelland, *The Origins of the Romantic Movement in Spain* (Liverpool: Institute of Hispanic Studies, 1937), p. 206.

60. Tieje (1913), pp. 236, 239, 242. Even more curiously, Tieje goes on to give copious examples from prefaces to seventeenth-century fiction that disprove his thesis. For McKillop, see his p. 7.

61. The following quotations and citations can be found in Magendie, pp. 125 ff.; Tieje (1913), pp. 236, 239, 242; Showalter, pp. 28, 17; and Barnett, pp. 7, 23.

62. For de Mouhy, this is the translation by Green, "The Eighteenth-Century French Critics ...," p. 180; for Johnson, see especially his analysis of Shakespeare's "genius" in the Preface to Shakespeare, but see also his praise of Pope's "Imagination" in any number of places, especially in the section on "Eloisa to Abelard" and in the summary of Pope's characteristics.

63. The "anonymous" author of *Amours de Lintason et de Pallinoé*, as quoted by Tieje (1913); for Mackenzie, Boyle, and Manley, see Barnett; for Soubligny's preface, see Showalter, pp. 163–64, and Mylne, p. 26n., who notes that Ian Watt, pp. 18-20, dismisses this "realistic" development in English fictional names. For much more on the huge subject of "plain truth" and style in general, see Chap. X below.

64. Huet, *Traité de l'origine des romans*, quoted in Magendie, p. 126.

65. For Fielding, see the Preface to *Joseph Andrews;* for Sorel, see his *De la Connaissance des bons livres* (1672), especially Chap. IV, as well as Paulson, *Satire and the Novel*, p. 14; and for Johnson, see *Rambler* No. 4, par. 2.

66. All these, and others, can be found in Magendie, pp. 118-57. The last phrase is from Bishop Huet, e.g.

67. Le sieur Viard, in the *Avis* to his *Dorisandre*. See Magendie, p. 132.

68. See Mylne, p. 10n. Showalter, pp. 27-37, has much on du Plaisir in a fine analysis of the contemporaneous criticism of seventeenth-century French fiction and its search for rules. D'Argens in *Les Lettres juives* (1738), a work of fiction in the Marana-Montesquieu tradition, has more theories about the roman, theories close in fact to those of Fielding.

69. Barnett, pp. 91-97.

70. For Griffith and Cumberland, see Barnett, p. 119, p. 156; the "chortler," H. Lawrence, author of *The Contemplative Man*, I, 213-14, is quoted by Paulson, *Satire and the Novel*, p. 8.

71. Showalter makes this claim for both French and English fiction (p. 65). He is, I think, more nearly correct in believing that prefaces were no real indication of what was happening to the novel, that a particular novelist cannot be trusted to analyze his or her own technique or aims (pp. 63-64). See Tieje (1912) for the same theory, with evidence.

72. See the standard bibliographies, some listed in note 33 above, for translations out of one language into the other. But see also Georges May, "The Influence of English Fiction on the French Mid-Eighteenth-Century Novel," *Aspects of the Eighteenth Century* (Baltimore: Johns Hopkins Univ. Press, 1965), pp. 265-81; Daniel Mornet, "Les Enseignements des bibliothèques privées (1750-1780)," *Revue d'histoire littéraire de la France*, 17 (1910), 457; James R. Foster, *History of the Pre-Romantic Novel in England* (New York: MLA, 1949); H.W. Streeter, *The Eighteenth-Century English Novel in French Translation: A Bibliographical Study* (New York: Institute of French Studies, 1936); and studies of individual novelists, especially Scudéry, Scarron, Prévost, Rousseau, and Behn, Defoe (*Crusoe* only), Sterne, and Richardson.

73. See Maurice Bardon, *"Don Quichotee" en France au XVIIe et au XVIIIe sièlcle, 1605-1815* (Paris: Champion, 1931), 2 vols.; and James Fitzmaurice-Kelly, *Cervantes in England* (London: Frowde, 1905). For only one of many short statements of the influence of Cervantes, see Paulson, pp. 29-33.

74. For most of these statistics and other facts, see note 72 above. Novak, "Some Notes

toward a History of Fictional Forms," *Novel*, 6 (1973), 120-33. Compare Georges May: "nowhere else is a comparative approach more legitimate" (note 72 above). Tieje's two long articles (1912, 1913) talk of far more than just English fiction, and Paulson's *Satire and the Novel* shows a wide acquaintance with the fiction of the Continent, as does Foster, *The History of the Pre-Romantic Novel in England.*

75. Wagenknecht, *Cavalcade of the English Novel* (New York: Holt, 1943), p. 69.

76. Steeves, *Before Jane Austen*, p. 1; and Watt, p. 9. Watt's subtitle is, of course, "Studies in Defoe, Richardson and Fielding."

77. Raleigh, *The English Novel* (London: John Murray, 1894) treats Defoe as a precursor and Richardson as the first novelist, but Raleigh does recognize (p. 140) that La Fayette and Marivaux preceded Richardson as novelists.

78. Paul Morillot, *Le Roman en France depuis 1610 jasquà nos jours* (Paris: Masson, n.d.), p. 1. Morillot, p. 14, was in fact almost quoting Bishop Huet, *Essai sur l'origine des Romans* (1670), who presented d'Urfé as the first to claim the roman from "barbarism" and to supply it with "rules."

79. See especially P. G. Walsh, *The Roman Novel* (Cambridge: The University Press, 1970), who makes this his thesis. But see also J.P. Sullivan, *The Satyricon of Petronius* (Bloomington: Indiana Univ. Pres, 1968), pp. 93 ff. Even an older standard survey, J. Wright Duff, *A Literary History of Rome in the Silver Age* (1927; rpt. New York: Barnes and Noble, 1960), p. 153, while calling *The Golden Ass* a "romance" places *The Satyricon* with the "novels" largely because of its realism but also because of its satire.

80. Paulson, pp. 29-32, who concludes that the "novel is born out of an act of satire," and Boris Eichenbaum as quoted by Robert Scholes, "The Contributions of Formalism and Structuralism," p. 144. Paulson does go on to say that *Don Quixote* is "one kind" of novel.

81. The "modern novelist" is A.E.W. Mason, in *The Future of the Novel*, p. 50. In the rest of the paragraph, for Tillyard, see his *The Epic Strain in the English Novel* (Fair Lawn, N.J.: Essential Books, 1958); for Ortega, see his *Meditations on Quixote*, (1914), trans. E. Rugg and D. Marin (New York: Norton, 1961), p. 161; for Kahn and Shroder, see Davis, ed., *The Novel*, pp. 46, 47; and for Warren, see Wellek and Warren, *Theory of Literature*, p. 77. Nearly every one of these critics qualifies his opinion of course; and of course other such dogmatic statements can be found about a single origin for the novel, one such being that of George Sherburn: "the nouvelle [was] the true source from which the later long novel emerges" [quoted by W.H. McBurney, *Four Before Richardson* (Lincoln: Univ. of Nebraska Press, 1963) p. xiv].

82. Somewhere Eliseo Vivas argues that "the 'novel' that James perfected had to be abandoned just as the imagists and the free verse poets had to find new forms of expression."

83. The definition of "evolution" used here is the one employed by certain other critics, notably Shroder, p. 57: "Brunetière's theory ... confused evolution and progress." William Park, "What Was New about the New Species of Writing," *Studies in the Novel*, 2 (1970), 112-30, claiming to be an antievolutionist, suggests "mutation" as a more suitable term than "evolution" and goes on to attack the "branches, roots, stems, trunks" theories that have made a "botanized garden" of the novel. It is interesting to discover Boris Eichenbaum employing "evolution" in Shroder's sense also and yet to find Robert Scholes in his brilliant survey of Russian formalism and more recent Russian and French structuralism, written seven years after *The Nature of Narrative*, quoting Eichenbaum favorably (note 12 above), p. 144. Scholes, however, still prefers the term "diachronic" to "evolutionary" thinking and sums up Eichenbaum's thesis thus: for him, "the novel is a 'syncretic' form, which is made up of other elementary forms" (p. 144). For Novak, below, see note 74 above. For Showalter, stressing the French novel, see p. 5: "The novel tried to incorporate them all."

84. For Certantes see *Don Quixote* (II, 47) in the Spanish edition of Cervantes in 7 vols. (Madrid: Spanish Royal Academy, 1916-23): "la épica tan bien puede escribirse en prosa como

en verso"; and Aubrey F.G. Bell, "The Epic Theme" in *Don Quixote,* Chap. 4 in Bell's *Cervantes* (New York: Collier Books, 1961; 1st ed. 1947). Byron's statement is in *Don Juan* (XII.9). For a more detailed survey of this question, see Percy G. Adams, "The Epic Tradition and the Novel," *Southern Review,* 9 (1973), 300-310, and of course the books by Tillyard (note 81 above), H.T. Swendenberg, *The Theory of the Epic in England, 1650-1800* (Berkeley and Los Angeles: Univ. of California Press, 1944), and Donald M. Foerster, *The Fortunes of Epic Poetry* (Washington: Catholic Univ. of America Press, 1962).

85. Beattie (1783), speaking of *Tom Jones,* "Not since the days of Homer has the world seen a more artful epick fable," quoted with approval by R.S. Crane, *Critics and Criticism,* ed. Crane (Chicago: Univ. of Chicago Press, 1952), p. 616; Thackeray, also speaking of *Tom Jones,* "the great comic epic," in his essay "Hogarth, Smollett and Fielding," in *The English Humorists of the Eighteenth Century.* For Hegel, see note 2 above; and for Gyorgy Lukacs, see his *The Theory of the Novel* (Cambridge, Mass.: MIT Press, 1971; 1st pub. about 1938 in Russia).

86. For Ortega, see note 81 above; for Tillyard, see *The Epic Strain,* p. 58; and for Cleanth Brooks, see *Fugitives' Reunion: Conversations at Vanderbilt,* May 3-5, 1956, int. Louis D. Rubin, Jr., ed. Rob Roy Purdy (Nashville: Vanderbilt Univ. Press, 1959).

87. Such an interpretation is that given by the Fugitives (see note 86 above), one of whom, Donald Davidson, defined the epic as "intended for oral performance and oral currency." Others of the group did, however, include the *Aeneid.* See also Charles R. Beye, *The "Iliad," the "Odyssey," and the Epic Tradition* (Garden City, N.Y.: Doubleday Anchor Book, 1966), pp. 241-43, for "the fashion today." This also is the tradition favored by Kellogg and Scholes in *The Nature of Narrative,* published also in 1966.

88. For the changing view of the epic, see Swedenberg, *The Theory of the Epic,* p. 306. Here Swedenberg concludes that as with other forms of literature "epic" has evaded definitions. See also Foerster, *The Fortunes of Epic Poetry;* Brian Wilkie, *Romantic Poets and Epic Tradition* (Madison: Univ. of Wisconsin Press, 1965), who concludes wisely that "the epic is not and never really has been a genre; it is a tradition"; and H. J. Hunt, *The Epic in nineteenth-Century France* (Oxford: The univ. Press, 1941), who concludes that today the epic will find prose a more acceptable medium than verse (p. 45).

89. René Le Bossu, *Traité du Poème épique* (Paris: Nyon, 1708; 1st pub. 1675). See Fielding, *Joseph Andrews and Shamela,* ed. Martin C. Battestin (Boston: Houghton Mifflin, 1961), p. xxxi.

90. For the great influence in seventeenth-century France of Ariosto and the epic in general, see Magendie; and for suggestions about its continuing effect on French eighteenth-century writers of fiction, see Mylne, p. 6. See also Joseph Cottaz, *L'Influence des théories du Tasse sur l'épopée en France* (Paris: Italia R. Foulon, 1942).

91. Lyall H. Powers, "The Influence of the *Aeneid* on Fielding's *Amelia,*" *MLN,* 71 (1956), 330-36.

92. See note 89 above.

93. For Voltaire's attack on Achilles, see his *Essai sur la poésie épique,* first in English (1727), note 59 above. For a twentieth-century version of this analysis, see also Simone Weil's *The Iliad, or the Poem of Force* (in Beye, p. 249).

94. Frye, in his analysis, found in "Specific and Continuous Forms" in *The Anatomy of Criticism,* insists that "the prose romance, then, is an independent form of fiction to be distinguished from the novel" but that, paradoxically, a "pure" example is "never found." For his most recent analysis of "romance" and "novel," see his *The Secular Scripture: A Study of the Structure of Romance* (Charles Eliot Norton Lectures, 1974-75) (Cambridge.: Harvard Univ. Press, 1976). For more on this subject, see Chap. IV below.

95. Vinaver, *The Rise of Romance* (Oxford: Clarendon, 1971), pp. 15, 34, and Guyer, *Chrétien de Troyes: Inventor of the Modern Novel* (New York: Bookman Assocs., 1957).

96. Quoted in Lionel Stevenson, p. 19.

97. The classic statement of this opinion is that of Richard Chase, *The American Novel and Its Tradition* (Garden City, N.J.: Doubleday Anchor, 1957); an analysis of this theory is by Nicolaus Mills in "American Fiction and the Genre Critics" (*Novel*, 1969).

98. James, "The Art of Fiction," in *Henry James Selected Fiction*, ed. Leon Edel (New York: Dutton, 1953), p. 598.

99. Magendie, pp. 16-23; Mylne, p. 59; Huet, *Traité de l'origine des romans*, as quoted by Magendie, p. 17.

100. For these examples and others, see H.F. Watson, *The Sailor in English Fiction and Drama, 1550-1800* (New York: Columbia Univ. Press, 1931); and James Foster, *History of the Pre-Romantic Novel*, especially pp. 45-74; as well as E.A. Baker's early volumes.

101. For this, and other suggestions, see John Dunlop, *The History of Prose Fiction*, 2 vols. (Loudon: G. Bell and Sons, 1896), I, 96-113. For very recent discussions of the "romance" tradition in eighteenth-century British literature, especially in the novels of Fielding and Smollett, see Henry Knight Miller, *Henry Fielding's "Tom Jones" and the Romance Tradition* (Victoria: Univ. of Victoria English Literary Studies, 1976); and Melvyn New, " 'The Grease of God': The Form of Eighteenth-Century English Fiction," *PMLA*, 91 (1976), 235-43. Although these two do not always agree on definitions, they do agree on the lively existence of "romance" in eighteenth-century England, while Miller's opening chapter is an excellent survey of the tradition itself. What neither says directly, but each implies, is that "romance" not only has many varieties but that it is normally found in a mixed state—with comedy, epic, "history," satire, for example. New's wise insistence on this point—as with Defoe's economics and romance—leads to a "dilemma' not unlike that found by Georges May. What neither New nor Miller emphasizes enough, however, is that Henry James is right in believing "romance" and "novel" are inseparable: *Tom Jones*, as Miller shows well, can be placed in the romance tradition, but it is still a novel derived from many literary forms.

102. For the influence of Cicero on theories of history from the Renaissance through the eighteenth century, see George H. Nadel, "Philosophy of History before Historicism," *History and Theory*, 3 (1964), 291-316, who discusses some of the theorists listed here and concludes with this three-point "law" of history.

103. For Bayle's campaign, see note 48 above. For Voltaire's judgments on ancient and modern historians, much like those of Bayle, see J.B. Black, *The Art of History* (1926; rpt. New York: Russell and Russell, 1965) pp. 58-61. In the next sentences, for Boyle and Jenner, see their prefaces in Barnett, pp. 3, 122-23, and—more defense of fiction over history—*Three Seventeenth-Century Prefaces*, ed. Charles Davies, Augustan Reprint Society, no. 42 (Los Angeles: William A. Clark Memorial Library and Univ. of California, 1953), the three being by Boyle, Sir George Mackenzie, and Nathaniel Ingelo. For Lenglet-Dufresnoy, see his *De l'usage des romans*, 2 vols. (Amsterdam: chez la veuve de Pillras, 1734), I, Chap. 2; and for him, Baculard, and Restif, see May, "Le Roman ou l'histoire," in *Dilemme*, pp. 139-61. For more on the relations between seventeenth-century historical fiction and ancient history, see especially Alexis Chassang, *Histoire du roman et de ses rapports avec l'histoire dans l'antiquité grecque et latine (Paris: Didier, 1862)*.

104. Nadel, pp. 307-9.

105. For more on this currently popular subject, see J. Paul Hunter, "Biography and the Novel," *Modern Language Studies*, 9 (1979), 68-84; and for some of the information in this paragraph, see Nadel, pp. 306-7, especially; J.B. Black, pp. 17, 31-34; J. Hillis Miller, "Narrative and History," *Journal of English Literary History*, 41 (1974), 455-73; May, both his article, "L'Histoire a-t-elle engendré le Roman" and his book *Dilemme;* Paulson, "Satire and History," in *Satire and the Novel*, pp. 150-57, who argues that in the eighteenth century the historian and the fictional satirist had the same goals; Sidney J. Black, "Eighteenth-Century 'Histories' as a Fictional Mode," *Boston University Studies in English* 1 (1955), 38-45, whose article is much out of date but who does recognize that the novelist and the historian both turned to the "general

experiences of mankind"; Herbert Davis, "The Augustan Conception on History," in *Reason and the Imagination*, ed. J.A. Mazzeo (New York: Columbia Univ. Press, 1962), pp. 213-29; Thomas Preston, "Historiography as Art in Eighteenth-Century England," *TSLL*, 11 (1969), 1209-21; Lawrence J. Forno, "The fictional letter in the Memoir Novel . . . ," *SVEC*, 81 (1971), 149-61, who follows May closely in saying that "The evolution of the novel has been traced from authentic memoirs . . . to pseudo-memoirs . . . to memoir-type novels"; Lester A. Segal, "Nicholas Lenglet Du Fresnoy and Historiography," *SVEC*, 18 (1972), 69-119; Mylne's book and other work on the letter-novel; Jacques Rustin, "L'Histoire 'véritable' dans la littérature romanesque du XVIIIe siècle français," 18 (1966), 89-102; Patricia Meyer Spacks, *Imagining a Self: Autobiography and the Novel in Eighteenth-Century England* (Cambridge: Harvard Univ. Press, 1976); Jean Rousset, "Prévost romancier: la forme autobiographique," *MLN*, 80 (1965), 289-300; and two fine chapters by Stewart in *Imitation and Illusion*.

106. Lesage, in the 1726 ed. of *Le Diable boiteux*, as quoted by Showalter, p. 50; Fielding, in the Preface to *Joseph Andrews;* James, "The Art of Fiction," in *Selected Fiction*, ed. Edel, p. 587; and Conrad, in "Henry James: An Appreciation" (1905), in *Notes on Life and Letters* (Garden City: Doubleday, 1921). Frank Kermode is only one to stress this fact; see his "Novel, History and Type," *Novel*, 1 (1968), 231-38. Note Kellogg and Scholes in *Nature of Narrative* saying that "the rise of scientific history parallels the rise of the novel" (p. 213).

107. Some of this and other information can be found in May, *Dilemme*, pp. 110-16; Mylne, pp. 125-43. F.C. Green, *French Novelists*, pp. 82-86; W.H. Rogers, "Fielding's Early Aesthetic and Technique,*SP*, 40(1943), 529-51, rpt. in "Fielding: A Collection of Essays, ed. Ronald Paulson (Englewood Cliffs, N.J.: Prentice-Hall, 1962), pp. 125-45: Leonard Lutwack, "Mixed and Uniform Prose Styles in the Novel," who contrasts Richardson and Fielding and finds the dramatic to be one of three styles used by Fielding; Mark Kinhead-Weekes, *Samuel Richardson: Dramatic Novelist* (London: Methuen, 1973);Ira Koningsberg, *Samuel Richardson and the Dramatic Novel* (Lexington: Univ. of Kentucky Press, 1968); Northrop Frye, "The Rhythm of Decorum: Drama," in *Anatomy of Criticism*, who makes analogies between fiction and drama; W.C. Cross, "The Novel versus the Drama," in *The English Novel*, pp. 56-63; Viola Hopkins, "Visual Art Devices and Parallels in the Fiction of Henry James," *PMLA*, 76 (1961), 561-74; W.H. McBurney, ed. *Four before Richardson*, pp. xxvi-xxxiv, on Mrs. Davys and Mrs. Haywood and Restoration comedy; James J. Lynch, *Box, Pit and Gallery* (Berkeley: Univ. of California Press, 1953), pp. 215-18, especially, which shows how the drama permeated the eighteenth-century novel.

108. Note, for example, Mylne, pp. 63-65, on Lesage's characters, and p. 118 on Marivaux's; or May, *Dilemme*, pp. 111-15, on the influence of La Bruyère's characters on *Le Diable boiteux* and on Marivaux; or Fielding's references to the characters of Theophrastus, Horace, and La Bruyère as he praises the characters in his sister's *David Simple* (preface to *David Simple*, 1744).

109. For allegory and fiction, one can start with Angus Fletcher, *Allegory: The Theory of a Symbolic Mode* (Ithaca: Cornell Univ. Press, 1964); Edwin Honig, *Dark Conceit: The Making of Allegory* (New York: Oxford Univ. Press, 1966); or Frye's *The Anatomy of Criticism*. Any good bibliography for the eighteenth century will have books and articles by Homer O. Brown, Maximillian Novak, J. Paul Hunter, G.A. Starr (all on Defoe alone), John J. Richetti, Tieje (1913; "romantic" allegory), Showalter (pp. 49-50, e.g.), Magendie, V. Cherbuliez.

110. For the rise of journalism, see W.J. Graham, *The Beginnings of English Literary Periodicals: A Study of Periodical Literature, 1665-1715* (New York: Oxford Univ. Press, 1926), and his *English Literary Periodicals* (New York: T. Nelson and Sons, 1930); R.P. Bond, ed., *Studies in the Early English Periodical* (Chapel Hill: Univ. of North Carolina Press, 1957), and his *The Tatler: The Making of a Literary Periodical* (Cambridge: Harvard Univ. Press, 1971). There are also studies of individual journalists besides Addison, Steele, and Defoe—for example,

Robert N. Cunningham, *Peter Anthony Motteux,* 1663-1718 (Oxford: Blackwell, 1933); Robert Wieder, *Pierre Motteux et les débuts du journalisme en Angleterre* . . . (Paris, n.d.); Ned Ward, *The London Spy,* ed. Kenneth Fenwick (London: Folio Society, 1955); H.W. Troyer, *Ned Ward of Grub Street* (Cambridge: Harvard Univ. Press, 1946). For short fiction in periodical literature, see Donald Kay, *Short Fiction in "The Spectator"* (University, Ala.: Univ. of Alabama Press, 1975), with its excellent bibliography. For the character in early periodicals, consult Edward C. Baldwin, "The Relation of the Seventeenth-Century Character to the Periodical Essay," *PMLA,* 19 (1904), 75-114; W. Matthews, "The Character-Writings of Edward Ward," *Neophilologus,* 21 (1936), 116-34; and studies of the *Tatler* and *Spectator.* For long fiction serialized, consult Melvin R. Watson, *Magazine Serials and the Essay Tradition, 1746-1820* (Baton Rouge: Louisiana State Univ. Press, 1956); Roy M. Wiles, *Serial Publication in England before 1750* (Cambridge: Cambridge Univ. Press, 1957); and Robert D. Mayo, *The English Novel in the Magazines, 1740-1815* (Evanston: Northwestern Univ. Press, 1962). For journalism and rogue and criminal literature—the novel was "partially fertilized by certain naturalistic elements in popular journalism such as criminal narrative"—see John J. Richetti, *Popular Fiction,* pp. 22 ff. For studies of the influence of journalism on the technique and contents of the new novel, see a number of articles by Novak, especially "Imaginary Islands and Real Beasts: The Imaginative Genesis of *Robinson Crusoe,*" *Tennessee Studies in Literature,* 19 (1974), 57-78, in which Novak demonstrates how articles, often by Defoe himself, in *The Weekly Journal* and *The Mercurius Politicus* for 1718 and 1719 inspired certain sections of Defoe's first novel. Prévost also kept up with current events and as a result was able to use correct data for the French government's sending prostitutes, such as Manon, to Louisiana. Mme d'Aulnoy was only one other writer of fiction to ransack the newspapers, in her case reports of Spain for her *Mémoires de la cour d'Espagne* (1690) and her *Relation de voyage d'Espagne* (1691). See Percy G. Adams, *Travelers and Travel Liars, 1660-1800* (1962; rpt. New York: Dover, 1980), pp. 97-99. For Johnson and his travel reviews, see Walter Jackson Bate, *Samuel Johnson* (New York: Harcourt, Brace, Jovanovich, 1976), pp. 189-90.

111. Wain, "The Conflict of Forms in Contemporary English Literature," in *Essays on Literature and Ideas* (New York and London: Macmillan, 1963), rpt. in Davis, ed., *The Novel,* p. 292.

112. Aldridge, "Introduction: Shifting Trends in Narrative Criticism," *CL,* 6 (1669), 225-29.

113. Novak (note 74 above), p. 133, is quoting Lévi-Strauss, *The Savage Mind.*

114. Beasley, "English Fiction in the 1740's: Some Glances at the Major and Minor Novels," *Studies in the Novel,* 5 (1973), 155-76, as well as his book *Novels of the 1740's (Athens: Univ. of Georgia Press, 1982). See also Park, "What Was New about the 'New Species of Writing,'"* and *Richetti, Popular Fiction before Richardson,* pp. 1-23.

115. For Jakobson, here and below, see Scholes, "The Contributions of Formalism and Structuralism to the Theory of Fiction," p. 145; and *Russian Formalist Criticism,* ed. Lemon and Reis. For Hirsch, see his "Objective Interpretation" (note 18 above).

116. These are the words of Scholes, "The Contributions of Formalism and Structuralism . . . ," p. 143; see also Tzvetan Todorov, *Théorie de la littérature* (Paris: Seuil, 1965), pp. 197-211, who treats both Shevirev and Eichenbaum at length.

117. Jones, "Prose Fiction and Related Matters to 1832," *Bulletin of Bibliography* . . ., 21 (1956), 234-36.

118. That is true also for other excellent studies of French fiction of the eighteenth century, those by Showalter, Mays, Stewart, and F.C. Green, the last of whom cites five important contributing forms and modes—epic, history, tragedy, comedy, satire (p. 25).

119. Baker, III, 130-219.

120. Curley, *Samuel Johnson and the Age of Travel* (Athens: Univ. of Georgia Press, 1976).

121. Spengemann (New Haven: Yale Univ. Press, 1977).

122. For Penrose, Heawood, Parks, Chinard, Atkinson, and other such historians, including J.N.L. Baker and studies of the Grand Tour, see Chap. II below. For the rest of the paragraph, see Casson, *Travel in the Ancient World* (London: George Allen and Unwin, 1974); Zacher (Baltimore: Johns Hopkins Univ. Press, 1976); Batten (Berkeley and Los Angeles: Univ. of California Press, 1978); and Fussell (New York: Oxford Univ. Press, 1980).

123. Butor, "Travel and Writing," *Mosaic*, 8 (1974), 1-16, originally published in a different version in *Romantisme* (1972); Brée, "The Ambiguous Voyage: Mode or Genre," *Genre*, 1 (1968) 87-96; and Keene, *World within Walls: Japanese Literature of the Pre-Modern Era 1600-1867* (London: Secker and Warburg, 1977).

CHAPTER TWO

1. Claude Lévi-Strauss, *Tristes Tropiques* (New York: 1979), p. 102.

2. See Lionel Casson, *Travel in the Ancient World*, pp. 294-99.

3. Casson, p. 307, has stories of other early travels to the Holy Land.

4. For Adaman, the French bishop, see Sidney Heath, *In the Steps of the Pilgrims* (1911; rpt., London: Rich and Cowan, 1953), p. 17.

5. See Boies Penrose, *Travel and Discovery in the Renaissance 1420-1620* (Cambridge: Harvard Univ. Press, 1952), p. 16, for the *Crusader's Manual* by Marino Sanuto of Venice; Chap. XIV of *Mandeville* has the four routes; and for Petrarch see his *Itenerarium Syriacum*, ed. Giacomo Lumbuso, Serie quarta, IV (Roma, 1888), 390-403, and Zacher, *Curiosity and Pilgrimage*, p. 17.

6. For more on Wey and Wynkyn, see J.J. Jusserand, *English Wayfaring Life in the Middle Ages* (London: Unwin, 1897), pp. 395-99; Heath, p. 135; and George B. Parks, *The English Traveler to Italy* (Stanford: Stanford Univ. Press, n.d.), pp. 524-25. Parks has much information on the various routes across Europe to Rome and to the ports of debarkation for Beirut or Jaffa; he reprints the Wey-Wynkyn "Directions."

7. See Chap. I of Esther Moir, *The Discovery of Britain: The English Tourist* (London: Routledge and Kegan Paul, 1964), for more on early guides for Britain; E.S. Bates, *Touring in 1600: A Study in the Development of Travel as a Means of Education* (Boston: Houghton Mifflin, 1912), has a chapter on guidebooks and guides, pp. 35-59.

8. To Moir and Bates (note 7 above) add Clare Howard, *English Travelers in the Renaissance* (1914; rpt. New York: Burt Franklin, 1968), Chap. II; for France, see Albert Babeau, *Les Voyageurs en France* (1885; rpt., Genève: Slatkine Reprints, 1970), especially Chap. V; for some of Hakluyt's own instructions to seamen, see *The Principal Navigations ...* (London: Dent, 1913), V, 165-70, II, 214-27; for other collections and their instructions, see Awnsham and John Churchill, *A Collection of Voyages* (1704; rpt., London: Walthoe, 1732), I, lxix, and J.F. Bernard, *Recueil de Voiages ... au nord*, 10 vols. (Amsterdam: Bernard, 1725-1738), X, cxlv; for the *Philosophical Transactions*, see I (1665-66), 140-41, 147, 186; and for Careri, see his *Giro del mondo* (Naples, 1697-1700) in 6 vols., translated in part for Churchill, IV. Batten, pp. 84 ff., has more on guidebooks in the eighteenth century.

9. Sterne, *Tristram Shandy*, ed. James A. Work (New York: Odyssey, 1940), V, ii, VII, x. For most of the eighteenth century the Jaillot family had the government monopoly for French road maps.

10. Xenophon's *Anabasis* is accessible in the Loeb Classics; for Hsüan Tsang, see René Grousset, *In the Footsteps of the Buddha*, trans. Leon (Freeport, New York: Books for Libraries, 1970), and Percy Sykes, *A History of Exploration from the Earliest Times to the Present Day* (London; Routledge and Kegan Paul, 1949), pp. 24-36.

11. Lodovico di Varthema, *Itinerario di ... nello Egypto, nella Surria, ... Persia*, etc.

(Roma, 1510); for English translations, see *The Itinerary of . . . of Bologna from 1502-1508*, ed. Sir R.C. Temple (London; Argonaut, 1928), and *The Travels of . . .*, trans. J.W. Jones, ed. G.P. Badger (London: Hakluyt, 1863).

12. Álvar Núñez Cabeza de Vaca, *Relación* (1542), trans. Buckingham Smith as *Relation of Alvar Nunez . . .* (1871; rpt. Ann Arbor: Univ. Microfilms, 1970); for another trans., by A.F. Bandelier, of this account of the classic trip across southern North America, see *The Journey of . . .* (New York: Allerton, 1922); and for the South American travels, see *The Commentaries of Alvar Nunez . . .* from the original Spanish ed. of 1555, in *The Conquest of the River Plate*, ed. Luis L. Dominguez (London: Hakluyt, 1891), pp. 95-263. For de Soto, see E.G. Bourne, *Narratives of the Career of Hernando de Soto*, 2 vols. (New York: Allerton, 1922), and Hakluyt, "Virginia richly valued, by the description of the main land of Florida, her next neighbor. . . . " Written by a Portugal Gentleman of Elvas. . . . (London: Kyngston, 1609), in Peter Force, ed., *Tracts and Other Papers* (Washington: Force, 1846), IV, 1-136.

13. For Ascham, see his *Works*, ed. J.A. Giles, 3 vols. (London: J.R. Smith, 1864-1865), I, part II, 265, and especially 106; for Montaigne, see his *Journal de voyage en Italie par la Suisse et l'Allemagne*, ed. Charles Dédéyan (Paris: Société les Belles Lettres, 1946); for Coryat, see his *Coryat's Crudities Hastily gobled up in five Moneths travells in France, Savoy, Italy, Rhetia . . . Newly digested in the hungry aire of Odcombe in the County of Somerset, and now dispersed to the nourishment of the travelling Members of this Kingdome* (Glasgow: James MacLehose and Sons, 1905; 1st ed. London, 1611); then, Evelyn, *The Diary of John Evelyn*, ed. E.S. de Beer, 6 vols. (Oxford: Clarendon, 1955), and *A Selection from the Diary of John Evelyn* (London: Folio Soc., 1963); and Jouvin, *Voyageur d'Europe ou sont les voyages de France, d'Italie . . . 1672* (Paris, 1672), and the summary by Albert Babeau, pp. 148-55.

14. For the following accounts of water travel, see Edgar Prestage, *The Portuguese Pioneers* (London: Pioneer Histories, 1933); K.G. Jayne, *Vasco da Gama and His Successors, 1460-1580* (1910; rpt. New York: Barnes and Noble, 1970); E.G. Ravenstein, ed., *The Journal of the First Voyage of Vasco da Gama, 1497-1499* (London: Hakluyt, 1898); J.C. Beaglehole, *The Exploration of the Pacific* (London: Pioneer Histories, 1934); James A. Robertson, ed., *Magellan's Voyage around the World* (Cleveland: Arthur H. Clark, 1906); J.T. Medina, *The Discovery of the Amazon*, trans. and ed., B.T. Lee and H.C. Heaton (New York: American Geographical Soc., 1934) [for Orellana]; Francis Parkman, *Pioneers of France in the New World*, especially *La Salle and the Discovery of the Great West* (1901), and J.B. Brebner, *The Explorers of North America* (London: Pioneer Histories, 1933); Cecil Jane, ed., *Select Documents Illustrating the Four Voyages of Columbus*, 2 vols. (London: Hakluyt, 1930); S.E. Morison, trans. and ed., *Journals and Other Documents on the Life and Voyages of Christopher Columbus* (New York: Heritage, 1963); S.E. Morison, *Admiral of the Ocean Sea*, 2 vols. (Boston: Little, Brown, 1942); Sir Clements Markham, trans. and ed., *The Letters of Amerigo Vespucci* (London: Hakluyt, 1894), and F.J. Pohl, *Amerigo Vespucci: Pilot Major* (New York: Columbia Univ. Press, 1944); Sir Richard C. Temple, ed., *The World Encompassed [by] Sir Francis Drake* (London: Argonaut, 1926); H.R. Wagner, *Sir Francis Drake's Voyage around the World: Its Aims and Achievements* (San Francisco: J. Howell, 1926); Zelia Nuttall, trans. and ed., *New Light on Drake: A Collection of Documents Relating to His Voyage . . .* (London: Hakluyt, 1914); William Dampier wrote more than one travel book and all were collected and published in 1729; his first and best is *A New Voyage round the World* (London: Knapton, 1697), reissued many times; see, e.g., the Hakluyt rpt., ed. Sir Albert Gray (1927) with a new int. by Percy G. Adams (New York: Dover, 1968); Wafer, *New Voyage and Description of the Isthmus of Panama* (London: Knapton, 1699); for Cowley, Sharp, and William Hacke, *Collection of Original Voyages* (London: Knapton, 1699), and other buccaneers, see Knapton's complete ed. of Dampier in 1729, Vol. IV; for the literature on Anson, see Percy G. Adams, *Travelers*, pp. 167-70, 260, especially Chaplain Richard Walter, *Anson's Voyage round the World in the years 1740-44* (London: Knapton, 1748), rpt. with a new introduction by Percy G. Adams (Dover, 1974); and *The Journals of Captain James Cook on His Voyages of Discovery*, ed. J.C.

Beaglehole (Cambridge: Hakluyt, 1955-1967), in three vols., the third in two parts, and Beaglehole, *The Life of Captain James Cook* (Stanford: Stanford Univ. Press, 1974; London: Hakluyt, 1974), as well as the one-vol. ed. (Dover, 1971), with a new int. by Percy G. Adams.

15. See, e.g., R.T. Gunther, *Early Botanists and Their Gardens* (1922; rpt. New York: Kraus, 1971), p. 276.

16. For Willibald, see Sidney Heath, *In the Steps of the Pilgrims* (New York: Putnam's Sons, 1951), p. 27, and Parks, *The English Traveler to Italy*, pp. 69-73; for Conti, see R.H. Major, ed., *India in the Fifteenth Century* (London: Hakluyt, 1857); and for Cabeza de Vaca, see note 12 above.

17. For the Roman soldiers, see Casson, pp. 222-25; for Columbus, see note 14 above; for Tasso, see his letters to the comte Hercule de Contrari, *Lettera nella quale si paragona l'Italia a la Francia* (1581), and Babeau, pp. 41-47; for Lady Mary, see *Letters of the Right Honorable Lady M--y W----y M------e; written, during her travels in Europe, Asia and Africa ...* 3d ed. (London: T. Becker and P.A. DeHondt, 1763), 3 vols. in 1, as well as a Dublin ed. of the same year. For Smollett, see his *Travels through France and Italy*, ed. Frank Felsenstein (Oxford: Oxford Univ. Press, 1979); and for Sharp, see his *Letters from Italy* (London: R. Cabe, 1966). For much more on travels in letter form, especially by the Jesuits, see Chap. VI below.

18. For Evelyn, see note 13 above, and for Fielding, see his *The Journal of a Voyage to Lisbon* (London: Millar, 1755), in *The Complete Works of Henry Fielding, Esq.*, ed. W.E. Henley et al, 16 vols. (London: Heinemann, 1903), and in Everyman's Library (1932); for John Fielding's editing, see Percy G. Adams, *Travelers*, p. 87.

19. For Montaigne and Berkeley, see note 13 above and E.W. Manwaring, *Italian Landscape in Eighteenth Century England* (New York: Oxford Univ. Press, 1925), p. 12. Berkeley's *Journal of Travels in Italy* can be found in his *Works*, ed. A.A. Luce and T.E. Jessop (London and New York: T. Nelson, 1948).

20. For Ringrose, see Alexandre Exquemelin (Esquemeling, Oexmelin) and Basil Ringrose, *The Buccaneers of America* (1684; 1893; rpt. New York: Dover, 1966); this is a trans. of a Spanish trans. of the Dutch original of 1678 and has a new int. by Percy G. Adams.

21. For Dampier and Cook, see note 14 above; then Robert Challe, *Journal d'un voyage fait aux Indes Orientales*, 3 vols. (La Haye, 1721) and an excellent new ed. by Frédéric Deloffre and Melahat Menemencioglu, with int. and notes (Paris: Mercure de France, 1979).

22. For Coryat, see note 13 above; Nugent, *The Grand Tour; or, a Journey through the Netherlands, Germany, Italy, and France ...* (London: J. Rivington, 1778; 1st ed. 1749).

23. Ricci, *Histoire de l'expédition chrestienne au royaume de la Chine ...* traduite en françois par le S.D.F. de Riquebourg-trigault [Nicolas Trigault] (Lyon: Cardon, 1616). In English, see *China in the Sixteenth Century: The Journals of Matthew Ricci, 1583-1610* (New York: Random House, 1953).

24. For the baron de Lahontan, see Percy G. Adams, *Travelers*, pp. 55-63. His first pub., in 2 vols., *Nouveaux voyages de m. le baron de La Hontan dans l'Amérique septentrionale* (La Haye: les frères Honoré, 1703), was trans. into English the same year with two additions, one being "Dialogues with an American Indian." The next year appeared *Dialogues de m. le baron de Lahontan et d'un sauvage, dans l'Amérique* (Amsterdam: Veuve de Boeteman, 1704). These "dialogues," as we shall see in Chap. IX below, were most important during the eighteenth century.

25. Although there were many books by and about the Sherley brothers, see Anthony Nixon, *The Three English Brothers. Sir Thomas Sherley his Travels ... Sir Anthony Sherley his Embassage to the Christian Princes. Master Robert Sherley his wars against the Turkes* (London: John Hodgets, 1607); for Gramont, see Antonie (Anthony) Hamilton, *Mémoires de Chevalier de Gramont*, ed. Claire-Eliane Engel (Monaco: Eds. du Roche, 1958); Rousseau's wanderings, mostly on foot, begin in Book Two of *Les Confessions*, increase in Book Four, continue in Five and Six, reach their height in Seven when he is secretary to the ambassador at Venice, continue

in Eight (Paris, e.g.), cease in Nine and Ten, begin again in Eleven (England, e.g.), and continue in Twelve, the last book, where his eccentricities and resulting persecution drive him in and out of Switzerland.

26. For Smith, see his *A True Relation of . . . Virginia*, 1608, as found in *Travels and Works of Captain John Smith*, ed. Edward Arber (Edinburgh: J. Grant, 1910); for Chapelle and Bachaumont, see *Voyage de Mm. François le Coigneaux de Bachaumont et Claude-Enman Luillier Chapelle* (La Haye, 1732), 1st ed. in *Recueil de quelques pieces nouvelles et galantes* (1663); and for their imitators, see Babeau, p. 142; for Taylor, see *All the Works of John Taylor the Water Poet* (London: for the author, 1630); for Bashō, see Keene, *World within Walls*, and, for a start, Bashō's *Narrow Road to the Far North: A Haiku Journey* (New York: Kadanska International, 1974); for Regnard's fascinating life and works, see his *Oeuvres*, 2 vols. (Paris, 1854), introduced by two essays, one on his drama and life by Aldred Michiels, the other a "notice" by M. Beuchot; the two travel poems are in Vol. II.

27. Obviously no one person is qualified to do such a book, for there are thousands of major primary works alone to be read. The studies that come closest now are Percy Sykes, *A History of Exploration* (1934); J.N.L. Baker, *A History of Geographical Discovery and Exploration* (1937); Sir Raymond Beazeley, *The Dawn of Modern Geography*, 3 vols. (1897-1906); three books by the great French authority Charles de La Roncière, all of which concentrate largely on geography and exploration. Add to these the following: Casson for the ancients; Penrose, with his excellent bibliographies; Edward Heawood, *A History of Geographical Discovery in the Sixteenth and Eighteenth Centuries* (1912: rpt. New York: Octagon Books, 1969); Justin Winsor, ed., *Narrative and Critical History of America, 1884-1889*; S.E. Morison, *The European Discovery of America*, 2 vols. (New York: Oxford Univ. Press, 1971-74); books by Gilbert Chinard and Geoffroy Atkinson; books by D.B. Quinn, George Parks, Charles Batten, and Thomas Curley. Allison Lockwood has just done a much-needed survey of American travelers in Europe in the nineteenth century, called *Passionate Pilgrims* (East Brunswick, N.J.: Assoc. Univ. Presses, 1981). There are also fine studies of the Crusades, pilgrimages, the Grand Tour, false travel books, the imaginary voyage, the supernatural voyage, individual travelers such as Marco Polo, Cabeza de Vaca, Magellan, Drake, and a hundred others, as well as of travels to and in individual countries or parts of countries, even individual cities. The historian is handicapped because the bibliographies are both out of date and cover limited periods, as with E.G. Cox, *A Reference Guide to the Literature of Travel*, 3 vols. (Seattle: Univ. of Washington Press, 1935-38). Like Swift's Hack in the Preface to *A Tale of a Tub*, "I have been for some years preparing Materials towards" a history of the literature of travel to 1800; here for some pages is the abbreviated result.

28. For Chang Ch'ien and other far-traveled Asiatics before 700 A.D., see Sykes, pp. 20-34.

29. Casson, p. 95.

30. See Casson, pp. 39-43, for this intriguing manuscript as found in J. Pritchard, *Ancient Near Eastern Texts Relating to the Old Testament* (Princeton: Princeton Univ. Press, 1955, with a supplement, 1969).

31. For most of this paragraph, see the Loeb Classical Library, published by Harvard Univ. Press, and C.A. Robinson, *Introduction to Selections from Greek and Roman Historians* (New York: Rinehart, 1957), pp. xxxv-xxxvi, which has the quotation from Thucydides as trans. by Benjamin Jowett.

32. For Cicero and a fascinating chap. on ancient Greek and Roman vacationing, see Casson, pp. 138-48; for Luke and Paul, see Acts 27, e.g.; for Synesius the bishop coasting Asia Minor, see Casson, pp. 159-60; and for the relationship between Horace's clever, detailed, often amusing Satire five of Book One and the fragmentary poem of Lucilius about his trip to Sicily, see, e.g., Eduard Fraenkel, *Horace* (1957; rpt. Oxford: Clarendon, 1966), pp. 106-7.

33. Scholarship not only keeps pushing the "Renaissance" back in time but discovering that the medieval period, in spite of its conflict between *sapientia*, divine knowledge, and *scientia*, human knowledge, never lost its thirst for information, *curiositas*, or its bent to what has come to be called "humanism." Certainly the medieval period, like every age, delighted in travel. See, as examples, Jusserand; Zacher; R.W. Southern, *The Making of the Middle Ages* (New Haven: Yale Univ. Press, 1961); D.J. Hall, *English Medieval Pilgrimage* (London: Routledge and Kegan Paul, 1965); Jean Leclerq, *The Love of Learning and the Desire for God: A Study of Monastic Culture*, trans. Catharine Misrahi (New York: New American Library, 1962); Paul O. Kristeller, "The Medieval Antecedents of Renaissance Humanism," in *Eight Philosophers of the Renaissance* (Stanford: Stanford Univ. Press, 1964), pp. 147-65; and, for an excellent summary of travel to Asia between 1245 and 1345, Eileen Power, "The Opening of the Land Routes to Cathay," in *Travel and Travellers of the Middle Ages*, ed. A. P. Newton (1926; rpt. Freeport, New York: Books for Libraries Press, 1967), pp. 124-58.

34. For Suleyman and other Asiatic travelers, see Sykes, Chap. V.

35. Richard Hakluyt, *The Principal Navigations, Voyages . . . of the English Nation* (1907; rpt. London: Dent, 1910), I, 56-60. See also Baron A.F. Meyendorff, "Trade and Communication in Eastern Europe, A.D. 800-1200," in Newton, *Travel and Travellers*, pp. 119-20.

36. Meyendorff, p. 105.

37. Sykes, p. 59.

38. Jean, sire de Joinville, "Joinville's Chronicle of the Crusade of St. Lewis," in *Memoirs of the Crusades*, trans. Frank Marzials (London and New York: Dutton, 1910), pp. 135-327. Also, *Chronicles of the Crusades*, trans. M.R.B. Shaw (New York: Penguin, 1963).

39. For the next two paragraphs, see C.R. Beazeley; Eileen Power (note 33 above); Sykes; and Penrose. For individual travelers, see *The Journal of William of Rubruck . . . with two accounts of . . . John of Pian de Carpine*, ed. W.W. Rockhill (London: Hakluyt, 1900); C.R. Beazeley, *Carpini and Rubruquis* (London: Hakluyt, 1903); *The Book of Ser Marco Polo . . .*, ed. Sir Henry Yule, 3d ed., revised H. Cordier (London: Hakluyt, 1903); *Marco Polo: The Description of the World*, trans. and ed. A.C. Moole and P. Pelliot (London: Routledge, 1938); Sir Henry Yule, ed., *Cathay and the Way Thither*, revised H. Cordier, 4 vols. (London: Hakluyt, 1913-16), which is a collection of travel accounts by Europeans in "Cathay," including Odoric, Pegolotti, Jordanus, and ibn-Batuta; and ibn-Batuta, *Travels, A.D. 1325-1354*, trans. and ed. from the Arabic text, ed. C. Defremery and B.R. Sanguinetti, by H.A.R. Gibb (Cambridge: Hakluyt, 1958-).

40. See Parks, *The English Traveler to Italy*, pp. 277-621, for the countless travelers to Italy, from nobleman and envoys to pilgrims to soldiers, merchants, and students, for Italian universities were much admired through the fifteenth, sixteenth, and seventeenth centuries.

41. For fifteenth-century travel, see Beazeley, who goes to about 1420, Sykes, Power, and Roncière; the bibliography and information in J.H. Parry, *The Age of Reconnaissance* (London: Weidenfeld and Nicolson, 1963), are excellent.

42. For Clavijo, see A. Sancha, *Historia del Gran Tamorlan, e Itinerario . . . del Viaje . . .* (Madrid, 1782), and *Narrative of the Embassy of Clavijo to the Court of Timour*, ed. Sir Clements Markham (London: Hakluyt, 1859); the first printing of Clavijo was in Seville in 1582 but his story was told by Spanish historians in the time of Ferdinand and Isabella and was then trans. into other languages. See Beazeley, III, 332-33. Schiltberger was popular from the beginning, with a first ed. in Augsburg, c. 1460, and eleven other eds. by 1600. See Beazeley, III, 555, for more bibliographical information about him, including modern eds. in German and the Hakluyt trans.

43. Josafa Barbaro and Ambrogio Contarini, *Travels to . . . Persia*, ed. Lord Stanley of Alderley (London: Hakluyt, 1873); Zeno was well known because he was in the best collection of travel accounts of the sixteenth century—G.B. Ramusio, *Raccolta de navigazioni et viaggi* (Vincenzi, 1550-59).

44. For Stephano, see Mario Longhena, *Viaggi in Persia, India e Giava de Nicolo di Conti, Girolamo Adorno e Girolamo de San Stefano* (Milan, 1929), and the Hakluyt trans. of 1858, ed. Richard H. Major, which has both Conti and Stefano. See Note 11 above for the popularity of Varthema.

45. For these, see note 6 above and Penrose, p. 32; Breydenbach's *Peregrinatio in Terram Sanctam* (Mainz, 1486) is so described by Penrose, p. 32.

46. See note 14 above for some of these facts and for bibliographies.

47. For a bibliography covering most of this section's information, see the excellent essay, "The Geographical Literature of the Renaissance," by Penrose, pp. 274-326. Penrose was unable, however, to do justice to much excellent travel literature of the period—that of the Jesuit missionaries, for example, as well as that restricted to the continent of Europe—and he has little information for the Renaissance after 1610. Frobisher's voyages and those of Gilbert are in Hakluyt, V, 131-231. For Albuquerque, an especially intriguing person, see Elaine Sanceau, *Indies Adventure: The Amazing Career of Alfonso de Albuquerque* (London: Blackie and Son, 1936), and his *Commentaries*, trans. and ed. W.deG. Birch, 4 vols. (London: Hakluyt, 1875-83). Barents is in *The Three Voyages of William Barents*, ed. K. Beynen (London: Hakluyt, 1876).

48. For some of the information in this paragraph, see Parks, *English Travelers to Italy* (who goes to 1550) and Clare Howard (now much out of date). For Hoby, see *The Travels and Life of Sir Thomas Hoby. Written by Himself, 1547-64*, ed. Edgar Powell for the Camden Soc., Third Series, Vol. 4, 1902; and Howard, pp. 16, 47, 35c. For Paulet, see the *Copy-Book of Sir Amias Paulet's Letters written during his Embassy to France, A.D. 1577*, ed. O. Ogle (London: Roxburghe Club, 1866), and Howard, p. 44. Lippomano's journal is by his secretary and is in *Relations des ambassadeurs vénitiens sur les affaires de France au seizième siècle*, recueilliés et traduites par N. Tommaseo (Paris, 1838); see also Babeau, pp. 47-54.

49. Quoted in Bates, p. 386n.

50. Alvarez, *Ho Preste Joam das Indias* (Lisbon, 1540), and *The Prester John of the Indies: A True Relation . . . of the Portuguese Embassy to Ethiopia in 1520*, by Father Francisco Alvarez, trans. Lord Stanley of Alderley (1881), rev. and ed. C.F. Beckingham and G.W.B. Huntingford, 2 vols. (Cambridge: Hakluyt, 1961). For Covilhan, see Penrose, pp. 48-50, 284.

51. Tenreiro, *Itinerario* (Coimbra, 1560); F.M. Pinto, *Peregrinacam* (Lisbon, 1614), and *The Voyages and Adventures during his Travels . . .* Done into English by H. C[ogan] (London: F. Macock, 1653). See Penrose, p. 288, for the literature and bibliography of these two. Pinto was especially popular, often reprinted; the standard Portuguese ed. is ed. A.J. DaCosta Pimpao and E. Cesar-Pegado (Porto: Portucalense, 1944), 7 vols.

52. Jenkinson, in *Early Voyages and Travels to Russia and Persia*, ed. E.D. Morgan and C.H. Coote (London: Hakluyt, 1886), 2 vols; and in Hakluyt, III, 36-38, II, 1-30, 73-77, I, 397-99, 408-64. For Fitch, see Hakluyt, III, 281-315; and Arnold Wright, *Early English Adventurers in the East* (London: Melrose, 1907); also *Early Travels in India, 1583-1619*, ed. William Foster (London: Oxford Univ. Press, 121).

53. For bibliographical data and other facts in this paragraph, see Penrose, pp. 274-326, and, especially for America, Percy G. Adams, "The Discovery of America and European Renaissance Literature," *CLS*, 13 (1976), 100-116.

54. René de Laudonnière, *L'Histoire notable de la Floride* (Paris, 1586), trans. by Hakluyt; Jan Ribaut's journal, which does not exist in the original, was first translated into English in 1563 as *The Whole and True Discoverie of Terra Florida* and finally retranslated in 1582 by Hakluyt. See also Francis Parkman, *Pioneers of France in the New World* (Boston: Little Brown, 1907), pp. 33-151. For Jacques Le Moyne de Morgues, see *The New World: the first pictures of America, made by John White and Jacques Le Moyne and engraved by Theodore de Bry*, with contemporary narratives of the French settlements in Florida 1562-1567, and the English

colonies in Virginia, 1585-1590, a new and rev. ed. (New York: Duell, Sloan and Pearce, 1965); and *Settlements of Florida.* Compiled by Charles E. Bennett (Gainesville: Univ. of Florida Press, 1968).

55. *Voyages of Samuel de Champlain,* trans. from the French by Charles P. Otis (Boston: the Prince Society, 1880), 2 vols [1st ed., Paris, 1613]; and Marc Lescarbot, *Histoire de la Nouvelle France* (Paris, 1609), and *Nova Francia. A Description of Acadia, 1606.* trans. P. Erondelle, 1609. Int. H.P. Bigger (London: Routledge and Sons, 1928); also the trans. of W.L. Grant (Toronto: Champlain Soc., 1907, 1911, 1914), 3 vols.

56. For Hariot, see *The Roanoke Voyages 1504-1590,* ed. David B. Quinn (London: Hakluyt, 1955), and *Thomas Hariot, Renaissance Scientist,* ed. John W. Shirley (Oxford: Oxford Univ. Press, 1974).

57. *The Captivity of Hans Stade of Hesse ...,* ed. Richard F. Burton (London: Hakluyt, 1874); Schmidt, in *The Conquest of the River Plate,* ed. Louis L. Dominguez (London: Hakluyt, 1891).

58. For bibliographical data on the great collections of voyages of the Renaissance, see Penrose, pp. 274-326.

59. For Hakluyt, besides Penrose, see George B. Parks. *Richard Hakluyt and the English Voyages* (New York: American Geographical Soc., 1930), and *The Hakluyt Handbook,* ed. D.B. and A.M. Quinn (London: Hakluyt, 1974).

60. Purchas, *Hakluytus Posthumus or Purchas His Pilgrimes* (1625) (Glasgow: MacLehose and Sons, 1905), 20 vols.; Thévenot, *Relations de divers voyages curieux, qui n'ont point publiées, ou qui ont esté traduites d'Hacluyt, de Purchas, et d'autres Voyageurs Anglois, Hollandois, Portugais, ...* (Paris: Jacques Langlois, 1663), 4 vols. See a recent reminder about a seventeenth-century French collector of voyages before Thévenot, that is Pierre Bergeron, an admirer of Hakluyt. Bergeron traveled widely, propagandizing for French exploration, edited and revised the often-printed account of François Pyrard in 1619 as well as many other travels before publishing a collection of French voyages in 1634. See Robert O. Lindsay, "Pierre Bergeron: A Forgotten Editor of French Travel Literature," *Terrae Incognitae,* 6 (1976), 31-38.

61. For all this and more on the Jesuits and their significance as travel writers, see bibliographies such as those of Aloys de Backer and Carlos Sommervogel, *Bibliothèque de la compagnie de Jesus* (Bruxelles: O. Schepens, 1900), 9 vols., Robert Streit, *Bibliotheca missionum,* 11 vols. (Munster: Aschendorff, 1916), and E.G. Cox. Then turn to books such as Francis Parkman, *The Jesuits in North America in the Seventeenth Century* (Boston: Little, Brown, 1901); Geoffroy Atkinson, *Les Nouveaux horizons de la renaissance française* (Paris: Droz, 1935), with its year-by-year bibliography for France (pp. 434-79); Jean Baptiste Du Halde, *Description ... de la Chine,* 4 vols. (Paris: Lemercier, 1735), trans. into English by John Watts in 4 vols. in 1736 and in 2 vols. by Edward Cave in 1738-41; John Lockman, *Travels of the Jesuits into Various Parts of the World,* 2 vols. (London: n.p., 1735; 1743); *Lettres édifiantes et curieuses, écrites des missions étrangères, par quelques missionaires de la Compagnie de Jesus,* 20 vols. (Paris: Nicolas Le Clerc, 1717-28) [started by Le Gobien in 1702 and finished by Du Halde in 1776, in 34 vols.]; R.G. Thwaites, *Jesuit Relations and Allied Documents* (Cleveland: Burrows Bros. 1896-1901); Lawrence C. Wroth, "The Jesuit Relations from New France," *The Papers of the Bibliographical Society of America,* 30 (1936), 110-50; Virgile Pinot, *La Chine et la formation de l'esprit philosophique en France (1640-1740)* (Paris: Paul Guethner, 1932); George R. Healy, "The French Jesuits and the Idea of the Noble Savage," *William and Mary Quarterly,* 15 (1958), 143-67; and a fine survey article by John Parker, curator James Ford Bell Library, in *The Merchant Explorer,* Occasional Paper No. 17 (Minneapolis: Univ. of Minnesota Library, May 1977).

62. For Saris, see Penrose, pp. 208, 210, 322.

63. Pyrard de Laval, *Discours du voyage des François aux Indes Orientales ...* (Paris: Chez David Le Clerc, 1611); this book was much altered for the 2d ed. (Paris: Remy Dallin, 1615),

while the 3d ed. (1619) added a Maldive vocabulary; the 3d ed. trans. into English, is edited by Albert Gray for Hakluyt (1887-90) in 2 vols.

64. Thévenot (note 60 above).

65. Tavernier, *Six voyages en Turquie, en Perse et aux Indes* (1676). This important book was often reprinted in French, with supplements, and translated into English as *The Six Voyages . . . To which is added a new Description of the Seraglio . . .* (London: For Robert Littlebury and Moses Pit, 1678), with a supplement in 1680 by Moses Pit; Tavernier traveled widely in the East in various trips between 1638 and 1663. For Chardin, see his *Voyage en Perse et aux Indes Orientales* (1711), the first volume of which was published in English in 1686, after Chardin was knighted by Charles II, and supplemented in 1691; see *Sir John Chardin's Travels,* with intr. by Sir Percy Sykes (London: Argonaut, 1927).

66. Uring, *The History of the Voyages and Travels of Captain Nathaniel Uring* (London, 1726); and *The Voyages and Travels of . . .* , ed. Captain Alfred DeWar (London: Callell, 1928).

67. Defoe, *A General History of the Pyrates* (1724), ed. from the 4th ed. of Vol. I and the 1728 Vol. II by Manuel Schonhorn (Columbia, S.C.: Univ. of South Carolina Press, 1972), 2 vols. in one.

68. *Buccaneers of America* (note 20 above).

69. For Dampier and Wafer, see note 14 above; for Raveneau de Lussan, see his *Journal du voyage fait à la mer du sud* (Paris: Coignard, 1689, 1690), trans. for the *Works* of Dampier in 1724 and by M.E. Wilbur (Cleveland: Arthur H. Clark, 1930).

70. Woodes Rogers, *A Cruising Voyage round the World* (London: A. Bell and E. Lintot, 1712); see the 1928 ed. of G.E. Manwaring (1928; rpt. New York: Dover, 1970), with a new int. by Percy G. Adams. Edward Cooke's one-vol. ed. came out in 1711, within months of landing, and then it was expanded into two vols. after Rogers had published.

71. For Anson, see note 14 above.

72. See Heawood, pp. 162-165.

73. Heawood, pp. 172-73.

74. For Hennepin, see many books and articles by Jean Delanglez as well as Adams, *Travelers,* pp. 45-50.

75. Della Valle, *Viaggi de P. della Valle . . . (in 54 Lettere familiari) . . . all 'erudito . . . Mario Schipano . . .* (Roma: Biagio Diversin, 1652), 4 vols.; often reprinted, della Valle was published with Sir Thomas Roe in English (London: Pr. for J. Macock, 1665). See *The Travels of Pietro Della Valle,* ed. Edward Grey (London: Hakluyt, 1892), a rpt. of the 1665 (really 1664) English ed.

76. Sandys, *A Relation of a Journey begun An: Dom: 1610* (London: W. Barrett, 1615).

77. Shaw, *Travels or Observations Relating to Several Parts of Barbary and the Levant* (Oxford, 1738-46; London: A. Miller and W. Sandby, 1757).

78. Fallam's journal is in Clarence W. Alvord and Lee Bidgood, *The First Explorations of the Trans-Allegheny Region by the Virginians* (Cleveland: Arthur H. Clark, 1912); Colonel Chicken is in S.C. Williams, ed., *Early Travels in the Tennessee Country* (Johnson City, Tenn.: Watauga 1928).

79. Bruce, *Travels to Discover the Source of the Nile* (London and Edinburgh: Robinson, 1790), 5 vols.

80. Johan Nieuhof (John Nieuhoff), *An Embassy From the East-India Company of the United Provinces, To the Grand Tartar Cham Emperiour of China . . .* , trans. John Ogilby (London: John Macock, 1669). Nieuhof was author of another seminal travel book, this one on South America (1682).

81. Winthrop, *Some Old Puritan Love-Letters: John and Margaret Winthrop, 1618-1638.* ed. J.H. Twichell (New York, 1893); Lechford, *Plain Dealing: or, Newes from New-England* (London, 1642), in *Coll. Mass. Hist. Soc.,* 3d Series, III (1833), 55-128; Josselyn, *An Account of Two*

Voyages to New-England ... (London: Giles Widdowes, 1674), and *An Account of Two Voyages to New England* ... *1638, 1663* (Boston: W. Veazie, 1865), but most famous is his *New England's Rareties Discovered* (London: G. Widdowes, 1672).

82. Alsop, *A Character of the Province of Maryland* (London, 1666), rpt. ed. by N.D. Mereness (Cleveland, 1902); Lawson, *A New Voyage to Carolina* (1709), in John Stevens, *A New Collection of Voyages and Travels*, again separately that year and then in 1714 and 1718 as *The History of Carolina*. See the ed. of F.L. Harriss (Richmond, 1937).

83. Ligon, *A True and Exact History of the Island of Barbados* (London: H. Moseley, 1657); Bancroft, *An Essay on the Natural History of Guiana, In South America* ... (London: T. Becket, 1769).

84. For the Sherleys, see note 25 above; for Bonneval, see Peter Wilding, *Adventures in the Eighteenth Century* (New York: Putnam's, 1937), trans. into Franch as *Les Grands Adventuriers du XVIIIe Siècle* (Nevers, Paris: Editions Corréa, 1938).

85. In this paragraph, Roe (Rowe), usually badly mishandled, was published in the third vol. of della Valle (note 75 above) as well as in many collections—Purchas (1625), Thévenot (1663), Churchill (1732) (1744) (1752), and others. For Olearius, besides the two original eds., each in Schleswig, see a new partial trans. in English, *The Travels of Olearius in Seventeenth-Century Russia*, ed. S.H. Baron (Stanford: Stanford Univ. Press, 1967). For Spathary (Spafarik), a Greek, see Sykes, pp. 165-66, and Heawood, p. 127. For Gerbillon, learned and widely traveled, see J.B. Du Halde, *Lettres édifiantes et curieuses* ... (Paris, 1707-73), and Vol. II of Du Halde, *Description* ... (1735). Ides's first ed. was in Dutch, trans. from "barbarous and unintelligible Latin"; trans. also into German, French, and other languages, it was pub. in English as *Three Years Travels from Moscow overland to China* ... (London, 1706). Gui Tachard, *Voyage de Siam* ... (Paris, 1689). Louis Le Comte (Conte) wrote one of the most influential books on China ever published (1696); immediately trans. into English as *Memoirs and Observations* ... *Made in a Late Journey through the Empire of China, and Published in Several Letters* ... (London, 1697), it saw two other eds. in two years, the 2d being (London: Benjamin Tooke, 1698). Father Theodore Krump, a medical doctor, traveled North Africa with six other Jesuits in 1700-02 and published 1710. For many more of these embassies, by no means all, see the early sections of Babeau; Heawood, e.g., p. 133; and A.L. Sells, *The Paradise of Travellers* (Bloomington: Indiana Univ. Press, 1964).

86. Etienne de Flacourt, *Histoire de la Grande Isle Madagascar* (Paris: Lassenlin, 1658); the Bibliothèque Nationale has two copies of this scarce and seminal work, which records many eyewitness accounts. Léonard, who also wrote *Lettre sur un voyage aux Antilles*, a travel book much like his novels, has been written about by William M. Kerby, *The Life, Diplomatic Career and Literary Activities of Nicholas Germain Leonard*, thesis, London (Paris, 1925). For Byrd, below, see *Histories of the Dividing Line betwixt Virginia and North Carolina* (New York: Dover, 1967), a rpt. of W.K. Boyd's ed. of 1929, with additions and an int. by Percy G. Adams; see for Byrd's letters and diaries, many of which are concerned with travels, Richard Beale Davis in Davis, Holman, and Rubin, eds., *Southern Writing, 1585-1920* (New York: Odyssey, 1970), p. 96. For one of Young's travel vols., see *Travels in France during the Years 1787, 88, 89*, ed. Constantia Maxwell (Cambridge: Univ. Press, 1929).

87. For Olearius, Nieuhof, Roe, and Walter in this paragraph, see notes above. Torquato Tasso, *Lettera nella quale si paragona l'Italia a la Francia*, a letter to Hercule de Contrari (1581); see Babeau, pp. 40-47. Terry, *A Voyage to East-India* ... (London: Pr. for T.W., 1655); this is a much expanded version of the one found in Purchas. Rickman, *Journal of Captain Cook's Last Voyage* ... (rpt. Ann Arbor: Univ. of Michigan Press, 1967). For Ledyard, whose veracity has often been attacked, see Adams, *Travelers*, pp. 261-62.

88. Bernier's *Voyages* (1671-72, 1699) was almost as well known as the volumes by Chardin and Tavarnier. See Heawood, pp. 66-67. Engelbrecht Kaempfer, obviously a genius, wrote

Amoenitates Exoticae (1712), an account of his travels, especially in Japan; and then, after his death, appeared his great *History of Japan,* trans. J.G. Scheuchzer (London: Scheuchzer, 1727), again enlarged, in 1728 and trans. immediately into French as *Histoire Naturelle, Civile, et Ecclesiastique de l'Empire du Japon* (La Haye: P. Gosse, 1729), the best book on Japan for the seventeenth century. Hans Sloane, *A Voyage to the Islands Madera, Barbados, Nieves, ... and Jamaica ...,* Vol. I (London: Pr. by B.M. For the Author, 1707), Vol. II (1725).

89. Frézier, *Relation du voyage de la Mer du Sud aux côtes du Chily et du Pérou ... 1712, 1713 et 1714* (Paris: Nyon, 1716). For de Brahm, an intriguing traveler, see Percy G. Adams, "Travel Literature of the Seventeenth and Eighteenth Centuries: A Review of Recent Approaches," *TSLL,* 20 (1978), 499. For the rest of this paragraph, see Coxe, *Travels in Switzerland ... in a Series of Letters to William Melmoth* (London: T. Cadell, 1789, 1791); Crèvecoeur, *Voyage dans la Haute Pensylvanie et dans l'Etat de New York, par un membre adoptif de la Nation Oneida ...,* 3 vols. (Paris: Chez Maradan, 1801); Halley, *Miscellanea Curiosa,* 2d. ed. (London: R. Smith, 1708); Wales and Bayley and Solander—see Beaglehole's ed. of Cook, Note 14 above; Ray, *Observations Topographical, Moral, and Physiological: Made in a Journey through Part of the Low-Countries, Germany, Italy, and France: With a Catalogue of Plants Not Native of England* (London: John Martyn, 1673); Kalm, *Travels into North America* [1st. pub. 1753-61], trans. J.R. Forster (London, 1770-71; rpt. Barre, Mass: Imprint Soc., 1972).

90. For this paragraph, see de Brosses, *Lettres écrites d'Italie ... en 1739 et 1740,* 2 vol. (Paris: Levasseur, 1836); he later did the great *Histoire des Navigations aux Terres Australes ...* 2 vols. (Paris, 1756; rpt. Amsterdam, 1967), an influential book on French thought. For him, see also Babeau, pp. 184-88. *Journal of Andre Michaux,* in Thwaites, *Early Western Travels* (Cleveland: Clark, 1904), III, 25-104. For Martine and Durand, see Babeau, pp. 163-68, and *Voyage litt éraire de deux religieux bénédictins* (Paris, 1717-24), 2 vols. Locke, *Travels in France, 1675-1679,* ed. John Lough (Cambridge: Univ. Press, 1953). Lassels retired to France, where his book came out posthumously in 1670. François-Maximillian Misson de Valbourg—not to be confused with his brother Henri, another Huguenot refugee (note 94 below)—published first in France, his book being translated as *A New Voyage to Italy; Together with Useful Instructions for those who shall Travel thither* (London, 1695).

91. There are a number of studies of the Grand Tour in general or for a given period. Besides Howard, Bate, Babeau, and Parks, *The English Traveler to Italy,* see J.W. Stoye, *English Travellers Abroad 1604-1667* (London: Jonathan Cape, 1952); William Mead, *The Grand Tour in the Eighteenth Century* (Boston: Houghton Mifflin, 1914); Constantia Maxwell, *The English Traveller in France, 1689-1815* (London: Routledge, 1932); George B. Parks, "Travel as Education," in *The Seventeenth Century,* ed. R.F. Jones, et al (Stanford: Stanford Univ. Press, 1951), pp. 264-90; Paul F. Kirby, *The Grand Tour in Italy (1700-1800)* (New York: S.F. Vanni, 1952). Thomas Nugent in the eighteenth century even called his travel-guide book *The Grand Tour; or, a Journey through the Netherlands, Germany, Italy, and France ...* [1st ed. 1749] (London: J. Rivington and Sons, 1778), the 3d ed. in 4 vols.

92. For Boyle, see Howard (Note 8 above), pp. 158-68. For Seignelay below, see *L'Italie en 1671. Relation d'un voyage du marquis de Seignelay* [J.B. Colbert] (Paris: Didier, 1867); Babeau, followed by Howard, gives 1617 in the title when Seignelay's dates are 1653-90. Buffon, *Correspondence inédite de Buffon* (Paris: Hachette, 1860), 2 vols.; Sandys, see note 76 above. For Temple as traveler, see Clara Marburg, *Sir William Temple: A Seventeenth Century "Libertine"* (New Haven: Yale Univ. Press, 1932). Addison, *Remarks on Several Parts of Italy ... in the Years 1701, 1702, 1703* (1705), in *The Works of ... Addison,* with notes by Richard Hurd, D. D., ed. H.G. Bohn, 6 vols. (London: Bohn, 1856).

93. For this paragraph: Huygens's *Reyserverhael* is in the first ed. of his Works and can be found in *Les Journeaux de Christiaan Huygens (Journal de voiage à Paris et à Londres, Octobre 1660-Mai 1661; Du Voiage de Paris et de Londres, 1663)* ed. H.L. Brugmans (Paris, 1935); for

Franklin as traveler, see Percy G. Adams, "Franklin and the Travel-Writing Tradition," in *The Oldest Revolutionary: Essays on Benjamin Franklin*, ed. J.A. Leo Lemay (Philadelphia: Univ. of Pennsylvania Press, 1976), pp. 33-51; Mandelslo's *Deux lettres* are in *Relation du voyage de Moscovie, Tartarie, et de Perse . . . Traduite de l'Alleman du Sieur Olearius . . .* (Paris: Clouzier, 1656), and see Olearius, ed. Baron, p. 293n; Heawood, p. 65, combines the two trips in one.

94. For this paragraph: for the von der Trenck cousins, see *Memoirs of the Life of the Illustrious Francis Baron Trenck . . . Written by himself, and done from the original German* (London: W. Owen, 1747), and *The Life of Baron Friedrich Trenck (1726-94) . . . Trans. by Thomas Holcroft from German* (London: Pr. for G.G.J. and J. Robinson, 1788-93), 4 vols. [Holcroft's trans. was very popular, and the lives of both adventurers were popular all over Europe; their amazing memoirs, of themselves and of each other, are highly suspect]; Lebeau, *Avantures du sr C. Lebeau . . .; ou Voyage curieux et nouveau parmi les sauvages de l'Amérique septentrionale . . .* (Amsterdam: Uytwerf, 1738), 2 vols.; F. Misson (note 90 above) and Henri Misson, *Mémoires et observations faites par un voyageur en Angleterre* (1698), trans. John Ozell as *M. Misson's Memoirs and Observations in His Travels over England* (London: D. Browne, 1719); Brereton, *Travels in Holland, the United Provinces, England . . . 1634-1635*, ed. E. Hawkins (Chelham Soc. I, 1844), and see Stoye, pp. 242-47, for more on Brereton; for Fielding and Smollett, see notes 18 and 17 above, and Sterne, *A Sentimental Journey through France and Italy by Mr. Yorick*, ed. Gardner D. Stout, Jr. (Berkeley and Los Angeles: Univ. of California Press, 1971; 1st ed. 1768).

95. Rouvière, *Voyage du tour de la France* (Paris, 1713).

96. *The Journeys of Celia Fiennes*, ed. Christopher Morris (London: Cresset, 1949; 1st pub. incompletely in 1888); and *Mémoires de Pierre Thomas, sieur du Fossé*, 4 vols. (Rouen: F. Bouquet, 1876-1889); Macky, *A Journey through England in Familiar Letters from a Gentleman Here to his Friend Abroad* (London: Hooke, 1714), which had 5 eds. by 1732.

97. *The English Works of John Gower*, ed. G.C. Macaulay (London: K. Paul, 1900-1901), II, 253; and the quotation is from *Mandeville's Travels*, ed. M.C. Seymour (Oxford: Clarendon, 1967), pp. 119-20. See Zacher, pp. 141-42; Jusserand, pp. 387-89, who asserts that "every author who draws their portrait describes their taste for moving about at home, and their love of distant travel."

98. Gower, II, 253; Howard, p. xi, but on p. 22 she says that the English and Germans equal each other as ardent travelers; see Thomas Nugent in the mid-eighteenth century, who found the Germans everywhere he went on the Continent.

99. Casson, p. 122. But see also even his early chapters.

100. For the rest of the paragraph, see Zacher, Chap. II, for Petrarch and the Church Fathers; Carnochan, *Confinement and Flight* (Berkeley: Univ. of California Press, 1977); J.R.L. Anderson, *The Ulysses Factor* (New York: Harcourt Brace Jovanovich, 1970); and, for the German, C.M. Wieland, ed., *Der Teutsche Merken*, Oct. 1784.

101. Wilding, note 84 above. The quotation from Montesquieu is on Wilding's title page.

102. Voltaire, *Candide*, Chap. 26.

103. For John Cabot—his son Sebastian was perhaps even more to be called a Great Adventurer—see J.A. Williamson, *The Cabot Voyages and Bristol Discovery under Henry VII* (Cambridge: Hakluyt, 1962); for Dom de Castro, daring hero and friend of Francis Xavier, see Penrose, pp. 67-69, and Elaine Sanceau, *Knight of the Renaissance: D. Joao de Castro* (London: Hutchinson, 1949). For other adventurers in this paragraph, see notes above.

104. In this paragraph, for Psalmanazar, see Adams, *Travelers*, pp. 93-97; for Diego de Torres y Villaroel, see his *Vida*, written during 1743-44, appearing in Madrid in part in 1743 and in other parts in 1752 and 1758, with the complete works in 15 vols. in Madrid in 1794-99, and with a life by Antonio García Boíza (Madrid, 1949) done in English as *The Remarkable Life of Don Diego . . .*, trans. William C. Atkinson (London: Folio Soc., 1958); for the von der Trencks, see note 94 above; for Pöllnitz and Raspe, Adams, *Travelers*, pp. 81-82, 216, and the

notes to those pages; also for Pöllnitz, Q.D. Robson-Scott, *German Travelers in England 1400-1800* (Oxford: Blackwell, 1953), pp. 126-27. In his Epilogue, Wilding names other adventurers but none of these I have added here; nor does he name a host of other possible additions, e.g., the Hungarian Count Benyowski with his sentimental love affair in Kamchatka and his death in an abortive plan to colonize Madagascar (see Adams, *Travelers,* pp. 81-82). For more on Torres, see Chap. VII below.

105. Although the next three paragraphs are indebted to my *Travelers and Travel Liars,* they go before the period covered by that book, and where I thought it helpful, documentation has been added.

106. For *Mandeville,* see Josephine W. Bennett, *The Rediscovery of Sir John Mandeville* (New York: MLA, 1954); the ed. of *Mandeville* by Seymour; and Chap. VI of Zacher.

107. For Obregón and Combes, see Valentin de Pedro, *America en las letras españolas del siglo de oro* (Buenos Aires: Editorial Sudamericana, 1954), pp. 112-13, and G. Atkinson, *Les Nouveaux horizons de la renaissance française* (Paris: Droz, 1935), pp. 311-12; for Lahontan below, Adams, *Travelers,* pp. 54-62.

108. Mme d'Aulnoy, Misson, and Defoe are discussed in my *Travelers and Travel Liars.* For Courtilz, see Mylne, pp. 58-62; B.M. Woodbridge, *Gatien de Courtilz, Sieur du Verger* (Baltimore: Johns Hopkins Univ. Press, 1925); and Wilhelm Fuger, *Die Entstehung des historischen Romans aus der fiktiven Biographie in Frankreich und English* ... (Münschen, 1963). For the scholarly wars over *Drury,* see Rodney Baine, "Daniel Defoe and Robert Drury's *Journal,*" *TSLL,* 16 (1974), 479-91. See also for Leguat, G. Atkinson, "A French Desert Island Story of 1708," *PMLA,* 36 (1921), 511, and Philip B. Gove, *The Imaginary Voyage in Prose Fiction* (New York: Columbia Univ. Press, 1941), pp. 207-210; for d'Aulnoy, see R. Foulché-Delbosc, int. to Mme D'Aulnoy, *Travels into Spain* (London: Routledge and Sons, 1930); and for Defoe, see A.W. Secord, *Studies in the Narrative Method of Defoe* (Urbana: Univ. of Illinois Press, 1924), and other books by him and John Robert Moore.

109. *Journal des Savants* (VIII. 708). Its four "fakes" are *Jacques Sadeur* (1676; 6th ed. 1732), *François Leguat* (1707), *Glantzby* (1729), and Prévost's *Robert Lade* (1744). Note also that the longest serial in the *London Chronicle* before 1760 was of a travel book called *The Voyages and Adventures of Captain John Holmesby* (London, 1757), which by the *Chronicle* was considered real but which is called a "novel" by the *Critical Review,* 4 (1757), 395-402. See Gove, p. 346. For the methods, techniques, motives, and success of fabricators of travel literature of the seventeenth and eighteenth centuries, see Adams, *Travelers,* to which one could add very much for the Renaissance and Lucian's day.

110. Quoted in Atkinson, *Les Nouvelles horizons* ..., p. 30n (my translation).

111. In Shaftesbury, *Characteristics* (1711). See Sigworth, *Criticism and Aesthetics, 1660-1800,* pp. 184-85.

112. See, for elaborate evidence of the "outstanding emphasis on travel books of all kinds, pseudo memoirs, 'voyages,' 'shipwrecks,' and stories of piratical adventure," Robert D. Mayo, *The English Novel in the Magazines 1740-1815* (Evanston: Northwestern Univ. Press, 1962), p. 61, and p. 408, n. 37.

113. *Bibliothèque universelle* as quoted in a prefatory note to Gabriel Foigny's *Jacques Sadeur* [not a real travel book], Feb. 1786, I, 182. See Gove, pp. 23-26, for more evidence. For Wieland, see Note 100 above.

114. Frantz, *The English Traveller and the Movement of Ideas, 1660-1732, Univ. of Nebraska Studies,* 32-33 (1934; rpt. Lincoln: Univ. of Nebraska Press, 1967); see also note 85 above.

115. For Temple, see Marburg (note 92 above), pp. 56-71; for Locke, note that Frantz, p. 146, points out that Locke cites Peter Martyr, Garcilaso, Jean de Léry, and Thévenot; for the *Spectator,* see the index to R.P. Bond's five-volume ed. (Oxford: Clarendon, 1965).

116. For a well-documented account of d'Aulnoy's reputation in England, see Melvin D.

Palmer, "Madame d'Aulnoy in England," *CL*, 27 (1975), 237-53. Over 36 eds. of her works were printed there before 1750.

117. Bernard, X, cxiv.

118. *Précis du siècle de Louis XIV* (Paris: Renouard, 1818; 1st pub. 1748), p. 245 [my trans.].

119. Hakluyt, for example, added stories of gold and precious stones to "Virginia richly valued, ... " (note 12 above).

120. For La Salle, see Adams, *Travelers*, pp. 52-54, including his distortion of maps of North America, among them those of the king's cartographer Franquelin; for Drage, see Percy G. Adams, "The Case of Swaine Versus Drage: An Eighteenth-Century Publishing Mystery Solved," in *Essays in History and Literature Presented by Fellows of the Newberry Library to Stanley Pargellis*, ed. Heinz Bluhm (Chicago: Newberry Library, 1965), pp. 157-69.

121. For some of the information in this paragraph, see, e.g., for Hakluyt and the Royal Society, Percy G. Adams, "The Achievements of James Cook and His Associates in Perspective," in *Exploration in Alaska: Captain Cook Commemorative Lectures, June-November 1978*, ed. Antoinette Shalkop (Anchorage: Cook Inlet Historical Society, 1980), pp. 21-22; for the Jesuits as surveyors, see Heawood, pp. 137-41; for Manoa, see Penrose, p. 108; for Lahontan's river, see "Letter Sixteen" in his *Dialogues curieux*, ed. Gilbert Ghinard (Baltimore: Johns Hopkins Univ. Press, 1931), and Chinard's introduction as well as Adams, *Travelers*, pp. 56-58; for examples of distorted maps, see Henry P. Wagner, "Apocryphal Voyages to the North-West Coast of America," *Proceedings of the American Antiquarian Soc.*, N.S., 41 (1931), 190-96.

122. This story badly needs to be told. I have made a small attempt at it in papers to which the following two paragraphs are indebted: "The Achievements of James Cook ... " (note 121 above) and "Science and Early Travel to the Americas," a paper read at a meeting of the ACLS held in Victoria in 1977. A book on traveling medical doctors alone would be fascinating.

123. For only two of countless documented records of the marvels that passed for facts, see Clark B. Firestone, *The Coasts of Illusion* (New York: Harper and Brothers, 1921), and James Masterson, "Traveller's Tales of Colonial Natural History," *Journal of American Folklore*, 19 (1948), 51-67, 174-88.

124. Monardes, *Primera y segunda y tercera partes de la historia mediciniae ... de nuestras Indias Occidentales ...* (Sevilla, 1574). For Frampton (London, 1577), see Stephen Gaslee's ed., 2 vols. (London, 1925), and H.M. Jones, *O Strange New World* (New York: Viking, 1964; 1st ed. 1952), pp. 401-2.

125. For one example, see Bacon's use of Acosta: R.R. Cawley, *The Voyagers and Elizabethan Drama* (London: Oxford Univ. Press, 1938), p. 327.

126. Hakluyt, *Principal Navigations*, V, 165-70. See also Hakluyt's instructions for Arthur Pet and Charles Jackman, sent out by the Muscovy Company in 1580, in II, 214-27.

127. *Philosophical Transactions*, I (1665-66), 140-41, 147, 186. These had obvious effects; see, e.g., *Philosphical Transactions*, 18 (1694), 167, where Captain Narbrough is praised for following the "Directions."

128. Churchill (1704; rpt. 1732), I, xlix; and Bernard, X, cxlv.

129. For these academies, see Harcourt Brown, *Scientific Organizations in Seventeenth-Century France (1620-1680)* (1934; rpt. New York: Russell and Russell, 1967), pp. 1-17, 64-117; Roger Hahn, *The Anatomy of a Scientific Institution: The Paris Academy of Sciences, 1660-1803* (Berkeley: Univ. of California Press, 1971), Chap. I, and Hahn's excellent bibliography; William E. Knowles, *The Experimenters: A Study of the Accademia del Cimento* (Baltimore: Johns Hopkins Univ. Press, 1971); and the many histories of the Royal Society since the first by Thomas Sprat, *The History of the Royal Society* (London: J.R., for J. Martyn, 1667). For Evelyn, see note 13 above; for Boyle and other traveling scientists, see Brown, p. 99, Hahn, p. 106; for Huygens, see note 93 above; Sorbière, *Relation ...* (Paris: L. Billaine, 1664); Magalotti, *Travels of Cosmo III, Grand Duke of Tuscany, through England during the Reign of King Charles II* (1669) (London:

Mawman, 1821). All this, as well as the rest of the paragraph, is expanded in Adams, "The Achievements of Captain Cook. . . . "

130. For Ricci, see note 23 above and Henri Bernard, S.J., *Matteo Ricci's Scientific Contributions to China,* trans. E.C. Werner (Peiping: Henri Vetch, 1935); Tachard, *Voyage de Siam* (1686); for Leibnitz, see Frank E. Manuel, *The Eighteenth Century Confronts the Gods* (Cambridge; Harvard Univ. Press), p. 102. R.F. Jones, *Ancients and Moderns: A Study of the Rise of the Scientific Movement in Seventeenth-Century England* (1959; rpt. St. Louis: Washington Univ. Studies, 1961), p. 88, believes that "our modern scientific utilitarianism is the offspring of Bacon begot upon Puritanism," a conclusion obviously too narrow. Nowhere in this seminal book does Jones make use of travel writers. For a broader conclusion, see Peter Gay, *The Party of Humanity* (London: Knopf, 1964), p. 45.

131. For the Rites controversy, see Manuel; *The Merchant Explorer* (1977), pp. 24-28 especially; William D. Appleton, *A Cycle of Cathay* (New York: Columbia Univ. Press, 1951), pp. 3-65; Arnold H. Rowbotham, "The Impact of Confucianism on Seventeenth-Century Europe," *Far Eastern Quarterly,* 4, 1945, 224-42. For Jesuit bias about the Canadian Indian, see Healy (note 61 above).

132. Manuel, p. 58, p. 15, and especially p. 19. See also Frantz, pp. 72-120, and Atkinson, *Nouveaux horizons,* pp. 221-71.

133. See Leibnitz, *Novissima Sinica* (1697), for his system of natural theology; also Donald F. Lach, "Leibnitz and China," *Journal of the History of Ideas,* 6 (1945), 436-55; Bayle, *Dictionnaire historique et critique* (1697), s.v. "Spinoza"; Marburg, *Temple,* pp. 50-60; Homer E. Woodbridge, *Sir William Temple: The Man and His Work* (New York: MLA, 1940), pp. 276-84.

134. Muriel Dodds, *Les Récits de Voyages Sources de l'Esprit des Lois de Montesquieu* (Paris: Champion, 1929), is most helpful but by no means exhaustive for Montesquieu. See also the notes to the first vol. of *De l'Esprit des loix* in *Oeuvres complètes de Montesquieu,* ed. Jean Brethe de la Gressaye (Paris: Société les belles lettres, 1950); for *Les Lettres persanes,* see discussions below, especially in Chap. IV. See also R.W. Frantz's chap., "The Traveller and the Science of Government," pp. 120-39.

135. See note 1 above.

136. Stafford has done much with this fascinating side of the travelers, but much is yet to be done, especially with the earlier travelers like Breydenbach and those found in de Bry. See Stafford, "Rude Sublime: The Taste for Nature's Colossi . . . ," *Gazette des Beaux Arts* (Avril, 1976), pp. 113-26, only one of her excellent studies.

CHAPTER THREE

1. Strabo, in Loeb ed. of Strabo, trans. H.L. Jones, and quoted in William Nelson, "The Boundaries of Fiction in the Renaissance: A Treaty Between Truth and Falsehood," *ELH,* 36 (1969), 33.

2. Norman Friedman, in a review in *Style,* 9 (1977), 215, of Guido Almansi, *The Writer as Liar: Narrative Technique in the "Decameron"* (London: Routledge and Kegan Paul, 1977).

3. Kamber, in *British Journal of Aesthetics,* 17 (1977), 335-45; Nelson in *ELH,* 36 (1969), 30-58, and his *The Dilemma of the Renaissance Storyteller* (Cambridge: Harvard Univ. Press, 1973). All references to Nelson will be to the article of 1969.

4. Mylne, Stewart, and Showalter, in Chap. I above. For British fiction, see, e.g., McKillop, *Early Masters.* See also, for only one other necessary analysis of history's opinions about lying and art, R.J. Clements and Joseph Gibaldi, *Anatomy of the Novella: The European Tale Collection from Boccaccio and Chaucer to Cervantes* (New York: New York Univ. Press, 1977), especially pp. 16-19.

5. Nicolson (Chap. II above) and Atkinson, *The Extraordinary Voyage in French Literature*

before 1700 (New York: Columbia Univ. Press, 1920), and *The Extraordinary Voyage in French Literature from 1700 to 1720* (Paris: Champion, 1922).

6. Gove (Chap. II above).

7. Spence, *Letters from the Grand Tour*, ed. Slava Klima (Montreal: McGill-Queen's Univ. Press, 1975), p. 223. Although the present chapter owes a small debt to my *Travelers and Travel Liars: 1660-1800*, I hope that any reader will soon see both the reason for including the chapter here and the fact that it makes an original and necessary linking of the novel and travel literature.

8. From article "Calius," note D., as loosely trans. from Paul Hazard, *La Crise de la Conscience Européene, 1680-1715* (Paris: Boivin, 1935), pp. 109-10.

9. Note first, however, that Hume arged in "Of the Delicacy of Taste and Passion" that "nothing is so improving to the temper as the study of the beauties, either of poetry, eloquence, music, or painting," and, second, that Richard Kamber (note 3 above) is only one to believe that Hume "was speaking loosely and with deliberate exaggeration" (p. 335). But see Hume in "Of the Standard of Taste" saying that "Many of the beauties of poetry and even of eloquence are founded on falsehood and fiction. . . . " Patricia Meyer Spacks, ed., *Late Augustan Prose* (Englewood Cliffs, N.J.: Prentice-Hall, 1971), p. 239.

10. For more information on Plato, Solon, Lucian, etc., see Nelson, pp. 30-34 especially. Lucian's position was taken also by the Emperor Julian.

11. The medievalist is John Hurt Fisher, "Truth versus Beauty: An Inquiry into the Function of Language and Literature in an Articulate Society," *The Humanity of English*, NCTE 1972 Distinguished Lecture (NCTE, 1972), p. 3; the Renaissance scholar is Nelson.

12. Nelson, p. 31.

13. For Plato and, below, Cicero, Quintilian, Plutarch, and St. Augustine, see Nelson, pp. 31-35.

14. Sidney, "An Apologie for Poetry."

15. Quoted in Walter R. Davis, *Idea and Art in Elizabethan Fiction* (Princeton: Princeton Univ. Press, 1969), p. 36. See also his discussion of Sidney, p. 44.

16. Vives, *Opera Omnia* (Valencia, 1782), II, 517-31. A summary and commentary are provided by Nelson, pp. 55-57.

17. Nelson, p. 57.

18. Dryden, "A Parallel of Poetry and Painting," *Of Dramatic Poesy and Other Essays*, ed. George Watson (New York: Dutton, 1964), pp. 193-94, 186-87.

19. Shaftesbury, in Oliver F. Sigworth, ed., *Criticism and Aesthetics 1660-1800* (San Francisco: Rinehart, 1971), p. 184.

20. Swift, "To Stella; 1720."

21. See note 2 above, e.g., and add, say, Arthur Heiserman, *The Novel before the Novel* (Chicago: Univ. of Chicago Press, 1977), and Tieje (1913).

22. For one account of Bayle's attack, see Stewart, p. 15.

23. Marivaux, in "Avis au lecteur" to *Les Aventures^{xxx}, ou les Effets surprenants de la sympathie* (Paris, 1713); and for Bellegarde, see Mylne, p. 14.

24. Trans. from Voltaire's *Le Siècle de Louis XIV* (Paris: Garnier-Flammarion, 1966), II, 213.

25. *The Complete Letters of Lady Mary Wortley Montagu*, ed. Robert Halsband (Oxford: Univ. Press, 1965), I, 293.

26. For Diderot, see Mylne, p. 215; the modern critic is Joseph Margolis, *The Language of Art and Art Criticism* (Detroit: Wayne State Univ. Press, 1965), Chap. II. For an answer to Margolis, see F.E. Sparshott, "Truth in Fiction," *The Journal of Aesthetics and Art Criticism*, 26 (1967), 3-9; see also George Levine, "Realism, or, In Praise of Lying . . .," *CE*, 31 (1970), 355-65, who argues that the novelist's "fiction is a fiction—a lie," that, e.g., the late Eliot and all of Hardy "masquerade" as truth. For only one more, see J.M. Cameron, "Problems of Literary History,"

New Literary History, 1 (1969), 7-20, who solves the problem of true and false in fiction by arguing that fiction is neither the one nor the other since there is "no real situation" with which it can be compared.

27. Lucian, *True Story* (or *True History*), in *Lucian Selected Works*, trans. Bryan P. Reardon (New York: Bobbs-Merrill, 1965), p. 220.

28. *The Acts and Monuments of John Foxe*, ed. Josiah Pratt (London: Religious Tract Soc., 1887), III, 268, as quoted in Jusserand, pp. 206-7; and Zacher, p. 152.

29. For von Harff, Varthema, and Pinto in this paragraph, see, for only two explanations, Penrose, pp. 28, 29-32, 70-72, and Monroe Z. Hafter, "Towards a History of Spanish Imaginary Voyages," *ECS*, 8 (1975), 263-85. Other fictitious or partly fictitious Renaissance travel accounts are by, or attributed to, Andres Laguna, *Viaje de Turquia* (1557); Pierre Olivier Malherbe (c. 1600); Pedro Ordóñez de Cevallos, *Viaje del Mundo* (1614); the sieur de Feynes (1615); Vincent le Blanc, whose travels began when he was shipwrecked in 1568 and who was published only in 1649 (English, 1660), after his death [see Hafter, p. 272; Atkinson, *The Extraordinary Voyage ... before 1700*, pp. 25-33; and Penrose, pp. 218-22].

30. Biddulph, in *The Travels of Certain Englishmen into Africa, Asia, ... Jerusalem* (London: Pr. for Thomas Haveland, 1609), pp. 115-43. See also Richard Beale Davis, *George Sandys, Poet-Adventurer* (London: Bodley Head, 1955), p. 69n.

31. For only one study of the real distortions in Jesuit missionary accounts, of their biases, and of the editing given them by superiors at home, see George R. Healey, note 61, Chap. II above. For a chap. on religious and other biases of travel writers, see Adams, *Travelers* (for Macaulay, p. 195), as well as R.W. Frantz.

32. Butler, *Characters and Passages from Note-Books*, ed. A.R. Waller (Cambridge: Cambridge Univ. Press, 1908), p. 64.

33. Shaftesbury, "Advice to an Author," in *Characteristics* (1711), excerpted in Sigworth, ed., *Criticism and Aesthetics*, p. 184.

34. Ward, *The London Spy*, ed. K. Fenwick (London: Folio Society, 1955), p. 33.

35. Jacquin, *Entretiens sur les romans. Ouvrage moral et critique. Dans lequel on traite des origines des Romans et de leur différentes espèces ...* (Paris: Duchesne, 1755), p. 191; see also pp. 46, 251, 348.

36. Bernard, I, cxlv.

37. For these and many other travel writers completely or partially fake, and still others that were called liars, see Adams, *Travelers;* Gove; and a fine summary for the eighteenth century in Batten, pp. 52-64.

38. Nichols in Hakluyt, IV, 23.

39. Uring, "Advertisement to the Reader," *The Voyages and Travels of Captain Nathaniel Uring*, (see Chap. II, note 66, above). For late eighteenth-century followers of this tradition among travelers in Europe, see Batten, p. 45.

40. For a study of, and bibliography for, all three, see P. Loubriet, "Les Guides de voyages au début de xviiie siècle et la propagande philosophique," *SVEC*, 32 (1965), 269-327.

41. John Bulkeley and John Cummins, *A Voyage to the South Seas. By His Majesty's Ship Wager* (London: T. Twig, 1743). See Adams, *Travelers*, p. 260, notes 10, 11, for a bibliography of the eight most important books to come from Anson's voyage.

42. Jeffreys, *The Natural and Civil History of the French Dominion in North and South America* (London: Pr. for T. Jeffreys, 1760), p. 161; Adair, *Adair's History of the American Indians* [1775], ed. S.C. Williams (Johnson City, Tenn.: Watauga Press, 1930), pp. xxxiii and, e.g., xxxvi.

43. By Mylne, p. 16.

44. See Mylne, pp. 4-18, and Stewart, "Nothing but the Truth," pp. 170-93, for fine treatments of the subject. Stewart, p. 269, says that most French readers of novels in the early eighteenth century "asked nothing better than to be fooled and that the abundance of prefaces

dedicated to claims of veracity arose from a desire to humor this initially amenable attitude." He quotes F.C. Green, *French Novelists*, p. 63, who agrees that readers were willing to be deceived "within reasonable limits."

45. *The Works of Thomas Nashe*, ed. R.B. McKerrow (Oxford: 1958), I, 11.

46. Sorel, *La Bibliothèque française* (Paris, 1664), and Guéret, *La Promenade de Saint-Cloud* (Paris: Librairie des Bibliophiles, 1888), p. 37. For these and other such statements, see Stewart, pp. 27-30.

47. For more on these three and other examples from French fiction, see Showalter, pp. 44-45, 50, 163, et seq. Stewart, pp. 6-9, e.g.; and Frédéric Deloffre, "Le Probleme de l'illusion romanesque et le renouvellement des techniques narratives de 1700 à 1715," *La Littérature narrative d'Imagination* ... (Paris: Presses Universitaires de France, 1961), pp. 115-33.

48. See Richardson's letter to Warburton, 19 April 1748, in *Selected Letters of Samuel Richardson*, ed., John Carroll (Oxford: Clarendon, 1964), p. 85. For more on Richardson's attitude, see Elizabeth Bergen Brophy, *Samuel Richardson* (Knoxville: Univ. of Tennessee Press, 1974), pp. 31-32, and McKillop, *Early Masters*, pp. 42-44.

49. James, *The Art of Fiction* (1884), and Fielding in *Tom Jones* are both cited by Watt, p. 286.

50. See Chap. IV below for the scholarly argument as to whether or not Behn really saw Surinam. For other examples of such seventeenth-century claims, see Tieje (1913), p. 231, whose essay supports many of the points this chapter makes for the early novel.

51. For Villedieu, see B.A. Morrissette, *The Life and Works of Marie-Catherine DesJardins* [Mme de Villedieu] (Saint Louis: 1947), and a short treatment in Mylne, pp. 36-38; for d'Aulnoy, see Adams, *Travelers*, pp. 97-100, and Foulché-Delbosc; for Courtilz, see B.M. Woodbridge, *Gatien de Courtilz, Sieur de Verger: Etude sur un Précurseur du Roman Réaliste en France* (Baltimore: Johns Hopkins Studies in Romance Literature and Language, 1925), and for a short treatment, Mylne, pp. 38-40.

52. See Spiro Peterson, ed., *The Counterfeit Lady Unveiled, p. 7. For the text of this "history," see pp. 11-102.*

53. For a fine analysis of these and other such stories, see John J. Richetti, *Popular Fiction before Richardson*, Chap. III.

54. See Crébillon's preface to *Les Egarements du coeur et de l'esprit* (1736 ff.) and, for a fine essay on Diderot, Mylne, pp. 192-220.

55. McKillop, *Early Masters*, pp. 5-6, quotes the entire passage and then, I think, misinterprets it when he says (p. 5) that "At best" Defoe only grudgingly admitted that "feigned narrative may both teach and delight." Defoe's whole career, in fact, points to the opposite conclusion. For the old-fashioned approach to Defoe the unconscious artist who was forced by his environment to be a liar, see Baker, III, 224 ff.; for the later emphasis on the conscious artist and the creator of illusion, see excellent essays by Maximillian Novak, "Defoe's Theory of Fiction," *SP*, 61 (1964), 650-58, and Homer O. Brown, "The Displaced Self in the Novels of Daniel Defoe," *SEC*, ed. H.E. Pagliaro, 4 (1975), 69-95, first pubd. in *ELH*, 38 (1971). For still more on Defoe's attitude to the "possible propriety" of lying, see the appendix to G.A. Starr, *Defoe and Casuistry* (Princeton: Princeton Univ. Press, 1955).

56. Beasley, "English Fiction in the 1740's," pp. 157-71.

57. John J. Burke, Jr., "History without History: Henry Fielding's Theory of Fiction," in *Essays on Fielding and Others in Honor of Miriam Austin Locke*, ed. Donald Kay (University: Univ. of Alabama Press, 1977), pp. 45-65. We shall return to this subject in Chap. IV, since Fielding and his contemporaries were in the romance tradition as well as the realistic, whether mimetic or "philosophical," and since Fielding in the preface to his *Voyage to Lisbon*, as well as Defoe (see McKillop, *Early Masters*, p. 7), argued the rewards of history and travel accounts, Herodotus, e.g., over those of prose fiction.

58. Henri-François de La Solle, *Mémoirs de deux amis, ou Les Aventures de Méssieurs Barnival et Rinville* (Londres, 1754), p. xxx, and François Béliard, *Zélaskim histoire amériquaine ou les Aventures de la Marquise de P^xxx (Paris: Chez Mérigot, 1765)*.

59. See note 103 of Chap. I above for these three defenders of the novel over history. For still other perspectives on the useful lie, the allegorical or general truth, see D.W. Smith, "The Useful Lie in Helvétius and Diderot," *Diderot Studies,* 14 (1971), 185-95, and L.G. Crocker. "The Problem of Truth and Falsehood in the Age of Enlightenment," *Journal of the History of Ideas,* 15 (1953), 575-603. Helvétius and Diderot, Smith concludes, seem to have supported the notion of some useful lies but to abhor the "mensonge" in general. Neither of these articles treats the novel or aesthetics directly.

60. May, *Le Dilemme,* p. 145.

61. Pierre-François Guyot Desfontaines, preface to *Histoire de Dom Juan de Portugal* (Paris, 1724), and Prévost, *Le Pour et Contre* (Paris: Didot, 1733-40), vi, 352-53.

62. For more about omitting or changing names in French fiction, see Stewart, pp. 277-80.

63. For Correvon, see "Lettre à Mme D^xxx sur les romans," *Bibliothèque françoise, ou Histoire Littéraire de la France* (Amsterdam: Bernard, 1728), XII, 47, as quoted by Stewart in a fine essay on this tradition in France as part of the total attempt at illusion (pp. 24-29). For Fielding, see *Tom Jones* (XIII.i), where Fielding was, he said, quoting "a genius of the highest rank," that is, Pope in *Peri Bathous,* Chap. V.

64. See especially the excellent essays by Alter, "The Modernity of Don Quixote: or The Mirror of Knighthood and the World of Mirrors," *Southern Review,* 9 (1973), 311-33; and Fuentes, "*Don Quixote* or the Critique of Reading," *Wilson Quarterly,* 1 (1977), 186-203. Then add Clements and Gilbaldi, *Anatomy of the Novella,* and E.C. Riley, *Cervantes's Theory of the Novel* (Oxford: Clarendon, 1962).

65. *Obras completas,* ed. A.V. Prat (Madrid: Aguilar, 1956), p. 1115, and quoted by Clements and Gibaldi, p. 19.

66. Fuentes, p. 199.

67. For the following information, see *The Travels,* ed. Badger, pp. x, xxi, 1-3, and Penrose, pp. 28-32, 306.

68. See Chardin's *Travels,* ed. with int. by Sykes.

69. For Exquemelin, see his *The Buccaneers of America,* Dover ed.; for Dampier and Wafer below, see the Dover ed. of *A New Voyage round the World* and *A New Voyage and Description of the Isthmus of Panama,* ed. L.E.E. Joyce (London: Hakluyt, 1934). Consult Batten, pp. 44-45, 58-60, for examples of such affirmations after 1750, among them *George Cartwright and His Labrador Journal,* ed. C.W. Townshend (Boston: Estes, 1911) of the 1790s, and Henry Swinburne, *Travels through Spain* (London: Elmsly, 1779).

70. Raleigh, *The Discoverie . . . of Guiana,* ed. V.I. Harlow (London: Argonaut, 1928; 1st ed. 1596). Zacher, p. 153, cites this example in his chapter on *Mandeville.*

71. Timberlake, *A True and Strange Discours . . .* (London: Pr. for the Author, 1603); see his opening sentence in a book that had at least twelve eds. in a hundred years.

72. Biddulph, p. 5 of Preface.

73. For Defoe, see McKillop, *Early Masters,* p. 7; for Fielding, see John J. Burke (note 57 above), who has an opinion somewhat different from mine, since he does not refer to Fielding's *Voyage to Lisbon.* Note also Fielding's *Champion* essays, which satirize the faults of travel literature, especially No. 112 for 31 July 1740: ". . . tho a Traveller, I have no strange, and surprising Discoveries to make . . . I don't take upon me to make People stare . . . like our own Sir John Mandeville." See Augustan Reprint Society, no. 67, ed. S.J. Sackett (Los Angeles: William Andrews Clark Memorial Library, 1958), p. 12.

74. For the *Critical Review,* see Batten, p. 27, who quotes the *Critical Review* for other such opinions; for Davys, see the first sentences of her preface to *The Works of Mrs. Davys* (London: Pr. by H. Woodfall, 1725).

75. Batten's fine study of eighteenth-century travel literature is in fact called *Pleasurable Instruction* and begins with much on the conflict between, the combination of, utile and dulce; one must remember, however, that the conflict and combination existed along before, in Herodotus, in "Mandeville," in Varthema, in Pinto, even in all the Jesuit letters.

76. For Defoe, Challe, and Smollett and the ' 'techniques of fiction," see Chap. VII below and Roger Francillon, "Robert Challe, L'Authenticité du *Journal de voyage aux Indes Orientales,*" *RHL,* 79 (1979), 940-46.

77. Brunel, *Voyage d'Espagne, Curieux, Historique, et Politique. Fait en l'année 1655* (Paris: Ninville, 1666; 1st ed. 1665), p. 3.

78. Swinburne, p. v.

79. For these and other such controversies, see Adams, *Travelers,* Chap. IX.

80. For Bergeron and Le Blanc, see Atkinson, *Extraordinary Voyage . . . before 1700,* p. 27; for Defoe and Crèvecoeur, see Adams, *Travelers,* pp. 111-14, 129-31.

81. "Translator to Reader," *The Life of Baron Frederick Trenck . . .,* trans. Holcroft.

82. See Stewart, p. 276, for more on this and similar devices.

83. See Batten, pp. 54-55, for a discussion of Moore's *View.*

84. Prévost, *The Life and Entertaining Adventures of M. Cleveland, Natural Son of Oliver Cromwell,* 5 vols. (London: T. Astley, 1734), p. xi. Prévost was apparently aware of the English edition of the first volume of Chardin (1686; 1691), the editor of which offered Tournefort as another, later, traveler to verify Chardin's facts (p. xxvii of 1927 ed.).

85. For this and other examples of travelers unfairly thought to have created marvels, see Adams, *Travelers,* Chap. XI.

86. Taylor, *The Life and Extraordinary History of the Chevalier John Taylor [the author's father],* 2 vols. (Dublin: D. Chamberlain, 1771; 1st ed. 1761).

87. Denis Veiras d' Alais, *Histoire des Sévarambes* (Part 1, 1677, in Paris; Part 2, 1678, 1679); first pubd. in part in English as *The History of the Sevarites or Sevarambi . . .* (London: Pr. for Henry Broome, 1675). See Atkinson, *Extraordinary Voyages . . . before 1700,* for bibliographical details.

88. For Shaftesbury, see note 19 above; for Fielding, speaking facetiously in part, *Tom Jones,* p. 645 of the Modern Library ed., or the opening sentence of XII.xiii: "The elegant Lord Shaftesbury somewhere objects to telling too much truth; by which it may be fairly inferred that, in some cases, to lie is not only excusable but commendable."

89. J.R. Moore, *Defoe in the Pillory and Other Studies* (Bloomington: Univ. of Indiana Press, 1939), p. 135.

90. See Adams, *Travelers,* pp. 100-104, for a discussion heavily indebted to Atkinson, *Extraordinary Voyage from 1700 to 1720,* pp. 36-67.

91. See R.W. Frantz, "Gulliver's 'Cousin Sympson,'" *HLQ,* 1 (1938), 329 ff.

92. Picasso, in "Art as Individual Idea," *The Arts,* 3 (1923), 315-26, and often quoted, as by Richard Ellman and Charles Feidelson, Jr., eds., *The Modern Tradition* (New York: Oxford Univ. Press, 1965), p. 25.

CHAPTER FOUR

1. Louis Aragon, *J'Abats mon jeu* (Paris: Editeurs français réunis, 1959), p. 48.

2. For these details and much more about *Lade,* see Gove, pp. 310-11; Claire Engel's chapter "Chacun sa vérité" in her *Figures et aventures du XVIIIᵉ siècle: voyages et découvertes de l'abbé Prévost* (Paris: Editions "Je Sers," 1939), pp. 197 ff.; and, say, Stewart, pp. 202-5. Note that Cox's bibliography of travels is uncertain about Lade and simply says, "'No English original is listed.' Hiersemann—The French translator was Prévost." (Cox, I, 79). Engel speaks often of Prévost's "imagination," p. 197, e.g.

3. William Bonner, *Captain William Dampier Buccaneer-Author* (Stanford: Stanford Univ.

Press, 1934), pp. 177-78; and R.W. Frantz, "Swift's Yahoos and the Voyagers," *MP*, 29 (1931), 49-57.

4. Dampier, *Voyages and Descriptions*, in *Dampier's Voyages*, ed. John Masefield (London: E. Grant, 1906), II, 161; and Wafer, *A New Voyage*, ed. Winship, pp. 112-13.

5. For Drury, still puzzling scholars, see J.R. Moore, *Defoe's Sources for "Robert Drury's Journal"* (Bloomington: Univ. of Indiana Press, 1943); A.W. Secord, *"Robert Drury's Journal" and Other Studies* (Urbana: Univ. of Illinois Press, 1961); Rodney M. Baine, "Daniel Defoe and Robert Drury's Journal," *TSLL*, 16 (1974), 479-91; and Adams, "Travel Literature of the Seventeenth and Eighteenth Centuries."

6. Nelson (note 3 in Chap. III above), p. 46; Murray W. Bundy, *The Theory of Imagination in Classical and Medieval Thought*, Univ. of Illinois Studies in Language and Literature, No. 12 (Urbana: Univ. of Illinois Press, 1927); Tieje (1913), who says, p. 239, 239n., novelists then exhibited a "wayward allegiance" to the "imagination" although "Non-fictionists apparently believed in the imagination." See, however, William Rossky's dissenting views in "Imagination in the English Renaissance," *Studies in the Renaissance*, 5 (1958), 49-73. Then return to the now outdated, but still indispensable, essay by Donald F. Bond, " 'Distrust' of Imagination in English Neo-Classicism," *PQ*, 14 (1925), 54-69, often anthologized, which demolishes such theories as those of Tieje and concludes that the majority opinion after 1660 (as at other times) was that for the creative writer "there were two essential elements—imagination ... and judgment."

7. Tolkien, *Tree and Leaf* (London: Allen and Unwin, 1964), p. 43. For Coleridge, Blake, and others on "imagination," see Frye, *Secular Scripture*, pp. 36, 175, e.g., who seems in perfect agreement with Tolkien while employing the term "creative imagination." If this hasty treatment of a heated academic dispute seems naive, I must add that the approaches of Tolkien and Frye seem to be sane attempts to clean up the waters once so muddied by Coleridge's famous essay on fancy and imagination.

8. See, e.g., Ben E. Perry, *The Ancient Romans* (Berkeley: Univ. of California Press, 1967); P.G. Walsh; Walter R. Davis; Arthur Heiserman; and, say, Margaret Schlauch, *Antecedents of the English Novel 1400-1600* (London: Oxford Univ. Press, 1963), who, unlike Heiserman or Davis, is of the "mimetic," "philosophic realism" school of Auerbach and Watt.

9. Stevick, "Lies, Fictions, and Mock-Facts," *Western Humanities Review*, 30 (1976), 1-12.

10. Thibaudet, "... Le Roman de l'aventure," *Nouvelle revue française*, 13 (1919), 610 ff. (quoted in Gove, p. 161); Green, *Dreams of Adventure, Deeds of Empire* (New York: Basic Books, 1979), p. 22.

11. The first critic is Steeves, p. 21; the second is Patrick Brantlinger, "Romances, Novels, and Psychoanalysis," *Criticism*, 17, pp. 15-40, who does say, however, that romance is not necessarily inferior to novel.

12. For Chapelain, see, e.g., Magendie, p. 121; for the other facts, see Chap. I above.

13. Macky, *A Journey through England* (London: J. Pemberton, 1724), II, iii, was provoked to this tirade by the French-Protestant Henri Misson's *Memoirs and Observations in His Travels over England* (1719), which, he said with many English people of the time, was "stuffed with the greatest Absurdities imaginable." Compare Ascham's 1570 attack in *The Schoolmaster* on fiction imported from Italy—"enchantments of Circe."

14. Augustan Reprint Society, no. 95 (Los Angeles: William Andrews Clark Memorial Library, 1962), pp. 14, 19.

15. See his "A Letter on the Novel," part of the *Conversation about Poetry* (1800), trans. in Howard E. Hugo, ed., *Aspects of Fiction: A Handbook* (Boston: Little, Brown, 1962), pp. 192-93. In this Letter Schlegel charges that "only pedants would ask for labels."

16. In this paragraph, see Freedman, p. 60; Kraft, "Against Realism: Some Thoughts on Fiction, Story, and Reality," *CE*, 31 (1970), 344-54; and Chap. I above.

17. Frye, *Secular Scripture,* and Hunter's review, pp. 531-33, in "Studies in Eighteenth-Century Fiction," *PQ,* 56 (1977), 498-539.

18. Miller, p. 20. Nevertheless, Miller retains the distinction between "novel" and the old "romance," that of Greece and the Middle Ages and not that of La Calprenède, Scudéry, or the eighteenth century. For just one on Defoe, see Martin Green, p. 82: "*Robinson Crusoe* is basically a romance"; Green, however, like Miller, often hedges. Elsewhere, for example, he says that "the posture of Robinson Crusoe was antithetical to that of Amadis de Gaul." For Richardson, see Margaret Dalziel, "Richardson and Romance," *Journal of Australasian Language and Literature Association,* No. 33 (May 1970), 5-24, who, like many others, reminds us that Richardson condemned the seventeenth-century French romances but employed many of the elements, the "stock situations," of "romance." For good older approaches to all this—more to sentimentality than to romance—see J.R. Foster; and Servais Etienne, *Le Genre Romanesque en France* (Paris, 1922). Finally, note René Girard's contention in *Mensonges romantiques et vérité romanesque* (Paris: Grasset, 1961), p. 25, that we are ignorant today of the meaning of "romantisme": "let terme désigne les romans de chevalrie et il désigne *Don Quichotte.*"

19. Doody, "*Don Quixote, Ulysses,* and the Idea of Realism," *Novel: A Forum in Fiction,* 12 (1979), 197-98. See p. 202 for his summary of the limitations of Watt's approach.

20. See Paulson, *Satire in the Novel,* p. 29, and his quotation of Ortega for this theory also. F.R. Karl, *The Adversary Literature: The English Novel in the Eighteenth Century: A Study in Genre* (New York: Strauss and Giraux, 1974), p. 40n., quotes Georges May's conclusion that there was no sharp distinction between the romance and the early novel.

21. Dorothy Richardson, in *The Future of the Novel,* pp. 90-91. See also in the same volume the novelists Waugh (p. 84) and Swinnerton (p. 45).

22. See Chap. I above; see also Addison, *Spectator* 315 (1712); Davys, Preface to her *Works* (1725). Wallace Jackson, *The Probable and the Marvelous: Blake, Wordsworth, and the Eighteenth-Century Critical Tradition* (Athens: Univ. of Georgia Press, 1978), is of little use here, since its emphases are on poetry and the late eighteenth century.

23. Karl, p. 48, says this of *Oroonoko.* Karl's hesitation is only one example of the conditioning that has come with Auerbach and Watt and that is found again in statements such as this: "A clearcut distinction between novel and romance came about ultimately because the novel's unique power of illusion functions best when its realism is undisturbed by other elements" (Showalter, p. 349).

24. For most of these travelers, see Chap. II above; for Muralt's opinions of English and French, see his *Lettres sur les anglois et les françois,* with 7 eds. in 3 years, and François Jost, *La Suisse dans les lettres français . . .* (Fribourg: Eds. Universitaires, 1956).

25. Newcastle (London: A. Maxwell, 1666); see "To the Reader." See also her "The Tale of a Traveller," a realistic "novel" of a man who searches everywhere for happiness before finding it at home, as well as "The Experienced Traveller," "The Observer," "Of Three Travellers," "The Travelling Spirit," and the eighth book of *Natures Pictures Drawn by Fancies Pencil to the Life* (London: F. Martin, 1656), the heroine of which is named Travelia; each is a realistic or a fantastic travel tale.

26. Bonner, p. 64; Smollett, *Travels through France and Italy,* Letter XXVIII. For Smollett on Keyssler and for much more on this tension between dulce and utile in travel books, see Batten, Chap. III.

27. The "student" is Hans Galinsky, "Exploring the 'Exploration Report' and Its Image of the Overseas World: Spanish, French, and English Variants of a Common Form Type in Early American Literature," *EAL,* 12 (1977), 7; for Curley and Batten, see Chap. II above.

28. See Chap. X below for Godwin and his successors.

29. Magendie, pp. 130, 262-73; Tieje (1913), p. 218n. Magendie, p. 266, argues that even in novels not in the picaresque tradition "gross and vulgar scenes," scenes of "ugly realism," are

"more frequent than one might think," and he cites drunken, riotous scenes and ludicrous, ugly people and incidents among corsairs and highwaymen in those novels not related to *Don Quixote* or *Le Roman comique.*

30. Magendie and others—Showalter (p. 10), for example—stress Gomberville's imaginative or superficial local color, while Morillot, *Le Roman en France,* pp. 50-54, stresses the detailed description of this costume. Showalter also emphasizes the "increasing skill with which Challe, Marivaux, and Prévost used local geography" and reminds us (101) that Challe was a voyager himself, was in the Canary Islands, and remembered that Gomberville made imaginative use of them.

31. Alex Gelley, "Setting and a Sense of the World in the Novel," *Yale Review,* 62 (1973), 186-202. See also, for a similar treatment of the landscape as "internal reality," Royal A. Gettmann, "Landscape in the Novel," *Prairie Schooner,* 45 (1971), 239-44.

32. Besides Frye, *Anatomy of Criticism,* see Ronald T. Swigger, "Fictional Encyclopedism and the Cognitive Value of Literature," *CLS,* 12 (1975), 351-67.

33. See the Preface by J.W. Jones to the Hakluyt *Varthema* (1893).

34. For the full title see the large one-volume ed. of Manuel Schonhorn, 1972, II, 381; and for many more such travel book titles for imaginary voyages, see Nicolson, *Voyages to the Moon,* and Gove, especially pp. 198 ff.

35. Lucian, pp. 223-35, 240-228.

36. *The Golden Ass of Apuleius,* trans. William Adlington (1566) (London: Lehmann, 1946).

37. For Mandeville, see Chap. II above, especially Bennett, *The Rediscovery of Sir John Mandeville* (1954).

38. For the use made of travel literature by More and others, see Adams, "The Discovery of American and European Renaissance Literature," p. 110 and notes 64, 65; for Rabelais and the "sieur de Combes," in the next sentence, see Arthur A. Tilley, "Rabelais and Geographical Discovery," in *Studies in the French Renaissance* (New York: Barnes and Noble, 1968; 1st pub. 1922), pp. 46-49, and Atkinson, *Nouveaux horizons,* pp. 311-12, but Atkinson is not correct here in believing that the "roman de voyage" was not "cultivated" in the Renaissance.

39. Rouillard, *The Turk in French History, Thought, and Literature (1520-1660),* No. 13 of *Etudes de la littérature étrangère et comparée* (Paris: Boivin, 1938). See especially pp. 516-596, although Rouillard in pp. 170-270 concentrates on sixteenth- and seventh-century travel accounts, their popularity and their influence, especially those of Johannes Boemus (pub. six times in France alone between 1539 and 1547); Antoine Geuffroy (1542, 1543, 1546); Pierre Belon (4 eds. by 1558), the botanist whose account may be more attractive than Chardin's 100 years later; the Hungarian Georgiewitz (1544), who was a slave in Turkey for thirteen years and whose account had "a phenomenal European popularity"; and Guillaume Postel (1560), a professor of Hebrew and Greek whose two trips to Islamic countries helped produce one of Montaigne's favorite books; and all those of the early seventeenth century when "There was never a period of more than three years . . . without a new publication or re-edition of a book" dealing with Turkey.

40. For these facts and others about Rabelais, see Roullard, pp. 516-22.

41. Rouillard, p. 534. For the full analysis of Gomberville's Turkish local color, see pp. 533-41.

42. Rouillard, pp. 546-71. The title of the roman: *Ibrahim, ou l'Illustre Bassa* (Paris: Sommaville, 1641), in 4 vols.

43. Cawley, *The Voyagers and Elizabethan Drama* (London: Oxford Univ. Press, 1938), and *Unpathed Waters* (Princeton: Princeton Univ. Press, 1940).

44. Whitney, "Spenser's Use of Travel Literature in the *Faerie Queene,*" *MP,* 19 (1921-22), 143-62.

45. See note 51 of Adams, "The Discovery of America."

46. For more on the foreign-observer type of novel, see Martha P. Conant, *The Oriental Tale in England in the Eighteenth Century* (New York: Columbia Univ. Press, 1908), and G.L. Van Roosbroeck, *Persian Letters before Montesquieu* (New York: Institute of French Studies, 1932), as well as a number of articles published since Van Roosbroeck, including three by A.S. Crisafulli, one being "L'Oservateur oriental avant *les Lettres persanes,*" *Lettres romanes,* 8 (1954), 91-113. J. Robert Loy's 1961 Meridian ed. of *The Persian Letters,* with its excellent introduction and notes, helps much with Montesquieu's methods and especially with his use of his travel book sources. Muriel Dodds, note 134 of Chap. II above, deals with the travel sources for *L'Esprit des loix.*

47. Loy's ed. of *The Persian Letters* cites all of these and more, but it does not mention the long list of oriental travelers before 1660—Boemus, Belon, and Postel, for example.

48. See the "Reflections" on *Les Lettres persanes* that Montesquieu provided for the 1754 ed. and that are translated in the eds. of Loy and George R. Healey (1964).

49. Besides Conant, see especially R.S. Crane and H.J. Smith, "A French Influence on Goldsmith's Citizen of the World," *MP,* 19 (1921), 83-92, who show not only how indebted Goldsmith was to d'Argens but inform us how much d'Argens depended on real travel accounts such as "Du Halde, Chardin, Kemper, Hyde, Picart, and Vertot" (p. 84). Du Halde (1734) was translated into English in 1735, but Budgell in No. 18 of the *Bee* (1733) had already made his letters popular in England after seeing Du Halde's prospectus of 1733. See also A.L. Sells, *Les Sources françaises de Goldsmith* (Paris: Champion, 1924), pp. 88 ff.

50. Newcastle, *Natures Pictures Drawn by Fancies Pencil,* pp. 220-72: "The Eighth Book."

51. See note 90, Chap. III above.

52. Adams, *Travelers,* p. 121.

53. Steeves, p. 16; Wagenknecht, p. 19; Bernbaum, "Mrs. Behn's Biography a Fiction," *PMLA,* 28 (1913), 432-53.

54. See three articles by H.D. Benjamins in *De West-Indische Gids* (1919, 1920, 1927); H.D. Hargreaves, "Of Mrs. Behn's *Oroonoko,*" *Bulletin of the New York Public Library,* 74 (1970), 437-44; and especially Wylie Sypher, "A Note on the Realism of Mrs. Behn's *Oroonoko,*" *MLQ,* 3 (1942), 40-45. George Guffey, "Aphra Behn's *Oroonoko:* Occasion and Accomplishment," in Guffey and Andrew Wright, *Two English Novelists: Aphra Behn and Anthony Trollope* (William Andrews Clark Memorial Library Seminar Papers, 37) (Los Angeles: Clark Library, 1975), pp. 1-41, summarizes the critical argument over Behn's claim of firsthand observation and decides that the argument has detracted from a proper study of the novel itself.

55. Much of this is found in Edward D. Seeber's revealing article "*Oroonoko* in France in the Eighteenth Century," *PMLA,* 51 (1936), 953-59; and Mornet, "Les Enseignements des bibliothèques privées (1750-1780)," *RHLF,* 17 (1910), 449-96.

56. Jean Sgard, *Prévost Romancier* (Paris: Jose Corti, 1968), p. 531, is only one to show the great influence of Prévost, including that on Chateaubriand.

57. For studies of Chateaubriand's imaginative recourse to books about America, see J. Bédier, *Etude Critique* (Paris, 1903), pp. 127 ff; Gilbert Chinard, "Notes sur le voyage de Chateaubriand en Amérique," *MP,* 4 (1915), 269-349; and Adams, *Travelers,* pp. 85-86, 199. Chateaubriand's *Voyage en Amérique* was not published until thirty-five years after his return from the New World, and in it he claimed, contrary to possibility, that he went down the Ohio and Mississippi rivers.

58. For Head and Timberlake, see H.F. Watson, *The Sailor in English Fiction and Drama* (New York: Columbia Univ. Press, 1931); and C.W.R.D. Moseley, "Richard Head's 'The English Rogue': A Modern Mandeville?" *YES,* 1 (1971), 102-107.

59. Santo Stephano, *Account of the Journey of Hieronomo Santo Stephano, in India in the Fifteenth Century,* trans. and ed. R.H. Major (London: Hakluyt, 1857), p. 5.

60. Varthema, ed. Badger (1863), pp. 202-3. Head's hero discovers only the next morning that the new wife is a child.

61. Head, *The English Rogue: Described in the Life of Meriton Latroon* ... (London: Henry Marsh, 1665; rpt. Boston: New Frontier Press, 1961), p. 245.

62. See William H. McBurney, Int. to *Four before Richardson* (Lincoln: Univ. of Nebraska Press, 1963), pp. xx-xxi, for the similarities between *The Jamaica Lady,* perhaps by Ward's friend William Pittis, and the *Trip to Jamaica* by Ward.

63. Secord, *The Narrative Method of Defoe,* pp. 112-64. The *Voyages and Travels of J. Albert de Mandelslo* was included in Adam Olearius, *Voyages and Travels of the Ambassadors* (1662), a copy of which Defoe owned (Secord, p. 119). For more on Olearius and Flacourt, see notes 85, 86, Chap. II above.

64. See Maximillian Novak, int. to *Of Captain Misson,* Augustan Reprint Society, no. 87 (1961). Richetti, "Travellers, Pirates, and Pilgrims," in his *Popular Fiction before Richardson,* pp. 60-118, has a long section on Defoe's Avery and Defoe's Misson but without stressing their origins in travel accounts.

65. De Lussan, *Journal du voyage fait à la Mer du Sud* (Paris, 1689), and Dampier, *New Voyage,* Dover ed., p. 45.

66. For these facts, see Manuel Schonhorn, "Defoe's *Four Years Voyage of Captain George Roberts* and *Ashley's Memorial,*" *TSLL,* 17 (1977), 93-102.

67. See the review by Rogers of Earle, *The World of Defoe,* in *TLS,* Jan. 21, 1977. Benton J. Fishman, "Defoe, Herman Moll, and the Geography of South America," *HLQ,* 36 (1972-73), 227-38.

68. Baker, "The Geography of Daniel Defoe," in *The History of Geography: Papers by J.N.L. Baker* (New York: Barnes and Noble, 1963), first presented as a lecture in 1929; Fishman (note 67 above); Jane H. Jack, "*A New Voyage round the World:* Defoe's Roman à Thèse," *HLQ,* 24 (1961), 323-36. See also Adams, *Travelers,* pp. 114-15.

69. Baker (note 68 above), pp. 169-70; Adams, *Travelers,* p. 115.

70. The best of these treatments of Defoe's *New Voyage* is still Baker's since it put that novel in perspective by associating it with Defoe's other geographical novels. Both Fishman and Jack add much on Defoe's economic plans: Fishman stresses Moll's *Compleat Geographer;* and Jack adds Lionel Wafer and Exquemelin as sources for Defoe's floods and sinking rafts, although she has not read Baker and says that Wafer and the other buccaneers "twice crossed South America" when they crossed only the relatively narrow Isthmus of Panama. Bonner, *Dampier,* has chapters on Defoe and Swift that are of little help.

71. For an excellent essay on Smollett's rendering into fiction his own experiences and those of other travelers, including especially those sailors with Anson's *Wager*—Commodore Jack Byron, e.g.—see George M. Kahrl, *Tobias Smollett: Traveler-Novelist* (Chicago: Univ. of Illinois Press, 1945), pp. 12-28. Kahrl concludes that *Roderick Random* "has the convincing quality of an eyewitness account" and that "Smollett interpreted his experience [in *Random*] more like a traveler than a novelist." See also L.A. Wilcox, *Anson's Voyage* (New York: St. Martin's Press, 1970), p. 45, who quotes *Roderick Random* for an authentic account of life below decks, "a realistic rendering of Smollett's own experiences, that of an eye-witness, not a novelist."

72. Shebbeare, *Lydia, or Filial Piety. A Novel,* 4 vols. in 2 (London: J. Scott, 1755), Chaps. 14 and 28; the sea voyage occupies most of vol. I, chaps. 3-28.

73. (Paris: Ganeau, 1732), 2 vols.

74. Lesage employs a number of Lahontan's terms and spellings—"jongleur," "Onuntio." G. Chinard, *L'Amérique et le rêve exotique dans la littérature française au XVII᷎ et au XVIII᷎ siècle* (Paris: Droz, 1934), pp. 271-79, tells the story of Beauchêne, argues that he was not real, points to Lesage's use of Lahontan, Dampier, Exquemelin, perhaps J.-B. Labat, but does not

know of Beauchene-Gouin or of Woodes Rogers's essay on him. See Rogers, *A Cruising Voyage,* Dover ed., pp. 86-88. Chinard's essay is not cited by recent historians of the French novel, who, if they referred to it, would perhaps not hesitate to agree that *Beauchêne* is a fabrication, a "roman" in the Defoe tradition. Gove, pp. 288-91, believes that A. Fateux, "Les Aventures de chevalier de Beauchêne," *Caniers des dix,* 2 (1937), 7-33, proved "convincingly ... that 'l'on peut sans aucune hésitation continuer à ranger parmi les romans *les Aventures de Robert Chevalier.*' " Stewart, p. 327, while believing that "The hero is apparently historical," reminds us (p. 74) that in the third part of *Beauchêne* "Lesage was openly referring to the work as a novel." Professor Roseann Runte of Dalhousie University read a fine paper on *Beauchêne* at a meeting of the American Society for Eighteenth-Century Studies in Washington, D.C., in April 1981. In it she stressed the imaginative reworking that Prévost gave his sources.

75. Prévost, *Voyages du capitaine Robert Lade en différentes parties de l'Afrique, de l'Asie et de l'Amérique* ... (Paris, 1744), in 2 vols.; Engel, p. 197, compares Prévost's method to that of Chateaubriand in *Atala,* after him, and to that of Defoe, in *Crusoe,* before him. Prévost translated George Lillo's play *George Barnwell, or The London Merchant,* which Lillo had dedicated to the chief merchant of London, Sir John Eyles, whom Prévost served as secretary.

76. For her massive evidence for Prévost's use of travel literature here and elsewhere, see Engel, one of whose chapters is entitled (p. 197) " 'Chacun sa vérité': La vérité de l'abbé Prévost." Prévost's hoax was of course suspected in his own day and uncovered before Engel. See, e.g., Joseph Ducarré, "Une 'supercherie littéraire' de l'abbé Prévost: Les Voyages de Robert Lade," *RLC,* 16 (1936), 465-76.

77. *Mercure de France* (Nov. 1744), p. 135, as quoted in Stewart, p. 113 (my trans.) Stewart's good summary of Prévost's methods in *Lade,* pp. 113, 203-5, does not make use of Engel.

78. See Penrose, p. 289, and Keith Huntress, ed., *Narratives of Shipwrecks and Disasters, 1586-1860* (Ames: Iowa State Univ. Press, 1974) for this and other information. Robert Marx in *Shipwrecks of the Western Hemisphere* (New York, 1971), Huntress (p. xx) points out, lists some 7,000 shipwrecks in the Western Hemisphere alone and claims to know of 28,500 of them.

79. Huntress, pp. xvi-xvii. Huntress, pp. xviii ff., devotes considerable space to Poe's use of such shipwreck stories in *The Narrative of Arthur Gordon Pym,* stories Poe found in R. Thomas, *Remarkable Shipwrecks* (1835).

80. See Penrose, p. 289, for more.

81. Head, Chaps. XXIII and LXVI.

82. Claude-Prosper Jolyot de Crébillon, Préface to *Les Egarements du coeur et de l'esprit, ou Mémoirs de M. de Meilcoeur* (Paris: Prault fils, 1736).

83. *Don Quixote,* Part II, Book iii, Chap. 63. She is taken from a Moorish brigantine attempting to raid the coast near barcelona.

84. See Richard Beale DAvis, *George Sandys, Poet-Adventurer* (London: The Bodley Head, 1955), pp. 60, 53-54.

85. Samuel Purchas, *Hakluytus Posthumus or Purchas His Pilgrimes* (Glasgow: Maclehase, 1905-1907), VI, 108-109. See also IX, 278, and IX, xi. For this and some of what follows, see the excellent essay by G. Starr, "Escape from Barbary: A Seventeenth-Century Genre," *HLQ,* 19 (1965), 35-52. Then look at Richetti, *Popular Fiction before Richardson,* pp. 104-118; J.D. Fage, *A History of Africa* (London: Hutchinson, 1978), pp. 183-86; Stanley Lane, *The Barbary Corsairs* (London, 1890); Sir Godfrey Fisher, *Barbary Legend: War, Trade, and Piracy in North Africa, 1415-1830* (Oxford: Clarendon, 1957); Charles Tailliart, *L'Algérie dans la littérature française,* 2 vols. (Paris, 1925).

86. Starr, note 85 above.

87. Tyler, *The Algerine Captive; or, The Life and Adventures of Doctor Updike Underhill: Six Years a Prisoner Among the Algerines* (Walpole, New Hampshire: David Carlisle, 1797), viii, x, xi, xii. And see the Int. by Claude E. Jones to the Augustan Reprint Society edition, no. 64,

as well as the fine essay on *The Algerine Captive* by William Spengemann, *The Adventurous Muse*, pp. 119-38.

88. Secord, *The Narrative Method of Defoe*. For the island portion, see especially pp. 32-49, 53-63. Friedrich Wackwitz, *Entstehungsgeschichte von D. Defoes "Robinson Crusoe"* (Berlin: Mayer and Muller, 1909), one of the German scholars so interested in Crusoe, treats possible inspirations for the island story such as those of Peter Surano and Henry Neville's *The Isle of Pines* (1668). See Secord's comments, pp. 22-23, and for his bibliography of sources, pp. 240-43.

89. Most of the following account of Crusoe, Rogers, Selkirk, and the Crusoe myth is taken from my introduction to the Dover rpt. of Rogers, *Cruising Voyage*. It should be supplemented by Secord, Novak, Hunter, Starr, Homer Brown, and others.

90. Ulrich, *Robinson und Robinsonaden: Bibliographie, Geschichte, Kritik* . . . (Weimar, 1898), 2 vols; vol. I is the bibliography. See also his *Defoes Robinson Crusoe: die Geschichte sines Weltbuches* (Leipsig: Reisland, 1924) and his review of Secord in *Englische Studien*, 59 (1925), 457-67.

91. See Schonhorn, "Defoe's *Four Years Voyages* . . . and *Ashton's Memorial,*" and Gove, p. 246, p. 252.

92. Bonner, pp. 192-96, 207-14, and Gove, 266-68, provide evidence.

93. Williams, *The Journal of Penrose, Seaman* (Bloomington: Univ. of Indiana Press, 1969). Originally published in 1815 in London by John Murray, but badly bowdlerized, it was translated into German and republished in English in 1825, even more bowdlerized. Howard Dickason, who discovered the manuscript in England, published it as the author wrote it, and then he did a study of the author, *William Williams: Novelist and Painter of Colonial America* (Bloomington: Univ. of Indiana Press, 1971), three of the five sections of which treat the novel. I am indebted to Dickason and to my review of the two books [see *American Literature* (1972), 478-83], which attempts to demonstrate that *Penrose*, rather than being an autobiography, is a fireside Robinsonade.

94. See William Dunlop, *The History of Fiction* (Edinburgh: 1816); Hugo Friedrich, *Abbe Prévost in Deutschland* (Heidelberg: 1929); E. Guilhon, *L'abbé Prévost en Hollande* (The Hague: Wolters, 1933); Sgard, pp. 499-502, and his bibliography; and Foster, *Pre-Romantic Novel*, pp. 68-73 especially.

95. Stewart, p. 210; Foster, p. 53, for Prévost and Defoe's *Tour*. On p. 204 Stewart states the general opinion, "Prévost was certainly himself a connoisseur of travel literature, having exploited, plagiarized, and imitated it in *Mémoires d'un homme de qualité*, *Manon Lescaut*, and *Cleveland.*"

96. Chinard, *L'Amérique et le rêve exotique*, p. 303 [my trans.] But see Mylne, p. 81, for the opinion that some of the New Orleans details are inaccurate.

97. Engel, preface and p. 198, and Chinard, *Le Rêve exotique*.

98. Vernière, "L'abbé Prévost et les réalités géographiques, à propos de l'episode Américain de *Cleveland*," *Revue historique littéraire de la France*, 73 (1973), 626-35. Vernière finds Prévost using the maps of Sanson (1713), Delisle (1718), and Nolin (1720) as well as John Smith, Robert Beverley's *History and Present State of Virginia* (1715), de Soto in Garcilaso, and others such as François Coreal, *Voyages* . . . (Amsterdam: Bernard, 1722). Vernière could, in his excellent essay, have found all of Coreal's information in the *Atlas Geographus*.

99. See Chinard, *Le Rêve exotique*, pp. 167-87, 287-301, especially p. 300, and Adams, *Travelers*, pp. 54-63, for the Adario tradition, Lahontan in general, and his invented geography and Indian tribes. The Noplandes, as told about by Mme Riding, are in Vol. IV of *Le Philosophe anglais, ou Histoire de M. Cleveland* (Amsterdam, 1783) and *The Life and Entertaining Adventures of M. Cleveland* . . . (London: T. Astley, 1734), IV.

100. The episode of the colony from La Rochelle is in *Cleveland* (1783), I, 284 ff., and Vol. I of the English, 1734, ed. It is treated by Engel, pp. 112-18, Chinard, *Le Rêve exotique*, pp. 283-86, and now at length by Jacques Décobert, "Au proces de l'utopie, un 'roman des illusions

perdues': Prévost et la 'Colonie Rochelloise,' " *Revue des sciences humaines,* 39 (1974), 493-504. Engel did not seem to know the fireside nature of *Leguat* or that Misson wrote it or where "Eden" was. She does also refer to the 1689 *Quelques mémoires servant 'a l'instruction pour Etablissement de l'Isle d'Eden.* See Gove, p. 283-84, on the "colonie Rochelloise" and Prévost's later discussion of it in his Preface.

101. One good version of this story is in Boyde Somerville, *Commodore Anson* (London: Heinemann, 1934), pp. 301-2.

102. These two nonexistent places are discussed in Prévost's *Oeuvres choisies* (Amsterdam, 1784), XXXV, 267-80, 351-57. Loysell's island, which he claimed in 1730 to have found in 1718, was very rich and near Bermuda. For the oft-told and influential story of Henry Neville's *Isle of Pines* (1668)—there are two real ones by that name now, one in the West Indies, one part of New Caledonia in the Pacific—see Gove, pp. 128-29, and, to come up to date, A.O. Aldridge, "Feijoo, Voltaire, and the Mathematics of Procreation," *Studies in Eighteenth-Century Culture,* ed. Harold E. Pagliaro, 4 (1975), 131-39.

103. Sgard, pp. 104 ff., 165.

104. Grandchamp, 4th ed., 2 vols. (Cologne: Pierre Marteau, 1710), I, 116-18; Olivier, *L'Infortuné Napolitain, ou Les Avantures et mémoires du signor Rosselly* (Bruxelles: André Rovieli, 1704), pp. 188-191.

105. For Ramsey, see Tieje (1912), p. 430; for the *Peruvian Tales,* see Tieje (1913), p. 249; for Aragon, see the headnote to this chapter.

106. Amory, *Buncle* (London: J. Noon, 1756), pp. 163-270 especially, and *Several Ladies* (London: J. Noon, 1755), pp. 112 ff.

107. See E.A. Baker, V, 146.

108. For a good sampling of Beckford's use of travel writers, see *Three Gothic Novels,* ed. E.F. Bleiler (New York: Dover, 1966), which has its information in notes.

109. See B.G. McCarthy, *The Later Women Novelists, 1744-1818* (Cork Univ. Press, Oxford: B.H. Blackwell, 1947), pp. 154-59, for more on Smith, as well as Florence M.A. Hilbish, *Charlotte Smith: Poet and Novelist* (Philadelphia: n.p., 1941), especially pp. 295-86. Ramond de Carbonnières, *Observations faites dans les Pyrénées* (Paris: Belin, 1789). Ramond, so important to the English novelists, was a remarkable writer and scientist. He translated the geologist William Coxe's important but rather dull book (1779) on Switzerland as *Lettres de William Coxe sur la Suisse* and after each "Lettre" added a long "Observations du traducteur," which is colorful, lyric, alive with images. See. e.g., Henri Beraldi, *Cent ans aux Pyrénées* (Paris, 1898), who claims that Ramond gave birth to the Pyrenees (pp. 1 ff.).

110. J.M.S. Tompkins, "Ramond de Carbonnières, Grosley and Mrs. Radcliffe," *RES,* 5 (1929), 294-301 (the quoted words are those of Tompkins, p. 297). These parallels can be found in Ramond, chaps. 1, 2, 5, and *Udolpho,* vol. 1, chaps. 1, 3. Although Ramond is the chief inspiration for Radcliffe's wild, grand, sublime mountain scenes, she also knew the late eighteenth-century painters, Salvator Rosa, e.g.

111. Tompkins used Grosley, *New Observations on Italy and its Inhabitants* (1769); the original French was published in 1764. The quotation about Hannibal is from *Udolpho,* I, i; see Grosley (1769), I, 35 ff. For this and much more, see Tompkins, pp. 298-301, including parallel passages and the fact that Radcliffe needed Grosley for *The Italian* also.

112. Hester Lynch Piozzi (Mrs. Thrale), *Observations and Reflections made in the Course of a Journey through France, Italy, and Germany* (London: A. Strahan and T. Cadell, 1789). Radcliffe did not use either Piozzi's spellings for Italian places nor those of Brydone. For example, in *The Italian* she spells the grotto near Naples "Puzzuoli"; Piozzi has it "Pozzuoli." See E.A. Baker, V, 192-204, who claims much more for Mrs. Piozzi than he should and not enough for Radcliffe's use of travel books in general.

113. Brydone, in 2 vols. (London: W. Strahan, 1776).

114. For the very popular *The Italian,* see the ed. called *The Confessions of the Black Penitents* (London: Folio Soc., 1956), p. 13 for fireworks, pp. 46 ff. for one convent scene, pp. 60-61 for a mountain villa with appropriate scenery.

115. For a discussion of Brydone as a "painter" of nature, see Batten, pp. 102-5. See also George B. Parks, "The Turn to the Romantic in the Travel Literature of the Eighteenth Century," *MLQ,* 25 (1964), 22-33; but then see in Chap. X below the long discussion of earlier travelers and their ecstatic descriptions of mountain scenery.

116. See Lynne Epstein, "Mrs. Radcliffe's Landscapes: The Influence of Three Landscape Painters on Her Nature Descriptions," *Hartford Studies in Literature,* 1 (1969), 107-20, and the essays of Stafford.

117. See Foster, *The Pre-Romantic Novel,* pp. 98-99, who refers us to H.V. Hong, "Thomas Amory: Eccentric Literary Philosopher," Univ. of Minnesota dissertation (1938).

118. Garcilaso, first translated into French in 1634, went through many eds. Graffigny makes mistakes in customs and terms as well as in chronology: "Hamas," p. 142 of Paris, 1752 ed., is defined as "Mot générique des bêtes" when it really refers to the famous South American llama. E.A. Baker, V, 140-41, thinks Graffigny's novel "a remarkable anticipation of Bernardin de St. Pierre in its ecstatic word-paintings of tropical scenery." Graffigny often names Garcilaso in her notes. See Showalter, pp. 144-45, for the anachronism with which the *Lettres* begins: The heroine, Princess Zilia, survives the sixteenth-century Spanish conquest and is taken to eighteenth-century France.

119. Mouhy (Paris: Duchesne, 1753), in 6 vols. Among the terms footnoted: A "Boursac" is a "magicien" (p. 48); "Houbchonc" is a "philosophe" (p. 67); a "Grichemik" is the first slave of the emperor's bedchamber (p. 89).

120. Béliard, *Zélaskim histoire amériquaine ou les Aventures de la marquise de p***** ... (Paris: Chez Mérigot, 1765), 4 vols. For only one account of the "allumette," a composite one by a Frenchman, see Michel Guillaume St. Jean de Crèvecoeur, *Le Voyage dans la haute Pensylvanie et dans New York* (Paris: Chez Maradan, 1801), in 3 vols., note 2 to Chap. VII of Vol. I.

121. Roddier, pp. 182-88. See also Adams, *Travelers,* pp. 93, 117, 126, 199, 232.

122. For H.G. von Bretschneider, see Scott-Robson, pp. 184-86, who has much on sentimental travelers in England; and A.N. Radischev, *A Journey from St. Petersburg to Moscow* (St. Petersburg, 1790).

123. See Note 105 above.

124. Berington, *The Memoirs of Signior Gaudentio di Lucca* (1737; rpt. New York: Garland, 1973), int. by Josephine Grieder.

125. Lee M. Ellison, "Gaudentio Di Lucca: A Forgotten Utopia," *PMLA,* 50 (1935), 598. See Gove, pp. 295-300, for eighteenth-century eds. and comments.

126. Case, *Four Essays on Gulliver's Travels* (Princeton: Princeton Univ. Press, 1945); J.R. Moore, "The Geography of Gulliver's Travels," *JEGP,* 40 (1941), 214-28; Bracher, "The Maps in Gulliver's Travels," *HLQ,* 8 (1944), 59-74.

127. Here Bracher, p. 73, is using words very similar to those of Moore, pp. 227-28.

128. Probyn, "Gulliver and the Relativity of Things: A Commentary on Method and Mode with a Note on Smollett," *Renaissance and Modern Studies,* 18 (1974), 63-76; and Richetti, *Popular Fiction before Richardson,* pp. 60-61. Each of these scholars refers to my *Travelers and Travel Liars* as evidence that Swift satirized travel literature. Nowhere, however, did I attempt to support a conclusion other than the one presented here: To attack abuses in religion and learning, as Swift did, is not necessarily to attack religion and learning; to use the form of the epic in *The Rape of the Lock* is not necessarily to attack the epic, which to Pope was the supreme form of literature; and to use the form of travel literature or to make fun of travel exaggerations or lying travelers is not to condemn all travel literature necessarily. See also the older article by Edward Stone, "Swift and the Horses ...," *MLQ* 10 (1949), 367-76.

129. See Bonner, pp. 158-65, for some of this, although Bonner concentrates on the influence of Dampier when Swift was working in a well-established tradition.

130. Marburg, *Sir William Temple*, pp. 56-71, treats Temple and the travelers at great length. By reading them, he said, we learn that "the fundamental moral beliefs . . . are shared by all men."

131. These facts and more can be found in Bonner, pp. 158-60.

132. Moore, "The Geography of Gulliver's Travels," p. 227.

133. To all this, add Lucius Hubbard, *Notes on . . . James Dubourdieu and His Wife, A Source for "Gulliver's Travels"* . . . (Ann Arbor: Ann Arbor Press, 1927), and Philip Gove, "Gildon's 'Fortunate Shipwreck' as Background for *Gulliver's Travels,*" *RES*, 18 (1942), 470-78. Arthur Sherbo, "Swift and Travel Literature," *MLS*, 9 (1979), 114-27, helps to set the record straight by returning to an evaluation different from that of certain others cited here.

134. Cohan, "Gulliver's Fiction," *Studies in the Novel*, 6 (1974), p. 9 especially.

135. Since the "optimists," like the "moderns" of the Renaissance—Columbus, More, Ronsard, Vives, Erasmus, Las Casas, Bacon—kept close to travelers and the information of travelers, their opponents, to counter their arguments, were often forced to resort to the same sources, as Montaigne, Swift, Voltaire, and Johnson did. The fairest studies of optimism as it relates to Voltaire—or perhaps anyone else—are two articles by George R. Havens, his Introduction to *Candide* (New York: Holt, 1934), pp. xxix-lii, and his "The Nature Doctrine of Voltaire," *PMLA*, 40 (1925), 852-62, and a section of A.O. Lovejoy, *The Great Chain of Being* (Cambridge: Harvard Univ. Press, 1936), pp. 208-26. But Lovejoy often displays bias against the philosophy of Plotinus, Archbishop King, Pope, and Jenyns, believes Pope acquired his ideas from Bolingbroke, and does not note that Voltaire was himself an optimist of sorts in earlier years.

136. For the inn-hotel motif in travels and fiction and the interpolated stories it permitted, see Chap. VIII below.

137. For Garcilaso and Ralegh, as well as Rousseau, see G.R. Havens, Introduction to *Candide* (1934). For relationships among Coreal, Ralegh, and Rousseau, see Adams, *Travelers*, pp. 118-28.

138. The entire letter is translated in *Voltaire: Candide or Optimism*, ed. Robert M. Adams (New York: Norton, 1966), pp. 175-76; it was written in response to a review of *Candide* in the *Journal encyclopédique*. The review, also translated, is in Robert Adams, p. 142.

139. Père Charlevoix, *Histoire du Paraguay*, 3 vols. (Paris, 1756). For Montesquieu's use of Charlevoix, as well as of Garcilaso, see Dodds, p. 297.

140. The following discussion of Rasselas is heavily dependent on Curley, *Samuel Johnson and the Age of Travel*, pp. 147-82. For only a few other special studies of Johnson's reading from travel accounts, see Donald Lockhart, "The Fourth Son of the Mighty Emperour: The Ethiopian Background . . . ," *PMLA*, 78 (1951), 516-28; Gwin Kolb, "The Structure of *Rasselas,*" *PMLA*, 66 (1951), 698-717; J.R. Moore, "Rasselas and the Early Travellers to Abyssinia," *MLQ*, 15 (1954), 36-41; and articles by Ellen Leyburn and Arthur Weitzman. See Curley's notes to his chap. 5. Add to all this, however, the accounts of the Jesuits in Abyssinia, especially those by Alvares, Pedro Páez, and Antonio Fernández. Job Ludolf's expanded *A New History of Ethiopia* (London, 1682) includes much from Téllez, including a map more accurate than those maps published by Gastaldi or, in the late seventeenth century, by Dapper. See, e.g., Heawood, pp. 144-53.

141. For his *Lobo* (1735), Johnson translated from the French the text of Joachim Le Grand (1728), who not only had added from other travel accounts but had supplied some fifteen dissertations on subjects largely religious. See Curley, pp. 56-57, and Johnson, *A Voyage to Abyssinia by Father Jerome Lobo* (London: Elliot and Kay, 1789). Lobo traveled in East Africa during the second quarter of the seventeenth century, but his Portuguese account did not

appear until 1660. See Penrose, p. 284, and the forthcoming edition of Johnson's *Lobo* in the Yale Johnson, ed. by Joel J. Gold. For some observations on *Rasselas* as a travel book, see Carey McIntosh, *The Choice of Life: Samuel Johnson and the World of Fiction* (New Haven: Yale Univ. Press, 1973), pp. 193-97, including the importance of travel to conversation.

142. Gregory, whose knowledge was used by Téllez and Ludolf, had his name placed on the map of Abyssinia in Ludolf's *History*. See that map reproduced in Heawood, p. 147.

143. Berington, *Gaudentio di Lucca,* pp. 174-75.

CHAPTER FIVE

1. Ive, *A Voyage from England to India* (London: Dilly, 1773), p. vii.

2. René Wellek, *A History of Modern Criticism* (New Haven: Yale Univ. Press, 1950), p. 2.

3. See the conclusion of Brée, "The Ambiguous Voyage," p. 88: "... no image is more basic to literature"; and Frye, *Secular Scripture,* p. 56, for only one of his many assertions of this fact.

4. Spengemann, *Adventurous Muse,* p. 6, quotes another version of the famous statement made by Howells at the end of his life, as does Jean Rivière, "L'Education du réaliste par le voyage: William Dean Howells et l'Europe," in *Le Voyage dans la littérature anglo-saxonne,* Actes de Congrès de Nice (1971) (S.A.E.S., 1972), p. 117; for Butor, see his "Travel and Writing."

5. Paulson, *Satire and the Novel,* p. 109; for Coleridge, see *The Complete Works,* ed. W.C.T. Shedd (New York: Harper and Bros., 1853), IV, 380.

6. Frye, *Secular Scripture,* p. 53; for Kusch's attractive essay, including his bibliography, see "The River and the Garden: Basic Spatial Models in *Candide* and *La Nouvelle Héloïse*," *ECS,* 12, (1978), 1-15.

7. Frye, pp. 30, 56, 97, 173-74, 45, 42-43. See also his earlier, seminal essay, "The Mythos of Summer: Romance," often anthologized.

8. Vinaver, p. 15. Vinaver, however, goes on to blame the eighteenth century for the "fallacy" when surely the twentieth century, after Percy Lubbock, is most responsible.

9. Hume, "Romance: A Perdurable Pattern," *CE,* 36 (1974), 129-46; Vogel, "A Lexicon Rhetoricae for Journey Literature," *CE,* 36 (1974), 185-89; and Friedman, *Form and Meaning in Fiction* (Athens: Univ. of Georgia Press, 1975).

10. These are, of course, Frye's terms. The same kinds of explanation are given for twentieth-century science fiction by Frye, *Secular Scripture,* p. 180, e.g., or by, say, Willis E. McNelley, "Archetypal Patterns in Science Fiction," *CEA Critic,* 35 (1973), 15-20, who speaks of such Jungian archetypes as quest, rites of passage, alienation, return. One must remember too that such discussions will work just as well for all early science fiction, from Lucian to Thomas More to Bishop Godwin, Cyrano, and Defoe.

11. Tasso, quoted by Nelson, pp. 55-56; the 1750 "reader," quoted by Batten, p. 131n., who takes it from the *Monthly Review,* 4 (1750), 63; and Charles Garnier, ed., *Voyages imaginaires, songes, visions* ... (Amsterdam and Paris, 1787-89), XII, 5, as found in Gove, pp. 43-45 [my translation].

12. Major, ed., *India in the Fifteenth Century;* see also Pero Tafur, *Travels and Adventures of Pero Tafur* (1435-39), ed. Malcolm Letts (London: Broadway Travels, 1926).

13. Erskine (?), *The Travels and Adventures of Mad―――de Richelieu, Cousin of the Present Duke of that Name. Who made the Tour of Europe, dressed in Men's Cloaths, attended by her Maid, Lucy as her Valet de Chambre. Now done into English from the Lady's own Manuscript* ... (London: M. Cooper, 1744), 3 vols. There was a Dublin ed. of 1743-44.

14. Quoted by Fussell, *Abroad,* pp. 15-16.

15. See Adams, "The Anti-Hero in Eighteenth-Century Fiction," for more.

16. Richard Beale Davis, *Sandys*, p. 43; for Sandys, see note 76, Chap. II above.

17. See note 75, Chap. II above.

18. For Regnard, see note 26, Chap. II above.

19. Le Beau, *Avantures ... ou Voyage curieux et nouveau parmi les sauvages de l'Amérique septentrionale ...* (Amsterdam: Uytwerf, 1738), 2 vols. See also Chinard, *Le Rêve exotique*, pp. 306-12, who is the only significant scholar so far to question the existence of Le Beau. Chinard points out that the *Voyage* is like its contemporary Prévost's *Cleveland* and a sentimental foreshadowing of Chateaubriand's *Atala*.

20. Simon Patrick, *The Parable of the Pilgrim* (London, 1667), pp. 324-25, quoted by Curley, p. 50, who has a fine two-page statement about the relationship between fiction and travel literature in the eighteenth century (pp. 49-51).

21. Frye, *Secular Scripture*, p. 120.

22. See J. Frank Dobie, *Coronado's Children Tales of Lost Mines and Buried Treasures of the Southwest* (Dallas: Southwest Press, 1930).

23. *The New Found Land of Stephen Parmenius. The life and writings of a Hungarian poet drowned on a voyage from Newfoundland, 1583.* Ed. and trans. with commentaries by David B. Quinn and Neil M. Cheshire (Toronto: Univ. of Toronto Press, 1972). Martire frequently used such expressions; see *The Decades of the New World*, trans. Eden (1959) (Ann Arbor: Univ. Microfilms, 1966), p. 17a especially, but also pp. 208, 211, 212.

24. For the importance of utopian fiction in the seventeenth and eighteenth centuries, there is a huge bibliography. See Gove, as well as a recent fine review article, Raymond Trousson, "Utopie et roman utopique," *Revue des sciences humaines*, 39 (1974), 367-78.

25. Zacher, p. 154, who finds *Mandeville* "the first 'travel book' of its kind to combine a pilgrimage itinerary with an account of wordly exploration." Actually Odoric of Pordenone, a source for *Mandeville*, seems just as curious and just as bent on exploration as he sets out on his pilgrimage.

26. Haywood, in McBurney, *Four before Richardson*, p. 184.

27. This paragraph, dependent on one in my "The Discovery of America and European Renaissance Literature," p. 107, is based on *Hernando Cortés Five Letters 1519-1526*, trans. J. Bayard Morris (New York: Norton, 1962); *Hernan Cortés Letters from Mexico*, trans. and ed. by A.R. Pagden and with a fine int. by J.H. Elliott (New York: Grossman 1971); Bernal Díaz del Castillo, *The True History of the Conquest of New Spain*, trans. A.P. Maudslay (London: Hakluyt, 1908-16), 5 vols.; and the excellent treatment by Irving A. Leonard, *Books of the Brave* (New York: Gordian Press, 1964).

28. Leonard, p. 39.

29. For Bonneval, see Wilding, *Great Adventurers*.

30. Among them are *Mémoires du Comte de Bonneval ...* (Londres: aux dépens de la Compagnie, 1737) and *Nouveaux Mémoires du C. de B. depuis son départ de Venise jusqu'à son exil à l'île de Chio* (La Haye: van Duren, 1737), which is really the third vol. of the *Mémoires*. See also Stewart, p. 317.

31. Haywood, *Philidore and Placentia*, in *Four before Richardson*, ed. McBurney, pp. 157-231, espeically the tale told by the "Christian eunuch," pp. 194-208; for Varthema, see note 11, Chap. II above.

CHAPTER SIX

1. Dampier, preface to *A New Voyage*.

2. For Spengemann and Batten, see notes 121, 122, Chap. II above.

3. Batten, pp. 92, 97 ff., 54 ff. See also George B. Parks, "The Turn to the Romantic in the Travel Literature of the Eighteenth Century," *MLQ*, 25 (1964), 22-33. Batten, pp. 4-5, also

suggests that sometimes the eighteenth century distinguished between its travel accounts and those older, romantic, untrustworthy ones.

4. Tallmadge, in *Exploration*, 7 (1979), 1-16. This is the best short treatment of the subject, the first really to appear after Walter Veit, speaking at one of the many conferences during the Captain Cook bicentennial and citing Rotunda and Vladimir Propp, called for a structural analysis that would discover "constancies in the relationship between themes, motifs and symbols which govern the travel story as a distinct genre of literature." See Veit, ed., *Captain James Cook: Image and Impact* (Melbourne: Hawthorn, 1972), p. 11.

5. The first opinion is that of George Sherburn, in Sherburn and D.F. Bond, eds. *Restoration and Eighteenth Century*, p. 1067; the second is that of E. Millicent Sowerby, in *Catalogue of the Library of Thomas Jefferson* (Washington: Library of Congress, 1952-59), IV, 85-356. Batten, pp. 132-35, notes these and a variety of other opinions about how to classify writing about travel.

6. Hunter, "Biography and the Novel," *MLS*, 9 (1979), 68-74. See also Donald Stauffer, *The Art of Biography in Eighteenth-Century England* (Princeton: Princeton Univ. Press, 1941).

7. Anderson, *Over the Alps* (London: Hart-Davis, 1969), p. 33.

8. For the influence of spiritual autobiographies in English, see Richetti, *Popular Fiction before Richardson*, H.O. Brown, and G.A. Starr, *Defoe and Spiritual Autobiography* (Princeton: Princeton Univ. Press, 1965); and for the influence of real seventeenth-century autobiographies on French fiction, see short statements by Stewart, p. 19, and Mylne, p. 45.

9. For an excellent summary of Defoe's use of a persona in most of his more than 500 books, tracts, newspapers, and fake sermons, see J.R. Moore, "Defoe's Persona as Author: The Quaker's Sermon," *SEL*, 11 (1971), 507-16.

10. May, "Autobiography and the Eighteenth Century," in *The Author in His Work: Essays on a Problem in Criticism*, ed. Louis L. Martz and Aubrey Williams (New Haven: Yale Univ. Press, 1978); the review is in *The Scriblerian*, 12 (1980), 196. See also May, *Autobiographie* (Paris: Presses Universitaire de France, 1979).

11. Forno, "The Fictional Letter in the Memoir Novel: Robert Challe's *Illustres françaises*," *SVEC*, 81 (1971), 150. Forno, like May and Mylne, whose books he follows, does not refer to any of the great autobiographies before 1600.

12. V.S. Pritchett, "An Ocean Between," *New Statesman*, Mar. 19, 1971. pp. 383-84, is only one who with George Sherburn places travel literature under autobiography. See also Catharine M. Parke, "Imlac and Autobiography," *SEEC*, 6 (1976); and Allan Wendt, Int. to Samuel Johnson, *A Journey to the Western Islands* ... and James Boswell, *The Journal* ... (Boston: Houghton Mifflin, 1965), p. xi especially, who concentrates on the theory that the *Journal*, for example, "must be read as a chapter in the *Life of Johnson*"; October 9, 1980, at the seminar of "The Unknown Samuel Johnson" held at the Univ. of Alabama, in a paper entitled "Travels to the Unknown: *Rasselas* and *A Journey to the Western Islands of Scotland*," Edward Tomarken argued that Johnson's *Journey* is not a travel book but "historical autobiography." The student with more than 100 autobiographies in the seventeenth century is Dean Ebner, *Autobiography in Seventeenth-Century England* (The Hague: Mouton, 1971), who has one sentence on Courthope's travels and in his "Epilogue" has another sentence on "Autobiographies of travel" (pp. 97, 155).

13. Pascal, *Design and Truth in Autobiography* (Cambridge: Harvard Univ. Press, 1960); Spengemann, *The Forms of Autobiography: Episodes in the History of a Literary Genre* (New Haven: Yale Univ. Press, 1980); Pike, "Time in Autobiography," *CL*, 28 (1976), 326-42; Misch, *Geschichte der Autobiographie*, I (Bern: Franke, 1949-50), II, III, IV (Frankfurt: Schulte-Bulmke, 1955-69); Weintraub, *The Value of the Individual: Self and Circumstances in Autobiography* (Chicago: Univ. of Chicago Press, 1978); Ebner, note 12 above; Delaney, *British Autobiography in the Seventeenth Century* (London: Routledge, 1969). The quotation is from Ebner, p. 11.

Spengemann, Pike, and Pascal are only three to speak of "true" autobiography. For an excellent, select annotated bibliography, see Spengemann, *The Forms of Autobiography*, pp. 170-245, especially pp. 186, 194 for his and Pike's limited definitions. Weintraub's is perhaps the best recent book on autobiography, especially for its earlier forms and practitioners.

14. Banks, *The "Endeavour" Journal of Joseph Banks*, ed. J.C. Beaglehole, 2 vols. The Trustees of New South Wales in Association with Angus and Robertson, 1962. Besides Boswell's *Corsica* and *Hebrides*, there are his journals of his Continental Grand Tour after 1663, e.g., *Boswell on the Grand Tour: Germany and Switzerland 1764*, ed. Frederick A. Pottle (London: Heinemann, 1963).

15. Pascal, p. 182—his definition of "true" autobiography.

16. See, e.g., Joan Webber, *The Eloquent "I": Style and Self in Seventeenth-Century Prose* (Madison: Univ. of Wisconsin Press, 1968).

17. Spacks, *Imagining a Self: Autobiography and Novel in Eighteenth-Century England* (Cambridge: Harvard Univ. Press, 1976), p. 22. See also Pascal, "The Autobiographical Novel and the Autobiography," *Essays in Criticism*, 19 (1959), 134-50, who has a more limited approach; and Spengemann, *The Forms of Autobiography*, pp. 210-13, for a bibliography.

18. Spengemann, *The Adventurous Muse*, p. 269n.

19. Batten, *Pleasurable Instruction*, shows it well in Chap. II.

20. See Boswell, *Life of Johnson*, ed. R.W. Chapman, a new ed. corrected by J.D. Fleeman (London: Oxford Univ. Press, 1970), p. 403; see also Johnson's continued pleasure, as recorded by Boswell, in reading Boswell's unpublished, very personal journal of the tour of the Hebrides.

21. Spengemann's *Adventurous Muse* is a fine beginning. One of his theses is the slow evolution from impersonal first-person travels to those more personal ones in America culminating in R.H. Dana, but my own reading of travel literature finds its subjective element much more prominent before, say, Mrs. Sarah Kemble Knight than his thesis will allow; nor is his reading of certain Renaissance travelers—the third Letter of Columbus or Cabeza de Vaca—the same as mine. Spengemann, p. 38: "If the development of the travel-narrative from Columbus to Bradford appears as a shift in the locus of authority from the traveler's home to the traveler himself, the history of the genre from Bradford to Richard Henry Dana describes the traveler's increasing susceptibility to the experiences of travel." But then see p. 46: Traveler Timothy Dwight is not so interesting as Renaissance travelers because he lacks "the more heroic, personal element which makes ocean voyage literature so entertaining. . . ."

22. See Zacher, *Curiosity and Pilgrimage*, for this and certain other facts given here about the Middle Ages, including the thesis that by the fourteenth century curiosity about the physical world had, contrary to the wishes of the Church, become a chief motive for travel. For numerous accounts of curious early medieval travels, see Hakluyt, II, 402-60.

23. See Spengemann, *Adventurous Muse*, pp. 9-12. Ingulphus is in Hakluyt, II, 406-8; for Joinville, see note 38, Chap. II above; William of Rubruquis is most accessible in The *Travels of Sir John Mandeville*, ed. A.W. Pollard (1905; rpt. New York: 1964), pp. 326-62, and see note 39, Chap. II above.

24. The latest fine analysis of *Mandeville*, and especially of its personal autobiographical nature, is that of Zacher, pp. 130-57; but see Bennett also for a defense of it as "romance of travel." For citations below, see the ed. by M.C. Seymour of the Cotton MS (Oxford: Clarendon, 1967).

25. Zacher, p. 155.

26. For Pyrard, see Note 63, Chap. II above. Pyrard was much reprinted in one form or another and included in Purchas, Harris, Prévost, and *The World Displayed* (1774-78). Terry, chaplain to Ambassador Roe, wrote *A Voyage to East-India* that was partly published in Purchas, but in 1655 Terry rewrote it and added and altered much (London: T.W., 1655), in 547 pp.

27. Pinto, *Peregrinacam* (Lisbon, 1614) is without doubt one of the most widely read of travelers, and rightly so. See the first English ed., *Travels for the Space of one and twenty years in The Kingdoms of Ethiopia, China, . . . , Japan, . . . five times suffered shipwreck, was sixteen times sold, and thirteen times made a Slave.* Done into English by H.C. Gent. [Henry Cogan] (London: Macock, 1653). This ed. is in one vol. of 326 pp., only a small part of the original, which is ed. in Portuguese in 1744 by A.J. DaCosta Pimpao in 7 vols.

28. Percy G. Adams, Int. to Dampier, *New Voyage,* Dover ed.

29. Giovanni Francisco Gemelli Careri [Doctor of Civil Law], *Giro del Mondo,* 6 vols. (Roma, 1699-1700), first trans. into English and pub. in Churchill (1704), IV, 1-607. The circumnavigation was made between 1693 and 1698. See also his just-as-personal travel letters of 1686 written on a journey to Paris, England, the Low Countries, and Vienna, found also in Churchill.

30. For the *Voyages Fameux Du Sieur Le Blanc, Marsellois. . . .* redigez fidellement sur ses Mémoires et Régistres, par Pierre Bergeron (Paris: Gervais Clousier, 1648), see especially G. Atkinson, *Extraordinary Voyage* (1920), pp. 25-34.

31. Dunton (London: Richard Newcome, 1691).

32. See Dunton, ed., *The Athenian Gazette: or Casuistical Mercury . . .* , 10 vols. (London: Pr. for John Dunton, at the Raven in the Poultry, 1691-93), or—for more, and high, praise of travel—Dunton, *The Athenian Oracle* (London: Knapton, 1728), IV, 324-25. See also the only full-length study, Stephen Parks, *John Dunton and the English Book Trade* (New York: Garland, 1976), which can be supplemented by Paul Hunter's enjoyable article, "The Insistent I," *Novel,* 13 (1979), 19-37, which is about Dunton entirely: "As autobiography, and as a great many other things, the *Life and Errors* deserves the consideration of literary history . . ." (p. 25).

33. See Stephen Parks, p. 50. Any reader of the *Voyage* and Sterne will very shortly recognize the similarities—the digressive-progressive method, the playful attitude, the travel metaphors, the unacknowledged borrowings, the personal tone. See Wilbur Cross, *Life and Times of Laurence Sterne* (New Haven: Yale Univ. Press, 1925), I, 132-33, for Sterne's admission that he borrowed "many of his ideas" from Dunton's Kainophilus.

34. This popularity can be traced in such works as G.F. Singer, *The Epistolary Novel* (1933; rpt. New York: Russell and Russell, 1963); Howard Anderson, et al., *The Familiar Letter in the Eighteenth Century* (Lawrence: Univ. of Kansas Press, 1966); Edme Boursault, *Lettres nouvelles, avec treize lettres amoureuses d'une Dame à un cavalier* (Paris, 1699), trans. Eliza Haywood, *Works,* III; Robert A. Day, *Told in Letters* (Ann Arbor: Univ. of Michigan Press, 1966); Charles E. Kany, *The Beginnings of the Epistolary Novel in France, Italy, and Spain* (Berkeley: Univ. of California Press, 1937), with much on letters in third-person novels in Europe; K.G. Hornbeak, *The Complete Letter-Writer in English, 1568-1800,* Smith College Studies in Modern Languages, XV, Nos. 3-4 (Northampton, Mass., 1934).

35. F.C. Green, *Minuet,* pp. 365-430; Mylne, p. 265, and especially her Chap. IX.

36. Foster, *The Pre-Romantic Novel,* p. 114; and see Baker, V, 93, borrowing from Singer, p. 318, the fact that in the decade 1760-69 "more than thirty novels were published in the form of letters" in England.

37. See Mayo, for example, pp. 86-88, 102, and Marr, *Eighteenth-Century Essayists,* pp. 249-50.

38. For these and others, see Singer and Boursault in note 34 above; W.L. Cross, *The Development of the English Novel* (New York: Macmillan, 1925), pp. 22-24; *Letters of Eloisa to Abelard,* trans. J. Hughes from a French version (Amsterdam, 1693), used by Pope, and popular, with four eds. by 1722 in London; and *Letters of a Portuguese Nun,* ed. E. Prestage (London, 1893).

39. See Hornbeak (note 34 above) and William E. Sale, Introduction to *Pamela* (New York: Norton, 1958), p. v.

40. *Select Documents Illustrating the Four Voyages of Columbus,* ed. Cecil Jane (London: Hakluyt, 1930-33). For more details, see Jane's Int., or S.E. Morison, *Admiral of the Ocean Sea,* 2 vols. (Boston: Little, Brown, 1942).

41. For more on this subject, see Penrose, pp. 291-95, and C.R. Markham, Int. to *The Captivity of Hans Stade,* ed. Burton, pp. lxxvii-xci; for Vespucci, see *The Letters of Amerigo Vespucci* (London: Hakluyt, 1894).

42. *The Letters of Hernando Cortés* (London: Broadway Travellers, 1928).

43. Hakluyt, VIII, 15-19.

44. Hakluyt, II, 270-81. There are many more such letters in Hakluyt and Purchas.

45. For a discussion of this and other merchant correspondence of the sixteenth century, see John Parker, *The Merchant Explorer,* No. 19 (Minneapolis: Univ. of Minnesota Library, 1979), pp. 15-16.

46. For a fine essay on these Jesuit annual letters, see John Parker, *The Merchant Explorer,* No. 17 (1977).

47. F.C. Danvers and Sir William Foster, ed., *Letters Received by the East India Company from Its Servants in the East, 1602-1617,* 6 vols. (London: Samson Low and Co., 1896-1902).

48. Coryat is in the fourth vol. of Purchas (1905); William Biddulph, *The Travels of certain Englishmen into Africa, Asia. . . . And into Syria . . . Jerusalem. . . . Begun in the yeere of Jubile 1600. . . .* (London: Thomas Hameland, 1609); Timberlake (London: Thomas Arvher, 1603).

49. See John Harris, *Navigantium atque Itinerarium Bibliotheca, or A Complete Collection of Voyages and Travels . . .* (London: T. Woodard, et al., 1744), I, 856-73.

50. C.N. Robinson and John Leyland, "Seafaring and Travel," *The Cambridge History of English Literature,* ed. A.W. Ward and A.R. Waller (New York: Macmillan, 1939), pp. 109-10. Robinson and Leyland note at length how Purchas could not resist a "Euphuistic" addition to and embellishment of Cavendish's letter. See also D.B. Quinn, ed., *The Last Voyage of Thomas Cavendish* (Chicago: Univ. of Chicago Press, 1975).

51. For della Valle, see note 75, Chap. II above. Besides two eds. in Rome before 1664, there were at least six in three other countries by the end of the century.

52. Mandelslo was first pub. in German with Olearius's own account, *Des Hoch Edel-gebornen Johan Albrechts von Mandelslo . . .* (Schlesswig, 1658) and put into French as "Deux Lettres" in *Relation du voyage de Moscovie, Tartarie, et de Perse.* Traduite de l'Alleman du Sieur Olearius . . . (Paris: Clouzier, 1656), and into other languages, including English, trans. J. Davies (London, 1662) [with Olearius]. This last edition, which was owned by Defoe, was taken over by collectors, e.g., Churchill and Harris. For English travel letters of those decades, see the bibliography in Frantz, *English Traveller and the Movement of Ideas, pp. 161-69.*

53. See note 29 above; Churchill, VI, 43-141 (1732).

54. For Muralt, see the ed. of Charles Gould (Paris: Champion, 1933).

55. By 1655 the publisher was proudly announcing a fourth vol.—"never before published"—to go with the three of earlier eds. (London: Moseley, 1655). Quotations here are from this ed. George Kahrl, pp. 101-18, discusses the popularity of real and fabricated travel letters in the eighteenth century, especially for Smollett's time, and notes the historical significance for Howell.

56. Healey, Int. to *The Persian Letters* (New York: Bobbs-Merrill 1964), p. vii.

57. Terry, *A Voyage to East-India. Wherein Some Things are taken notice of in our passage thither, but many more in our abode there. . . . Mix't with some Parallel Observations and inferences upon the storie, to profit as well as delight the Reader . . .* (London: T.W., 1655). See "To the Reader" and the full title as well as the many "digressions" on morality, religion, and customs obviously added by the author when, as rector at Greenford in Middlesex County, he rewrote and ended with a volume several times the length of his original book.

58. Booth, *The Rhetoric of Fiction* (Chicago: Univ. of Chicago Press, 1961); see the chap.

"The Unreliable Narrator," although the words are those of Frank D. McConnell, "Towards a Syntax of Fiction," *CE*, 36 (1974), 151.

59. For an analysis of Suzanne's awareness and dependability, as well as of Diderot's authorial interruptions and coloring of incidents, see Georges May, *Diderot and "La Religieuse"* (New Haven: Yale Univ. Press, 1954), and Mylne, pp. 198-214.

60. Franz K. Stanzel, "Second Thoughts on Narrative Situations in the Novel: Towards a Grammar of Fiction," *Novel*, 11 (1978), 247-64. Stanzel, like so many others, disagrees with Booth's well-known "Perhaps the most overworked distinction is that of person" (*Rhetoric of Fiction*, p. 150). See also Kate Hamburger, *The Logic of Literature* (Bloomington: Indiana Univ. Press, 1973), trans. from 1957 *Die Logik der Dichtung*, and Michel Butor, "L'Usage des pronoms personnels dans le roman," *Repertoire*, 2 (1964), 61-72. See Batten, pp. 40-41, 134-45, for examples of attempts by eighteenth-century travel writers to avoid appearances of autobiography by employing "we," even "you" in the case of Samuel Derrick and Samuel Ireland. The question of the difference between the fictional and nonfictional narrators, as well as between the "implied" and the "second" self, is treated at length—if not to everyone's satisfaction—by John Kilham, "My Quarrel with Booth," *Novel*, 1 (1968), 267-72.

61. One of the best analyses of reader-persona relationship is that of Bruce Morrissette, "The Alienated 'I' in Fiction," *Southern Review*, 10 (1974), 15-30.

62. See, e.g., *The East India Company Journals of Captain William Keeling and Master Thomas Bonner, 1615-1617*, ed. Michael Strachan and Boies Penrose (Minneapolis: Univ. of Minnesota Press, 1971).

63. Johnson, *Journey*, ed. Wendt, p. 110. Spon, *Voyage d'Italie* (1678-80), and Wheler, *Journey into Greece* (1682). See Wendt's ed. of Johnson and Boswell, p. 405, for the "irreconcilable contrarieties" in their two versions.

64. For Kilham on Montaigne and Addison, see p. 271 (note 59 above). Montaigne's "c'est moi que je piens" is in his one-page "Au Lecteur," written about 1580; see his *Essays and Selected Writings*, a bilingual ed., ed. Donald M. Frame (New York: Columbia Univ. Press, 1963).

CHAPTER SEVEN

1. The anonymous critic was referring scathingly to J.R. Joly's *Aventures de Mathurin Bonice* (Paris: Guillot, 1783-87), in 6 vols.; quoted in Gove, p. 376 [my trans.]

2. See Shklovsky, "La Construction de la nouvelle et du roman," in *Théorie de la Littérature*, ed. Tzvetan Todorov (Paris: Seuil, 1965), pp. 170-96. Jonathan Culler, *Structuralist Poetics* (Ithaca, N.Y.: Cornell Univ. Press, 1975), p. 223, e.g., and Robert Scholes, "The Contributions of Formalism and Structuralism . . . ," pp. 142-43, are only two who emphasize the importance of Shklovsky to studies of structure.

3. Propp, *Morphology* . . . (Bloomington: Indiana Univ. Press, 1958); for a brief suggestion of Propp's tremendous influence, see Culler, pp. 207-24.

4. See Seymour Chatman's summary in "The Structure of Fiction," *University Review* (Kansas City), 37, No. 3 (1971), pp. 199-214.

5. Todorov, *The Poetics of Prose*, especially pp. 35-36, 135-36, 137.

6. Crane, in *Critics and Criticism: Ancient and Modern* (Chicago: Univ. of Chicago Press, 1952), p. 621; Frye, *Anatomy of Criticism*, pp. 52-53.

7. Curley, p. 50.

8. Spengemann, *Adventurous Muse*, p. 72; the quotation is from Richetti, *Popular Fiction before Richardson*, p. 62.

9. "The Epistle Dedicatorie in the First Edition, (1589)," Hakluyt, I, 1.

10. Magendie, p. 222; for Nashe and Lyly and their followers, see, e.g., Jean Loiseau, "Deux attitudes élisabethaines devant le voyage Lyly (*Euphues*) et Nash (*Jack Wilton*)," in *Le*

Voyage dans la littérature anglo-saxonne, Actes du Congrès de Nice (1971) (S.A.E.S., 1972), pp. 13-19; and Hunter, *Occasional Form,* p. 144. Note that while Richetti does say that travel fiction in the eighteenth century was often by a narrator imbued with the notion of providence, he nevertheless believes in "The popularity of the travel narrative and of these 'novels' organized around travel" for the eighteenth century (p. 63).

11. Hunter, *Occasional Form,* p. 155.

12. Knight, *The Journal of Mme Knight,* ed. Theodore Dwight (New York: P. Smith, 1935). For a fine essay on Knight, her "two voices," and her "growth" as she journeys back roads in New England, see Spengemann, *Adventurous Muse,* pp. 39-45; see also Peter Thorpe, "Sarah Kemble Knight and the Picaresque Tradition," *CLA,* 10 (1966), 114-21; for Challe, see note 21, Chap. II above; for Boswell, see note 12, Chap. VI above; for Smollett, *Travels through France and Italy,* in 2 vols (London: Printed for R. Baldwin, 1766), and in 1 vol., ed. Frank Felsenstein (Oxford: Clarendon, 1979).

13. See, e.g., François Jost, "La Tradition de Bildungsroman," *CL,* 21 (1969), 97-115, who employs all these terms and others, such as *kunstlerroman,* and who is reluctant to let *bildungsroman* be used for any novel outside Germany.

14. As Victor Brombert also believes in *The Hero in Literature* (Greenwich, Conn.: Fawcett, 1969), p. 13.

15. Lukacs, *Theory of the Novel,* trans. Anna Bostock (Cambridge: MIT Press, 1971).

16. These are the words of Graham Good in a review of Lukacs in *Novel,* 6 (1973), 177.

17. Richter, *Fable's End: Completeness and Closure in Formal Fiction* (Chicago: Univ. of Chicago Press, 1974), p. 30. Richter's second chapter, "The Eighteenth-Century Rhetorical Novel," treats the structure of *Rasselas* and *Candide* and defends the conclusion of each as an example of closure.

18. William Baffin, *The Voyages of William Baffin,* 1612-1622, ed. Sir Clements Markham (London: Hakluyt, 1881); Drage [Theodore Swaine-Drage], *An Account of a Voyage for the Discovery of a North-West Passage by Hudson's Streights . . . in the Year 1746 and 1747 . . .* (London, 1748), 2 vols. For the intriguing story of Swaine and Drage being the same man and of that man's involving Benjamin Franklin in the search for a Northwest Passage, see note 120, Chap. II above.

19. See Elaine Sanceau, *Knight of the Renaissance: D. Joao de Castro* and Jan Huyghen van Linschoten, *The Voyage of . . . to the East Indies,* ed. from the trans. of 1598 by A.C. Burnell and P.A. Tiele (London: Hakluyt, 1885), 2 vols.

20. See Batten, p. 95, for one statement of this fact.

21. Coryat, I, 122-48, but see also his "Epistle Dedicatorie" and his "The Epistle to the Reader," I, 1-16; for Howell, see Chap. VI above; Nugent, like Howell, had many eds., of which see the preface to the first ed. of 1749 or to the third (London: J. Rivington and Sons, et al., 1778), 4 vols.

22. McBurney, *Four before Richardson,* p. xxvii.

23. Shaftesbury, *Characteristics,* ed. John M. Robertson (Indianapolis: Bobbs-Merrill, 1964), pp. 217-34.

24. Magendie, p. 270, cites a number of works of long fiction that have explanations of the advantages to be derived from such travel.

25. See Magendie, p. 270.

26. See, e.g., J.A. Worth, Int. to *Tristram Shandy* (New York: Odyssey, 1940), p. xlvi. All references to the novel itself are to this text.

27. All this is in Vol. VII; the quotations are on pp. 534-35; and for the popular guide-travel account by Piganiol, see Worth, p. 519, and—at some length—Van R. Baker, "Sterne and Piganiol de la Force: The Making of Volume VII of *Tristram Shandy,*" *CLS* 13 (1976), 5-15.

28. For these fictional Grand Tours, see Rufus Putney, "The Plan of *Peregrine Pickle,*"

PMLA, 60 (1945), 1051-63; Kahrl, pp. 38, 94, etc.; and especially S.B. Rice, "Smollett's 'Travels through France and Italy' and the Genre of Grand Tour Literature," Diss., Univ. of Arizona, 1968.

29. For a brief note on the subject, see Ann F. Woodhouse, "Eighteenth-Century English Visitors to France in Fiction and Fact," *MLS*, 6 (1976), 37-42.

30. For Montaigne, see note 64, Chap. VI above; for Montesquieu, see C.J. Beyer, "Montesquieu et le relativisme esthétique," *SVEC, 24 (1963), 171-82.*

31. Addison and Steele, like Montesquieu, knew many travel accounts, those of Ligon to the Barbados and Chardin to Persia and Dampier around the world, for example, but Addison depended heavily on his own Grand Tour, as in *Spectators* 21, 45, 83.

32. These are terms used by Paul Fussell, *The Rhetorical World of Augustan Humanism* (Oxford: Clarendon, 1975), p. 264.

33. Misson (note 1 above).

34. Olivier (Bruxelles: Rovieli, 1704), pp. 188-91.

35. Addison, *Remarks on Several Parts of Italy . . .* , in *Works*, ed. Henry G. Bohn (London: Henry G. Bohn, 1861), p. 373; 1st ed. 1704.

36. For Smith, who trans. *Manon Lescaut*, see note 109, Chap. IV above, and add Baker, V, 189-90.

37. Paulson, *Satire and the Novel*, p. 135.

38. Frye, *Secular Scripture*, p. 120.

39. Butler, *Characters*, ed. A.R. Waller (Cambridge: Cambridge Univ. Press, 1908), p. 469.

40. Of the many eds. of the rebellious Jesuit Baltasar Gracián's *El Criticón*, see his *Obras*, ed. Arturo del Hoyo, 4th ed. (Madrid: Aguilar, 1960). The long novel was translated into English as *The Critic* by Sir Paul Rycaut, the great traveler-historian (London: Henry Brome, 1681). The trans. here is by Virginia R. Foster, *Baltasar Gracian* (Boston: Twayne, 1975), p. 74.

41. Paulson, *Satire and the Novel*, p. 135, develops this idea.

42. Ibid., p. 178.

43. Ibid., p. 171.

44. See, consecutively, John F. Sena, "Smollett's Persona and the Melancholic Traveler: An Hypothesis," *ECS*, 1 (1968), 354; Robert D. Spector, "Smollett's Traveler," in *Tobias Smollett: Bicentennial Essays Presented to Lewis M. Knapp*, ed. G.S. Rousseau and P.G. Bouce (New York: Oxford Univ. Press, 1971), p. 238; and Paulson, *Satire and the Novel*, pp. 190-94.

45. Rice, "The Satiric Persona of Smollett's *Travels*," *Studies in Scottish Literature*, 10 (1972), 33-47. Quotations below are from pp. 36, 5, 39; that from Keirnan is in *The Cankered Muse* (New Haven: Yale Univ. Press, 1959), p. 18.

46. For these facts, see Adams, *Travelers*, pp. 90-92; Martz, pp. 31-32, 68-71; and especially Kahrl, pp. 80-95.

47. Batten, *Pleasurable Instruction*, pp. 22-23, 130-31, and, especially, "*Humphrey Clinker* and Eighteenth-Century Travel Literature," *Genre*, 7 (1974), 392-408. Here Batten answers those students of Smollett who find no form in *Humphrey Clinker* or fail to note the real source of the form.

48. Batten, *Pleasurable Instruction*, p. 23, quoting Robert Chambers, *Smollett: His Life and a Selection from His Writings* (Edinburgh: W. and R. Chambers, 1867), p. 130.

49. For this and much more, see Kahrl, pp. 132-47; Batten, "*Humphry Clinker . . .*," p. 397; Howard M. Jones, Int. to *The Expedition of Humphry Clinker*, ed. Charles Lee (London: Dent, 1943); Kahrl, "Captain Robert Stobo," *Virginia Magazine of History and Biography*, 49 (1941), 141-51, 254-68. Thomas Preston, in a paper read March 1982 at a meeting of the ASECS in Houston, adds much new information about this matter.

50. Batten, "*Humphry Clinker . . .*," p. 404. See also Kahrl's chap. on *Humphry Clinker*.

51. Rice, "Satiric Persona," p. 35; and Paulson, *Satire and the Novel,* p. 192.

52. Sheldon Sacks, *Fiction and the Shape of Belief* . . . (Berkeley: Univ. of California Press, 1967), p. 271; and Batten, "*Humphry Clinker* . . . ," p. 394.

53. Geoffrey M. Sill, "Defoe's Tour : Literary Art or Moral Imperative?" *ECS,* 11 (1977), 83, who is arguing that Pat Rogers, with his aesthetic approach in "Literary Art in Defoe's *Tour,*" *ECS,* 6 (1972-73), 153-85, does violence to the old economic approach of G.D.H. Cole in the int. to his ed. of the *Tour* (London, 1927).

54. Hackos, "The Metaphor of the Garden in Defoe's *A Tour* . . . ," *PLL,* 15 (1979), 247-62.

55. For Rogers, see note 53 above; see also Rogers, "Defoe as Plagiarist: Camden's *Britannia* and *A Tour* . . . ," *PQ,* 52 (1973), 771-74, and his "Defoe at Work: The Making of a *Tour* . . . , Volume I," *BNYPL,* 78 (1975), 431-50.

56. It has been pointed out that "Parts of *Moll Flanders* reverse the travels [Defoe] later outlined in the *Tour.*" See J.R. Moore, *Defoe,* p. 280.

57. *Literary History of the United States,* ed. Robert E. Spiller et al., 3d ed. revised (New York: Macmillan, 1972), p. 1465.

58. Arms, "Howells' English Travel Books: Problems in Technique," *PMLA,* 82 (1967), 10-16.

59. Sandra Rosenberg, "Travel Literature and the picaresque novel," *Enlightenment Essays,* 2 (1971), 40-47, after calling for a definition of the "genre" called "travel literature," without noting the great academic debate over "picaresque," using only three eighteenth-century British novels, and yet offering some keen impressionistic insights, thinks, e.g., that "The particular form of fiction the travel-book most resembles is the picaresque novel."

60. Parker, *Literature and the Delinquent: The Picaresque Novel in Spain and Europe, 1599-1753* (Edinburgh: Edinburgh Univ. Press, 1967). See Frank Kurand's review in *Novel,* 1 (1968), 190-93.

61. Miller, *The Picaresque Novel* (Cleveland: Case Western Reserve Univ. Press, 1967). For a most liberal treatment, see Christine J. Whitbourn, *Knaves and Swindlers: Essays on the Picaresque Novel in Europe* (New York: Oxford Univ. Press, 1974), which is reviewed by the illiberal Parker in *CL,* 29 (1977), 83-85.

62. Frohock, "The Failing Center: Recent Fiction and the Picaresque," *Novel,* 3 (1969), 62-69, who quotes Walter Allen and, as a conservative more liberal than Parker, Miller, or Robert Alter in *Rogues Progress,* wants us to see that the Renaissance Spanish world is not ours and should not determine our picaresque. See also his "The Idea of the Picaresque," *Yearbook of Comparative and General Literature* (1967), pp. 43-52.

63. Ulrich Wicks has written much on the picaresque, but see especially his "The Nature of the Picaresque Narrative: A Modal Approach," *PMLA,* 89 (1974), 240-49, with its bibliography; Watt, *Rise of the Novel,* p. 94; Guillén, *Literature as System* (Princeton: Princeton Univ. Press, 1971), 71-106, wrote this essay as a speech in 1961 and revised it here. See also A.D. Deyermond, *Lazarillo de Tormes: A Critical Guide* (London: Grant and Cutler, 1975).

64. Paulson, *Satire and the Novel,* p. 241, who argues that after Fielding English writers "tend to soften the picaresque."

65. These three elements are chosen from among many for the sake of making our points about travel literature and the novel. Other elements are of great interest to readers, of course, but to avoid a discussion of them here does not affect our conclusions. One fine survey of the eight elements he finds can be found in Wicks, note 63 above.

66. For this fact and for much of what follows in this paragraph, see Richard Bjornson, "The Picaresque Novel in France, England and Germany," *CL,* 29 (1977), 124-48.

67. The quotations here are from Bjornson, who has numerous other examples. And one can add other novels from the eighteenth century—*Gil Blas, Moll Flanders, Le Paysan parvenu, Roderick Random.*

68. Bjornson, pp. 132-33.

69. See ibid., and Hubert Rausse, "Zur Geschichte des spanischen Schelmenromans in Deutschland," *Munstersche Beitrage zur neuren Literaturgeschichte,* 8 (1908), 33-39.

70. See J.H. Scholte, *Der Simplicissimus und sein Dichter. Gesammelte Aufsatze* (Tübingen, 1951), p. 71, e.g.; Richard Newald, *Die Deutsche Literatur . . . 1570-1750* (München: C.H. Beck'sche, 1951), p. 375; and Mirco Mitrovich, *Deutsche Reisende und Reiseberichte im 17. Jahrhundert. Ein kultur-historischer Beitrag* (Urbana: Univ. of Illinois Press, 1963), pp. 202-204. For these sources I wish to thank my colleague John Osborne.

71. For this paragraph and much more, see my "The Anti-Hero in Eighteenth-Century Fiction," pp. 46-47, and my *Travelers,* pp. 216-17.

72. Paulson, *Satire and the Novel,* has a fine treatment of this tradition for the novel, pp. 220-26, 175-76, 192n.

73. See Showalter, e.g., for the *Diable* tradition in France, pp. 49-50, 187-88.

74. Smollett, *The History and Adventures of an Atom* (1769), and Sterne, *Tristram Shandy,* Vol. IV. But see *Tristram,* III, xxxiv, for my Father's having "collected every book and treatise . . . upon noses with as much care as my honest uncle Toby had done those upon military architecture."

75. See *The Complete Memoirs of That Notorious Impersonator Will. Morrell,* in Peterson, ed., *The Counterfeit Lady Unveiled . . . ,* pp. 299-372, and his short bibliography, p. 299.

76. See, e.g., I.L. McClelland, *The Origins of the Romantic Movement in Spain* (Liverpool: Institute of Hispanic Studies, 1937), pp. 261-81.

77. See especially Russell P. Sebold, *Novela y Autobiografía en la "Vida" des Torres Villaroel . . .* (Esplugues de Llobregat: Editorial Ariel, 1975); and Sabine Kleinhaus, *Von der "novela picaresca" sur burgerlichen autobiographie: Studie zur "Vida" des Torres Villaroel* (Meisenheim am Glan: A. Hain, 1975).

78. Pike, "Time in Autobiography," *CL,* 28 (1976), 337.

79. Walpole, in a letter to his friend Horace Mann, Jan. 28, 1754. See *The Travels and Adventures of Three Princes of Sarendip. Inter-mixed with Eight Delightful and Entertaining Novels. Translated from the Persian into French, and from thence done into English . . .* (London: Chetwood, 1722). The 1557 original was pub. at Venice. See Thomas G. Renner, ed., *Serendipity and the Three Princes* (Norman: Univ. of Oklahoma Press, 1965), as trans. from the Italian by A. and T. Borselli.

80. Consecutively: E. Simon, "The Function of the Spanish Stories in Scarron's *Roman comique,*" *L'Esprit créateur,* 3 (1963), 130-36; F.A. de Armas, *The Four Interpolated Stories in the "Roman Comique": Their Sources and Unifying Function* (Chapel Hill: Univ. of North Carolina Press, 1971); J.W. Scott, "The 'Digressions' of the *Princesse de Clèves,*" *French Studies,* 11 (1957), 315-21; Watt, *Rise of the Novel,* p. 268; and Knight, "The 'Digressive' Tales in Fielding's *Tom Jones* and the Perspective of Romance," *PQ,* 54 (1975), 258-74. See also Howard Weinbrot, "Chastity and Interpolation: Two Aspects of *Joseph Andrews,*" *JEGP,* 69 (1970), 26n, who summarizes the defense of the Old Man story in *Tom Jones;* and especially Paul Hunter, *Occasional Form,* pp. 151-60, for an excellent treatment of the question in general and for Fielding in particular. For France, see Mylne, pp. 56-64, e.g.; and Stewart, pp. 136 ff.

81. Korkowski, "*Tristram Shandy,* Digression, and the Menippean Tradition," *Scholia Satyrica,* 1 (1975), 3-16. See also J. Paul Hunter, "Response as Reformation: *Tristram Shandy* and the Art of Interruption," *Novel,* 4 (1970), 132-46; and M.V. Deporte, "Digressions and Machines in *A Tale of a Tub* and *Tristram Shandy,*" *HLQ,* 34 (1970), 43-57.

82. Rosenberg, "Digressions in Imaginary Voyages," *The Varied Pattern: Studies in the Eighteenth Century,* ed. Peter Hughes and David Williams (Toronto: Hakkert, 1971), pp. 21-39.

83. See Chap. IX below for this story.

84. Ray, *Observations* (1673), pp. 113-31.

85. Careri, in Churchill (1704), IV, 520-23.

86. Martire, *Decades* (1533), trans. Richard Eden (London: Powell, 1559; rpt. Ann Arbor: Univ. Microfilms, 1966), p. 17; and Lescarbot, *Nova Francia*, pp. 157-61.

87. For Adario, see Chap. IX below.

88 For these examples and others, see Adams, *Travelers*, pp. 199-201.

89. Varthema, pp. 240-42, 144-46.

90. Challe, ed. Deloffre, pp. 328, 420 ff., e.g.; Coreal (Paris, 1722), p. 70, and the chap. "Of the Customs and Religion of the Creoles and Spanish."

91. Foigny, *La Terre Australe connue* . . . , 2d ed. (Vannes: Vernevil, 1676), pp. 84-124.

92. J.H. Maubert de Gouvert, *Lettres Iroquoises*, Nouvelle ed., Revue et corrigée (Irocopolis: Chez les Vénérable [sic], 1755), 1st ed. 1752. See also P.A. de Saint Foise Arcq, *Lettres d'Osmon* (Constantinople, 1753), pp. 146-74, which uses Igli, also to confound European intellectuals.

93. R.M. Lesuire, *Les Sauvages de l'Europe* (Berlin, 1760), and *Les Amants françois, ou Les Délices de l'Angleterre* (Londres: Duchesne, 1780).

94. Fiennes, p. 79.

95. Montaigne, p. 314.

96. Smollett, *Travels*, ed. Felsenstein, pp. 76-78.

97. Alvarez, trans. Stanley (Hakluyt, 1961), I, I, 145-47, 149-51.

CHAPTER EIGHT

1. Johnson was with Boswell in Dr. Taylor's post chaise, as reported by Boswell in the *Life* for September 19, 1777; Fielding, in *Joseph Andrews* (I.i).

2. Tomashevsky, in Lemon and Reis, *Russian Formalist Criticism*, interpreted by Scholes in "The Contributions of Formalism and Structuralism to the Theory of Fiction." The quotation is from Scholes.

3. See Chap. VII above.

4. Alan Frost, "Captain James Cook and the Early Romantic Imagination," in Walter Veit, ed., *Captain James Cook: Image and Impact*, p. 102. Frost finds Cook an exception who sets a pattern for the "Romantic imagination."

5. Brée, "The Ambiguous Voyage," pp. 87-96.

6. See note 1 above.

7. Hester Thrale Piozzi, *Anecdotes of the Late Dr. Johnson* (Cambridge: Harvard Univ. Press, 1932), p. 177.

8. Placing characters in a stage coach has of course been noted as a popular device in the eighteenth-century novel, for example, by E.A. Baker, V, 103, who is speaking of Mackenzie's *The Man of Feeling*, and by Foster, *History of the Pre-Romantic Novel*, p. 23, speaking of Mrs. Mary Manley. But no one has yet demonstrated how important the device was in other ways or how it is a necessary device in the best travel books written about journeys on land. The treatment here closely follows my article, "The Coach Motif in Eighteenth-Century Fiction," *MLS*, 8 (1978), 17-27.

9. See Joan Parks, *Travel in England in the Seventeenth Century* (London: Oxford Univ. Press, 1925), pp. 74-80.

10. For information in this and the following paragraph, see Parks; Harvey S. Firestone, *Man on the Move: The Story of Transportation* (New York: Putnam's, 1967); Beatrice Saunders, *The Age of Candelight: The English Social Scene in the Seventeenth Century* (Philadelphia: Dufour eds., 1961); *Encyclopaedia Britannica*, s.v. "Berlin," "Carriages," "Coaching," "Driving," "Cart," "Wagon"; Esther Moir, *The Discovery of Britain: The English Tourist* (London: Routledge and Kegan Paul, 1964), Chap. 1; D.J. Dyos and D.H. Aldercroft, *British Transport* (Leicester: Leicester univ. Press, 1969), pp. 29-36 especially; A. Lytton Sells, *The Paradise of Travellers;* Peter

Bray, ed., *Transport through the Ages*. With drawings by Barbara Brown (London: Arthur Barker, 1971); J.W. Stoye, *English Travellers Abroad, 1604-1667* (London: Cape, 1952); J.H. Markland, "Some Remarks on the Early Use of Carriages in England," from *Archaeologia: or Miscellaneous Tracts Relating to Antiquity* (a speech read February 22, 1821, at the Inner Temple); Rosamund Bayne-Powell, *Travels in Eighteenth-Century England* (London: John Murray, 1951); and Constantia Maxwell, *The English Traveller in France 1698-1815* (London: Routledge and Sons, 1932). These, and other such sources, must be compared and used with caution, especially Bayne-Powell and Maxwell.

11. *The Diary of John Evelyn*, ed. de Beer, p. 135, for April 19, 1744; for Montagu on French roads and especially on the splendid Paris-Orleans road, see his diary as quoted in Stoye, p. 33.

12. See Firestone, p. 65.

13. Regnard, *Oeuvres*, I, 10-20.

14. Misson, *Mémoires et observations ... en Angleterre*, trans. John Ozell (London: D. Browne et al., 1719), p. 39.

15. Brunel, note 77, Chap. III above.

16. Palmer, *A Four Months Tour through France*, 2 vols. (London: 1776), I, 160-68.

17. Manley, *A Stage-Coach Journey to Exeter Describing the Humours on the Road, with the Characters and Adventures of the Company. In Eight Letters to a Friend. To which is added The Force of Love: or, The Men's Complaint*. By the Hon. Colonel Pack (London: J. Roberts, 1725), 1st version 1696. Foster, *Pre-Romantic Novel in England*, p. 23n., is convinced that Manley was imitating d' Aulnoy's *Travels in Spain*, which was also used by Defoe in *Captain Carleton;* and Foster points out that Smollett in Chap. I of *Fathom* refers to the 1753 ed. of *The Stage-Coach, Containing the Character of Mr.[sic] Manley, and the History of his Fellow Travellers*.

18. Byrd, *Another Secret Diary of William Byrd of Westover, 1739-1741*, ed. Maude E. Woodfin and Marion Tinling (Richmond, Va.: Dietz, 1942). pp. 286-90.

19. See II.x and III.xci, e.g., of Scarron, *Le Roman comique*, ed. Emile Magne (Paris: Garnier, n.d.). The third part is not by Scarron but was added after his death.

20. Marivaux, *La Voiture embourbée* (1714), in *Oeuvres complètes*, 12 vols. (Paris: V ve Duchesne, 1781), XII, 143-280.

21. Thomas l'Affichard, *Le Voyage interrompu* (1737), in *Voyages imaginaires, Romanesques, Merveilleux. ...* 30 vols. (Amsterdam and Paris: Rue et Hôtel Serpents, 1788), XXX, 1-163.

22. Gimat de Bonneval, *Le Voyage de Mantes, ou Les Vacances De 17 ...* (Amsterdam: no pub., 1753).

23. Baretti, *A Journey from London to Genoa* (London, 1770), I, 3-13. The comparison is made by Kahrl, p. 55.

24. Smollett, *The Expedition of Humphrey Clinker* (New York: Rinehart, 1950), p. 100.

25. Lucian, "Hired Companions," in *Lucian: Selected Works*, trans. Bryan P. Reardon (New York: Bobbs-Merrill, 1965), p. 213.

26. Settle, in Peterson, ed., *The Counterfeit Lady Unveiled and Other Criminal Fiction ...*, pp. 291-373.

27. *Coryat's Crudities* (1905), II, 1, 350, 377 (for the letter he carried to Wotton).

28. For some of these facts about literary inns, see George Long, *English Inns and Road-Houses* (London: Laurie, 1937), especially pp. 59-68.

29. *Coryat's Crudities*, II, 174-75, 360-61, 62, 106, 140-41, 150, and, for the Three Kings, I, 211-13.

30. Moryson, *An itinerary ... containing his ten yeeres travell. ...* (London, 1617; rpt. Glasgow: James MacLehose and Sons, 1907-1908). in 4 vols., I, 362. Stoye, who has almost nothing on the inns frequented by travelers, does refer to this incident (p. 111), cites the source incorrectly as Vol. II, and says that Moryson admitted here his lack of proficiency in each of

the three languages; actually Moryson was sure of his own fine talents and very critical of those of the other Englishman.

31. Moryson, I, 384.

32. Jodocus Sincerus (Zinzerling), *Itinerarium Galliae* ... (Lugduni, 1616). For more on this francophile, see Babeau, pp. 75-79.

33. Goelnitz, *Ulysses belgico-gallicus* ... (Lugduni, 1631). See Babeau, pp. 79-84.

34. Evelyn, *A Selection from the Diary,* ed. Philip Francis (London: Folio Soc., 1963), p. 28; the date is April 20, 1644.

35. Brunel, Chap. I.

36. Ray, *Observations* ... (1673); and Regnard, *Voyage de Flandre et de Hollande,* in *Oeuvres* (1854), I, 1-20.

37. Babeau, Chap. I.

CHAPTER NINE

1. Arnold Bennett, *The Journals of Arnold Bennett* (1931).

2. See Frye's sixth phase of Romance, the lonely old man, the hermit, with a story to tell, in *The Anatomy of Criticism,* pp. 192-206. For an excellent treatment of Fielding's use of *Télémaque,* structurally and thematically; see Paul Hunter, *Occasional Form,* pp. 133-40.

3. For *Epigone,* see Alexandre Ciornascu, "*Epigone,* le premier roman d l'avenir," *Revue des sciences humaines,* 39 (1974), 441-48; for Sadeur and more, see Atkinson (before 1700), p. 61.

4. Frye, *Anatomy of Criticism,* pp. 195-97, speaks of the importance of such characters as Spenser's Satyrane, the "salvage man," "a Renaissance favorite," or Friday—"children of nature, who can be brought to serve the hero...."

5. For interesting notes on possible origins of Friday, see Paul Hunter, "Friday as a Convert: Defoe and the Accounts of Indian Missionaries," *HLQ,* 14 (1963), 243-48.

6. Bissell, *The American Indian in English Literature of the Eighteenth Century* (New Haven: Yale Univ. Press, 1925); Fairchild, *The Noble Savage: A Study in Romantic Naturalism* (New York: Columbia Univ. Press, 1928; New York: Russel and Russel, 1961); Chinard, *L'Amérique et le rêve exotique.* See also August Viatte, *Histoire littéraire de l'Amérique francqise des origines 'a 1950* (Québec: Presses Universitaires Laval, 1954); Viatte's "La Littérature française d'Amérique au XVIIe et XVIIIe siècle," *Revue de la Littérature Comparée,* 25 (1951), 5-11, is a good summary of Chinard, especially the sections in Chinard on travelers such as du Tertre, Labat, and Chastellux, with some additions on Lescarbot.

7. For Dr. Chanca, see *Select Documents Illustrating the Four Voyages of Columbus,* trans. and ed. Cecil Jane, 2 vols. (London: Hakluyt, 1930), I, 70, and for the heated debate after 1519 between Chanca's followers—Oviedo, Quevedo, Sepúlveda—and Bartolomé de Las Casas, start with the works of Lewis Hanke. See Adams, "The Discovery of America and European Renaissance Literature." Martire, pp. 17a, 208, 211, 212.

8. For the drawings by John White and Jacques Le Moyne, see, besides de Bry, Paul Hulton and D.B. Quinn, *The American Drawings of John White, 1577-1590,* 2 vols. (London: British Museum, 1964), and Charles E. Bennett, compiler, *Settlement of Florida* (Gainesville: Univ. of Florida Press, 1968), which has Le Moyne's drawings.

9. Père Jean-Baptiste du Tertre, *Histoire générale des Isles de S. Christophe, de la Guadeloupe, de la Martinique et autres dans l'Amérique* (Paris: Jacques et Emmanuel Langlois, 1654). This one-volume work was followed by two vols., *Histoire générale des Antilles* ... (Paris: Thomas Jolly, 1667), and four vols. in 1671. See Chinard, pp. 54-58, for a discussion of the well-known debate about whether the Protestant minister Rochefort stole du Tertre's manuscript for his *Histoire Naturelle et Morale des Isles Antilles* (Rotterdam, 1658).

10. Typical of the hundreds of articles on this subject is A.L. Dickett, "The Noble Savage

Convention . . . in Lawson's *A New Voyage to Carolina,*" *North Carolina Historical Review,* 43 (1966), 413-29.

11. Bissell, pp. 1-2.

12. *Tsonnonthonian* (London: J. Knox, 1763), 2 vols. See Foster, "A Forgotten Noble Savage, Tsonnonthonian," *MLQ,* 14 (1953), 348-59. This novel was trans. into French; See Chinard, *Le Rêve exotique, p. 445.*

13. Foster, "A Forgotten Noble Savage," p. 348.

14. Columbus's old man is in Martire, p. 17; Jean de Léry, partly to refute his Roman Catholic colleague André Thevet (1557), wrote *Histoire d'un voyage fait en la Terre de Bresil* (La Rochelle, 1578); Lescarbot, *Nova Francia,* pp. 157-61; for the Rites controversy, which left Defoe unconvinced of the wisdom of Confucius and which affected many other thinkers such as Addison, Voltaire, and Diderot, see Appleton, *A Cycle of Cathay;* Arnold W. Rowbotham, *Missionary and Mandarin* (Berkeley: Univ. of California Press, 1942); G. Alan Nelson and Michael Rewa, "Enlightenment Sinophilia: Defoe's Dissent," *Enlightenment Essays,* 5 (1974), 26-43.

15. See especially the article "Kondiaronk" in the *Dictionary of Canadian Biography,* II, and the article "Adario" in the *Handbook of American Indians,* I, 13. Cadwallader Colden, *The History of the Five Indian Nations* (London: T. Osborn, 1747), p. 86, spells Adario's tribe *Deonondadies* and puts him at a meeting with the French at Albany in 1684. For more on Lahontan and Adario, see Chinard, *L'Amérique et le Rêve exotique,* pp. 179-87, and Atkinson, *Extraordinary Voyage . . . from 1700 to 1720,* pp. 31-35.

16. See Desfontaine's Preface. Tieje (1912) relates this book to Foigny's *Sadeur,* Veiras's *Histoire des Sévarambes,* and *Oroonoko.*

17. Bricaire's *Le Sauvage de Taiti aux Français* (1770), Voltaire's *Les Oreilles du comte de Chesterfield et le chapelain Goudman* (1775), and other such fictions are treated briefly by John Dunmore, "The Explorer and the Philosopher," in Veit, ed., *Captain James Cook,* pp. 54-66. Chinard, better than Fairchild or Bissell, recognized the relationship between Adario and Tahiti when he edited the *Supplément au voyage de Bougainville . . .* (Baltimore: Johns Hopkins Univ. Press, 1935). There are far too many Adarios to name them all here. For example, see the Igli of more than one novel, such as that by Arcq, *Lettres d'Osman* (1753), and the Abaqui Indian Iglou of Prévost's *Cleveland;* and travelers borrowed the character, even the name, as Thomas Ashe borrowed both for a southern American Indian a hundred years after Lahontan (see Adams, *Travelers,* p. 198).

18. For all this and more on Franklin and the stories like his, see Adams, "Benjamin Franklin and the Tradition of Travel Literature"; Bissell, p. 75, has one of the three Franklin tales.

19. Davys, *The Works of . . .* (London: H. Woodfall, 1725), II, 69-70.

20. See also *The Highland Rogue* (1723; rpt. New York: Garland, 1973), with an int. by Josephine Grieder.

21. Magendie, pp. 20-21.

22. See Watson, p. 58; Samuel C. Chew, *The Crescent and the Rose* (New York: Oxford Univ. Press, 1937); and Godfrey Fisher, *Barbary Legend,* whose bibliography shows how dependent on travel books is his work.

23. Exquemelin and Ringrose, *The Buccaneers of America* (Dover), pp. 229-30.

24. As Starr, "Escape from Barbary," p. 49, points out.

25. McBurney, in Int. to *Four before Richardson.*

26. Atkinson, *Les Nouveaux horizons,* p. 438; and Starr, "Escape from Barbary," p. 35.

27. For Temple, Defoe, and the Rites controversy, see note 14 above; For the Jesuits in South America, see Philip Carasman, *The Lost Paradise: The Jesuit Republic in South America* (London: Sidgwick and Jackson, 1975); Maxime Haubert, *La Vie quotidienne au Paraguay sous*

les Jésuites (Paris: Hachette, 1967); and Jacques Décobert, "Les Missions Jésuites du Paraguay devant la philosophie des lumières," *Revue des sciences humaines,* 38 (1973), 17-46.

28. See this and more in J.M. Reid, *Traveller Extraordinary* (London: Eyre and Spothswood, 1968).

29. Ward, *A Trip to New-England. With a Character of the Country and People, both English and Indians* (London, 1699), in *Five Scripts commonly attributed to Edward Ward,* pub. for the Facsimile Text Soc. (New York: Columbia Univ. Press, 1933). H.W. Troyer, *Ned Ward of Grub Street* (Cambridge: Harvard Univ. Press, 1946), is surely right in believing that Ward never made a trip to New England and that, with the help of real travelers such as John Josselyn (1672), Ward wrote a fictional, satiric travel book (p. 21).

30. Bissell, p. 135.

31. Foster, *The Pre-Romantic Novel,* p. 51.

32. Ligon, *True and Exact History of the Island of Barbados* (1657), p. 55.

33. Mocquet, *Voyages en Afrique, Asie, Indies Orientales et Occidentales, fait par Jean Mocquet, garde du Cabinet des singularitez du Roy aux Tuilleries* (Paris, 1616; Rouen: Jacques Cailloue, 1645), p. 150. See Chinard, *L'Amérique et le rêve exotique,* p. 26, who retells the story.

34. Chinard, p. 27, incorrectly thinks that Steele worked with Mocquet; he also thinks that Prévost did (see below).

35. Parks, "Tudor Travel Literature: a Brief History," in *The Hakluyt Handbook,* ed. D.B. Quinn (London: Hakluyt, 1974), I, 121. Here Parks quotes J.A. Williamson for the same opinion (1933).

36. See Batten, p. 101, for this quotation from the *Universal Magazine* (1798).

37. Kahrl, *Smollett,* p. 54.

38. See Ward, *Five Travel Scripts;* for d'Aulnoy and for Montesquieu's use of her "haughty" Spaniards in the *Lettres persanes,* see Paul Ilie, "Exomorphism: Cultural Bias and the French Image of Spain from the War of Succession to the Age of Voltaire," *ECS,* 9 (1976), 375-90. Ilie's fine article depends, however, on secondary sources in the eighteenth century—Hume and the dictionary writers, e.g.—and not on the travel writers themselves.

39. For recent works on this subject, see Adams, "Travel Literature of the Seventeenth and Eighteenth Centuries: A Review. . . ." See also Lynn Altenbernd, "The Idea of National Character: Inspiration or Fallacy," *America: Exploration and Travel,* ed. Steven E. Kagle. (Bowling Green, Ohio: Bowling Green State Univ. Press, 1979), and Chap. VII above.

CHAPTER TEN

1. Lowes, p. 313.

2. Mylne, pp. 54-55.

3. Auerbach, p. 432, is here thinking mostly of Saint-Simon, who wrote his memoirs after 1739.

4. Manley, preface to *The Secret History of Queen Zarah* (1709-11).

5. For this now vast subject, see F.P. Wilson, *Seventeenth-Century Prose: Five Lectures* (Berkeley: Univ. of California Press, 1960); Robert Adolph, *The Rise of Modern Prose Style* (Cambridge: MIT Press, 1968); Louis T. Milic, "Against the Typology of Prose Styles," in *Essays on the Language of Literature,* ed. Seymour Chatman and Samuel L. Levin (Boston: Houghton Mifflin, 1967); Ian A. Gordon, *The Movement of English Prose* (London: Longmans, 1966); Brian Vickers, Francis Bacon and Renaissance Prose (Cambridge: Cambridge Univ. Press, 1968); *Joan Webber, Contrary Music: The Prose Style of John Donne* (Madison: Univ. of Wisconsin Press, 1963). All these should be added to the studies of Kroll, Williamson, Thomson, and others, none of whom considers travel writers of Europe from 1500 to 1800.

6. Manley, preface to *Queen Zarah.*

7. Pope, *Notes to the Iliad,* Book VI [my italics in last sentence].

8. For the "many voices," including Defoe's own, and for Dobrée, see E. Anthony James, *Defoe's Many Voices: A Rhetorical Study of Prose Style and Literary Method* (Atlantic Highlands, N.J.: Humanities Press, 1972).

9. Thomson, *Classical Influences on English Prose* (1956; New York: Collier Books, 1962), pp. 277-92.

10. Osselton and Parks, in *The Hakluyt Handbook,* ed. Quinn, I, 23-30, 97-133.

11. Osselton and Parks, pp. 27, 30, 130.

12. Lowes, p. 316.

13. Watson, pp. 12-23.

14. Frantz, pp. 48-68.

15. Sprat, *The History of the Royal Society* (London, 1667), p. 113.

16. See Adams, *Travelers,* pp. 268-69, notes 4, 6, 9. J.R. Moore like myself, is one who did not, for example, find that only after 1660 "the average voyager strove to see clearly and record objectively." Joseph M. Levine, "Ancients and Moderns Reconsidered," *ECS,* 15 (81), 72-90, finds that this theory of R.F. Jones, and of his disciple Frantz, is "now seriously dated." The fact that the Ancients were strong enough to carry on a war with the Moderns and to enlist most of the great Moderns on their side might indicate that it is simplistic to think that a great revolution occurred in prose style, at least in England, after the formation of the Royal Society an entire generation before the height of the Ancient-Modern debate.

17. Givner, "Scientific Preconceptions in Locke's Philosophy of Language," *JHI,* 23 (1962), p. 354.

18. Knox, "On the Manner of Writing Voyages and Travels," in *Essays Moral and Literary* (5th ed.; London: Dilley, 1784), pp. 113-18.

19. Montaigne, *Essays,* Temple Classics, I. 256 (Bk. I, Chap. 25).

20. See Frantz, p. 18, for the Royal Society's praise of Narbrough, and pp. 60-62 for Martin and Dampier as "disciples."

21. Varthema, pp. 2-3.

22. For this "Commission," see Hakluyt, II, 97-98; for Hakluyt on Chancellor, see I, 28-29, and on Carpini and William of Rubruquis, p. 31. Frantz cites other such claims from Beste, Lane, Ralegh, Keymis, and John Smith.

23. For Dampier and the *Buccaneers,* see the Dover eds., p. 1, pp. xlvi-xlvii, respectively.

24. My trans. See Atkinson, *Extraordinary Voyage . . . before 1700,* pp. 92-93, for the public, in part, accepting the book as truthful at first.

25. Jenkinson in Hakluyt, I, 409, 440.

26. Hawks in Hakluyt, VI, 283.

27. Frantz, pp. 49-50, 62-65, quotes Frobisher and Hawkins for a plain style, along with other travel writers perhaps not so plain; and he cites Martin and of course Dampier, as well as Josselyn in New England. Martin, *A Journey to the Western Islands of Scotland* (1703), ed. Donald J. MacLeod (Stirling: Makay, 1934); Frobisher is quoted from George Best, *A True Discourse . . .* (1578) (London: Hakluyt, 1867), but his letter is found also in Hakluyt, V, 220, inserted there in Best's long account; Hawkins in *The Hawkins Voyages . . . ,* ed. C.R. Markham (London: Hakluyt, 1878).

28. Newberry in Hakluyt, III, 271, 272, 274.

29. Fiennes, ed. Morris, p. xxxvii.

30 Fiennes, p. 93.

31. J. Bayard Morris, trans. and ed., *Hernando Cortés Five Letters (1519-1526),* p. xli. See, e.g., a twenty-seven–word sentence (in good trans.) on pp. 48-49 and others on pp. 108, 128-29, and elsewhere.

32. Hakluyt, VI, 351; my italics point to the abundance of subordinate clauses. For other

sentences just as complex, see pp. 340, 342; but see, p. 350, a paragraph of three sentences of ten lines and only three dependent clauses altogether.

33. Hakluyt, VI, 164-96. For quick confirmation, see pp. 188-89, 194-95.

34. For only three of these: Keymis in Hakluyt, VII, 358, 361; Moryson, I, 26-27; Montaigne, pp. 225, 342.

35. All these examples, including several poems, are taken from some four books on America by Smith and can be found in the selections in Davis, et al., *Southern Writing*, pp. 20-29.

36. As Frantz does, pp. 54-57.

37. For one of many balanced "plain-style" passages in Sandys, see his wonderful account (p. 14) of Sunday street dancing and music and holiday clothes for the island of Chios.

38. See Frantz, pp. 54-55, 57.

39. Frantz, pp. 49, 61, and elsewhere.

40. Lithgow, *The Totall discourse of the rare adventures and painefull peregrinations of long nineteene yeares travayles* (London, 1614, 1632; Glasgow, 1906); the leaned Heylin, lecturer and Anglican apologist, did not publish for more than thirty years, and then from notes; see his *A Full Relation of Two Journeys: the one into the mainland of France* (1656). Stoye, *English Travellers Abroad*, p. 18, correctly, I think, speaks of the "sprightly" eccentricities of Lithgow and Coryat.

41. Alsop, *A Character . . . of Mary-Land* (London, 1666), has often been reprinted. Frantz, p. 57, quotes an early sentence from a reprint in Cleveland, 1902, p. 33; see also the edition by John G. Shea (1880), as well as C.C. Hall, ed., *Narratives of Early Maryland, 1638-1689* (1910).

42. Lemay, *Men of Letters in Colonial Maryland* (Knoxville: Univ. of Tennessee Press, 1972), p. 48.

43. Fox, *North-West Fox: or Fox from the North-West Passage* (London, 1635). See also *The Strange and Dangerous Voyage of Captain Thomas James in his Intended Discovery of the North-West Passage . . .* (London, 1633). *CHEL*, IV, 123-24, makes the same point about Fox, citing even more of his language and noting that in spite of his witty sneers he was a collector of voyages himself.

44. *The Relation of a Voyage to Guiana . . . Performed by Robert Harcourt* (London, 1609). See also a version in Purchas and, the most complete, a revised ed. of 1626. *CHEL*, IV, 113, quotes him.

45. Keymis, *A Relation of the second Voyage to Guiana, performed and written in the yeere 1596. . . .* In Hakluyt, VII, 358-62, especially.

46. Hakluyt, VII, 339. See Lowes, p. 314, who omits the first sentence and words after "which" and uses the Glasgow, 1903-5, Hakluyt, X, 418.

47. Galinsky (note 27, Chap. IV above), p. 17.

48. My trans., following that found in *Voyages of Samuel de Champlain*, trans. C.P. Otis, 2 vols. (Boston: The Prince Soc., 1878), II, 210-11, and the one done for The Champlain Society and partially reproduced in Robert E. Spiller, ed., *The Roots of National Culture to 1830* (New York: Macmillan, 1935), p. 34.

49. See *Voyages*, trans. Otis, II, 245.

50. Lescarbot, *The History of New France*, trans. [with my emendations] W.L. Grant, 3 vols. (Toronto: The Champlain Soc., 1907, 1911, 1914), II, 299. Lescarbot's personal account starts in II, 289. See, for a slightly different trans., *Nova Francia. A Description of Acadia, 1606*, trans. P. Erondelle, 1609, int. H.P. Bigger (London: Routledge, 1928), pp. 73-74. Hakluyt was responsible for Erondelle's trans., which follows the first French ed. of 1609.

51. Commander Charles N. Robinson, R.N., and John Leyland, in *CHEL*, IV, 98.

52. Raleigh, *The English Novel*, p. 134; Bonner, *Dampier*, Chap. VIII: Echeruo, "*Robinson Crusoe, Purchas His Pilgrimes* and the 'Novel,' " *English Studies in Africa*, 10 (1967), 167-77.

53. Kahrl, *Smollett*, p. 84, quotes this passage from the preface to Smollett's *Compendium*

(1756). See also Kahrl, pp. 152-53, for a long paragraph on Smollett's debt to travels in style: "... there is a recognizable similarity between the style of travel books and that of Smollett." Kahrl believes Defoe and Smollett owe much to the voyagers's "simple," "direct narrative style" (p. 152).

54. Batten, *Pleasurable Instruction*, p. 79, who cites three examples.

55. Gove, pp. 171-72. See *Quarterly Review*, 17 (1817), 464, and a review of Bell in the *Critical Review*, 53 (1789), 175-83, both cited by Gove.

56. Davis, ed., *The Novel*, p. 264. That Davis is correct is seen, e.g., by turning to Rahv's essay in Davis and reading his attack on the theories brought to novelistic style by critics trained on poetry—Ransom and Leavis, e.g.—and by this statement," ... the norms of the novel are scarcely those of ornamentation...." (pp. 114-17).

57. Richardson, *A Collection of the Moral and Instructive Sentiments. ...* (London: Pr. for S. Richardson, 1755), p. 73. For this and much more, see E.B. Brophy, *Samuel Richardson: The Triumph of Craft* (Knoxville: Univ. of Tennessee Press, 1974), pp. 38-49.

58. Grandchamp, *La Guerre d'Italie* (1702; Cologne: Pierre Marteau, 1710), p. 2. For this fact, see Showalter, p. 17 [my trans.].

59. Stewart, p. 78, for a different purpose cites Lesage, Prévost, and others such as Challe, Mouhy, and Rousseau, the last of whom sounds much like Richardson in his plea for simplicity.

60. For a fine discussion of the style of *Gil Blas*, see Mylne, pp. 53-55.

61. Mylne, pp. 88, 96. See also the theory of Sgard, *Prévost*, that Prévost tried to be simple in style but was innately ornamental.

62. For *Marianne*, see Mylne, pp. 14-24, and Showalter, p. 45.

63. Lutwack, in Davis, ed., *The Novel*, pp. 255-56. Lutwack contends that Fielding's ' "Homerican" language and essay style in *Tom Jones* simply "point up the unsuitability in the novel of the 'elevation of style' used in more traditional forms of narrative writing," a thesis that of course tends to ignore the importance of romance and epic to the novel as Lutwack and others would define it.

64. Lutwack, p. 257.

65. Richardson writes at length of his own style and technique in "Hints of Prefaces," in *Clarissa, Preface, Hints ..., and Postscript*, ed. R.F. Brissenden, Augustan Reprint Soc., no. 103 (Los Angeles: Clark Memorial Library and Univ. of California, 1964). See, for a good summary of Richardson's opinions about his style, Brophy, pp. 38-43.

66. On the development of Marivaux's style and on Laclos's opinions about his variety, see Mylne, pp. 107-12, 235-36.

67. Montesquieu, *The Persian Letters*, trans. Healy, p. 7.

68. Careri, as in Prévost, *Histoire générale des voyages* (1753), XI, 558-61; E.G.R. Taylor, *The Original Writings and Correspondence of the Two Richard Hakluyts*, 2 vols. (London: Hakluyt, 1935), II, 482; see also F.M. Rogers, "Hakluyt as Translator," in *Hakluyt Handbook*, ed. Quinn, I, 37-47.

69. Rouillard, pp. 189-95.

70. Neither Pyrard de Laval's 1611 nor his 1615, enlarged, ed. has the vocabulary; but the third, 1619, does; after which it was often reprinted. For the problem about Drury's vocabulary, see J.R. Moore, *Defoe in the Pillory ...* (Bloomington: Indiana Univ. Press, 1939), and his *Defoe's Sources for "Robert Drury's Journal"* (Bloomington: Indiana Univ. Press, 1943); A.W. Second, *Robert Drury's Journal and Other Studies* (Urbana: Univ. of Illinois Press, 1961); and Adams, *Travelers*, p. 113 and p. 253, n. 27.

71. Long, p. xvii.

72. The bibliography for the subject of Europe's interest in a common, or simplified, language is enormous. The following paragraph, a terse statment of a fascinating story, is based on the following studies: L. Couterat et L. Leau, *Histoire de la langue universelle* (Paris: Hachette,

1903); Albert L. Guérard, *A Short History of the International Language Movement* (New York: Boni and Liveright, n.d.); 2 articles by Emile Pons, "Les Langues imaginaires dans le voyage utopique. Un Précursor: Thomas Morus," and "Les Langues imaginaires dans le voyage utopique: les 'jargons' de Panurge dans Rabelais," *RLC*, 11 (1931), 185-218; Edward Seeber, "Ideal Languages in the French and English Imaginary Voyage" *PMLA*, 60 (1945), 586-97, which is good although Seeber did not know of Godwin's use of Ricci; and much the best, Paul E. Cornelius, *Languages in Seventeenth- and Early Eighteenth-Century Imaginary Voyages* (Genève: Droz, 1965). Cornelius has information about other debts Godwin especially owed to travelers. Marjorie Nicolson's seminal *Voyages to the Moon* has nothing on the question of languages on the moon and other superterrestrial places.

73. Rouillard, pp. 516-22, points to travel writers whom Rabelais could have known.

74. Behn, *Oroonoko; or, The Royal Slave* (1688; rpt. New York: Norton, 1973), pp. 55, 56, 49.

75. One need simply compare Rouillard's findings about Turkey and Persia in French seventeenth-century fiction with, say, Magendie's opinion (p. 271, e.g.) about the almost complete lack of local color in that fiction, an opinion often repeated by students of the eighteenth century.

76. Defoe, *The Life, Adventures and Piracies of the Famous Captain Singleton* (London: Dent, 1906), pp. 160, 80.

77. See Stewart, pp. 62-63, for yet more examples for France.

78. J.-F. Lafitau, *Moeurs des sauvages américains* . . . , 2 vols. (Paris: Saugrain l'aîné, 1724).

79. Ward, *A Trip to Ireland* and *A Trip to North-Wales*, both in *Five Travel Scripts*, pp. 8, 3; see also his *A Trip to Jamaica*, p. 12, for samples of Irish brogue and, p. 10, for a sailor's dialect.

80. See *The Jamaica Lady*, pp. 140, 112, 142, in that order; for the great popularity of Ward's *Jamaica*, see Troyer, and McBurney, ed., *Four Before Richardson*, p. xx. For Behn, see Note 74 above.

81. *The Merry Wanderer*, in *The Works of Mrs. Davys*, 2 vols. (London: H. Woodfall, 1725), I, 162-63. Also in Augustan Rpt. Soc. Pub. No. 54, ed. Robert A. Day.

82. L'Affichard, in *Voyages imaginaires* . . . , XXX, 23 [the novels in this volume are not voyages imaginaires in Gove's sense; e.g., this very realistic fiction is followed by another, Marivaux's *La Voiture embourbée*].

83. Gary N. Underwood, "Linguistic Realism in *Roderick Random*," *JEGP*, 69 (1970), 32-40. See also Lutwack, p. 261, whose analysis of dialect styles in fiction is apparently unsound historically. See also N.C. Starr, "Smollett's Sailors," *American Neptune*, 32 (1972), 81-99.

84. Gage, p. 234.

85. Père de Charlevoix, *Histoire et description générale de la Nouvelle France* (Paris, 1744), VI, 6-7; see also Viatte, "La Littérature française," p. 29. In "Smollett among the Indians," a forthcoming article, Thomas R. Preston demonstrates Smollett's knowledge of and use of Colden in *Humphrey Clinker*.

86. Shebbeare, *Lydia* (1755), p. 10; see also Colden, *The History of the Five Indian Nations* (London, 1747), pp. 65, 68, 201, for similar metaphors. Colden, p. xiii, has an analysis of Indian eloquence and explains how the translation does poor justice to it. Bissell, pp. 89-96, and Foster, pp. 91-94, treat this novel at length without noting the Colden original; Foster, p. 92, in fact, thinks Shebbeare got his idea for Cannassatego from a Creek chieftan named Calcathony in Edward Kimber's novel, *History of . . . Mr. Anderson*, "a poor imitation of Defoe's *Colonel Jacque* supposed to be based on its author's American travels. . . ." Note that Shebbeare also borrowed the name of another Indian chief, Decanessora, from Colden, pp. 2-3, to be the rival of Cannassatego and that the object of their affection is Yarico, out of the tradition stemming from travelers Moquet and Ligon (see Chap. IX above).

87. See Bissell, pp. 24-31, and Viatte, "La Littérature française," p. 29.

88. Crèvecoeur, *Voyage*, Chaps. VII, VIII, and IX of Vol. I.

89. Lowes, pp. 321, 314, 313.

90. Quoted by Lowes, p. 313; *Friedrich Martens vom Hamburg Spitzbergische oder Groen-landische Reise-Beschreibung gethan im Jahr 1671* (Hamburg, 1675). The trans. used by Coleridge and Lowes is that found in a vol. including Narbrough, Wood, Tasman, and Martens (spelled Marten there) and entitled *An Account of Several Late Voyages and Discoveries to the South and North* (London, 1694). The quotations are on p. 121.

91. Philips, in Lowes, p. 574; not Anson himself, as Lowes says, p. 316.

92. Lowes, p. 317; Fernández de Oviedo y Valdes, *General History of the Indies*, in Purchas, 20 vols. (1617; Glasgow, 1905-1907), XV, 168. Oviedo, the great Spanish traveler-historian of the New World, published his second vol., *La Historia general . . . de las Indias*, in Seville in 1535.

93. Anderson, *Over the Alps*, p. 24.

94. Quoted by Anderson, p. 24.

95. Dennis, *Miscellanies in Verse and Prose* (1693), pp. 133-34. Elizabeth Manwaring, *Italian Landscape in Eighteenth Century England* (New York: Oxford Univ. Press, 1925), pp. 5-6, as with other such descriptions in the seventeenth and eighteenth centuries, is unable to understand how people before the period of "Romanticism" or before the great landscape painters could enjoy such scenes of grand nature.

96. Addison, *Works* (1856), I, 483-84.

97. Ibid., pp. 485-86, 510-11. For other such passages on nature, see especially pp. 414-15, 421, 427, 438-40, 507; see also Clarence DeWitt Thorpe, "Two Augustans Cross the Alps: Dennis and Addison on Mountain Scenery," *SP*, 32 (1935), 463-88, and D.F. Bond's review in *PQ*, 15 (1936), 171-72.

98. Quoted in Manwaring, p. 12.

99. Letter of 24 Oct. 1730. Quoted also in Douglas Grant, *James Thomson: Poet of the Seasons* (London: Cresset, 1951), p. 117.

100. These are the words of Stafford, ' 'Toward Romantic Landscape Perception: Illustrated Travels and the Rise of 'Singularity' as an Aesthetic Category," *Art Quarterly*, 1 (1977), 118, n.3.

101. These are of course only a few of the poets whose imagery gleaned from travels has been studied. See, e.g., Milton Rugoff, *Donne's Imagery* (1939), and Theodore Banks, *Milton's Imagery* (1950).

102. Goethe, *Die Leiden des jungen Werthers*, ed. Ernst Feise (New York: Oxford Univ. Press, 1914), p. 52.

103. Eric M. Steel, *Diderot's Imagery* (New York: Haskell House, 1966), pp. 184-88, 261 n.

104. Manley, 2d ed., 2 vols. (1709), I, 83.

105. Hunter, *Occasional Form*, p. 143.

CHAPTER ELEVEN

1. Eliot, "The Dry Salvages," quoted also by Paul Fussell, *Abroad*, p. 56.

2. Paris: Le Mercier, 1735.

3. Only the first volume of Sloane's *Voyage* (1707) was parodied, since the second volume appeared in 1725. For the whole story, see David Nokes, "Who Was Esdras Barnivelt?" *Scriblerian*, 8 (1975), 55.

4. See Gove, pp. 316-18, for a bibliography showing the popular success of Coyer; see Chap. II above for the many editions of Chaplain Walter's account of Anson, only one of several written by people accompanying Anson.

5. Linguet, *Voyage au labirinthe du Jardin du Roi* (La Haye: Chez les Libraires associés, 1755).

6. McIntosh, pp. 193-97.

7. By Denise Fauconner, in *Le Voyage dans la littérature Anglo-Saxonne,* Actes du Congrès de Nice (1971) (S.A.E.S., 1972), pp. 182-203.

8. See Emile Henriot, *Les Livres du second rayon, irréguliers et libertins* (Paris: Grasset, 1948); and Jacques Barchilon, *Le Conte merveilleux français de 1690 à 1790* (Paris: Champion, 1975), pp. 125-28.

9. For Sartre and quotations from him, see his "An Explication of *The Stranger,*" first pub. in *Situations I* (Paris: Gallimard, 1947), then trans. Annette Michelson and rpt. in *Camus, A Collection of Critical Essays,* ed. Germaine Brée for Twentieth Century Views (Englewood Cliffs, N.J.: Prentice-Hall, 1962), pp. 108-21, p. 118 especially.

10. Franklin, *Discoverers, Explorers, Settlers: The Diligent Writers of Early America* (Chicago: Univ. of Chicago Press, 1979), p. 2.

11. See note 1, Chap. II above.

12. See Veit, *James Cook: Image and Impact,* p. 14.

13. In a paper read at a session of MLA in New York, December 1981. For Lady Mary's travel letters, see Chap. II, note 17, above.

14. See the letters "De Ceuta [on the coast of Morocco], ce 7 août, 1633," and "à Avignon, le lundi gras 1642."

15. These are the words of Robert Rogers, *The Double in Literature* (Detroit: Wayne State Univ. Press, 1970), p. 161, who speaks of Strether.

16. Mylne, p. 268.

17. For both Sitwell and Douglas, see Fussell, *Abroad,* pp. 204, 123.

18. Note that Gove, p. 175, Starr, "Barbary Captivities," p. 40, and Rosenberg, "The Imaginary Voyage in Prose Fiction," p. 23n., agree that the "Imaginary Voyage" is "impossible" to define.

19. Tallmadge, pp. 6-9. Despite my academic disagreement with Tallmadge, I find his essay the most helpful and inspiring of short treatments of travel literature; although he speaks only of "exploration reports," much of what he says applies to other kinds of travel accounts.

20. Wilson, *The Literary Travelogue: A Comparative Study with Special Relevance to Russian Literature from Fonvizin to Pushkin* (The Hague: Martinus Nijhoff, 1973). Wilson treats a verse travel book in spite of his definition and shows the clear influence of Sterne in Russia. See Butor on "Travelogues."

21. All of these are in Chap. II above except Twardeski; for him, see Reuel Wilson.

22. Lalande, *Journal d'un voyage en Angleterre, 1763,* ed. with int. by Hélène Monod-Cassidy for *SVEC* (Oxford: The Voltaire Foundation, 1980); samples of the drawings are reproduced by Monod-Cassidy.

23. Todorov, *The Poetics of Prose,* p. 35.

24. Kermode, "Novel, History and Type," *Novel,* 1 (1968), 231-38.

25. For Fiedler and Wain, see Chap. I above; for Ortega—the "novel" has "certainly entered its last phase"—see his "Notes on the Novel," pp. 53-54; for Sullivan, see his "Where Have All the Flowers Gone?" *Sewanee Review,* 78 (1970), 654-64. Sullivan's thesis is that the "novel" has been "rooted in a sense of community," a sense that has deteriorated.

26. Butor, "Travel as Writing," pp. 14-15.

27. Harris, *Navigantium* (1744), p. ii.

28. Merton, "From Pilgrimage to Crusade," *Cithara,* 4 (1964), 4.

29. Here Johnson is quoting Lord Essex favorably; see Boswell's *Life,* ed. Chapman, p. 306. For Voltaire on "extraordinary Persons," see Batten, p. 72.

30. Brée, "The Ambiguous Voyage," p. 94.

31. Mosher, "Herzog's Quest," in *Le Voyage dans la littérature anglo-saxonne,* Actes de Congrès de Nice (1971) (S.A.E.S., 1972), p. 171.

32. Green, p. 225.

33. Naipaul, p. 86, as quoted by Green, p. 336.

34. Anderson, p. 33.

INDEX

Names in brackets indicate the author in whose work the fictional character appears: Friday [Defoe].

A